PRAISE FOR DRUGS AS W

"Well-documented ... not just opinion ... I'n
this book and read it ... I really encourage everybody to get online and order this book right away!"

–**Joe Madison**, a radio host who has been selected as one of *Talkers* magazine's top ten most influential talk radio personalities for ten consecutive years and he is the only African-American to be listed in the "talented tenth."

"I really think [*Drugs as Weapons Against Us*] is a fascinating compendium of ... what the CIA was doing ... regarding manipulating our minds ... targeting a lot of famous celebrities, musicians. [John Potash is] an author I really recommend you read ... definitely read *Drugs as Weapons Against Us*."

–**Sean Stone**, host of *Buzzsaw* on The Lip TV, as well as an actor, film director, producer and screenwriter. Sean is the son of film director, Oliver Stone.

"This is a marvelous book!"

–**John B. Wells**, former weekend radio host of "Coast to Coast AM," 2012-2014, who has appeared on dozens of international radio stations and currently hosts "Caravan to Midnight."

"In my first radio interview, Frank Zappa told me the CIA was distributing LSD to the hippies. [*Drugs as Weapons Against Us* is] Unbelievable! Just a compelling story!"

–**Allan Handelman**, syndicated "Rock Talk" radio host who spent three years on *Talkers* magazine's "Heavy Hundred" most influential American radio hosts.

"Awesome guest [John Potash] ... is going out on a limb. This is a book that if you're interested in the manipulation of the population, you're going to want to get. This is the kind of book I just crave."

–**Joyce Riley**, nationally syndicated radio host of "The Power Hour."

"[John Potash] has done a wonderful job of research and a wonderful job of presenting [his] facts."

–**Rob McConnell**, nationally syndicated Canadian radio host of "The X Zone."

"When Lennon met semi-privately with media guru Marshall McLuhan in late 1969, McLuhan let Lennon know he was a 'useful fool,' and The Beatles were [used] for psychological warfare ... in popularizing drugs. Lennon stormed out but came back a few hours later to learn more. [*Drugs as Weapons Against Us*] is exhilarating and well-researched ... with startling revelations ... definitely worth the read!"

–**Richard Syrett**, nationally syndicated Canadian radio host of "The Conspiracy Show."

(more→)

“The CIA have used drugs as weapons against Americans ... to control people or pacify dissension against the official status quo—the government’s war policies.... We should not delude ourselves that U.S. Intelligence has repented and would never repeat these operations.... Many people still look at the rapid rise of the hallucinogenic use among these popular Sixties rock stars such as The Beatles, Rolling Stones and Jimi Hendrix as positive contributions – I don’t – to the Sixties idealism. It wasn’t about the world’s possibility for peace, love and global cooperation – that’s naïve. Nevertheless, we barely consider the possibility that such pacifist views were the intention of U.S. Intelligence agencies, and the CIA and its moneyed interests had a role in creating the Sixties subculture and [leading them to] dropping out and leaving behind radical dissent and protest. [John Potash has] covered so much in [his] research ... we appreciate his work.”

--**Gary Null,** radio host on New York City’s WBAI 99.5 FM, and syndicated to Pacifica Radio stations in Los Angeles and elsewhere, as well as the Progressive Radio Network.

“The book is amazing!”

–**David Clyde**, radio host of “The Wild Side,” 990AM WBOB, Rhode Island.

“I just got the book a couple days ago and I can’t wait to read it. I really can’t.”

–**Bill LuMaye**, WPTF, 680AM/850AM Raleigh, Duram, Chapel Hill, NC. Listed in *Talkers* magazine Top 250

“This book is magnificent!”

–**Pam Africa**, Chairwoman of the International Concerned Family and Friends of Mumia Abu-Jamal.

“Rob Dew, our News Director, said he finished [reading Drugs as Weapons Against Us] and he said it’s excellent.”

–**Darrin McBreen**, Infowars Nightly News host.

Drugs as Weapons Against Us

The CIA's Murderous Targeting of SDS, Panthers, Hendrix, Lennon, Cobain, Tupac, and Other Activists

John L. Potash

Drugs as Weapons Against Us: The CIA's Murderous Targeting of SDS, Panthers, Hendrix, Lennon, Cobain, Tupac, and Other Activists

Published by:
Trine Day LLC
PO Box 577
Walterville, OR 97489
1-800-556-2012
www.TrineDay.com
publisher@TrineDay.net

Library of Congress Control Number: 2014947508

Potash, John L.
Drugs as Weapons Against Us: The CIA's Murderous Targeting of SDS, Panthers, Hendrix, Lennon, Cobain, Tupac, and Other Activists
—1st ed.
p. cm.
Epud (ISBN-13) 978-1-937584-93-1
Mobi (ISBN-13) 978-1-937584-94-8
Print (ISBN-13) 978-1-937584-92-4
1. Drug abuse -- Political aspects -- United States. 2. Psychotropic drugs -- United States -- History -- 20th century. 3. Social history -- 1960-1970 -- United States. 4. LSD (Drug). 5. Counterculture. 6. United States -- Central Intelligence Agency. I. Potash, John L. II. Title

First Edition
10 9 8 7 6 5

Printed in the USA
Distribution to the Trade by:
Independent Publishers Group (IPG)
814 North Franklin Street
Chicago, Illinois 60610
312.337.0747
www.ipgbook.com

There's something happening here
What it is ain't exactly clear
There's a man with a gun over there
Telling me I got to beware
I think it's time we stop, children, what's that sound
Everybody look what's going down

– Stephen Stills

If you look back, many things that we thought were accidents turned out were not accidents. The entire LSD movement itself was sponsored originally by the CIA, to whom I give great credit. I would not be here today if it had not been for the foresight and prestige of the CIA psychologists, so give the CIA credit for being truly an intelligence agency.

– Timothy Leary
High Times, February 1978

Sidney Cohen: *Would you mind not calling it a cell? Let's call it a cluster!*
Timothy Leary: *All right. [Room laughs] Our undercover agents in Los Angeles were very cool about, uh, and yet they did more in a very laid-back way, uh, and it's every bit as public as some of the other, you know, the buses running around the country*

– https://www.youtube.com/watch?v=_qaumQvMWBA

The basic thing nobody asks is why do people take drugs of any sort? Why do we have these accessories to normal living to live? I mean, is there something wrong with society that's making us so pressurized, that we cannot live without guarding ourselves against it?

– John Lennon

If you think dope is for kicks and for thrills, you're out of your mind. There are more kicks to be had in a good case of paralytic polio or by living in an iron lung. If you think you need stuff to play music or sing, you're crazy. It can fix you so you can't play nothing or sing nothing.

– Billie Holiday

Junk is the ideal product... the ultimate merchandise. No sales talk necessary. The client will crawl through a sewer and beg to buy.

– William S. Burroughs

Words are the most powerful drugs used by mankind.

– Rudyard Kipling

Jerry held his guitar and picked some random licks. I spoke from an LSD haze. "LSD changes perception. Music transcends the musician. You are the vehicle for communication."

Garcia stopped and stared at me.

"I practice," *Garcia declared.* "Anyone can do that."

That shut me up and he returned to the guitar.

– Rhoney Gissen Stanley,
Owsley and Me: My LSD Family

Contents

Preface

I came to write about this subject from personal experience. I've been working as a counselor for twenty-five years, largely in the field of addictions. I studied psychology as an undergraduate. Some may think I came into my views with an anti-drug agenda from early on, but it was much the opposite. I abused drugs in high school and my first year of college before weaning off them, but I still positively coupled them with leftist activism.

I grew up in Baltimore with an immediate family that always had leftist sympathies. My father organized doctors against the Vietnam War. My mother was a public defender with a leftist perspective (leftist meaning, for example, anti-war, anti-pollution, anti-poverty and pro-civil rights). Her father was a successful activist lawyer whose work led to the FBI starting a file on him. He did decades of free work for the NAACP, and he successfully represented several Black Panthers in New York.

During my freshman year of college, I started getting more interested in leftist activism. Then I took LSD about a half-dozen times. I never had the proverbial "bad trip," but I did see my grades drop drastically afterwards. A classmate I befriended later in college took about the same amount of acid in his sophomore year and had the same experience. That classmate and I discussed our prior ability to write at least a full page of an essay in our heads word for word before committing it to paper. We both lost that ability after our LSD experiences. While our grades came back up after about a year or more following our last hits of acid, we both still couldn't remember more than one sentence at a time for our class papers. This caused me to drop the activism for a few years, until I felt that I had regained my normal mental capacity.

LSD also negatively affected my confidence and emotional control for many months, if not years, after the acid trips. I wrestled in college, and I saw another upper-classman wrestler try to come back to the team after a hiatus from school during which he ate dozens of hits of acid. He ended up so anxious before each match that he had to vomit. This weakened him, and he couldn't perform half as well as he did in practice, leading him eventually to quit. Both personally and professionally throughout the following decades, I would see this weakening in emotional control amongst many former acid users.

In college, after leaving drug abuse behind, I started reading some of the activist books from my grandfather's library. Initially, I had a hard time not coupling the use of LSD and other drugs positively with the leftist activism of the Sixties. Thus, I repressed my negative experience with acid, writing a senior paper in college that partly glorified the drug. It took a while to fully come to terms with LSD's negative effects. Similarly, I have met a number of people who were politically active in the Sixties and appear to repress acid's negative effects on them. On the other hand, one or two activists have introspectively and openly discussed their negative LSD experiences with me.

My earliest years of work started making me aware of the power structure around alcohol and other drugs, even before doing addictions work. I tended bar at a restaurant owned by powerful people. The owners worked in the state government and were also connected to the Mafia. I then worked as a probation officer and saw high-level drug traffickers let off of major charges, while low level dealers and users received jail time. Coworkers told me about the vast amount of money laundering going on through the local restaurants. In 1989 I started working as an addictions counselor—work that I continued in Baltimore, Washington D.C. and New York City. In New York I completed a Masters in Social Work and started counseling on a broader range of mental health issues.

I began conducting the research for this book in 1990. I came across many "alternative" media articles that glorified LSD and other drugs. I read various books that discounted the negative effects of acid, despite the authors' quoting interviewees who said they thought their mental abilities were hurt by it. While in graduate school at Columbia University in the mid-1990s, I poured over articles in the medical school library. I uncovered a number of articles that discuss how LSD can cause mild-to-severe cumulative damage to our minds.

My profession and my outside research enlightened me on the obvious damage that abuse and/or addiction to THC, heroin, cocaine, ecstasy and amphetamines can cause people. I have learned from personal and professional experience how regular marijuana use can cause pronounced apathy and have other negative consequences, particularly in teenagers. I've also seen how "spice" (synthetic marijuana) is making people delusional. I've seen how heroin and cocaine addiction can ruin lives, while ecstasy use can cause memory problems and lead to depression.

I believe in legalizing the hemp plant, of which marijuana is a variety, as well as in legitimatizing the use of medical marijuana, but I also see how the over-prescribing of medical marijuana is rampant. Such "weed" use tends to keep people distracted and diverted. This might be fine in a better world, one where an oligarchy didn't consistently erode our rights, take more of our money and time, and constantly take and destroy innocent lives.

Through my work and my writing I have heard familiar repetitive stories regarding drug dangers. Addicts have to steal, deal drugs or prostitute to support their habits. I've seen long-term acidheads whose anxiety had gotten so bad that they woke up most mornings nauseated and vomiting from it. Heroin, cocaine and methamphetamine users share needles and contract HIV and hepatitis.

Involved with both creative writing and social activism outside of work, I was exposed to some of the content of this book before it entered more mainstream awareness, allowing me a personal perspective. For example, while sitting in a Washington D.C. street in protest of the first Gulf War of 1991, I was told by a member of the Christic Institute about the Senate's 1989 Kerry Report revealing CIA drug trafficking. These details became more widely known through the investigative reporting of the late Gary Webb.

Reading poetry locally and at larger forums such as the Lollapalooza Music Festival, I befriended musicians who told me about the rampant heroin use amongst "alternative" band members. Drug dealers that I met in various venues, both as a counselor and socially, described how the drug traffickers above them appeared to have government connections. Traveling musicians conveyed stories coming out of Seattle about Kurt Cobain's possible murder. Women in New York told me about "rolling" (getting high) on ecstasy with top male rap groups.

Throughout much of this book I repeat the idea that drug trafficking oligarchs promote drugs to us by associating them with top musicians and leftist activist leaders. It's similar to the obvious sales technique of having a beautiful, scantily clad woman on a new car. It can be hard not to get similarly excited by a musician's passionate drug references. It took me a long time to realize what a visceral titillation it can be. However, while the *music* may hold strong in songs glorifying heroin or acid, the lyrics start to leave a sour taste for me personally, knowing how transiently exciting escapes through drugs can bring on so many major problems.

Besides studying counseling in graduate school, I also took classes in community organizing and social movements, working briefly through a grant I applied for to complete a project in East New York. This experience along with my trying to fit social activism in among my full-time counseling work drove home two main points. First, I saw the importance of having a clear mind for devising tactics and strategies in working against powerful groups. Secondly, I saw how little time is available for balancing activism, full-time work, and other aspects of life. Drug use takes up too much time for activism, while also fogging the ability to best accomplish activist goals.

Work in the counseling field led to discussion with coworkers who had lived through the various events detailed in this book. Black residents of Harlem, Washington and Baltimore all described the seemingly sudden deluge of heroin that flooded their neighborhoods in the late 1960s, during the Vietnam War. The immediate and huge increase in crime then kept people off their porches and behind locked doors. In the 1980s, the wave of crack cocaine resulting from U.S. meddling in Central America had an even worse effect on their neighborhoods.

Some older whites described their anti-Vietnam War activism changing into an immersion in what some called the "hippie movement," with everyone tripping from the late 1960s onwards. Even some black activists described being scared off by political arrests during their "Friends of the Panthers" work, only to join the more hedonistic hippie movement. LSD use, synonymous with this movement, led to former activists and many more experiencing subtle to severe problematic effects, lasting from weeks to years.

I don't use these stories as evidence for the theses herein. But I did use them as leads to see if such evidence existed. This led to two decades of research, culminating in this book. I have exhaustively documented it with over 1400 notes, which I encourage you to explore.

In 1994 I came upon evidence of FBI Counterintelligence Program (Cointelpro) targeting of the rap icon Tupac Shakur. This information compelled me to take a turn in my research and writing, resulting in my previously published book, *The FBI War on Tupac Shakur and Black Leaders*. Working on the Tupac book opened many doors to a wealth of information on underground activism and institutionalized political targeting involving Cointelpro, the Black Panthers and other activist groups of various ethnicities working with the Panthers. This invaluably enhanced my commitment and the wealth of information brought to writing *Drugs as Weapons Against Us*.

I want to again thank Tupac's lawyers, manager, associates and Black Panther extended family for so graciously sharing much private information with me about his activist life, and death at the age of 25. Also thank you to all of those working, professionally or otherwise, in the media, and in activist groups, for helping to get word out on that book. The premature deaths of Tupac and a number of other stars covered herein are tragic. Also tragic are the early deaths of too many of their associates. That so many of Tupac's associates died under mysterious circumstances suggests a continued U.S. intelligence cover-up of Tupac's murder, which could provide material for another whole book. Space precludes it all being mentioned here.

Many readers may have their own preconceptions of what happened in these various historical contexts, and, because the events involved beloved musicians, people may get very passionate about their opinions. If this applies to you, I hope you can carry your passion into the notes and see the sources of the material. While I don't claim to hold the ultimate truth on any one matter, I urge you to keep an open mind. Some of my sources are the CIA's own Operation MK-Ultra documents. CIA Director Richard Helms had ordered these shredded in the early 1970s, but 30,000 pages remained untouched in the CIA's finance department records. I'm hoping my sources create a healthier debate over these issues.

In this book, I do not discuss the abuse or overuse of prescription medications. I have little to say about the time-honored abuses of alcohol. I've had a hard enough time creating a book of readable length in just covering "illicit" drugs. Tomes can be written on all of these other substances along the same veins traced here. Other researchers are urged to do so, as much of this book's content may be just the tip of the iceberg.

My next book is a novel.

John L. Potash
Baltimore, Maryland
May 1, 2015

Chapter One

Opium Traders Achieve Global Predominance

As early as 3400 b.c., the Sumerians used the opium poppy, which they called the "joy plant," for its euphoric effects. In *The Politics of Heroin: CIA Complicity in the Global Drug Trade,* University of Wisconsin Professor Alfred McCoy explains that most opium, and its derivative heroin, still comes from poppies grown in the northern section of former Sumerian lands and adjoining territories. Today, this includes a narrow 4,500-mile stretch of mountains extending along the southern tier of Asia, from Turkey through Iran, Afghanistan and Pakistan to India, an area known as the "Golden Crescent." That same stretch of mountains then extends to the world's second largest area of poppy cultivation in the "Golden Triangle," where Myanmar (formerly Burma), Thailand and Laos come together adjacent to Vietnam.[1]

From as early as 1500 A.D., opium and other drugs played a crucial role in the rise of industrialized powers. Professor Carl Trocki, of Queensland University, Australia, provided this summary of the opium trade:

> Accumulations of wealth created by a succession of historic drug trades have been among the primary foundations of global capitalism and the modern nation-state itself. Indeed, it may be argued that the entire rise of the west, from 1500 to 1900, depended on a series of drug trades.[2]

Professor Peter Dale Scott of the University of California at Berkeley concurred:

> All empires since the Renaissance have been driven by the search for foreign resources, and nearly all, including the British, the French, and the Dutch, used drugs as a cheap way to pay for overseas expansion.[3]

Access to an abundance of opium poppies by Western industrialized countries brought centuries of problems to the East, particularly in China. There, in the early 1500s, the Chinese had only used opium medicinally and in oral form. During this time the Portuguese fleet initiated the smoking of opium in China, discovering that the effects of smoking opium were instantaneous. The Chinese, however, considered the practice barbaric and subversive.[4]

In the early 1700s, the Dutch took over trade with China and the islands of Southeast Asia, while popularizing the use of a tobacco pipe for opium smoking. In 1729, the Emperor Yung Cheng issued an edict prohibiting the smoking of opium and its domestic sale, except under license for use as a medicine.[5]

By 1750, the British East India Company had taken control of several opium-growing regions of India, and by the 1790s had developed a monopoly on the opium trade. China's new emperor, Kia King, then banned opium completely. This failed to stop the British East India Company from increasing their smuggling and sale of opium in China, which grew from 15 tons a year in the earlier 1700s to 3,200 tons a year by 1850.[6]

American University Professor Clarence Lusane argued that once Britain had developed its empire, it used opium as an important new political tool for conquest. The British, he wrote, used opium to help addict and control the Chinese people en masse, increasing British profits in China and allowing them easier access to China's resources.[7]

Statements of high-level Chinese officials support this argument. In 1836, mandarin Hsu Nai-tsi, vice president of the Sacrificial Court, informed the emperor that opium, originally ranked among the medicines, was now being inhaled. Hsu called the practice "destructive ... injurious," and despite its ban in 1799, the foreign "barbarian merchants" helped it "spread throughout the entire empire." Mandarin Chun Tsu, a member of the Board of Rites, found that within the Chinese army, "a great number of the soldiers were [opium] smokers; so that, although their numerical force was large there was hardly any force found among them." Chu proclaimed the Chinese needed to oppose the "covetous and ambitious schemes" of the British with their opium sales.[8]

By 1839, the British East India Company's shipments of opium to China reached 1,400 tons per year. The Chinese premier tried to outlaw foreign ships from bringing opium into Chinese ports for sale. Chinese officials confiscated 15,000 chests containing 95 tons of opium from foreign merchants, including 10 tons from the American firm Russell & Co. They dissolved the opium in a trench of water with salt and lime.[9]

British soldiers during the Second Opium War. When China tried to ban the sale of opium, England launched two successful "Opium Wars" against China on behalf of its opium merchants.

Unwilling to lose the political power opium had given it, Britain attacked China in the first Opium War, which lasted three years until 1842. China then signed a peace treaty giving Hong Kong to Britain. China kept opium illegal, but stopped confiscations. However, when Chinese officials tried to enforce the prohibition of British opium sales, tensions led to the second Opium War (1856-1858). Once more China lost and had to comply with British demands to legalize the opium trade.[10]

In 1865, Scotsman Thomas Sutherland started the Hongkong Shanghai Banking Company (later HSBC). A senior Chinese government official had issued a warrant for future HSBC board member Thomas Dent in 1839, to close his opium warehouses. This helped spark the first Opium War. France's *Le Monde Diplomatique* said that "HSBC's first wealth came from opium from India, and later Yunan in China." Yunan is in the Golden Triangle area. The first Opium War forced China to cede Shanghai to Western powers, transforming it from a fishing village to China's largest, most modern city with a network of opium smoking dens. Prof. Alfred McCoy would eventually call Hong Kong "Asia's heroin laboratory," and HSBC would become the world's second largest bank.

By 1900 China had an estimated thirteen million opium addicts. Six years later, 27% of all adult males in China smoked opium. This astounding rate of addiction has never since been equaled. Other Asian countries developed similar public addiction issues when forced to participate in the drug trade by European powers. Corrupt, foreign-supported leaders in these countries may have also been motivated to make money on the side through taxing opium sales.[11]

However, the opium-trafficking families of the U.S. and Europe made the most money, as they bought most of the 35,000 metric tons of raw opium being produced in 1906 and sold it at a premium once it was processed. This was 85% of the world opium production that year and more than four times as much from any other single source in history. Most of this opium production took place in southern China, adjoining the area considered the Golden Triangle of opium production in Laos, Thailand, Burma (now Myanmar) and Vietnam.[12]

British rulers appeared to also use opium against British citizens who struggled to better their living conditions. Famous British resident Karl Marx coined the term "opiate of the masses" about opium abuse and addiction keeping people politically asleep. The timing of the ill effects of the industrial revolution—worker displacement, starvation and rioting in the early 1800s—suggests that British rulers promoted opiates to help quell the masses of poor and struggling workers, many of whom joined protests.[13]

After a particularly turbulent eight years of rioting and protest, in 1819 British Parliament passed the Six Acts, turning Britain into a police state. These acts prevented public meetings, restricted newspapers, sped up the judicial process and restricted access to firearms. Within ten years, street patrols of police were introduced. In 1827, the first commercial batches of the opium derivative morphine were produced[14]

Opium distribution for medicinal and recreational use in industrialized European countries led to problems among their own poor and working classes. Professor Lusane cited Karl Marx in *Capital*, which stated that in 1861, 26 percent of deaths among English children resulted from their working-class parents treating the children's ailments with opiate medicines. As Prof. Al McCoy also reported, mass addiction to opium became a significant feature of the late 1800s in England.[15]

U.S., British Traffic Opium As Workers Organize

Starting in the 1700s, the British East India Company acquired a number of partners among American families from New England. The opium merchants' power and loyalty extended to their American partners, and the American anglophiles showed their continued commitment to Britain by becoming part of the reported 15% of Americans who fought for the British as Loyalists during the American Revolutionary War.[16]

In his book, *Pipe Dream Blues: Racism and the War on Drugs*, Professor Clarence Lusane argues that British aristocracy and many of America's wealthiest families used alcohol and drugs as weapons, not only in the East, but also in Africa and in the Americas, with New England families dominating the rum trade. Lusane notes that prior to European influence, Africans traditionally drank only palm wine. Other intoxicants were used medicinally and in moderation. European traders introduced rum, tobacco and opium to Africa for economic gain, swindling African traders when gathering captured slaves, and also introduced rum in the Americas to lead a large percentage of Native Americans into dysfunction.[17]

The American families smuggling opium into China alongside the British included the prominent Russell family of Connecticut. The Russells intermarried with other rich families, including the Pierponts, the family that later spawned tycoon Julius Pierpont "J.P." Morgan. Over a half-dozen of the richest families, including the Cabots, Cushings, Astors, and Perkinses, gained huge wealth in the opium trade and went on to attain positions of power in the U.S. In just one single year (1840) these New Englanders brought 24,000 pounds of opium into the U.S.[18]

The Russell family helped found Yale University, and in 1833, one of the Russells founded Yale's elite secret society, Skull and Bones. A member of the Cabot opium-trafficking family founded Harvard's Porcellian Club, called the Porc or Pig Club by critics. The Russell Company unabashedly used the skull-and-bones pirate symbol in its international opium shipping. In 1856, a Skull and Bonesman, Daniel Coit Gilman, co-incorporated the Russell Trust Association, the opium-trafficking Russell family's fund, which then started bestowing money to Skull and Bones members. The Russell Trust reportedly granted each Skull and Bonesman $15,000, the equivalent of $255,000 in 2010 dollars, upon their graduation. In time, many of these Bonesmen rose to the ranks of the most powerful people in the world.[19]

Mss:766 1820-1891

Russell & Company. Russell & Co.
Records, 1820-1891: A Finding Aid

Baker Library

Harvard Business School, Boston, MA 02163
April 2011
© 2011 President and Fellows of Harvard College

Descriptive Summary

Repository: Baker Library, Harvard Business School
Call No.: Mss:766 1820-1891
Creator: Russell & Co.
Title: Russell & Co. records, 1820-1891
Quantity: 4 linear ft. (25 vols., 3 boxes, 7 mapcase folders)
Abstract: The Russell & Co./Perkins & Co. collection contains letter books, order and purchase books, invoices, shipping orders and other financial material relating to the China trade merchant firms.

Provenance:

Gift of Shewan, Tomes & Co., 1929, 1932.

Access Restrictions:

Appointment necessary to consult collection.

Preferred Citation:

Cite as: Russell and Co./Perkins and Co. Collection. Baker Library Historical Collections. Harvard Business School.

Historical Note:

Perkins & Co. was established in 1803 as a branch of the Boston based merchant trading firm J. & T.H. Perkins & Co., owned by merchant brothers James and Thomas Handasyd

Harvard Business School's library provides documentation of Russell & Company's takeover of the Perkins family's opium trading. The Russells became the dominant American family joining British families in the vastly profitable opium trade.

In 1874, a British chemist turned the opium derivative, morphine, into heroin. By 1898, the Bayer Company of Germany introduced heroin as a commercial product. Bayer introduced its milder pain reliever, aspirin, one year later. Both drugs were mass-marketed on a similar scale, with heroin being touted as a "non-addictive" cure for adult ailments and infant respiratory diseases. Other companies followed suit and mass marketed heroin throughout Europe and America, with the American Medical Association's approval of heroin as a non-addictive morphine substitute.[20]

The next thirty years were a time of great political upheaval in the United States. Socialist and anarchist newspapers thrived both in the cities, particularly among recent immigrants, and in the rural areas where homegrown leftist activists gained a readership. This widespread radical leftist political activism came on the heels of the American Industrial Revolution, which followed a few decades after Europe's Industrial Revolution.

In the European countries, the newly rich industrialists stood in opposition to the old money of the royal families. Columbia University sociologists Richard Cloward and Frances Fox Piven described how these European industrialists and royal families competed for the workers' allegiance. This gave the workers more leverage to gain concessions, such as better workplace conditions and national health care.

Piven and Cloward noted the marked difference between European and American labor history. When the industrialists rose up in the U.S. after the 1860s Civil War, there was no aristocracy standing in opposition to them. As workers in the factories tried to organize for better wages and conditions, the industrialists initially used violence against them, but soon employed more sophisticated strategies.[21]

The opium-trafficking families ramped up their importation of drugs by the end of the 1800s. Companies marketed much of the imported opium and its first derivative, morphine, in medicines. But at least a quarter of imported opium was intended for smoking. By 1900 over 1% of the U.S. population was addicted to opium. Addiction to opium, particularly heroin, rose "at alarming rates" in 1903, in parallel with a rise of worker activism.[22]

During this time period, women organized for the right to vote. In the 1870s, police arrested Susan B. Anthony and Sojourner Truth for their efforts in this cause. In 1890, the National American Woman Suffrage Association was created to promote women's voting rights. Many of these activist women also fought for anti-lynching laws and formed groups fighting for better working conditions.[23] By the 1890s and early 1900s women made up two-thirds to three-quarters of opium addicts.[24]

Opium Profiteers Buy Media, Push War

Yale University Professor David Musto wrote that opiate addiction reached its peak in the early 1900s, rising to a level never since equaled in this country. The opiate-addict population nearly doubled the rate of addiction today. It is unknown how many only "abused" opiates without developing a full-fledged addiction. Abuse alone could generally be enough to fill up users' free time and disincline their political and social activism.[25]

At the turn of the century, cocaine addiction became almost as widespread as opiate addiction. This appeared to have its genesis in 1886 when, during the early stages of the Progressive Movement, the Georgia counties of Atlanta and Fulton passed alcohol prohibition legislation. In response, a Georgia pharmacist, John Pemberton, developed Coca-Cola, a non-alcoholic version of French Wine Coca. He developed the original formula for Coca-Cola, containing 2.5 mg of cocaine per 3.3 ounces of fluid. The syrup had 5 ounces of coca leaf per gallon of syrup, an addictive amount for those with the susceptibility. This formula was sold as a headache cure and stimulant.[26]

A wealthy Atlanta pharmacist, Asa Candler, bought exclusive rights to the Coca-Cola formula and incorporated Coca-Cola in 1892. Manufacturers sold cocaine in a wide range of patent medicines, tonics, elixirs and fluid extracts at that time. Asa Candler and his wealthy investors put massive amounts of money into advertising his new drink for sale in popular drug-store fountains all over the U.S. and Canada. It soon became America's most popular drink.

By 1902, cocaine-related products provided many ways to access the drug on a daily basis. This led to an estimated 200,000 cocaine addicts in the United States. Between 1900 and 1907, U.S. coca leaf imports tripled. Hundreds of early Hollywood silent films depicted scenes of drug use and trafficking.[27]

Meanwhile, leftist workers organizing for better work conditions gained help from investigative magazines that exposed corrupt companies. Together, these organizers and writers helped bring the reform-minded president Theodore Roosevelt into office in 1901. Roosevelt, who also founded the Progressive Party in 1912, helped gain the passage of anti-trust laws to break up the robber barons' monopolies over certain industries. When these tycoons bought out all their competition in an industry, they could raise prices as high as they liked. During the Roosevelt administration, many laws and regulations were instituted to give the average American a "Square Deal," or a chance to make a fair living without getting robbed by the rich.[28]

Professor Musto detailed how the Progressive Movement of the late 1800s and early 1900s brought about "federal laws ... improving the nation's morals and resisting the selfish actions of the rich and powerful." Most pertinently, it led to the prohibition of opium for non-medicinal purposes by 1914, and the more problematic prohibition of alcohol a few years later.[29]

In seeming reaction to these progressive political developments, the Rockefeller and J.P. Morgan families bought out all the top investigative magazines that contributed to American political reform.[30] By 1915, J.P. Morgan also bought out the major newspapers. The Congressional Record revealed that in 1915, J.P. Morgan's "'steel, shipbuilding and powder interests' had purchased control of twenty-five great newspapers ... to control generally the policy of the daily press of the United States."[31]

Control of the media aided the Rockefellers, the J.P. Morgan family, and their fellow intermarried, wealthy families. In 1917, they swayed public opinion and influenced the United States to aid England in World War I. While tens of thousands of Americans died after the U.S. entered the war, these wealthy families made huge profits from moneylending, steel manufacturing for armaments, and oil sales for trucks, tanks, railroads and airplanes.[32]

Media Promotes "Red Scare"

Control of the media aided the creation of the first "Red Scare." Researchers say the Russian Revolution of 1917 scared the wealthiest in all the capitalist countries. The Russian Revolution took land from the wealthy and redistributed it to the poor. It took ownership of the factories and gave it to councils of workers. In response, to make sure nothing fomented in the U.S, the corporate owners, including the Rockefellers, Russells, Morgans, Vanderbilts, Carnegies, Harrimans and Bushes, helped propagate a Red Scare through the media. Their tactics led to the Sedition Act of 1918, which criminalized many behaviors formerly seen as merely unpatriotic. Legislators also passed laws directed at immigrants, leading to imprisonment and deportation of people for radical or anarchist political beliefs.[33] Evidence supports the case that U.S. intelligence framed Italian anarchist organizers Nicola Sacco and Bartolomeo Vanzetti before their trial and execution.[34]

In 1919 and 1920, U.S. Attorney General, A. Mitchell Palmer, and his young functionary J. Edgar Hoover, started a mass arrest of immigrant workers nationwide. These were known as the "Palmer Raids." Hoover led the "Alien Radical" division of the vastly expanded Bureau of Investigation (soon the Federal Bureau of Investigation, or FBI). Estimates of the numbers of Italian, Russian and other immigrants arrested for "radical subversion" in one massive dragnet ranged from 3,000 to 19,000 persons.[35]

Some of the still-independent press complained, as did some members of Congress. The Immigration Act of 1920 initially sought to help victims of the Palmer Raids. It ended up making possession of radical literature, and even sympathy for activist causes, punishable offenses for immigrants, referred to as "aliens." Criminal syndicalism charges started in most states, and were used to repress socialist and anarchist political organizing. In 1903 the State Militias had been organized by Congress into what would become the National Guard, for additional peacetime repression.[36]

Yet again, toward the end of the 1940s, U.S. intelligence, politicians and journalists created a second Red Scare. The U.S. House of Representatives Un-American Activities Committee (HUAC), along with a similar Senate committee led by Senator Joe McCarthy, held hearings to root out Communists, suspected Communists, and "fellow travelers." Many were jailed, thousands more were blacklisted, even for leftist leanings, making it impossible for them to find jobs in their fields, most notably in the film industry and the arts. The FBI visited employers and warned them not to hire such people.[37] They also interrogated friends and relatives of suspected "pinko" targets. The CIA appeared to attack such targets out of concern for anyone infringing on their own attempt to mold people's hearts and minds.[38]

A government memorandum showed CIA plans to set a particular example of two Communist activists. Julius and Ethel Rosenberg were convicted of treason for giving atomic secrets to the Soviet Union. They became the only people executed for treason during peacetime. Later, published evidence supported the possibility of their innocence.[39] These events demonized Italian and Jewish leftist communities and left them fearful of participating in activism.[40]

Politicians further directed legislation at workers' organizations, such as the Industrial Workers of the World, nicknamed the Wobblies. The Wobblies used sitdown strikes to gain many workers' rights. Starting in 1917, the U.S. Justice Department and War Department, with many high posts held by the Rockefellers, Harrimans and Bush tycoons, ordered troops to invade Wobbly headquarters, broke up Wobbly meetings, and took Wobblies hostage without charges. The Postmaster suspended scores of second-class mailing permits for progressive newspapers and magazines, based on minor infractions, while the Justice Department closed down socialist newspapers and deported the Italian immigrant publisher of the top anarchist paper.[41]

Opium's Role in Genocidal Eugenics, Nazi Atrocities

In 1902, Daniel Coit Gilman, the man who incorporated the Russell Trust Association for America's top opium-trading family, moved on from his assistance to opium traffickers and accepted the first presidency of the newly founded Carnegie Institution of Washington. One of Gilman and the Carnegies' first projects was the genocidal "eugenics" agenda. Award-winning syndicated columnist Edwin Black wrote about the Eugenics Movement exhaustively in his book, *War Against the Weak*. Black had his manuscript for the book peer-reviewed and corrected before publication. He noted that the word "eugenics" derived from the Greek for "well born."[42]

Black described how the Rockefellers, Harrimans, Carnegies, and the J.P. Morgan family used their money and influence to pass laws in a majority of American states that led to the sterilization of poor people and immigrants. The wealthiest enlisted military researchers to invent biased IQ tests, called Alpha and Beta tests. These tests used wealthy white cultural examples from the early 1900s, such as asking what was missing from a tennis court or bowling alley. The tests purported to prove that "47% of whites generally, 70% of Jews and 89% of Negroes were deserving of elimination." Asian and Latino immigrants were also targeted as inferior.[43]

Officials further used sly and unsavory means to kill poor Americans. Incoming patients at certain hospitals were fed milk from tubercular cows, resulting in a thirty- to forty-percent annual death rate. Such hospitals and institutions were often the only ones in poor areas, like the Illinois Institution for the Feebleminded in the Chicago area in Lincoln, Illinois.[44]

Ivy League universities, as well as Stanford, Johns Hopkins and others, received funding from eugenicists to lend legitimacy to the fraudulent pseudoscience. The *Journal of the American Medical Association* supported eugenics in many of its articles, aiding the passage of sterilization legislation in 27 states. These states also passed legislation against mixed-race marriages.[45] The Eugenics Movement had its founding national office at Cold Spring Harbor Laboratory in Long Island, New York.[46]

Black's extensive research exposed that during the 1920s, the rising fascist revolutionary, Adolph Hitler, regularly communicated with American eugenicists. The Carnegies and Rockefellers helped fund eugenics institutions in Europe, particularly in Germany, to spread genocidal racist ideology.

In 1928, the Ford Company and the Rockefellers interlocked their companies with the giant German chemical company I.G. Farben (which included heroin-introducer Bayer). All three companies played major roles in Nazi Germany. I.G. Farben gave massive funds for Hitler's election, helped him initiate and wage his wars, and ended up running the largest concentration camp—Auschwitz. Also, the U.S. Justice Department eventually cited Rockefeller's Standard Oil for exclusively providing their sought-after synthetic rubber process to Nazi Germany's navy. Black further documented that the Ford Company used slave labor from the Buchenwald concentration camp.[47]

London's *Guardian* reviewed U.S. documents and found the Harriman and Bush families joined these other groups in helping fund the rise of the Nazis. George H.W. Bush's father, Prescott Bush, managed the elite British-American banking venture, Brown Brothers Harriman. BBH worked behind the back of the British government on behalf of the government's opponents, the British royalty. Former Brown Brothers partner Montagu Norman, a Bank of England Governor, was reportedly a Hitler supporter. The bank also worked behind the back of President Franklin Roosevelt's administration. BBH and Bush-Harriman steel and shipping companies kept up joint ventures with German steel mogul, Fritz Thyssen. In his autobiography, *I Paid Hitler,* Thyssen boasted of helping finance Hitler's rise to power.[48] Brown Brothers Harriman's Silesian Steel owned German steel and coalmines, and their Hamburg-Amerika shipping line spread pro-Nazi propaganda in the U.S. and Germany.[49]

IBM also offered huge support to the Nazis. Edwin Black's bestseller, *IBM and the Holocaust,* detailed how IBM first used its Hollarinth punch cards to systematize the extermination of Europe's Jews, gypsies, Communists, socialists, anarchists and homosexuals. IBM employees conducted door-to-door censuses, and processed all of the information onto punch cards. These cards acted as the key codes to the earliest versions of computers, and kept the data necessary for identifying and speeding up the execution of so many people. Six million Jews and five million people from these other groups were killed on the spot or sent to one of at least 300 concentration camps. There, Nazis etched tattoos on prisoners' arms with numbers corresponding to their punch card numbers.[50]

Other U.S. major banks and corporations also aided Nazi Germany. Chase Bank helped the Nazis exchange the money stolen from Jewish bank accounts. General Motors supplied Hitler with tens of thousands of inexpensive military Blitz trucks and worked with Rockefeller's Standard Oil and I.G. Farben to build advanced ethyl plants for the Nazis.[51]

Throughout WWI and WWII, the Russell Opium Trust-funded Skull and Bones folks were omnipresent in power positions. They included Skull and Bonesman Henry Stimson, who served as President W.H. Taft's Secretary of War, President Hoover's Secretary of State, and President Franklin Roosevelt's Secretary of War. Roosevelt selected the aging Stimson to appease the Republicans by making his cabinet more bipartisan after entering WWII.[52]

Henry Stimson took direct control of the atomic bomb development, overseeing the Manhattan Project.[53] He pushed President Harry Truman to drop the atomic bomb on the Japanese twice in several days, against the wishes of most military commanders who said it was by no means necessary.[54] Such actions appeared indicative of the continued Eugenics extermination philosophy.[55]

Oligarchs Foster the CIA

Within the WWII intelligence group, the Office of Strategic Services (OSS), were members of America's wealthiest families, including J.P. Morgan's sons, the Mellons, Vanderbilts and Duponts.[56] Later, other key Skull and Bones members gained important positions in U.S. intelligence including Prescott Bush, father of President George H.W. Bush. These families played the major role in helping pass the legislation titled the National Security Act of 1947. This act founded the Central Intelligence Agency and gave the CIA preeminence among the other fourteen-plus intelligence agencies developed thereafter.[57]

The highest-ranking CIA whistleblower, former Assistant Deputy Director Victor Marchetti, was a 14-year CIA veteran. Marchetti joined British magazine editor Frances Saunders in finding that virtually the entire CIA leadership and middle ranks were filled with members of the white, Protestant, wealthiest families, with the most connections coming from the Rockefeller family and Foundation. It remained that way into the 1970s with few exceptions. Brothers Allen and John Foster Dulles were close friends with the Rockefellers. John headed the Rockefeller Foundation before becoming President Dwight Eisenhower's Secretary of State (1953-61). Allen would become the longest serving CIA Director (1953-61).[58]

Nearly one quarter of a million federal documents released in the post-WWII time period exposed the facts that the CIA, along with MI6, its British equivalent, hired Nazi war spies and other war criminals following the war. These included five key associates of infamous Nazi leader, Adolph Eichmann, and top Nazi spy, Renald Gehlen. The CIA helped Gehlen and his advisors retain their leadership in West Germany's intelligence network. A *New York Times* article revealed that the CIA gave at least two of these Nazis citizenship. Many Nazi war criminals were charged with mass murders. Yet MI6 also hired many Nazi agents, including one responsible for killing close to 100 British agents.[59]

Researchers in the 1980s revealed other extensive aspects of CIA/Nazi work. Award-winning investigative reporter Christopher Simpson's 1988 book, *Blowback: America's Recruitment of Nazis,* listed hundreds of government archival files and thousands of documents, among its copious citations, describing a half-dozen U.S. intelligence operations protecting and employing Nazis. One, code-named "Sunrise," was comprised of former Nazi spies. Another, of Nazi scientists, was code-named "Paperclip." Simpson named Robert Lovett, Allen Dulles and OSS agent Frank Wisner as U.S. intelligence leaders who pushed the hiring of Nazis to do CIA work in the U.S., Europe, Latin America and the Middle East. Simpson summarized, "hundreds, and perhaps thousands, of such recruits were SS [Nazi elite guard] veterans."[60]

A whistleblowing former chief prosecutor of the Justice Department's Nazi War Crimes Unit, John Loftus, reported that under Operation Sunrise, CIA director Allen Dulles helped smuggle some 5,000 Nazi Gestapo and SS agents to South America for U.S. intelligence work.[61] As detailed later, these Nazis would help the CIA create vast drug trafficking networks in Central and South America.

Super-Rich Control Media at Home & Abroad

U.S. intelligence abided by the famous dictum of Nazi propagandist Joseph Goebbels, who said the aim was not about controlling people physically but controlling their hearts and minds. British magazine editor Frances Saunders reviewed troves of buried archival U.S. intelligence documents that explained their goals. In a 1950 "NSC Directive," the U.S. intelligence umbrella group, the National Security Council, described it as

> psychological warfare ... [through] propaganda ... to influence [people's] thoughts and actions ... [so that] the subject moves in the direction [controllers] desire for reasons which he believes to be his own.[62]

U.S. intelligence leaders developed such extensive control over American media that they boasted about it. In the late 1940s, the CIA's

Frank Wisner, at the Office of Policy Coordination, oversaw 302 people on their payroll. The Office conducted psychological warfare operations through its "Propaganda Assets Inventory." Wisner boasted he could, "play the media like a mighty Wurlitzer [music organ]." Wisner supervised an increasing staff that rose to 2,812 locally in 1952, along with 3,142 overseas contract personnel. The budget also rose in that period from \$4.7 million to \$82 million.[63]

While it is unknown exactly what Frank Wisner's employees were doing, various investigators shed some light on their work. Watergate muckraking reporter Carl Bernstein wrote a seminal 1977 exposé on the media. Despite his earlier '70s Watergate fame, only *Rolling Stone* magazine published this revealing article. Bernstein wrote that a Senate Intelligence Committee forced CIA Director George H.W. Bush, to admit, "more than 400 journalists had lived double lives, maintaining covert relationships with the CIA." Others in the CIA told Bernstein the number was far higher. Bernstein listed the Senate Committee findings that owners of virtually all of the leading media companies worked with the CIA. They also had top executives, editors and journalists on the CIA payroll willing to reprint CIA-written articles verbatim under their names.[64]

How America's Most Powerful News Media Worked Hand in Glove with the Central Intelligence Agency and Why the Church Committee Covered It Up

THE CIA AND THE MEDIA

BY CARL BERNSTEIN

In 1953, Joseph Alsop, then one of America's leading syndicated columnists, went to the Philippines to cover an election. He did not go because he was asked to do so by his syndicate. He did not go because he was asked to do so by the newspapers that printed his column. He went at the request of the CIA.

Alsop is one of more than 400 American journalists who in the past twenty-five years have secretly carried out assignments for the Central Intelligence Agency, according to documents on file at CIA headquarters. Some of these journalists' relationships with the Agency were tacit; some were explicit. There was cooperation, accommodation and overlap. Journalists provided a full range of clandestine services—from simple intelligence-gathering to serving as go-betweens with spies in Communist countries. Reporters shared their notebooks with the CIA. Editors shared their staffs. Some of the journalists were Pulitzer Prize winners, distinguished reporters who considered themselves ambassadors-

Watergate muckraker Carl Bernstein described the U.S. Senate Church Committee's findings that well over 400 members of the media, mostly its owners and editors, lived dual lives while working for the CIA.

The CIA's control of the media appeared to increase each year. Before his retirement, veteran CIA agent Ralph McGehee obtained a CIA memo in 1991 claiming the Agency had representatives in every media outlet in the country that helped to spin and censor the news.[65]

The Rockefeller and J.P. Morgan interests had already bought control of the most influential newspapers and investigative magazines. Ben Bagdikian, Dean of the University of California/Berkeley Journalism School, set forth the ways in which multinational corporate owners continued to gain even tighter controls over public information in his book *The Media Monopoly*, describing how the ever-consolidating world of media ownership approached near-monopolization by a few companies.[66]

He explained that most major media outlets have directors on their company boards who also sit on the boards of major multinational corporations. For example, the Board of Directors of *Time* magazine and the industry standard-bearer *New York Times* also sit on corporate boards involved in defense contracting, oil, and pharmaceuticals, as well as banks, finance and insurance companies. Under law, "The director of a company is obliged to act in the interests of his or her own company."[67] Thus, the directors of media further the interests of the interlocked multinational companies.

In the 1970s and 1980s, to further tighten the elite's control of public information, U.S. intelligence gained direct ownership over the vast majority of magazine and journal information sources. One of their own publications, *Armed Forces Journal International,* revealed that the Pentagon (military intelligence) published 371 magazines in 1971, making it sixteen times larger than the nation's next biggest publisher. This number increased to 1,203 different periodicals by 1982.[68] These 1200 magazine and journal titles straddled many areas of life, controlling information that could make it to the pages of news, fashion and sports magazines crowding book chain outlets.

In 1975, a Senate intelligence committee issued a report revealing the taxpayer-funded CIA owned outright "more than 200 wire services, newspapers, magazines, and book publishing complexes," according to Professor Michael Parenti in his book, *Inventing Reality,* and *Washington Post* reporter Morton Mintz in his book, P*ower, Inc.* Mintz quoted a Senate Select Committee on Intelligence Activities 1976 report that showed how the CIA promoted its own propaganda. It said a book written "by one CIA operative was reviewed favorably by another CIA agent in the *New York Times*."[69]

Dan Rather, one of the best-known media insiders, described the media's conservative censorship in stark terms. Rather's career included reporting for United Press International, working as the CBS Southern Bureau chief and then a position as anchorman on the *CBS Evening News* in 1981. He remained in that position until 2005. In 2002, the British Broadcasting Corporation interviewed Rather about the media's aid in the suppression of dissent in the United States. Rather said, "What you have here is a miniature version of what you have in totalitarian states."[70]

As detailed later, this kind of control over people's access to information would allow American rulers to manipulatively promote certain dangerous drugs. It would further hide the use of Nazis in various U.S. intelligence-related operations. And, it would influence people to fight wars to control other countries' drug crops, while leading people to believe they were fighting for freedom and democracy.

Notes

1 Alfred McCoy, *The Politics of Heroin: CIA Complicity in the Global Drug Trade* (New York: Lawrence Hill Books, 1972/1991), pp. 3, 20. McCoy started his investigation in 1971. As a 25-year-old Yale graduate student, McCoy traveled to the Vietnam area during the U.S. war there. On Sumerians, see PBS, "The Opium Kings: Opium Throughout History," *Frontline*, http://www.pbs.org/wgbh/pages/frontline/shows/heroin/etc/history.html.

2 Carl Trocki, *Opium, Empire and the Global Political Economy: A Study of the Asian Opium Trade 1750-1950 (Asia's Transformations)* (London: Routledge, 1999).

3 Peter Dale Scott, *Drugs, Oil and War: The United States in Afghanistan, Colombia and Indochina* (New York: Rowman and Littlefield, 2003), p. 27.

4 PBS, "The Opium Kings: Opium Throughout History," *Frontline*, http://www.pbs.org/wgbh/pages/frontline/shows/heroin/etc/history.html.

5 PBS, "The Opium Kings: Opium Throughout History," *Frontline*.

6 PBS, "The Opium Kings: Opium Throughout History," *Frontline*. McCoy, *The Politics of Heroin*, p. 4.

7 Clarence Lusane, *Pipe Dream Blues: Racism and the War on Drugs* (Boston: South End Press, 1999), pp. 28, 30.

8 Joyce Kolko and Gabriel Kolko, *The Limits of Power* (New York: Harper & Row, 1972), p. 157, cited in McCoy, *The Politics of Heroin*, pp. 85-86. For an early 20th century book that describes the China problem in even starker terms, see Samuel Merwin, *The Drugging of a Nation: The story of China and the opium curse; a personal investigation, during an extended tour, of the present conditions of the opium trade in China and its effects upon the nation* (New York: F.H. Revell, 1908), http://archive.org/details/druggingnationst00merwiala.

9 Maurice Agulhon and Barat Fernand, *C.R.S. Marseille* (Paris: Armand Colin, 1971), pp. 145-46, cited in McCoy, *The Politics of Heroin*, p. 86.

10 *La Marseillaise* (Marseille newspaper), November 13, 17, 21 and December 10, 1947; cited in McCoy, *The Politics of Heroin*, p. 88.

11 Jean-Louis Conne, "Maritime Business and the Opium Trade; HSBC: Chinese for Making Money," *Le Monde Diplomatique* (English edition), February, 2010. http://mondediplo.com/2010/02/04hsbc. McCoy, *The Politics of Heroin*, p. 263. HSBC second largest, 2014. http://www.relbanks.com/worlds-top-banks/assets. Regarding 27% of all adult males in China smoking opium: International Opium Commission, Report, vol. 2 pp. 44-66; U.S. Department of Commerce, Statistical Abstract 1915, p. 713. In McCoy, p. 88 n38.

12 McCoy, *The Politics of Heroin*, p. 495, "World Non-Medicinal Opium Production 1906-1989," Figures were compiled from several sources. International Opium Commission, Report of the International Opium Commission: Shanghai, China, February 1-26, 1909 (Shanghai: *North China Daily News*, 1909), p. 356; "Statistics of Trade in Opium: A. Import," League of Nations, Advisory Committee on the Traffic in Opium and Other Dangerous Drugs, Annual Reports of Governments on the Traffic in Opium and Other Dangerous Drugs for the year 1935, vol. 11 (Geneva: League of Nations, 1937), pp. 46-47; Average of two U.S. government agency estimates, U.S. Congress, Senate, Committee on Appropriations, Foreign Assistance and Related Programs Appropriations for Fiscal Year 1972, 92nd Cong. 2nd sess. (Washington, DC: U.S. Government Printing Office, 1971), pp. 578-84; U.S. Cabinet Committee on International Narcotics Control (CCINC), World Opium Survey 1972 (Washington, DC: CCINC, 1972), pp. 11, 138-39; U.S. State Department, Bureau of International Narcotics Matters, International Narcotics Control Strategy Report, March 1990 (Washington, DC: U.S. Government Printing Office, March, 1990), p. 19.

13 See history of Luddites and the workers' protests: http://www.victorianweb.org/history/riots/luddites.html.

14 Roberto Mangabeira Unger, *Free Trade Reimagined: The World Division of Labor and the Method of Economics* (Princeton, NJ: Princeton University Press, 2007). On Six Acts, police, and morphine, Patricia Hollis, *Class and conflict in nineteenth-century England, 1815-1850*, Birth of modern Britain series, International Library of Sociology and Social Reconstruction (London:

Routledge, 1973). Morphine was first extracted in 1805. It was first commercially produced by Merck Pharmaceutical company in Germany in 1827. McCoy, *The Politics of Heroin*, pp. 5-6.

15 Lusane, *Pipe Dream Blues*, p. 31. McCoy, *The Politics of Heroin*, p. 5.

16 Ray Raphael, *A People's History of the American Revolution* (New Press: 2012), p. 393. Paul H. Smith, "The American Loyalists: Notes on Their Organization and Numerical Strength," *William and Mary Quarterly*, Vol. 25, No. 2 (1968), pp. 259-77.

17 Lusane, *Pipe Dream Blues*, p. 28.

18 The Russells were amongst the dozen people who founded Yale University in the early 1700s. On intermarriage of Russells and Pierponts, see "Birth of Yale," *The Yale Standard*, March 3, 2012, http://www.yalestandard.com/histories/birth-of-yale/. Regarding the other families who smuggled opium, see PBS, "The Opium Kings: Opium Throughout History."

19 For $15,000, see Alexandra Robbins, *Secrets of the Tomb: Skull and Bones, the Ivy League, and the Hidden Paths of Power* (Boston: Little Brown, 2002). For inflation conversion, see the inflation calculator at http://www.westegg.com/inflation/infl.cgi. On Gilman, see "Daniel Coit Gilman, A Biography; Fabian Franklin Tells the Life Story of a Great Educational Organizer and Administrator," *New York Times*, May 21, 1910, http://query.nytimes.com/mem/archive-free/pdf?res=9F0CEFDA1530E23325752C2A9639C946196D6CF. On Cabot, see Francis Cabot Lowell (1775-1817) "Papers: Guide to the Collection," Massachusetts Historical Society. Also see, Robert Thomas Jr., "Thomas Cabot, 98, Capitalist and Philanthropist, is Dead," *New York Times*, June 10, 1995, http://www.nytimes.com/1995/06/10/obituaries/thomas-cabot-98-capitalist-and-philanthropist-is-dead.html?src=pm. Note that most Ivy League schools had similar clubs started by these wealthiest opium-trafficking families. It's unknown if they also set up beneficial trusts as the Russells did, but their families gained similar vast power in governmental affairs.

20 See *Encyclopedia Britannica* online: http://www.britannica.com/EBchecked/topic/263607/heroin.

21 This author's explanation of Piven and Cloward's "Dissensus Politics" comes from having Cloward as a professor for several classes as well as a one-on-one tutorial at Columbia University (1995-1998), and conducting a long personal interview with Frances Fox Piven (Spring, 1998). In 2000, they won an American Sociological Career Award for the Practice of Sociology. Piven was also President of the American Sociology Association, 2006-07.

22 On 1% statistic, see Harold Doweiko, *Concepts of Chemical Dependency* (New York: Brooks Cole, 8th Ed., 2011), p. 159. On 1903, see *Frontline*: "The opium kings: Opium throughout history," URL at note 4.

23 "One Hundred Years of Suffrage: An Overview," complied by E. Susan Barber, on National American Woman Suffrage Association Collection Home Page, http://memory.loc.gov/ammem/naw/nawstime.html.

24 Harold Doweiko, *Concepts of Chemical Dependency*, p. 159.

25 David F. Musto, *American Disease: Origins of Narcotic Control* (New Haven: Yale University Press, 1973), p. 5; Estimates among experts appear to differ somewhat. David T. Courtwright, *Dark Paradise: Opiate Addiction in America before 1940* (Cambridge: Harvard University Press, 1982), Chap. 1, "The Extent of Opiate Addiction," pp. 9-34. On abuse and addiction, this writer has worked in the field of addictions for over twenty years. The view is partly based on the psychiatric standard in the Diagnostic and Statistical Manual-IV, http://www.sis.indiana.edu/DSM-IV-Criteria.aspx.

26 On Pemberton and cocaine in original Coca-Cola, see SAMSHSA TIP 33: cites Coca-Cola Bottling of Shrevebport, Inc et al. vs. The Coca-Cola Company, a Delaware Corporation, 769 F. Supp. 671, www.neurosoup.com/addctions/history_of_cocaine_use.html. On addictive amount see www.aana.com/peerassist.aspx. On headache cure and stimulant, see http://www.washingtontimes.com/world/20040419-093635-4754r.html. Also see Michael R. Liebowitz, *The Chemistry of Love* (Boston: Little, Brown, & Co., 1983).

27 Jill Jonnes, *Hep-Cats, Narcs, and Pipe Dreams: A History of America's Romance with Illegal Drugs* (New York: Scribner, 1996), http://www.pbs.org/wgbh/pages/frontline/shows/drugs/buyers/socialhistory.html#ixzz1bY37bnwl. Foul play surrounded many aspects of Candler's

dealings with Coca-Cola. Researchers suggested that Candler's problems with Charley Pemberton resulted in Pemberton's early death not long after the sale.

28 Ben Bagdikian, *The Media Monopoly* (Boston: Beacon Press, 5th ed., 1997), p. 211.

29 David Musto, "The History of Legislative Control over Opium, Cocaine, and Their Derivatives," http://www.druglibrary.org/schaffer/history/ophs.htm. Goode, 2005, p. 97 from www.umsl.edu/~keelr/180/drughistory.html. On Harrison Act corrupted, doctors arrested, see Stephen Kandall, "Women and Addiction in the United States, 1850-1920," http://www.nida.nih.gov/PDF/DARHW/033-052_Kandall.pdf. Edward M. Brecher and the Editors of Consumer Reports Magazine, eds., *The Consumers Union Report on Licit and Illicit Drugs* (New York: Little Brown and Co.), 1973.

30 Bagdikian, *The Media Monopoly*, p. 211.

31 *New York Times*, February 14, 1917; Congressional Record of February 9, 1917, page 2947, as entered by Representative Oscar Callaway of Texas, http://query.nytimes.com/mem/archive-free/pdf?res=9504E7DA1538EE32A2575 7C1A9649C946696D6CF.

32 Martin Horn, "A Private Bank At War: J. P. Morgan & Co. and France, 1914-1918," *Business History Review* Vol. 74, No. 1 (2000), pp. 85-112. Roberta Allbert Dayer, "Strange Bedfellows: J. P. Morgan & Co., Whitehall and the Wilson Administration During World War I," *Business History* Vol.18, No. 2 (1976), pp. 127-51

33 David D. Cole, "Enemy Aliens," *Stanford Law Review* Vol. 54, No. 5 (2003), pp. 953-1004; doi:10.2307/1229690.

34 Robert D'Attilio, "Sacco-Vanzetti Case," *Encyclopedia of the American Left*, ed. Mari Jo Buhle, Paul Buhle and Dan Georgakas (Chicago: University of Illinois Press, 1992), pp. 667-70.

35 *Encyclopedia of the American Left*, p. 647. Ward Churchill and Jim Vander Wall, *Agents of Repression: The FBI's Secret Wars Against the Black Panther Party and the American Indian Movement* (Boston: South End, 1988), pp. 21-23.

36 *Encyclopedia of the American Left*, p. 648.

37 Richard M. Fried, *Nightmare in Red: The McCarthy Era in Perspective* (Oxford University Press, 1990).

38 See, for example, Victor Navasky, *Naming Names* (New York: River Run Press, 1991). On blacklisted musicians such as Pete Seeger, see www.writing.upenn.edu/~alfilreis/50s/seeger-bio-2.html.

39 Frances Stonor Saunders, *The Cultural Cold War: The CIA and the World of Arts and Letters* (New York: New Press, 2000), pp. 180-83, 291. The Rosenberg children's adopted father, Abel Meeropol, a folk musician, had written Billie Holiday's classic song "Strange Fruit," about rampant lynchings from trees in the South; http://www.law.umkc.edu/faulty/projects/ftrials/rosenb/ROS_BMER.HTM. Saunders's citations on Rosenbergs include Douglas Dillon to State Department, 5/15/53, (CJD/DDE). Charles Taquey to C.E. Johnson, Psychological Strategy Board, 3/29/53 (CJD/DDE), and C.D. Jackson to Herbert Brownell, 2/23/53 (CJD/DDE). On blacks and the arts, see C.D. Jackson to Nelson Rockefeller, 4/14/55 (CDJ/DDE). For evidence of taped sessions stating that U.S. intelligence fraudulently manufactured its key evidence against the Rosenbergs: Walter and Miriam Schneir, *Invitation to an Inquest* (New York: Doubleday, 1965), http://www.nbooks.com/articles/archives/1966/feb/03/the-strange-trial-of-the-rosenbergs/?pagination=false.

40 D'Attilio, "Sacco-Vanzetti Case," *Encyclopedia of the American Left* , pp. 667-70.

41 Paul Buhle, "The Red Scare," and Joyce R. Kornbluh, "Industrial Workers of the World," *Encyclopedia of the American Left*, pp. 357, 646-48. On Post Office Department denying second-class mailing to IWW, see "International News," *The Maoriland Worker*, Wednesday September 28, 1921, p. 4, http://paperspast.natlib.govt.nz/cgi-bin/paperspast?a=d&d=MW19210928.2.19.2.

42 Black's editors had nominated him for the Pulitzer Prize ten times. Edwin Black's parents escaped Nazis as teens and were "Partisans" fighting from the forests, along with many others. Edwin Black, "Introduction to the 1984 Edition," *The Transfer Agreement: The Dramatic Story of the Pact Between the Third Reich and Jewish Palestine* (Washington, DC: Dialog Press, 2009), p. xxii.

43 Edwin Black, *War Against the Weak: Eugenics and America's Campaign to Create a Master Race* (New York: Four Walls Eight Windows, 2003), pp. 75, 81-84, 103-04.

44 Edwin Black, *Nazi Nexus: America's Corporate Connections to Hitler's Holocaust* (Washington, DC: Dialog Press, 2009). Black, *War Against the Weak*, pp. 254-55. Black's sources include: Neal Black, *Animal Health: A Century of Progress*, Ch. 4; BBC, "Cattle TB Threatens Farmers," June 27, 2002; State of Illinois Board of Administration, *Volume II: Biennial Reports of the State Charitable Institutions: October 1, 1914 to September 30, 1916* (State of Illinois, 1917), p. 695; "Superintendent Leonard's Report to Board of Administration," *Institutional Quarterly* Vol. 7 (1916), pp.117-18. The director of this institution and others like it proudly referred to them as "slaughterhouses": Martin A. Elks, "The 'Lethal Chamber': Further Evidence for the Euthenasia Option," *Mental Retardation* Vol. 31, No. 4 (August 1993), p. 201.

45 "The New Format," *Eugenical News* Vol. XVII (1932), p. 16. Referenced in Black, *War Against the Weak*, p. 300 n81.

46 Black, *War Against the Weak*, p. 47. James Watson, known as co-discoverer of the DNA double helix, worked at Cold Spring Harbor from the mid-1900s to the new millennium. Reporters quoted him as making the erroneous, racist statement, "Blacks are genetically less intelligent." Black, *War Against the Weak*, p. 426; CNN, "Nobel Prize-Winning Biologist apologizes for remarks about blacks," October 19, 2007, http://www.cnn.com/2007/WORLD/europe/10/18/nobel.apology/.

47 That company's interlocking board of directors included: Edsel Ford of the U.S. and Carl Bosch of Ford Germany, along with Walter Teagle of Rockefeller's Standard Oil. Other directors included Jewish banker Paul Warburg of the Federal Reserve; *Moody's Manual of Investments* (1930), Anthony Sutton, *Wall Street Rise of Hitler* (GSG & Associates, 1976), Ch. 2; Edwin Black, *IBM and the Holocaust* (New York: Three Rivers Press, 2001), pp. 337, 420-21. On Ford, see Edwin Black, "GM and the Nazis: Part 4," http://www.whale.to/b/black_gm.html. Originally in Edwin Black, *Internal Combustion: How Corporations and Governments Addicted the World to Oil and Derailed the Alternatives* (New York: St. Martin's Press, 2006). On Black's meticulous peer review process, see http://h-net.msu.edu/cgi-bin/logbrowse.pl?trx=vx&list=h-holocaust&month=0202&week=b&msg=CLsUq0I7pif6wz7tL9MPRg&user=&pw=.

48 Ben Ari and Duncan Campbell, *The Guardian* (London), 9/25/04. Document citations found in Webster Tarpley and Anton Chaitkin, *George Bush: The Unauthorized Biography* (San Diego, CA: Progressive Press, 2004), pp. 2, 6-44, include "Office of Alien Property Custodian, Vesting Order No. 248." The order was signed by Leo T. Crowley, Alien Propert Custodian, executed 10/10/42; F.R. Doc. 42-11568; Filed 11/6/42; 7 Fed. Reg. 9097 (11/7/42). Fritz Thyssen, *I Paid Hitler*, 1941, reprinted (Port Washington, NY: Kennikat Press, 1972), p. 133. Thyssen said that his contributions began with 100,000 marks given in October 1923 for Hitler's attempted "putsch" against the constitutional government. On Brown Brothers Harriman and Montagu Norman, see Andrew Boyle, *Montagu Norman* (London: Cassell, 1967); Sir Henry Clay, *Lord Norman* (London: McMillan & Co., 1957), pp. 18, 57, 70-71; John A. Kouwenhouven, *Partners in Banking ... Brown Brothers Harriman* (Garden City, NY: Doubleday & Co., 1969).

49 Most of this material is in both Ari and Campbell, *The Guardian* (London), 9/25/04 and Tarpley and Chaitkin, *George Bush*, pp. 26-44. On Morgan Chase Bank aid of Nazis, see Tim Reid, "Files Show CIA Gave Jobs to Nazi Criminals," *The Times* (London), 5/14/04, reprinted at http://blog.zmag.org/rocinante/archives/000392.html. Note on Henry Ford from James Pool and Suzanne Pool, *Who Financed Hitler?* (New York: Dial Press, 1978), Ch. 3, as cited in Jonathan Vankin, *Conspiracies, Cover-ups and Crimes* (New York: Dell, 1992), p. 292. Tarpley and Chaitkin include a picture of the Library of Congress/Law Department's copy of the U.S. government WWII "vesting order" #248, seizing the Union Banking Corporation as a front for Fritz Thyssen and his Nazi Steel Trust, see pictures between pp. 114-15.

50 Edwin Black, *IBM and the Holocaust* (New York: Three Rivers Press, 2001). On 300 concentration camps, see *Memories of the Camps*, aired originally on *Frontline*, PBS, 1985. Originally edited partly by Alfred Hitchcock, after footage taken in 1945 by filmmakers who accompanied the troops when they liberated the concentration camps.

51 A U.S. Senate investigating committee found that the Nazis admitted that they couldn't have taken over other countries without this performance-boosting gasoline additive. Edwin Black,

Internal Combustion: How Corporations and Governments Addicted the World to Oil and Derailed the Alternatives (New York: St. Martin's Press, 2006). General Motors "humanitarian" efforts continued long after the war. GM led a criminal conspiracy to monopolize and undermine mass transit in dozens of American cities; sixteen months after the end of World War II, FBI Director J. Edgar Hoover got a memo outlining GM's work to develop shadow company National City Lines in 1937.

As suggested by a theme in the 1980s movie *Who Framed Roger Rabbit*, General Motors helped create the front company National City Lines, with five uneducated bus drivers, the Fitzgerald brothers, owning it. General Motors led Mack Truck, Phillips Petroleum, Standard Oil of California and Firestone Tires in operating behind the scenes as major preferred stockholders of National City Lines. The company bought trolley car systems in more than sixteen states and pulled the tracks from the streets. They then trashed or burned the cars and replaced them with more expensive and environmentally-hazardous motor buses.

52 Susan Dunn, "When Partisans Became Partners," *New York Times*, 12/1/12; http://www.nytimes.com/2012/12/02/opinion/sunday/can-bipartisanship-work-it-did-in-1940.html.

53 Sean L. Malloy, *Atomic Tragedy: Henry L. Stimson and the Decision to Use the Bomb Against Japan* (Ithaca, NY: Cornell University Press, 2010).

54 Alexandra Robbins, *Secrets of the Tomb: Skull and Bones, the Ivy League, and the Hidden Paths of Power* (Boston: Little, Brown, 2002). John Bonnett, "Jekyll and Hyde: Henry L. Stimson, Mentalite, and the Decision to Use the Atomic Bomb on Japan," *War in History* Vol. 4, No. 2 (1997), pp. 174-212. *Washington Blog*, "The Real Reason America Used Nuclear Weapons Against Japan (It Was Not to End the War or Save Lives)," October 14, 2012. This article gives quotes and sources of most of the top military leaders from that time period: http://www.washingtonsblog.com/2012/10/the-real-reason-america-used-nuclear-weapons-against-japan-to-contain-russian-ambitions.html.

55 ABC News.com, "State Secret: Thousands Secretly Sterilized: N.C. Woman Among 65,000 Sterilized by Gov't, Often Without Their Knowledge, in 20th Century," 5/15/05. ABC News' Keith Garvin originally reported this story for *World News Tonight* on 4/23/05: http://abcnews.go.com/WNT/.

56 Saunders, *The Cultural Cold War*, pp. 34-35.

57 Tarpley and Chaitkin, *Bush*, pp. 15, 31, 66-7. The authors cite the following references in the endnotes for those pages: On Lovett and BBH, see Kouwenhouven, *Partners in Banking*. On Prescott Bush's father Sam on War Industries Board helping Rockefellers, see Gen. Hugh S. Johnson to Major J.H.K. Davis, 6/6/18, file no. 334.8/168 or 338.451 in U.S. National Archives, Suitland, MD. On Prescott and U.S. intelligence, in 1962 he founded a National Strategy Information Center with future CIA Director William Casey, "that got into trouble for financing publications issued by a CIA front company engaged in disinformation campaigns"; reference Bob Callahan, "Agents for Bush," *Covert Action Information Bulletin*, #33, in Jon Vankin, *Conspiracies, Cover-ups and Crimes* (New York: Dell, 1992), pp. 232, 348.

58 Victor Marchetti and John D. Marks, *The CIA and the Cult of Intelligence*, pp. 44-46, 266-69, 315. British magazine editor Frances Stoner Saunders, also backs this claim: Saunders, *The Cultural Cold War*, pp. 41, 142-45.

59 Book review of *U.S. Intelligence and the Nazis*: Thom J. Rose, "Files Show Nazi Criminals' U.S. Intel Role," *United Press International*, 5/13/04. Tim Reid, "Files Show CIA Gave Jobs to Nazi Criminals," *The Times* (London), 5/14/04, Overseas News, p. 20. Elizabeth Olson, "Documents Show U.S. Relationship with Nazis During Cold War," *New York Times*, 5/13/04, p. 5. Sarah Helm, "MI6 Protected Nazi Who Killed 100 British Agents," *The Times* (London), 5/14/05, www.timesonline.co.uk.

60 Christopher Simpson, *Blowback: The First Full Account of America's Recruitment of Nazis, and Its Disastrous Effect on Our Domestic and Foreign Policy* (New York: Weidenfeld and Nicolson, 1988). Simpson was also a visiting scholar at the Institute for Policy Studies and research director for famed French film director Marcel Ophuls's film on Nazi Klaus Barbie. On Paperclip and similar coded operations, see pp. 35-36, 38-39, 73. On recruits as ex-SS, p. xv. On Lovett and Dulles, pp. 4, 8,

92-93, 100, 104. On U.S., Europe, Latin American and Middle East, see, for example, Italy pp. 88-94; Egypt/Middle East, pp. 244, 248, 260; Latin America, pp. 179-80, 186, 189, 194.

61 Note that one of Loftus's books making some of these claims was nominated for a Pulitzer Prize: John Loftus, *The Belarus Secret* (New York: Knopf, 1982). Loftus later published a fuller, uncensored version of this book, when his security obligation of non-disclosure had expired, as *America's Nazi Secret* (Walterville, OR: TrineDay, 2010). Also, *Publishers Weekly* noted that Loftus and co-author Mark Aarons interviewed some 500 former intelligence officers of various nationalities for *The Secret War Against the Jews: How Western Espionage Betrayed the Jewish People* (New York: St. Martin's Griffin, 1997). The authors included 115 pages of references.

During his investigations of the post WWII Justice Department, John Loftus also found that a circle of elite families, mostly in the U.S. but also in England, actually had bankrolled the Nazis from their inception. In *The Secret War Against the Jews,* Loftus noted that these elite families included the Rockefellers, Harrimans, and Bushes, and they worked with the German industrialist Fritz Thyssen, whose memoir was *I Paid Hitler* (reprint Port Washington, NY: Kennikat Press, 1972). Loftus said the financiers took advantage of the fact that WWI impoverished Germany, which allowed them to pay for vast propaganda and a mercenary army of Brownshirts for Hitler. See John Loftus and Mark Aarons, *The Secret War Against the Jews* (New York: St. Martin's Press, 1994) and Thyssen, *I Paid Hitler,* p. 133.

62 National Security Council Directive, 10 July 1950, quoted in *Final Report of the Select Committee to Study Governmental Operations with Respect to Intelligence Activities* (Washington: United States Government Printing Office, 1976). Cited in Saunders, *The Cultural Cold War,* p. 4, nn. 5, 6.

63 Saunders, *The Cultural Cold War,* p. 41. Also see Lisa Pease, "The Media and the Assassination," in eds. James Di Eugenio and Lisa Pease, *The Assassinations: Probe Magazine on JFK, MLK, RFK, and Malcolm X* (Los Angeles: Feral House, 2003), p. 300. On Wisner's "Wurlitzer," Joseph Crewden, "Worldwide Propaganda Network Built by the CIA," *New York Times,* 12/26/77, p. 1.

64 Carl Bernstein, "The CIA & the Media," *Rolling Stone,* October 20, 1977. On more than 400, see p. 55. On virtually all leading media companies, p. 56. On Senate Intelligence Committee forcing the disclosure, p. 65. On "far" more than 400, see CIA "officials most knowledgeable about the subject say that figure of 400 American journalists in on the low side," p. 66. On "living double lives," see one-time CIA Deputy Director William Bader and others saying "reporters had been involved in almost every conceivable operation," p. 66. On reprinting CIA-written story under another name, see example of Cy Sulzberger, p. 59. On some first worked for media, some CIA, p. 63. On work as "covert operations" vs. "foreign intelligence," p. 66. On CIA spy work on Americans locally, see Seymour Hersh, "Huge C.I.A. Operation Reported in U.S. Against Antiwar Forces, Other Dissidents in Nixon Years," *New York Times,* 12/22/74, p. A1. On blacks, Seymour Hersh, "CIA Reportedly Recruited Blacks for Surveillance of Panther Party," *New York Times,* March 17, 1978, p. A1, A16, quoted in Huey P. Newton, *War Against the Panthers* (New York: Harlem River Press/Writers and Readers Publishing, 1996), p. 90.

65 On McGehee, a former 25-year CIA operative, he obtained documents from 1991 through the Freedom Of Information Act (FOIA) in which the CIA's Public Affairs Office (PAO) said, "PAO now has relationships with reporters from every major wire service, newspaper, news weekly, and television network in the nation. This has helped turn some 'intelligence failure' stories into 'intelligence success' stories ... In many instances, we have persuaded reporters to postpone, change, hold, or even scrap stories," from Lisa Pease, "The Media and the Assassination," in *The Assassinations,* p. 311.

66 Bagdikian, *The Media Monopoly,* pp. 210-11. This was also noted in the film *America: Freedom to Fascism* (2006) by the director of the hit comedy *Trading Places* (1983), Aaron Russo. Russo was diagnosed with cancer and died young, after refusing one of the Rockefeller's attempts to "coopt" him by asking him to join the Council on Foreign Relations.

67 Bagdikian, *The Media Monopoly,* pp. ix, 24-25. Other researchers have elaborated on how the top corporations control the general political state of the nation, partly through their dominance

in the National Association of Manufacturers. For example, see an essay by Alex Carey, "Managing Public Opinion: The Corporate Offensive" (University of New South Wales, 1986, mimeographed), pp. 1-2. This essay had also been referenced in Noam Chomsky and Edward Herman, *Manufacturing Consent: The Political Economy of the Mass Media* (New York: Pantheon Books, 1988), p. 342n. Bagdikian cited a 1979 study by Peter Dreier and Steven Weinberg that listed the *New York Times* interlocked Board of Directors as including Merck, Morgan Guaranty Trust, Bristol Meyers, Charter Oil, Johns Manville, American Express, Bethlehem Steel, IBM, Scott Paper, Sun Oil, and First Boston Corporation. Time, Inc. (before becoming Time Warner) "had so many interlocks it almost represented a Plenary Board of directors of American business and finance, including Mobil Oil, AT&T, American Express, Firestone Tire and Rubber Company, Mellon National Corporation, Atlantic Richfield, Xerox, General Dynamics, and most of the major international banks. It's interesting to note that Bagdikian did not set out to find this information. During a sabbatical to study the media industry, Bagdikian set out to research another topic before he found out about the ever-consolidating media ownership.

68 "DOD Kills 205 Periodicals; Still Publishes 1,203 Others," *Armed Forces Journal International*, August 1982, p. 16, in Chomsky and Herman, *Manufacturing Consent*, p. 20.

69 On first Senate intelligence report quote, Michael Parenti, *Inventing Reality: The Politics of the Mass Media*, (New York: St. Martins Press, 1986), p. 233. This information is also referenced in Morton Mintz and Jerry Cohen, *Power Inc.* (New York: Bantam Books, 1976), p. 364. On the *Times* exposé, Joseph Crewden, "Worldwide Propaganda Network Built by the CIA," *New York Times*, December 25, 26, 27, 1977. On CIA agents in *New York Times* reviewing CIA books, see Senate Select Committee on Intelligence Activities, *Final Report*, April 1976, cited in Mintz and Cohen, *Power, Inc.*, p. 364. Also see *Columbia Journalism Review*, July/August 1976, pp. 36-37 and David Wise and Thomas Ross, *The Invisible Government* (New York: Bantam, 1965), pp. 134-35, 267; both cited in Parenti, *Inventing Reality*, p. 233, n. 28.

70 A clip of Dan Rather saying this was included in *Why We Fight* (Sony, 2005), director Eugene Jarecki. This film won the Grand Jury Prize for documentary at the Sundance Film Festival. Rather's quote was reprinted at www.mediaresearch.org/cyberalerts/2002/cyb20020517_extra.asp.

Albert Hoffman and Gordon Wasson

Chapter Two

How the CIA Used LSD as a Weapon

Seventy-six LSD subjects (24% of 320) reported one or more long-term adverse reactions to LSD exposure (Table 6) (US Army 1980). All complaints from subjects were reported as "adverse effects" even though these events had occurred on average 19 years earlier.

– US Army Medical Department, US Army Health Services Command, Project Director LTC David A. McFarling, MC. "LSD Follow-up Study Report, October 1980."[1]

Project MK-Ultra was the CIA's umbrella name for at least several projects that used psychedelic drugs against the enemies of the American ruling oligarchy. This was revealed by Martin Lee and Bruce Shlain, who interviewed hundreds of people and read thousands of declassified government documents, books and articles for their book *Acid Dreams, The Complete Social History of LSD: The CIA, the Sixties and Beyond.* Although CIA Director Richard Helms destroyed all of the CIA's MK-Ultra files in 1973, he missed the financial department's files. It is those files and other source material that provided Lee, Shlain and other researchers with information on the project.[2]

One such researcher, Professor Alfred McCoy, the author of *The Politics of Heroin,* later wrote about the CIA projects that led up to MK-Ultra. In his book, *A Question of Torture,* McCoy wrote that Dr. Kurt Plotner and other Nazi scientists tested mescaline on concentration camp prisoners during World War II. The *New York Times* wrote that the U.S. Justice Department printed a 600-page secret report in 2006 about the U.S. government's operations saving Plotner and thousands of other Nazis.

Writers such as retired Air Force colonel Walter Boyne, a former director of Washington's Air and Space Museum, wrote an *Air Force Magazine* article about "Project Paperclip" (better known as Operation Paperclip) that saved at least 700 Nazi scientists. The Joint Chiefs of Staff started these operations in 1945, and the CIA continued them, saving what was originally estimated as "10,000 Nazis" from various professions, though the Justice Department report found a somewhat lower number of Nazis saved. The operations gave these Nazis employment with the U.S. government, ostensibly to fight Communism during the Cold War.[3]

Hank Albarelli Jr., a veteran journalist who also had served in President Jimmy Carter's administration, wrote several articles as well as a book about Operation Paperclip and MK-Ultra, exposing the fact that the Operation transferred over 1,600 Nazi scientists to the U.S. to work in the former eugenics office, known as Cold Spring Harbor Laboratory, as well as in the Brookhaven nuclear laboratory and on Plum Island, the site of biological weapons experiments. Nazi scientists brought with them their research on psychedelics into offices shared with CIA scientists. They also regularly met with Swiss Sandoz scientist Albert Hoffman.[4]

The many inhumane exploits of these Nazi scientists who later worked in MK-Ultra programs are well known. CIA-employed Nazi scientist Herbert Gerstner had programmatically killed German children.[5] America's "father of space medicine," Hubertus Strughold, tested psychedelics on concentration camp victims at Dachau, and he conducted experiments that involved shooting victims, injecting them with gasoline, crushing them to death, and freezing them to death in ice water.[6]

In 1938, Albert Hoffman created Lysergic acid diethylamide (LSD) while working for a Swiss company, Sandoz, a subsidiary of the Nazi I.G. Farben cartel. The Swiss pharmaceutical industry had previously handled much of the European opium traffic. Sandoz then supplied LSD to Nazi doctor Joseph Mengele who first experimented with it on concentration camp victims.[7]

In 1943, Albert Hoffman tried his first experiment with LSD on unwitting patients at a Swiss hospital; he then experimented on university students and laboratory workers. At least one of them committed suicide by jumping from a high window. A later Independent Commission of Experts in Switzerland found that Sandoz, as well as the Swiss pharmaceutical company Ciba, acted in collaboration with I.G. Farben in Nazi atrocities. During WWII, Farben fired all the Jews employed in its companies and replaced them with Nazi supporters. They also collaborated on the manufacturing of Zyklon B and other lethal gasses used in concentration camps.[8]

Gordon Wasson, who had been working as a vice-president of J.P. Morgan and Company, reported that he and several scientists began working for the CIA several years after it had formed.[9] Wasson traveled the world with CIA scientists in search of poisonous and psychedelic mushrooms that they gathered and sent to Albert Hoffman at Sandoz.[10] In the late 1950s, Wasson published an article in *Life* magazine promoting psychedelic mushrooms.[11]

CIA-employed American and former Nazi scientists started Operation Bluebird, which used drugs, electroshock, hypnosis and psychosurgery to control people during interrogation. Dr. Charles Savage headed this program at the Naval Medical Research Institute in Bethesda, Md.

The U.S. Army made former Nazi Friedrich Hoffman (no relation to Albert) the "Chief of Agents" (drugs) at Maryland's Edgewood Chemical Arsenal, where seven other former Nazi scientists also worked. Hoffman, Dr. Savage and fellow scientists gave LSD to unknowing soldiers at Edgewood in the 1950s. They then coupled the LSD with other techniques in a project called Artichoke. Their experiments included keeping prisoners, who were drug-treatment patients in Lexington, Kentucky, tripping for 77 days straight.[12]

The U.S. Army also worked with the CIA in running similar experiments in their Chemical Warfare Laboratories, sharing their research with British and Canadian scientists. The CIA claimed they researched LSD because of an unverified report that the Soviet Union had bought up the world supply.[13] However, only three months before, CIA Director Helms had said the Soviets were five years behind the U.S. in LSD research.[14]

Similarly, a group of conservative politicians formed the Committee on the Present Danger and propagandized the myth of Soviet technical superiority in nuclear weapons. They warned of imminent danger from a Soviet Union nuclear attack. In reality, the Soviet Union developed nuclear arms years after the U.S. The Soviet arsenal never came close in size to America's. The CIA also falsely claimed the Russians might put LSD in the U.S. water supply. In fact, it was the CIA that researched and successfully found a way to make LSD work in a water supply.[15]

MK-Ultra Widens Use of LSD & Other Drug Weapons

Within several years, the CIA combined many of its mind-altering drug programs under the title MK-Ultra. At the time, future CIA Director Richard Helms was an assistant deputy, in charge of covert operations, and supervised Dr. Sidney Gottlieb, who ran the program. Gottlieb had worked on other projects that obtained substances from the U.S. Army Special Operations, and he continued to direct the testing of LSD and other substances as potential incapacitants, and for the purpose of assassination. Two other areas of MK-Ultra focus included cancer-causing compounds and radiation warfare, the latter of which was almost completely blacked out of CIA documents.[16]

The CIA put LSD in the drinks of thousands of unsuspecting people from the 1950s onwards. Jonathan Marks, Director of the Bureau of Intelligence and Research at the U.S. State Department, described how the CIA started dosing individuals in 1952.[17] The CIA leaders came from some of the wealthiest families, and they considered leftists their political opponents. The CIA eventually would develop a hit list of leftist leaders to dose, damage and discredit (presumably with an extremely large amount of LSD at one time). Marks stated that the involuntary dosing with LSD caused one Argentine leftist professor, an early victim, to act in highly irrational ways that discredited him for several years.[18] As will be discussed in more detail, one of the largest populations of saved Nazis was in Argentina.

Syracuse University math professor William A. Pierce was targeted by the CIA's MK-Ultra for speaking out against the McCarthy era purging of leftist academics. Pierce's Math Department chair fired two members of his department for alleged activities in "controversial" political groups. Pierce said he was considered a "left-winger," due "partly to my membership in peace groups and opposition to the Cold War, but it was primarily my criticism of FBI investigations." The House Un-American Activities Committee investigated Professor Pierce. Pierce moved to Oklahoma State University, where he published a letter criticizing unreasonable psychiatric hospitalizations. A few days later, a police officer and sheriff's deputy arrested Pierce for false reasons, involuntarily committed Pierce, and placed him under the care of influential MK-Ultra doctor Louis Joylin West. Pierce would never teach again.[19]

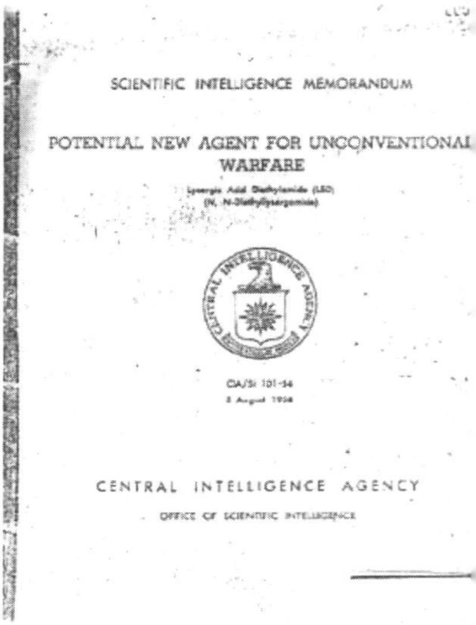
SCIENTIFIC INTELLIGENCE MEMORANDUM

POTENTIAL NEW AGENT FOR UNCONVENTIONAL WARFARE

CENTRAL INTELLIGENCE AGENCY

Around 1950 the CIA began a number of program merged under the title MK-Ultra, using drugs as "un conventional weapons." The drug used most frequent was LSD.

By 1953 the CIA had ordered 10 kilos of LSD from Sandoz for $240,000. Having already tested LSD many times since 1949, the CIA knew this supply offered one hundred million doses. The CIA asked the Eli Lilly pharmaceutical company to try to synthesize LSD. By mid-1954, Eli Lilly broke Sandoz's formula and assured the CIA that in a matter of months LSD would be available in tonnage quantities.[20]

U.S. intelligence superspy Captain Alfred Hubbard served with the CIA-forerunner Office of Strategic Services (OSS). Hubbard worked with British psychiatrist Humphrey Osmond in experiments with LSD and mescaline on patients in Canada, even though Hubbard had no medical or scientific credentials.[21] By 1953, psychiatrists had begun using LSD across North America, utilizing low doses on patients in special mental health treatment centers. Soon, similar LSD centers sprung up in Germany, Holland, France, Italy, Czechoslovakia and some Scandinavian countries.[22]

Dr. Osmond used large doses of LSD on patients at Weyburn Hospital in Canada, reportedly to cure their alcoholism. Hubbard opened three treatment centers in Canada for the same purpose. The centers claimed a 50% success rate and began using "high dose" treatment with LSD in the U.S. Whether their 50% success rate was true or not (later medical reviews said it wasn't), Hubbard and Osmond had other plans with LSD, or "acid." They said they wanted to transform the belief systems of world leaders to "further the cause of world peace." Their actual goal appeared the same as their U.S. intelligence employer's—to damage leftist leaders' minds and increase American rulers' global dominance.[23]

Dr. Humphrey Osmond coined the term "psychedelic," meaning "mind-manifesting." Osmond's work to popularize acid led him to enlist *Brave New World* author Aldous Huxley as a proponent of psychedelics. *Brave New World,* published in 1932, was listed by many literary organizations as one of the most important novels of the century. Osmond first gave mescaline to Huxley in May of 1953. Huxley wrote about the experience in *The Doors of Perception*. Osmond continued his LSD experiments at Princeton University.[24]

While Huxley worked on another book, Hubbard supplied him with his second mescaline trip, before introducing LSD later in the year. Captain Hubbard impressed Huxley with his connections to the top echelons of American business and government, which Huxley believed was due partly to Hubbard's fortune made as a uranium entrepreneur.[25] Huxley promoted psychedelics in his last books, despite the themes of *Brave New World,* which warned of rulers keeping people content with their lot through the use of escapist drugs.

LSD, MDA & Murders of Whistleblower, Tennis Star

In the early 1950s, a push began for mental hygiene departments that were closely intertwined with eugenics. William Welch, a founding leader of the Committee of Mental Hygiene, was also chairman of the Eugenics Record Office board of scientific directors, and scientific director for top eugenics funder John D. Rockefeller.[26] This movement enabled Dr. Sidney Gottlieb to run MK-Ultra psychedelics experiments through contracts with many institutions. It began with jails, but soon included drug treatment agencies and mental institutions. The directors of the National Institute of Mental Health and the National Institutes of Health used their agencies to help channel funds to these institutions for the known purpose of testing drugs on subjects.

By 1953, in what appeared to be purposeful targeting, MK-Ultra doctors started damaging more prominent people with their MK-Ultra drugs. After a divorce in that year, Harold Blauer, a once-highly-seeded, 42 year-old, Jewish professional tennis player, went inpatient for depression. Despite progress he made in talk therapy, doctors at the Rockefeller-funded New York State Psychiatric Institute ordered MDA for him as part of a military experiment on him without his knowledge. MDA (code name EA 1298) is an ecstasy pre-curser drug, and the Army Chemical Corps, stationed at Maryland's Edgewood Arsenal, supplied it. Dr. Paul Hoch, a member of the still-extant Eugenics Society, and Blauer's hospital physician, ordered the drug, well aware it would damage Blauer, as Hoch had previously published a paper on that very subject. When Blauer had a bad reaction and attempted to refuse a fourth injection of the drugs, Dr. Hoch ignored him. A fifth injection of the drugs killed Blauer.[27] It should be remembered that eugenics deemed 70% of Jews deserving death.[28]

Dr. Hoch worked for the Army and as a CIA consultant. He gave LSD to psychiatric patients and then lobotomized them to compare the effects of acid before and after the surgery. In one experiment a patient was given a local anesthetic and told to describe what he saw as the doctor removed chunks of his cerebral cortex. Hoch is quoted as saying, "It is possible that a certain amount of brain damage is of therapeutic value." In 1955 Hoch became New York State Commissioner of Mental Hygiene.[29]

Two years earlier, in 1953, Dr. Sidney Gottlieb used LSD as a weapon on an important CIA scientist named Frank Olson. Olson headed key biological warfare experiments at Camp Detrick (now Fort Detrick) in Maryland. U.S. intelligence considered Olson a serious security risk after he began telling people close to him that he wanted to leave the CIA. Olson had helped guide Air Force testing of anthrax-like spores on people in Antigua and Alaska. Less dangerous spores were tested in San Francisco and many other cities. The family of one man claimed these spores caused their father's death in a case that was taken to the Supreme Court.[30]

U.S. intelligence first interrogated Olson in 1949, but had darker plans for him by 1953. Those closest to Olson reported he became very disturbed about the Air Force's use of biological weapons he had worked upon in the Korean War from 1950-53.[31] Olson also voiced strong misgivings about taking part in some of the early MK-Ultra experiments in Germany where he had joined other CIA and Nazi scientists, including concentration camp experimenters, in interrogating agents from the Soviet Union and East Germany. These interrogations involved the use of LSD and other drugs. They also involved fatal torture. Olson's close friend and former military scientist colleague, Norman Courneyer, said Olson returned from that trip to Germany very distraught. In a documentary film, *Code Name Artichoke,* Courneyer relates that, in 1953, Olson told him that witnessing people tortured to death led him to prepare to resign from his CIA post.[32]

Hank Albarelli wrote an 800-page book on Frank Olson's murder at the hands of the CIA. Alabarelli conducted hundreds of personal interviews and sifted through decades of government documents. Albarelli's book, *A Terrible Mistake,* presented overwhelming evidence that the highest levels of the CIA wanted to silence Olson. They not only wanted to stop him from speaking out on the operations cited above but also, and more particularly, for his exposing of Project SPAN, an operation involved in the 1951 aerosol spraying of LSD on the town of Pont-St. Esprit, France, which resulted in several deaths and many injuries.[33]

Two CIA sources, among others, confirmed to Albarelli that MK-Ultra Director Sidney Gottlieb targeted Frank Olson with LSD and another interrogation drug at a retreat near Camp Detrick on November 19, 1953. After the interrogation, Olson remained highly confused and disturbed.[34] The CIA then sent Olson to New York to see a Columbia University professor, Harold Abramson, MD. Abramson was also a major in the Army, working as a part-time consultant for the Army Chemical Corps as part of Operation Artichoke, which officially became part of MK-Ultra in April of 1953.[35]

On November 28, nine days after his interrogation, Frank Olson fell from a 10th floor room of the Statler Hotel in New York. A CIA agent was found in his room moments later. Albarelli's book and the film *Code Name Artichoke* present overwhelming evidence that CIA agents threw Olson out of that window. According to notable forensic doctors, Olson suffered blunt trauma to the head that killed him before he was thrown from the window.

Also of interest, Francois Spirito and longtime CIA spy Pierre Lafitte were the last people with Olson just before his death. MK-Ultra Deputy Director Robert Lashbrook left Olson with Spirito and Lafitte at the end of the night. They escorted Olson up to his room, shortly before Olson came falling out the tenth floor window. Award-winning journalist Sally Denton and former National Security Council staff member Roger Morris found that Pierre Lafitte also played a major role in the opium-trafficking network that included Meyer Lansky and in which the CIA "ultimately colluded."[36]

During his time off from Columbia University, Dr. Abramson ran MK-Ultra experiments at Cold Spring Harbor Laboratory on Long Island in New York.[37] Did research at this location, formerly the official eugenics headquarters, continue where it had left off, using more sophisticated tactics in the targeting of groups the oligarchs and CIA considered undesirable? According to Hank Albarelli: "Abramson, throughout the 1950s, was well known in select circles for staging almost weekly LSD sorties at his Long Island estate. The gatherings were said to be so popular that guests had to be turned away."[38] MK-Ultra agents appeared to duplicate Abramson's model in the 1960s.

Canadian Doctor Uses LSD for Torture

Dr. Ewen Cameron, an important Canadian academic working with LSD, had headed the Canadian, American, and the World Psychiatric Associations before his death. While working at McGill University, Cameron administered LSD in frequent doses and delivered massive electroshock treatment in conjunction with repeatedly playing tape-recorded messages to "depattern" and then recondition people he diagnosed with schizophrenia. Cameron also injected LSD into patients with depression and put them through electroshock treatment, many times at far higher doses than was standard.[39]

Dr. Cameron's methods were later discredited, and nine of his subjects sued the American government for a million dollars each when it was learned that Cameron had been working with the CIA's MK-Ultra program. Plaintiffs said they never agreed to participate in Cameron's scientific experiments and still suffered from the trauma up into the 1990s.[40] The CIA settled out of court for substantial amounts of money.

One of Cameron's victims was the wife of a prominent Jewish leftist politician, David Orlikow. After Orlikow's wife, Val, gave birth to their daughter, she suffered from postpartum depression. The *Winnipeg Free Press* described what happened next. "She was sent to Montreal for several treatment stints, totaling three years, under the care of psychiatrist Ewen Cameron. She was made an unwitting guinea pig in secret brainwashing experiments financed by the CIA that used frequent shock treatments at far stronger than standard levels. She was the subject of 14 experiments with LSD ... the damage to her mind was permanent."[41]

Dr. Cameron had also been a member of the Nuremberg Tribunal (1945-1948) that passed judgment on Nazi war criminals. To many, the Nuremberg "trials" appeared a sham, at least in part. For example, Mary M. Kaufman prosecuted the case against I.G. Farben, which ran murderous experiments on prisoners at the Auschwitz concentration camp. Kaufman said, "We were hampered by the [U.S.] State Department throughout." She also said she was shocked to find one I.G. Farben defendant out of jail. The defendant told her: "The judge let me out so I could go over some evidence." She said, "What he had done, in fact, was to go with an assistant to the place where the I.G. Farben files were kept and indicate which files should be destroyed. Which was promptly done! The judges ... were motivated by a tremendous anti-Semitism ... [and] getting their hands on German real estate."[42]

The Nuremberg Tribunal heard the cases against Nazi war criminals and set the International Code of Ethics, including an international ban on torture. Yet, the U.S. subsequently allowed the CIA and other intelligence agencies to act outside of the Code. Many Nuremberg defendants got off easy or completely, despite what Kaufman described as a mass of evidence against them. I.G. Farben's Director, Otto Ambrose, received an eight-year sentence. U.S. intelligence, under Operation Paperclip, commuted it to three. Upon release, Ambrose was hired by major American chemical company W.R. Grace.[43]

Table 1. Common Pharmaceutical Agents, Close Analogs, and Simulant or Control Agents Used in the Edgwood/Aberdeen Experiments.[1]

Agent/Simulant Name	*Agent Class*
Antipyrine	Analgesic (PDR[2], Auralgan)
Atropine (methylnitrate, sulfate salts)	Anticholinergic (PDR, Lomotil)
Banthi (Banthine bromide, Methantheline bromide)	Anticholinergic (drug not available in the US)
Benzetimide	Anticholinergic
Dibutoline	Anticholinergic
Methscopolamine (bromide salt)	Anticholinergic (PDR)
Methylatropine	Anticholinergic
Scopolamine (hydrobromide)	Anticholinergic (PDR)
THA (Tetra Hydro Amino Acrodim) (Tacrine)	Anticholinergic (PDR)
5-HTP (5-Hydroxytryptophane)	Antidepressant
Regitine (Phentolamine)	Antihypertensive
Prolixin	Antipsychotic (PDR, as Fluphenazine)
Thorazine	Antipsychotic (PDR)
Adrenaline (epinephrine)	Bronchodilator (PDR)
Methacholine (mecholyl)	Cholinergic
Mylaxen (Hexafluronium bromide)	Cholinergic
Pilocarpine	Cholinergic (PDR)
Prostigmine (Neostigmine)	Cholinergic (PDR)
Succinylcholine	Cholinergic (PDR)
Urecholine	Cholinergic (PDR)
2-PAM Chloride	Cholinesterase Reactivator
Amyl Nitrate	Cyanide Antidote
Fluorescein	Dye
Indo-Cardio-Green Dye (Indocyanine Green)	Dye
Ammonium Chloride	Salt
Saline	Salt
Sodium Bicarbonate (NaHCO3)	Salt
Alcohol (ethanol)	Sedative
Amobarbital (Amytal)	Sedative
Chloral Hydrate	Sedative
Meprobamate	Sedative (PDR)
Nembutal	Sedative (PDR)
Secobarbital Sodium	Sedative
Seconal	Sedative
Valium (Diazepam)	Sedative (PDR)
Caffeine	Stimulant
Dexedrine	Stimulant (PDR)
Ritalin	Stimulant (PDR)
MDA (methylenedioxyamphetamine)	Stimulant, incapacitating agent
Niacinamide (Niacin, Vitamin B3)	Vitamin
Thiamine (HCl) (Vitamin B12)	Vitamin

[1]Data provided by Department of Defense, Health Affairs, Deployment Health Directorate, 2006.
[2]PDR – listed in the Physicians Desk Reference, Medical Economics Company, Inc.

Under the auspices of MK-Ultra and linked government programs, the military used soldiers at Edgewood Arsenal as guinea pigs in testing dozens of drugs for unconventional warfare.

At locations such as Edgewood Arsenal and U.S. Air Force bases, American and ex-Nazi MK-Ultra scientists gave LSD to more than one thousand soldiers. At Edgewood, records of these soldiers were tracked from 1955-75. Early on, the records made it clear to MK-Ultra officials that LSD caused lasting damage in their research subjects.[44] An officer reported volunteering for an experiment with a substance he was told was akin to alcohol. After receiving two LSD doses, he ended up feeling permanently damaged. Over the next eleven years he suffered extreme anxiety, depression and violent behavior. He retired early from the Air Force in 1968.[45]

Another soldier, a U.S. Army sergeant, "suffered hallucinations, memory loss, incoherence, and severe personality changes as well as uncontrollable violence. These effects destroyed his family and impeded his working ability. He never knew why until the Army asked him to participate in a follow-up study." After suing for compensation, he lost a Supreme Court decision. But in 1991, his Congressman sponsored a bill that helped him receive $400,000 compensation from the government for the damage LSD had done to him.[46]

LSD Studies Reveal Mild Cerebral Damage, Psychosis

While the Army eventually released a report on the Edgewood experiments, the CIA never released the conclusions of any other studies conducted throughout the 1950s and 1960s. However, individual reports and over a dozen research studies have revealed problems associated with therapeutic and recreational LSD use, including mild cerebral damage.

Research by two physicians in 1970 determined LSD use didn't necessarily cause "an acute psychotic reaction" in people without "marked schizoid or sociopathic traits." However, it "fostered a gradual retreat from reality and affective pain, leading to a chronic, egosyntonic psychotic syndrome which was relatively resistant to inpatient treatment."[47]

Another study noted mental health problems in a majority of subjects studied when LSD was legal to use in therapy. The study's authors found that LSD led to prolonged psychoses in a quarter of their subjects; in another quarter, it caused a decrease in the ability to cope with anxiety, even weeks after use. The authors concluded that, "this was most notable in periods of stress, when it was necessary to mobilize resources to counter anxiety. Instead of functioning effectively, they experienced depersonalization and a return to visual hallucinations, and were much more incapacitated than they had been before the LSD experience."[48]

One man whose LSD use initiated long-term psychosis was Mark Vonnegut, the son of best-selling novelist Kurt Vonnegut (*Slaughterhouse Five*). Mark Vonnegut reported previously "tripping" on LSD four times without any problems, but the fifth time led to immediate and lasting psychosis. Vonnegut ended up in a mental institution for a year. He wrote about this harrowing time of his life in a memoir, *Eden Express*.[49]

An overview of 46 existing studies, published in 1968, reported many harmful reactions lasting beyond the intoxication stage of acid. These included "paranoia ... megalomaniacal delusions ... prolonged or intermittent LSD-like psychosis." LSD use also resulted in "psychotic depressions usually associated with agitation and anxiety." The studies further found that longer-term LSD use often led to "chronic anxiety reactions associated with depression, somatic symptoms, difficulty in functioning and a recurrence of LSD-like symptoms," along with "acute panic states."[50]

A 1966 study by Max Rinkel stated, "Dangers are many times multiplied by their illegitimate use. People who have taken LSD obtained on the black market can become psychotic often weeks or months after the ingestion of LSD. They are being admitted to the hospital in ever-increasing numbers." While this quote may be an overstatement of the problem, Rinkel died of a heart attack shortly after publication of this study, and Sandoz laboratory discontinued their provision of LSD to researchers.[51]

The American Psychiatric Association produced a position statement on LSD at a meeting in June of 1966. After ten years of use in their therapy sessions with patients, they cautiously admitted the dangers of LSD use, stating, "The indiscriminate consumption of this hazardous drug can and not infrequently does lead to destructive physiological and personality changes." Cornell University Professor Donald Louria stated that LSD "must be listed as one of the most dangerous drugs in the pharmacopeia of man ... well-adjusted persons can be thrown into acute psychosis requiring days or weeks of hospitalization. This is true even in the hands of an experienced physician who carefully selects his patients."[52]

Researcher Conrad Schwarz reviewed 46 studies of LSD in a presentation to the North Pacific Society of Psychiatry. One of the five discussion points of this meta-study remains key. The author commented on the findings of LSD users' "personality deterioration toward a nonactivist role in society." Conservative think-tank leaders later commented on their success at spreading the use of LSD to cultivate a "dropped out" society of young Americans.[53]

Schwarz's meta-study further brought up the danger of contaminants and impurities in LSD. One common additive to LSD is strychnine, an animal poison that can cause some mild brain damage. While some say this is an urban myth, respected researchers Lee and Shlain report strychnine as a common additive in the 1960s, and forensic textbooks report it remains an LSD contaminant today.[54]

At least four studies, conducted between 1966 and 1976, support evidence of LSD, street-bought or not, causing possible brain damage. A 1969 study by William McGlothlin et al. found "evidence of moderate impairment of abstract abilities ... suggestive of minimal brain damage," though the experimental design could not determine whether it was definitively causal. A 1972 study by I.D. Accord noted that the subjects who had previously taken LSD showed "some mild, but measurable cerebral dysfunction regarding abstract abilities." A 1973 study by Accord and Barker began "to indicate that there may be a causal relationship between the use of hallucinogens and brain damage." And a study that Margarete DiBenedetto conducted in 1976 on the brains of subjects who had discontinued LSD use three to twelve months prior to testing also suggested some possible cerebral damage.[55]

Notes

1 See pdf of paper, "Chemical Warfare Agent Experiments Among U.S. Service Members," https://www.hsdl.org/?view&did=466161, including: US Army Medical Department, US Army Health Services Command, Project Director LTC David A. McFarling, MC. "LSD Follow-up Study Report, October 1980, 158 pp. Pages 23-25 of this paper show how at least 24% of subjects reported long-term adverse effects of LSD when surveyed nineteen years later. Also see *Bad Trip to Edgewood* (1993) on over 7,000 soldiers tested with various psychedelic drugs from 1955-75, with thousands reporting long-term adverse effects: http://www.youtube.com/watch?v=g0kILxvfgu8.

2 Martin Lee and Bruce Shlain, *Acid Dreams: The Complete Social History of LSD: The CIA, the Sixties, and Beyond* (New York: Grove Press, 1994). Lee cofounded the media watchdog group Fairness and Accuracy In Reporting (FAIR) in the 1980s. He had also contributed at numerous mainstream media outlets and published several books, as had Shlain. Lee also co-authored *Unreliable Sources: A Guide to Detecting Bias in News Media*, and wrote articles for *Newsday*, the *San*

Francisco Chronicle, Spin and the *Village Voice*. Shlain authored *Oddballs and Baseball Inside Out*. He further wrote for the *New York Times, Rolling Stone*, and others.

3 Alfred McCoy, *A Question of Torture: CIA Interrogation, from the Cold War to the War on Terror* (New York: Metropolitan, 2006), pp. 21-22. For U.S. Justice Department report, see Judy Feigin, "The Office of Special Investigations: Striving for Accountability in the Aftermath of the Holocaust," ed. Mark M. Richard, Former Deputy Assistant Attorney General, Criminal Justice Division, December 2006, http://documents.nytimes.com/confidential-report-provides-new-evidence-of-notorious-nazi-cases?ref=us#p=1. For 10,000 figure original estimation, see p. 6 of this report (says "V" at bottom of page though). For *New York Times* article on report, see Eric Lichtblau, "Nazis Were Given 'Safe Haven' in U.S, Report Says," *New York Times*, November 13, 2010, http://www.nytimes.com/2010/11/14/us/14nazis.html?pagewanted=1&_r=2. For other accounts, David Black, *Acid: The Secret History of LSD* (London: Vision, 1998) p. 27; Lee and Shlain, *Acid Dreams*, p. 6. For 9,000, see Stephen Lendman, "MK-ULTRA: The CIA's Mind Control Program," *Baltimore Chronicle*, 2/16/10. On *Air Force Magazine* article covering Operation Paperclip, see Walter Boyne, "Project Paperclip," *Air Force Magazine: Online Journal of the Air Force Association*, Vol. 90, No. 6 (June 2007), http://www.airforcemag.com/MagazineArchive/Pages/2007/June%202007/0607paperclip.aspx.

4 See, for example, Nazi Friedrich Hoffman. H.P. Albarelli Jr., *A Terrible Mistake: The Murder of Frank Olson and the CIA's Secret Cold War Experiments* (Walterville, OR: TrineDay, 2009), pp. 173, 359. Hank Albarelli Jr., "Operation Paperclip: CIA's Denial of Protecting Nazi is Blatant Lie—Part 1" and Part 2, 12/7/2010, http://www.voltairenet.org/CIA-s-Denial-of-Protecting-Nazis.

5 Hank Albarelli Jr., "Operation Paperclip: CIA's Denial of Protecting Nazi is Blatant Lie—Part 1 and Part 2," 12/7/2010, http://www.voltairenet.org/CIA-s-Denial-of-Protecting-Nazis.

6 Lee and Shlain, *Acid Dreams*, p. 6.

7 A. True Ott, "Bush continues family tradition of doing business with I.G. Farben" *Idaho Observer*, January 2009. On Swiss pharmaceutical industry handling opium, Brian Inglis, *The Forbidden Game: A Social History of Drugs* (New York: Scribner, 1975), Ch.11, apparently referring to the Swiss pharmaceutical companies refining the opium.

8 Albarelli, "Operation Paperclip." For original Swiss report on Sandoz, see "Switzerland, National Socialism and the Second World War: Final Report," Independent Commission of Experts Switzerland – Second World War, 2001, http://www.uek.ch/en/schlussbericht/synthesis/ueke.pdf.

9 On Wasson with J.P. Morgan, "Medicine: Mushroom Madness," *Time*, June 16, 1958. On Wasson working for the CIA, Albarelli, *A Terrible Mistake*, p. 359.

10 Albarelli, *A Terrible Mistake*, p. 359. Note that this writer believes that Albarelli, while writing an excellent book with great research, makes the common mistake of assuming Wasson was being honest in just "loving mushrooms and mushroom study." This was a common ploy of these federal agents, who would call themselves the "Johnny Appleseed" of acid, or write memoirs saying they "Turned on the World" (Michael Hollingshead). Their actions should be judged, not their rhetoric. Most of them were knowingly doing CIA MK-Ultra or British MI6 Tavistock work.

11 Lee & Shlain, *Acid Dreams*, p. 72.

12 Stephen Lendman, "MK-ULTRA," *Baltimore Chronicle*, 2/16/10. On Hoffman as Chief of Agents, Albarelli, "Operation Paperclip," 12/7/10, http://www.voltairenet.org/article167692.html. On seven other Nazi scientists working with Hoffman, see Linda Hunt, *Secret Agenda: The United States Government, Nazi Scientists, and Project Paperclip, 1945 to 1990* (New York: St. Martin's Press—Thomas Donne Books, 1991). Lendman said Operation Bluebird also had the name Project Chatter under Dr. Savage. Lendman said that notorious Nazi Joseph Mengele also used mescaline on men, women and children in WWII concentration camp experiments. On Lexington, KY prisoners: Albarelli, *A Terrible Mistake*, p. 235.

13 Alfred McCoy, *A Question of Torture*, p. 23.

14 Lee & Shlain, *Acid Dreams*, p. 34. They cite [CIA] Memorandum for Mr. J. Lee Rankin, General Counsel, President's Commission on the Assassination of President Kennedy, "Soviet Brainwashing Techniques," June 26, 1964.

15 Lee & Shlain, *Acid Dreams*, p. 21

16 David Black, *Acid: The Secret History of LSD* (London: Vision, 1998), p. 28. The previous operation Gottlieb had worked in was titled MK-Naomi. On MK-Ultra's other areas of focus, cancer-causing agents and radiation, see H.P. Albarelli, *A Terrible Mistake*, pp. 292-93.

17 Lee & Shlain, *Acid Dreams*, pp. 19, 28. Also: Jonathan Marks, *The Search for the Manchurian Candidate* (Times Books: 1979; Norton Paperback:1991), p. 96. Marks's source is CIA-contracted agent George White's diary, entry date June 9, 1952.

18 On psychedelic hit list of leftist leaders, see Martin Lee and Bruce Shlain, *Acid Dreams*, pp. 35, 44-45, 52-53. Lee and Shlain cite a CIA document from June 9, 1954, *Project MK-ULTRA, The CIA's Program of Research in Behavior Modification*, Joint Hearing before the Select Committee on Intelligence and the Subcommittee on Health and Scientific Research of the Committee on Human Resources, United States Senate, August 3, 1977. Marks wrote about an Argentinean leftist professor who was involuntarily dosed with a psychedelic by a stranger who stuck him with a pin, leading to his discrediting for several years. Marks, *The Search for the Manchurian Candidate*, p. 111. Marks failed to give this professor's name, possibly because he wanted anonymity.

19 Greg Guma, "Crimes of the Surveillance State: A Victim's Story," *Global Research*, September 12, 2013, http://www.globalresearch.ca/crimes-of-the-surveillance-state-a-victims-story/5349529.

20 Lee and Shlain, *Acid Dreams*, p. 27.

21 Lee and Shlain, *Acid Dreams*, pp. 87-88.

22 Lee and Shlain, *Acid Dreams*, p. 56.

23 Lee and Shlain, *Acid Dreams*, pp. 44, 50, 56.

24 Lee and Shlain, *Acid Dreams*, pp. 45-46, 54-55. Aldous Huxley, *Brave New World* (New York/London: Harper Collins, 1932, 1946). On *Brave New World* as one of century's top novels, see *100 Best Novels* (Random House, 1999). This ranking was by the Modern Library Editorial Board.

25 Lee and Shlain, *Acid Dreams*, p. 48.

26 Lee and Shlain, *Acid Dreams*, p. 38. On Welch and eugenics see, Edwin Black, *War Against the Weak: Eugenics and America's Campaign to Create a Master Race* (New York: Four Walls Eight Windows, 2003) pp. 93-94, 138. For Welch and mental hygiene history, see Johns Hopkins School of Public Health website, Dr. Wallace Mandell, "The Realization of an Idea," http://www.jhsph.edu/departments/mental-health/about/origins.html.

27 Lee and Shlain, *Acid Dreams*, pp. 37-38, citing "Inspector General's Report of Inquiry in the Facts and Circumstances surrounding the Death of Mr. Harold Blauer at the New York State Psychiatric Institute (NYSPI) and Subsequent Claims and Actions," DAIG-IN 27-75, 1975. For another detailed account, see Hank Albarelli, *A Terrible Mistake* (Walterville, OR: TrineDay, 2009), pp. 159-63. Also see Tyner, *Probe, Mind Control*, p. 2. On Hoch as member of Eugenics Society, see *Eugenics Quarterly*, Special Issue, June 1959, Proceedings of the International Conference, Afternoon Session Chairman, Paul Hoch, MD, http://www.ncbi.nlm.nih.gov/pmc/articles/PMC2972827/pdf/eugenrev00227-0012.pdf.

28 Edwin Black, *War Against the Weak: Eugenics and America's Campaign to Create a Master Race* (Thunder's Mouth Press, 2004) pp. 75, 81-84, 103-04. Also see Black, *Nazi Nexus: America's Corporate Connections to Hitler's Holocaust* (Washington, DC: Dialog Press, 2009).

29 John Marks, *The Search for the Manchurian Candidate: The CIA and Mind Control, The Secret History of the Behavioral Sciences* (New York: W.H. Norton, 1979), p. 123. Cited in Lee and Shlain, *Acid Dreams*, p. 38. Note that this author couldn't find the quote in a 1991 edition of the Marks book, apparently edited out of this later printing. Note that much information on Hoch also appears in Albarelli, *A Terrible Mistake*, pp. 160-63.

30 Leonard Cole, *Clouds of Secrecy: The Army's Germ Warfare Tests over Populated Areas* (Totowa, NJ: Rowan and Littlefield, 1988). Note that this book has a Foreword by Senator Alan Cranston. On San Francisco, see pp. 75-104.

31 Olson's wife, as well as Olson's colleague Norman Courneyer, said this. Olson's son Eric and Courneyer stated this on camera for the documentary, *Code Name Artichoke: The CIA's Secret*

Experiment on Humans (2002), shown on World Link TV, *Spotlight*, http://www.youtube.com/watch?feature=player_embedded&v=ThqUt6fozhc#. On other sources regarding American use of biological weapons in Korea and elsewhere, see William Blum, *Rogue State* (Monroe, ME: Common Courage Press, 2000); Stephan Endicott and Edward Hagerman, *The United States and Biological Warfare: Secrets From the Early Cold War and Korea* (Bloomington, IN: Indiana University Press, 1998).

32 *Code Name Artichoke: The CIA's Secret Experiment on Humans.*

33 Albarelli, *A Terrible Mistake*, pp. 686-95.

34 *Code Name Artichoke: The CIA's Secret Experiment on Humans.*

35 U.S. Senate Select Committee to Study Governmental Operations with Respect to Intelligence Activities, report no. 94-755, 94th Cong., 2d Sess. [hereinafter "Church Committee Report"] (Washington, DC: GPO, 1976), p. 390; http://www.aarclibrary.org/publib/contents/church/contents_church_reports_book1.htm. "MKULTRA was approved by the DCI [Director of Central Intelligence] on April 13, 1953," and Operation Artichoke melded into MK-Ultra, according to memorandum from Richard Helms to CIA Director Allen Dulles.

36 Sally Denton and Roger Morris, *The Making of Las Vegas: The Money and the Power* (New York: Vintage, 2001), pp. 103-04; referenced in Albarelli, *A Terrible Mistake*, p. 435.

37 Lee and Shlain, *Acid Dreams*, p. 31. Also see "Medicine: Artificial Psychoses," *Time*, Dec. 19, 1955. Note that Cold Spring Harbor Laboratory's website now calls the start of eugenics as "genetics" research, but names the eugenics founding director, Charles Davenport, and the Carnegie Institution.

38 Albarelli, *A Terrible Mistake*, p. 629.

39 Lee and Shlain, *Acid Dreams*, pp. 23-24. Also see, for example, Allison Mayers, "Moving tribute: Local artist turns to dance to further explore her grandmother's torment at the hands of the CIA," *Winnipeg Free Press*, 2/4/10.

40 Howard Witt, "CIA Brainwashing Suit Settled," *Chicago Tribune*, October 5, 1988, http://articles.chicagotribune.com/1988-10-05/news/8802040759_1_brainwashing-experiments-dr-ewen-cameron-canadians.

41 Allison Mayers, "Moving tribute: Local artist turns to dance to further explore her grandmother's torment at the hands of the CIA," *Winnipeg Free Press*, 2/4/10.

42 "Interview With a Nuremberg Prosecutor," *Covert Action Information Bulletin (CAIB)*, Number 25 (Winter 1986), pp. 24-25. Note *CAIB* was started by acclaimed CIA agent whistleblower, Phil Agee, who also wrote the book, *Inside the Company: CIA Diary* (New York: Farrar, Strauss and Giroux, 1975). CAIB later changed its name to *Covert Action Quarterly*, before ceasing publication around 2005. Also see, on Kaufman as Nuremberg prosecutor, Obituary, Mary M. Kaufman, *Orlando Sentinel*, September 12, 1995, http://articles.orlandosentinel.com/1995-09-12/news/9509110428_1_hunton-temple-mount-mazar.

43 "J. Peter Grace and Project Paperclip," *Covert Action Information Bulletin (CAIB)*, Number 25 (Winter 1986), p. 28. *CAIB* cites ABC-TV *News Closeup*, "Escape from Justice: Nazi War Criminals in America," January 16, 1980.

44 See pdf of paper, "Chemical Warfare Agent Experiments Among U.S. Service Members," https://www.hsdl.org/?view&did=466161. "Seventy-six LSD subjects (24% of 320) reported one or more long-term adverse reactions to LSD exposure (Table 6) (US Army 1980). All complaints from subjects were reported as 'adverse effects' even though these events had occurred on average 19 years earlier." It includes: US Army Medical Department, US Army Health Services Command, Project Director LTC David A. McFarling, MC., "LSD Follow-up Study Report, October 1980," 158 pp. Pages 23-25 of this paper show how at least 24% of subjects reported long-term adverse effects of LSD when surveyed 19 years later. Also see, *Bad Trip to Edgewood* (1993) on over 7,000 soldiers tested with various psychedelic drugs from 1955-75, with thousands reporting long-term adverse effects: http://www.youtube.com/watch?v=g0kILxvfgu8.

45 Stephen Budiansky, Erica E. Goode and Ted Gest, "The Cold War Experiments Radiation tests were only one small part of a vast research program that used thousands of Americans as guinea

pigs," *U.S. News and World Report*, 1/16/94.

46 Stephen Lendman, "MK-ULTRA," *Baltimore Chronicle*, 2/16/10. On Hoffman as Chief of Agents: Albarelli, "Operation Paperclip," 12/7/10. Also see William Gibson, "Army Won't Fight Bill for Victim of LSD Experiment," *Sun Sentinel* (Florida), July 11, 1991, http://articles.sun-sentinel.com/1991-07-11/news/9101250505_1_experiments-edgewood-arsenal-nazi. On Lendman's *Baltimore Chronicle* article, http://www.voltairenet.org/article167692.html.

47 George S. Glass, MD and Malcolm B. Bowers Jr., MD, "Chronic Psychosis Associated with Long-Term Psychotomimetic Drug Abuse," *Archive of General Psychiatry—Vol. 23*, August 1970, pp. 100, 103. Note this is not to be confused with the old myth that taking seven hits of LSD makes someone legally insane.

48 William A. Frosch, MD, Edwin S. Robbins, MD and Marvin Stern, MD, "Untoward Reactions to Lysergic Acid Diethylamide (LSD) Resulting in Hospitalization," *New England Journal of Medicine*, Vol. 273, No.23, December 2, 1965, p. 1238.

49 Mark Vonnegut, *Eden Express* (New York: Delta, 1998). First published by Praeger Press in 1975.

50 Conrad J. Schwarz, "The Complications of LSD: A Review of the Literature," *Journal of Nervous and Mental Disease*, 1968, Vol. 146, no. 2., p. 181. Note this paper was first presented at the annual meeting of the North Pacific Society of Psychiatry and Neurology, Vancouver, B.C. April 6-8, 1967. It includes references to 46 studies on LSD conducted from 1960-67.

51 On Rinkel's death: http://oasis.lib.harvard.edu/oasis/deliver/~med00074. On Sandoz discontinuing their supply of LSD to researchers: Lee, *Acid Dreams*, p. 151.

52 Schwarz, "Complications of LSD," *Journal of Nervous and Mental Disease*, 1968, Vol.146, no. 2, pp. 181-82. Schwarz cited: American Psychiatric Association, "Position Statement on LSD," *Amer. J. Psychiat.*, 123, 1966, p. 353. Donald Louria is quoted on p. 182 of Schwarz: from D. Louria, *Nightmare Drugs* (New York: Pocket Books, 1966), p. 47.

53 Schwarz, "Complications of LSD," *Journal of Nervous and Mental Disease*, 1968, Vol. 146, no. 2, p. 184. See Hudson Institute consultant Herman Kahn: Lee & Shlain, *Acid Dreams*, p. 197.

54 Schwarz, "The Complications of LSD," *Journal of Nervous and Mental Disease*, p. 182. Lee & Shlain, *Acid Dreams*, p. 188. Joseph A. Prahlow, *Forensic Pathology for Police, Death Investigators, Attorneys, and Forensic Scientists* (New York: Humana Press, 2010), p. 296. Note that the Center for Disease Control states that strychnine can cause brain damage from low oxygen following its ingestion: http://www.bt.cdc.gov/agent/strychnine/basics/pdf/facts.pdf.

55 W.H. McGlothlin, D.O. Arnold, and D. X. Freedman, "Organicity Measures Following Repeated LSD Ingestion," *Archives of General Psychiatry*, 21, 1969, p. 708; L.D. Accord, "Hallucinogenic Drugs and Brain Damage," *Military Medicine* 137, 1972, p. 19; L.D. Accord and A.B. Barker, "Hallucinogenic Drugs and Cerebral Deficit," *Journal of Nervous and Mental Disease*, 156 (4), 1973, p. 283; M. DiBenedetto, "Electrodiagnostic Evidence of Subclinical Disease State in Drug Abusers," *Archives of Physical and Medical Rehabilitation*, 57, 1976, p. 65.

Sidney Gottlieb, director of the CIA's MK-Ultra, traveled worldwide to dose opponents with LSD and other drugs.

Chapter Three

CIA Drug War on Asian & African Leaders

After World War II, a civil war broke out in China, and in 1949 the Chinese People's Liberation Army, led by Communist Mao Zedong (also written Mao Tse-tung), overthrew the old, U.S.-backed colonialist government. Mao introduced food crops to replace the poppy fields and led a massive detoxification campaign that eliminated demand in the world's largest addict population. Those who refused to give up their addiction were sent to labor camps.[1]

The Kuomintang (Nationalist) leader at the time of Mao's revolution, Generalissimo Chiang Kai-shek, retreated to the island of Taiwan while Nationalist Chinese generals and many thousands of troops also retreated to Burma, adjoining China's southern border. In the following years, the Burmese Army drove some of these troops into Laos. In both Burma and Laos, these generals cultivated vast new poppy fields similar to the ones they had presided over in China. From 1950 onwards, the U.S. military and intelligence also aided Chiang and his generals' attempts to regain control of China.[2]

By 1950, weapons manufacturing companies in the U.S. gathered politicians to form the Committee on the Present Danger. Under the leadership of Paul Nitze and Dean Acheson, they influenced President Truman to pass National Security Council Directive 68 that called for military containment of the Soviet Union. The National Broadcasting Corporation aired a weekly television program to promote it. This initiated the anti-Communist Red Scare, or Cold War, that lasted for over three decades.[3]

The fight against the "Red Menace" was first played out in Korea, a country bordering Communist China's northeast. By the end of World War II, the Japanese had controlled Korea for over fifty years. After WWII, Korea was divided in half, with the Soviet Union occupying North Korea and the U.S. occupying South Korea. Around 1950, border skirmishes between the two territories ended up with American soldiers fighting for South Korea and Red Chinese soldiers sent in to defend North Korea. Red

Scare propaganda helped President Truman recruit many more American soldiers to fight the North Korean Communists in the Korean War.

By mid-1950, the U.S. Air Force was dropping 800 tons of napalm per day on North Korea.[4] An American insider and Asian investigators said the U.S. also dropped biological weapons on Korea.[5] One source estimated that 8-9 million Koreans died in the war, about 20% of their population.[6]

That war appeared to be more than just a fight over political ideologies. Journalist Larry Collins wrote in the *New York Times*:

> The CIA ties to international drug trafficking date to the Korean War. In 1949, two of Chiang Kai-shek's defeated generals, Li Wen Huan and Tuan Shi Wen, marched their Third and Fifth Route armies and families and livestock, across the mountains to northern Burma. Once installed, the peasant soldiers began cultivating the crop they new best, the opium poppy.
>
> When China entered the Korean War, the CIA had a desperate need for intelligence on that nation. The agency turned to the warlord generals, who agreed to slip some soldiers back into China. In return, the agency offered arms. Officially, the arms were intended to equip the warlords for a return to China. In fact, the Chinese wanted them to repel any attack by the Burmese.[7]

In brief, the U.S. followed a CIA directive to arm these longtime opium-trafficking generals partly for a counter-revolution in China. Professor Alfred McCoy backed Collins's assertion that the CIA also helped arm the Chinese Nationalist generals in Burma to protect their opium crops from attacks by the Burmese Army. The CIA supported the Nationalist Chinese while they became the opium barons of the Golden Triangle area of Burma, Thailand and Laos. According to McCoy: "CIA activities in Burma helped transform [its] Shan states ... into the largest opium growing region in the world."[8]

In late 1952, towards the end of the Korean War, the Nationalist Chinese generals once loyal to Chiang Kai-shek and the U.S. led thousands of Nationalist Chinese mercenaries to help them expand their territory in Burma. The Burmese Army pushed back and found American consultants' dead bodies on the battlefield. In March of 1953, four months before the end of the Korean War, Burma took its case of Nationalist Chinese and American aggression before the U.N. Burma won a resolution for the Nationalist Chinese generals and soldiers to be deported to Taiwan. Professor McCoy detailed how the U.S. Ambassador to Thailand, a senior advisor to the CIA, helped orchestrate a fake exodus of Nationalist generals and soldiers (impersonated by tribal boys) that actually left all the generals and most of the mercenary Nationalist Chinese soldiers where they were: in Burma, protecting their opium fields.[9]

France, U.S. Fight for Vietnam-Area Opium

Many of the wealthiest American families already had a hand in the opium trade. Now family members and employees in leadership positions at the CIA helped them increase this role. They did so in conjunction with their opposition to Communist influence in countries worldwide. Professor McCoy, in *The Politics of Heroin*, points out how, when France was still digging itself out from war in 1947, various factors, including the CIA covertly intervening, helped topple the Communist party from power and brought about a permanent realignment of politicians in Marseille, France.[10]

Just after World War II, the newly created CIA provided arms, money and other support to help the Corsican Mafia take control of Marseille ports from the labor unions and Communist Party. The CIA aided the Mafia in drug trafficking too, and soon Marseille was the opium-trafficking capital of the industrialized world. This was spotlighted in a Hollywood movie, *The French Connection*. Heroin laboratories opened in Marseille in 1951, only months after the Corsicans gained control over the waterfront.[11]

The French had fights over opium trafficking both locally and abroad. The future North Vietnamese leader, Ho Chi Minh, was educated in France, before helping found the French Communist Party. In Marseilles, dock workers fought for higher pay and better working conditions, striking in 1947 and 1950. A CIA agent was quoted as saying he supplied a leader of the American Federation of Labor with up to $2 million to pay off Corsicans to break strikes and bring in replacement workers from Italy. Corsican gangsters threw any Communist leaders who opposed them into the harbor.[12]

In South Vietnam, the French and U.S. gave money and arms to local leaders in a war with each other for control of the country. French intelligence, the Deuxieme Bureau, spent a great deal of money strengthening their already existing groups, such as the Binh Xuyen. The CIA gave millions of dollars to Prime Minister Ngo Dinh Diem and his Vietnamese army.[13]

UC-Berkeley Professor Peter Dale Scott documented the importance of drugs in America's Vietnam War. In *Drugs, Oil and War* he wrote, "In 1959 ... the local drug trade was threatened by political developments," which pulled the U.S. into its first U.S. Marine presence in Vietnam within a year. Scott's research also found the CIA supporting the Kuomentang Nationalist Chinese Party in their goal of reconquering China, and in their drug trade with corrupt officials in Thailand and Hong Kong.[14]

Professor McCoy detailed how in 1959, "Field Marshal Sarit [Thanarat of Thailand] unleashed a full military assault on the opium trade." Troops "swept the country, raiding the opium dens, seizing their stocks, and confiscating opium pipes." Sarit then made a declaration of drug eradication to the Thai people.[15]

Two weeks later, seemingly on behalf of the American oligarchy's drug traffickers, the CIA raised this as a crisis in neighboring Laos, saying it required increasing American military intervention over the next decade (and triggering the war in neighboring Vietnam). Agent John Stockwell, like other whistleblowers, took part in the drug trafficking for his employer throughout that area and Indochina before he quit the CIA.[16]

Asian Opium Used to Repress Asian Opposition Movements

The opium traffickers who comprised part of America's wealthiest ruling oligarchy had good reason to covet the poppy fields of the region around Vietnam. Along with its potential for cash, they wanted the opium to help suppress leftist liberation movements at home and abroad. So, in tandem with using the money garnered from opium sales to buy support against the Communist North Vietnamese, they flooded American inner cities with heroin. They appeared to do this to repress antiwar activists and people of color struggling for equal rights.

In his landmark book *The Politics of Heroin*, Professor Alfred McCoy detailed the manner in which American-supported South Vietnamese leaders were able to traffic heroin with U.S. intelligence aid. McCoy also chronicled later how South Vietnamese heroin was directly imported into New York and other cities.

Around the time Ho Chi Minh and the Communist Viet Minh were about to win an overwhelming victory in the 1954 Vietnamese elections, the American oligarchs and their political allies countered by supporting a political split in that country. The Communists posed the threat of ridding the country of opium dealings, as Mao Zedong had done after the Communist revolution in China.[17] McCoy quoted the infamous "Pentagon Papers" leaked by government official Daniel Ellsburg to the press. The conclusion: South Vietnam "was essentially a creation of the United States," and, "Without U.S. aid in the following years ... South Vietnam ... could not have survived."[18]

McCoy cited military reports on the development of major heroin trafficking from this U.S. intelligence-created South Vietnamese government. One report from a U.S. Army provost marshal stated that high-ranking members of the South Vietnamese government were "the top 'zone' in a four-tiered heroin pushing pyramid."[19] The CIA aided the South Vietnamese government and the neighboring Laotian government in fighting the growing movement of people in both countries struggling for a more egalitarian communist society. The Academy Award-winning documentary *Hearts and Minds* presented South Vietnamese leaders saying the CIA forced their government to do CIA bidding, such as arranging deliveries from other opium-producing countries like Burma to areas where Laotian and Vietnamese people sided with the Communists against U.S. goals.[20]

The CIA also trained the Hmong people. From "1960-1974, the CIA maintained a secret mercenary army of 30,000 Hmong tribesmen in the mountains of northern Laos, participants in a covert operation that remains the largest single operation in the agency's forty-year history," to fight Communist insurgents throughout Laos.[21] The Hmong cultivated opium-producing poppy fields, the opium was processed into heroin, and the CIA had its charter airline, Air America, transport the heroin.[22]

Many historical records, such as a diverse array of South Vietnamese interviewed in *Hearts and Minds* and McCoy's hundreds of interviews in Vietnam, present the huge South Vietnamese resistance to America's division and control of Vietnam. In further response, U.S. intelligence repressed the Vietnamese militarily through Operation Phoenix, which assassinated Communist South Vietnamese by the tens of thousands.

The CIA expanded its use of heroin to repress activists and potential activists in China and other Asian countries. McCoy wrote, "Still enjoying tacit CIA support for their counterinsurgency work [against the government of Communist China], [ousted] Nationalist Chinese military caravans [in Burma] continued to move almost all of Burma's opium exports into northern Thailand, where they were purchased by a Chinese [organized crime] syndicate for domestic distribution [inside China] and export to Hong Kong and Malaysia." These Chinese Nationalist CIA assets were used as part of what news organizations labeled the 1967 Opium War against Communists in Burma, partly to gain further control of their poppy fields.[23]

During U.S. military missions in Indochina, the CIA set up a vast opium-trafficking system through Laos.[24] Within a dozen years, the country would have one of busiest airports in the world despite having a population under three million and its third-world status. With the other two countries around Vietnam, Burma and Thailand, Southeast Asia became the source of about 70% of the of the world's opium for heroin production by 1970.[25]

U.S. Use of Guns & Drugs on African Leftists, Lumumba

European countries conquered the African continent in the late 1800s through military innovations developed during their industrial revolution, dividing Africa into various territories at the Berlin Conference of 1884-85. By 1905, Europeans controlled virtually all of Africa, except Ethiopia and Liberia, the country founded by freed American slaves. While

Britain and France controlled the most African nations, Germany, Spain, Italy, Belgium and Portugal also controlled African territories.

These European countries exported much of Africa's natural resources of gold, rubber, sugar, diamonds and oil while exploiting African labor. Researcher Thomas Peckenham, in *The Scramble for Africa,* quoted many verified accounts of European brutality against the Africans. Peckenham said, and other researchers agreed, that blacks in Africa were slaves in every way except by name. European colonizers used decades of starvation, mutilation and mass murder to ensure servitude.[26]

World War II left European armies depleted, allowing local leaders in Africa to organize independence movements. Libya, under joint control of Italy, Britain and France, gained independence in 1951. Egypt ultimately freed itself from Britain in 1953. Sudan fought off British control in 1956, and Tunisia gained freedom from French rule in that same year. Morocco gained independence from France and Spain in 1956 as well. The socialists and nationalist groups leading the movements were tired of being exploited by industrialized countries.

U.S. intelligence worked in collaboration with British and other European intelligence agencies to stop African independence. These independence movements cost the wealthy corporate owners in their countries hundreds of millions of dollars (billions in present values). Intelligence agencies used guns and drugs against the African independence movements, in both open and surreptitious actions.[27]

The CIA's use of drugs for this purpose remains a part of their covert operations, with few details revealed. CIA documents state how the agency used LSD to aid interrogation on an operational basis from the mid-1950s through the early 1960s. As previously mentioned, the CIA also used LSD against foreign leftist leaders. A CIA document noted that the CIA's administration of LSD "to high officials would be a relatively simple matter and could have significant effect at key meetings, speeches, etc."[28] The agency planned to slip odorless, tasteless LSD, "to socialist or left-leaning politicians in foreign countries so that they would babble incoherently and discredit themselves in public."[29]

The CIA certainly wasn't looking to cause mind expansion. Their own documents said the acid could "produce serious insanity for 8-18 hours and possibly longer." ABC News showed CIA documents citing how CIA MK-Ultra's Dr. Sidney Gottlieb carried LSD overseas to dose leftist foreign diplomats and statesmen. Egyptian President Gamal Abdal Nasser, one of Africa's most outspoken leaders, was on the hit list.[30] The CIA concealed exactly how and if the leaders on that hit list were dosed, but did they give these leaders massive LSD doses in an attempt to also cause subtle brain damage?

The assassination of the Congo independence leader Patrice Lumumba represents a well-documented example of U.S. and European attacks on African independence leaders with MK-Ultra scientists' aid. The U.S. became the first country to recognize the claims of Belgium's King Leopold II to the territories of the Congo Basin. Brutal economic exploitation under Leopold II resulted in millions of Congolese deaths. The U.S. acquired a stake in the Congo's minerals. The U.S. military used uranium from Congolese mines for manufacturing atomic weapons.[31]

As various African countries began to gain their independence, the Belgian Congo's Patrice Lumumba organized the Mouvement National Congolais in 1958. The Congolese people elected the 34-year-old to be their Prime Minister in 1960. In his acceptance speech, Lumumba said the Congo's independence "put an end to the humiliating slavery which was imposed on us by force."[32]

About ten weeks after Prime Minister Lumumba took office, Colonel Joseph Mobutu led a coup d'etat, backed by Belgian officers still in the Congolese army.[33] Many reports implicate the CIA in helping orchestrate this coup. The Congressional Church Committee found that CIA director Allen Dulles ordered Lumumba's assassination.[34] The CIA's MK-Ultra director Sidney Gottlieb aided this assassination, devising a poison resembling toothpaste, and he flew to the Congo with it. Lumumba was assassinated in January of 1961.[35] Details on the role of the poison in the assassination remain unknown.

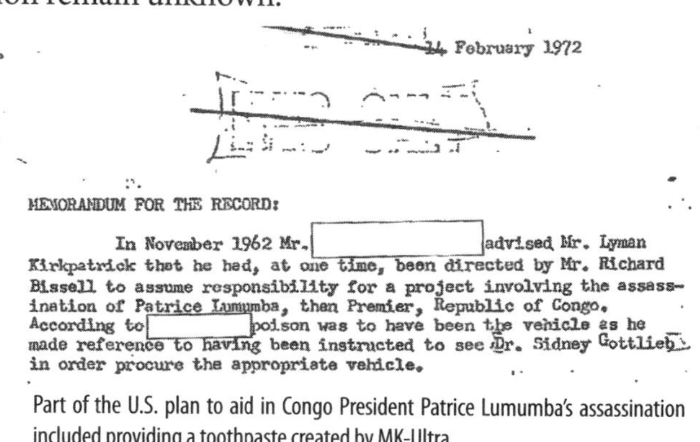

14 February 1972

MEMORANDUM FOR THE RECORD:

In November 1962 Mr. [ ] advised Mr. Lyman Kirkpatrick that he had, at one time, been directed by Mr. Richard Bissell to assume responsibility for a project involving the assassination of Patrice Lumumba, then Premier, Republic of Congo. According to [ ] poison was to have been the vehicle as he made reference to having been instructed to see Dr. Sidney Gottlieb in order procure the appropriate vehicle.

Part of the U.S. plan to aid in Congo President Patrice Lumumba's assassination included providing a toothpaste created by MK-Ultra.

Notes

1 On largest addict population, estimated at 40 million Chinese addicts, and mass detox, see C.P. Spencer and V. Navaratnam, *Drug Abuse in East Asia* (Kuala Lumpur: Oxford University Press, 1981), pp. 50-51, 154-55. On Mao replacing poppy fields, "The World Opium Situation," U.S. Bureau of Narcotics and Dangerous Drugs (Washington, DC: U.S. Government Printing Office, October 1970), p. 13. Also see U.S. Drug Enforcement Administration, Office of Intelligence, International Intelligence Division, "People's Republic of China," *Drug Enforcement* (Fall 1974), pp. 35-36; cited in Alfred McCoy, *The Politics of Heroin: CIA Complicity in the Global Drug Trade* (New York: Lawrence Hill Books, 1972/1991), pp. 123, 163.

2 On Chiang Kai-Shek, see Jay Taylor, *The Generalissimo: Chiang Kai-shek and the Struggle for Modern China* (Cambridge, Massachusetts: Belknap Press of Harvard University Press, 2009). On Nationalist Chinese generals and troops, see McCoy, *The Politics of Heroin*, pp. 162-71.

3 Jerry Sanders, *Peddlers of Crisis: The Committee on the Present Danger and the Politics of Containment* (Boston: South End Press, 1999).

4 "Napalm on North Korea," *Le Monde Diplomatique*, 12/10/2004, http://monde-diplomatique.de/pm/2004/12/10/a0034.text. This French article, translated by a Google program, cites the *New York Times*, July 31, August 2 and September 1, 1950, regarding the note of 800 tons a day dropped. The article examines a book by a professor emeritus of University of Chicago, Bruce Cummings, *North Korea, Another Country* (New York: New Press, 2003).

5 Hank Albarelli, *A Terrible Mistake: The Murder of Frank Olson and the CIA's Secret Cold War Experiments* (Waterville, OR: Trine Day, 2009), pp. 196-98.

6 Richard Rhodes, "The General and World War III," *The New Yorker*, June 19, 1995, p. 53. Also see Brian Wilson, "Korea and the 'Axis of Evil,'" *Global Research*, October 12, 2006.

7 Larry Collins, "The CIA Drug Connection is as Old as the Agency," *New York Times*, December 3, 1993, http://www.nytimes.com/1993/12/03/opinion/03iht-edlarry.html?pagewanted=all.

8 McCoy, *The Politics of Heroin*, p. 162.

9 Interview with William vanden Heuvel, New York City, June 21, 1971; vanden Heuvel was executive assistant to Ambassador Donovan and had noted this incident in his personal journal. Hugh Tinker, *Union of Burma* (London: Oxford University Press, 1957), pp. 53-54. Interview with Rev. Paul Lewis, Chiang Mai, Thailand, September 7, 1971; at the time of this interview, Rev. Lewis was acting as a mail link for many of these separated Lahu families and received two to three letters per week from Taiwan. All cited in McCoy, *The Politics of Heroin*, pp. 173-76.

10 McCoy, *The Politics of Heroin*, p. 54

11 McCoy, *The Politics of Heroin*, chapters 1-2.

12 McCoy, *The Politics of Heroin*, p. 61.

13 McCoy, *The Politics of Heroin*, pp. 155-56.

14 Peter Dale Scott, *Drugs, Oil, and War* (New York: Rowman and Littlefied, 2003), pp. 50-51.

15 Prasert Rujirawong, "Kanluk Supfin" ["Abolishing Opium Smoking"], in Khana Ratthanontri, *Prawat lae phonngan khong jomphon Sarit Thanarat, phim nai jgan phraratchathan pleong sop phon jomphon Sarit Thanarat* [The Life and Works of Field Marshal Sarit Thanarat, Published on the Occasion of the Cremation of Field Marshal Sarit Thanarat] (Bangkok: Prime Minister's Office, 1964). Cited in McCoy, *Politics of Heroin*, p. 190.

16 http://wn.com/john_stockwell_on_george_bush,_the_cia,_and_drug_trafficking.

17 Mike Gravel, ed., *The Pentagon Papers*, 5 vols. (Boston: Beacon Press, 1971), vol. 1, pp. 221-22; referenced in McCoy, *The Politics of Heroin*, pp. 193-94.

18 Gravel, *The Pentagon Papers*, vol. 2, p. 22.

19 "The Drug Abuse Problem in Vietnam," *Report of the Office of the Provost Marshal*, U.S. Military Assistance Command Vietnam (Saigon, 1971), p. 6.

20 Interview with William Young, Chiangmai, Thailand, September 14, 1971, McCoy, *The Politics of Heroin*, pp. 300-01. Peter Davis, *Hearts and Minds* (BBS Productions, Rainbow Releasing, 1974).

21 *New York Times*, 6/6/71, p. 2. Also see *Evening Star* (Washington, DC), 6/19/72. On CIA support of other military leaders in region: Interview with Elliot K. Chan, Vientiane, Laos, 8/15/71; Chan was a USAID police adviser to the Royal Laotian government. Also Interview with an agent, U.S. Bureau of Narcotics and Dangerous Drugs, New Haven, CT, 11/18/71. All referenced in McCoy, *The Politics of Heroin*, pp. 286-89.

22 Interview with Gen. Ouane Rattikone, Vientiane, Laos, 9/1/71; interview with Gen. Thao Ma, Bangkok, Thailand, 9/17/71; Don A. Schanche, *Mister Pop* (New York: David McKay, 1970), pp. 240-45. On CIA training and aiding its secret Hmong army, see John Lewallen, "The Reluctant Counterinsurgents: International Voluntary Services in Laos," in Adams and McCoy, *Laos: War and Revolution*, pp. 361-62. USAID admitted to using "humanitarian" refugee operations for military-

type work in a report: U.S. Congress, Senate, Committee of the Judiciary, *Refugee and Civilian War Casualty Problems in Indochina*, 91st Cong., 2nd session (Washington, DC: U.S. Government Printing Office, 1970), pp. 22-24. All referenced in McCoy, *The Politics of Heroin*, pp. 304-07.

23 McCoy, *The Politics of Heroin*, pp. 287, 333, 360-61.

24 Scott, *Drugs, Oil, and War*, pp. 50-51.

25 On 70%, Report of the United Nations Survey Team on the Economic and Social Needs of the Opium-Producing Areas in Thailand (Bangkok: Government Printing, 1967), pp. 59, 64, 68; *New York Times*, September 17, 1963, p. 45; June 6, 1971, p. 2. All cited in Alfred McCoy, *The Politics of Heroin*, p. 285. On Laos population: https://www.google.com/#q=population+of+laos. On "busiest airports" see James Parker, *Codename Mule: Fighting the Secret War in Laos for the CIA* (Naval Institute Press/Naval Institute Special Warfare, 1995), cited in Claire Bobbyer and Andrew Spooner, *Vietnam, Cambodia and Laos* (Footprint Handbooks, 4th ed, 2013), p. 492.

26 Thomas Peckenham, *The Scramble for Africa: White Man's Conquest of the Dark Continent from 1876-1912* (New York: Avon, 1992).

27 Patrick Bond, *Looting Africa: The Economics of Exploitation* (London: Zed Books, 2006), p. 2. Also see Michael Watts, "Empire of oil: Capitalist Dispossession and the scramble for Africa," *Monthly Review*, September 2006.

28 Martin Lee and Bruce Shlain, *Acid Dreams: The Complete Social History of LSD: The CIA, the Sixties, and Beyond* (New York: Grove Weidenfeld, 1985), pp. 19, 28.

29 Lee and Shlain, *Acid Dreams*, pp. 29, 35, 190.

30 Lee and Shlain, *Acid Dreams*, pp. 35, 44-45, 52-53, CIA document from June 9, 1954, *Project MK-ULTRA, The CIA's Program of Research in Behavior Modification*, Joint Hearing before the Select Committee on Intelligence and the Subcommittee on Health and Scientific Research of the Committee on Human Resources, United States Senate, August 3, 1977.

31 Georges Nzongola-Ntalaja, "Patrice Lumumba: the most important assassination of the 20th century. The US-sponsored plot to kill Patrice Lumumba, the hero of Congolese independence, took place 50 years ago today," *The Guardian* (London), 1/17/2001, http://www.guardian.co.uk/global-development/poverty-matters/2011/jan/17/patrice-lumumba-50th-anniversary-assassination.

32 Chukwunyere Kamalu, *The Little African History Book – Black Africa from the Origins of Humanity*, p. 115; Ludo De Witte, *The Assassination of Lumumba*, trans. by Ann Wright and Renée Fenby (London, New York: Verso, 2002). Joseph Kasa-Vubu was declared President. At the Independence Day Ceremony, Belgian King Baudouin praised the progression of the Congo under his country's reign, alluding to the "genius" of his great-granduncle Leopold II. In *his* speech, Lumumba said, "For this independence of the Congo we gave our strength and our blood." Some sources also claim Lumumba added: "We are no longer your monkeys!" referring to a common slur used against Africans by Belgians.

33 P. Johnson, *A History of the Modern World* (London: Weidenfeld, 1991). One report said that as Prime Minister Lumumba made a decision to raise the pay of all government employees except for the army. Many of the military officers were Belgian, to which the lower-level Congolese army soldiers took offense.

34 In August of 2000, the Senate committee released this interview, which was with then-US National Security Council minute keeper Robert Johnson. Johnson quoted Eisenhower. FOIA declassified documents on Lumumba on the CIA website. Also see, "Patrice Lumumba: 50 Years Later, Remembering the U.S.-Backed Assassination of Congo's First Democratically Elected Leader," *Democracy Now!* Jan. 21, 2011. John Stockwell, *In Search of Enemies: A CIA Story* (W.W. Norton, 1978), p. 105.

35 Kevin Whitelaw, "A killing in Congo," *US News and World Report*, July 24, 2000, http://www.usnews.com/usnews/doubleissue/mysteries/patrice.html; Martin Kettle, "President 'ordered murder' of Congo leader," *The Guardian* (London), August 10, 2000, http://www.guardian.co.uk/Archive/Article/0,4273,4049783,00.html. Also see John Stockwell, *In Search of Enemies: A CIA Story* (1978), p. 105.

Clare Booth Luce and her husband Henry Luce, owner of Time Inc. Clare claimed that LSD "saved our marriage."

Chapter Four

CIA Drug Targets: Paul Robeson, Writers, Elvis

Henry Luce, the founder of *Time* and former *Life* magazines, was a close friend of CIA Director Allen Dulles, who held that position from 1953-61. So it is not surprising that when Luce needed to fill the position of vice-president for Time Inc., the largest media company in the U.S., he chose Dulles's CIA associate, Charles Douglas (C.D.) Jackson.

C.D. Jackson was the co-author of a CIA-sponsored study recommending the reorganization of the American intelligence services.[1] Research confirms he had a huge historical role in shaping U.S. intelligence, particularly regarding culture manipulation. During Jackson's decades-long career at Time Inc., he took several breaks for U.S. intelligence leadership work. He was deputy chief of the Psychological Warfare Division, and functioned as outside director of CIA covert operations. He later worked as Special Adviser to President Eisenhower for Psychological Warfare, and more closely enmeshed the media propaganda unit with the covert operations unit of the CIA. Jackson used Time Inc.'s publications for psychological manipulation of society at home and abroad.[2]

Jackson embodied the violently anti-Semitic, racist, anti-leftist belief system typical of the wealthiest oligarchical families with whom he helped start the CIA. The rabid anti-Communist agenda they carried out, which barred thousands of people from work, exemplified Jackson and his Psychological Warfare Division's opinion and influence.[3] Jackson's psychological warfare operations also targeted black cultural leaders. One of his propaganda projects financed black musicians, writers and actors who didn't comment on U.S. racism, eroding the livelihood of activist black writers and performing artists.[4]

One of C.D. Jackson's activist targets was the African-American singer Paul Robeson, who overcame institutionalized racism while becoming the most accomplished black entertainer of the first half of the 20th century. An extensive report from military intelligence to FBI Director Hoover detailed the close intelligence surveillance of Robeson and his wife as early as 1951, according to an FBI memo discussing his friend Richard Wright.[5]

Paul Robeson held concerts for the Freedom Riders of northern whites and blacks who came down to help Martin Luther King and the Student Nonviolent Coordinating Committee's Civil Rights work in 1960.

Robeson had achieved much in a wide variety of endeavors by the 1930s. After becoming an All-American football player at Rutgers University, he went on to graduate from Columbia Law School. He starred in plays and then movies, while also receiving honors as a world-renowned singer. Robeson's activism included raising money against Spain's fascist Generalissimo Francisco Franco during the Spanish Civil War in the mid-1930s. Robeson told President Truman that if he refused to sponsor anti-lynching legislation to stop the ongoing murders of southern blacks, they would arm themselves for self-defense.[6]

Singer Paul Robeson sang for workers rights and civil rights before he was dosed with large amounts of a psychedelic and given dozens of excessively high-dose electro-convulsive shock treatments which effectively ended his career.

British intelligence had been looking at Robeson's activities as early as 1935. In 1943, the CIA's predecessor, the Office of Strategic Services, opened a file on him. In 1947, Robeson was nearly killed in a car crash after someone tampered with his car's left wheel. Senator Joseph McCarthy's anti-Communist hearings sabotaged his acting and singing career in the U.S. in the 1950s.[7] After Robeson refused to cooperate with the HUAC/McCarthy hearings, the government blacklisted him.[8]

Robeson spoke more than twenty languages, including Russian, Chinese, and several African languages. When the government returned Robeson's passport in 1958, he decided to live in the Soviet Union, where he said he experienced less racism. Robeson was on close terms with Jawaharlal Nehru, Jomo Kenyatta, and other Third World leaders. He always planned to return to the U.S. to help lead the emerging civil rights movement.[9]

While Robeson was in the Soviet Union, he arranged a trip to Cuba for a meeting with President Fidel Castro and revolutionary leader Ernesto "Che" Guevara, scheduled for two years after Castro's revolution and two weeks before the failed U.S. "Bay of Pigs" invasion of Cuba. In lectures, interviews, and articles, Robeson's son, Paul Robeson Jr., detailed how U.S. and British intelligence orchestrated a chemical attack on his father, partly to stop

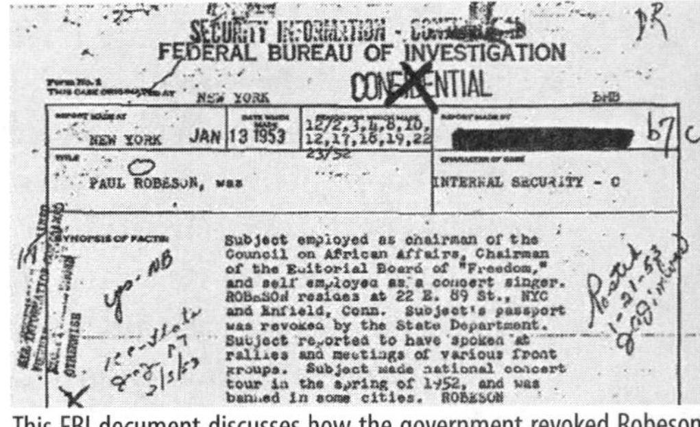

FEDERAL BUREAU OF INVESTIGATION

CONFIDENTIAL

NEW YORK

REPORT MADE AT	DATE WHEN MADE	PERIOD FOR WHICH MADE	REPORT MADE BY
NEW YORK	JAN 13 1953	12/2,3,4,8,10, 12,17,18,19,22 23/52	[redacted] b7c

TITLE	CHARACTER OF CASE
PAUL ROBESON, was	INTERNAL SECURITY - C

SYNOPSIS OF FACTS: Subject employed as chairman of the Council on African Affairs, Chairman of the Editorial Board of "Freedom," and self employed as a concert singer. ROBESON resides at 22 E. 89 St., NYC and Enfield, Conn. Subject's passport was revoked by the State Department. Subject reported to have spoken at rallies and meetings of various front groups. Subject made national concert tour in the spring of 1952, and was banned in some cities. ROBESON

This FBI document discusses how the government revoked Robeson' passport in the 1950s, before Paul Robeson Jr. said the CIA's MK-Ultr targeted his father, and himself, with psychedelic drugs.

him from jeopardizing the U.S. invasion of Cuba. As British intelligence-linked psychiatrists worked closely with the CIA on MK-Ultra, the CIA targeted Robeson with LSD.[10]

At the time, Paul Robeson was staying at a hotel in Russia. A large group of anti-Soviet Americans connected to the U.S. government had a large party in the rooms next door to Robeson's. Some of the Americans talked Robeson into joining the party where they gave him a drink that caused him to experience the symptoms of an LSD trip (note, Robeson said it was either a large dose of LSD or the more potent BZ, in different speeches). When Robeson's son went to check on his father the next day, someone also dosed his drink with a hallucinogenic. Robeson Jr. said that when he came down from his trip he was able to function again and help his father when he came out of the hallucinogenic trip.[11]

Several days later, Paul Robeson re-experienced the hallucinogenic trip and depressive symptoms. Doctors and associates talked his wife into having him go into a psychiatric hospital near London, where they kept him for two years and gave him fifty-four electric convulsive treatments at levels much higher than those used today. His son found that this, along with drug therapy used at the British hospital, matched the CIA's Project MK-Ultra "mind depatterning" technique.[12] Within months of Robeson's treatments, another leftist artist, writer Ernest Hemingway, also experienced the same damaging treatments while U.S. intelligence closely spied on him.[13]

When Paul Robeson Sr. came back to the United States, someone dosed his drink yet again. Robeson felt he couldn't fully recover from the more recent incident. He kept himself out of the public eye until his death fifteen years later, to avoid tarnishing his legacy. The CIA had effectively neutralized him.[14]

Robeson's son subsequently lectured about his father's targeting. He also told Julia Wright he believed that her father, the renowned African-American novelist Richard Wright, a close friend and political ally of Paul Robeson, was similarly targeted with LSD. With the 1940 publication of *Native Son*, Wright had become the first best-selling African-American novelist. While a mass of evidence supports the contention that U.S. intelligence targeted Wright due to his leftist political activism, adequate evidence for the use of psychedelics in that targeting has yet to appear, though it seems clear that intelligence-manipulated media played a role in an organized attempt to discredit him.

Richard Wright continued his literary success with the bestseller *Black Boy: A Record of Childhood and Youth*, published in 1944. In 1945, an article about Wright in Time-owned *Life* magazine showed a picture of unidentified adults putting a glass (of something) to a young boy's lips, with an outrageous caption: "At the age of 6, Richard Wright became a drunkard." Wright's FBI files contained a 1951 military intelligence memorandum to FBI Director Hoover discussing surveillance of Wright's meetings with Paul Robeson.

In 1960, Richard Wright spent many hours discussing strategy with Martin Luther King. In November of 1960, Wright also made a long speech discussing tactics U.S. intelligence was using in America, in Paris where he resided, and against his friend Patrice Lumumba in the Congo. It was filmed and first broadcast on November 28 on Radio Television Francaise as the first of four installments.

On the same day as the November broadcast, Richard Wright mysteriously died in a French hospital after being admitted for an ongoing mild stomach ailment. Doctors had just given Wright an otherwise clean bill of health during that hospital admission. Ollie Harrington said Wright had forewarned him of French and U.S. intelligence carrying out his murder during such a hospital stay and had developed procedures to protect himself. Harrington said this was the first time Wright strayed from those procedures. Authorities said Wright died of a heart attack and, despite family suspicions of murder, no autopsy was done.[15]

Beats & LSD: Ginsberg and Burroughs

U.S. intelligence's goal of controlling people's hearts and minds also played out with white artists who influenced the white majority. U.S. intelligence sought to manipulate, control, damage or silence such figures when they opposed the wealthy oligarchy's bigoted, hypercapitalist agenda.

The Beatniks, or Beats, wrote popular poems and books with radical political content that countered racism, anti-Communism, and the war industry. Although Senator Joseph McCarthy had been discredited in 1956, people still feared the anti-Communist witchhunts. Just after McCarthy's discrediting that year, Beat poet Allen Ginsberg published two famous poems with radical leftist sentiments.

In his poem "Howl," Ginsberg described many of "the best minds of my generation … protesting the narcotic tobacco haze of Capitalism, who distributed Supercommunist pamphlets in Union Square." In "America," Ginsberg glorified top leftist historical groups, figures and causes, asking when the U.S. …

> will be worthy of your million Trotskyites? … I feel sentiments about the Wobblies … You should have seen me reading Marx … save the Spanish loyalists … Sacco and Vanzetti must not die … I am the Scottsboro boys.

Psychiatrists who had worked for the U.S. Navy and U.S. intelligence gave Allen Ginsberg his first LSD dose in 1959, as part of the CIA MK-Ultra experiments.[16] Acid, the popular term for LSD, diverted Ginsberg and some other Beats. Ginsberg's friend Jack Kerouac wrote the highly acclaimed classic *On the Road* in the early 1950s, and later *The Dharma Bums*. In the latter book, Kerouac created a lead character who took psychedelic drugs.[17]

Within a few years, Allen Ginsberg partly weaned himself away from psychedelics. Ginsberg started feeling depressed about his drug "trips." In 1961 he visited eminent Jewish philosopher Martin Buber in Israel, and an Indian swami who influenced him away from acid. While in Japan in mid-1963 he wrote a poem titled "The Change" about leaving psychedelics behind.[18]

Another Beat writer, William S. Burroughs, took an immediate dislike for psychedelics. Burroughs was no prude about drugs, and had written several books related to his heroin addiction. He was hooked on heroin and wrote about it while living in Tangiers, producing *Naked Lunch,* a literary blockbuster. The U.S. tried to ban *Naked Lunch,* but many called it a work of allegorical genius. *Naked Lunch* beat the ban, selling well.[19]

Burroughs's fame grew as large as his Beat generation friend Jack Kerouac's. In their book *Acid Dreams,* Lee and Shlain noted Burroughs's comments on psychedelics. Looking back on the era, Burroughs eventually said, "LSD makes people less competent." About the forces behind LSD, he added, "You can see their motivation for turning people on [to acid]. Very often it's not necessary to give it more than just a little push. Make it available and the news media takes it up, and there it is. They don't have to stick their necks out very much."[20]

In 1964, Burroughs sent a warning to readers with the opening passages of his book *Nova Express*. By that time the CIA-manipulated press and operations had made LSD a popular "underground" phenomenon in the U.S. Burroughs didn't buy it, saying:

> At the immediate risk of finding myself the most unpopular character of all fiction – and history is fiction – I must say this: Bring together stay of news – Inquire onward from state to doer – Who monopolized Immortality? Who monopolized Cosmic Consciousness? Who monopolized Love Sex and Dream? Who monopolized Time Life and Fortune?

So Burroughs invoked LSD, an acronym for Love, Sex and Dream, while also alluding to the three top magazines of the day in the next sentence. Burroughs understood these magazines also served as message machines for the CIA.

Burroughs continued:

> Listen: Their Garden of Delights is a terminal sewer ... Their Immortality Cosmic Consciousness and Love is second-run grade-B

> shit ... Stay out of the Garden of Delights ... Throw back their ersatz Immortality ... Flush their drug kicks down the drain – They are poisoning and monopolizing the hallucinogenic drugs – learn to make it without any chemical corn.[21]

CIA and Oligarchy Move to Control Rock & Roll

The wealthiest oligarchy and their U.S. intelligence apparatus faced a number of threats to their influence over people's hearts and minds. The most serious emerged in the 1950s in the form of movies and music, particularly popular youth music. The FBI eventually admitted having started files on musicians such as Elvis Presley in the mid-'50s and other musicians thereafter, but never fully disclosed the reasons.[22]

In the early '50s, Allan Freed, a half-Latino Jewish disc jockey in Cleveland was credited with introducing rock music to large white audiences. White crooners such as Perry Como dominated pop radio at the start of that decade. Freed was the first large-city deejay to introduce danceable black rhythm and blues musicians to white audiences at a time when most stations only allowed white musicians' songs. Freed was credited with coining the term "rock and roll," which he borrowed from a black slang term for sex. Freed, under the moniker Moondog, drummed pencils and howled to songs. He inspired other small stations nationwide to develop his R&B format, soon forcing large stations to follow suit.[23]

By 1952 Freed's soaring influence could not be denied. That year, 25,000 people, two-thirds of them white, came to a 10,000-seat arena for Freed's first concert.[24] A few years later, Jewish mobster Morris Levy signed a deal with Allan Freed and influenced him to accept a huge salary as a deejay at WINS, one of New York City's top music stations. Freed's program became #1 within months.[25]

Levy and former OSS agent John McCaw appeared to use Allan Freed for more nefarious reasons. McCaw attended meetings of the U.S. intelligence umbrella group, the National Security Council, as he served on their Advisory Council.[26] After Freed helped make WINS the country's most popular music station, McCaw implemented changes at the station in 1957 that shaped the rock music world. WINS led the nationwide promotion of the Top 40 music format. This format helped large money interests gain the most dominant influence and control over top music sales through promotion money and radio play menus.[27] It would further aid censorship of political songs by barring them from radio play.

Levy, an associate of the Genovese Mafia family, owned top New York jazz clubs and song publishing rights. The Genovese family, started by Vito Genovese and U.S. intelligence collaborator Charles "Lucky" Luciano, were the first of the five Mafia families to break the code of not dealing drugs and were the first family to work with U.S. intelligence. The Italian Mafia took over from the Jewish mobsters who had dominated the drug trade in the 1920s.[28] With the help of Freed's popularity, Levy started the jazz and rock record label, Roulette Records, in 1956. An Assistant U.S. Attorney claimed that Roulette Records was also a way station for heroin trafficking around that time.[29]

Powerful forces started a continuous assault on Freed the following year. In 1958, when violence occurred outside a Boston arena at a Freed show, authorities indicted Freed for inciting a riot. This became a common accusation against leftist musicians and activists.[30] Although charges were dropped against Freed, McCaw fired him in 1958. On the day Freed was fired, a gunman looked for him in the WINS studio before Freed escaped. It was alleged that the gunman was an upset concert promoter.[31]

Allan Freed went to work for WABC, but researchers believe Freed was set up there and scapegoated when Orrin Hatch's congressional committee focused exclusively on him in the "payola" scandals in 1959. The term implied a "pay to play" bribe for certain songs. Morris Levy, the source of much of the payola money to play his records, was never called to testify. Fredric Dannen, author of the bestselling book, *Hit Men,* said these deals weren't illegal then, and were only considered misdemeanors thereafter. Nonetheless, the scandal effectively ended Freed's career around 1960. He died of alcoholism five years later.[32]

Elvis Enlisted and Drugged

Elvis Presley was apolitical, but socially radical for his time, defying racism and segregation. Elvis embraced African-American music and popularized rhythm and blues before virtually any other white music star of his era. He countered segregationist attitudes by expressing great admiration for black musicians and broke segregation rules in regularly attending black-only shows and events both before and after he was famous. At least a dozen black celebrities, from Muhammad Ali to Fats Domino, whom Elvis called the real "King of Rock and Roll," defended their friend Elvis against accusations of racism, as did investigating black magazines.[33]

Reports of Elvis's racism stemmed from *Sepia* magazine reprinting a rumor in 1957. A writer from another magazine, *Jet,* investigated the rumor that year and stated that it was unfounded. Furthermore, while Elvis profited off a racist music marketplace that segregated black music, he credited black musicians with creating rock.[34]

Some also considered Elvis's emotional communication revolutionary when radio first played him. One-time American Indian Movement leader

John Trudell experienced murderous U.S. intelligence attacks that killed his whole family. In the 1980s Trudell turned to music. On his Jackson Browne-produced debut CD, *AKA Grafitti Man,* Trudell included a song about Elvis titled "Baby Boom Che." Trudell said that in this song he felt Elvis was revolutionary in terms of freeing men to express their emotions openly.[35]

Television shows censored Elvis's wildly erotic, hip-shaking dancing. Many of Elvis's concerts were banned and radio station owners forced deejays to ban his music. Fans responded by, for example, throwing a brick through a station window with a note on it saying, "We'll tear up this town" if the deejays don't play his music.[36]

Biographers said Colonel Tom Parker started giving Elvis pills before he was drafted and controlled Elvis for the rest of his drug-shortened life.

As noted, the FBI admitted starting a file on Elvis Presley by the mid-1950s. Colonel Tom Parker talked Elvis into a management deal in 1955 when Elvis was twenty years old and already a star. In 1948, Tom Parker had received the rank of Colonel in the Louisiana State Militia, which was involved in major U.S. intelligence covert operations.[37] Elvis's former manager, Memphis radio deejay Bob Neal, reportedly couldn't accommodate Elvis's success and let Parker take over some duties.

Parker took complete control over Elvis Presley's management and his life. Did Parker do this on behalf of U.S. intelligence? In the late 1950s the Army drafted Elvis and mainly stationed him in Germany from 1958-60.[38] As previously noted, MK-Ultra was conducting operations with former Nazi intelligence at their military bases in Germany. A close associate of Elvis said Parker introduced Elvis to amphetamines early on, and Elvis started using them heavily while in the Army.[39] Researchers claimed that "the Elvis Presley who emerged from the army in 1960 would bear little resemblance to the Elvis who entered the service in 1958."[40]

John Lennon, who was watching Elvis's career closely, would later state on BBC Radio One: "When Elvis died, people were harassing me for a comment. I'll give it to you now. Elvis died when he went into the army. That's when they killed him, that's when they castrated him. The rest of it was just a living death."[41]

Writers described the vast control Colonel Parker took over Elvis Presley for the rest of the entertainer's strange life.[42] Parker wouldn't let Elvis perform a live concert until 1967, a hiatus of almost a decade.[43] Parker also only permitted the star to perform in films that were all of

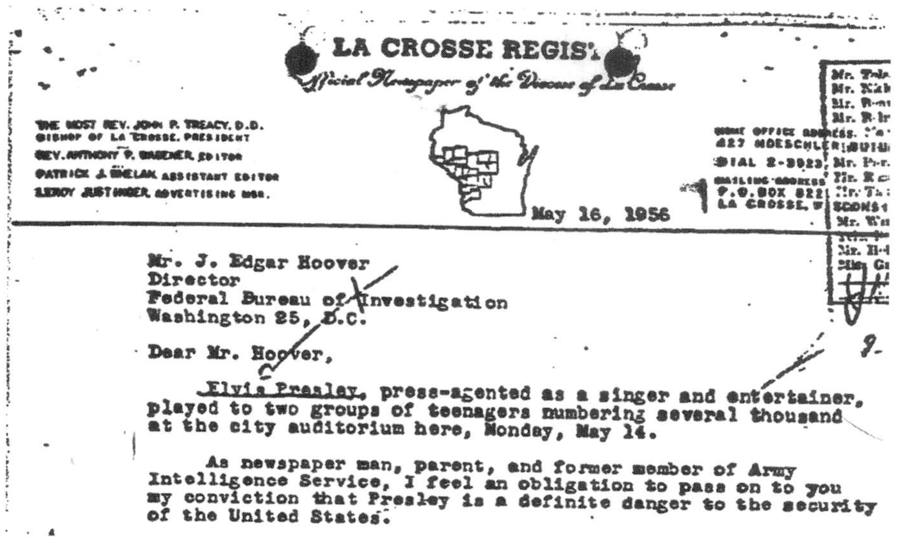
LA CROSSE REGIS[illegible]
Official Newspaper of the Diocese of La Crosse

THE MOST REV. JOHN P. TREACY, D.D. BISHOP OF LA CROSSE, PRESIDENT
REV. ANTHONY F. WAGENER, EDITOR
PATRICK J. WHELAN, ASSISTANT EDITOR
LEROY JUSTINGER, ADVERTISING MGR.

HOME OFFICE ADDRESS: 427 MOESCHLER BUILDING
DIAL 2-3923
MAILING ADDRESS: P.O. BOX 822 LA CROSSE, WISCONSIN

May 16, 1956

Mr. J. Edgar Hoover
Director
Federal Bureau of Investigation
Washington 25, D.C.

Dear Mr. Hoover,

Elvis Presley, press-agented as a singer and entertainer, played to two groups of teenagers numbering several thousand at the city auditorium here, Monday, May 14.

As newspaper man, parent, and former member of Army Intelligence Service, I feel an obligation to pass on to you my conviction that Presley is a definite danger to the security of the United States.

This document from his FBI file shows that they had started watching Elvis at least as early as 1956, when he was only 21 years old. The surveillance continued until his death.

a similar superficial type, forcing Elvis to turn down many film offers, including *West Side Story, A Star is Born,* and *Midnight Cowboy*.[44] Some said Parker gained assistance in controlling Elvis from Joe Esposito, Elvis's tour manager, whom he met during his tour of duty in West Germany in 1958.[45]

Many say that Parker and Esposito, along with several other of the "Memphis Mafia" who worked with Elvis, at least allowed, if not encouraged, his increasingly dangerous drug problem. In the 1960s and 1970s, Elvis's addiction led to multiple near-death overdoses and concerts where reports stated he could barely function.[46] If Colonel Parker and his associates worked for U.S. intelligence, as their control of Elvis suggests, the wealthiest had power over a music star with influence over millions of fans.

Bloated, overweight, 42-year-old Elvis Presley was found dead on the floor of his bathroom in 1977. Before the autopsy was complete and toxicology was known, medical examiner Jerry Francisco declared cardiac arrhythmia as the cause of death. Within months, two lab reports said that "polypharmacy" was heavily implicated.[47] Elvis's doctor George Nichopoulos had written prescriptions for 10,000 doses of amphetamines, sedatives and narcotics in Elvis's name for the eight months before the singer's death. Dr. Nichopoulos's license was suspended for three months. In the 1990s the state medical board revoked the doctor's license for overprescribing.[48] Was Nichopoulos working for U.S. intelligence before losing his immunity in the 1990s?

Notes

1 Carl Bernstein, "The CIA and the Media," *Rolling Stone*, 10/20/77, p. 63.

2 Jackson further headed CIA front groups, such as the Congress of Cultural Freedom, which obtained vast amounts of money to influence all facets of the arts. Frances Stonor Saunders, *The Cultural Cold War: The CIA and the World of Arts and Letters* (New York: The New Press, 1999), pp. 116-17, 146-49, 152-53. See citations that include C.D. Jackson, "Notes of meeting," 3/28/52 (CDJ/DDE) and Dwight D. Eisenhower, quoted in Blanche Wiesen Cook, *The Declassified Eisenhower: A Divided Legacy of Peace and Political Warfare* (New York: Doubleday, 1981). C.D. Jackson to Henry Luce, 3/28/58 (CDJ/DDE), C.D. Jackson to Abbott Washburn, 2/2/53 (CDJ/DDE) and Lawrence de Neufville, telephone interview, Geneva, March 1997. Note that CDJ/DDE stands for C.D. Jackson Papers and Records, Dwight D. Eisenhower Library, Abilene, Kansas.

3 See, for example, Victor Navasky, *Naming Names* (New York: River Run Press, 1991). On blacklisted musicians such as Pete Seeger, see www.writing.upenn.edu/~alfilreis/50s/seeger-bio-2.html.

4 On blacks and the arts, see C.D. Jackson to Nelson Rockefeller, 4/14/55 (CDJ/DDE). In this letter Jackson warned his CIA colleagues not to get the "smarty pants" idea of using these artists as intelligence sources. Saunders, *The Cultural Cold War*, pp. 180-83, 291.

5 U.S. Dept of Justice, Federal Bureau of Investigation, Washington, D.C. Liaison Office, Heidelberg, Germany, Date: 1/8/52, To: John Edgar Hoover, Director, Federal Bureau of Investigation, From George A. Vannoy, Subject: Richard Wright [REDACTED], Security Matter-C encls. Cc-Paris (encl), 67C, 67D per Army. Region XX, 66th CIC Detachment, APO [illegible] U.S. Army, 4 December 1951, File: XX-F-489.

6 Paul Robeson Jr. in *Encyclopedia of the American Left*, pp. 654-56.

7 Jeffrey St. Clair and Alexander Cockburn, "Nature & Politics: Did the CIA Poison Paul Robeson?" www.eatthestate.org, Volume 3, #33, 5/12/99. Also see it at http://www.ratical.org/ratville/JFK/JohnJudge/CIA-Robeson.html.

8 Paul Robeson Jr. in *Encyclopedia of the American Left*, pp. 654-6.

9 St. Clair and Cockburn, "Nature & Politics: Did the CIA Poison Paul Robeson?" See note 7 for websites.

10 On Castro being on CIA "hit list" for dosing with LSD, see Lee & Shlain, *Acid Dreams*, pp. 35, 44-45, 52-53, CIA document from June 9, 1954, *Project MK-ULTRA, The CIA's Program of Research in Behavior Modification*, Joint Hearing before the Select Committee on Intelligence and the Subcommittee on Health and Scientific Research of the Committee on Human Resources, United States Senate, August 3, 1977. Also see Paul Robeson, Jr., "The Paul Robeson Files," *The Nation*, 12/20/99, www.frankolsonproject.org/Articles/Robeson,%20Nation.html. Robeson Jr.'s article for *The Nation* says his father was dosed with BZ, but his direct lectures state it was LSD. He repeated these accounts and described them in detail on the *Democracy Now!* radio show; http://www.democracynow.org/1999/7/1/did_the_cia_drug_paul_robeson. Julia Wright met with Paul Robeson Jr. as he was being interviewed on a radio program in Philadelphia. She read the transcript from that recorded talk at the Richard Wright Centennial Celebration in Paris, where this author also interviewed her, on June 18, 2008.

11 To hear Paul Robeson Jr's incredible direct account, http://voxunion.com/realaudio/coupradio/RobesonJr.mp3.

12 Personal Interview, Julia Wright, 6/18/08, Paris. At least one study in 2007 showed that ECT, even in its more refined uses today, can cause "permanent amnesia and cognitive deficits," though most medical authorities disagree with this finding. PRNewswire-USNewswire, "Electroconvulsive Therapy Causes Permanent Amnesia and Cognitive Deficits, Prominent Researcher Admits," *Forbes*, 12/21/06, http://www.prnewswire.com/news-releases/electroconvulsive-therapy-causes-permanent-amnesia-and-cognitive-deficits-prominent-researcher-admits-57223302.html. For the research article discussed, see Harold A. Sackheim et al., "The Cognitive Effects of Electroconvulsive Therapy in Community Settings," *Neuropsychopharmacology* 32 (2007), pp. 244-54, http://www.nature.com/npp/journal/v32/n1/pdf/1301180a.pdf.

13 Peter Beaumont, "Fresh claim over role the FBI played in suicide of Ernest Hemingway," *The Guardian/The Observer* (London), 7/2/11, http://www.guardian.co.uk/books/2011/jul/03/fbi-and-ernest-hemingway.

14 Paul Robeson Jr., http://voxunion.com/realaudio/coupradio/RobesonJr.mp3.

15 Ann Rayson, "Richard Wright's Life," *Modern American Poetry*, http://www.english.illinois.edu/maps/poets/s_z/r_wright/wright_life.htm. Richard Wright, *A Father's Law* (New York: Harper Perennial, 2008), Introduction by Julia Wright with Timeline, pp. 16-17. This author possesses a copy of the *Life* magazine "drunkard" photograph, article/picture undated. On FBI discussion of their surveillance of Wright's meetings with Paul Robeson: U.S. Dept of Justice, Federal Bureau of Investigation, Washington, D.C. Liaison Office, Heidelberg, Germany, Date: 1/8/52, To: John Edgar Hoover, Director, Federal Bureau of Investigation, From George A. Vannoy, Subject: Richard Wright [REDACTED], Security Matter-C encls. Cc-Paris (encl), 67C, 67D per Army. Region XX, 66th CIC Detachment, APO [illegible] U.S. Army, 4 December 1951, File: XX-F-489. On Wright speech and strategizing with MLK: Addison Gayle, *Richard Wright: Ordeal of a Native Son* (Garden City, NY: Anchor/Doubleday, 1980), pp. 298-99, Ollie Harrington, *Why I Left America and Other Essays* (Jackson, MS: University of Mississippi Press, 2010), pp. 15-16. African-American newspapers, such as the *Chicago Defender*, printed much content from this speech: Gayle, *Richard Wright*, p. 273. Michael Fabre, *The Unfinished Quest of Richard Wright* (Chicago: University of Illinois Press, 1993), pp. 516-19. On Wright's last days and aftermath: Harrington, *Why I Left America*, p. 25. Also film, *Richard Wright-Black Boy*, dir. Madison Davis Lacy; co-producers include: Mississippi Educational Television, the Independent Television Service, Madison Davis Lacy and the British Broadcasting Corporation (BBC), 1994. It first aired on PBS in 1995.

16 Martin Lee and Bruce Shlain, *Acid Dreams: The Complete Social History of LSD: The CIA, the Sixties, and Beyond* (New York: Grove Press, 1994), p. 58.

17 Jack Kerouac, *On the Road* (New York: Viking Penguin, 1957); *The Dharma Bums* (New York: Viking Penguin, 1958).

18 Lee and Shlain, *Acid Dreams*, p. 112.

19 See transcripts from trial of Burroughs for charges of obscenity in writing *Naked Lunch*: http://realitystudio.org/texts/naked-lunch/trial/. Also Ted Morgan, *Literary Outlaw: The Life and Times of William S. Burroughs* (New York: Avon, 1988).

20 Lee and Shlain, *Acid Dreams*, pp. 81-82, 282.

21 Lee and Shlain, *Acid Dreams*, p. 82.

22 See, for example, Alex Constantine, *The Covert War Against Rock* (Los Angeles, Feral House, 2000), p. 12 on U.S. intelligence focus on music. Constantine also stated that samples of FBI files on Elvis, Jimi Hendrix and Jim Morrison can be found in their reading room. Also see Fenton Bressler, *Who Killed John Lennon* (New York: St. Marks, 1989), p. 9.

23 Frederic Dannen, *Hit Men* (New York: Vintage Books, 1991), pp.42-43, 46. On Freed widely credited with coining the term "rock and roll" from the black community's slang for sex, see "Allan Freed" at www.history-of-rock.com/freed.htm. It cites the Dominoes' "Sixty Minute Man," for the slang. This source also told of small stations imitating Freed, and actually used the words, "eventually forcing large stations to follow suit." On ethnicity, see http://www.jewornotjew.com/profile.jsp?ID=941.

24 On 25,000 people showing up, http://groups.msn.com/Teddyboyrock/biographyofallanfreed.msnw. This source cites a book on Freed by John A. Jackson, *Big Beat Heat: Allan Freed and the Early Years of Rock and Roll* (New York: Schirmer, 1995). Jackson has written many books on music, and this book was made into an NBC movie.

25 On Levy and Freed, see Fredric Dannen, *Hit Men*, pp. 37-38, 42-46, 164 n, 272-99. That Paramount Pictures paid Allan Freed $29,000 a day to make a teen movie in 1957 exemplified Freed's immense success in the music world, http://groups.msn.com/Teddyboyrock/biographyofallanfreed.msnw, from John A. Jackson, *Big Beat Heat*.

26 Constantine, *The Covert War Against Rock*, pp. 19-22.

27 Rick Sklar, *Rocking America: How the All-Hit Radio Stations Took Over* (New York: St.

Martin's Press, 1994) pp.11, 17, 19. Cited in Constantine, *Covert War Against Rock*, pp. 19-22.

28 Selwyn Raab, *Five Families: The Rise, Decline, and Resurgence of America's Most Powerful Mafia Empires* (New York: St. Martin's Press, 2006). On Genovese family history of working with U.S. intelligence, see Constantine, *Covert War Against Rock*, pp. 19-22. On Mafia, particularly Genovese, and U.S. intelligence collaboration in WWII and then drug trafficking, see Alfred McCoy, *The Politics of Heroin: CIA Complicity in the Global Drug Trade* (New York: Lawrence Hill Books, 1991), pp. 30, 35-37, 73-74. Also see Clarence Lusane, *Pipe Dream Blues: Racism and the War on Drugs* (Boston: South End Press, 1991), pp. 38-42. McCoy is a professor of Southeast Asian History at University of Wisconsin-Madison and Lusane is a professor at University of the District of Columbia. On Jewish gangs, see U.S. Congress, Senate, Committee on Government Operations, Organized Crime and Illicit Traffic in Narcotics, 88th Cong., 1st and 2nd sess. (Washington, DC: U.S. Government Printing Office, 1964) pp. 4, 913; cited in McCoy, *The Politics of Heroin*, p. 28.

29 On charge of Roulette for heroin traficking, Dannen, *Hit Men*, p. 53.

30 On Boston inciting riot charge, "Allan Freed" at www.history-of-rock.com/freed.htm, also in http://groups.msn.com/Teddyboyrock/biographyofallanfreed.msnw. Also see Jackson, *Big Beat Heat*.

31 On gunman looking to kill Freed in the music studio after McCaw fired him, Sklar, *Rocking America*, p. 46, cited in *Covert War Against Rock*, pp. 19-22. Rick Sklar's wife was at the scene when a gunman came to the station looking for Freed that day.

32 Constantine, *Covert War Against Rock*, pp.19-22. Fredric Dannen, *Hit Men*, pp.37-38, 42-46. Dannen said that "payola" wasn't illegal at that time, Congress only made it a misdemeanor thereafter, and noone besides Freed was penalized.

33 Peter Guralnick, *Last Train to Memphis: The Rise of Elvis Presley* (Little, Brown: 1994).

34 Michael T. Bertrand, *Race, Rock, and Elvis* (University of Illinois Press: 2000). Jody Cook, Graceland National Historic Landmark Nomination Form [PDF], United States Department of the Interior, 2004. Also see http://www.elvis.com.au/presley/elvis_not_racist.shtml.

35 John Trudell, *AKA Grafitti Man* (Rykodisc, 1992). Also see David Hadju, "Hustling Elvis," *New York Review of Books*, 10/9/03. Also has note of Elvis memorizing *Rebel Without a Cause* scenes.

36 Linda Martin and Kerry Seagrave, *Anti-Rock: The Opposition to Rock 'n' Roll* (New York: Da Capo Press, 1993), p. 66; as example, authors cite *Variety* 204:1, September 5, 1956.

37 Adam Victor, *The Elvis Encyclopedia* (Gerald Duckworth & Co Ltd.), pp. 384–95. One other major U.S. intelligence covert operation in which the Louisiana State Militia, also called the Louisiana Army National Guard, was documented to have played a major role was Martin Luther King's assassination. Martin Luther King's friend and family attorney, William Pepper, claimed in his book *Orders to Kill* that the 20th Special Forces Group played a significant role in the assassination. Pepper wrote that the 20th SFG participated in "'behind the fence' [covert] operations. This group was made of reservists from Alabama, Mississippi, Florida and Louisiana"; William Pepper, *Orders to Kill: The Truth Behind the Murder of Martin Luther King, Jr.* (New York: Warner Books, 1995), p. 414.

38 Martin and Seagrave, *Anti-rock*, pp. 66-67.

39 Michael Lollar, "Parker's Shadowy Past New to Memphis Mafia," *The Commercial Appeal* (Memphis, TN), 3/18/05.

40 Martin and Seagrave, *Anti-rock*, pp. 67-68.

41 Phil Strongman, *John Lennon: Life, Times & Assassination* (Liverpool, England: Bluecoat Press, 2010), p. 216.

42 David Hadju, "Hustling Elvis," *New York Review of Books*, 10/9/03.

43 Martin and Seagrave, *Anti-rock*, pp. 67-68.

44 Hadju, "Hustling Elvis." Also see interview with Elvis tour manager Joe Espisito at http://www.elvispresleynews.com/JoeEsposito.html.

45 Joe Espisito at http://www.elvispresleynews.com/JoeEsposito.html.

46 Alan Higginbotham, "Doctor Feelgood," *The Observer* (London), August 11, 2002. Peter Guralnick, *Careless Love: The Unmaking of Elvis Presley* (Back Bay Books, 1999).

47 Guralnick, *Careless Love*.

48 Higginbotham, "Doctor Feelgood."

Chapter Five

MK-Ultra East? Civil Rights,LSD and Leary

In 1957 and 1958, American college students organized to protest in ways never seen before concerning issues of racial equality and free speech, and against the often mandatory participation in the Reserve Officer Training Corps (ROTC).[1] Students organized large demonstrations involving thousands of people and, in 1959, started the pacifist Student Peace Union, a nationwide group on dozens of campuses.[2]

In 1960, the Students for a Democratic Society (SDS) first convened in Michigan, demonstrating for labor and civil rights issues. In the 1960s, SDS members became Freedom Riders to combat racial inequality in the South, joining forces with the Student Nonviolent Coordinating Committee (SNCC) to desegregate buses, register southern blacks to vote, and for other civil rights. Mostly-white SDS increased in numbers nationwide.[3]

In the early 1960s, civil rights demonstrations and marches began exploding onto newspaper front pages in the U.S. and abroad. On the 1st of October of 1962, in Oxford, Mississippi, mobs killed two residents and a French journalist, while injuring 375, in an unsuccessful attempt at stopping the integration of the University of Mississippi. In Birmingham, Alabama, fire marshals used firehoses on civil rights demonstrators. The high-pressure water hoses caused broken legs and caved in rib cages. Arrests were made by the hundreds. [4]

Top Spies Promote, Distribute Acid

Besides dosing leftist leaders, when the civil rights movement and student activism began gaining ground, the CIA's MK-Ultra used its media assets and agents to promote LSD to the masses. After writing the definitive book on the politics of heroin, Professor Alfred McCoy studied CIA interrogation. He found that from 1953 to 1963, the CIA received funding of $25 million for mind-control research, with MK-Ultra supervising 149 projects and 33 subprojects.[5] With researchers finding that LSD led many to "personality deterioration toward a nonactivist role in society," conservative Hudson Institute think-tank consultants would later reveal their purpose of having "social control" over many young people and creating a "dropped out" society.[6]

The previously mentioned superspy and uranium entrepreneur, Captain Al Hubbard, worked for the Treasury Department, the Federal Narcotics Bureau and the Food and Drug Administration at the same time the latter two organizations assisted the CIA's drug-testing programs.[7] During the 1960s Hubbard worked for the major defense-contracting company Teledyne.[8] Top CIA personnel involved in MK-Ultra knew Hubbard well.[9] By the late 1960s, Hubbard worked for the Stanford Research Institute. It received funding from Britain's version of MK-Ultra, the Tavistock Institute, as well as the U.S. Army, to work on "chemical incapacitants." The Stanford Research Institute's director admitted he was at war with leftist protesters.[10]

Captain Alfred Hubbard straddl several government agencies th also worked with MK-Ultra, as spread LSD around the world allegedly benevolent reasons.

From an early period of MK-Ultra, Hubbard carried out tasks similar to those carried out by MK-Ultra Director Sidney Gottlieb. Author Hank Albarelli reported: "Throughout the 1950s, Hubbard received large shipments of LSD directly from Sandoz in Switzerland, with Agency [CIA] approval."[11] With unlimited access, Hubbard flew around North America and Europe supplying distributors with vast amounts of LSD.[12]

British psychiatrist Humphrey Osmond had joined forces with Hubbard in the early 1950s, shortly after Hubbard tried his first hit of LSD. Osmond received CIA funds for his work in Canada with LSD.[13] An associate of Hubbard's said that with Osmond's help, Hubbard had influenced, "a prime minister, assistants to heads of state, UN representatives and members of the British parliament," to participate in LSD sessions. Hubbard said, "My job was to sit on the couch next to the psychiatrist and put the people through it, which I did."[14] These targets were likely an expansion of the number of leftists on the CIA's original acid hit list for possible mental damage.

Researcher Martin Lee said Hubbard gave LSD to thousands of people from all walks of life—policemen, statesmen, captains of industry, church figures and scientists. Hubbard had such vast influence he even obtained papers from the Vatican granting him permission to use LSD within the context of the Catholic Church, using it on certain priests. (Were these "liberation" theologists or similarly activist leftists?)[15] Hubbard brought large stashes of acid to a Los Angeles psychiatrist who introduced it to philosopher Alan Watts, researchers Sidney Cohen, Keith Ditman and Arthur Chandler.

A Hubbard-supplied psychiatrist also gave LSD to influential writers like Anais Nin and entertainers Jack Nicholson, James Coburn, Lord Buckley and Cary Grant. [16] Time Inc., with its strong U.S. intelligence connections, promoted positive quotes by these public figures, and published generally positive articles with quotes from "expert" psychiatrists about LSD.[17]

While Time/Life's owner, Henry Luce, was a close friend of CIA Director Allen Dulles,[18] Time's Vice President C.D. Jackson continued to work for U.S. intelligence, particularly regarding culture manipulation in the Psychological Warfare Division. Jackson also headed various CIA front groups, like the Congress of Cultural Freedom, which obtained approximately $200,000 for administrative costs in 1951 (equivalent to $1.7 million in 2011) and tens of millions of dollars from the CIA over the next seventeen years to influence all facets of the arts.[19]

Through his acid promotion activities, Al Hubbard gained the title of the "Johnny Appleseed" of LSD. This title was common in mainstream media, the nickname suggesting that undercover agents such as Hubbard were well meaning. In the same period, high-level CIA whistleblowers countered any good intentions of the agents involved in CIA tasks, reporting that the CIA carried out genocidal operations globally.[20]

From approximately 1955 until 1966, undercover MK-Ultra agents employed prostitutes to dose people. CIA agent George Hunter White and others paid drug-addicted prostitutes in both New York and San Francisco to pose as non-professionals. They would pick up men and bring them back to safe houses where the men would be unknowingly dosed with LSD. It remains uncertain if these were actual targets or test subjects, but the fact that these operations were run in areas of leftist activism suggests the former.[21]

Civil Rights: Freedom Riders & SDS

In conjunction with increasing white student activism, civil rights demonstrations gained more national support. The leftist national organization, Students for a Democratic Society (SDS), grew dramatically each year. Starting with 250 members, by 1964 membership grew to 2,500.

As early as 1962, professors at Brandeis University (near Boston), organized for university reform that could help spread leftist ideas and leftist activism. Top leftist sociologist, Herbert Marcuse, taught there and helped bring together a conference with other leftist professors including Paul Goodman, and SDS leaders such as Tom Hayden. SDS members wrote about it in their school newspapers.[22]

A PBS special noted President John Kennedy's moves towards integration: "In 1962 President Kennedy sent hundreds of U.S. marshals to enforce a court order to admit African American James Meredith to the University of Mississippi. The marshals encountered fierce resistance from violent segregationists. In a melee, two people were killed and dozens injured."

White activists came from the North to aid SNCC and Martin Luther King Jr.'s organization in the South. Southern racists continued their reaction to these inroads with ever-increasing violence towards civil rights organizers, soon bombing organizers' homes and offices. Blacks rioted in response.[23] Between June and October of 1964, twenty-four Black churches were bombed in Mississippi alone.[24] Segregationists set off so many bombs in Birmingham, Alabama, it became known as "Bombingham."

It remains uncertain what role U.S. intelligence played in these racist attacks. A professor's book, *The Informant*, detailed the work of undercover FBI agent, Gary Rowe, who was "in the vicinity of just about every conflagration of racial violence in the virulently segregated Alabama of the early 1960s. He was around for beatings, bombings, ultimately even murder." The book said he almost never arrested anyone and kept several top Klansmen from getting arrested after their brutal crimes. With the CIA leadership's vehemently racist history regarding the eugenics movement, did undercover agents take an active role in fomenting these racist attacks?[25]

In 1963, King led a civil rights march to Washington D.C. where he delivered his famous "I Have a Dream" speech. Folk singer Bob Dylan played at that event and influenced young whites to get involved in civil rights activism. Within a few years, Dylan sidelined himself from activism after using psychedelics and taking on the motto "Better Living through Chemistry." The temporary but increasing blurriness of this once brilliant mind can be heard in interviews from late 1965 to 1968. (Note that Dylan also had a serious motorcycle accident in July of 1966. Proof of U.S. intelligence directly targeting Dylan is lacking.)[26]

One of the largest civil rights groups was the Congress of Racial Equality (CORE). While activists founded CORE in Chicago, the New York chapter was considered indistinguishable from the Chicago national office, due to so many CORE leaders living in New York. A large wave of white leftist students joined in 1961. They became Freedom Riders that summer and the following few summers.[27]

The civil rights movement and white student support brought major changes for the cause. In 1963 alone, Americans held 1,412 demonstrations. More and more white Northern students traveled down South for the Freedom Rides to register black voters. The white segregationist backlash culminated in the 1964 murders of three SNCC members—two Jewish activists from New York, Michael Schwerner and Andrew Goodman, along with a black activist from Mississippi, James Chaney. Evidence suggests that police aided the Ku Klux Klan in killing them.[28]

Brit Doses U.N. Members, Controls Timothy Leary

The increase of activism coincided with an increase of U.S. intelligence's spread of LSD. Along with American agents who worked on spreading LSD, help came from MI6, the British version of the CIA. While a former MI6 agent claimed MI6 supervised the CIA's work promulgating LSD and other drug use, the truth of this can't be ascertained.[29] As previously noted, Britain's Tavistock Institute ran a congruent operation with the CIA's MK-Ultra regarding the use of acid as a spy weapon.[30]

Britain's Michael Hollingshead dosed many unsuspecting foreign leaders through his job at the United Nations. Hollingshead threw parties at his Fifth Avenue apartment where he invited people from the U.N, reportedly covering his entire apartment with LSD so anyone who touched anything got a dose of acid involuntarily.[31] In a memoir, Hollingshead said he was on a "crusade to launch LSD on the world!" as if for the love of humanity.[32]

Hollingshead's links to the CIA and British intelligence suggest the more insidious shared motives of the CIA's Dr. Sidney Gottlieb and Richard Helms. Hollingshead said that in 1961 he worked as executive secretary of the Institute for British American Cultural Exchange, "a semi-official British propaganda agency in the field of international cultural relations where creating propaganda was a primary task." British police detective Dick Lee called Hollingshead's organization the "British Council," which was heavily funded by King George VI in 1940, while also working partly for the British government in "cultural propaganda," much like the CIA.[33]

Hollingshead admitted he got funding for his group from the Rockefeller Institute. This Institute channeled CIA funds for MK-Ultra projects at universities. Nelson Rockefeller sat on the National Security Council in the early 1950s, which decided to okay CIA funding for these MK-Ultra projects.[34]

Michael Hollingshead further revealed that CIA asset Lionel Trilling served on his Institute for British American Cultural Exchange's board of directors. For her book, *The Cultural Cold War*, Frances Stonor Saunders interviewed key people who verified that Trilling knowingly accepted CIA aid for his work over many years and was highly involved in CIA work. Trilling recommended the director for a CIA front group, the Fairfield Foundation, and he worked on acquiring funds for the American Committee for Cultural Freedom. Saunders found that the CIA's Psychological Strategy Board supervised the American Committee for Cultural Freedom. She also found the Fairfield Foundation was meant to be a cover for CIA funding of artists and writers, paying for Trilling's trips to Poland, Rome, Athens and Berlin.[35]

In 1961, Michael Hollingshead, with CIA approval, bought a gram of LSD. This amount allowed him to make 10,000 hits of the drug, which he did with the help of a physician associate in New York. Hollingshead went to Harvard University with a mayonnaise jar full of these doses, which he distributed liberally.[36]

In 1964, when William S. Burroughs printed his warnings about LSD, the CIA's MK-Ultra projects already had vast covert programs to promote its use on both American coasts. On the East Coast at Boston's Harvard University, Psychology Professor Timothy Leary ran experiments (also conducted at other schools nationwide) where professors received grants to pay students to take psychedelic drugs. A group called the Human Ecology Fund gave Leary and other professors the money for this work.[37]

MK-Ultra scientists gave depositions about the start of the Human Ecology Fund. The CIA started it in 1959 at Cornell University Medical School in New York City as a covert funding source for various MK-Ultra projects. Besides Cornell and Harvard, it involved other prestigious universities near hotbeds of student activism, such as Stanford University near Berkeley, California, and Johns Hopkins University in Baltimore, Maryland, where student-led civil rights activism had made considerable headway.

Harvard, Stanford, Hopkins and Yale had all been hotbeds for eugenics, suggesting why they spearheaded these experiments. Harvard, Stanford and Cornell Medical Schools became epicenters for MK-Ultra activities, paying student volunteers to take part in experiments with psychedelics, from mushrooms to LSD. Many of the volunteer students had poor, ethnic immigrant backgrounds and were in need of the money to help pay their way in school. [38] In total, the CIA allocated $7-13 million for 44 colleges and universities to conduct this research (twelve hospitals and 24 other institutions received MK-Ultra funds and conducted similar experiments).[39]

Up to this time, Prof. Leary had done tests only with psilocybin (mushrooms). Leary hadn't tried LSD and said he wasn't eager to begin, as he believed one psychedelic was like all others. Researcher Martin Lee detailed how in 1961, Hollingshead first convinced Leary to try acid with him, after Leary's initial refusal.

Lee noted that Hollingshead gave Leary about six times the normal dose of acid, which had Leary "tripping" for three days. The experience led Leary to consider Hollingshead his guru. Leary's closest Harvard Psilocybin Project associates, Richard Alpert and Ralph Metzner, were upset to see Leary in a helpless state and blamed Hollingshead for having "blown [Leary's] mind" in the destructive sense. Lee described Hollingshead as very witty, and the potbellied Brit eventually convinced doubters Alpert and Metzner, along with other Harvard associates, to sample the acid from his mayonnaise jar. Soon after they started using LSD as part of their research.[40]

This fell in line with CIA MK-Ultra goals regarding LSD. The United States Senate's Church Committee would eventually investigate and publish a little-known report detailing MK-Ultra. It stated that one goal of MK-Ultra was to manipulate foreign leaders after dosing them with LSD. The Senate Select Committee's report cited a memorandum from the Director of Security to [MK-Ultra subproject] Artichoke, Subject: "ARTICHOKE Restatement of Program." It stated that the CIA was using LSD "in order to develop means for the control of the activities and mental capacities of individuals whether willing or not."[41] This source also cited the use of LSD on unwitting Americans. This and other evidence indicates MK-Ultra similarly worked against American cultural and political leaders at home.

Through Timothy Leary, Hollingshead met top jazz artists such as white trumpet player Maynard Ferguson. Hollingshead smoked a joint with Ferguson and his wife, and told them about acid. By the end of the night Hollingshead had the Fergusons sampling his mayonnaise jar supply.[42]

In an interview later in life, Leary admitted that within a year of his first acid trip, "I was working as an intelligence agent since 1962. I was a witting agent of the CIA."[43]

Leary & MK-Ultra Push Acid on East Coast Icons

Harvard University expelled Leary and Alpert in 1963 for taking too much LSD with the subjects of their experimentation. The two professors immediately started a grassroots nonprofit group called the International Federation of Internal Freedom (IFIF) and Leary's "guru" Hollingshead joined them in this venture. They opened offices in Boston, New York, Los Angeles and headquarters in Mexico near Acapulco. Mexico expelled them after six weeks, but not before the group acquired 3,000 dues-paying members.[44]

IFIF quickly found new benefactors and participants. Peggy Mellon Hitchcock opened IFIF's New York office, and her brother, William Mellon Hitchcock, rented IFIF his 4,000-acre estate in Duchess County, N.Y. for only $500 a month. At the center of the estate was Millbrook, a sixty-four-room mansion, where Leary lived and set up shop. They started a major expansion of the weekly LSD parties that MK-Ultra scientist Harold Abramson had thrown at his Long Island home.

Much evidence supports the notion that the CIA's MK-Ultra guided IFIF. William Hitchcock's uncle, Andrew Mellon, was a wealthy Pittsburgh financier (Mellon Bank), and Hitchcock's grandfather, William Larimer Mellon founded Gulf Oil (later Chevron), one of the largest oil companies in the world.[45] During the 1940s, the Mellon family held U.S. intelligence posts in Madrid, London, Geneva and Paris.[46] Paul Mellon worked for the Special Operations Executive in London while his sister, Alisa (once known as the world's richest woman), was married to his OSS London chief.[47] Europe OSS operations chief Allen Dulles supervised them at that time. Later Dulles supervised all of U.S. intelligence as CIA Director, overseeing eight-plus years of MK-Ultra, until President John F. Kennedy replaced him in 1961.[48]

Martin Lee noted how "certain influential members of the Mellon family maintained close ties with the CIA. Mellon family foundations have been used repeatedly as conduits for Agency funds. Notably, Richard Helms was a frequent guest of the Mellon patriarchs in Pittsburgh during his tenure as CIA director (1966-1973)."[49]

Lee referred to William Mellon Hitchcock as the black sheep of the family, but William's actions stayed in line with those of his sister Peggy. While Timothy Leary, Hollingshead and Alpert lived in Bill Hitchcock's mansion, Hitchcock stayed a half-mile away in a private four-bedroom house. As a millionaire and member of one of the country's wealthiest families, he threw many parties for his elite social circles. Despite a $65,000/month allowance from his trust fund, Bill Hitchcock also still worked each morning, talking with Swiss and Bahamian bankers. The CIA used both for covert operations such as laundering cocaine money with the Bank of Credit and Commerce International (BCCI). He kept in close contact with New York brokers and investors, inviting them over to Leary's parties two hours north of New York City, where he helped initiate many, most likely his enemies, to acid.[50]

Timothy Leary with William Mellon Hitc cock. Leary admitted working for the C while Hitchcock's family owned Mellon Ba and Gulf Oil and held several U.S. intelligen posts. Hitchcock and his sister funded t world's largest LSD-trafficking group.

At the Millbrook mansion, Hollingshead apparently had access to various new CIA drugs and used Alpert as a guinea pig. When Alpert went to sleep early one night with a cold, Hollingshead injected him with the short-acting superpsychedelic DMT. After, while Alpert was still high on the DMT, Hollingshead gave him 800 micrograms of LSD. Later, Alpert believed he could fly and jumped out of a second-story window, ending up with a broken leg.[51]

Several top government psychiatrists and physicians regularly passed through or set up an office at Millbrook. Max "Feelgood" Jacobson worked in the White House. At Millbrook, Jacobson injected people with psychedelics.[52] He would later give regular injections to members of artist Andy Warhol's "Factory" in New York City.

Other intelligence agents reported mentoring Leary at this time. Top spy Alfred Hubbard frequently spoke to Leary and supplied drugs to him.[53] MK-Ultra psychiatrist Humphrey Osmond was yet another MK-Ultra figure who set up shop at Millbrook.

Martin Lee called Millbrook the "Psychedelic Central for the whole East Coast." It attracted jazz musicians including Steve Swallow and Charles Lloyd. Philosopher R.D. Laing joined the party, as did cartoonist Saul Steinberg and left-wing satirist Paul Krassner. Krassner said Hollingshead guided his trip.[54]

Paul Krassner later gave acid to fellow secular Jewish comedians Groucho Marx and Lenny Bruce.[55] Bruce, an extremely popular young comedian, had leftist political alliances, particularly about integration and civil rights. Bruce developed a heroin habit and ended up dying of a heroin overdose.

NASA scientist Steve Groff created a new military incapacitating agent: JB-118; its action was similar to that of the Army's BZ. Both were potent superhallucinogenics that made users feel they were in free fall, and gave them bizarre visions. Millbrook resident Ralph Metzner said Millbrook attendees took these drugs. They proceeded to see things that were not there, along with walking into furniture and doors.

Another Millbrook visitor named Arthur Kleps swore that Hollingshead placed a few thousand micrograms of pure Sandoz acid in some brandy by his bed. Kleps ended up founding the Neo-American Boohoo Church in 1966. He declared LSD a sacrament and sought protection under the law similar to Native Americans' sacrament of peyote. A judge ruled against the Boohoos, saying that a group with "Row, Row, Row Your Boat" as its theme couldn't be taken seriously enough to qualify as a church.[56]

Researcher Lee reported that Leary, Hollingshead and their associates tried to "program" people's trips in "ways analogous to that of the CIA and the military." While Lee assumed Hollingshead's associates and the CIA had different goals, the work of Humphrey Osmond and Al Hubbard indicates the opposite.[57] These MK-Ultra figures, along with Hollingshead and Bill Mellon Hitchcock, make it clear that U.S. and British intelligence had their own covert psychedelic guinea pig farm at Millbrook. They accomplished domestically the same task that MK-Ultra directors Gottlieb and Hubbard had conducted abroad with their "psychedelic hit list."

Timothy Leary and his CIA associates also ran an advertising campaign for acid. Leary linked LSD to sex. He first called it a shortcut to mystical enlightenment. Later he talked about it as a new form of radical politics, to appeal to activists, calling it "erotic politics." He also called it a "cure for homosexuality" and said it led women to have several hundred orgasms during an LSD session. TV film crews regularly appeared at Millbrook, broadening Leary's propaganda worldwide.[58]

Hubbard's regular partner, MK-Ul psychiatrist Humphrey Osmond, s up shop in Mellon Hitchcock's ma sion, where Leary held constant a parties during the mid-'60s, attra ing many from New York City.

Eventually, Duchess County parents got upset when their teens visited Millbrook. They got local sheriff, and future Watergate conspirator, G. Gordon Liddy to break down Millbrook's door, arresting Leary amongst a group watching a film of a waterfall. The Supreme Court overturned Leary's arrest, purportedly because he wasn't read his rights. After the arrest, Liddy set up a roadblock and submitted people to strip-searches, ending the Millbrook scene in 1967.[59] It's uncertain how many activists and potential activists tripped there before it closed.

Notes

1 Kenneth Cloke, *A Brief History of Civil Liberties Protest Movements in Berkeley – From TASC to SLATE to FSM* (1957-1965) (Santa Monica, CA: CDR Press, 1994), pp. 20-27.

2 Kirkpatrick Sale, *SDS: The rise and development of the Students for a Democratic Society ...* (New York: Vintage, 1973), p. 16. For more on Student Peace Union, see Maurice Isserman, *If I Had a Hammer* (New York, Basic Books, 1987), pp. 195, 198.

3 Sale, *SDS*, pp. 22-23, 28-36. Sale's *SDS* is probably the most comprehensively researched account of the Students for a Democratic Society.

4 Nick Bryant, "Black Man Who Was Crazy Enough to Apply to Ole Miss," *Journal of Blacks in Higher Education* 53 (Autumn 2006), pp. 60-71.

5 Alfred McCoy, *A Question of Torture: CIA Interrogation, from the Cold War to the War on Terror* (New York: Metropolitan, 2006), pp. 28-31. Note that this $25 million would be $193 million in 2014 dollars. McCoy cites: Central Intelligence Agency. Memorandum for: The Record, Subject: Discussion with ... Chief ... Division, and ... Chief of ... on Utilization of ... Assets, August 9, 1960, [Sgd.] Sidney Gottlieb, Deputy Chief, TSD/Research Branch, File: Subproject 121 MKUltra, Box 4, CIA Behavior Control Experiments Collection, National Security Archive, Washington. McCoy also cited John Ranleigh, *The Agency: The Rise and Decline of the CIA* (New York: Simon and Schuster, 1986), pp. 204-08, 575-76, 778; and Harvey Weinstein, *Psychiatry and the CIA: Victims of Mind Control* (Washington, DC: American Psychiatric Press, 1990).

6 Conrad J. Schwarz, "The Complications of LSD: A Review of the Literature," *Journal of Nervous and Mental Disease* Vol. 146, No. 2 (1968), p. 184. See Hudson Institute consultant Herman Kahn; Martin Lee and Bruce Shlain, *Acid Dreams: The Complete Social History of LSD: The CIA, the Sixties, and Beyond* (New York: Grove Press, 1994), p. 197.

7 Martin Lee and Bruce Shlain, *Acid Dreams: The Complete Social History of LSD: The CIA, the Sixties, and Beyond* (New York: Grove Press, 1994), pp. 44-45, 52-53.

8 Lee and Shlain, *Acid Dreams*, p. 53.

9 H.P. Albarelli, *A Terrible Mistake: The Murder of Frank Olson and the CIA's Cold War Experiments* (Waterville, OR: Trine Day, 2009), pp. 238-39, 292. See top CIA MK-Ultra psychologist John Gittinger's statement of knowing Hubbard on site. And see George White and Sidney Gottlieb discussing him at length.

10 Lee and Shlain, *Acid Dreams*, p. 198. Also Jim Keith, *Mass Control: Engineering Human Consciousness* (Kempton, Illinois: Adventures Unlimited, 1999, 2003), p. 111.

11 Albarelli, *A Terrible Mistake: The Murder of Frank Olson and the CIA's Cold War Experiments*. Waterville, Or: Trine Day, 2009, pp.238-9, 292. See top CIA MK-Ultra psychologist John Gittinger's statement of knowing Hubbard on site. And see George White and Sidney Gottlieb discussing him at length.

12 Lee and Shlain, *Acid Dreams*, pp. 49-50.

13 Jim Keith, *Mass Control*. Keith cites an interview of Dr. Colin Ross, 4/6/97 on CKLN-FM 88 in Toronto, Canada, conducted by Wayne Morris. Note that Keith published a second version of his book titled, *Mass Control, World Control*, which reportedly sold around 50,000 copies. He reportedly died in uncertain circumstances related to breaking his knee by falling from a stage at the Burning Man festival in 1999.

14 Lee and Shlain, *Acid Dreams*, p. 50.

15 Lee and Shlain, *Acid Dreams*, p. 51.

16 Lee and Shlain, *Acid Dreams*, pp. 57, 61-62.

17 Lee and Shlain, *Acid Dreams*, p. 57.

18 Carl Bernstein, "The CIA and the Media," *Rolling Stone*, 10/20/77, p. 63.

19 Frances Stonor Saunders, *The Cultural Cold War: The CIA and the World of Arts and Letters* (New York: The New Press, 1999), pp. 106, 116-17, 129, 146-49, 152-53. See citations that include, C.D. Jackson, 'Notes of meeting,' 3/28/52 (CDJ/DDE) and Dwight D. Eisenhower, quoted in Blanche Wiesen Cook, *The Declassified Eisenhower: A Divided Legacy of Peace and Political Warfare (New York: Doubleday,1981)*. C.D. Jackson to Henry Luce, 3/28/58 (CDJ/DDE), C.D. Jackson to Abbott Washburn, 2/2/53 (CDJ/DDE) and Lawrence de Neufville, telephone interview, Geneva, March 1997. Note that CDJ/DDE stands for C.D. Jackson Papers and Records, Dwight D. Eisenhower Library, Abilene, Kansas.

20 See Victor Marchetti and John Marks, *The CIA and the Cult of Intelligence* (New York: Dell, 1974). Phil Agee, *Inside the Company: CIA Diary* (New York: Bantam, 1975). John Stockwell's speech with graphics on YouTube: http://www.youtube.com/watch?v=KcsTdrOLQ_U&feature=mfu_in_order&list=UL.

21 Lee and Shlain, *Acid Dreams*, pp. 32-35. For copious information on George White, his associates and safehouses, see Albarelli, *A Terrible Mistake*, pp. 574-79, 694-97, which gives street addresses for the CIA safehouses. On areas of activism: in NYC they were located in Greenwich Village; in San Francisco, around Telegraph Hill. See Prof. William Domhoff, "Why San Francisco Is (Or Used to Be) Different: Progressive Neighborhoods Had a Big Impact," http://www2.ucsc.edu/whorulesamerica/local/san_francisco.html.

22 Kirkpatrick Sale, *SDS*, pp. 86, 663-64.

23 Frances Fox Piven and Richard A. Cloward, *Poor People's Movements: Why They Succeed and How They Fail* (New York: Vintage, 1978), pp. 238, 242. PBS, *American Experience*, "About the Film: The Kennedys and Civil Rights," http://www.pbs.org/wgbh/americanexperience/features/general-article/kennedys-and-civil-rights/.

24 Piven and Cloward, *Poor People's Movements*, pp. 244-48.

25 Michael Ollove, "The FBI's Mole in Klan was Horrifyingly Brutal as the Rest," *Baltimore Sun*, 6/5/05.

26 While Dylan came back closer to his old lyric-writing form in his later years, the, at least temporary, descent of his acid-addled brain can be seen starting in 1965 in interviews such as this one: http://www.youtube.com/watch?v=DcPoZZVm3Dk.

27 http://corenyc.org/nycore.htm.

28 Piven and Cloward, *Poor People's Movements*, pp. 244-48. For more on Chaney, Goodman and Schwerner, see, Seth Cagin and Phillip Dray, *We Are Not Afraid* (New York: Bantam Books, 1989).

29 James Casbolt, "MI6 are Lords of the Global Drug Trade," http://www.politicsandcurrentaffairs.co.uk/world-events/44044-mi6-lords-global-drug.html.

30 Jim Keith, *Mass Control.* Note that the British founded Tavistock in 1921.

31 Lee and Shlain, *Acid Dreams*, p. 98

32 Michael Hollingshead, *The Man Who Turned on the World* (London: Abelard-Schuman, 1974).

33 Hollingshead, *The Man Who Turned on the World.* On Dick Lee's statement, Dick Lee and Colin Pratt, *Operation Julie: How the Undercover Police Team Smashed the World's Greatest Drugs Ring* (London: W.H. Allen, 1978), p. 68, http://www.britishcouncil.org/history-1940-royal-charter.htm. The importance of King George VI's funding comes from the royalty's close connection with the British East India Company Opium traffickers in Britain and the U.S. This collaboration included work with Brown Brothers Harriman and funding the Nazi regime in Germany, behind the backs of Britain's Prime Minister Winston Churchill and President Franklin Roosevelt.

34 McCoy, *A Question of Torture*, p. 31. Saunders, *The Cultural Cold War*, pp. 135, 144.

35 On Trilling on Board of Directors of Hollingshead's organization, the Institute for British American Cultural Exchange, see Hollingshead, *The Man Who Turned on the World.* Saunders, *The Cultural Cold War*, pp. 151, 241, 357-58, 395, 438. Saunders has excellent sources. For example, on CIA's Psychological Strategy Board supervising the American Committee on Cultural Freedom, see National Security Council Directive, March 1950, quoted in Scott Lucas, "The Psychological Strategy Board," *International History Review* Vol. 18, No. 2 (May 1996). A British magazine's cultural critic, Saunders poured through loads of primary document sources to reveal many pages of U.S. and British intelligence agency work in her book, *The Cultural Cold War.* She found decades of CIA collaboration with Britain's MI6 revealed in much of this work. Saunders, *The Cultural Cold War*, pp. 167, 174.

36 Lee and Shlain, *Acid Dreams*, pp. 82-83.

37 On Leary, Lee and Shlain, *Acid Dreams*, pp. 73-76. On CIA & Human Ecology funding of schools nationwide, Weinstein, *Psychiatry and the CIA*, pp. 130, 179-80; referenced in McCoy, *A Question of Torture*, pp. 29-31. Also see Nicholas M. Horrock, "80 Institutions Used in C.I.A. Mind Studies: Admiral Turner Tells Senators of Behavior Control Research Bars Drug Testing Now," *New York Times*, August 4, 1977.

38 Albarelli, *A Terrible Mistake*, pp. 193, 234, 272, 288. Lee and Shlain, *Acid Dreams*, pp. 87, 197n. Also see Dr. William Henry Wall Jr., *From Healing to Hell* (New South Books, 2011), and Price H. David, "Buying a Piece of Anthropology Part 1: Human Ecology and Unwitting Anthropological Research for the CIA," *Anthropology Today* Vol. 23, No. 3, pp. 8-13. While it hasn't been verified by other sources, one activist said that Yale University ran special programs for gifted New Haven black teenagers; that program included giving them LSD: personal interview with George Edwards, former New Haven Black Panther, in 2001.

39 Weinstein, *Psychiatry and the CIA*, pp. 130, 179-80. Referenced in McCoy, *A Question of Torture*, pp. 29-31. Also see, Nicholas M. Horrock, "80 Institutions Used in C.I.A. Mind Studies: Admiral Turner Tells Senators of Behavior Control Research Bars Drug Testing Now," *New York Times*, August 4, 1977.

40 Lee and Shlain, *Acid Dreams*, pp. 82-84.

41 Church Committee Report, p. 393, http://www.aarclibrary.org/publib/contents/church/contents_church_reports_book1.htm.

42 Lee and Shlain, *Acid Dreams*, pp. 83-84.

43 Bowart's interview of Leary is found reprinted in many places, such as in Bowart's obituary review of Leary: http://www.raven1.net/mcf/hambone/tlcia.html. It's also found in fragments in Keith, *Mind Control*, pp. 108-09.

44 Lee and Shlain, *Acid Dreams*, pp. 96-98. Also see Hollingshead, *The Man Who Turned on the World.*

45 Lee and Shlain, *Acid Dreams*, p. 97. Dan Fitzpatrick, "Mellon Family's Legacy Lives On," *Pittsburgh Post-Gazette*, June 30, 2007.

46 Saunders, *The Cultural Cold War*, p. 34.

47 Lee and Shlain, *Acid Dreams*, p. 97.

48 Saunders, *The Cultural Cold War*, p. 35. Also on Dulles, see Marchetti and Marks, *The CIA and the Cult of Intelligence*, p. 53.

49 Lee and Shlain, *Acid Dreams*, p. 246.

50 Lee and Shlain, *Acid Dreams*, pp. 99-100.

51 Lee and Shlain, *Acid Dreams*, pp. 101-02.

52 Lee and Shlain, *Acid Dreams*, p. 102.

53 Lee and Shlain, *Acid Dreams*, pp. 87-8, 102.

54 That included uncontrollable laughing for an hour that he couldn't stop, even with thinking of depressing subjects such as Vietnam. He laughed so hard he threw up: Lee and Shlain, *Acid Dreams*, p. 103.

55 Lee and Shlain, *Acid Dreams*, p. 102.

56 Lee and Shlain, *Acid Dreams*, pp. 103-05.

57 Lee and Shlain, *Acid Dreams*, p. 109.

58 Lee and Shlain, *Acid Dreams*, pp. 113-14.

59 Liddy found people watching a film of a waterfall and arrested Leary, who was wearing only a shirt, Lee and Shlain, *Acid Dreams*, pp. 117-18.

Augustus Owsley Stanley III

Chapter Six

MK-Ultra West? Berkeley Protests, Kesey & Owsley

At the University of California-Berkeley in 1957, student activists formed the campus political party SLATE, which promoted the right of students to protest for racial equality, free speech, and voluntary, rather than the then-mandatory, male participation in the Reserve Officer Training Corps (ROTC).[1] Besides civil rights, people were protesting Senator Joe McCarthy's Red Scare about Communism at that time.[2]

In 1959 the House Un-American Activities Committee conducted a public interrogation of leftist activists in San Francisco. These diverse activists included a Cal-Berkeley sophomore, a popular local antiwar radio deejay, several members of the Longshoremen's Union, and some members of the Communist Party. Berkeley's student newspaper, *The Daily Cal,* printed a front-page article calling for students to protest the House Un-American Activities Committee hearings, recommending that people use the tactic of laughing loudly at HUAC's ridiculous questions and statements. The Longshoremen's Union and others also came out to protest and picket the events.[3]

Television journalists filmed the events at the City Hall for the evening news. So many protesters turned up at one event that police trained fire hoses on them, flooding the inside of the building. After a raucous three days of hearings and protests, HUAC subpoenaed the film from the San Francisco television stations covering the events. A HUAC researcher edited the film with narration, adding some fictional elements and speeches by members of HUAC, titling it *Operation Abolition.*[4]

According to articles about this movie, more than eight million people viewed it nationwide. Some groups agreed with its intention of locking up the Communists. Others used it to organize people against the HUAC trials. In another movie, *Berkeley in the Sixties,* activists said that their colleges showed *Operation Abolition* to students in an effort to warn them not to be duped by Communists. It had the opposite effect, leading many leftist students to transfer to Berkeley in order to "be where the action is."[5]

In the early 1960s, Berkeley student activists became involved in civil rights work. In what the Student Nonviolent Coordinating Committee dubbed "Freedom Summer" in 1964, a number of Berkeley students went on Freedom Rides to Mississippi. When they got back to Berkeley's campus that fall, they set up tables to raise money and educate students about these civil rights groups.

Like many colleges, the University of California at Berkeley did not allow fundraising for any political parties except the Democratic and Republican school clubs. Students and faculty were also upset about loyalty oaths (to the U.S. government) required of faculty. Faculty faced negative academic pressure if they tried to discuss socialist or anarchist history and ideas with students. For some, refusing to take the oath led to dismissal, and to debates about academic freedom.

In mid-September of 1964, one of the deans announced a ban on political tables that students often manned at the corner of Bancroft and Telegraph Avenues. A protest ensued that erupted into 3,000 people sitting around a police car to stop the arrest of activist Jack Weinberg, while also using the car as a podium for speeches. That December, upset about the administration singling out student leaders for punishment, several thousand students took over Sproul Hall in a last-ditch tactic to reopen negotiations with the Berkeley administration on political free speech and actions on campus.[6]

Mario Savio, a Berkeley student who had joined the civil rights Freedom Riders that summer, stood on the Sproul Hall steps and told a large rally that the university was acting like a factory that considers its students merely raw materials for processing into standardized personnel. Savio recommended a radical solution:

> There's a time when the operation of the machine becomes so odious, makes one so sick at heart, that you can't take part, you can't even tacitly take part, and you have to put your body upon the gears and the wheels, upon all the apparatus, and you've got to stop it. You've got to indicate to the people who run it, the people who own it, that unless you're free, the machine will be prevented from working.[7]

On cue from there, the demonstrators marched into the administrative offices of Sproul Hall and occupied its four floors.[8] District attorney, and Ronald Reagan's future U.S. Attorney General, Edwin Meese III got permission from Governor Edmund Brown Sr., and arrested some 800 students at 2 A.M., before releasing them several hours later. The University of California brought charges against the organizers, so students held larger protests that all but shut down the Berkeley campus.

In January 1965, the administration of the new acting chancellor finally backed down. The school established provisional rules for political activity on the Berkeley campus, allowed open discussion for members of all political groups at Sproul Hall during certain hours of the day, and permitted tables for leafleting. That spring, the students and organizers started the Vietnam Day Committee. This group helped spark the anti-Vietnam War movement nationwide.[9]

Magic Bus Promotes LSD in Harlem, South

Once again, an increase of MK-Ultra operations coincided with this same area of increased activism. In the late 1950s, aspiring writer Ken Kesey attended Stanford University's prestigious writing program. Kesey had also been an alternate on the 1960 U.S. Olympic wrestling team and had stated he had never even been drunk on beer, much less done any drugs at that time.[10] As an impoverished student while at Stanford, Kesey participated in one of MK-Ultra's Human Ecology Fund LSD experiment programs at Menlo Park Hospital in 1960. Writer Robert Hunter, who later gained fame as a lyricist for the Grateful Dead, also participated. Kesey and Hunter each earned $20 ($150 in 2012 dollars) every time they took a dose of LSD.

Writer Ken Kesey was paid to try LSD as part of an MK-Ultra-financed hospital-based study, before working at the same hospital and "stealing" it for his regular acid parties in Northern California.

When the experiment was over, Menlo Park Hospital offered Kesey a job in the psychiatric unit to work with the doctor who gave him the LSD. From his experiences there, Kesey wrote his first published novel, 1962's *One Flew Over the Cuckoo's Nest*. It was later made into a movie.[11] With his literary acclaim, Kesey's open use of LSD put the drug in a positive light. Kesey's fame also soon attracted other writers to his home.

Starting in the early 1960s, Kesey began throwing parties regularly at his home near Stanford. He was given the keys that opened the psychiatrist's office at Menlo Park, enabling him to "steal" (Kesey's word) LSD for his parties, where he served "electric chili" laced with LSD to his guests, many of whom were artists and writers. Did the Stanford/Menlo Park CIA program use Kesey in a special project, likely without his complete knowledge, encouraging him to throw parties like those CIA scientist Dr. Harold Abramson held weekly in his Long Island home, and which Leary would start in 1963?[12]

These parties would expand into ever-larger gatherings that would be dubbed "Acid Tests." That at least three high level CIA MK-Ultra scientists attended these parties (discussed below) suggests that they were a West Coast version of Timothy Leary's CIA-attended acid parties at William Mellon Hitchcock's Millbrook estate.

Kesey's parties eventually became "Acid Tests," where the Wa locks (later the Grateful Dead) played music and people we knowingly and unknowingly dosed with acid-filled punch.

Kesey coined the term "Merry Pranksters" to describe the growing crew of people hanging out at his place and made himself the leader of this group.[13]

An uncertain number of key people appeared to push Kesey's and the Merry Pranksters' LSD promotion. Augustus Owsley Stanley III (best known as Owsley) came from a wealthy and powerful Kentucky "blue blood" family. His father was a government attorney; his grandfather was a governor and then a U.S. Senator from Kentucky. Owsley had dropped out of the University of Virginia while studying engineering.[14] In 1958, at the age of 21, he enlisted in the Air Force and served for 18 months.[15] His behavior afterwards suggests he did continuing undercover work for Air Force intelligence and MK-Ultra.

Owsley Stanley traveled west to attend school briefly at the University of California-Berkeley where at least one writer said he first started a methedrine (amphetamine or "speed") laboratory. He began manufacturing mass quantities of LSD in 1963. After he paired with Berkeley science prodigy Tim Scully, Scully did the manufacturing.

After *One Flew Over the Cuckoo's Nest* was published, Kesey stopped working at the hospital and started getting acid from Owsley and Scully. They provided a bountiful supply of both LSD and amphetamines to Ken Kesey and often attended his parties. After Kesey wrote his second novel, he decided to do a promotional trip by traveling cross-country on a bus to the World's Fair being held in Queens, New York, in the summer of 1964. The Pranksters decked out an old school bus with bunk beds and electronic equipment, and painted it in swirling patterns with Day-Glo colors. Scully reportedly set up the stereo and speakers on the bus.[16] This might help attract people in black neighborhoods they visited, particularly areas of civil unrest in the South and Harlem just after the riots, to join their party on the bus.

Someone convinced Neal Cassady to join the Pranksters. Cassady was the inspiration for a freewheeling character in Jack Kerouac's best-selling novel *On the Road*. Cassady had just served two years at San Quentin prison for possession of a single joint of marajuana.[17] While ingesting large amounts of amphetamines, Neal Cassady drove the bus, and many journalists wrote about it. Kesey left his wife to watch their three children in California while he enjoyed the bus trip that was later glorified in music by The Who and the Beatles, with the songs, "Magic Bus" and "Magical Mystery Tour," respectively.

At the start of the trip Kesey stopped to pick up Ken Babbs at the El Toro Marine base where Babbs was completing his term of service.[18] A decorated Marine helicopter pilot, one of the first in Vietnam, Babbs had attended the Stanford Writing Program with Kesey in the late 1950s, and they became friends.[19] Along with the book *On the Bus*, a documentary film about the journey, *Magic Trip*, reported much about this bus trip.[20]

Though the supposed purpose of the trip was to go to New York, the bus took a long detour south. During the ever-increasing Freedom Summer civil rights campaigns, the bus swung through a number of southern towns bringing loads of acid.[21] Evidence indicates they tried to get some of the Freedom Rider activists "tripping."

In his book *On the Bus*, Paul Perry described the former struggling New York comedian Wavy Gravy, whom friends also knew as Hugh Romney.[22] The book included a picture of Wavy Gravy's business card that read "Goon King Brothers Dimensional Kreemo, Rudy Kloptic" (another alias). Wavy Gravy's Goon King Bros. was a psychotropic-substance delivery service in San Francisco that he started before meeting Kesey's group. Was this U.S. intelligence work that included Owsley Stanley and Tim Scully? Whether Owsley and Scully knowingly worked for the CIA could never be confirmed, but they would both soon work with the heavily CIA-linked group, William Mellon Hitchcock's Brotherhood of Eternal Love.[23]

Warlocks/Grateful Dead manager Hank Harrison said acid trafficker Augustus Owsley Stanley III, left, partnered with Mellon Hitchcock and fought with Harrison regarding influence over Jerry Garcia, right.

The Pranksters' circuitous route took them through Houston, New Orleans, Mississippi, Alabama and Florida. They went to segregated beaches and tried to go to black-only swimming areas, acting as if they were well-meaning civil rights movement integrationists. They went to jazz clubs and picked up a jazz artist whom they got to trip with them. Ken Babbs appeared to be leading the troupe's itinerary by the time they headed for Pensacola, Florida, where Babbs's Marine buddy had a place. That friend still served, and was in uniform. Babbs apparently still had connections to the military. Were these harmless connections to the military, or might Babbs have been working as an undercover MK-Ultra agent?[24]

The bus picked up Babbs's brother, John, who they said helped orchestrate the trip. John "went missing" and then hitchhiked back to the bus. This happened so many times that others nicknamed him "Sometimes Missing." With Ken Babbs later-seen propagation of the CIA's MK-Ultra goals, it's a wonder if John Babbs was consulting with U.S. intelligence handlers. Police stopped the bus at various times, but always let them go. Ken Babbs would also later talk an inspecting FBI agent out of arresting anyone in his drug-filled home.[25]

When the bus finally arrived in New York, its first stopping point was not the World's Fair, but Harlem.[26] Residents of Harlem had recently rioted over civil rights issues.[27] Promoting acid to rebellious blacks seemed important to the Pranksters, as they would later promote acid to blacks in the Watts neighborhood of Los Angeles just after the riots there.

Eventually the Pranksters did visit the World's Fair in Queens, New York. There the Pranksters met with Beat writers Allen Ginsberg and Jack Kerouac. The gathering, which was filmed, shows Ginsberg and Kerouac happily greeting Cassady, but no one else. Ginsberg reportedly had been having sex with bisexual Neal Cassady off and on for 21 years. Ginsberg, Kerouac and Cassady kept to themselves, separate from the Pranksters. Kerouac didn't enjoy the group and got Cassady to leave the party early, taking him back to Kerouac's Massachusetts home.[28]

Next, the bus traveled up to former Harvard professor Timothy Leary's rented Millbrook, NY estate. Kesey saw this as a great opportunity for two acid-taking leaders to meet. But acid failed to glue the two. Leary had started a three-day acid trip in his home, and didn't come out to meet Kesey.[29]

Kesey, Ken Babbs, Wavy Gravy and the Merry Pranksters returned to the San Francisco Bay area and continued to promote acid at Kesey's ranch and beyond. They drove their multi-colored, Day-Glo bus all around Northern California promoting LSD. The timing, coinciding with Freedom Summer, seems more than happenstance. At the nearby UC-Berkeley campus, students were organizing and protesting as part of the Berkeley Free Speech Movement.

Clearly, during two of the biggest leftist mobilizations of students, the civil rights Freedom Summer and the Berkeley Free Speech Movement, MK-Ultra-linked LSD promoters worked hard to spread the drug amongst them. U.S. intelligence had already launched FBI Counterintelligence Program (Cointelpro) tactics against Martin Luther King Jr. and the civil rights movement in the South. The CIA's Operation Chaos joined the FBI's Cointelpro targeting. Also, MK-Ultra was extremely active at Stanford University, forty miles south of Berkeley.[30]

Student accounts of the Free Speech Movement at Cal-Berkeley suggest that certain Pranksters targeted the radical leftists of Berkeley's campus. For example, Denise Kaufman described how she had just enrolled at Berkeley when she "discovered LSD and the free-speech movement within a few days of each other."[31] Kaufman also told of how one day she was standing in front of Sproul Hall next to tables with information about the Communist party and Socialists. She said she was arrested standing next to Berkeley Free Speech Movement leader Mario Savio. She said that within days she met Ken Kesey and the Pranksters when they had just returned from their cross-country bus trip. Kaufman later became one of the Pranksters.[32]

Activists invited Kesey to address a large anti-War rally, but he appeared to have been led to play the same role as Timothy Leary, who had a "tune in, turn on and drop out" message. Kesey brought both Pranksters and pro-War Hell's Angels with him on the bus to that event. When it was Kesey's turn to speak, he played "Home on the Range" on a harmonica and then asked the crowd: "Do you want to know how to stop the war? Just turn your backs and say fuck it." He then walked away.[33] Kesey and the Pranksters brought many student activists back to their La Honda home for acid parties.[34] In *Acid Dreams,* Lee and Shlain discuss this, stating: "Kesey's scene was all the rage in the Bay Area. Among others, it attracted people who were involved with the Free Speech Movement that arose on the Berkeley campus of the University of California in the fall of 1964."[35]

Police didn't arrest Kesey for years, either on his drug-raddled bus tour or at his home parties, where distribution of illegal drugs was rampant, and neighbors complained about the noise from Kesey's loudspeakers blaring in his back yard. In one instance, police cars arrived with red lights flashing but never came in, while the party lasted two days.[36] This suggests U.S. intelligence asked the police to hold off. According to *On the Bus*: "Finally, in April 1965, Kesey and 14 Pranksters were arrested," at Kesey's home. Most of the charges were for marijuana possession except for Kesey's, who was charged with "operating a premises where marijuana was furnished, and with resisting arrest." Kesey got out on bail and then had over a dozen court appearances before he received a suspended sentence.

MK-Ultra Scientists Attend Acid Tests, Target Activists

After leaving the Marines, Ken Babbs had a business card that read "Ken Babbs, Intrepid Trips, Inc." Other Pranksters, such as Lee Quarnstrom and Ron Bevirt, had similar picture ID cards, stating membership in Babbs's Intrepid Trips, Inc. On the back of the cards was a picture of Uncle Sam, as seen on WWII recruitment posters, with the legend: "Can YOU Pass the Acid Test?" The Acid Tests were a series of parties where Pranksters served Kool-Aid fruit punch spiked with LSD. Acclaimed writer Tom Wolfe would later write a book about it: *The Electric Kool-Aid Acid Test.*[37]

Kenn Babbs held his first "Acid Test" party in 1965 at a 400-acre farm he owned in Santa Cruz.[38] The Warlocks, Army veterans Jerry Garcia and

Bob Weir's band, performed at the party. Before the end of that year, the band changed its name to the Grateful Dead. A Prankster stated that no one came to their first show but fellow Pranksters.[39] This suggests that the Warlocks/Grateful Dead first started playing only for these events. To help make the Acid Tests more alluring, Owsley Stanley and Tim Scully designed advanced sound equipment for the rock group. *Rolling Stone* magazine said this advanced sound system was the likely reason the Grateful Dead broke out of the San Francisco scene.[40]

The Warlocks first manager, Hank Harrison, said that an important struggle arose early on regarding influence over the band. Harrison described himself as a student of a leading leftist community organizer named Saul Alinsky. He stood in opposition to the band's top benefactor, Augustus Owsley Stanley III, who Harrison said was very right-wing. Harrison said that Owsley had teamed up with William Mellon Hitchcock as early as 1964. Billy Hitchcock's Mellon family, as described earlier, was one of the country's wealthiest families who held many U.S. intelligence posts. Hitchcock provided unlimited financial and technological resources to the band. In opposition to Owsley, Harrison preached moderation in all drug use. Harrison's managerial position was cut short in 1965, after six months, and Owsley gained the upper hand in influencing the band. Nonetheless, Harrison continued as a consultant and roommate of longtime Grateful Dead bass player Phil Lesh until 1972.

Harrison also described the understated roles of two extremely wealthy women. He said that Owsley's girlfriend, Melissa Cargill, aided his work. Her family's Cargill Company had been listed as America's largest family-owned company. Harrison reported that Cargill was a chemist and that both she and Owsley were taught and continually advised by Professor Alexander "Sasha" Shulgin, who also worked for Dow Chemical Company. Harrison said Shulgin's "advising" often included hanging out with Owsley on the side or back of the stage at Grateful Dead shows for years. Shulgin synthesized and popularized MDMA (ecstasy), as well as the "super-psychedelic" STP for Dow and the MK-Ultra-collaborating U.S. Army Chemical Corps. Harrison added that William Mellon Hitchcock's sister Peggy helped fund their Brotherhood of Eternal Love acid manufacturing and promotion group.

Pranksters held the second Acid Test on December 4, 1965, at a house owned by a black man who lived near San Jose State University. The Pranksters held it the same night as the Rolling Stones concert in San Francisco. They passed out fliers at the Stones' show asking "Can YOU pass the Acid Test?" and got about 400 people to the party drinking their acid-spiked punch. Once again, the Grateful Dead played all night there. Police eventually stopped the music, but no one was arrested.[41] The Pranksters and Grateful Dead went on to serve huge bowls of Kool-Aid spiked with LSD to increasingly large numbers of people all over California (and the bowls eventually became trashcans full of "electric" Kool-Aid). Anyone who attended the shows and got thirsty dancing to the band was dosed without fully knowing they would be tripping. The Pranksters and Grateful Dead appeared to target impressionable students and black neighborhoods of unrest, including San Francisco State University and the black Watts neighborhood of Los Angeles.

As previously mentioned, journalist Hank Albarelli wrote a lengthy book on the history of MK-Ultra, *A Terrible Mistake*. Albarelli had worked in President Carter's White House and for the Department of the Treasury. He quoted John Gittinger, a CIA Technical Services Staff scientist with a dozen years at the Agency, who helped organize MK-Ultra's Human Ecology cover program in universities. Gittinger had even interviewed Dr. Sidney Gotlieb, to screen him for the position of CIA MK-Ultra director.[42]

Under deposition in a lawsuit brought by victims of a Canadian MK-Ultra doctor, Gittinger admitted that he and two of his fellow CIA Chemical Division scientists traveled from the East Coast and attended a number of Acid Test parties. Gittinger recalled how at one of these parties, U.S. intelligence "superspy" Alfred "Hubbard and some doctor ... two bald-headed, portly guys in dark suits walking into the middle of all this madness ... people began melting away from them ... At least when we went to these things we made an effort to blend in with things." The "effort to blend in" suggests that Gittinger and his colleagues were spying on the events. Did these high level CIA scientists spend this large amount of time traveling to the West Coast because they helped orchestrate these Acid Tests?[43]

High-level CIA MK-Ultra scientist John Gittinger stated in a legal deposition that he and two other CIA scientists attended at least several Acid Tests.

Meanwhile, anti-War activists increased their organizing on the West Coast. On a weekend in mid-October of 1965, 14,000 protesters marched on the Oakland Army induction center. Writers called it the first major San Francisco Bay area anti-Vietnam War demonstration. The police turned protesting marchers away the first day, and Hell's Angels turned the marchers away the second day. At the end of the second day of action at the induction center, many protesters were lured to a Longshoreman's Hall. The Longshoremen are a particularly radical labor union. Overall, 400-1,200 people came to the Hall for "the birth of a scene," with a group of rock bands and psychedelic lights.[44]

Kesey Tries to Pull Plug on Acid Tests and Is Jailed

After a third Acid Test with about 300 people on Muir Beach near San Francisco, Ken Kesey stated that the Acid Tests were over, as he wasn't happy with them anymore. In short order, police arrested Kesey a second time for possession of marijuana.[45] Several nights after Kesey's arrest, Ken Babbs, Stewart Brand and others held an even bigger Acid Test. Babbs and Brand had spent considerable time organizing a three-night event they called the "Trips Festival," which was a major step up from the former Acid Tests. It was held at the Longshoremen's Hall.[46]

Stewart Brand reported a particularly interesting military history. In one interview, Brand said he, like Babbs, was in the military ROTC at Stanford from 1960-62, and "taught Basic Training at Fort Dix, New Jersey. I did serve half a year at the Pentagon as the Army's senior photographer." In another interview, which is also on film, Brand added that at Fort Dix, "I was running basic training as a Second Lieutenant there. And then my weekends were in the Lower East Side in New York hanging out with artists ... messing with psychedelic drugs." Brand further said that "with the Merry Pranksters ... there were a number of ex-military people ... [including Kesey's] number two, Ken Babbs ... that gave us a common language and a set of understandings."[47]

Journalist Hank Albarelli reprinted CIA MK-Ultra scientist John Gittinger's report that he and at least two of his colleagues attended the Trips Festival. Researchers Lee and Shlain noted that the Trips Festival was three days long and included advanced technology for its time, such as closed circuit television cameras set up all over, so people could see themselves dancing. Grateful Dead lead guitarist Jerry Garcia said there were several thousand attendees each day. Music promoter Bill Graham described acid everywhere. "They had ices spiked with acid, available to all, children as well. There were big tubs on the balcony and downstairs."[48]

Ken Kesey's first marijuana arrest had resulted in probation with a three-year jail sentence hanging over his head if arrested again.[49] Friends bailed Kesey out after his second marijuana arrest, and he fled the country for Mexico. Sources stated: "with Kesey in Mexico, Babbs was the man in charge. He took the bus to Los Angeles for a series of Acid Tests. With the help of Wavy Gravy, the Pranksters put on four Acid Tests."[50] Besides holding a test in a Unitarian Church, the Los Angeles Acid Tests notably included one in a garage in the black Watts area, just after one of the largest riots in American history.[51] Was it more than coincidence that Ken Babbs and his tripped-out, easily led Pranksters tried to push acid at the two locations of the nation's first two major black riots, Harlem on the bus trip, and Watts?

With the Grateful Dead playing, the Watts Acid Test dosed many without their knowledge. After people got heated up dancing, they drank from one of the several 30-gallon drums of Kool-Aid fruit punch. People received massive doses of acid in that punch. Someone purportedly miscalculated the right amount of Kool-Aid for a normal trip and people who followed the instructions got six hits of LSD per cup instead of one.[52] Wavy Gravy described the scene: "People would be dancing for about three hours to the Grateful Dead, and then they'd be looking for something wet. Well, 'wet' was about 300 micrograms a swallow. That was pretty intense for some people, but if they wanted to go outside, there was nowhere to go because Watts was still smoldering from the riots."[53]

Along with the CIA's MK-Ultra scientists, local police and state narcotics agents also attended the events that appeared to be larger human-guinea-pig experiments. Witnesses said people harassed the police without a response.[54] During an Acid Test at a movie studio in Los Angeles, the Pranksters added only dry ice to the Kool-Aid to make it bubble, but drug-free. *Life* magazine photographed the Pranksters for its cover. As noted, Time/Life's owner and vice-president had an intertwined leadership with the CIA, suggesting that *Life* purposely published a picture where no one was tripping or crazy looking, as one of many articles trying to promote LSD.[55] *Time* magazine also highlighted the LSD phenomenon. Magazines such as *Look, The Reporter, Cosmopolitan, The Saturday Evening Post,* and *The Ladies Home Journal* followed suit.[56]

By the early fall of 1966, Ken Kesey, now a fugitive, planned an Acid Test Graduation at another Trips Festival. He planned to pop up on stage and tell people to go "beyond acid," then climb through a ceiling escape door and be whisked away by helicopter. However, police arrested Kesey shortly before the event. Authorities apparently didn't want a counterculture, rebel role model changing his mind and preaching against acid use.[57] Kesey eventually made the Acid Test Graduation event happen when he got out of jail, though pictures showed that between three to six dozen people participated.[58] Shortly after, a court sentenced Kesey to a prison work farm, followed by a three-year house arrest at his brother's farm in Oregon that definitively ended his "acid graduation" message.[59]

Ken Kesey said that by 1969, sixty-one people lived with him in a barn in Oregon. He said they all went to Woodstock without him that year when he found a candle burnt down just before it could catch the surrounding hay on fire. He kicked most of them out after that. Years later, Allen Ginsberg got the CIA records stating that the CIA was paying for those acid experiments to "try to make people insane—to weaken people and put them under the control of interrogators." Kesey said he thought the CIA didn't want to have people tripping again, as the CIA "didn't like the look" in LSD users' eyes. Of course, a mass of evidence dispels this notion. Kesey said he only did drugs on "religious occasions" in his later years.[60]

Notes

1 Kenneth Cloke, *A Brief History of Civil Liberties Protest Movements in Berkeley – From TASC to SLATE to FSM* (1957-1965) (Santa Monica, CA: CDR Press,1994) pp .20-27.

2 See, for example, Lisa Pearl Rosenbaum, "The Honorable Scars of the McCarthy Era," book review of *A Granddaughters Rite of Passage: Tales from the McCarthy Era*, printed in *Tikkun*, 1/25/11; http://www.tikkun.org/tikkundaily/2011/01/25/the-honorable-scars-of-the-mccarthy-era/.

3 These details come from various sources, including a viewing of the film *Operation Abolition* (1960), Dir. Fulton Lewis III and Writer, J. Edgar Hoover, and various archived histories of the time. This was Douglas Wachter, whose father, Saul Wachter, actively organized with the Communist Party's Northern California chapter. These included some in the Longshoremen Union and the Communist Party. HUAC also interrogated a popular Pacifica radio deejay named William Mandel.

4 The film *Operation Abolition* started with a narrator talking about a pamphlet shown on the screen. He says, "This pamphlet, and numerous others like it, play a major role as artillery in one phase of the Communist war to destroy our nation. It is a war the Communists call ..." Here the narrator's voice goes into spooky echo effect: "Operation Abolition," like he was Boris Karloff introducing a horror film.

5 Mark Kitchell, *Berkeley in the Sixties* (1990), Germany, Kitchell Films. Note that this film was nominated for an Academy Award for Best Documentary and won the Sundance Film Festival Audience Award in 1990.

6 Kenneth Cloke, *A Brief History of Civil Liberties Protest Movements in Berkeley – From TASC to SLATE to FSM (1957-1965)* (Santa Monica, CA: CDR Press, 1994). Jo Freeman, *At Berkeley in the 60s: The Education of an Activist, 1961-1965* (Bloomington: Indiana University Press, 2004). Students surrounded the car for 32 hours before police dropped the charges against Weinberg.

7 Martin Lee and Bruce Shlain, *Acid Dreams: The Complete Social History of LSD: The CIA, the Sixties, and Beyond* (New York: Grove Press, 1994), p. 127.

8 See example of writer David Solomon. He worked for the CIA-precursor OSS. Then he worked heavily with top U.S. intelligence LSD trafficker, Ron Stark. Solomon wrote articles promoting marijuana and LSD in "alternative" forums such as *Playboy* magazine. David Black, *Acid: The Secret History of LSD* (London: Vision/Satin Publication, 1998), pp. 65-66, 78-79.

9 Among the many useful sources on the Berkeley protests: Todd Gitlin, *The Sixties: Years of Hope, Days of Rage* (New York: Bantam, 1987). The demonstration remained civil, with students studying, watching movies, and listening to Joan Baez and other singers who came in to give support. Teaching assistants held "freedom classes."

10 Terry Gross, "Ken Kesey on Misconceptions of the Counterculture," recorded in 1989. Played on National Public Radio, April 12, 2011; http://www.npr.org/templates/transcript/transcript.php?storyId=139259106.

11 Mark Christensen, *Acid Christ: Ken Kesey, LSD, and the Politics of Ecstasy* (Tucson, AZ: Schaffner Press, 2009), p. 53. On Hunter, also see Lee and Shlain, *Acid Dreams*, p. 143n.

12 Lee and Shlain, *Acid Dreams*, p. 120. Some of the other known attendees included artist Roy Seburn, dancer Chloe Scott, and writers Robert Stone (*Dog Soldiers, A Flag for Sunrise*) and Larry McMurtry (*Hud, Terms of Endearment*), though it's uncertain how many of them took the acid.

13 Paul Perry, *On the Bus: The Complete Guide to the Legendary Trip of Ken Kesey and the Merry Pranksters and the Birth of the Counterculture* (New York: Thunder's Mouth Press, 1990), pp. 55-77. Note, this books credits "Flashbacks" in the book to Ken "The Intrepid Traveller" Babbs.

Forewords by Hunter S. Thompson and Jerry Garcia.

14 Elaine Woo, "Owsley Stanley, Counterculture Producer of LSD, Dies at 76," *Los Angeles Times*, March 14, 2011; http://www.radiowest.ca/forum/viewtopic.php?p=12804712.

15 Owsley Stanley blog posting; March 17, 2006.

16 Fraser, Andrew (2011-03-14). "Owsley 'Bear' Stanley dies in North Queensland car crash," *The Australian*, News Limited, http://www.theaustralian.com.au/news/nation/owsley-bear-stanley-dies-in-north-queensland-car-crash/story-e6frg6nf-1226021149610. On Scully, see *Rolling Stone* magazine No. 53, March 7, 1970 issue, and Bill Weinberg, "Farewell to the Chief: Ken Kesey's Long Strange Trip," http://www.american-buddha.com/farewellchiefkesey.htm. On methedrine lab, Alice Echols, *The Scars of Sweet Paradise: The Life and Times of Janis Joplin* (New York: Metropolitan/Henry Holt, 1999), p. 77.

17 Lee and Shlain, *Acid Dreams*, p. 122.

18 Perry, *On the Bus*, p. 57. The Who's "Magic Bus" alludes to it. The Beatles' *Magical Mystery Tour* album title song is a reference to this bus trip. It's unknown who, if anyone, influenced the bands to glorify this bus trip.

19 Lee and Shlain, *Acid Dreams*, p. 120. A documentary film about the cross-country bus trip, Alex Gibney and Alison Ellwood, *Magic Trip: Ken Kesey's Search for a Kool Place* (Magnolia Pictures, 2011), reported that en route, Babbs stole the affections of a woman with whom Kesey had been romantically linked: Fetchin Gretchin. On Babbs as decorated Marine helicopter pilot, Jeff Baker, "Ken Babbs, a Kesey crony and Merry Prankster, turns novelist," *Oregon Live*, April 9, 2011, http://www.oregonlive.com/books/index.ssf/2011/04/dexter_review_kesey_crony_a_pr.html.

20 Alex Gibney and Alison Ellwood, *Magic Trip: Ken Kesey's Search for a Kool Place* (Magnolia Pictures, 2011).

21 Gibney and Ellwood, *Magic Trip*.

22 Perry, *On the Bus*, p. 122.

23 Perry, *On the Bus*, pp. 124, 140, 151. Personal interviews Hank Harrison, November 2014.

24 Gibney and Ellwood, *Magic Trip*. For map of Kesey/Pranksters' bus path through the deep South, see Perry, *On the Bus*, p. 45.

25 Perry, *On the Bus*, p. 178.

26 Gibney and Ellwood, *Magic Trip*.

27 Gitlin, *The Sixties*, p. 168.

28 They walked into the Dupont Chemical Company's tent with a sign over it, "Better Living Through Chemistry": made sense. Gibney and Ellwood, *Magic Trip*. Bob Dylan repeated that phrase within a year or two. "The *Rolling Stone* 500 Greatest Songs of All Time," Rock List Music.

29 Ellwood, *Magic Trip*.

30 Robert Justin Goldstein, *Political Repression in Modern America: From 1870 to 1976* (University of Illinois Press, 2001), p. 456. Seymour Hersh (December 22, 1974). "Huge CIA Operation Reported in US Against Antiwar Forces, Other Dissidents in Nixon Years". *New York Times*, December 22, 1974. Verne Lyon, "Domestic Surveillance: The History of Operation CHAOS", *Covert Action Information Bulletin*, Summer 1990. William Pepper, *An Act of State: The Execution of Martin Luther King* (New York: Verso, 2008).

31 Perry, *On the Bus*, p. 124.

32 Perry, *On the Bus*, pp. 125-26.

33 Perry, *On the Bus*, pp. 129, 136-39.

34 Perry, *On the Bus*, p. 145.

35 Lee and Shlain, *Acid Dreams*, p. 126.

36 Perry, *On the Bus*, pp. 142-43.

37 Tom Wolfe, *The Electric Kool-Aid Acid Test* (Farrar, Straus and Giroux, 1968).

38 Perry, *On the Bus*, p. 141.

39 On only Pranksters at first acid test, Ellwood, *Magic Trip*. On Garcia as U.S. Army veteran, see http://www.rollingstone.com/music/artists/jerry-garcia/biography. On manager Hank

Harrison saying name change in months, see interview by authors, Max Wallace and Ian Halperin, *Love and Death: A New and Explosive Investigation into the Murder of Kurt Cobain* (New York: Atria Books, 2004) p.27.

40 *Rolling Stone* magazine No. 53, March 7, 1970.

41 On Owsley, Hitchcocks and Cargill, personal interviews, Hank Harrison, 11/2014. On Cargill Company, Andrew Murphy and Scott DeCarlo, "America's Largest Private Companies," *Forbes*, November 16, 2011. Also on Cargill, see the memoir by the third member of their longtime love triangle, Rhoney Gissen Stanley, *Owsley and Me: My LSD Family* (Rhinebeck, NY: Monkfish, 2013). Second Acid Test, Perry, *On the Bus*, pp. 115, 142. The man whose San Jose house was the site of the second Acid Test was called "Big Nig" by the Pranksters

42 H.P. Albarelli, *A Terrible Mistake: The Murder of Frank Olson and the CIA's Secret Cold War Experiments* (Walterville, OR: TrineDay, 2009), p. 297.

43 Albarelli, *A Terrible Mistake*, pp. 291-92, 794.

44 Alice Echols, *Scars of Sweet Paradise* (New York: Henry Holt, 1999), p. 117. On Gittinger at Longshoreman's Hall, see Albarelli, *A Terrible Mistake*, p. 291.

45 Perry, *On the Bus*, p. 115.

46 Perry, *On the Bus*, pp. 115-16.

47 On ROTC and Pentagon, Walter Isaacson, "Stewart Brand Responds," *Medium.com*, December 27, 2013, https://medium.com/@walterisaacson/stewart-brand-responds-f857b2e8da26. For other information, see Brand interview, "Big Think Interview with Stewart Brand," *Bigthink.com*, December 11, 2009, http://bigthink.com/videos/big-think-interview-with-stewart-brand. It includes a video of the interview. Also note that Whole Earth Catalogue publisher and purported environmentalist Brand supports genetically modified foods and nuclear power in this interview.

48 On Gittinger, Albarelli, *A Terrible Mistake*, p. 291. On rest, Lee and Shlain, *Acid Dreams*, p. 143. Graham quote: Christensen, *Acid Christ*, p. 153.

49 Perry, *On the Bus*, pp. 142-44.

50 Perry, *On the Bus*, pp. 116, 168-69.

51 Perry, *On the Bus*, pp. 151, 161. Gitlin, *The Sixties*, p. 168.

52 Perry, *On the Bus*, pp. 161, 163-64.

53 Prankster Wavy Gravy, in Perry, *On the Bus*, p. 164.

54 Perry, *On the Bus*, p. 164.

55 Perry, On the Bus, p. 167.

56 Jonathan O. Cole, M.D. & Martin M. Katz, Ph.D., "The Psychomimetic Drugs: An Overview," *Journal of the American Medical Association* Vol. 187, No. 10, 3/7/64, at www.psychedelic-library.org/colekatz.htm.

57 Perry, *On the Bus*, p. 119.

58 Perry, *On the Bus*, p. 119.

59 Lee and Shlain, *Acid Dreams*, p. 251.

60 Terry Gross, "Ken Kesey on Misconceptions of the Counterculture," recorded in 1989. Played on National Public Radio, April 12, 2011, http://www.npr.org/templates/transcript/transcript.php?storyId=139259106.

Chapter Seven

Opium's Golden Triangle & Vietnam War-Era Assassinations

Evidence supports the contention that the wealthiest oligarchs who influenced U.S. intelligence had opponents assassinated when necessary. In Vietnam, the American oligarchs saw a chance to gain more control over the opium cash crops that their families had a history of trafficking. Besides the obvious profit motive from opium trafficking, a little-known vast profit incentive also came from laundering drug profits. Also, with blacks increasingly rioting over civil rights in the 1960s, the oligarchy would have had the added motive of sedating and dividing poor black communities with heroin, the way their progenitors had conducted the Opium Wars on China, as discussed earlier.

President John F. Kennedy and his brother Robert F. Kennedy were said to have evolved away from their more right-wing early political stances. JFK tried to dismantle the CIA and close down MK-Ultra. Many also say he changed his mind on the Vietnam War, which would have enraged the opium traders.

Over a five-year period in the 1960s, gunmen assassinated the four most influential opponents of the Vietnam War: President John F. Kennedy, Malcolm X, Martin Luther King Jr. and Senator Robert F. Kennedy. The oligarchy had the top motive and means for these assassinations. Other books have explored detailed evidence regarding U.S. intelligence's possible assassinations of JFK, Malcolm X, MLK and RFK on behalf of the oligarchs.[1] The oligarchy's motive for assassinating the Kennedys deserves a new look with respect to both the Vietnam War and MK-Ultra.

Opium for Oppression and Corporate Profits

Activists fought tirelessly for African Americans' civil rights, and their small but increasing successes began occurring from the late 1950s to the late 1960s. In their award-winning book, *Poor People's Movements,* sociologists Frances Piven and Richard Cloward make a strong case that riots and other forms of mass disruption had the biggest influence on leading the ruling powers to pass civil rights legislation. While Malcolm X (El-Hajj Malik El-Shabazz) and MLK didn't start the riots, U. S. intelligence's research indicated that the rioters had the most respect for these two leaders, who arguably raised their awareness of oppression as a reason to riot.[2]

While the John F. Kennedy and Lyndon Johnson administrations enacted civil rights legislation, U.S. intelligence appeared to increase the distribution of heroin into black neighborhoods of American cities to help stop the riots. The wave of heroin that flooded into pockets of unrest in the 1960s served as a tool of oppression against activists and the rioters. Not only did it addict thousands and ruin their lives, it also sidetracked civil rights activists who became wary of entering poor black communities due to the vast increase in violence caused by the drug influx and fights over drug turf. Lyndon Johnson's Attorney General, Ramsey Clark, would later say that he believed "the government uses drugs to sedate and divide the masses."[3]

A former U.S. Assistant Secretary of Housing and Wall Street insider, Catherine Austin Fitts, explained a little-known aspect of illicit drugs' huge effect on the U.S. stock market. Fitts, who worked in the first President Bush's administration, had a high-level background on Wall Street. She was managing director and a member of the board of directors of Dillon Read & Co, considered one of the "Wall Street dynasties." She was also former president of The Hamilton Securities Group and later started The Solari Group, Inc.[4]

Fitts revealed that the CIA and Department of Justice admitted to creating "a memorandum of understanding that permitted the CIA to help its allies and assets to traffic in drugs and not have to report it." She stated that the U.S. competed with other countries in how best to accumulate cash immediately after World War II. Top researchers agree that the CIA used military transport airline Air America, as well as other airlines, to help traffic Golden Triangle opium worldwide over the following decades.[5]

Fitts referred to money made from illicit drug sales as "narco dollars." She said, "The power of narco dollars comes when you combine drug trafficking with the stock market," detailing how narco dollars exponentially increase the value of a company's stock. She continued, "The 'POP' is a word I learned on Wall Street to describe the multiple of income at which a stock trades. If a stock like PepsiCo trades at 20 times its income, that means for every $100,000 of income it makes, its stock [total market capitalization] goes up $2 million. The people who own the company and all sizes of investors make money from the stocks going up."

Fitts added that banks also make huge money from cash influxes, in lending it with compounded interest. For example, if someone gets a $120,000 home mortgage loan at 4.5% interest over 30 years, they actually end up paying the bank over $218,000 by the end of the loan term. Through these types of loans, as well as credit card loans, banks gain huge economic power.[6]

According to Fitts, banks and many other companies "launder" money from drug sales in their company's income to increase their stock market value. Laundering means taking the cash from drug dealers and listing it in their income reports. She said that restaurants and other companies dealing in cash also launder drug money. These restaurants and banks take money from the drug dealers and get a percentage of it before giving it back to the dealers as "clean" money. They easily hide these transactions in their accounting books. With a plausible 20-times increase in the stock value of the company that owns the restaurant, it's easy to return the money to the drug dealer in other ways that launders it of its source from the illegal drug trade, and hides it from the Internal Revenue Service.[7]

Global sources have documented the ever-increasing amount of money laundered over the last half century. These sources include Antonio Maria Costas, the head of the United Nations Office of Drugs and Crime.[8] The *Washington Post* would later report an admission by the CIA's own Inspector General that the CIA has trafficked drugs, as will be discussed.[9]

CIA Targets President John F. Kennedy

John F. Kennedy started his presidency with a conservative pledge to build more missiles in the wake of of his "missile gap" campaign. Later in his term he promoted more liberal policies including his evolving position on nuclear arms, in signing the first Limited Test Ban Treaty with the Soviet Union's Nikita Khrushchev.[10] Of key importance, Kennedy also called for a pullback of all troops from Vietnam.

Researchers have shown strong proof of JFK's decision to pull out of Vietnam. For example, researcher John Judge's mother worked for the government department that published the data on future troops assigned for deployment in Vietnam for the following years. In 1963, her publication reported zero troops for the coming year, as the pullout was supposed to be final in 1964. Also, University of Texas Prof. James Galbraith, son of a Kennedy advisor, stated on a British news show that the historical record includes official position statements and tapes documenting that Kennedy and his Secretary of Defense, Robert MacNamara, had made the formal decision by October of 1963 to pull all troops out of Vietnam by the end of 1965.[11]

When President Kennedy took office, he fired CIA Director Allen Dulles and appointed John McCone as CIA Director. Dulles, a former lawyer for the Rockefellers, had championed the MK-Ultra program and McCone ended the program. Richard Helms, the CIA's Deputy Director for Covert Operations, who was second in command under Dulles, took matters into his own hands and ran MK-Ultra behind McCone's and Kennedy's backs. But in 1963, CIA inspector general John Earman accidentally stumbled upon the MK-Ultra project. McCone tried unsuccessfully to defund the program, but Richard Helms continued it until at least 1973.[12] With Kennedy's presidency cut short on November 22, 1963, he had little time to stop the programs of Helms and others still loyal to Allen Dulles and the Rockefeller-Harriman-Morgan oligarchy.

It seems Helms first tried to get to Kennedy with MK-Ultra doctors. Lee and Shlain state that Max "Dr. Feelgood" Jacobson, MD, regularly visited Timothy Leary's headquarters on William Mellon Hitchcock's Millbrook estate, where he worked with known MK-Ultra operatives, such as psychiatrist Humphrey Osmond. Dr. Jacobson also worked as JFK's personal physician. Dr. Jacobson administered "vitamin" injections that left Kennedy "flushed and excited, leading some to speculate the shots included methamphetamine and/or cocaine." Other sources reported that these shots did in fact include amphetamines. Regular amphetamine injections lead to severe physiological withdrawal symptoms.[13]

Besides President Kennedy's efforts to defund MK-Ultra, the ruling oligarchy would have also wanted to eliminate him due to his work targeting key drug-trafficking partners—at least four Mafia kingpins. President Kennedy and his brother, Attorney General Robert F. Kennedy, were developing legal cases against New Orleans Mafia boss, Carlos Marcello, as well as Florida Mafia boss Santos Trafficante Jr., Chicago boss Sam Giancana, and mobster Johnny Roselli. Professor Alfred McCoy documented how Trafficante had taken over the work of top New York mobsters, Meyer Lansky and Charles "Lucky" Luciano, who worked with US intelligence in heroin trafficking. Professor Peter Dale Scott documented Marcello's narcotics smuggling from Latin American countries with U.S. intelligence support.[14]

The *Boston Globe* presented an important 50-year restrospective of JFK assassination research, stating that those four mobsters had

MORI DocID: 1451843

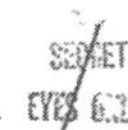

problem and were willing to pay a price of $150,000 for its successful accomplishment. It was to be made clear to Roselli that the United States Government was not, and should not, become aware of this operation.

6. The pitch was made to Roselli on 14 September 1960 at the Hilton Plaza Hotel, New York City. Mr. James O'Connell, Office of Security, was present during this meeting and was identified to Roselli as an employee of Maheu. O'Connell actively served as Roselli's contact until May 1962 at which time he phased out due to an overseas assignment. His initial reaction was to avoid getting involved, but through Maheu's persuasion, he agreed to introduce him to a friend, Sam Gold, who knew the "Cuban crowd." Roselli made it clear he did not want any money for his part and believed Sam would feel the same way. Neither of these individuals were ever paid out of Agency funds.

7. During the week of 25 September, Maheu was introduced to Sam who was staying at the Fontainebleau Hotel, Miami Beach. It was several weeks after his meeting with Sam and Joe, who was identified to him as a courier operating between Havana and Miami, that he saw photographs of both of these individuals in the Sunday supplemental "Parade." They were identified as Momo Salvatore Giancana and Santos Trafficant, respectively. Both were on the list of the Attorney General's ten most-wanted men. The former was described as the Chicago chieftain of the Cosa Nostra and successor to Al Capone, and the latter, the Cosa Nostra boss of Cuban operations. Maheu called this office immediately upon ascertaining this information.

8. In discussing the possible methods of accomplishing this mission, Sam suggested that they not resort to firearms but, if he could be furnished some type of potent pill, that could be placed in Castro's food or drink, it would be a much more effective operation. Sam indicated that he had a prospective nominee in the person of Juan Orta, a Cuban official who had been receiving kick-back payments from the gambling interests, who still had access to Castro, and was in a financial bind.

00013

2

The four top assassinations of the 1960s, JFK, Malcolm X, MLK, and RFK, all against war in the opium-growing area around Vietnam, had a mix of U.S. intelligence and Mafia involvement. This document shows the CIA Office of Security's work with the Mafia regarding Castro.

at least been working with the CIA to assassinate Castro, which Robert F. Kennedy tried to stop: "recently released RFK files" showed that he "put a stop to what he considered an insane initiative by the CIA to subcontract out the job to American gangsters." Yet "those efforts continued, but with different mobsters, and out of view of the Attorney General. Other recently released files also confirm that Marcello, Trafficante, Giancana, and Rosselli were all involved, at varying levels, in the CIA-Mafia plots to get Castro."[15]

New Orleans District Attorney Jim Garrison was made famous in Oliver Stone's movie *JFK*, based on Garrison's book *On the Trail of the Assassins*. In reviewing that book, the *New York Times* summarized Garrison's analysis: "the C.I.A., motivated by disgust with Kennedy's withholding of air cover during the Bay of Pigs invasion [of Cuba] and his reported decision to withdraw troops from Vietnam, executed Kennedy in a coup d'etat." The aforementioned *Boston Globe* article also stated that one week after JFK's assassination, Robert Kennedy sent loyalist William Walton to Moscow to tell Soviet leader Nikita Khrushchev of his belief that "domestic hard-liners, rather than foreign agents, were responsible." Here RFK was referring to right-wing oligarchs, the CIA and anti-Castro Mafia. Government documents included Marcello's eventual confession to his involvement.

The *Boston Globe* said that a 1975 Senate "subcommittee was the first offical body to openly question the lone-gunman narrative," calling Giancana and Rosselli to appear before it. Each was murdered before he could give testimony. In addition, researchers Ed Haslam and Judith Vary Baker presented ample evidence that she worked with accused JFK assassin Lee Harvey Oswald and David Ferrie on a U.S. intelligence project while Ferrie and Oswald were also working for Marcello's crime ring.[16]

President Kennedy continued on his path against the desires of the oligarchy and his generals' advice, and many argue that his presidency was cut short by that opposition. For example, James Douglas's highly regarded *JFK and the Unspeakable* highlights Kennedy's decision to pull out of Vietnam as a major reason for his assassination. UC-Berkeley Professor Peter Dale Scott's *Deep Politics and the Death of JFK* specifically posits that Kennedy's imminent withdrawal of the U.S. military from Vietnam was a threat to American-coordinated international drug-trafficking forces, and the primary reason for his assassination. In *Deep Politics*, Scott revealed that organized crime aided the CIA and America's notorious drug-trafficking families, who were concerned about losing their huge profits, in orchestrating Kennedy's assassination in Dallas.[17]

Malcolm X & MLK Oppose Vietnam War: Assassinated

Malcolm X and Martin Luther King Jr. were two of black America's most important leaders in the 1960s. Internationally, Malcolm X had commented that African independence leaders had developed socialist policies. These leaders formed a group they called the Organization of African Unity. Malcolm X was the only American allowed in their meetings.[18]

Malcolm X had split with the Nation of Islam (NOI) by 1964.[19] Malcolm formed the Organization of Afro-American Unity based in New York to expand his work for civil rights and social justice to non-religious and non-black activists who weren't part of the NOI. Malcolm X maintained his position of militant self-defense while he began directly collaborating with Martin Luther King's group and other civil rights movement leaders.[20]

Malcolm X had an impact on the American oligarchy and U.S. intelligence's use of drugs as political weapons in two ways. First, Malcolm X helped develop a very effective addiction treatment and peer support program in the Nation of Islam, which he described in *The Autobiography of Malcolm X*.[21] Malcolm X did not allow drug use among his group's members and he helped influence others against drug use. Secondly, according to the late Columbia University professor Manning Marable, Malcolm X was the first prominent African-American leader, and arguably the first American leader, to oppose the Vietnam War.[22] Gunmen assassinated Malcolm X (then calling himself El-Hajj Malik El-Shabazz) on February 21, 1965.

An FBI memorandum of March 1968 discussed their long-range goals. These included the goal to: "Prevent the rise of a 'messiah' who could unify, and electrify, the militant black nationalist movement. Malcolm X might have been such a messiah. He is the martyr of the movement today. Martin Luther King, Stokely Carmichael and Elijah Muhammed all aspire to this position. Elijah Muhammed is less of a threat because of his age. King could be a very real contender for this position should he abandon his supposed 'obedience' to 'white liberal doctrines' (nonviolence)."[23] This and other documents show how Malcolm X had clearly emerged as U.S. intelligence's top threat.[24]

Martin Luther King Jr. won a Nobel Peace Prize in 1964 after close to a decade of non-violent civil rights organizing, during which he spearheaded many marches and rallies to end segregation and gain voting rights denied to many poor blacks in the American South.[25] Later, according to CIA documents and FBI agents, the government's goal was to destroy the increasingly radical King, who had grown more complacent about blacks' riotous responses to injustice, saying, "A riot is the language of the unheard." The CIA made MLK their number-one black activist target.[26]

William Pepper worked as a journalist in Vietnam, an experience that led to anti-War activism beside King, and the two once tried to start a new political party together. Almost thirty years later, William Pepper published a book, *Orders to Kill* (and later *Act of State*), about his investigation of MLK's assassination, detailing U.S. intelligence documents, government whistleblowers, and other evidence supporting the suspicion that the oligarchy had U.S. intelligence assassinate Martin Luther King. By that time, King's sons and daughters had grown up to become accomplished leaders in their own right.[27]

In his introduction to *Orders to Kill*'s 1998 edition, MLK's son, Dexter Scott King, said U.S. intelligence orchestrated the assassination of his father in 1968 for several reasons. Their primary motive was to stop MLK's civil rights work and anti-Vietnam war organizing. The exhaustive evidence regarding this motive included the fact that U.S. intelligence orchestrated MLK's assassination on the exact one-year anniversary of his first official speech against the Vietnam War at New York's Riverside Church on April 4, 1967. They appeared to want to send a message against anti-War organizing. This magnifies the importance of the war to control the Golden Triangle opium-cultivating region.[28]

Pepper and others found government-documented evidence that a dozen government intelligence agencies coordinated their plotting against King before his death. Many witnesses and much evidence support how they worked with police and contracted with the Mafia to aid the fatal shooting of MLK in Memphis.[29] MLK's widow Coretta Scott King and their children had William Pepper, who had become an attorney, represent them in a lawsuit, partly to help publicize Pepper's findings. The King family filed a lawsuit against Lloyd Jowers and his government intelligence co-conspirators in MLK's assassination. Jowers owned the boarding house from where the assassin's shots reportedly came. The suit came to trial in 1999, and the King family won their case in court. The King family placed the entire trial transcript on the King Center's website.[30]

The Mafia figures U.S. intelligence contracted to aid this assassination were steeped in drug trafficking. Myron Billet told a U.S. House of Representatives Subcommittee on Assassinations that in January of 1968 he witnessed several CIA and FBI agents offer the heads of New York's top Mafia families $1 million to aid in the assassination of MLK. The New York Mafia rejected the offer. Carlos Marcello's New Orleans crime family accepted it. Carlos Marcello trafficked vast amounts of morphine and cocaine into the U.S. His Memphis crime associate Frank Liberto, who aided more directly in the operation, was also reportedly involved in drug trafficking.[31]

CIA Role in Robert F. Kennedy Assassination

Ross MacLean, a Canadian psychiatrist who worked at Hollywood Hospital in Vancouver, collaborated with federal agent and acid distributor Captain Al Hubbard. Dr. MacLean treated Senator Robert F. Kennedy's wife Ethel with LSD-assisted therapy in 1965. Robert Kennedy had moved to an increasingly leftist political agenda, particularly after his brother's assassination. The targeting of his wife for LSD therapy by the Canadian MK-Ultra psychiatrist parallels the targeting of Jewish leftist Canadian politician David Orlikov's wife, Val, by MK-Ultra psychiatrist Ewen Cameron. Unlike Ethel Kennedy, Val Orlikov's situation received long-term "treatment" that included high-dose shock treatment causing severe long-term damage to her mind.[32]

Robert Kennedy apparently saw some good in his wife's treatment. Given subsequent evidence of how MK-Ultra likely helped orchestrate RFK's assassination, it is ironic that RFK first defended LSD. Kennedy interrogated government psychiatrists and stated, "Perhaps we have lost sight of the fact that [LSD] can be very, very helpful in our society if used properly."[33] CIA representatives hid from Kennedy their research results on thousands of soldiers at Edgewood Arsenal from 1955-1975, showing that LSD had caused lasting damage in many of their research subjects.[34]

By 1968, U.S. intelligence considered Robert Kennedy a serious risk to the interests of the ruling oligarchy who wanted to win the Vietnam War and gain control over the opium-producing poppy fields. As early as February of 1966, then-Senator Kennedy publicly broke with the administration of President Lyndon Johnson in calling for settlement of the Vietnam War. By 1968, especially after the Tet Offensive of the North Vietnamese, many said that RFK stood fully against the Vietnam War.[35] Martin Luther King family attorney William Pepper said Robert Kennedy also made overtures to staunchly antiwar MLK to become his Vice-Presidential candidate if RFK won in the primaries.[36]

Bullets took the life of Robert F. Kennedy on June 6, 1968. By the end of March of that year, the sitting president, Democrat Lyndon Johnson, had announced he would not run for re-election. On the night of June 6, RFK had just won the California presidential primary, the country's largest, and most expected him to go on to win the presidency. After giving a victory speech to a large crowd in a California hotel, RFK was led out through a kitchen pantry, where he was assassinated. The Los Angeles Police Department investigative report on the RFK assassination stated Sirhan Sirhan, alone, fired eight shots in that pantry and killed the presidential candidate, before being wrestled to the ground by Kennedy's security.

A mass of evidence contradicts this. Los Angeles coroner Thomas Noguchi administered the autopsy. Understanding the gravity of the case, he invited national expert coroners to oversee his work. Noguchi declared that all three of the bullets striking Kennedy entered from the rear, in a flight path from down to up and right to left. Powder burns around the entry wound indicated the fatal bullet was fired from less than one inch from the head and no more than two to three inches behind the right ear. A photograph showed Noguchi at a press conference shaping his hand into a gun within an inch of his head to show from where the assassin must have shot.[37]

Many witnessed RFK's assassination. These witnesses claimed Sirhan Sirhan, who was eventually convicted of the assassination, stood in front of Kennedy firing his gun, but never got closer than two feet from RFK.[38]

Also, the Los Angeles Police Department's Rampart Division had multiple photographs of the shooting they hid from public view and eventually "lost."[39] William Harper, a criminologist with 35 years of experience that included U.S. intelligence work, was brought in to examine the evidence by Sirhan's defense attorneys. Harper testified in court and wrote a long affidavit supporting the coroner Noguchi and other witnesses' accounts that someone else fired a gun from behind RFK and within an inch of him. Harper also found that the bullets fired did not match Sirhan's gun and, in fact, had come from two different guns.[40] LAPD radio logs, eyewitnesses and media groups reported sightings of fleeing suspects other than Sirhan Sirhan, who was held at the scene.[41]

One pair of researchers who investigated RFK's assassination, William Turner and Jonn Christian, had strong journalistic credentials along with military and intelligence experience. Turner worked for ten years as an FBI agent before writing for high-circulation magazines. He also published two books on the FBI. Christian had served as a Navy airman and then worked as a broadcast newsman for ABC until 1966. Their book, *The Assassination of Robert F. Kennedy: The Conspiracy and Coverup*, was the first to state that the CIA assassinated RFK. Turner and Christian claimed U.S. intelligence used hypnosis and drugs to produce the mental state that led Sirhan Sirhan to fire a gun at Robert Kennedy.[42]

The CIA history of research that started as Operation Artichoke and developed into Operation MK-Ultra found success with hypnosis and drugs in the early 1950s. CIA documents dated 11/26/51 and 6/8/54 support this. The documents noted that the CIA scientists used heavy "amounts of scopolamine." Former Carter White House staffer-turned-journalist, H.P. Albarelli Jr., reported on two ultra-secret CIA behavior modification and hypnosis programs initially called ZR/ALERT and ZR/AWAKE, "creating hypnotically-controlled operatives to carry out Agency-directed tasks."[43]

Two more researchers agreeing with Turner and Christian's findings included *Probe* magazine editors James DiEugenio and Lisa Pease, who perused thousands of government documents from the RFK assassination records released.[44] These documents and interviews informed their conclusion that Sirhan Sirhan was a hypnotized patsy. Official agencys have ignored these findings.

DiEugenio and Pease also cited top eyewitness, CBS News employee Donald Schulman, who told radio reporter Jeff Brant that after Sirhan started firing, "a Caucasian gentleman stepped out and fired three times; the security guard hit Kennedy all three times." His and similar statements were confirmed in a related 1975 court hearing. The guard standing in that position just to the right and behind RFK was Thane Eugene Cesar. Cesar admitted pulling a gun out. The LAPD never tested his gun to see if it was fired. Cesar worked for Ace Guard Services. It's telling that LAPD criminalist DeWayne Wolfer, who may have helped cover up evidence concerning RFK's assassination, became president of Ace some years later.[45]

Another researcher, Shane O'Sullivan, originally produced the 2007 documentary *RFK Must Die: The Assassination of Bobby Kennedy* for *BBC Newsnight. RFK Must Die* presented evidence in agreement with the main points of these other researchers. The O'Sullivan documentary showed an interview with world-renowned hypnosis expert Dr. Herbert Speigel of Columbia University Medical School. Dr. Spiegel testified in court that Sirhan Sirhan was among the 5-10% of people found to be highly hypnotizable.[46]

Martin Luther King family attorney William Pepper eventually took on the Sirhan case and hired a Harvard Medical School psychiatrist, hypnosis expert Daniel Brown, to spend sixty hours interviewing Sirhan. The Associated Press said Professor Brown found Sirhan remembered being led by an attractive woman in a polka dot dress who pinched him. Pepper's court filings state someone placed Sirhan under hypnosis with the aid of drugs, so that the pinch caused him to realize he had a gun and to start firing it, thinking he was at a shooting range. Only under hypnosis did Sirhan remember seeing another gun fire shots and other details of what happened at RFK's assassination.[47]

Turner and Christian cited the FBI summary report that included interviews of seven witnesses who claim seeing the woman in the polka dot dress flee the scene, along with a man believed to be another shooter. Eyewitnesses Sandy Serrano and a couple identified as "the Bernsteins" gave interviews to police officer Sergeant Paul Sharaga stating that the woman in the polka dot dress exclaimed, "We shot him—we shot him!" Serrano asked, "Who did you shoot?" The woman replied, "Senator Kennedy." This bizarre pronouncement suggests that the fleeing woman was also under hypnosis. Furthermore, the multiple shooters would explain why six people were shot at the scene of Kennedy's assassination.[48]

And finally, a British Broadcast Corporation televised news report linked with Shane O'Sullivan's work presented several former CIA associates identifying three senior CIA agents at the Los Angeles hotel where RFK was assassinated. The BBC said these operatives had no authority inside the U.S.; they were supposed to be in Vietnam at the time. But one of these CIA operatives, David Morales, admitted to friends: "I was in Dallas when we got the son of a bitch, and I was in Los Angeles when we got the little bastard."[49]

Notes

1 William F. Pepper, *Orders to Kill: The Truth Behind the Murder of Martin Luther King, Jr.* (New York: Warner Books, 1998). James Douglas, *JFK and the Unspeakable: Why He Died and Why It Matters* (Mary Knoll, NY: Orbis Books, 2008). Note that the latter has been hailed as "by far the most important book yet written on the subject" by Gaeton Fonzi, former Staff Investigator, U.S. House Select Committee on Assassinations. James Douglas, "The Murder and Martyrdom of Malcolm X," in James DiEugenio and Linda Pease, eds., *The Assassinations: Probe Magazine on JFK, MLK, RFK, and Malcolm X* (Los Angeles: Feral House, 2003). William Turner and Jonn Christian, *The Assassination of Robert F. Kennedy: The Conspiracy and Coverup* (New York: Thunder's Mouth Press, 1978, 1993). Also see John Potash, *The FBI War on Tupac Shakur and Black Leaders: U.S. Intelligence's Murderous Targeting of Tupac, MLK, Malcolm, Panthers, Hendrix, Marley, Rappers and Linked Ethnic Leftists* (Baltimore, MD: Progressive Left Press, 2007).

2 Richard Cloward and Frances Fox Piven, *Poor People's Movements: Why They Succeed, How They Fail* (New York: Vintage, 1978). Pepper, *Orders to Kill*, p. 446.

3 Personal Interview, at conference "Beyond Terror," held by the Maryland Institute College of Art, 1991, Baltimore, MD.

4 On Fitts's résumé, see http://solari.com/about-us/catherine/. On Dillon Read as one of Wall Street Dynasties, see Charles Geisst, *The Last Partnerships: Inside the Great Wall Street Money Dynasties* (New York: McGraw Hill, 2001), http://books.google.com/books?id=tE2RMBKGItgC&printsec=frontcover&source=gbs_ge_summary_r&cad=0#v=onepage&q&f=false. Also see her hosting of a drug forum reprinted by *New York Times*: http://www.nytimes.com/2001/12/11/national/05DPTRAN.html?pagewanted=all.

5 On CIA Inspector General reporting CIA drug trafficking, Dale Russakoff, "Shifting Within Party to Gain His Footing," *Washington Post*, A1, A8, 7/26/04. Catherine Austin Fitts, "Narco Dollars for Beginners; How the Money Works in the Illicit Drug Trade; Part II: The Narco Money Map, *Narco News Bulletin*, October 31, 2001. For other researchers on Air America, see Alfred McCoy, *The Politics of Heroin: CIA Complicity in the Global Drug Trade* (New York: Lawrence Hill, 1976/1991), and Christopher Robbins, *Air America* (Avon Books, 1985).

6 See Catherine Austin Fitts, "Narco Dollars for Beginners; How the Money Works in the Illicit Drug Trade; Part II: The Narco Money Map, *Narco News Bulletin*, October 31, 2001. http://www.narconews.com/narcodollars2.html. On compounding interest computations, http://en.wikipedia.org/wiki/Compound_interest. On POP, see http://www.investopedia.com/terms/p/publicofferingprice.asp.

7 See Catherine Austin Fitts, "Narco Dollars for Beginners; How the Money Works in the Illicit Drug Trade; Part II: The Narco Money Map, *Narco News Bulletin*, October 31, 2001, http://www.narconews.com/narcodollars2.html.

8 Rajeev Sayel, "Drug Money Saved Banks in Global Crisis, Says UN Adviser," *The Guardian/The Observer* (London), December 12, 2009, http://www.guardian.co.uk/global/2009/dec/13/drug-money-banks-saved-un-cfief-claims.

9 On CIA Inspector General reporting CIA drug trafficking, Dale Russakoff, "Shifting Within Party to Gain His Footing," *Washington Post*, A1, A8, 7/26/04. Catherine Austin Fitts, "Narco Dollars for Beginners; How the Money Works in the Illicit Drug Trade; Part II: The Narco Money Map, *Narco News Bulletin*, October 31, 2001. For other researchers on Air America, see McCoy, *The Politics of Heroin* and Christopher Robbins, *Air America* (Avon Books, 1985).

10 Richard Reeves, *President Kennedy: Profile of Power* (New York: Simon and Schuster, 1993), p. 550. Some say that the Soviet's military helped Leonid Brezhnev depose Khrushchev within a year. Few Americans knew of Kennedy's back-channel mail correspondence with the Soviet Union's leader, Nikita Khrushchev. When Kennedy made a special appeal to Khrushchev for help regarding the Cuban Missile Crisis, the Soviet leader complied and turned his missiles around. Both leaders struggled against their militaries, and Kennedy paid Khrushchev back with a famous speech at American University in 1963, announcing an end to the Cold War with the Soviet Union. It was the only American presidential speech the Soviets printed in full on the front page of their national newspaper. Few American mainstream media outlets covered this monumental speech. Douglas, *JFK and the Unspeakable*. Also see U.S. Dept of State, Office of the Historian, http://history.state.gov/milestones/1961-1968/LimitedBan.

11 John Judge, former research director for Congresswoman Cynthia McKinley, an Atlanta Democrat, announced this at the John F. Kennedy Assassination Conference in November 18, 2011, and confirmed it in a personal interview. On Galbraith, see *Nightly News with Vincent Brown*. The section on this subject of Kennedy's Vietnam withdrawal begins at about 2:20 of this video: http://www.youtube.com/watch?v=OPNd8Y-3-jM. Also see the first two parts of this very interesting interview of Prof. Peter Dale Scott directly supporting Galbraith, http://www.youtube.com/watch?v=tQDoTdYTeDk and http://www.youtube.com/watch?v=BQn-Ygk8UdM.

12 Martin Lee and Bruce Shlain, *Acid Dreams: The Complete Social History of LSD: The CIA, the Sixties, and Beyond* (New York: Grove Press, 1994), pp. 33-34.

13 Quote from Lee and Shlain, *Acid Dreams*, p. 102. On shots including amphetamines, see Thomas C. Reeves, *A Question of Character: A Life of John F. Kennedy* (New York: Free Press, 1991), cited in Mark Roberts and Jeff Vandermeer, *The Thackery T. Lambshead Pocket Guide to Eccentric and Discredited Diseases* (New York: Bantam, 2005), p. 279.

14 On Trafficante, Luciano and Lansky working with U.S. intelligence, McCoy, *The Politics of Heroin*, pp. 35-37, 73-74. On legal cases against these Mafia figures, Bryan Bender and Neil Swidey, "JFK 50 Years Later: Robert F. Kennedy saw conspiracy in JFK's assassination," *Boston Globe*, November 24, 2013. Peter Dale Scott and Jonathan Marshall, *Cocaine Politics: Drugs, Armies and the CIA in Central America* (Los Angeles: University of California Press, 1998), pp. 52-53.

15 Bender and Swidey, "JFK 50 Years Later."

16 Bender and Swidey, "JFK 50 Years Later." Ronnie Dugger, "Reverberations of Dallas," *New York Times*, January 29, 1989. Edward T. Haslam, *Dr. Mary's Monkey: How the Unsolved Murder of a Doctor, a Secret Laboratory in New Orleans and Cancer-causing Monkey Viruses are Linked to Lee Harvey Oswald, the JFK assassinations and Emerging Global Epidemics* (Walterville, OR: TrineDay, 2014). Judith Vary Baker, *Me and Lee: How I Came to Know, Love and Lose Lee Harvey Oswald* (Walterville, OR: TrineDay, 2011).

17 Peter Dale Scott, *Deep Politics and the Death of JFK* (Berkeley: University of California Press, 1996). For an overview, see http://www.history-matters.com/pds/DP3_Overview.htm. The Bundys were another family who were members of Skull and Bones who pushed for the Vietnam War. They also co-authored Henry Stimson's memoirs, and whitewashed the Kennedy assassination. As detailed earlier, Skull and Bones was founded and forever funded by the opium trafficking Russell family trust. Webster and Tarpley, *George Bush: The Unauthorized Biography*, p. 127. Also Douglas, *JFK and the Unspeakable*.

18 FBI Memo, 9/17/64 in Clayborne Carson, *Malcolm X: The FBI File* (New York: Carroll and Graf, 1991), pp. 289, 299.

19 Malcolm X, as told to Alex Haley, *The Autobiography of Malcolm X* (New York: Ballantine, 1965), pp. 316, 322, for example.

20 See Corretta Scott King, *My Life with Martin Luther King, Jr.*, revised edition (New York: Henry Holt, 1993), p. 238. Cited in Douglas, *Assassinations*, p. 403. Also see PBS's *American Experience*, "Malcolm X : Make It Plain," archival footage of Malcolm pledging his group's support for Martin Luther King in an interview. Ossie Davis discussed Malcolm's day-long strategy meeting with other civil rights leaders. And in an interview Pacifica radio held with Mississippi-based Fannie Lou Hamer, she said Malcolm was her best friend and mentored her during her civil rights work.

21 Haley, *The Autobiography of Malcolm X*, pp. 259-62.

22 Manning Marable on radio program, *Democracy Now!* 5/21/2007, http://www.democracynow.org/2007/5/21/manning_marable_on_malcolm_x_a.

23 Carson, *Malcolm X*, p. 17.

24 On FBI document, FBI memorandum, March 4, 1968. In Carson, *Malcolm X*,p. 17. On 5,000 lynchings, Piven and Cloward, *Poor People's Movements*, p. 186. On bombings, see p. 243. Also see Kenneth O'Reilly, *Racial Matters: The FBI's Secret Files on Black America, 1960-1972* (New York: Free Press, 1989), pp.112, 217, cited in Ward Churchill and Jim Vander Wall, *The COINTELPRO Papers: Documents from the FBI's Secret Wars Against Dissent in the United States* (Boston: South End Press, 1991), p. 170.

25 Frances Fox Piven and Richard A. Cloward, *Why Americans Don't Vote* (New York: Pantheon, 1989).

26 Carson, *Malcolm X*, p. 17. Piven and Cloward, *Poor People's Movements*, pp. 244-48. Researchers documented a nationwide series of riots after police brutalized black leaders at some of the peaceful demonstrations. The largest of the riots were in New York, Chicago, Maryland, Philadelphia and New Jersey in the first half of 1964. Whether primarily responding to riots or sincere about civil rights, President John F. Kennedy initiated the Civil Rights Act just before his assassination in November of 1963. This took away many barriers to southern blacks voting. Congress passed the Act and President Johnson signed it in July of 1964. On effort to "destroy King," see memorandum in CIA file for Chief, Security Research Staff, from Allan Morse, one Jay R. Kennedy report. 6/9/65, p.7, in this writer's possession Thanks to New Haven Black Panther founding member, George Edwards, for providing copies of these documents, originally obtained in a FOIA filing by filmmaker, Lee Lew-Lee. Also see, Wallace Turner, "FBI Taps Called Plan to Discredit Dr. King," *New York Times*, Monday, May 21, 1973, p. A18. Pepper, *Orders to Kill*, pp. 294-95.

27 Pepper, *Orders To Kill*. See Foreword by Dexter Scott King.

28 This poor people's march was called an "extremely explosive situation." Memorandum from Howard Osborn, Director of Security to Deputy Director of Support. 3/27/68, copy in this writer's possession. Also, the fact that MLK was assassinated on the exact anniversary of his official anti-Vietnam War announcement attests to that stance as a major reason for his assassination. See more on this tactic below.

29 See both Pepper, *Orders to Kill* and *An Act Of State: The Execution of Martin Luther King* (New York: Verso, 2003). Also see Carson, *Malcolm X*, p. 17; Pepper, *Orders to Kill*, p. 82. Also, DiEgenio and Pease, *The Assassinations*, "MLK," pp. 432-529.

30 See www.thekingcenter.org and click on "News and Information" and then click on "Trial Transcript."

31 On Billet and New York Mafia, Pepper, *Orders to Kill*, pp.145-46, and much of book on Marcello and MLK. On Marcello and cocaine trafficking, John Davis, *Mafia Kingfish* (New York: McGraw-Hill, 1989), p. 36, in Scott and Marshall, *Cocaine Politics*, p. 54. On Liberto and drug trafficking, see admitted MLK assassination co-conspirator Lloyd Jowers, stating this about Liberto in Pepper, *Act of State*, p. 93 and Jim Douglas, "The Martin Luther King Conspiracy Exposed in Memphis," *Probe Magazine*, Spring 2000, http://www.ratical.org/ratville/JFK/MLKconExp.html. Both cited in Peter Dale Scott, "The Assassinations of the 1960s as Deep Events," *History Matters*, Oct. 17, 2008, http://www.history-matters.com/essays/jfkgen/AssassinationsDeepEvents/AssassinationsDeepEvents.htm#_ftn63. University of California-Berkeley Professor Peter Dale Scott noted that patsy James Earl Ray's brother, John Ray, said that James Earl Ray was involved in a marijuana delivery in Mexico in 1967. Professor Scott also detailed how Ray further made a ten-day visit to Lisbon, Portugal, just before his arrest for the King assassination. He tried to join the only mercenary army there, which was Aginter Press. Scott, a global expert on the politics of drug trafficking, said that Aginter Press was part of a "CIA-Mafia-Narcotics-Connection." On marijuana delivery, John Larry Ray and Lyndon Barsten, *Truth at Last: The Untold Story Behind James Earl Ray and the Assassination of Martin Luther King, Jr.* (Guilford, CN: Lyons Press, 2008), p. 99. On James Earl Ray in Lisbon, HSCA Report, MLK, Appendix, Volume XIII, p. 254.

32 Lee and Shlain, *Acid Dreams*, p. 93. Allison Mayes, "Moving tribute: Local artist turns to dance to further explore her grandmother's torment at the hands of the CIA," *Winnipeg Free Press*, 2/4/10, http://www.winnipegfreepress.com/arts-and-life/entertainment/arts/moving-tribute-83526407.html?path=/arts-and-life/entertainment/arts&id=83526407&sortBy=oldest&viewAllComments=y.

33 Lee and Shlain, *Acid Dreams*, p. 93.

34 See "Chemical Warfare Agent Experiments Among U.S. Service Members," http://www.whattheproblemis.com/documents/ra/ra_Chemical_Warfare_Agent_Experiments_Among_US_Service_Members.pdf. It includes: US Army Medical Department, US Army Health Services Command, Project Director LTC David A. McFarling, MC. "LSD Follow-up Study Report, October 1980, 158 pp. Pages 23-25 of this paper show how at least 24% of subjects reported long-term adverse effects of LSD when surveyed 19 years later. Also see *Bad Trip to Edgewood* (1993) on over 7,000 soldiers tested with various psychedelic drugs from 1955-75, with thousands reporting long-term adverse effects, http://www.youtube.com/watch?v=g0kILxvfgu8.

35 See http://www.jfklibrary.org/JFK/The-Kennedy-Family/Robert-F-Kennedy.aspx. for early position and growing opposition to Vietnam War. See excerpt of book by Thurston Clarke, "The Last Good Campaign," *Vanity Fair*, June 2008, http://www.vanityfair.com/politics/features/2008/06/rfk_excerpt200806 Also, to get a sense of how antiwar, anti-pollution, and leftist/progressive Kennedy was becoming: Remarks of Robert F. Kennedy at the University of Kansas, March 18, 1968.

36 William Pepper, "An Act of State: The Execution of Martin Luther King," talk given at Modern Times Bookstore, San Francisco, CA," 2/4/03, www.ratical.org/ratville/JFK/WFP020403.html.

37 *Los Angeles Herald-Examiner*, 5/13/74, cited in Turner and Christian, *The Assassination of Robert F. Kennedy*, p. 162. See picture in *Citizine* magazine's excellent coverage of RFK assassination, at http://www.citizinemag.com/politics/politics_0506_rfk_twhite.htm.

38 See, for example, sworn statement to Vince Bugliosi by eyewitness Martin Patruski, 12/12/75, and Turner and Christian, *The Assassination of Robert F. Kennedy*, pp. 350-51. Also Lisa Pease, "The RFK Plot Part 1: The Grand Illusion," in DiEugenio and Pease, *The Assassinations*, pp. 550-51.

39 James DiEugenio, "The Curious Case of Dan Moldea," in DiEugenio and Pease, *The Assassinations*, pp. 619-21. DiEugenio cites Bill Klaber and Phil Melanson, *Shadow Play: The Murder of Robert F. Kennedy, the Trial of Sirhan Sirhan, and the Failure of American Justice* (New York: St. Martin's, 1997), pp. 301-10. At least one photographer, Scott Enyart, took multiple pictures as he followed Kennedy from his victory speech into the kitchen pantry of the hotel where Kennedy was shot. Enyart said he continued taking photos during the shooting. The LAPD confiscated Enyart's film and failed to ever release the evidence to the public. Enyart's decades-long lawsuit for his film finally led the LAPD to admit they still had it, but then said it was lost while transporting it to the courthouse in 1996. Bill Boyarsky, *Los Angeles Times*, 7/9/96.

40 On official LAPD investigative report, see copy of it in Turner and Christian, *The Assassination of Robert F. Kennedy*, Appendix, pp. 376-77. On Harper's affidavit, see copy of it in same, pp. 378-79. On Harper's U.S. intelligence work, he was in the CIA precursor OSS: Pease, "RFK Plot Part I," *The Assassinations*, p. 565. Pease cited researchers' findings of different types of bullets used at the scene, pp. 556-62. For example, see witness Martin Patrusky's signed statement in Turner and Christian, *The Assassination of Robert F. Kennedy*, p. 350; cited in Pease, "RFK Plot Part I," p. 550. William Harper said the bullets he examined weren't fired from the same gun": Pease, "RFK Plot Part I," p. 555-57, 560-61.

41 Reports first cited at least two shooting suspects as well as several people shot. Turner and Christian, *The Assassination of Robert F. Kennedy*, pp. 167-68, sourcing a KFWB transcript, and Paul Hope, "Senator Felled in Los Angeles; 5 Others Shot," *The Evening Star*, 6/5/68. Both cited in Pease, "The RFK Plot Part II," *The Assassinations*, pp. 534, 602-03. These reports were quoted from LAPD files, radio broadcasts and even Intelligence Division log entries, with witness names and dates provided: Pease, "RFK Plot Part I," *The Assassinations*, pp. 544-45.

42 Turner and Christian, *The Assassination of Robert F. Kennedy,* see "About the Authors." On Bugliosi, see pp. 10, 243-44.

43 Declassified CIA document, "'ARTICHOKE,' Special Comments," 11/26/52. And CIA document dated 6/8/54, cited in Lee and Shlain, *Acid Dreams,* pp. 7-8. It stated: "We're now convinced that we can maintain a subject in a controlled state for a much longer time than we heretofore had believed possible." Regarding Albarelli accumulating over 30,000 documents, personal email correspondance on 4/29/14. On ZR/ALERT and ZR/WAKE, see H.P. Albarelli Jr., *A Secret Order: Investigating the High Strangeness and Synchronicity in the JFK Assassination* (Walterville, OR: TrineDay, 2013), p. 253.

44 Pease, "The RFK Plot Part 1: The Grand Illusion," in DiEugenio and Pease, *The Assassinations.* Pease and DiEugenio started their magazine in the wake of Oliver Stone's film *JFK,* which helped bring enough support.

45 Turner and Christian, *The Assassination of Robert F. Kennedy,* pp. 161, 165-66. Schulman's testimony and statements, along with similar witness statements, were introduced at official hearings in Los Angeles Superior Court in late 1975. Pease cited Schulman first making part of this statement in a radio interview on 6/5/68 and then repeating it in the District Attorney's office in 1971; *Assassinations,* p. 545. Cesar first said he had told a police sergeant about his .22 gun when he was interviewed after the assassination, but then he said he must have been mistaken as he had already sold it. His revised statements were cited by Turner and Christian from a reporter's transcript, "Room 113, Bureau of Investigation, DA's Office, 524 North Spring St., Los Angeles," 7/14/71, pp. 47-48. On Wolfer, see, for example, Pease, "The RFK Plot Part II," and DiEugenio, "The Curious Case of Dan Moldea," in *The Assassinations,* pp. 606, 617.

46 *RFK Must Die: The Assassination of Bobby Kennedy,* Dokument Films (2007), director/writer Shane O'Sullivan. Note that this film was produced by Sullivan and originally shown in parts starting on *BBC Newsnight,* 11/20/2006. Pease, "The RFK Plot Part 1," in DiEugenio and Pease, *The Assassinations.*

47 Associated Press, "Convicted RFK Assassin Says Girl Manipulated Him," CBS News, 4/28/12, http://www.cbsnews.com/2102-201_162-20058498.html?tag=contentMain;contentBody. Also see, "Bobby Kennedy assassin claims he was manipulated by pretty girl in a polka dot dress," *The Daily Mail* (UK), 4/29/11, http://www.dailymail.co.uk/news/article-1381917/Bobby-Kennedy-assassin-Sirhan-claims-manipulated-seductive-girl.html.

48 Lonny Worthey, interview 6/7/68, unpaginated in FBI Summary Report by Special Agent Amedee Richards, Jr., 8/1/69, not declassified until a FOIA request in 1976. Susanne Locke interviewed 6/7/68, pp. 405-5, FBI Summary report. Cathy Sue Fulmer, interview 6/8/68, unpaginated section of Summary Report. Sandra Serrano, interview 6/8/68, in Summary Report pp. 464-67. Darmell Johnson, 6/7/68, pp. 406-09. Thomas Dipierro, interviewed 6/8/68, pp. 432-34. George Green, interviewed 6/7/68, unpaginated section of Report. All in Turner and Christian, *The Assassination of Robert F. Kennedy,* pp. 68-73. Lisa Pease, as well as Turner and Christian, further cited other physical evidence from the RFK file photos and the FBI's report on them. The photos showed two bullet holes in the wall and a third bullet that was removed from a doorframe. The FBI also ran strings through many ceiling panel bullet holes. Published photos include LA coroner Thomas Noguchi and LAPD pointing to the various bullet holes at the scene: Turner and Christian, *The Assassination of Robert F. Kennedy,* photo pages 10-12. Credits for these photos were 6/5/68, Official LAPD photo, AP Wirephoto, Los Angeles County Coroner's Office, and Official FBI Photos taken under supervision of Special Agent Al Grenier and verified by Special Agent William Bailey. On bullets and victims, Pease, "The RFK Plot Part 1: The Grand Illusion," *The Assassinations,* pp. 540-43. On other witnesses seeing more suspects, see, for example, LAPD interview of Roy Mills, 8/9/68. Joe Klein, interviewed by LAPD, 7/3/68. Pease, *The Assassinations,* p. 545. Also Turner and Christian, *The Assassination of Robert F. Kennedy,* pp.180-81, 316-17. The Los Angeles Police Department's Rampart Division proceeded to tamper with and then destroy most of the evidence within a year of the assassination, despite an official legal appeal by Sirhan. Sgt. Sharaga took the reports of Serrano and the Bernsteins, while detailing much else that went mostly unreported in

mainstream media at the assassination scene. Art Kevin's taped interview with Sharaga, KMPC radio, L.A., 12/20/74, cited in Turner and Christian, *The Assassination of Robert F. Kennedy,* pp. 76-77. On destroyed evidence, see Deputy Chief Daryl Gates's interview on NBC network, 8/22/75, pp. 178-79. On bullet photos and bullet fragments sent to Rampart, Pease, *The Assassinations,* p. 554. On multiple people shot, see "RFK Assassination: Newly Discovered Footage Backs Up Doctor's Story About Aiding Kennedy," *CBS News,* June 5, 2013, http://www.cbsnews.com/8301-505263_162-57587756/.

49 "CIA Role Claim in Kennedy Killing: New video and photographic evidence that puts three senior CIA operatives at the scene of Robert Kennedy's assassination has been brought to light," *BBC News,* 11/20/06, http://news.bbc.co.uk/1/hi/programmes/newsnight/6169006.stm.

CHAPTER EIGHT

CIA Acid Fests Counter Protests

Reflecting upon the Sixties, a surprising number of counterculture veterans endorsed the notion that the CIA disseminated street acid en masse so as to deflate the political potency of the youth rebellion.

– Martin Lee and Bruce Shlain, *Acid Dreams: The Complete Social History of LSD: The CIA, the Sixties, and Beyond.*[1]

A top CIA-connected think tank, the Rand Corporation, headquartered in Santa Monica, California, "played a crucial role in designing strategies for counter-revolution and pacification" both in Vietnam and against anti-War Americans. A 1962 Rand report revealed that LSD could lead those in left-wing organizations to "resign or become inactive."[2]

Evidence shows that the CIA's MK-Ultra operations first dosed various leaders in politics and the arts, then had their media assets spotlight these leaders in a sophisticated way to make them well-known counterculture figures. They often coupled them with undercover agents in propaganda campaigns to promote LSD to leftists.

In February of 1965, President Lyndon Johnson initiated Operation Flaming Dart, a major expansion of U.S. involvement in the Vietnam War. It included the bombing of North Vietnam as well as the first use of U.S. ground troops to fight the Viet Cong in South Vietnam.[3] The Students for a Democratic Society (SDS) at the University of Michigan held the first anti-War teach-in, and other SDS chapters began to follow suit.

In October of 1965, UC-Berkeley students, led by Free Speech veteran organizers including Jerry Rubin and Mike Rossman, held one of the nation's largest events—an all day teach-in to protest the Vietnam War. Throughout the next fourteen months, Berkeley activists recruited more and more anti-War protesters for rallies and campus strikes.[4]

Berkeley students inspired other student actions nationwide. Many students joined SDS. By October of 1965, SDS had grown into a massive organization of leftest students with 10,000 members and chapters in 89 schools. By the end of that school year it added 5,000 more members and nearly doubled its chapters to 172 schools.[5]

The psychological handling of writer Ken Kesey to lead youth to acid went astray when Kesey urged people to "graduate" from LSD. By the end of 1966, Kesey, seen as the figurehead of the Acid Tests, moved from California and the UC Berkeley area to Oregon. Ken Babbs and other Pranksters moved with Kesey. They eventually changed Kesey's mind about stopping acid and urging others to stop using it. They also would promote acid in their Day-Glo bus at events such as Woodstock.[6]

While some of the Pranksters moved with him, a few key people involved in the Acid Tests stayed in the San Francisco Bay Area. These included top LSD trafficker Owsley Stanley and chemist Tim Scully. Within a year, these two and their cohorts had vastly expanded the size of the Acid Tests. While Owsley had manufactured a lot of acid before the mid-1960s, with Scully he set up a larger LSD laboratory in Richmond, California in the spring of 1966. Top MK-Ultra scientists attended Owsley's Acid Test parties. Also, former Grateful Dead manager/advisor Hank Harrison said Owsley and Scully worked with William Mellon Hitchcock by 1965. This and other evidence suggests that Owsley was working undercover for the CIA in helping set up the Acid Tests as LSD promotion events for MK-Ultra in a way that would make LSD production appear as a "grassroots phenomenon."[7]

Media Aids Suspected Agents Organizing Acid Fests

Owsley had a network of acid dealers who helped expand San Francisco's LSD scene. Allan Cohen dealt acid for Owsley, "turned on" brothers Ron and Jay Thelin to acid, and then worked with them when they started The Psychedelic Shop. Cohen also became an editor of the Psychedelic Rangers newspaper, *The Oracle*.[8]

John Starr Cooke, founder of the Psychedelic Rangers, promoted heavy acid dosing of people worldwide. Cooke regularly met with his connected in-laws, including Sherman Kent, who was CIA Director Allan Dulles's right-hand man.

Similar to Owsley's setting up Acid Tests with top CIA MK-Ultra scientists in attendance, John Cooke, a man with multiple links to U.S. intelligence, started the Psychedelic Rangers. Cooke had a close relationship with his sister and brother-in-law, Alice and Roger Kent, the latter a major figure in the California Democratic Party. Cooke also regularly partied with Roger's brother, Sherman Kent. Researchers Lee and Shlain said Sherman Kent headed the

"CIA's National Board of Estimates (a powerful position), and served as CIA director Allen Dulles's right-hand man during the Cold War." Cooke also "made the acquaintance of a number of CIA operatives while traveling in Europe."[9]

Cooke's governmental connections were legion. During the '60s, Cooke worked out of Mexico where he met with researcher Andrija Puharich, who ran "parapsychology and drug experiments for the U.S. military in the late 1950s, and Seymoure Lazare, a wealthy business associate of William Mellon Hitchcock." Cooke's funding sources were unknown, but they were lavish, affording him the ability to send off six of his Psychedelic Rangers to "various psychedelic hotspots in North America and Europe."[10]

The Psychedelic Rangers carried out MK-Ultra-type operations, following Cooke's directions to damage leftists with LSD. Lee and Shlain described how, "Following Cooke's master plan, the Psychedelic Rangers targeted selected individuals for high-dose LSD initiations." One Psychedelic Ranger, Michael Bowen, claimed "he furnished acid to a number of well-known figures, including comedian Dick Gregory." Gregory was the nation's most popular black comedian and an ardent civil rights activist. Other intelligence agents convinced top jazz musician Charles Mingus to try acid.[11]

In 1966, Cooke sent Michael Bowen to settle in Haight-Ashbury, and the two maintained constant communication. Bowen helped start a psychedelic newspaper, *The Oracle,* in San Francisco around the time of the Berkeley activism. Bowen had *Oracle* organizers at his house where they set up Acid Test type events—a Love Pageant Rally in 1966 and then, the first Human Be-In. They dubbed it a "Pow Wow, Gathering of Tribes." Michael Bowen and *The Oracle* reportedly held the Human Be-In in January of 1967 in order to "psychedelicize" the radical political left. If William S. Burroughs and a number of research articles are correct, they sought to do the CIA's bidding in making the radical left less competent.[12]

With Kesey and his Pranksters gone, *The Oracle* staff members and others, such as members of the Grateful Dead, took over the organizing of these massively expanded Acid Tests. Timothy Leary preached his acid-worshipping philosophy, while Michael Bowen and his *Oracle* organizers invited key leftist leaders, including Berkeley Vietnam Day organizer Jerry Rubin, comedian Dick Gregory, and socialist Beat poet Allen Ginsberg for the Human Be-In.[13]

Cooke and Bowen followed the lead of Captain Al Hubbard and Michael Hollingshead. They pretended to turn people on to acid to make the world better. But details of their operations show they were most likely undercover agents following the MK-Ultra game plan of damaging leftists' minds.

As Lee and Shlain described, Michael Bowen and his organizers followed "Cooke's master plan." The Psychedelic Rangers "gave people 2,000 to 3,000 micrograms (more than ten times the usual dose) during a single session in an effort to bring about a rapid and permanent transformation of psychological disposition." In other words, they overdosed them to damage them and make them easier to manipulate, as the U.S. Congressional House Select Committee said was MK-Ultra's goal with foreign leaders.[14]

The Oracle LSD promoters quoted Timothy Leary. By the mid-1960s, as student activism increased nationwide, Leary traveled the country urging young folks to "turn on, tune in, and drop out." Here Leary meant dropping out of society, including dropping activism. *Oracle* editor Ron Thelin repeated Leary in summarizing the paper's editorial slant. He said it was "to show that LSD provides a profound experience.... To get everyone to turn on, tune in, and drop out."[15]

With his famous slogan, ex-Harvard psychology professor Timothy Leary regularly implored crowds of potential activists to abandon society, rather than join civil rights and anti-War mobilizations.

With undercover agents throughout the San Francisco Bay area and other cities, U.S. intelligence could heighten their LSD promotion propaganda operations in another important way. Journalists John Stauber and Sheldon Rampton wrote a book about the public relations industry that reported how major public relations firms created "astroturf," manufacturing fake grassroots groups and propaganda to make their messages appear to come from passionate individuals, rather than huge wealthy institutions. The whole LSD and other drug movement, from Owsley and Bowen in San Francisco, to suspected agents in the East Village neighborhood of New York City, and even the Psychedelic Rangers' European "psychedelic hotspots," appeared to be part of this astroturf network.[16]

The Human Be-In organizers continually tried to appear grassroots, even using low-tech, homemade posters, while attaining mass media coverage. But their true aim was to help drug people both nationwide and globally.[17]

The organizers had Hell's Angels bikers working security at the Be-In—the same Hell's Angels who fought against activists marching in protest of the Vietnam War. Biker gangs' history shows a large percentage of membership is ex-military. Hell's Angels also did contract work for U.S. intelligence.[18]

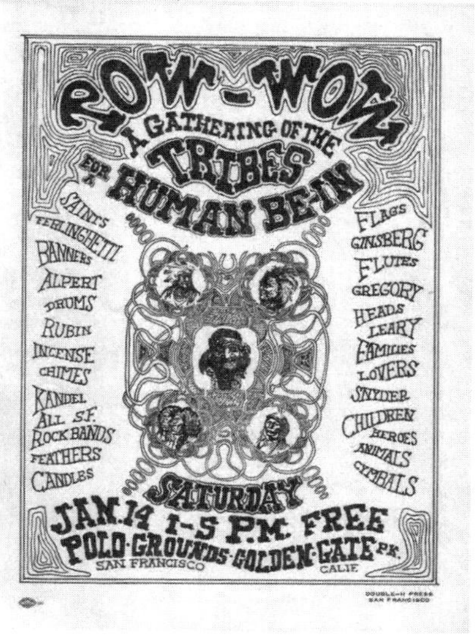

Cooke's Psychedelic Rangers organized the first Human Be-In, which gathered an estimated 25,000 in Golden Gate Park, many of whom were initiated into tripping by the featured speaker, Timothy Leary.

The Human Be-In was held on Polo Field at Golden Gate Park on January 14, 1967. Timothy Leary sat on the stage, dressed from head to toe in white, with his hands together as if in a prayer. His constant presence was a reminder to eat acid as part of the spiritual communal ritual. The Grateful Dead and other San Francisco rock bands played music at the Be-In and increased the bandwagon effect to encourage "tripping."[19]

Descriptions of the event reported that only Jerry Rubin and Allan Ginsberg talked about protesting the Vietnam War, and they were largely ignored. The Human Be-In created an overriding theme around the false myth of "expanding consciousness." Leary and others pushed the myth that eating acid had this desirable effect. A high percentage of the crowd of over 25,000 men, women and children were initiated into taking LSD at that event, including activists drawn in by anti-War speakers like Rubin.[20]

Timothy Leary continued his refrain after the event. In a press conference with philosopher Allan Watts and writers Allan Ginsberg and Gary Snyder, Leary presented himself as a perfect spokesman for those trying to suppress anti-War activists. Leary said, "The choice is between being rebellious and being religious. Don't vote. Don't politic. Don't petition. You can't do *anything* about America politically." He criticized student activists as "young men with menopausal minds," if they didn't focus primarily on "expanding their consciousness" with psychedelics.[21]

After this Be-In, organizers held similar events in Chicago, New York and other locations. While actual numbers are hard to determine, attendees remember a hundred Be-Ins held across the country. SDS had mobilized student activists around the Berkeley-inspired anti-Vietnam War protests on numerous college campuses. In seeming reaction, U.S. intelligence-linked LSD promoters used vast resources to duplicate their acid promotion at Be-Ins and other huge events nationwide.[22]

CIA Creates San Francisco Acid Wasteland

By 1966, the Student Nonviolent Coordinating Committee (SNCC) had cast out whites and took on the new name, Student National Coordinating Committee. By October of 1966, Huey Newton and Bobby Seale started the Black Panther Party for Self Defense in Oakland. In the spring of 1967, Martin Luther King Jr. broke with other traditional black leaders in announcing his opposition to the Vietnam War. At the same time, young people began to move politically more to the radical left. In the black community many were radicalized by Malcolm X's death.[23]

Race riots broke out nationwide, especially in the northern black communities, as a response to the killings of civil rights leaders and bombing of black churches in the South. As previously mentioned, King refused to criticize these racial eruptions, saying, "Riots are the language of the unheard."[24]

White youths ejected from SNCC went elsewhere. New York University sociologist Todd Gitlin, who had led the national SDS earlier, said some activists turned to marijuana and then acid as it began to pervade the southern communities in which they were organizing.[25]

During 1966 SDS grew exponentially, and by June of 1967 had an estimated 30,000 members.[26] An anti-War demonstration in Washington DC that year attracted about 70,000 people, while student teach-ins and anti-War protests erupted at schools from Berkeley to Harvard.

CIA think tanks, like the Rand Corporation in California and the Hudson Institute in New York, developed a number of plans for popularizing their chemical agent against the anti-War uprising. U.S. intelligence used its expanding media assets to help draw many to the San Francisco Bay area. FAIR cofounder Martin Lee said, "In 1967, when the grassroots acid scene was floodlit by the mass media ... young people started turning on in greater numbers than ever before ... the media catalyzed the widespread use of LSD."[27] Undercover MK-Ultra agents merely awaited the arrival of their test subjects.

Lee and Shlain interviewed a former CIA contract employee who said, "(CIA) personnel helped underground chemists set up LSD laboratories in the Bay Area during the Summer of Love to 'monitor' events in the acid ghetto." Writers asked why the CIA would do this. They wouldn't be trying to enforce the law, since police already had many undercover narcotics agents in the Haight.[28]

Lee and Shlain responded, "A CIA agent who claims to have infiltrated the covert LSD network provided a clue when he referred to Haight-Ashbury as a 'human guinea pig farm.'" Supporting this description, CIA MK-Ultra scientist Dr. Louis Joylon West rented a place in the heart of Haight-Ashbury for "monitoring" purposes.[29]

In a very long footnote, Lee and Shlain described other interesting aspects of Dr. West. West had examined Jack Ruby, the murderer of President Kennedy's purported assassin, Lee Harvey Oswald. West determined Ruby was "insane" because Ruby didn't agree with West's quick diagnosis of insanity. Dr. West also started a center for violence reduction. It made news when West proposed that very young black males receive psychosurgery and chemical castration as "pre-delinquent" children. West clearly had the same bigoted mentality as his superiors who started genocidal eugenics in the same offices later occupied by MK-Ultra scientists.[30]

Congregations of politically-left white activists organized with black, Latino and other ethnic activists in urban areas nationwide. The multiracial Congress of Racial Equality (CORE) had 53 chapters, mostly in large cities, and then became part of the anti-War movement, especially after King made his famous anti-War speech in April of 1967.[31] The number of CIA undercover agents and MK-Ultra scientists in San Francisco, a center for activism, illustrates the way in which U.S. intelligence appeared to create psychedelic wastelands of burnt minds among idealistic young adults.

During the summer of 1967, mainstream media provided a "Summer of Love" blitz. *Time* magazine had a cover story on "The Hippies: Philosophy of a Subculture." It should be remembered that Time Inc.'s Vice-President, C.D. Jackson, rotated in and out of his government position as head of Psychological Warfare.[32]

The Summer of Love media blitz also included a very popular song, "San Francisco (Be Sure to Wear Flowers in Your Hair)" by John Phillips of The Mamas and The Papas. Scott McKenzie's recording of the song entered the *Billboard* magazine music charts in May and reached Number 4 on the charts by the end of the summer.[33] Phillips reportedly wrote the song to help bring people to what had been called the first of many widely promoted and heavily attended multiple-band rock music events: the Monterey Pop Music Festival. Between 55 and 90 thousand people came to listen and party at the three-day event.[34]

Along with the music fest, the constant national media coverage of the Haight-Ashbury neighborhood led huge masses of people to visit that small section of San Francisco in the summer of 1967.[35] It's unknown how many who went there were initiated into LSD use.

Owsley Stanley became the largest acid dealer in the country by that summer. Estimates of his acid sales started at about several hundred thousand hits a year, and grew through the 1960s.[36] Owsley reportedly started the first amphetamine (speed) laboratory in the Bay area.[37] Reports also stated he had dealers distributing both drugs from Haight-Ashbury to Berkeley.[38]

At that time, Owsley and U.S. intelligence were coming out with more than just acid and speed. Dow Chemical made new drugs for the U.S. Army Chemical Corps that worked hand-in-hand with CIA MK-Ultra scientists. In 1964 Dow developed STP, a hallucinogenic, as a possible incapacitating agent for use by the U.S. Army Chemical Corps. The CIA used it for behavior modification experiments. STP, referred to as "Serenity, Tranquility, Peace," was quite the opposite. People described using STP as akin to "being shot out of a gun" for an intense three-day "trip." Owsley started manufacturing STP, and "shortly thereafter the drug was in the hippie districts of San Francisco and New York."[39]

At the onset of the Summer of Love, someone organized a solstice celebration. Five thousand tablets of STP were given out at that event. Many tripped for three straight days from the superhallucinogen, and San Francisco emergency units were filled with people afraid they would never come down. Doctors thought their patients were suffering from extended LSD trips and gave them Thorazine, but that drug potentiated the effects of the STP.[40]

Another drug that dealers began to sell in San Francisco was PCP ("Angel Dust"). MK-Ultra psychiatrists had been testing PCP on psychiatric patients, and the CIA stockpiled it as a "nonlethal incapacitant." Some chemists also started adding speed and strychnine (a poison) to LSD at this time.[41]

In "San Francisco," Scott McKenzie had sung, "If you're going to San Francisco, you're going to meet some gentle people there."[42] A quickly reporting grassroots news group, the Communications Company, gave a different account of what the drug ethos had led to:

> Pretty little 16-year-old-middle-class chick comes to the Haight to see what it's all about & gets picked up by a 17 year-old street dealer who spends all day shooting her full of speed again and again, then feeds her 3000 mikes [of LSD] & raffles off her temporarily unemployed body for the biggest Haight Street gang bang since the night before last.[43]

Lee and Shlain described how a similar culture was cultivated in New York City. A leading nuclear strategist, Herman Kahn, walked through Saint

Mark's Place in the East Village neighborhood of New York. He worked for the Hudson Institute that specialized in classified research on national security issues and also did MK-Ultra work. He observed the dropped-out flower children whose brains and bodies were damaged by the CIA-initiated psychedelics, stimulants and depressants. Kahn apparently marveled over his aid in MK-Ultra's success.

A fellow Hudson Institute consultant who once lectured on LSD described Kahn's motivations, saying, "He was primarily interested in social control." Kahn made a prediction about what his and the other CIA-tied think tanks tried to engender. He wrote that by the year 2000, this acid subculture would lead to an alternative "dropped-out" country within the United States.[44]

At the end of 1967, some well-meaning federal agents not linked with MK-Ultra arrested Owsley at his tabbing factory.[45] Owsley had a large stash of LSD and STP with a street market value of $10 million. Despite this vast amount of drugs, reports note that Owsley was quickly released from jail. Owsley continued his work as he fought his trafficking charge in court. Owsley only ended up serving jail time when he was arrested again in New Orleans after a concert as part of a nineteen-member crew working with the Grateful Dead.[46]

Owsley eventually got a $3,000 fine and a three-year prison sentence. This appeared to be part of a show to make him appear anti-establishment. Owsley served only two years in a federal prison.[47] By then, U.S. intelligence already had a much larger LSD trafficker running operations worldwide: Ronald Hadley Stark.[48]

MK-Ultra LA? Suspected Agent Rock Scene Births Hippies

"Papa John" Phillips comes into question regarding his song beckoning youth to San Francisco for the first outdoor multi-band rock concert, the Monterey Pop Music Festival. The Festival featured early, pre-stardom performances by Jimi Hendrix, Janis Joplin, and The Who, along with performances by the Byrds, the Grateful Dead, Otis Redding, Frank Zappa and The Mamas and The Papas, which Phillips led. Phillips cofounded the Monterey Pop Fest, which drew the largest crowds ever to the spy- and drug-infested San Francisco area of Haight-Ashbury. As it turned out, Phillips had a military intelligence background himself, and hailed from a Los Angeles neighborhood that at least rivaled, if not surpassed, the Haight-Ashbury scene regarding spies, drugs and suspicious musicians.

In his book, *Weird Scenes Inside the Canyon: Laurel Canyon, Covert Ops & the Dark Heart of the Hippie Dream*, David McGowan details a fascinating account of how John Phillips appeared to work for U.S. intelligence.

McGowan compiled the histories of several dozen rock stars who lived in the Laurel Canyon neighborhood of Los Angeles—an astounding aspect of one neighborhood in and of itself. McGowan reported that virtually all of these musicians and many of their partners or associates hailed from military intelligence families. These military intelligence-linked musicians and associates, many of whom also came from extreme wealth, included: Phillips (Mamas and Papas), Frank Zappa, David Crosby (Byrds; Crosby, Stills and Nash), Stephen Stills (Buffalo Springfield; Crosby, Stills and Nash), Jim Morrison (Doors), Mike Nesmith (Monkees), Corey Wells (Three Dog Night), Graham Parsons (Byrds, Flying Burrito Brothers) and Dewey Bunnell (America).[49]

McGowan detailed how John Phillips could be considered one of several leaders of the Laurel Canyon scene (with Frank Zappa and David Crosby). John's father, Claude Phillips, was a Marine Corps officer and engineer who worked out of Quantico Marine Corps Base. Claude Phillips was also commissioned to Haiti for years, and then Nicaragua, before returning to Alexandria, Virginia, within an hour's drive of Quantico. John Phillips attended the Annapolis-based Naval Academy before, reportedly, dropping out and then finding himself working with a retired Naval officer and four retired Army generals on a charter boat.[50]

John Phillips also married Susan Adams, a descendant of President John Adams, before John ended up in Havana, Cuba in 1958, at the time of Castro's revolution against the U.S-supported dictator, Fulgencio Batista. Phillips said he appeared on a live Havana variety television show at the time. Phillips dabbled in music while also spending two weeks in Jacksonville, Florida, the location of the Naval Air Station and Naval Station Mayport, at the coincidental time of the Cuban Missile Crisis.[51]

Two months after the Cuban Missile Crisis, Phillips left his wife, with whom he had a 5-year-old child, to marry an 18-year-old Michelle Gilliam. Gilliam's stepmother and mentor, Tamar Hodel, had previously been made pregnant by her father, Dr. George Hodel. The government had charged Dr. Hodel with "offering his young daughter to influential friends at an orgy." By all accounts, Michelle Gilliam Phillips appeared to be groomed for a bizarre, hypersexual lifestyle with her new 27-year-old husband, who started courting her when she was 16. Over the next few years, Michelle Phillips reportedly had sex with many in the Laurel Canyon scene during their marriage. John's eldest daughter, actress McKenzie Phillips (*One Day at a Time*), accused her father of raping her on her wedding night, the outset of a ten-year sexual "relationship" with her father.[52]

John and Michelle Phillips joined with "Mama Cass" Elliot and Denny Doherty to form The Mamas and The Papas. John Phillips claimed that they spent their first formative weeks as a band on a drug-fueled Caribbean adventure in St. Johns, where they "snorkeled on acid" for several weeks in early 1963. They then went to St. Thomas and sang for "drunken Marines and sailors on their way home from Vietnam." They came back to settle in the Laurel Canyon area of Los Angeles, where John and Michelle were soon able to afford to buy a mansion. The Mamas and The Papas first album came out in late 1965 and rose to the top of the music sales charts fast. The group would end up selling nearly 100 million albums.[53]

Starting in the mid-1960s, John and Michelle Phillips, Cass Elliot, Frank Zappa and David Crosby were some of the musicians who held huge drug and sex-filled parties in their Laurel Canyon mansions. These parties drew music stars such as the Beach Boys and other Laurel Canyon bands mentioned above, along with many bands outside Laurel Canyon. It further attracted many Hollywood celebrities that also drew visitors, such as Warren Beatty, Peter and Jane Fonda, Jack Nicholson, Candice Bergen, Marlon Brando, Roman Polanski, Sharon Tate, Abigail Folger, Dennis Hopper, Larry Hagman and, oddly enough, the murderous cult leader Charles Manson. These parties introduced many to LSD, cocaine, heroin and other drugs.[54]

McGowan detailed how an older artist, Vito Paulekas, worked with the musician leaders in appearing to birth the style and culture that evolved into the "hippie scene." Paulekas, born in 1913, presented himself as a "beatnick" clay sculptor and dancer. He had attempted armed robbery in his younger years, receiving a 25-year prison sentence before being released to serve in a branch of the U.S. Navy during World War II. Paulekas was also a first cousin of Winthrop Rockefeller's wife, Bobo. Winthrop's father, John Rockefeller, had funded eugenics and MK-Ultra projects. Arkansas elected Winthrop as their first Republican Governor since post-Civil War Reconstruction. Paulekas married and fathered two kids in the 1950s, before divorcing and, at the age of 48 in 1961, marrying an 18-year-old girl named Susan Shaffer.[55]

Susan changed her name to Szou and opened a clothing boutique on the ground floor of a three level building at the mouth of Laurel Canyon "which has been credited by some scenesters with being the very first to introduce hippie fashions." Upstairs, Vito Paulekas raised their first of several children. On the bottom floor, Vito gave clay-modeling lessons, which included nude models, to Beverly Hills patrons and Hollywood actors. Vito also held dance classes there.[56]

In 1963, Vito Paulekas took on a 29-year-old sidekick named Carl Franzoni who, as the nephew of an important Italian Cardinal, came from one of the wealthy elite families of Italy that would support fascist leader

Benito Mussolini for two decades. Paulekas and Franzoni gathered a group of 35 young dancers, some men but mostly women, who were called "Vito's Freaks." The identities of most of these young dancers remain elusive, but Pamela Des Barres wrote an infamous memoir, *I'm With the Band,* reporting how as a teenager she and other Vito dancers showed up at many of these Laurel Canyon bands' shows. Writer Dave McGowan noted that a young Chicago vice cop named Elmer Valentine opened the first Sunset Strip Whiskey-a-Go-Go nightclub in 1964, and then several others on the Sunset Strip soon after. Des Barres said these clubs always let their dance troupe in for free. They gave the bands an instant crowd and popularity, as people came to see the beautiful young people dancing in the audience.[57]

Vito Paulekas and Carl Franzoni reportedly collected some of their dancers in their communal home by what author Barry Miles described as operating, "the first crash pad in LA, an open house to countless runaways where everyone was welcome for a night, particularly young women." By the mid-1960s, Vito, his wife Szou, and Carl moved their communal home to a vast mansion and estate called The Log Cabin. They shared the rent in that location with the staff of the previously mentioned psychedelic newspaper *The Oracle,* started by the U.S. intelligence-linked "Psychedelic Rangers." A one-hit wonder band, the Fraternity of Man, also lived there, while regular visitors included Timothy Leary and musician Ravi Shankar. Frank Zappa moved into the mansion in 1968.[58]

More insidiously, these dancers, many still in their teens like Pamela Des Barres, participated in the drug-filled sex parties at the musicians' Laurel Canyon mansions. They helped introduce countless celebrities and musicians to acid. Des Barres observed that Vito Paulekas and Frank Zappa "never got high. They were both ringmasters who always wanted to be in control."[59] Record producer Kim Fowley and others described the beauty of Vito's dancers: "Vito was in his fifties, but he had four-way sex with goddesses." Besides Des Barres, McGowan described dancer Rory Flynn as "Canyonite Errol Flynn's statuesque daughter."[60]

Errol Flynn was likely lured to the area to live closer to work. But Los Angeles's Laurel Canyon neighborhood housed a large number of people working for U.S. intelligence, since the U.S. Air Force had run its Lookout Mountain Laboratory film studio there since 1947. Flynn and other film luminaries, such as John Ford, Jimmy Stewart, Howard Hawks, Ronald Reagan, Bing Crosby, Walt Disney, Hedda Hopper and Marilyn Monroe, signed secrecy agreements while working at that studio. Lookout Mountain "produced some 19,000 classified" movies at its Laurel Canyon location until at least 1969.[61]

McGowan noted that Frank Zappa's father, Francisco, started his work as a chemist assigned to MK-Ultra facility Edgewood Arsenal. The elder

Zappa spent the rest of his life employed by the U.S. military intelligence establishment. Younger Frank went to the Arsenal Complex's Edgewood School, and his family's elite connections included his mother having famed composer Edgard Varese call him for his 15th birthday. McGowan reported that Frank Zappa was only twenty-two years old when he partnered with a Marine electronics expert making guided missiles to open a first-class recording studio. It had a custom-built five-track tape recorder when most independent recording studios featured just mono or, at best, two-track recording. By 1963, Zappa played a bicycle as a musical instrument on the nationally televised *Steve Allen Show*. An international arms dealer named Herb Cohen, who had been in the Congo at the time of the CIA-orchestrated coup against Patrice Lumumba, then became Zappa's manager. Cohen later managed Linda Ronstadt, the band Alice Cooper and Tim Buckley.[62]

Regarding Vito Paulekas, writer Carl Gottlieb described how, "Vito and his Freakers were an acid-drenched extended family of brain-damaged cohabitants." In his book *Hippie,* Barry Miles wrote, "Vito, his wife Szou, Captain Fuck [Carl Franzoni] and their group of about thirty-five dancers ... [called] themselves Freaks, they lived a semi-communal life and engaged in sex orgies and free-form dancing whenever they could ... Vito and his Freakers were the first hippies in Hollywood ... perhaps the first hippies anywhere." Nationally released films and other media popularized Vito, Carl and the Freakers, including *Mondo Bizarro* (1966), *Something's Happening (aka The Hippie Revolt)* released in 1967, and *You Are What You Eat,* featuring David Crosby, Frank Zappa and Tiny Tim (1968). Carl Franzoni later turned up working on *The Gong Show,* produced by Chuck Barris, who wrote a memoir purporting to have worked as a CIA assassin while chaperoning couples who won trips on another of his shows, *The Dating Game.*[63]

Others also appeared to step in the position of spreading the "hippie" culture nationwide. For example, Stephen Gaskin taught at San Francisco State University, giving courses on subjects such as "witchcraft," until his job ended in 1967. Gaskin then began lecturing on his own, with as many as 1,500 "pure hippies" reportedly showing up for his weekly talks from 1967 to late 1970 or early 1971 (sources differ).

In February 1971, Gaskin traveled with several hundred people in 25 "colorfully painted buses," along with 35-50 vans and campers, to churches in 42 states for four months. But as with Vito Paulekas's 35-member dance troupe, who were able to afford years of communal work with no discernable jobs, how did 300 acid-taking people support themselves traveling nationwide for four straight months? Who could afford twenty-five buses to paint?

Several factors suggest that the prime suspect with the deepest pockets, U.S. intelligence, helped orchestrate this "acid-taking hippie culture" promotional tour. Similar to the Laurel Canyon musicians, Stephen Gaskin had volunteered for the Korean War and spent three years in the U.S. Marine Corps fighting in Korea. From 1967 to the start of 1971, the four most important years of the anti-War protests, Gaskin was known as an "acid guru," regularly lecturing at the "Family Dog rock hall, regularly drawing thousands." After spending money supporting four months of nationwide travel, the group bought a farm of over 1,000 acres at $70/acre ($411/acre in 2014 dollars).

Granted, the commune, called The Farm, reportedly did charitable work helping various disaster-stricken Central American countries and U.S. cities. Furthermore, after its vast promotional psychedelic bus tour, it also reportedly banned synthetic psychotropic drug use by its commune residents. Still, in the 1980s, The Farm contracted with President Ronald Reagan's Federal Emergency Management Agency (FEMA) on radiation detectors, and then reportedly did much lucrative work with Homeland Security under George W. Bush in 2004.[64]

Notes

1 Martin Lee and Bruce Shlain, *Acid Dreams: The CIA, the Sixties, and Beyond* (New York: Grove Press, 1994), p. 282.

2 William McGlothlin, "Long-lasting Effects of LSD on Certain Attitudes in Normals: An Experimental Proposal," Rand Corporation Study, May 1962, quoted in Lee and Shlain, *Acid Dreams*, pp. 197, 199.

3 Ronald Bruce Frankum, *Like Rolling Thunder* (New York: Rowman and Littlefield, 2005).

4 Todd Gitlin, *The Sixties: Years of Hope, Days of Rage* (New York: Bantam, 1987), p. 209. The students had mistakenly invited acid-addled Ken Kesey as one of their many speakers, shortly before the students planned to march on an army base in nearby Oakland, California. As Sixties activist-turned sociologist Todd Gitlin described it, "Kesey, who showed up in Day-Glo regalia ... announced, 'you're not gonna stop this war with this rally, by marching ... That's what *they* do,'" before he started playing "Home on the Range" with his harmonica.

5 Kirkpatrick Sale, *SDS: The rise and development of the Students for a Democratic Society* (New York: Vintage, 1973), pp. 198-99, 664.

6 Lee and Shlain, *Acid Dreams*, pp. 251, 265-66.

7 Lee and Shlain, *Acid Dreams*, p. 146.

8 Lee and Shlain, *Acid Dreams*, p. 148.

9 Lee and Shlain, *Acid Dreams*, p. 157.

10 Lee and Shlain, *Acid Dreams*, p. 158

11 Lee and Shlain, *Acid Dreams*, pp. 102, 158-59. On Gregory as ardent civil rights activist, see Howard Zinn, *You Can't Be Neutral on a Moving Train* (Beacon Press, 1994; rev. ed. 2002), p. 58.

12 Lee and Shlain, *Acid Dreams*, pp. 157-60, 282.

13 Lee and Shlain, *Acid Dreams*, pp. 158-60.

14 Lee and Shlain, *Acid Dreams*, pp. 158-59. Also, Church Committee Report, p. 391, http://www.aarclibrary.org/publib/contents/church/contents_church_reports_book1.htm.

15 Lee and Shlain, *Acid Dreams*, p. 149.

16 John Stauber and Sheldon Rampton, *Toxic Sludge is Good For You! Lies, Damn Lies and the Public Relations Industry* (Monroe, ME: Common Courage Press, 1995), pp. 13-14.

17 Lee and Shlain, *Acid Dreams*, pp. 159-61.

18 ATF agent Larry Shears in court, on Channel 23, Los Angeles, CA, news broadcast, 12/17/71. Drew McKillips, "Amazing Story by Hell's Angels Chief," *San Francisco Chronicle*, 12/12/72, p.1. "ATF Agent Says He Was Part of Coast Plot to Kill Cesar Chavez," *New York Times*, 1/2/72, p.31. All referenced in Alex Constantine, *The Covert War Against Rock* (Los Angeles, CA: Feral House, 2001), pp. 55-59. George Bush Sr. oversaw U.S. intelligence when the Hells Angels twice attempted to kill the Rolling Stones, and Barger got paroled early due to a Republican senator. Karen Brandel, "Angels in Arizona," *Tucson Weekly*, 8/15/96, p. 1. A.E. Hotchner, *Blown Away: A No-Holds-Barred Portrait of the Rolling Stones and the Sixties Told by the Voices of the Generation* (New York: Fireside, 1990), p. 320. On Newton, see Edward J. Epstein, *Agency of Fear: Opiates and Political Power in America* (New York: G.P. Putnam's Sons, 1977), pp. 201-201, 207, 213-215. Cited in Huey Newton, *War Against The Panthers* (New York: Harlem River/Readers and Writers, 1991), pp. 50-52.

19 Lee and Shlain, *Acid Dreams*, pp. 160-61.

20 Lee and Shlain, *Acid Dreams*, pp. 160-62.

21 Lee and Shlain, *Acid Dreams*, p. 166.

22 Personal Interview with attendee Warren Green, 9/30/13.

23 On SNCC, see Gitlin, *The Sixties*, p.168. On MLK, William Pepper, *Orders To Kill: The Truth Behind the Murder of Martin Luther, Jr.* (New York: Warner Books,1998). See Foreword by Dexter Scott King.

24 Frances Fox Piven and Richard Cloward, *Poor People's Movements: Why They Succeed, How They Fail* (New York: Vintage, 1979), p. 248 On MLK quote, see Lewis Killian, *The Impossible Revolution?* (New York: Random House, 1968), p. 109.

25 Gitlin, *The Sixties*, p. 168.

26 Kirkpatrick Sale, *SDS*, p. 664.

27 Lee and Shlain, *Acid Dreams*, p. 200.

28 Lee and Shlain, *Acid Dreams*, p. 188.

29 Lee and Shlain, *Acid Dreams*, pp. 188-89.

30 Lee and Shlain, *Acid Dreams*, pp. 189-90.

31 August Meier and Elliott Rudwick, *CORE: A Study in the Civil Rights Movement, 1942-1968* (Urbana: University of Illinois Press, 1973, 1975).

32 "Youth: The Hippies," *Time*, July 7, 1967, http://content.time.com/time/magazine/article/0,9171,899555,00.html. For the *Time* cover photo and a page from the article, see https://sites.google.com/site/rusieadi/the-hippies/aaaa.

33 Jay Stevens, *Storming Heaven: LSD and the American Dream* (New York: Grove Press, 1998), p. 344.

34 Christoph Grunenberg and Jonathan Harris (2005), *Summer of Love: Psychedelic Art, Social Crisis and Counterculture in the 1960s* (Liverpool University Press, 2005), p. 347. Phillips would later be accused of rape by his daughter. She said he raped her when she was around 18 years old. She then ended up having a 10-year sexual relationship with him. Actress McKenzie Phillips (TV show, *One Day at a Time*) accused her father John Phillips. See Russell Goldman, "McKenzie Phillips Confesses to Ten-Year Sexual Relationship with her Father," *ABC News*, September 23, 2009, http://abcnews.go.com/Entertainment/mackenzie-phillips-sexual-affair-dad/story?id=8647172.

35 P. Braunstein and M.W. Doyle, eds., *Imagine Nation: The American Counterculture of the 1960s and '70s* (New York: 2002), p. 7.

36 Lee and Shlain, *Acid Dreams*, p. 240. Also see Aidin Vaziri, "Owsley Stanley: '60s Counterculture Icon Dies," *San Francisco Chronicle*, 3/14/11.

37 Lester Grinspoon and Peter Hedblom, *The Speed Culture: Amphetamine Use and Abuse in America* (Boston: Havard Paperback Series, 1975), p. 25. Also see Alice Echols, *The Scars of Sweet Paradise: The Life and Times of Janis Joplin* (New York: McMillan, 2000), p. 77.

38 Barry Miles, *Hippie* (New York: Sterling, 2005).

39 Lee and Shlain, *Acid Dreams*, p. 187. Kirkpatrick Sale, *SDS*, pp. 430-34.

40 Lee and Shlain, *Acid Dreams*, p. 187.

41 Lee and Shlain, *Acid Dreams*, p. 188.

42 Stevens, *Storming Heaven: LSD and the American Dream* (New York: Grove Press, 1998), p. 344.

43 Stevens, *Storming Heaven*, p. 341. Also in Lee and Shlain, *Acid Dreams*, p. 186.

44 Lee and Shlain, *Acid Dreams*, p. 197.

45 Lee and Shlain, *Acid Dreams*, p. 240.

46 *Rolling Stone* magazine No. 53, March 7, 1970.

47 Eli Rosenberg, "The King of LSD Owsley Stanley's Colorful Legacy," *The Atlantic*, 5/15/2011, http://www.theatlanticwire.com/entertainment/2011/03/king-lsd-sixties-pioneer-owsley-stanleys-colorful-legacy/35836/.

48 Lee and Shlain, *Acid Dreams*, p.281.

49 David McGowan, *Weird Scenes Inside the Canyon: Laurel Canyon, Covert Ops & the Dark Heart of the Hippie Dream* (London: Headpress, 2014) pp. 8-9, 11-21.

50 McGowan, *Weird Scenes Inside the Canyon*, pp.16, 202.

51 McGowan, *Weird Scenes Inside the Canyon*, p. 202

52 McGowan, *Weird Scenes Inside the Canyon*, pp. 203-07

53 McGowan, *Weird Scenes Inside the Canyon*, pp. 205-07. McGowan noted that this backup band of studio musicians included the right-wing Glen Campbell.

54 On celebs, McGowan, *Weird Scenes Inside the Canyon*, pp. 207-08. On Beach Boys and Manson, p. 209. McGowan also noted that the same studio musicians were used for most of the Laurel Canyon bands.

55 McGowan, *Weird Scenes Inside the Canyon*, pp. 62-66.

56 McGowan, *Weird Scenes Inside the Canyon*, pp. 66-67.

57 On Carl Franzoni, "Vito's Freaks" and Elmer Valentine, see McGowan, *Weird Scenes Inside the Canyon*, pp. 67-71. Pamela Des Barres, *I'm with the Band: Confessions of a Groupie* (Chicago: Chicago Review Press, 1987). After diary entry October 8, 1966, in Google books.

58 McGowan, *Weird Scenes Inside the Canyon*, p. 73.

59 Barney Hoskyns, *Waiting for the Sun: A Rock and Roll History of Los Angeles* (New York: Backbeat Books, 1996, 2009), p. 113.

60 McGowan, *Weird Scenes Inside the Canyon*, p. 62. Similar to Crosby, Zappa and other musicians, biographer Charles Higham claimed that Rory's actor father was bisexual and worked as a Nazi spy, though other authors debate this claim. Charles Higham, *Errol Flynn: The Untold Story* (No Imprint, 1980). Also, Charles Higham, "The Missing Errol Flynn File," *The New Statesman*, April 17, 2000, http://www.newstatesman.com/node/137421. For refutations, see Tony Thomas, *Errol Flynn: The Spy Who Never Was* (Citadel, 1990) and Buster Wiles, *My Days with Errol Flynn: The Autobiography of a Stuntman* (Roundtable, 1988). Wikipedia says that Thomas and Wiles argue that Flynn was notorious in Hollywood as a womanizer and was a left-wing supporter of the Spanish Republic in the Spanish Civil War and of the Cuban Revolution, even narrating a documentary entitled *The Truth About Fidel Castro Revolution* shortly before his death. The pro-Castro documentary appears legitimate, and this writer remains unsure of whether "Flynn as Nazi spy" is legitimate, an intelligence smear campaign, or pure sensationalism.

61 McGowan, *Weird Scenes Inside the Canyon*, pp. 55-57. McGowan cites Peter Kuran, *Trinity and Beyond: The Atomic Bomb Movie* (Documentary film, 1995), narrated by William Shatner. Note that some sources state Lookout Mountain studio remained in operation long after 1969. Also see, "Secret Film Studio: Lookout Mountain," Nevada National Security Site, http://www.nv.doe.gov/library/factsheets/DOENV_1142.pdf.

62 McGowan, *Weird Scenes Inside the Canyon*, pp. 14, 80, 216-19.

63 David Crosby and Carl Gottlieb, *Long Time Gone: The Autobiography of David Crosby* (New York: Doubleday, 1988). Cited in McGowan, *Weird Scenes Inside the Canyon*, pp. 62-63. On hippie films, p. 73.

64 Douglas Martin, "Stephen Gaskin, Hippie Who Founded Enduring Commune, Dies

at 79," *New York Times*, July 2, 2014, http://www.nytimes.com/2014/07/03/us/stephen-gaskin-hippie-who-founded-an-enduring-commune-dies-at-79.html. Michael Niman, "Out to Save the World, Life at The Farm," *High Times*, February 1995, http://www.thefarm.org/general/hightime.html. Steve Chawkins, "Stephen Gaskins Dies at 79, Founder of The Farm Commune," *Los Angeles Times*, July 5, 2014, http://www.latimes.com/local/obituaries/la-me-stephen-gaskin-20140706-story.html. Jim Windorf, "Sex, Drugs and Soybeans," *Vanity Fair*, April 5, 2007, http://www.vanityfair.com/politics/features/2007/05/thefarm200705.

Chapter Nine

Dentist Doses Beatles; Rolling Stones Framed

In Great Britain, British MI6 and the Tavistock Institute worked with psychiatrists in a program similar to MK-Ultra. It allowed psychiatrists in England to experiment freely with acid during the 1950s and 1960s, dosing up to 1,500 patients. Their findings were that acid tended to induce schizophrenia only in those predisposed to it. More than fifty of these induced schizophrenic patients disagreed and sued them. While the result of that case is unknown, the U.S. government paid $750,000 to each of nine patients to settle a similar case, and the Canadian government has also paid dozens of compensation claims.[1]

By the mid-1960s, the CIA sent its MK-Ultra Deputy Director, Robert Lashbrook, to its London station. Lashbrook had at least two key assignments. One was disbursing Human Ecology Fund grants in England to promote LSD there. Researchers like famed writer A.E. Hotchner, a longtime editor of Ernest Hemingway's books, said Lashbrook's other assignment was to have undercover agents give LSD to British musicians, with and without their knowledge.[2]

Hotchner interviewed MK-Ultra agent Steve Abrahms, whom Lashbrook recruited when Abrahms attended Oxford University in the early 1960s. Abrahms said Human Ecology Fund agents "released acid to rock groups." Abrahms further said, "CIA agents were distributing acid all over the place."[3]

British propaganda agent Michael Hollingshead, a top man in the British American Cultural Exchange, had given Timothy Leary his first acid hits. Hollingshead traveled back and forth from New York to London before his major move back to London in the fall of 1965.[4] Upon his permanent move back, Hollingshead brought 5,000 hits of LSD with him. Hollingshead said he wanted to start "a drug-based religion for influential British cultural figures."[5] Similar to top MK-Ultra LSD distributors, Hollingshead purported benevolent motives for distributing acid, but his dosing of U.N. officials without their knowledge was in line with MK-Ultra's leftist hit list.

Before the end of 1965, Hollingshead started the World Psychedelic Center in the fashionable Kings Road district of London, where

"LSD-dipped fingers of bread were handed out gratis, much as today's supermarkets offer free samples of cookies or salad dressing."[6] Throughout the 1960s, Hollingshead brought well-known psychiatrists to his Center, along with famous artists and musicians, including Ian Sommerville and filmmaker Roman Polanski, along with musicians Donovan, Eric Clapton, Paul McCartney, and the Rolling Stones. Hollingshead used pirate radio from ships off the coast, the only music radio station to play rock, to further promote acid.[7] A few years later, Michael Hollingshead also held parties where anyone thinking they were drinking straight punch was dosed.[8]

With this in mind, Michael Hollingshead's travels back and forth across the Atlantic Ocean in 1965 deserve more scrutiny.[9] His goal, to get influential British cultural figures tripping, would surely include the Beatles lead singer/songwriter John Lennon. But, similar to most of Hollingshead's actions that decade, it fell perfectly in line with the plans of known CIA MK-Ultra agents working in London.[10]

John Lennon founded the band that evolved into the Beatles in Liverpool, England during the late 1950s. Lennon took them to Hamburg, Germany in 1960, where they gained more popularity. Germans flocked to their shows despite young Lennon deriding older crowd members, asking, "What did you do during the war? Bloody Krauts!"[11]

Lennon brought the Beatles back to Liverpool, where the band morphed and then solidified into the famous four of Lennon, McCartney, Harrison and Starr, drawing a nationwide following. By 1963, British television featured them opening for other top-billed bands playing the Prince of Wales theater. Before the last song, Lennon derisively addressed upper-class members of the audience, including the Queen and other royals: "For this number, we'd like to ask your help. Will the people in the cheaper seats clap your hands? And the rest of you, just rattle your jewelry." In response to Lennon's class-conscious rebelliousness, the *Daily Telegraph* compared the Beatles to Adolph Hitler, and their concerts to Nuremberg rallies.[12]

In 1964, John Lennon continued his antics when first touring America. A reporter asked, "Would you sing something now?" and Lennon responded, "We need cash first." The reporter continued, "How do you account for your success?" Lennon quipped, "A good press agent." A second reporter asked, "When do you rehearse?" Lennon replied, "We don't." Paul McCartney chimed in, "Yeah, of course we do." Lennon injected, "Paul does, we don't." On that tour, Lennon also made a political statement by publicly refusing to play segregated southern concerts. Despite skipping these shows, the Beatles accounted for 85% of all American singles record sales that year.[13]

With Lennon's actions and superstardom, U.S. and British intelligence surely hid early documents in their closely kept file on Lennon when they later revealed only a few hundred pages. Psychiatrists had already prescribed Lennon amphetamines and barbiturates. Lennon said he had been, "on one drug or another since Hamburg [and] had rarely faced the world straight." It is likely British intelligence knew this, perhaps even been involved in it the way it was suspected regarding Elvis, leading them to think Lennon might accept LSD.[14]

In early 1965, Lennon's Beatles bandmate, guitarist George Harrison, was a patient of a young dentist named John Riley. On a February night in 1965, Dr. Riley had his patient Harrison and John Lennon over for dinner. The two Beatles came with their partners to Riley's house in Hyde Park Square, London. George's girlfriend, model Pattie Boyd, described the situation, saying they knew Riley "quite well and had been to a few clubs with him in the past." The 24-year-old Lennon came with his 25-year-old wife, Cynthia.[15]

MK-Ultra agent Steve Abrahms said his job was to get British musicians tripping in the mid-'60s. George Harrison is seen here with girlfriend Pattie Boyd, who said Harrison's dentist inexplicably dosed Harrison's and Lennon's coffee for their first acid trips.

John Riley's 21-year-old Playboy Club employee girlfriend escorted the Beatles pair and their partners into Riley's candle-lit dining room. Once seated, Cynthia Lennon, who also described the incident, noticed four cubes of sugar arranged along the mantelpiece.[16]

After finishing their meals, Pattie Boyd said that "we had a lovely meal," but needed to leave to catch a friend's band. "As we prepared to leave, Riley's girlfriend jumped to her feet and said, 'You haven't had any coffee yet. It's ready, I've made it and it's delicious.'"

The four stayed and drank the coffee, and then Lennon said, "We must go now. Our friends are going to be on soon, it's their first night."

"You can't leave," said Riley.

"What are you talking about?" asked Lennon.

"You've just had LSD. It was in the coffee."

Lennon erupted, "How dare you fucking do this to us!"

"Do what?" asked Harrison and Boyd, not knowing what LSD was.

"It's a drug!" said Lennon with his hand on his head, very distraught, as he nor any of the Beatles band members had ever tried the drug before.

As the drug began taking effect they all felt strongly they had to get out of there. John Riley said they couldn't leave. Riley then insisted on driving. The four ignored Riley and got into their car, "which looked like it was shrinking. All the way to the club the car felt smaller and smaller, and by the time we arrived we were completely out of it," said Pattie Boyd.

"The club was on an upper floor," Boyd continued, "and we thought the lift was on fire because there was a little red light inside. As the doors opened, we crawled out and bumped into Mick Jagger, Marianne Faithfull and Ringo [Starr, the Beatles' drummer]. John told them we had been spiked." Boyd said that hours later they decided to go home. "This time George drove at no more than 10mph but if felt like 1,000mph ... It was very frightening and we never spoke to the dentist again."[17]

Cynthia Lennon said that when they got back home, "John was crying and banging his head against the wall. I tried to make myself sick, and couldn't. I tried to go to sleep and couldn't. It was like a nightmare that wouldn't stop, whatever you did. None of us got over it for about three days."[18]

Several people published accounts of this event, but Pattie Boyd's and Cynthia Lennon's firsthand takes seem the most accurate. No one appeared to know the motives for John Riley's bizarre action or why he would risk drugging his celebrity friend and patient, George Harrison, especially since Harrison had never even heard of the drug yet. But surely there is a reason why he would risk his reputation, his professional career and possibly a criminal charge or lawsuit in drugging these famous musicians, who were already wealthy enough to possibly sue him.

John Riley, a dentist for the stars, had a meteoric rise despite mediocre means. Riley's father worked as a British constable, a beat cop, in the 1950s. This constable sent his son to the very expensive Northwestern University Dental School in Chicago, Illinois, where Riley studied cosmetic dentistry. The Rileys bypassed extremely inexpensive dental schools in England. Staunchly conservative Northwestern also housed the Naval Reserve Officer Training Corps.[19] Riley "returned to London as one of Britain's most accomplished cosmetic dentists and quickly became first choice for actors, models, and singers" such as George Harrison.[20]

Did British intelligence talk to one of their front-line cops, Riley, about his son getting a special intelligence assignment, as happened in the father-son police targeting of other political musicians?[21] Riley's lining up of the sugar cubes showed his intention to dose only the Beatles and their partners. Why else would the sugar be so conspicuously arranged except to make sure they were the ones spiked with acid to go into the four's coffee. Accounts also have Riley offering to drive them all, since they were tripping, further suggesting he hadn't taken the acid.[22]

It would seem only someone working for British intelligence would take such actions against alleged friends, knowing he was immune to repercussions from these wealthy, influential musicians. Many reports link John Riley's LSD to Michael Hollingshead, who carried out MK-Ultra-type actions for British intelligence before LSD was more popularized.[23]

British intelligence, in collaboration with the CIA's MK-Ultra, appeared to have two goals in targeting John Lennon. First, this would dampen the cognitive abilities of the most intellectual Beatle, who could counter the British elite's conservative agenda. Secondly, Lennon was a clear leader of the Beatles. The LSD use would make it easier for them to manipulate Lennon, and they would also have a more easily manipulated band to help them popularize LSD. This would help them divert more young idealistic civil rights and antiwar activists to drugs.

Beatles Promote Acid Before Stopping Use

After John Lennon and George Harrison had a bad experience with their first trip, people around them apparently tried to sway them back to LSD and think of it in a more positive light. Harrison eventually said he thought Paul McCartney and Ringo Starr should also trip. Ringo first tried LSD at a party held by Byrds band members David Crosby and Roger McGuin.[24] The Beatles and London *Daily Mirror* journalist Don Short had rented a mansion in Benedict Canyon in California on their 1965 American tour. Paul wouldn't trip, but Ringo did. Benedict Canyon lied seven miles from Laurel Canyon, where researcher Dave McGowan said Byrds bandmembers Crosby and McGuin lived near the Lookout Mountain Air Force film studio as suspected U.S. intelligence assets.[25]

Beatles biographer Steve Turner said, "Paul didn't take LSD until late 1966, after the release of their album *Revolver*. He took it at the Eaton Row, London, home of Tara Browne, the socialite and heir to Guinness money, who was soon to die and be immortalized in the Beatles' song, "A Day in the Life." Browne was the man who "blew his mind out in a car."[26]

In 1966, John Lennon made more rebellious public comments without much discretion, such as: "Christianity will go, it will vanish and shrink ... We are more popular than Jesus now. Jesus was all right, but his disciples were thick and ordinary." In response, American southern radio and TV stations organized "Beatle-burning" rallies, and 35 radio stations banned Beatles songs. Lennon tried to apologize, explaining that he thought God was in all of us, but his songs were permanently banned in apartheid South Africa. Death threats began to arrive, and the KKK started holding protest rallies at Beatles shows.[27]

John Lennon had begun getting more overtly political by at least 1966. Lennon said he and his bandmembers were against the U.S. involvement in the Vietnam War. Lennon would repeat these opinions for international reporters. When reporters in Japan asked what he was looking for next, he answered, "Peace." Questioned about Vietnam, he said that the Beatles thought about the war every day, and "we don't agree with it. We think it's wrong ... That's all we can do about it—say we don't like it."[28]

American musicians and others tried to influence the Beatles to use more LSD. British propaganda agent Micheal Hollingshead had brought to England "three hundred copies of *The Psychedelic Experience: A Manual Based on the Tibetan Book of the Dead*, by Timothy Leary, Richard Alpert and Ralph Metzner; two hundred issues of the *Psychedelic Review*; and two hundred copies of *The Psychedelic Reader*, edited by Gunther Weil. Copies of these books were placed in the hands of the Beatles by Peter Asher's friend Barry Miles, who was now managing the Indica Bookshop in Southhampton Row."[29] Peter was the brother of Paul McCartney's girlfriend, actress Jane Asher.

U.S. and British intelligence appeared to gain unwitting help in popularizing LSD from the Beatles and other top British musicians. Hollingshead's World Psychedelic Center in London introduced LSD to top musicians Donovan Leitch, Rolling Stones guitarist Keith Richards, and the Yardbirds.[30] By fall of 1967, the Beatles ended up stopping their promotion of their latest album, *Sgt. Pepper's Lonely Hearts Club Band*, earlier than planned in favor of a new project. It's not certain who or what influenced them, but they began recording a new album and making a film based on it: *Magical Mystery Tour*.

This album and film provides an example of how the world's most popular band, like other bands, promoted LSD, and how intelligence-enmeshed mainstream media amplified such promotion. The Beatles based the project on Ken Kesey and the Merry Pranksters' psychedelic bus trip.[31] A report from Owsley's final home before he died said that Owsley Stanley supplied the Beatles with acid during their shooting of *Magical Mystery Tour*.[32] Paul McCartney later said, "Those were psychedelic times ... *Magical Mystery Tour* was the equivalent of a drug trip, and we made the film based on that."[33] The *Magical Mystery Tour* soundtrack stayed #1 on the sales charts for eight weeks.

When Beatles members and others got tired of acid, the media appeared to give that little attention. George Harrison reportedly "stopped taking LSD after his first visit to San Francisco in August 1967. While he was there he visited Haight-Ashbury [where] ... Head shops openly sold drug paraphernalia. Grateful Dead and Jefferson Airplane lived in old Victorian houses on neighboring streets." Harrison walked down Haight Street and was flocked by brain-damaged hippies who behaved as if he was a prophet sent from heaven. Harrison said it disgusted him and changed his mind about LSD, deciding to stay away from it.[34]

In a December 1970 interview with *Rolling Stone* magazine publisher Jann Wenner, Lennon described some of his history with LSD. He described himself as becoming "cracked" on it and "unstable." He said this was especially true in comparison to Paul McCartney, who he said "is a bit more stable than George and I ... I think LSD profoundly shocked him, and Ringo. I think maybe they regret it." Lennon also said he started having "many [bad trips]. Jesus Christ. I stopped taking it because of that. I just couldn't stand it." Later, a friend and publicist, Derek Taylor, along with Lennon's second wife, Yoko Ono, convinced him acid was okay to use again.[35]

John Lennon's LSD use caused him many problems. He had become irrational enough to consider trepanning, drilling a hole in his head to expand his consciousness.[36] Lennon also said he thought he was losing his mind. Lennon would later make negative comments about the LSD culture. He talked about *The Tibetan Book of the Dead*, an LSD tripping guide by Timothy Leary, as "that dumb Leary book."[37]

FBI Asset Gives Jagger First LSD Hit, Frames Stones

Nobel Prize winning novelist Earnest Hemingway's editor, A.E. Hotchner, later developed into a renowned historian, and wrote an important account of the second best-selling band of the 1960s, the Rolling Stones. Hotchner's book, *Blown Away: A No-Holds-Barred Portrait of the Rolling Stones and the Sixties Told by the Voices of the Generation*, provides plenty of evidence detailing how the CIA, and its British counterpart MI6, used drugs and murders to target the Rolling Stones.

After working in small London clubs, the Rolling Stones blues covers became chart-topping hits in Britain in 1964.[38] By 1965, lead singer Mick Jagger and guitarist Keith Richards wrote their own chart-toppers, and had appeared on *The Ed Sullivan Show* and the Dean Martin television show in America. Their first international #1 song, "(I Can't Get No) Satisfaction" was followed by #1 hit "Get Off of My Cloud," and a string of others in the following years.[39]

U.S. and British intelligence used many tactics to manipulate and control the music world in order to influence the mass of youth rebelling against the Vietnam War. They appeared to influence top rock bands to inadvertently become role models to promote acid and heroin, among other drugs. The Rolling Stones lyricists Jagger and Richards had written nine chart-topping singles, and all fifteen of their singles released from 1964 on were in the top ten on the music charts.[40]

By 1967 in London where the Rolling Stones were based, activists debated LSD's role in radical leftist action. Some activists had argued for a "politics of ecstasy," saying acid would radicalize youth. Others opposed that view. Some said, "Don't give LSD to [Cuban revolutionary leader] Che Guevara, he might stop fighting." British psychiatrist David Cooper feared drugs might undermine political commitment. The right-wing Rand Corporation think tank put forth the same thesis, that drugs would undermine people's commitment to radical politics, and they committed a large amount of money to making that happen.[41]

Rolling Stones lead singer Mick Jagger had a relationship with singer Marianne Faithfull at this time. Faithfull said that before February of 1967, Jagger had resisted taking LSD. She said Jagger was suing a London newspaper, *The News of the World*, for libel for saying Jagger was participating in LSD orgies. Jagger, one of the most popular musicians in the world and one with a rebellious reputation, was telling millions he never used LSD, making a dent in MK-Ultra's goal of creating a bandwagon effect to get people tripping.[42]

On February 11, 1967, Keith Richards held a party at his Redlands estate in England. David Schneidermann, an admitted LSD dealer, was already working for British intelligence and the FBI when he came to this Rolling Stones party. He helped get Mick Jagger to take his first dose of LSD at that event.[43]

Schneidermann came to the party with a briefcase full of drugs. The next morning he urged those who stayed overnight, including George Harrison and his wife, to have some of his tea, which contained a hallucinogenic he called "white lightning." By all reports this was actually his brand of LSD, called "Sunshine." Mick Jagger drank the tea and had his first trip. They were all tripping for at least eight hours. By that evening, someone else joined the weekend festivities and pulled out a large bag of hashish and passed it around.[44]

Police raided the home that night. Schneidermann told police he couldn't open his briefcase, which was full of drugs, as it had undeveloped film in it. They allegedly took him at his word and let him and his drug supply go. They arrested Keith Richards for allowing cannabis to be smoked in his home and Mick Jagger for possession of prescription "pep" pills (a common type of amphetamine).[45]

David Schneidermann, here with Rolling Stone Keith Richards, reportedly worked for the FBI and MI5 when he gave Mick Jagger his first hit of LSD in 1967.

By this time, both U.S. and British intelligence were spreading LSD throughout England with the help of Michael Hollingshead. As also mentioned, CIA MK-Ultra Deputy Director Robert Lashbrook had many agents in London trying to get pop musicians on LSD. David Schneidermann (sometimes spelled Sniderman or Schneiderman) told his wife he was working for British agents who were also working with the FBI's Counterintelligence Program (Cointelpro). This admission made clear that Cointelpro and MI6 were working in close collaboration with the CIA's MK-Ultra program. Schneidermann made acid and sold it in England.[46]

Schneidermann's former girlfriend detailed his role as one of Lashbrook's MK-Ultra agents. She said, "They'd come up with some new kind of way to make acid," and Schneidermann would travel from California to England "to sell it." She added that Schneidermann "was a heavy drug user, but he had a quick wit. He was the perfect choice to infiltrate the Stones."[47]

Mainstream London newspaper, *The Daily Mail,* confirmed that FBI undercover asset Schneidermann, often called the Acid King, set up the Rolling Stones' Mick Jagger and Keith Richards for a high-profile drug bust.[48] The drug bust would spread the word that the two used drugs, and would subconsciously encourage others to emulate their idols and do the same. The bust could have also been for gaining a reverse psychology effect through the ever-increasing anti-establishment youth mantra: "If the government doesn't want you to do it, it must be good."[49]

A final, most prominent motive for the arrest was to impose legal restraints on the Rolling Stones. The Stones were second only to the Beatles among top-selling bands. Some of the Stones top-selling hits were already subversively questioning marketing techniques, such as the 1965 hit, "(I Can't Get No) Satisfaction," describing watching the TV "and that man comes on to tell me how white my shirts can be, but he can't be a man 'cause he doesn't smoke the same cigarettes as me."

When the legal cases of Mick Jagger and Keith Richards came to court, the judge showed his extreme bias by saying to the jury, "There is no defense to this charge." The jury found Jagger guilty in five minutes, and the judge remanded him to prison for three months. A jury also found Richards guilty, and he was sentenced to a year in prison. The *London Times* editor-in-chief said that this sentence for Jagger was "particularly surprising," as the Rolling Stone singer was a "first time offender," and "Jagger's is about as mild a drug case as can ever have been brought before the Courts."[50]

Jagger and Richards eventually appealed their sentencing and won their way out of prison, but remained on probation, which kept legal pressure on them.[51] Dave Schneidermann ended up in Hollywood, where he changed his last name to Jove and produced a television show.[52] The following years would find the Rolling Stones inadvertently promoting acid and other drugs, while also coming under attack after writing antiwar songs, as will be discussed.

Notes

1 Claire Dyer, *British Medical Journal,* November 4 1995. Cited in David Black, *Acid* (London: Vision/Satin Publications, 1998), pp. 65-67. Louis Porter, Vermont Press Bureau, "Evidence Suggest CIA Funded Experiments at State Hospital," *Rutland Herald,* November 30, 2008, http://www.rutlandherald.com/apps/pbcs.dll/article?AID=2008811300299.

2 On Lashbrook as MK-Ultra Deputy Director, see H.P. Albarelli, *A Terrible Mistake: The*

Murder of Frank Olson and the CIA's Secret Cold War Experiments (Waterville, OR: Trine Day, 2009), p. 282. On Lashbrook bringing MK-Ultra to London, see A.E. Hotchner, *Blown Away: A No-Holds Barred Portrait of the Rolling Stones and the Sixties Told by the Voices of the Generation* (New York: Fireside/Simon & Schuster, 1990), pp. 216-18.

3 Hotchner, *Blown Away*, pp. 216-18.

4 Phillip Norman, *John Lennon: The Life* (New York: Ecco/Harper Collins, 2008), p. 426.

5 Steve Turner, *The Gospel According to the Beatles* (London: Westminister John Knox Press), 2006, p.113.

6 Norman, *John Lennon*, p. 426.

7 Martin Lee and Bruce Shlain, *Acid Dreams: The Complete Social History of LSD, the CIA, the Sixties, and Beyond* (New York: Grove Press, 1994), p. 115.

8 Undercover police attended one of these parties and arrested him the next day, but only for having a little hash. Hollingshead then "sneaked" acid into prison where he got a top Russian spy named George Blake tripping. Blake had "penetrated the highest echelons of British intelligence and passed information to the Russian KGB." George Blake reportedly was worried that Hollingshead was a spy who had given him truth serum. Evidence supports both of these possibilities. But Blake then changed his mind. Blake had served 6 years of a 43-year sentence but, after tripping with Hollingshead, he miraculously escaped with a rope ladder. He was reportedly last heard from in the Moscow Soviet Foreign Ministry. Lee, *Acid Dreams*, p.116. Did Hollingshead manipulate George Blake into becoming a Timothy Leary of the Soviet Union?

9 Norman, *John Lennon*, p. 426.

10 Steve Turner, *The Gospel According to the Beatles* (London: Westminister John Knox Press, 2006), p. 113.

11 Phil Strongman, *John Lennon: Life, Times & Assassination* (Manchester, England: Bluecoat Press, 2010), pp. 40-41.

12 Strongman, *John Lennon*, p. 61.

13 Strongman, *John Lennon*, pp. 97-99.

14 Turner, *The Gospel According to the Beatles*, p. 124.

15 Pattie Boyd, "The Dentist Who Spiked My Coffee with Acid," *The Daily Mail* (UK), August 5, 2007, http://www.dailymail.co.uk/tvshowbiz/article-473207/Patti-Boyd-The-dentist-spiked-coffee-LSD.html

16 Norman, *John Lennon*, p. 422. Also see Pattie Boyd, *The Daily Mail*, Aug. 5, 2007.

17 Pattie Boyd, *The Daily Mail*, 8/5/07.

18 Norman, *John Lennon*, p. 422. Also, Turner, *The Gospel According to the Beatles*.

19 http://www.northwestern.edu/nrotc/docs/StudentRegulations%20NSTCINST%20 1533.2A%20AUG2011.pdf

20 Turner, *The Gospel According to the Beatles*, p.114.

21 Some father and son U.S. intelligence agents include Richard Held Jr and Sr in the FBI, Reggie Wright Jr and Sr in the Los Angeles Police Department and Richard McCaulley Jr and Sr. in the LAPD.

22 Pattie Boyd, *The Daily Mail*, 8/5/07.

23 Lee and Shlain, *Acid Dreams*, p. 180. Turner, *The Gospel According to the Beatles*.

24 http://www.beatlesbible.com/1965/08/24/lsd-los-angeles-byrds-peter-fonda/

25 Norman, *John Lennon*, pp. 426-27. Note that at least one researcher, David McGowan, suspects David Crosby as having CIA ties, partly due to his being part of one of the wealthiest early families linked to the drug trafficking oligarchy. David McGowan, *Weird Scenes Inside the Canyon: Laurel Canyon, Covert Ops, and the Dark Heart of the Hippie Dream* (London: Headpress, 2014), pp. 55-57, 207-09.

26 Turner, *The Gospel According to the Beatles*, p. 125.

27 Strongman, *John Lennon*, pp. 104-08.

28 Turner, *The Gospel According to the Beatles*, p. 162. Strongman, *John Lennon*, p. 108.

29 Turner, *The Gospel According to the Beatles*, p. 119.

30 Lee and Shlain, *Acid Dreams*, p. 180.

31 Wade Everett, *The Beatles as Musicians: Revolver through The Anthology* (London: Oxford University Press, 1999), p. 131. Also see, Turner, *The Gospel According to the Beatles*, p. 132. It's

unknown if Pete Townshend of The Who wrote their song "Magic Bus" as an allusion to Kesey and the Merry Pranksters' bus trip, but he did originally write the song around that time in 1965, http://en.wikipedia.org/wiki/Magic_Bus_(song).

32 Fraser, Andrew (2011-03-14). "Owsley 'Bear' Stanley dies in North Queensland car crash," *The Australian*, News Limited, http://www.theaustralian.com.au/news/nation/owsley-bear-stanley-dies-in-north-queensland-car-crash/story-e6frg6nf-1226021149610 .

33 Paul McCartney interviewed and quoted in Barry Miles, *Many Years From Now* (New York: Macmillan, 1998).

34 Steve Turner, *The Gospel According to the Beatles*, pp. 130-31.

35 "Rolling Stone Interview: John Lennon, Part 1," *Rolling Stone*, January 21, 1971, http://www.jannswenner.com/Archives/John_Lennon_Part1.aspx Jann Wenner. In 1968, John Lennon left his wife of several years, Cynthia Lennon, for his future wife Yoko Ono. Lennon said that at a time he thought he had lost all confidence and thought he should stop tripping again, Yoko joined in with his Apple press officer, Derek Taylor, in convincing Lennon to trip again. Several reports state that Yoko convinced Lennon to try heroin for the first time. See, for example, Norman, *John Lennon*, p. 187.

36 Turner, *The Gospel According to the Beatles*, p. 165.

37 Turner, *The Gospel According to the Beatles.*

38 A.E. Hotchner, *Blown Away: A No-Holds Barred Portrait of the Rolling Stones and the Sixties Told by the Voices of the Generation* (New York: Fireside/Simon & Schuster, 1990), pp. 72-75.

39 Mick Jagger, Keith Richards, Charlie Watts and Ronnie Wood, *According to the Rolling Stones* (Chronicle Books, 2003), p. 62.

40 Christopher Andersen, *Jagger*, introduction (New York: Delacorte Press, 1993).

41 Lee and Shlain, *Acid Dreams*, pp.199-200.

42 Hotchner, *Blown Away*, pp. 231-2.

43 Hotchner, *Blown Away*, pp. 232-37.

44 Hotchner, *Blown Away*, pp. 231-33. On "white lightning," see Bill Wyman and Bill Colmeman, *Stone Alone* (New York: Viking, 1990), pp. 404-05, referenced in Constantine, *The Covert War Against Rock*, p. 44.

45 Hotchner, *Blown Away*, pp. 237, 245.

46 Sharon Churcher and Peter Sheridan, "How the Acid King said he Did set up the Rolling Stones for MI5 and the FBI," *The Daily Mail* (UK), 10/24/10, http://www.dailymail.co.uk/news/article-1323236/The-Acid-King-confesses-Rolling-Stones-drug-bust-set-MI5-FBI.html. As will be discussed, in 1971 an unknown group of activists broke into an FBI office in the small town of Media, Pennsylvania near Swarthmore College outside of Philadelphia. They removed thousands of documents and exposed the FBI Counter Intelligence Program (Cointelpro), a vast program aimed at law-abiding citizens protesting against the Vietnam War and for civil rights and economic justice. The documents also showed the FBI's sophisticated tactics and collaborative work with local police and many mainstream media outlets nationwide. The activists' distribution of these documents forced Congress and mainstream media outlets to at least acknowledge some of these brutal FBI illegalities with Cointelpro. Ward Churchill and Jim Vander Wall, *The COINTELPRO Papers: Documents from the FBI's Secret Wars Against Dissent in the United States* (Boston: South End Press, 1991), pp. xi, 332.

47 Churcher and Sheridan, "How the Acid King ..." *The Daily Mail*, 10/24/10.

48 Churcher and Sheridan, "How the Acid King ..." *The Daily Mail*, 10/24/10.

49 Personal interviews with Columbia University student activists, April, 1998.

50 William Rees-Mogg, Editor in Chief, "Who Breaks a Butterfly on a Wheel?" *The Times* (London), in A.E. Hotchner, *Blown Away*, pp. 247-49.

51 Hotchner, *Blown Away*, pp. 237, 245.

52 Churcher and Sheridan, "How the Acid King ..." *The Daily Mail*, 10/24/10. His intelligence work apparently allowed him to produce that television show. A friend disclosed to London's *Daily Mail* that Schneidermann/Jove always carried a handgun and admitted killing a man messing with his car. He later was rumored to have murdered his TV show host, Peter Ivers, with whom he was angry for leaving his show.

Chapter Ten

Acid Damages Anti-War Left: SDS & Yippies

The widespread use of LSD, or similar drugs waiting in the psychedelic wings, could lead to a whole generation of psychedelic dropouts, incapable or uninterested in addressing themselves to the important sociologic problems that challenge our times. If this happened, the very structure of this democratic society would be threatened.

– Donald Louria, MD, Cornell University Medical School Professor, in his column for *The New England Journal of Medicine*, February 1968.[1]

By 1968, the U.S. military ramped up its war effort, drafting young Americans to war. Meanwhile, membership in Students for a Democratic Society (SDS) was enjoying a strong growth spurt, thanks in large part to the actions of the Columbia University chapter regarding the military draft. Columbia SDS first gained success on campus by educating and mobilizing a majority of students to successfully oppose the class ranking of students based on their academic standing. In the fall semester of 1967, the group also had gained support for their anti-Vietnam War effort by showing the campus proof of Columbia's involvement with both the Institute for Defense Analysis and the CIA.

Leading SDS historian Kirkpatrick Sale wrote in his definitive history, *SDS*, that despite this revelation, Columbia was going through the "doldrums that practically every chapter encountered at one time or another. Several of the former chapter leaders had graduated or dropped out. Drugs proved a more satisfying answer than politics for many, and certainly less frustrating. Not only did drug use lead many away from SDS, police also arrested SDSers for weed possession, which lessened their likelihood to continue their political work in having to worry about their legal problems."[2]

Columbia SDS leadership broke into two groups regarding the way it approached activism. One side was referred to as the "Praxis Axis," as it revolved around the *Praxis* theoretical paper insert as part of the national SDS newspaper, *New Left Notes*. Ted Kaptchuk, Ted Gold and Dave Gilbert led this more theoretically-oriented "Praxis Axis," which emphasized writing and debating leftist political theory to educate others. Mark Rudd and John Jacobs led the other group, labeled the "Action Faction," that sought more often to put theory into action. Kirkpatrick Sale said this kind of split happened in SDS chapters nationwide.[3]

The Action Faction picketed and then held a sit-in to protest Dow Chemical Company recruiters. Dow manufactured incendiary jellied gasoline—Napalm—dropped on vast swaths of Vietnam (and Dow made STP).[4] The Faction also threw a meringue pie in the face of a recruiting officer who came to promote the military to students.[5] SDS voted Mark Rudd chapter president.[6]

By late March of 1968, Rudd led a hundred people through the Roman pillars of the university's Low Library administration building. They delivered a petition against the school's involvement with the Institute for Defense Analysis. Columbia placed Rudd, Jacobs, Gold, and three other SDS leaders on probation for that action.[7]

When gunshots killed Martin Luther King Jr. in April 1968, there were black riots in cities nationwide. The BBC said rioters sent at least 100 American cities up in flames.[8] Back in New York, Columbia held a memorial for King. Mark Rudd interrupted the memorial, making a speech about how the school's Institute for Defense Analysis program researched riot control and that the school punished students for nonviolent demonstrations, King's trademark action. He also said Columbia opposed unionization of its largely black workforce and acquired Harlem land for a new gym.[9]

Mark Rudd led the Columbia SDS to some of the biggest campus occupations protesting the Vietnam War. He was highly respected before erratic behavior appeared after suspected agents dosed him.

The Action Faction of SDS then outvoted the Praxis Axis for a rally and march to the president's office opposing the probation of the six SDS leaders, with a contingency plan that few took seriously—to occupy and blockade the office. This SDS action on April 23rd sparked an unprecedented anti-War uprising. A percentage of SDS members occupied Low Library, and many more students poured in to join them. Eventually, students and New York street radicals took over five university buildings. The Praxis Axis faction of SDS ultimately followed the emotionally radicalized students.[10]

Columbia building occupiers included the only eight black Columbia undergraduates, radical blacks from outside the university, Latino activists, and some radical Columbia professors. Other radicals, including former SDS leader Tom Hayden, also joined the strikers occupying the buildings. Members of a radical New York City group, Up Against the Wall Motherfuckers (named for what police said to them at times), joined in occupying the buildings.[11] With access to university files, students were successful in finding more on Columbia's and other universities' collaboration with military actions in Vietnam.[12]

This uprising gained particular significance because New York was the media capital of the world. Reporters and photographers sent images of the strike around the country and the world that effectively inspired other student protests. On the eighth day of the strike, university officials called in a massive police raid to take the building occupiers out in the middle of the night. Media news footage showed police clubbing strikers whether they physically opposed the police or not. Police dragged students down marble steps. Some students staggered out of Low Library bloody from head to toe. Police injured two hundred students and arrested more than seven hundred. The school reopened on May 6, and police continued to arrest more than 250 students for protesting.[13]

Columbia in 1968 surpassed Berkeley in 1964 as the most significant student rebellion in U.S. history. Campuses everywhere were demonstrating, and SDS reportedly played some role in virtually every outbreak.[14] Newspapers, magazines, and television programs around the country discussed Columbia. *Fortune* magazine derisively called SDS the "Che Guevaras of our society ... [acting to] overthrow 'bourgeois' America."[15] The *New York Times,* which had a board member who was also a Columbia trustee, a common situation, derided the student protest as a "temper tantrum," without exposing any negative finding on Columbia support for the Vietnam War.[16]

After this, Congress passed bills to withdraw financial aid to students who "disrupt" universities. It also denied funds to 22 schools that banned military recruiters. The U.S. president could send federal troops into any situation without sanction. And activists who crossed state lines to participate "in a riot or committing any act of violence in furtherance of a riot" could get up to five years in prison and a $10,000 fine.[17]

Nonetheless, student takeovers of buildings broke out nationwide. Most were non-violent. Cuban revolutionary Che Guevara had said: one, two, many Vietnams. The SDS national office was saying: one, two, many Columbias.[18]

After Columbia SDS stopped construction of a gym on Harlem land, Columbia University withdrew from the Institute for Defense Analysis, its administration humiliated. This gained the SDS's Action Faction many new recruits. Four weeks after the first building takeover, they retook the same buildings to protest disciplinary action against four SDS leaders. Columbia threatened to suspend any student arrested, forcing students to decide between continuing their studies or starting full-time radical activism. Police arrested 160 people at the end of the second student takeover of the same buildings.[19]

In June of 1968, Robert F. Kennedy was assassinated. While SDS's national leadership didn't make any endorsement of Kennedy, "there were reports of SDSers willing to defect from radicalism if he became the Democratic presidential candidate." SDS cofounder Tom Hayden reportedly cried at RFK's casket.[20]

SDS Leaders Battle Infiltrators Amid Increasing Psychedelics

Future SDS leader Bernardine Dohrn joined the Columbia takeover while working as an activist lawyer in New York.[21] Dohrn began her activist leadership in Chicago. She had attended the University of Chicago Law School and got her law degree at a time when the average law class included fewer than 10% women.[22] While in college, she was the student leader of the National Lawyers Guild, the association of leftist lawyers.

The January 1967 San Francisco Human Be-In reportedly led Dohrn to help organize a similar event in Chicago in the spring of '67. It is not certain if Dohrn used LSD at that time.[23] One-time SDS leader Todd Gitlin said Dohrn painted her legs in psychedelic swirls for the Chicago Be-In. But Gitlin didn't name Dohrn as the organizer of that event, instead placing the event as the work of a "newly organized underground newspaper called the *Seed*."[24]

Whether the *Seed* was similarly linked to U.S. intelligence as San Francisco's *Oracle* was, isn't known. One source did say the *Seed* and the *Oracle* were two of the first tabloid newspapers to use special split-font inking on a web press. This suggests large initial funds and expertise for these upstart "underground" presses. They also had unusually large funding to be able to distribute some 40,000 copies nationally.[25]

SDS started turning towards psychedelics in 1967. The SDS national newspaper, *New Left Notes*, featured a headline article positively covering a "Human Be-In," held in New York, in its April issue. LSD-promoting groups such as Timothy Leary's League for Spiritual Discovery co-sponsored the Be-In. *New Left Notes* also published a November 1967 article by someone living in San Francisco's Haight-Ashbury, who said, "We left, lit our pipes and popped our acid ... we pumped the nation full of acid, pot ... Hippies are ... an act of rejection, a military vanguard, a hope for the future."

While another article, "Hippies on the East Village," was less flattering of New York's hippies, in June the SDS National Administrative Committee unanimously decided that the SDS National Office would become official members of the Grateful Dean fan club.[26]

Bernardine Dohrn gravitated towards the psychedelic hippie scene, but it didn't yet appear to affect her competence. She worked with Martin Luther King Jr. in the mid-1960s, organizing students around both antiwar activities and civil rights. When a gunman assassinated MLK in April of 1968, a friend said Dohrn cried a lot. After, she changed from her signature minidress into "riot gear" pants to participate in demonstrations that included vandalism. She also began talking about urban guerrilla warfare.[27]

In the summer of 1968, Dohrn traveled to Michigan State University to run for the national leadership position of Inter-organizational Secretary at the SDS national conference. One audience member used the McCarthy "red-baiting" tactic in asking Dohrn if she was a socialist. Dohrn upped the ante and heralded the new political sentiment by replying, "I consider myself a revolutionary communist."[28]

Bernardine Dohrn won her SDS position, as did her close political friend Mike Klonsky. A large, more socially conservative group within SDS had a dual affiliation with a national organization called the Progressive Labor Party. Kirkpatrick Sale said members of the Progressive Labor Party (PLP) continually created conflicts in chapters nationwide. They started long debates over small points of ideology. Some believe spies infiltrated the PLP. The fact that former PLP member Phillip Luce worked for the right-wing House Un-American Activities Committee soon after leaving the PLP supports this notion.[29]

Progressive Labor talked so much about students uniting with workers that the New York group Up Against the Wall Motherfuckers staged a mock marriage between a student and a worker at the SDS convention hall. PLP had positive ideas against the growing drug use amongst SDSers. But their straight-laced look—starched work shirts, coat-and-ties, fifties-short hair, and clean-shaven faces—also allowed easier agent infiltration. Many said PLP's members' ideological battles soured people on activism.[30]

Kirkpatrick Sale noted many old leftist groups at the June '68 SDS convention. These included Sparticists, Wobblies, Communists, International Socialists and Socialist Workers. While these groups also appeared overly sectarian, PLP had the largest student presence, and they opposed the SDS National Office regulars of Dohrn, Mike Klonsky, et al.

Aware that the FBI and police had infiltrated SDS, the National Office regulars created a workshop billed as devoted to the discussion of sabotage and explosives. They wanted to draw many of these undercover agents to that workshop so that they wouldn't attend SDS's serious workshops on activist strategy. An agent infiltrator later acknowledged that strategy's success.[31]

While the Progressive Labor Party members got one representative elected to the three National Secretary positions, the SDS National Office had virtually all of their candidates voted into the National Interim Committee, a group of the regional SDS leaders. The convention voted Mark Rudd as a first alternate to that Committee and used Rudd's publicity to make him a national fundraiser. By November, Rudd had raised over $3,000 in speaker's fees for SDS.[32]

MK-Ultra Agent Gives "Sober" Abbie Hoffman LSD

Another much smaller activist group, the Youth International Party, or YIPpies, started by Abbie Hoffman, arose with considerable media attention by 1968. Hoffman earned an undergraduate degree at Brandeis and a master's degree at the University of California-Berkeley, graduating in 1960. He and his wife Sheila married that year and had two children within the next two years. They both participated in leftist activism for civil rights and against the Vietnam War, and helped organize a delegation to go down south and participate in the Freedom Rides with the Student Nonviolent Coordinating Committee.

By 1965 they organized an anti-War protest and led radical talks by activists at a community center near their home outside of Boston.[33] Abbie Hoffman's stature as an activist grew. He edited a Boston area leftist newsletter, *The Drum*. Hoffman also rallied students to help get a third-party anti-nuclear, peace candidate, Harvard Professor H. Stuart Hughes, on the ballot for the U.S. Senate in Massachusetts. For that cause he gathered 17,000 signatures on a petition for what was reportedly the first progressive third-party campaign since 1948.[34]

In 1965, Hoffman balanced activism with writing and theater projects. The U.S. Army had drafted Hoffman's former roommate, Manny Schreiber, and had him work for MK-Ultra on a secret military project testing the effects of LSD on soldiers. Schreiber brought LSD home to Hoffman. At that time Hoffman had never even tried marijuana.[35]

Abbie Hoffman was introduced to LSD by a friend who worked for MK-Ultra. Hoffman's ongoing tripping had his activist wife leave him, and Hoffman's activism mutated to include "levitating the Pentagon."

After that introduction to acid, Abbie Hoffman started using drugs regularly. His wife Sheila, a constant partner in activism, divorced him in 1966, citing his drug use. Hoffman moved away from his kids in Boston, to the Lower East Side of Manhattan that year. That East Village area had a long history of activism and a growing bohemian population, but by 1967 agents helped make it another drugged-out wasteland like San Francisco's Haight-Ashbury.[36]

While there, Hoffman staged street-theater protests. One of his best known was in August of 1967, when he led fellow activists to the gallery of the New York Stock Exchange. He brought along about 100 or more real dollar bills mixed in with hundreds of fake dollar bills and threw them off the top floor of the stock exchange. Many of the traders frantically scrambled to pick up the bills, creating a metaphor for their rat-like scampering for money. Media groups gave it global coverage.[37]

In October, David Dellinger of the National Mobilization Committee to End the War in Vietnam (MOBE) asked Berkeley Free Speech veteran Jerry Rubin to help mobilize and direct a march on the Pentagon. 70,000 protesters gathered at the Lincoln Memorial to hear Dellinger, Dr. Benjamin Spock and others give speeches. Afterward an estimated 50,000, including Hoffman and poet Allen Ginsberg, marched to the Pentagon. Military police stopped the marchers outside the Pentagon. Showing the effects of too much acid, Hoffman and Ginsberg directed people to focus their psychic energy to levitate the Pentagon, at which point they said it would rise, turn orange, vibrate, and end the Vietnam War. Ginsberg led Tibetan chants to assist Hoffman.[38]

By the summer of 1968, Abbie Hoffman and his new wife, Anika, had teamed up with fellow heavy LSD users Jerry Rubin and Paul Krassner to form the Youth International Party. The Mobe, the Yippies and others organized a protest at the Democratic National Convention in Chicago. Activist groups like SDS and the Black Panthers didn't get directly involved in the organizing, but did send representatives. SDS sent some 500 members to recruit more people and politically educate the crowd. The Black Panthers had Bobby Seale speak at the protest on one of the five days.[39]

The day before the convention, the rock group MC5 ("Kick Out the Jams") and folk singer Phil Ochs played at a Festival of Life concert supporting the protest. There, people passed around acid in the form of spiked honey. Writers said Mayor Richard Daley sent police in en masse, and the Festival of Life became a festival of blood.[40]

Historians have called the militant reaction to the convention activism a police riot against protesters. Police clubbed and tear-gassed thousands of protesters, left hundreds bloodied, and arrested many. Police took seven leaders of the protest to court in a highly publicized "Chicago Seven" trial. Prosecutors added an eighth, Black Panther national cofounder Bobby Seale, although he had only given a speech and then left the protest. When Seale debated his inclusion in the court proceedings, the judge had him bound and gagged, as made more famous in the Crosby, Stills and Nash song, "Chicago."

Unknown to the Yippie leaders Abbie Hoffman and Jerry Rubin, who stood trial and gained national celebrity, Yippie steering committee member George Demmerle was an undercover FBI informant and had acted as Hoffman's bodyguard during the Chicago protest. U.S. intelligence appeared to put acid-fueled activists Hoffman and Rubin in a media spotlight as top Sixties activist icons, thoroughly linking LSD and activism.[41]

George Demmerle was one of a number of undercover operatives at the Democratic Convention and among the Yippies. CBS News obtained Army intelligence documents stating nearly one out of six demonstrators at the Chicago convention was undercover. These included, "Bob Pierson, a Chicago cop disguised as a biker who latched onto Jerry Rubin during the convention and became his bodyguard." Pierson started provocations such as throwing stones at police, pulling down flags, inciting protesters to stop traffic and starting fires in the street that helped police chiefs incite their men to physically attack the protesters.[42]

The exact number of undercover agents who worked with Demmerle to manipulate Hoffman, Rubin and other Yippies, influencing them to promote acid, remains unknown, but evidence indicates that U.S. intelligence did manipulate the Yippies and used them in this manner.[43] Peggy Hitchcock of the intelligence-involved Mellon Hitchcock family helped fund the Yippies, particularly the March to "levitate" the Pentagon.[44]

Meanwhile, President Richard Nixon had the CIA expand its Operation Chaos. The CIA's Chaos enacted strange trivial tactics like use itching powder against leftists, though it also aided U.S. intelligence-orchestrated arrests and assassinations. In the '50s, the CIA's benign sounding Technical Services Staff devised operations using LSD. Chaos trained many local police intelligence divisions who pulled off operations, including Bob Pierson's undercover work as Jerry Rubin's bodyguard.[45]

People protested the Democratic Party for President Johnson's authorization of the horrific carpet-bombing in Vietnam. Additionally, under an operation called the Phoenix Program, the U.S. military conducted assassinations of South Vietnamese civilians sympathetic to the Communists, and they dropped Napalm on innocent Vietnamese. Television news showed many of these images.[46]

But the Democrats were a party divided, with some standing for the war and others standing in opposition to it. The Republican Party was more solidly supportive of the military operations in Vietnam. In response to this, the acid-saturated Yippie leaders protested only the Democratic National Convention. No similar protest was staged at the Republican National Convention.[47] The melee at the Democratic convention was said to help Republican Richard Nixon win the presidential election of 1968 over Vice

President Hubert Humphrey, who was also saddled with Johnson's disastrous Vietnam policy. The press let Nixon get away with claiming that he had a "secret plan" to end the War, which actually outlasted Nixon's presidency.

Did U.S. intelligence use its mass of agents to orchestrate events at the Democratic National Convention to help achieve a desired electoral result?

FBI Agents Dose Mark Rudd & Columbia SDS

Once Richard Nixon got into office, he instituted draconian sentencing for drug-possession charges. President Nixon had many leading leftists arrested and jailed on minor drug charges. White Panther leader (and MC5 band manager) John Sinclair was given ten years in jail for two joints. Police put black anarchist bookstore owner Martin Sostre in jail for six years by planting weed in his store. Amnesty International helped get him released. Columbia SDS leader Mark Rudd was arrested on a drug-related charge through an undercover agent.[48]

In the fall of 1968, Mark Rudd toured campuses trying to use his previous year's celebrity status to raise money for SDS.[49] Shortly after, Bernardine Dohrn and Mike Klonsky worked with groups of people of color, including the Black Panthers; the Latino activists, the Young Lords; along with the Revolutionary Black Workers and dissenting G.I.s. Black Panther leaders declared solidarity and support for SDS, while the SDS National Office also expressed support for the Panthers. SDS's *New Left Notes* declared them the leading Black activist group.[50]

SDS's Chicago National Office began to experience U.S. intelligence attacks similar to those against the Panthers and Young Lords, albeit less brutal. For example, police purported getting a call of a shooting at the National Office and demanded to inspect the premises. Then firemen came behind stating a report of a fire. The police and firemen tried to barge into the office while SDSers physically tried to keep them out, thinking it was a police plot to ransack their premises. Police arrested Mike Klonsky and five other SDS leaders.[51]

In the summer of 1969, Dohrn, Rudd and and nine others formed a committee which released a paper they called the "Weatherman Statement." It attempted to distance itself from the Progressive Labor contingent and align SDS with youth and revolutionary groups of color. The Weatherman name came from Bob Dylan's 1965 political song, "Subterranean Homesick Blues": "You don't need a weatherman to know which way the wind blows." The Weatherman Statement focused on fighting U.S. imperialism as it waged war on Third World liberation movements at home and abroad.[52]

Progressive Labor used the smallest of differences to find fault in other groups under attack by the U.S. It criticized North Vietnamese leadership for trying to make agreements with the United States as part of peace efforts, instead of just continuing the war. It also attacked the Black Panthers with false accusations that they ignored the working class and waged war against whites.[53]

By that summer of 1969, many other sectarian groups with a history of U.S. intelligence infiltration joined in the SDS national convention. These infiltrators appeared to join collectively against the SDS leadership and two Black Panther members invited to talk at the convention. The Black Panther Party was a vanguard organization that served as a model for organizations formed by other ethnic communities. They were active in at least 45 cities nationwide by this time, though they had also closed membership in many of these cities because the FBI had heavily infiltrated so many of their chapters.[54]

The 1969 SDS convention had scheduled talks by lesser-known Panthers, including Rufus "Chaka" Walls, Minister of Information of the Illinois Black Panthers, who worked with SDS's National Office. Walls first criticized Progressive Labor and read a policy letter dismissing the group, approved by Panther National Chairman Bobby Seale. Walls also made a chauvinist remark about women's liberation as "pussy power," leading to many "boos" in the convention audience. It's uncertain where Chicago Panther leader Fred Hampton was on this occasion, but another Panther, Jewell Cook, continued a chauvinist line of comments. Cook said that the "position for you sisters is ... prone." This hurt the Weatherman contingent's appeal to convention delegates.[55]

The convention became very fractious, with boos and jeers at the Panthers and the Weatherman contingent. Interorganizational Secretary Bernardine Dohrn impulsively decided to walk away from it, and encouraged about 700 others to follow her. This effectively ended the Students for Democratic Society, which had close to 100,000 members by that time.[56]

U.S. intelligence waged a huge campaign against Dohrn and her comrades at that convention. Did acid use lead to Dohrn's impulsivity and loss of emotional control to enact that walkout? Sociologist and former SDS leader Todd Gitlin credited Dohrn's action with "dismantling ... the largest American organization anywhere on the Left in fifty years."[57] Still, Dohrn's Weatherman remained the de facto revolutionary cadre.

U.S. intelligence didn't have as much initial luck getting Columbia SDS leader and icon Mark Rudd, nor his fellow Columbia SDS leaders, to use acid. According to Lee and Shlain, Rudd

> declined numerous offers to turn on with the Crazies (a militant offshoot of the Yippies) on the grounds that it would interfere with his politics. The Crazies chided Rudd and his cohorts for being straight-laced and ignorant of the youth culture, but Rudd's crowd was not to be persuaded. Finally the Crazies took matters into their own hands and put acid in the wine at a Weather party without telling the hosts.

> Soon the place exploded into a frenzy of song and dance; afterwards the local leadership agreed that LSD was inherently revolutionary, and they [Rudd and other Columbia leaders] ordered every Weatherperson in New York to take the drug and get experienced.[58]

Historians Lee and Shlain apparently didn't realize, nor did Rudd and the other Columbia leaders realize, that undercover FBI asset George Demmerle was one of the Crazies' leaders. Lee and Shlain actually described Demmerle as one of many informants who received training at the FBI's "Hoover University" in Quantico Marine Base in Virginia. This elite academy taught them how to infiltrate left-wing organizations. These undercover agents "smoked pot and dropped acid with unsuspecting radicals." Lee said that New York radical circles knew Demmerle as "Prince Crazy," without connecting him with the Yippie offshoot group.[59]

George Demmerle testified as an undercover agent after he infiltrated Hoffman's Youth International Party anti-War group (the Yippies) and was also suspected of dosing Columbia's SDS.

Radical anti-War activist Jane Alpert detailed Demmerle's work with the Crazies. Alpert said Demmerle was thirty-eight-years old in 1968, and his face looked like worn out rubber. He tried to convince her to drop chemicals in manholes of New York's financial district in order to blow out the supply of electricity to major Wall Street corporations. She further said Demmerle founded the Crazies, and she saw him man the Crazies booth for many hours at the Woodstock music festival.[60] Demmerle later revealed his undercover identity when he testified in court against Alpert and other radicals in the mid-'70s.[61]

Abbie Hoffman eventually got clean and sober, identifying himself as an addict in recovery. Hoffman continued organizing protests in a more clear-headed way against the CIA, and against U.S. intervention in Latin America. Hoffman further organized successfully against nuclear reactors. In 1989 Hoffman was found dead of a reported suicide by barbiturate overdose at 52 years of age.[62]

Doctors Warned: LSD Is Threat to Democracy

As early as February of 1968, experts saw what rampant expansion of LSD usage was doing to America, and tried to warn their colleagues to help stop it. For example, Cornell University Medical School professor Donald Louria, M.D. wrote a column addressing this in the prestigious *New England Journal of Medicine*. Prof. Louria had a regular column, "Medical Intelligence," where he first gave an overview of the latest studies on LSD that indicated some substantiation to small benefits from the drug, but he dispelled the truth to claims of any larger benefits.[63]

Professor Louria discussed how "a variety of prolonged, even permanent, adverse reactions [from LSD use] are being reported increasingly often." Louria warned,

> Many of the proponents of the LSD experience, undaunted by the lack of documentation of benefits or the many tragedies caused by the drug, are irresponsibly and unconscionably promoting the use of LSD or other equally potent hallucinogens. Advancing facile arguments about individual freedom, trumpeting the alleged ecstasies, minimizing the dangers and depending on personal charisma, these psychedelic missionaries are attempting by every possible overt and *covert* [emphasis added] technique to inveigle young people into joining the hallucinogenic drug movement. Such proselytizing is extraordinarily difficult to counteract.

Louria also warned that laws against LSD had failed to stop its spread, which had "reached critical proportions in some areas of the U.S. and in some colleges." Louria then urged:

> As with other public health problems, a vigorous education campaign is mandatory if those unalterably committed to the potent psychedelic-drug experience are to be prevented from subverting the majority of young people who are uncommitted but educable. The medical profession must give itself fully to this educational effort but has not yet done so. If responsible persons, including physicians, fail or abrogate their educative obligations, an enormous increase in the use of LSD and other potent hallucinogens, with consequent medical and psychiatric tragedies, will almost inevitably occur.
>
> Even more important, the widespread use of LSD, or similar drugs waiting in the psychedelic wings, could lead to a whole generation of psychedelic dropouts, incapable or uninterested in addressing themselves to the important sociologic problems that challenge our times. If this happened, the very structure of this democratic society would be threatened.
>
> The recent writings of academicians, scientists, psychiatrists and beatnik philosophers suggest that the LSD problem must be recognized as an integral part of a much larger issue; this, put in its simplest form, is the question of whether man's mind and emotions in the 21st century should be unfettered or should be controlled by euphoria-producing or hallucinogenic drugs or carefully placed electrodes. This question may

seem to many hardly worthy of serious consideration, but serious it is, and its answer may well determine the future course of our civilization.[64]

Notes

1 Donald B. Louria, M.D. "Medical Intelligence: Current Concepts, Lysergic Acid Diethylamide," *The New England Journal of Medicine*, Vol. 278, No.8, February 1968, p. 437.

2 Kirkpatrick Sale, *SDS: The rise and development of the Students for a Democratic Society...* (New York: Vintage, 1973), pp. 272, 432. Regarding why the U.S. was in Vietnam, while the American ruling elite and the U.S. military reported wanting to protect South Vietnam from the northern Communists, many South Vietnamese wanted to join North Vietnam. The U.S. military started the Phoenix Program that sought to assassinate any of these South Vietnamese, dubbed "Viet Cong insurgents." While over a million North Vietnamese ended up dying in the Vietnam War, the U.S. Senate Church Committee would later find the Phoenix Program assassinated well over 20,000 South Vietnamese. Philip Sheldon, "20 Years After Victory," April 1995, Folder 14, Box 24, Douglas Pike Collection: Unit 06 - Democratic Republic of Vietnam, The Vietnam Archive, Texas Tech University. On Phoenix Program, see Church Committee Report, http://www.aarclibrary.org/publib/contents/church/contents_church_reports_book1.htm. Also see http://www.serendipity.li/cia/operation_phoenix.htm.

3 Kirkpatrick Sale, *SDS: The rise and development of the Students for a Democratic Society ...* (New York: Vintage, 1973), p. 434.

4 Sale, *SDS*, pp. 430-34.

5 Sale, *SDS*, p. 433.

6 Sale, *SDS*, p. 434.

7 Sale, *SDS*, p. 435.

8 "On this Day" BBC Home. 4/6/68. http://news.bbc.co.uk/onthisday/hi/dates/stories/april/6/newsid_2902000/2902487.stm.

9 Sale, *SDS*, p. 435.

10 Sale, *SDS*, pp. 435-36.

11 Partly from personal interview with one of the black undergraduates, met at the 100 year Celebration of Richard Wright Conference in Paris, April 2008. Also personal interview with Juan Gonzales at the first Media and Democracy Congress in San Francisco, 2006. And Sale, *SDS*, p. 437. On quotas on blacks, http://beatl.barnard.columbia.edu/learn/archives/WechslerText.htm. This and other articles tells how there were quotas on Jews and Italian Catholics only a decade or two earlier.

12 They found meeting minutes and letters in the president's office on planting fake articles in the *New York Times* to support Columbia's takeover of Harlem land. They found a University of Chicago president's advice on how the two schools could pretend to give up IDA research while still doing it. And, they found documents on U.S. universities' aid in CIA covert military operations. Sale, *SDS*, p. 437.

13 *Columbia Revolt* (1968, film, 50 minutes), Third World Newsreel (TWN).

14 Sale, *SDS*, pp. 440-41.

15 Sale, *SDS*, pp. 441-2.

16 Sale, *SDS*, pp. 442-43. Also see example of William "Dink" Smith who is on the Board of Regents of University of Georgia and is president of CNI, which publishes several dozen newspapers in Georgia, Florida and North Carolina, http://www.usg.edu/regents/members

17 Sale, *SDS*, p. 444.

18 Sale, *SDS*, pp. 444-46.

19 Sale, *SDS*, pp. 446-47.

20 Sale, *SDS*, p. 450.

21 Sale, *SDS*, pp. 446-7.

22 See Helda Garza, *Barred from the Bar (Women Then-Women Now)* (Chicago: Franklin Watts, 1996). Also see her website: *A History of Women and the Legal Profession,* http://www.american-buddha.com/lit.barredbar.6.htm.

23 Martin Lee and Bruce Shlain, *Acid Dreams: The Complete Social History of LSD, the CIA, the Sixties, and Beyond* (New York: Grove Press, 1994), p. 230.

24 Todd Gitlin, *The Sixties: Years of Hope, Days of Rage* (New York: Bantam, 1987), p. 212. Note that Gitlin was protesting the psychedelic onslaught diverting people from leftist activism.

25 Abe Peck, *Uncovering the Sixties: The Life and Times of the Underground Press* (New York: Citadel, 1991) http://www.enotes.com/topic/Chicago_Seed_(newspaper).

26 NLN News Service, "Human Be-In: Covers Meadows, Baffles Cops," *New Left Notes,* Vol. 2 No. 13, April 10, 1967. Note in this copy the No. is crossed out and 14 written in. On Leary's League for Spiritual Discovery, see Lee and Shlain, *Acid Dreams,* p. 161. On NAC approval of NO becoming part of Grateful Dead Fan Club, see *New Left Notes* reprint of "NAC Minutes," June 15, 1967.

27 Gitlin, *The Sixties,* p. 306. On Dohrn at Columbia, see Sale, *SDS,* p. 446.

28 Sale, *SDS,* p. 451. "Bernardine Dohrn, Bluhm Legal Clinic, Faculty Profiles, Faculty & Research, School of Law, Northwestern University," Law.northwestern.edu.

29 Phillip Abbott Luce, *The New Left* (New York: Dave McKay, 1966).

30 Sale, *SDS,* pp. 456, 462-63.

31 This agent infiltrator testified to Congress on the success of this. Sale, *SDS,* p. 456.

32 Sale, *SDS,* pp. 470, 482.

33 Marty Jezer, *Abbie Hoffman: American Rebel* (New Brunswick, NJ: Rutgers University Press, 1992), pp. 42-60.

34 Jezer, *Abbie Hoffman,* pp. 46-47, 51

35 Jezer, *Abbie Hoffman,* pp. 29, 69. Also Jonah Raskin, *For the Hell of It: The Life and Times of Abbie Hoffman* (Los Angeles: University of California Press, 1998), p. 48.

36 On divorce, Jezer, *Abbie Hoffman,* pp. 70-73. On Lower East Side psychedelic wasteland, see Lee and Shlain, *Acid Dreams,* p. 197

37 Cynthia Blair, "1967: Hippies Toss Dollar Bills onto NYSE Floor," in Fran Capo and Frank Borzellieri, *It Happened In New York* (New York: Two Dot, 2005). James Ledbetter, "The day the NYSE went Yippie," CNNMoney.com. Abbie Hoffman, *Soon To Be A Major Motion Picture: The Autobiography of Abbie Hoffman* (Perigree Books, 1980), p. 101.

38 See http://www.uic.edu/orgs/cwluherstory/jofreeman/photos/Pentagon67.html.

39 Lee and Shlain, *Acid Dreams,* pp. 215-22.

40 Lee and Shlain, *Acid Dreams,* p. 220.

41 Lee and Shlain, *Acid Dreams,* p. 223.

42 Lee and Shlain, *Acid Dreams,* p. 224.

43 Lee and Shlain, *Acid Dreams,* p. 203

44 Lee and Shlain, *Acid Dreams,* pp. 205, 219.

45 Lee and Shlain, *Acid Dreams,* p. 224-5.

46 Lee and Shlain, *Acid Dreams,* p. 227. See note 2 above for references about the Phoenix Program.

47 Lee and Shlain, *Acid Dreams,* p. 224.

48 Lee and Shlain, *Acid Dreams,* pp. 225-26. On Sinclair, see Patrick Cadogan, *The Revolutionary Artist: John Lennon's Radical Years* (Lulu, 2008).

49 Sale, *SDS,* pp. 509-10.

50 Sale, *SDS,* pp. 512, 516-17.

51 Sale, *SDS,* p. 533.

52 Sale, *SDS,* p. 558-59. "Subterranean Homesick Blues" from Bob Dylan, *Bringing It All Back Home* (Columbia Records, 1965).

53 Sale, *SDS,* pp. 510, 534-35.

54 Nathan Daniel Beau Connelly, "The Black Panther Party," *Encyclopedia of Chicago*

(Chicago: The Newberry Library, 2004), http://www.encyclopedia.chicagohistory.org/pages/142.html.

55 Sale, *SDS*, pp. 510, 566-67.

56 Gitlin, *The Sixties*, pp. 387-88.

57 Gitlin, *The Sixties*, pp. 387-88.

58 Lee and Shlain, *Acid Dreams*, pp. 230-31.

59 Lee and Shlain, *Acid Dreams*, p. 223. Also on Demmerle, including his labeling himself as Prince Crazy, see Peter Zimroth's interview and coverage of him in Peter Zimroth, *Perversions of Justice* (New York: Viking Press, 1974), pp. 63-67.

60 Jane Alpert, *Growing Up Underground* (New York: Citadel Press, 1990), pp. 199, 205.

61 Alpert, *Growing Up Underground*, p. 367.

62 Wayne King, "Abbie Hoffman Committed Suicide Using Barbiturates, Autopsy Shows," *New York Times*, April 19, 1989.

63 Louria, "Medical Intelligence," p. 435.

64 Louria, "Medical Intelligence," p. 437.

BRING
THE
WAR
HOME!
SDS
CHICAGO-OCT. 11
Paul Krassner

Chapter Eleven

Acid, Bombings Impair Weatherman Leaders

LSD makes people less competent. You can see their motivation for turning people on. Very often it's not necessary to give it more than just a little push. Make it available and the news media takes it up, and there it is. They don't have to stick their necks out very much.

– William S. Burroughs[1]

Students for a Democratic Society (SDS) members in Weatherman showed signs of a cerebral downturn in their behavior as their acid use increased. Included were some of the brightest and most courageous of the SDS leaders, including Bernardine Dohrn, Mark Rudd, Jeff Jones, Billy Ayers and Kathy Boudin. Dohrn was an attorney who graduated from the University of Chicago law school. Rudd had risen to the leadership position at Columbia for his inspiring speeches and tactics, with Jeff Jones by his side. Boudin, a bright, inspiring activist, was the daughter of a top radical New York lawyer.

Acid Dulls Education Efforts of Best and Brightest

When these top Weathermen, as the group came to be known, were with SDS they helped lead protest actions. They also tried to educate others through local chapter newsletters, as well as the national SDS newspaper *New Left Notes,* explaining why they took their radical stances. Other activists published in alternative magazines such as *Ramparts,* New York City's *Rat* and *The Guardian,* where non-SDS radical activists Jane Alpert and Sam Melville worked.[2]

The U.S. government put out a barrage of propaganda in the mainstream press to persuade people to support the war in Vietnam and the suppression of Black Liberation leaders. SDS and other activists had to use their limited resources to try to convince people otherwise. They had to be lucid, clear thinking, and knowledgeable about the issues. Acid impaired these abilities.

Several of the Weather contingent's leaders started taking an over-the-top anti-intellectual stand that mirrored their increased acid uptake. Bill Ayers initially had reservations about eating acid. He had taken a major role in the University of Michigan's Jesse James Gang and then became part of the nucleus of Weatherman leadership. The Jesse James Gang was Michigan SDS's version of Columbia's Action Faction. Writer Martin Lee said that a White Panther, Ken Kelley, who edited an underground newspaper, got Ayers to try LSD despite his having reservations about it, and Ayers continued to use it while he was with the Weathermen (a later action by Kelley would put into question his greater allegiance to the Panthers or the FBI).[3]

Ayers ran for the position of Education Secretary of what remained of the national SDS organization, now split in two, months after Dohrn led a walkout at the summer of 1969 convention. The Weathermen ran one SDS group; Progressive Labor ran the other. In his nominating speech, Ayers announced with pride that neither he, nor former SDS leaders Mark Rudd and Jeff Jones, had read a book in a year.[4]

The Weathermen first carried out ideas that Ayers proposed for expanding their adherents. Even sympathetic historians regarded these tactics as very futile and counterproductive. Weathermen marched with Vietnamese National Liberation Front flags through local parks comparing the first American Revolution to the need for current revolution. They also held "jailbreaks"—invading community colleges and high schools, gagging teachers and preaching to classrooms, leading to many Weatherman arrests. They further fought Progressive Labor activists and police with their fists and broken table legs.[5]

Weathermen interrupted other activist gatherings to announce their October '69 "National Action" in Chicago. This action involved Weathermen planning a riot in Chicago they would later call the "Four Days of Rage." They tried preaching to others to recruit more participants in the National Action. Many of these former SDS leaders acted with good intentions after visiting anti-imperialist fighters from Cuba to Vietnam, but their tactics appeared increasingly less effective in their initial year.

After Rudd's first experience with acid in the summer of 1969, his subsequent change of behavior was obvious. He began to promote the use of LSD to the rest of his New York activists, and frequently behaved irrationally. He toured the country "haranguing student audiences, and engaging Progressive Laborites and others who disagreed with him in bloody fistfights."

In general, he also displayed decreasing effectiveness at appealing to college students. In a September appearance at Columbia University, he paced back and forth away from the podium, brandished a chair leg and yelled at the students for being soft, bragging about his preparation for the revolution, saying, "I've got myself a gun—has everyone here got a gun? Anyone? No?! Well, you'd better fuckin' get your shit together."

After about twenty minutes a short, stocky SDS member got up and said Rudd had his turn and now he wanted to speak. Rudd glared at him and tried to punch the SDS member who pushed Rudd into the podium. Rudd, stunned, joined his friends on the side, gaining no Weatherman recruits that day.[6]

In September, the trial of the Chicago Democratic Convention protest leaders began. Chicago prosecutors accused the Chicago Seven (actually eight with Bobby Seale) of organizing the protests and creating the riotous atmosphere. Some SDS National Office leaders had attended the Chicago Democratic Convention and were arrested there.[7]

The Chicago Black Panthers' highly regarded leader Fred Hampton had organized well with the SDS National Office. But when Weathermen such as Mark Rudd started acting strangely after their acid use, Hampton's respect for them decreased. Earlier, Rudd made a speech at a Chicago event co-organized by Hampton, and spoke about the Four Days of Rage in an attempt to get the Panthers and white activists involved. Only one movement group, Youth Against War and Fascism, ever offered support. Hampton called Rudd "a 'motherfucking masochist' to his face and proceeded to deck him with a single blow."[8]

Acidheads' Dubious Anti-War Tactics: Days of Rage

The Weathermen apparently hoped to draw thousands to the Four Days of Rage in Chicago. But the first cold night they huddled around a bonfire to keep warm, and found they numbered only about two hundred. The total for the four days drew about six hundred participants. The hundreds wore motorcycle, football, and construction helmets, along with padded bras, pipes, first aid kits, and t-shirts with emergency numbers written on them. Bernardine Dohrn tried to rally them saying it was the second anniversary of Che Guevara's death.[9]

Historian Kirkpatrick Sale described how the acid-addled Weathermen went on a rampage chanting "Ho! Ho! Ho Chi Minh! Dare to struggle, dare to win!" They also shouted, "Bring the war hoooome!" and "Off the pigs!" They threw rocks and bricks through windows of posh apartment houses and smashed the windows of parked cars. They sometimes pummeled a solo policeman in their way. Police ran their cars through the Weathermen throng, indifferent to hitting them. Police also beat many of the protesters until they were mangled and bloody.[10]

On some days, Mark Rudd put on a fake moustache, suit and tie, and simply watched from the darkness. Police arrested Rudd with three other leaders on the fourth Day of Rage. The Weathermen smashed store and car windows before the police grabbed and brutalized them. All the leaders were arrested except Bill Ayers, Terry Robbins and Jeff Melish. The group faced $2.3 million worth of bail bonds and up to five-year jail sentences. But the longest jail time actually ended up being 112 days, because the most seriously charged went into hiding.[11]

One faction of the SDS leadership was not aligned with the Progressive Labor faction, nor the Weathermen. This group, Revolutionary Youth Movement II (RYM II) had Mike Klonsky and Noel Ignatin as its spokesmen. The Black Panthers and Young Lords, Chicago and New York-based Hispanic activists, supported RYM II as they held peaceful demonstrations in Chicago. After six Weathermen were shot and sixty-eight arrested during the Days of Rage, Weatherman canceled its planned actions—a rock concert, a march on the Chicago courthouse, and more "jailbreaks" (encouraging students to walk out of school), in order to rethink their mission and strategies.[12]

Historically, criticism of the Weathermen's actions must be tempered with an understanding of those violent times. By December 4 in Chicago, police had raided Black Panther leader Fred Hampton's home and murdered him in his bed. A mass of evidence suggested it was an FBI orchestrated assassination, one that also killed Illinois Panther leader Mark Clark.[13]

With the media accurately reflecting America's mass-murder of Vietnamese men, women and children, the Weathermen might be seen as simply reacting by the only means left, as past peaceful protests hadn't had much effect. Still problematic is the Weathermen's poor judgment on the best tactics for violent protests against the government-sanctioned genocide in Vietnam.

With the national SDS splintered, few were left to carry the mantle of protest on white college campuses. The Weathermen made national headlines with their October action, albeit with articles titled, "Radicals Go on a Rampage." But campus SDS chapters didn't know what to do about the split, so campus chapters splintered, fell apart or declared themselves independent. Most called the Progressive Labor SDS irrelevant, while one Wisconsin SDS chapter popularly mocked the Weathermen with the line: "You don't need a rectal thermometer to know who the assholes are."[14]

Acid-Addled Weathermen Laud Murderers

Many Weathermen stayed committed to fighting against the war in Vietnam and decided to use media attention to build their ranks with a national convention to be held in December of 1969. With numerous Weathermen still "underground" they decided to communicate the location of their convention by word of mouth alone. To avoid infiltration around this time, a number of Weather collectives instituted their own "acid tests." They made new members eat acid with them and then asked if they were agents.

It failed to work at times, as exemplified by one undercover FBI asset, Larry Grathwohl. During a two-day trip he said he was a "pig" (police or intelligence agent), but added that being in the Army, he was "a pig for what I did in Vietnam; because I stood by and saw brutality of what was being done to innocent people." He was accepted into a Cincinnati Weatherman collective and, several months later, fingered two New York female Weathermen for the FBI.[15]

Early in December of 1969, police arrested Charles Manson and his "hippie" followers for the July 1969 murders of actress Sharon Tate and four of her friends. Tate, a young film actress, was married to director Roman Polanski (*Chinatown*), and eight months pregnant with their first child. Attackers had stabbed her forty-nine times with a butcher knife. One attacker also notoriously left a fork stuck in Tate's belly. They smeared the walls of her Bel Air, California mansion with blood, writing "Piggies" and "Helter Skelter." These were titles of songs by the Beatles from their popular and sometimes politically radical *White Album*.

Charles Manson had a group of young girls living with him who were taking lots of acid. He convinced them to commit these murders. An underground Los Angeles newspaper named Manson "Man of the Year" and ran his picture with the word "hippie" as the caption. The Weathermen put Manson on a pedestal, saying he offed some "rich honky pigs."[16]

By mid-December, with the Weathermen still worried about too much agent infiltration, they let out that the Christmas weekend National Council would be held in Flint, Michigan. SDS historian Kirkpatrick Sale gave a detailed account of this event. Some four hundred attendees showed up in a giant ballroom in a black ghetto of Flint, which they decorated with huge psychedelic posters of Weatherheroes Fidel Castro, Eldridge Cleaver, Che Guevara, Ho Chi Minh, Lenin, Mao Zedong, Malcolm X and Fred Hampton.

At night they held mass meetings they called "wargasms." The agenda started with a group karate routine. It then proceeded with regular exercises, followed up by songs they had created with radical lyrics, such as one to the tune of the Beatles "Nowhere Man."[17]

Bernardine Dohrn and Mark Rudd's Weatherman faction faced many undercover agents, and was influenced to walk out of the 1969 SDS conference, dismantling the largest antiwar student group in U.S. history.

While the whole event appeared to reflect some of the more chaotic thinking of the organizers, within the context of the times, things were relatively rational until the nighttime speeches. Weatherleader Bernardine Dohrn began by describing Weatherman actions in the recent months. "We were in an airplane, and we went up and down the aisle 'borrowing' food from people. They didn't know we were Weathermen; they just knew we were crazy. *That's* what we're about, being crazy motherfuckers and scaring the shit out of honky America."

Mark Rudd was not to be outdone. He said, "It's a wonderful feeling to hit a pig. It must be really wonderful to kill a pig or blow up a building." In debates that continued down this road, the mostly white gathering ended up increasing its venom against all white people who weren't revolutionaries, until one Weatherman shouted to the audience, "All white babies are pigs!"

Bernardine Dohrn was a brilliant law student who led SDS in a clear-minded way. Then her acid-influenced irrational pronouncements at a Weatherman conference lauded Charles Manson and his murderous followers.

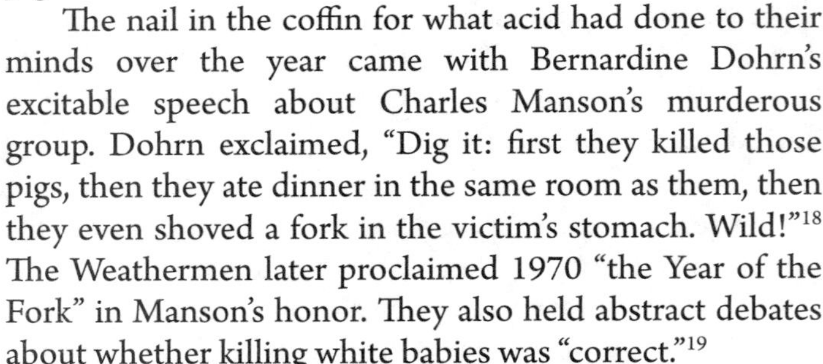

The nail in the coffin for what acid had done to their minds over the year came with Bernardine Dohrn's excitable speech about Charles Manson's murderous group. Dohrn exclaimed, "Dig it: first they killed those pigs, then they ate dinner in the same room as them, then they even shoved a fork in the victim's stomach. Wild!"[18] The Weathermen later proclaimed 1970 "the Year of the Fork" in Manson's honor. They also held abstract debates about whether killing white babies was "correct."[19]

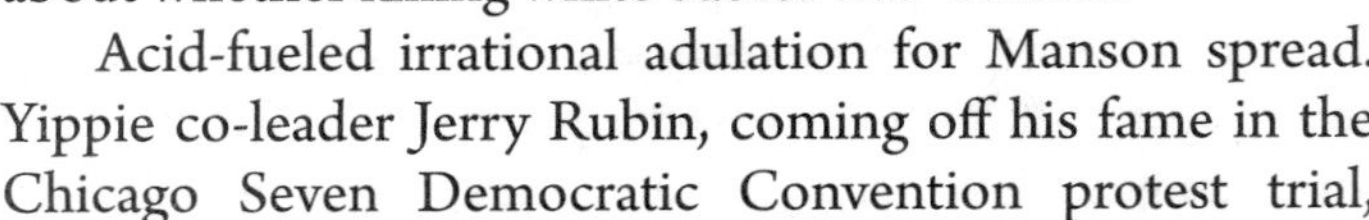

Acid-fueled irrational adulation for Manson spread. Yippie co-leader Jerry Rubin, coming off his fame in the Chicago Seven Democratic Convention protest trial, expressed his sentiments. Rubin said that when the accused murderer appeared on television, he fell in love with Manson's "cherub face and sparkling eyes."[20]

Researcher Martin Lee, in describing Weatherman's December National War Council, called it a "drug-crazed Wargasm conference." But he said that at the close of the four-day conference, the Weathermen "dropped acid and danced all night long," as if to indicate they had not eaten acid earlier. If, in fact, they were not on acid when they spoke, this suggests the lasting damage the acid did to their judgment. While dancing, Martin Lee said they burst into spirited chants, including the appropriate "Women Power!" and "Struggling Power!" but also "Sirhan Sirhan Power!" and "Charlie Manson Power!" The Sirhan cheer seemed very inappropriate, given that Robert Kennedy had evolved to oppose the Vietnam War.[21]

Kirkpatrick Sale said that in later months Bernardine Dohrn came to regret lauding Charles Manson. Sale stated that some Weathermen tried to stop using all drugs at this time. It's unknown how soon Dohrn and others did stop taking acid, but over the following years they did eventually regain much clarity that helped their anti-War and anti-racist activism. They conducted most of this activism while in hiding. All the Weathermen decided to go underground at this National War Council and to split up into revolutionary cells with eight to ten members.[22]

Activists Conduct Protest Bombings, Arsons Nationwide

By the end of 1969, activists inside and outside SDS and the Weathermen began using different militant tactics. Besides the rioting over civil rights issues, they also started setting buildings ablaze and conducting bombings. They focused these actions mostly on military-related buildings, while also targeting structures related to the government's murders of Black Panthers.

Kirkpatrick Sale wrote that the bombings actually started on college campuses in the spring of 1968 to protest the draft and the Vietnam War. He cited government statistics stating ten bombings occurred on campuses that spring. Protesters reportedly conducted eighty-four bombings in the spring of 1969 on campuses and ten more off-campus. Sale said, "In the 1969-70 school year, by an extremely conservative estimate, there were no fewer than 174 major bombings and attempts on campus, and at least seventy more off-campus incidents associated with the white political left, a rate of roughly one a day."[23]

By the end of 1969, police arrested some of these bombers, including a foursome: Jane Alpert, her boyfriend Sam Melville, Nate Yarrow and undercover agent George Demmerle on bombing charges. Yarrow's girlfriend, Patricia Swinton, had also taken part in the bombings and became a fugitive.

Bombings began in July of that year to protest U.S. violence against people of color in the Vietnam War, and U.S. government violence at home against the Panthers. The Weathermen later printed a book titled *Prairie Fire,* and Jane Alpert published a memoir, *Growing Up Underground.* Alpert and the Weatherman writers described how they bombed buildings owned by multinational companies that were bulwarks of American imperialist actions that brutalized third-world people of color. These bombers and others said they used the tactic of consistently calling administrators of the buildings in advance to insure they were cleared, to try and avoid any people getting hurt.[24]

Alpert's group is a good example of acid's effects on intelligent, committed activists who saw their own militancy increase while acid decreased their feelings of sanity and competency. Jane Alpert thought her activist boyfriend Sam Melville was going crazy after a period of acid use, when he talked about blowing up one of the only anti-War radio stations, WBAI. After Alpert told Melville her thoughts, he tore a mirror off the wall and almost hit her with it.[25]

Weeks later, Melville realized he was losing it, and said, "I don't seem to react well to drugs anymore." Informant George Demmerle hadn't been part of the group, but Melville accidentally got himself and others entrapped by Demmerle in a bizarre plan, after Melville told Demmerle almost everything about his bombings. Police arrested Demmerle before Demmerle revealed his agent status, and he testified against Melville and the others. (Demmerle and other undercover agents regularly encouraged bombings to gain activists' arrests.)[26]

Jane Alpert protested the bigoted justice system by refusing to accept the low bail set for her in New York when the Black Panther 21 had an early bail set at $100,000 each. The judge rescinded that bail allowance when two of the Panther 21 escaped to Algeria to join Eldridge Cleaver's Panther leadership there. Alpert finally agreed to leave jail on bail when one-time Harlem Panther leader Afeni Shakur sent her a note saying, "Revolutionaries belong in the streets, not in the jails."[27]

Several Weatherman cells followed suit with political bombings in late 1969. By 1970, they appropriately changed their name to the Weather Underground due to their status in hiding and to remove the sexist "man" part of their name. In 1974 they published *Prairie Fire: Political Statement of the Weather Underground,* in which they listed their long series of politically motivated bombings.

Bernardine Dohrn, Billy Ayers, Jeff Jones and Celia Sojourn wrote *Prairie Fire* and listed well over twenty political bombings they carried out "to retaliate for the most savage criminal attacks against black and Third World peoples, especially by the police apparatus." The Weather Underground and others also protested the government's forced draft of young American males to risk their lives carrying out this genocide.[28]

Prairie Fire listed bombings from October of 1969 to March of 1974. They included Chicago's Haymarket police statue twice and Chicago police cars after the police murders of Black Panther leaders Fred Hampton and Mark Clark. They also bombed the New York City police headquarters, the

Office of California prisons after the murder of Panther George Jackson in jail, and the Department of Corrections in Albany, New York after the police-guard mass murder of Attica prison inmates. Sam Melville helped organize the prisoners' several day takeover, and died in the Attica uprisings.

They further bombed in protest of "U.S. aggression and terror against Vietnam and the Third World," as well as "institutions that most cruelly oppress, exploit and delude the people." These included the "Harvard war research Center for International Affairs," the U.S. Capitol after the invasion of Laos, the Pentagon after the bombing of Hanoi and mining of the harbors of North Vietnam. Some other bombings they mentioned included the ROTC buildings, Vietnam War draft and recruiting centers, and the "ITT Latin America Headquarters, following the fascist counterrevolution in Chile in September 1973."[29]

Other activist groups joined the Weather Underground in bombing buildings owned by companies or agencies taking part in the government's murderous atrocities at home and abroad. They all reportedly called in advance to evacuate the buildings in order to spare bodily harm. They targeted ROTC buildings (197 acts of violence, from bombings to window breaking, including the destruction of at least nineteen buildings, an eight-fold increase over 1968-69 actions), government buildings (at least 232 bombings and attempts from January 1969 to June 1970, chiefly at Selective Service offices, induction centers, and federal office buildings). Activists also targeted corporate offices connected with American imperialism, such as the Bank of America, Chase Manhattan Bank, General Motors, IBM, Mobil, Standard Oil, and the United Fruit Company.[30]

The U.S. military's invasion of Cambodia in 1970, after already bombing the country for a year, sparked some of the biggest protests and reprisals. Sale described how five thousand people stormed the Justice Department building and needed to be turned away by massive doses of CN gas (a highly toxic riot-control agent). Both Attorney General John Mitchell and Weatherleader Billy Ayers said this "looked like the Russian Revolution." During nationwide protests, the National Guard shot twelve students in Buffalo and two in Santa Barbara, one fatally. In Berkeley, four thousand stormed an ROTC building with tear gas, bottles and rocks. At Harvard, several thousand took over Harvard Square, burning three police cars, and trashed banks and local stores. Students and street people caused $2 million of damage in several nights of demonstrations.[31]

While the Weather Underground had purposefully splintered into a multitude of cells around the country by 1970, they remained one of many guerilla groups. Other groups involved in such militancy included the New Year's Gang, the Quartermoon Tribe (Seattle), the Proud Eagle Tribe

(Boston), the Smiling Fox Tribe (New York City), an unnamed group around Columbia University, the John Brown Revolutionary League (Houston), the Motherfuckers (moved from New York to New Mexico) and various generally unofficial branches of the White Panthers. While the FBI murderously targeted the Black Panthers, they also targeted the Panther-inspired Puerto Rican Young Lords. Both the Panthers and Young Lords were in solidarity with these other groups.[32]

Temperature range: today 32-44; Saturday 28-42. Details on Page 39.

SUNDAY, DECEMBER 22, 1974 — 60 CENTS

HUGE C.I.A. OPERATION REPORTED IN U.S. AGAINST ANTIWAR FORCES, OTHER DISSIDENTS IN NIXON YEARS

Richard Helms — James R. Schlesinger — William E. Colby

The New York Times

FILES ON CITIZENS

Helms Reportedly Got Surveillance Data in Charter Violation

By SEYMOUR M. HERSH

Special to The New York Times

WASHINGTON, Dec. 21—The Central Intelligence Agency, directly violating its charter, conducted a massive, illegal domestic intelligence operation during the Nixon Administration against the antiwar movement and other dissident groups in the United States.

Investigative reporters eventually found out that the CIA was working with the FBI in targeting American dissidents inside the U.S.

In May of 1970, National Guardsmen fired 61 shots at random into a crowd of student protesters, from a distance that was longer than a football field, at Kent State University in Ohio. They killed four and wounded nine, paralyzing one from the neck down. Ten days later, white police officers also killed two black student protesters and wounded twelve more at Jackson State University in Mississippi, which garnered less media coverage.

These events sparked 169 bombings and burnings of ROTC and other military-linked buildings that month. Student strikes, violent protests, and takeovers led to the shutdown of over a third of the country's over thirteen hundred colleges and universities for a period of time. Some fifty schools shut down for the entire year. All the National Guardsmen at Kent State were subsequently exonerated for any wrongdoing.[33]

In February of 1970, a trial of the New York Panther 21 had begun with trial Judge John Murtagh presiding over it. A report said the Weathermen set off a bomb at the home of Judge Murtagh. They did this because of Murtagh's well-documented attempt to permanently imprison the New York Black Panther leaders, who were later acquitted of all charges.[34]

Two weeks after the bomb went off in Murtagh's home, a New York Weather Underground cell's bombs accidentally exploded in their temporary home. They had been staying in a Greenwich Village townhouse owned by Cathy Wilkerson's father, a radio station owner who was away on vacation. Wilkerson had taken the opportunity to assemble bombs there, resulting in the complete demolition of the four-story building.

The wife and ex-wife of actors Dustin Hoffman and Henry Fonda, respectively, lived nearby. They helped two naked Weather Underground women, Cathy Wilkerson and Kathy Boudin, get out of the rubble and into clothes. Wilkerson, Boudin and three others escaped. Another three Weather Underground members—Ted Gold, Terry Robbins and Diana Oughton—were blown up beyond initial recognition.[35]

Notes

1 Martin Lee and Bruce Shlain, *Acid Dreams: The Complete Social History of LSD, the CIA, the Sixties, and Beyond* (New York: Grove Press, 1994), p. 282.

2 Jane Alpert, *Growing Up Underground* (New York: Citadel Press, 1990), pp. 145, 185, 187.

3 Lee and Shlain, *Acid Dreams*, p. 231. Despite being a member of the White Panthers in 1969, with a supposed allegiance to the Black Panthers, Ken Kelley wrote articles smearing Black Panther national cofounder Huey Newton just after Newton's 1989 murder. Writing for *East Bay Express,* one of four Bay-Area alternative weeklies, Kelley began by quoting an elderly black woman he purported hearing "in an Oakland dentist's office. Reading about Newton's funeral in the *San Francisco Chronicle,* she encountered the quotation of a minister describing Newton as Black America's Moses. 'If he's our Moses,' she retorted, 'then give me that old Pharaoh Ramses any old day ... Huey Newton was just a plain old thug. Period. All these fools are trying to make him into a saint.'" Ken Kelley, "Huey: I'll Never Forget," *East Bay Express,* Sept. 15, 1989, Vol. 11, No. 49. Quoted in Hugh Pearson, *The Shadow of the Panther: Huey Newton and the Price of Black Power in America.* Another source said that this article by Kelley also claimed that Newton confessed to him of having personally murdered Kathleen Smith and having ordered the murder of Betty van Patter: http://en.wikipedia.org/wiki/Death_of_Betty_Van_Patter. Here, Kelley was named as Newton's PR agent, but Pearson said Kelley was only very briefly a PR agent for the Black Panthers.

4 Kirkpatrick Sale, *SDS: The Rise and Development of the Students for a Democratic Society...* (New York: Vintage, 1973), p. 580.

5 Sale, *SDS*, pp. 587, 601.

6 Sale, *SDS*, pp. 601, 628.

7 Sale, *SDS*, pp. 475-77.

8 Sale, *SDS*, p. 602. Top leftist intellectual, Professor Noam Chomsky felt extremely inspired by Fred Hampton, the 20-year-old Illinois Panther leader. Chomsky said he was one of the only white people to attend Hampton's funeral, flying from Boston to Chicago for it. Personal interview, Boston, April 2009.

9 Sale, *SDS*, pp. 603-04.

10 Sale, *SDS*, pp. 608-09.

11 Sale, *SDS*, pp. 608-13. One bizarre city official liked to join the police in such brutality. He ended up diving head first into a brick wall trying to grab an elusive demonstrator. The Chicago Press found the demonstrator guilty of murder before a real trial acquitted him.

12 Sale, *SDS*, p. 609.

13 Documents introduced as evidence in case of *Ibera Hampton, et al., Plaintiffs-Appellants*

v. Edward Hanrahan, et al., Defendants-Appellees (Nos. 77-1968, 77-1210 and 77-1370) Transcript at 33716. In Ward Churchill Jim Vander Wall, *Agents of Repression: The FBI's Secret Wars Against the Black Panther Party and the American Indian Movement* (Boston: South End, 1988), pp. 73, 403n. On FBI falsely telling police that the Panthers killed a cop and O'Neal drugging his punch, see *Me and My Shadow: Investigation of the political left by the United States government*, Executive Producer Tarabu Betserai, Pacifica Radio Archives, track 4. Hampton's drugging also comes from Hampton's mother's testimony that Hampton was talking on the phone with her and fell asleep mid-sentence, and from an FBI agent's trial admission. Also see former FBI Counterintelligence Agent, M. Wesley Swearingen's statements of how the FBI set up Hampton's murder: Wes Swearingen, *FBI Secrets: An Agent's Expose* (Boston: South End Press, 1992), pp. 88-89.

14 Sale, *SDS*, p. 615.

15 Sale, *SDS*, p. 625. Sale quoted the *Liberated Guardian*, 9/27/70, and the *Berkeley Barb*.

16 Lee, *Acid Dreams*, pp. 256-57.

17 Among other decorations, one wall of their meeing room had alternating black and red commemorative pictures of Fred Hampton. A banner showed many bullets, each bearing the name of a Weatherenemy—Alioto, Daley, the *Guardian*, Humphrey, Johnson, Nixon and Reagan. Included in those enemies was Sharon Tate, the pregnant victim of the Manson murders. Posters showed a rifle with a high-powered rifle sight labeled "PIECE NOW." From the ceiling hung a six-and-a-half foot cardboard machine gun. Sale, *SDS*, pp. 626-27.

18 Sale, *SDS*, p. 628.

19 Sale, *SDS*, p. 628, and Lee and Shlain, *Acid Dreams*, p. 257.

20 Lee and Shlain, *Acid Dreams*, p. 257.

21 Lee and Shlain, *Acid Dreams*, p. 258.

22 Sale, *SDS*, pp. 628-30.

23 Sale, *SDS*, p. 632.

24 Alpert, *Growing Up Underground*, pp. 225-33.

25 Alpert, *Growing Up Underground*, pp. 159, 180

26 Alpert, *Growing Up Underground*, pp.182, 223, 234-35. Also on Demmerle, see Peter Zimroth's interview and coverage of him in Peter Zimroth, *Perversions of Justice* (New York: Viking Press, 1974), pp. 63-67.

27 Alpert, *Growing Up Underground*, p. 234.

28 Bernardine Dohrn, Billy Ayers, Jeff Jones and Celia Sojourn, *Prairie Fire: Political Statement of the Weather Undergound* (Communications Co., 1974); for list of places bombed, p. 16.

29 Dohrn et al., *Prairie Fire*, p. 16. Lee and Shlain, *Acid Dreams*, p. 260.

30 Sale, *SDS*, p. 632.

31 Sale, *SDS*, p. 633. On Cambodia, see http://chnm.gmu.edu/hardhats/cambodia.html.

32 Sale, *SDS*, pp. 633-34.

33 Sale, *SDS*, pp. 635-37, 641.

34 Zimroth, *Perversions of Justice*, p. 52.

35 Sale, *SDS*, pp. 3-5.

Chapter Twelve

CIA Traffics Acid; Leary & Panthers; Woodstock

If U.S. intelligence bodies collaborated in an effort to drug the entire generation of Americans, then the reason they did so was to disorient it, sedate it, and de-politicize it.

– Prof. Carl Oglesby, 1966 SDS president in "The Acid Test and How It Failed," *The National Reporter*, Fall 1988.[1]

U.S. intelligence appeared to counter the threat of radical underground groups by targeting their mental functioning. They used ever more complex schemes to continue promoting acid use as part of radical protest. A prime example came with the Weather Underground's operation to free Timothy Leary.

Starting in the summer of 1969, the Weather Underground cells had thrown "themselves into Mao and Marx, they practiced karate and survived on brown rice diets ... accustomed property feelings needed to be rooted out, so that no one felt attached to 'personal' belongings ... individualism and selfishness had to give away to a collective spirit." Also important at this time was that "they tried abstinence from drugs, alcohol, even pets."[2] But some Weather cells, including the leadership cell of Bernardine Dohrn, Jeff Jones, Billy Ayers and others, still thought of acid guru Timothy Leary as a hero.[3]

Timothy Leary's top benefactor, Millbrook estate owner William Mellon Hitchcock, had taken a more active hand in LSD distribution. His Brotherhood of Eternal Love had become the top American acid trafficker in the country.[4] By 1967 Hitchcock financed the Brotherhood's LSD manufacturing and distribution group. The Brotherhood produced ten times more LSD than when they had previously worked with Owsley Stanley. Owsley's partner, Tim Scully, remained a Brotherhood chemist.[5]

Hitchcock stored much of his money in Castle Bank in the Bahamas, which was "set up by the CIA as a funding conduit for a wide range of covert operations in the Caribbean," according to Lee and Shlain. Castle Bank's founder, using a CIA proprietary company, Sea Supply, set up the Golden Triangle mercenary army, which cultivated fields of opium poppies. Sea Supply also supplied weapons to anti-Communist guerillas in that Golden Triangle area near Vietnam.[6]

With the increased militancy of anti-War protests came a huge increase in LSD production and distribution worldwide, supported by U.S. intelligence. Hitchcock's links to U.S. intelligence, along with his late 1960s acid trafficking, typified the continuance of MK-Ultra work. In the summer of 1969, a key figure, Ronald Hadley Stark, came into the Brotherhood of Eternal Love with a kilo of LSD (1.5 million doses). When police in Italy later arrested Stark in 1975, an Italian judge ended up releasing him because he "belonged to the American Secret Services."[7]

After Timothy Leary left Hitchcock's Millbrook estate in New York in the summer of 1969, Hitchcock gave Leary a $14,000 check and had him relocate near his Brotherhood of Eternal Love's Laguna Beach headquarters just south of Los Angeles. The Brotherhood provided for Leary's living expenses there and paid for his frequent travels to Berkeley, where they rented a second place for him.[8]

In September of 1969, police arrested Leary on a marijuana possession charge. Leary went to trial a number of months later, and his sentence made big news, with Leary going to a minimum-security prison. The Weather Underground planned a prison break for Leary. On September 20 of 1970, Leary jumped a fence and climbed into a van driven by Weathermen, before going to the hiding place of Bernardine Dohrn, Jeff Jones and others. The Weather Underground referred to a "bombing" connected to this, which might have been a small detonation for a distraction of some sort.[9]

The Weather leaders described Leary as a political prisoner who was "captured for the work he did in helping all of us begin the task of creating a new culture on the barren wasteland that has been imposed on us by Democrats, Republicans, Capitalists and creeps." They declared acid and weed would help make a better world in the future, but for now "we are at war ... peace is only possible in the destruction of US Imperialism."[10]

The Weather leaders got stoned with Leary and housed him for a while. Leary shaved the top of his head, dyed his hair and grew a moustache. He made proclamations through the Weather leaders' communications channels. Leary, changing for the times, no longer played the pacifist. He now said, "Shoot to Live ... To shoot a genocidal robot policeman in defense of life is a sacred act." Leary seemed to try to appeal to the Black Panthers' reaction to their genocide by the FBI and police.[11]

But Leary added, "World War III is now being waged by short-haired robots whose deliberate aim is to destroy the complex web of free wild life by the imposition of mechanical order ... Blow the mechanical mind with Holy Acid ... dose them ... dose them." He urged everyone to "stay high and wage the revolutionary war."

The Weather Underground helped Leary make this escape with a false passport. Leary and his wife flew to Algeria, where the Black Panthers in Exile had a chapter. Eldridge Cleaver, the former national Black Panther Minister of Information, headed the group with his wife, Kathleen, the former National Panther Secretary of Communications (spokeswoman). They accepted Leary, announcing at a "solidarity" press conference, "Dr. Leary is part of our movement."[12] The Weather Underground role in Leary's prison break helped Eldridge Cleaver accept him. Cleaver had previously announced his solidarity with SDS, the hippies, Yippies and Weathermen.[13]

The Cleavers needed to keep their security tight, and they trusted few, particularly since they didn't get any kind of safety promises from the Algerian government. U.S. intelligence spies remained a concern, and Leary attracted media attention. The Panthers frisked all visitors, even Leary's friends, and drugs were banned from Panther headquarters except on rare occasions when Eldridge Cleaver said it was okay. Leary tried to persuade Cleaver to "free yourself internally before you attempt to free yourself behaviorally."[14]

Not long into Leary's stay, Cleaver put Leary and his wife under house arrest. CIA agents had infiltrated the Cleavers' Panther encampment, and undercover FBI agents in the New York Panthers were sending poison pen letters to Cleaver. But Cleaver had his own reason to put the Learys under house arrest. Leary had smuggled 20,000 hits of LSD into Algeria with plans of turning Africans on to acid. Kathleen Cleaver said her husband went to the government and showed them the package of acid he had confiscated from Leary.[15]

The CIA reportedly aided Timothy Leary's travels to the Black Panthers-in-Exile Algerian chapter, where Minister of Information Eldridge Cleaver first welcomed him, but then expelled him for bringing a huge amount of LSD for proselytizing.

Eldridge Cleaver became disgusted with Leary's stoned escapades. He sent out a communiqué to the underground press saying, "Something is wrong with Leary's brain. We want people to gather their wits, sober up and get down to the serious business of destroying the Babylonian empire." Cleaver declared the psychedelic counterculture quasipolitical and dangerous. Lee and Shlain detailed Cleaver's communication about LSD as describing Leary's attempt to sell him on "drug induced totalitarianism." Cleaver concluded by saying, "To all those of you who looked to Dr. Leary for inspiration and leadership, we want to say to you that your god is dead because his mind has been blown by acid."[16]

Evidence indicates that much of Timothy Leary's prison break and travel to Algeria was a CIA propaganda and espionage operation. For one thing, Leary admitted knowingly working for the CIA since 1962. Secondly, Hitchcock and U.S. intelligence agent Ron Stark's Brotherhood of Eternal Love financed every step of it, giving the unwitting Weather Underground $25,000 to fund Leary's escape from prison. When that plan succeeded, Stark flew to the Brotherhood of Eternal Love's ranch in California and celebrated the operation's success.[17]

Researchers Lee and Shlain said that the Brotherhood also supplied a group of trained professionals to take Leary and his wife out of Algeria. Undercover CIA agents who had infiltrated Cleaver's Panthers in Exile, likely aided Leary's freedom and departure. When Cleaver put Leary under house arrest, the Brotherhood bought his freedom for another $25,000. A CIA-employed Algerian bureaucrat arranged exit visas for Leary and his wife.[18]

Upon leaving Algeria, Leary entered Switzerland, where authorities imprisoned him while reviewing his case. A mysterious benefactor and gunrunner, Michel-Gustave Hauchard, pampered Leary while he was detained. Hauchard had strong connections in the Swiss government to achieve Leary's release. Hitchcock met Leary in Europe, as did LSD's founding chemist, Albert Hoffman. Hoffman had worked for American intelligence, working with high-level CIA MK-Ultra agents. It is telling that Leary asked Hoffman if there was any evidence of brain damage caused by LSD. Hoffman said the dangers were only psychological and could be avoided with supportive conditions while tripping.[19]

This statement made Leary appear more a burnt-out, manipulated figurehead than a lifetime committed agent. California police busted Leary when he returned home in 1973, and a judge sentenced him to five years for escaping from prison, plus twenty from his earlier trial.[20] Leary then identified the Weathermen and their hideout for the FBI in 1974.[21]

Leary was sentenced to twenty-five years in prison, but in 1976 the government paroled Leary early for good behavior. Leary went on to do a college lecture circuit and even performed in nightclubs as a stand-up philosopher. He later did a college circuit debate tour with G. Gordon Liddy, President Nixon's operative busted for Watergate spying on Democrats, and the local sheriff who had arrested Leary at Millbrook in 1967.[22]

The original high-profile sentencing of Leary appeared to serve as a psychological operation and propaganda coup. It continued Leary's legend and the reverse psychology promotion of acid. Since most youth were anti-government at this time, busting Leary made it appear that the government didn't want youth to use acid. Actually, CIA agents and contacts remained the largest manufacturers and traffickers of acid. The U.S. intelligence's use of acid's subtle brain impairment to bring down the leftist rebellion continued in order to counter an onslaught of tactics to stop the Vietnam War.

Protesters Help End Vietnam War

Many groups helped to end the Vietnam War. One was a Baltimore-based clergy-linked peace movement. After standard marches, rallies and letter writing campaigns, the Baltimore group took a new approach to ending the drafting of young Americans to die in the Vietnam War. In October of 1967, Catholic priest Philip Berrigan, artist Tom Lewis, writer Dan Eberhart and Rev. James Mengel, entered a Selective Service Board office in Baltimore and poured blood on draft files. For this action they became known as the Baltimore Four.

While out on bail, Berrigan, his fellow priest and brother, Daniel, and seven other Baltimore activists took draft files from a Catonsville neighborhood of Baltimore and burned them in the parking lot with homemade napalm. They left a statement saying America's "religious bureaucracy ... is racist, is an accomplice in this war, and is hostile to the poor."[23] This action and some of these same activists helped organize one hundred similar actions nationwide, culminating in the Media, Pennsylvania, FBI office break-in and document theft that exposed the FBI's Counterintelligence Program (Cointelpro), U.S. intelligence's war on anti-War and civil rights activists.[24]

Meanwhile, U.S. military atrocities in Vietnam grew. An "elite" Tiger Force of U.S. troops tortured and executed prisoners. They threw prisoners into "tiger cages" built by Texas military contractor RMK-BRJ, the forerunner of Haliburton subsidiary KBR. The Tiger Force cut off executed prisoners' ears as souvenirs and made them into necklaces.

New York Times bestselling author Mike Davis reviewed more Vietnam War atrocities and quoted officers who had witnessed them. The U.S. military assault on the Vietnamese "grew to the routine slaughter of unarmed farmers, elderly people, even small children." As one former sergeant said, "It didn't matter if they were civilians. If they weren't supposed to be in an area, we shot them. If they didn't understand fear, I taught it to them." Women and children were regularly killed. "A 13 year-old girl's throat was slit after she was sexually assaulted ... an unarmed teenager was shot in the back ... and a baby was decapitated to remove a necklace." The latter incident finally got public attention and led to a five-year investigation. Eventually, members of President Gerald Ford's administration buried the case.[25]

Students and other young adults heard about many of these atrocities, and they saw friends come home in coffins or as amputees. They empathized with Vietnamese, feared being drafted and killed, and responded in various ways. They tried teach-ins, moved on to nonviolent rallies and marches, then to civil disobedience, then violent opposition.

Students and young adults posed an increasingly important threat to the oligarchy that supported the Vietnam War. The Alcohol, Tobacco and Firearms Division of the U.S. Treasury did an extensive survey on anti-War protest violence between January 1969 and June 1970, which

> established that there were no fewer than 40,934 bombings, attempts, and threats (by admittedly "conservative" estimate) during these fifteen and a half months, and of the 36% it was able to attribute, something like 8,255 incidents were related to "campus disturbances." By extrapolation, we can figure that of the other 64%, at least 13,000 incidents could be attributed to student activity, for a total of 21,000 incidents, or approximately 50 every day; of those, also by extrapolation, one can estimate some 2,800 were actual bombings, or approximately six a day for the entire period.[26]

Other researchers gave similarly large figures, and these actions inspired violent protest in many countries. Author Peter Zimroth cited the Assistant Secretary of the Treasury, who reported on compiled police sources documenting 4,000 explosive and incendiary bombings over a period of sixteen months. These acts resulted in "40 deaths, 384 injuries, almost $22 billion in property damage."[27] Violent anti-government protests increased in Spain, Italy, France, England, Germany, Mexico and many other countries from 1968-1970, as news from American media traveled globally.[28]

One other aspect of these events complicates the certain identification of the perpetrators of all these American war-protest actions. When investigators looked at the 1970 Kent State shootings, they found a witness, Dr. Elaine Wellin, who overheard uniformed and plainclothes officers around a ROTC building before and after it was set ablaze. Wellin overheard someone with a walkie-talkie say they should not send down the fire truck, as the ROTC building was not on fire *yet*. In that same incident, an FBI undercover agent fired a gun four times, which soldiers believed to be protester sniper fire, one minute before the Ohio National Guard commander ordered his guard to shoot at the protesters. This puts into question how many other incidents were orchestrated to bring down martial force against anti-War protesters and try to scare them away from their protest actions.[29]

Around May of 1971, war protesters tried another tactic. A group calling themselves the Mayday Tribe (or Above-ground Weather Underground) put out a call for a new civil disobedience action—the blockage of government all over Washington DC until the war was ended. Various anti-War activist collectives made their own decisions around blocking roads, bridges, and government offices with barriers and their bodies. The idea was to produce an action that created as much social chaos as possible while still maintaining the support of much of the general public.

About 25,000 took part in this action. The Nixon administration used approximately 14,000 police and national guardsmen to arrest 13,500 people. It was called the largest sweep-arrest in U.S. history, turning martial law on bustling Washington DC.[30]

A final tactic, "fragging" by soldiers, also helped to end the war. Fragging was a shorthand term for setting up a fragmentation hand grenade to explode and kill a soldier's own commanding officer or fellow soldier. A particularly large number of black soldiers joined other soldiers in conducting fragging against officers who tried to force them into combat zones, partly to oppose the war and partly to spare their own lives. Military lawyers estimated that only 10% of these fragging perpetrators ended up in court.

A Congressional investigation reported 1,016 incidents of fragging between 1969 and 1972. Historian David Cortwright noted that incidents of enlisted men assaulting their commanding officers with all sorts of weapons were likely in the thousands near the end of the war. By 1972, President Nixon began de-escalating the Vietnam War.[31]

Superspy Helps CIA Push Acid Globally

In the summer of 1969, the top acid trafficker in the world, Ronald Stark, came into the Brotherhood of Eternal Love with a kilo of LSD (1.5 million doses).[32] Ronald Hadley Stark started trafficking LSD on multiple continents. Stark had business contacts with the Japanese Mafia, who could smuggle acid into mainland China, the Soviet Union, and other Communist countries. British researcher David Black extensively detailed how Stark set up LSD laboratories and international trafficking operations.[33]

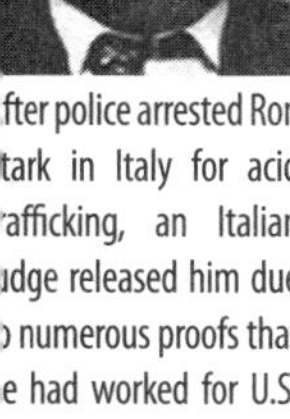

fter police arrested Ron tark in Italy for acid afficking, an Italian idge released him due o numerous proofs that e had worked for U.S. ntelligence since 1960.

Stark came to London at the same time as Cord Meyer, who had previously worked as Cultural Affairs Chief for the CIA in Washington. To researcher Black, Meyer coming to London appeared more than coincidence. In his book *Acid,* he extensively detailed Stark's work in the CIA and regarding Cord Meyer. Black wrote, "Meyer was the overseer of a world-wide operation to infiltrate international student organizations and promote various cultural foundations which were, in reality, CIA fronts." In 1967, someone leaked this to the American leftist *Ramparts* magazine, and the CIA "kicked Meyer upstairs to serve as the CIA station chief in London ... the same period Ron Stark arrived there."[34]

By the late 1960s, researchers discovered that the CIA was carrying out operations against Americans, contrary to its charter, which forbids it to spy domestically. Of course, the CIA's Operation Chaos and MK-Ultra worked with the FBI, while Operations such as "Merrimac" embraced various forms of domestic spying. The *New York Times* archived government documents describing Operation Chaos as the parent operation to Merrimac that targeted anti-War activists. Stark's activities exemplified the continuation of CIA MK-Ultra's operations in a widening global arena.[35]

By 1969, Stark worked on four continents, in at least a dozen countries. He went from dining with millionaires to hanging out in California hippie communes and elsewhere. In 1970, Stark acknowledged he worked for the CIA.[36]

There is plenty of evidence to support Stark's status as a U.S. intelligence MK-Ultra superspy. Though physically unimposing, he was described as an accomplished con artist who could speak ten languages fluently and talk circles around anybody. He was bisexual and used drugs and sex to manipulate people. Stark claimed a relationship to the Whitneys, one of America's richest families. He also maintained an expensive Greenwich Village apartment, understood international finance, claimed seats on many company boards, and assumed Hitchcock's role as banker and money manager of the Brotherhood.[37]

Ron Stark communicated on a regular basis with the American Embassy in London, which helped him set up his Belgium lab after the CIA shut down his Paris operation due to local investigators. He had 20 kilos of LSD (fifty million doses) at the Belgium location. Lee and Shlain report it was the largest amount of acid ever to come from one single underground source, and most of it was sold in the United States. When federal drug agents broke up the Brotherhood, Stark received all the money and property confiscated. Reportedly, Stark immediately started a new British LSD organization to take the Brotherhood's place.[38]

As corroborated by British researcher David Black, Lee and Shlain detailed how Stark maneuvered between Europe, Asia, Africa and America. Besides running several acid laboratories and trafficking it worldwide, he also ran a cocaine distribution ring in the San Francisco Bay area without his Brotherhood cohorts knowing about it. By the mid-1970s, Stark's British group set up acid factories in London and then Wales. Black's estimates differ from Lee and Shlain's claim about Belgium producing the most LSD with 50 million doses. British Inspector Dick Lee found that Stark's laboratories produced "over a hundred million dosages of LSD" in three years, before a police operation uncovered their activities, against British intelligence wishes.[39]

As the lead British detective to uncover this LSD operation, Inspector Dick Lee wrote a book about his investigation, *Operation Julie* (a name made famous in a song by The Clash). Inspector Lee said "a British chemical company supplied Red China with 400 million dosage units of LSD." Did these go to undercover agents working there to undermine Communist China? Did the Opium Wars turn into the Acid War? Inspector Lee received a warning from a high official that "he was not to do anything that might embarrass Her

Majesty's Government." Lee's superiors began boxing in his team's investigation, saying they weren't allowed to inquire about the LSD traffickers' Swiss banking accounts, nor their bank accounts in Germany and France. They also prohibited Lee from investigating anyone not already in custody by 1977.[40]

More evidence came forth regarding MI6 and the Tavistock Institute's close work with the CIA's MK-Ultra. Black stated that Ron Stark worked with an intelligence agent who also worked with Howard Marks, while Britain's MI6 was paying Marks as he was trafficking acid.[41] Scientist Steve Abrahms, of the Human Ecology Fund doing work in Britain, also exposed the high-level joint effort of various U.S. intelligence agencies regarding MK-Ultra: "Stark had told me he had worked for the Department of Defense and was seconded to the White House."[42]

When authorities arrested Ron Stark in Italy in 1975, they found interesting evidence amongst Stark's possessions that showed his numerous global government and cultural connections. Among Stark's belongings, police found letters headed, "Dear Ron," from an economic counselor at the American embassy in London. A draft letter from Stark to the American vice-consul in Florence talked about how conditions were not yet right for a coup in Italy. Other letters connected Stark to acid dealers in Amsterdam and Israel. Stark had a British passport with a different name, stamped by Lebanon, Holland and Sweden. Stark also had phone numbers for band members of well-known rock groups, including Rod Stewart's old band, Faces, the band Deep Purple, and the Grateful Dead.[43]

David Black further detailed how Stark worked as a "fixer in deals involving various Arab royal families." Stark represented Imam Moussa Sadr in business deals. Sadr had a 1,000-strong army protecting his cannabis plantations in Lebanon.[44]

And finally, Stark's documents verified his connection with Italy's Mafia and undercover agents.[45] According to a 300-page report issued by Italian and Belgian investigators, U.S. and other NATO intelligence forces targeted Italy from the 1950s on. The report, confirmed by the Italian Prime Minister in 1990, stated that England's MI6 and the CIA left "stay behind" armies across Europe that included many agents who had been loyal to Hitler, Mussolini and other fascist Axis-country leaders in World War II. These agents worked directly with the CIA and MI6, creating a parallel secret service to the Italian government's intelligence agencies.[46]

An Italian court sentenced Ron Stark to fourteen years in prison for his drug trafficking. Lee and Shlain described how, in 1978, the courts assigned Bologna magistrate Graziano Gori, "to investigate and clarify Stark's ties to the US, the Arabs, Italian terrorists, and other mysteries. A few weeks later Gori was killed in a car accident. The Italian government subsequently charged Stark with 'armed banditry' for his role in aiding and abetting terrorist activities, but he never stood trial on these charges."[47]

In April of 1979, Judge Giorgio Floridia ordered Stark released from prison. Floridia wrote that he released Stark due to "an impressive series of scrupulously enumerated proofs" that Stark was actually a U.S. intelligence agent. Floridia said these and many other "circumstances suggest that from 1960 onwards Stark belonged to the American secret services." An Italian parliamentary commission wrote a long report reviewing domestic terrorism in the 1960s and '70s. In a special section titled, "The Case of Ron Stark," they restated the CIA's use of Stark.[48] Judge Floridia also stated that Stark received regular payments from Fort Lee, "known to be the site of a CIA office," and that one of Stark's assistants also worked for U.S. intelligence.[49]

Acid Damage Diverts Millions; Woodstock

Many counterculture veterans endorsed the notion that the CIA disseminated massive amounts of street acid in order to "deflate the political potency of youth rebellion." These included the Beat generation writer William S. Burroughs and White Panther founder John Sinclair. Burroughs wrote about his addiction in his autobiographical novels, *Junkie* and *Naked Lunch*, before stating that LSD made people less competent and implying that was why U.S. intelligence tried to get people using it.[50]

Former acid enthusiast John Sinclair had started the White Panthers based on the socialist Black Panthers and also managed the rock group MC5. Sinclair agreed that the CIA could have been behind the whole acid movement to dampen the effectiveness of the anti-War movement. "It makes perfect sense to me," he said. "We thought at the time that as a result of our LSD-inspired activities great things would happen. And, of course, it didn't ... They were moving that shit around. Down on the street, nobody knew what was going on." Sinclair also said LSD blinded him from seeing that everyone didn't turn on to radical politics from acid.[51]

With their assets and growing control over mainstream media, the CIA had the means for many MK-Ultra operations. They expanded the size of their 1965 Acid Tests at the three-day long San Francisco Trips Festivals of 1966, where several thousand attended each day.[52] This increased to tens of thousands at the "Human Be-Ins" started in San Francisco.[53] And twice as many people attended the 1967 Monterey Pop Music Fest, when San Francisco was an acid wasteland filled with undercover CIA agents. An estimated 400,000 people attended the Woodstock Music Festival in upstate New York in 1969. Dealers made sure there was plenty of the Brotherhood's Orange Sunshine acid for the crowd. "Nearly everybody was blazed on something and unarmed policemen, clothed in bright red T-shirts with the words 'love' and 'peace' emblazoned across their chest ... let the dopers do their thing. Lumps of hash were there." Once someone is very stoned on these so-called "gateway" drugs, it's easier to talk them into trying a new drug such as acid.[54]

At Woodstock, many groups started, or infiltrated, by undercover agents attended: the Yippies, the Crazies (including at least one FBI informant, George Demmerle), Motherfuckers, White Panthers, and Weathermen. Attendee Jane Alpert detailed her conversation there with undercover agent George Demmerle, the Crazies founder. The Yippies' Bob Pierson, also an undercover agent, and suspected undercover agents in the Merry Pranksters attended.[55] Thirty-one bands played at Woodstock, including the Grateful Dead and other acid-rock bands. There weren't any political speeches at this festival except one unsuccessful attempt by Abbie Hoffman.[56]

Although known for conducting bombings, the Weather Underground and those in similar activist cells were trying to battle injustice by producing newsletters, books, teach-ins, and participating in rallies. This mass dissemination of LSD decreased their competency as they struggled against the oligarchy and its vast resources.

Acid use also became a staple of those who considered themselves "hippies." Former black activists have stated how police repression of their fellow activists led them to "drop out of activism and join the hippies." It's unknown how many other activists the hippie world lured with the attraction of free love and supposed stoned bliss. But with the vastly greater amount of acid produced and distributed by Stark's minions, the answer is likely at least tens of millions of people worldwide.[57]

One book, *Substance and Shadow,* cited Gallup polls reflecting this increased LSD use in the U.S. The poll found only 1% of college students responded to having tried LSD in 1967. That rose to 4% in 1969 and more than tripled to 14% by the end of 1970, peaking in the mid-'70s. Another report noted that by 1970, between one and two million Americans had tried LSD.[58]

Other surveys reported that among young adults, LSD use kept rising until 1979. That year, 25% of young adults, between 18 and 25, reported having used a hallucinogen (predominantly LSD) in their lifetime. Another study found that 16% of high school seniors had used a hallucinogen in 1975, while 25% used one by 1980, the last year before a decrease began among that age group.[59]

These survey results suggest that while Stark was in prison from 1975-79, his acid laboratories continued without him. The ongoing investigations of these laboratories and distribution rings by honest lower-level police officials, like British Inspector Dick Lee, were a factor in decreasing their activities.

By 1980, with conservative Republican Ronald Reagan capturing the White House, the feeling of a need to sabotage young minds may have decreased.

U.S. intelligence had duped millions of idealistic young adults into damaging themselves. Carl Oglesby, a 1966 president of the Students for a Democratic Society, wrote about LSD and '60s activism, summing it up well in an introspective article. After SDS, Oglesby worked as a journalist and then taught politics at the Massachusetts Institute of Technology and Dartmouth College. In a 1988 article, "The Acid Test and How It Failed," Oglesby said,

> What we have to contemplate nevertheless is the possibility that the great American acid trip, no matter how distinctive of the rebellion of the 1960s it came to appear, was in fact the result of a despicable government conspiracy.... If U.S. intelligence bodies collaborated in an effort to drug the entire generation of Americans, then the reason they did so was to disorient it, sedate it, and de-politicize it.[60]

Notes

1 Carl Oglesby, "The Acid Test and How It Failed," *The National Reporter*, Fall 1988, p. 10. See this excerpt on web at http://www.foreignpolicyjournal.com/2011/02/07/the-globalist-web-of-subversion/6/.

2 Kirkpatrick Sale, *SDS: The rise and development of the Students for a Democratic Society* (New York: Vintage, 1973), p. 584.

3 See their glorification of breaking Timothy Leary from jail in Bernardine Dohrn, Billy Ayers, Jeff Jones and Celia Sojourn, *Prairie Fire: Political Statement of the Weather Undergound,* (Communications Co., 1974), p. 16.

4 Martin Lee and Bruce Shlain, *Acid Dreams: The Complete Social History of LSD, the CIA, the Sixties, and Beyond* (New York: Grove Press, 1994), pp. 241-43.

5 Lee and Shlain, *Acid Dreams,* p. 242.

6 Lee and Shlain, *Acid Dreams,* pp. 245-6, 246n. Also see Peter Dale Scott, *Drugs, Oil, and War* (New York: Rowman & Littlefield, 2003), p. 122. Note that Hitchcock provided $5 million to Bahamian company Resorts International. Hitchcock attended their 1968 New Year's Eve party at which Richard Nixon was their guest of honor, as he launched his presidential run. The Resorts president donated $100,000 to Nixon's campaign.

7 Lee and Shlain, *Acid Dreams,* p. 281. Also see David Black, *Acid: The Secret History of LSD* (London: Satin/Vision, 1998), pp. 175, 186ff.

8 Lee and Shlain, *Acid Dreams,* p. 238.

9 Dohrn et al., *Prairie Fire,* p. 16.

10 Lee and Shlain, *Acid Dreams,* pp. 263-65. Dohrn et al., *Prairie Fire,* p. 16.

11 Lee and Shlain, *Acid Dreams,* p. 265.

12 Lee and Shlain, *Acid Dreams,* pp. 265, 267.

13 Lee and Shlain, *Acid Dreams,* p. 210.

14 Personal Interview with Kathleen Cleaver in New York in 2000, when she had this author join a group to discuss Congresswoman Cynthia McKinney present a Human Rights Bill and chair a Congressional meeting regarding the FBI's Cointelpro then and now. Also see Lee and Shlain, *Acid Dreams,* p. 267.

15 Personal Interview with Kathleen Cleaver, New York City, 2000 (see above) and January 5, 2014 by phone. In latter talk, Cleaver said Leary arrived to Panthers in Algeria uninvited and with a

member of the Yippies. Also, on "twenty thousand hits," see Lee and Shlain, *Acid Dreams*, p. 268. On "you've got to free yourself," Michael Zwerin, "Revolutionary Bust," *Village Voice*, February 11, 1971. On CIA infiltrating Panthers, CIA document, "Situation Information Report," February 12, 1971, and Seymour Hersh, "CIA Reportedly Recruited Blacks for Surveillance of Panther Party," *New York Times*, March 17, 1978. All cited in Lee and Shlain, *Acid Dreams*, p. 268.

16 Michael Zwerin, "Revolutionary Bust," *Village Voice*, February 11, 1971. Michael Zwerin, "Acid, Guns, and Love," *Vancouver Free Press*, February 24, 1971. CIA document, "Situation Information Report," February 12, 1971, and Seymour Hersh, "CIA Reportedly Recruited Blacks for Surveillance of Panther Party," *New York Times*, March 17, 1978. All cited in Lee and Shlain, *Acid Dreams*, p. 268

17 On $25,000, see Lee and Shlain, *Acid Dreams*, p. 264. On Stark celebrating success, see Black, *Acid*, p. 116. Note that British Police Inspector Dick Lee and writer Colin Pratt stated that the Brotherhood of Eternal Love gave the Weather Underground $50,000 to spring Leary from prison. Lee didn't comment on $25,000 given to Panthers in Exile to let Leary go, so this amount might have been added together by Lee and Pratt: Dick Lee and Colin Pratt, *Operation Julie: How the Undercover Police Team Smashed the World's Greatest Drugs Ring* (London: W.H. Allen, 1978), p. 78.

18 Lee and Shlain, *Acid Dreams*, pp. 264, 268, 269.

19 Lee and Shlain, *Acid Dreams*, p. 269.

20 Lee and Shlain, *Acid Dreams*, pp. 270, 273. Note that Joanna Harcourt-Smith then entered Leary's personal life, becoming his partner. Her father was a British aristocrat, her stepfather was one of Europe's richest men, and her uncle was London publisher, Simon Harcourt-Smith. A defense committee formed around Joanna Harcourt-Smith, attracting celebrities that included activist poet Allen Ginsberg, who soon grew to believe that Harcourt-Smith was a government agent. After Leary's arrest, Harcourt-Smith had a relationship with a known government informant who helped gain the arrest of two-dozen people.

21 Lee and Shlain, *Acid Dreams*, p. 273. On Leary informing on Weather Underground for FBI, "Tune In, Turn On, Rat Out," (Part of Timothy Leary's 1974 interview with the FBI), *Harper's Magazine*, September 1, 1999.

22 Lee and Shlain, *Acid Dreams*, pp. 292-93.

23 Sharon Erickson Nepstad, *Religion and War Resistance in the Plowshares Movement* (London: Cambridge University Press, 2008), p. 48.

24 Daniel Berrigan's wife, Elizabeth McAlister, in *Hit and Stay* (2013) documentary by Joe Tropea and Skizz Cyzyck.

25 Mike Davis, "Manifest Destiny: Necklace of Human Ears Through History," *San Francisco Chronicle*, 11/23/2003, http://www.sfgate.com/cgi-bin/article.cgi?f=/c/a/2003/11/23/INGUL36QMH1.DTL&ao=all. Davis cited a Toledo, Ohio newspaper, *The Blade*, for these quotes. Note that future George W. Bush Vice President Dick Cheney worked as Ford's Chief of Staff. Donald Rumsfeld served as Defense Secretary under both President Ford and President George W. Bush.

26 Sale, *SDS*, p. 632.

27 Peter Zimroth, *Perversions of Justice: The Prosecution and Acquittal of the Panther 21* (New York: Viking Press, 1974), pp. 44-45. Through extrapolation of the statistics, Sale concluded there were approximately 2,800 student-linked actual bombings during this 15-month period, about six a day around the country.

28 Stuart Christie, *Edward Heath Made Me Angry: The Christie File Part 3, 1967-1975* (London: ChristieBooks.com, 2004), pp. 122-24. "Memories of Massacre in Mexico." *Washington Post*, February 14, 2002. p. A21. "Ten Bloodiest Student Protests in History," Top Masters in Education: Your Online Guide for Masters in Education Degrees. http://www.topmastersineducation.com/student-protests/. Gianni Statera, *Death of a Utopia: The Development and Decline of Student Movements in Europe* (New York: Oxford University Press, 1975).

29 *The Project Censored Show* on *The Morning Mix*, "May 4th and the Kent State Shootings in the 42nd Year," Pacifica Radio, KPFA, 94.1FM, May 4, 2012 live at 8:00 A.M., archived online

at http://www.kpfa.org/archive/id/80293 and http://dl.dropbox.com/u/42635027/20120504-Fri0800.mp3. For Wellin on ROTC, see recording at 28:45. For article on Kent State shootings as U.S. intelligence orchestrated murder, see http://www.globalresearch.ca/kent-state-was-it-about-civil-rights-or-%E2%80%A8murdering-student-protesters/.

30 On social chaos, Mayday Tactical Manual, author's collection, p. 3. On "freaky people": Mark Goff, "Washington D.C. -Spring 1971," *The Bugle-American* (13-19 May 1971). The phrase "qualified martial law" was used by William H. Rehnquist, who was assistant attorney general at the time and was later named to the Supreme Court. Quoted in an American Civil Liberties Union report, *Mayday 1971: Order without Law* (July 1972), p. 14. The government reported conflicting arrest totals, ranging from 13,245 to 14,164; a discussion of these figures is in the same report, pp. 64-65. On Nixon and staff "shaken," and Helms' statement, the quotations are from Tom Wells, *The War Within: America's Battle over Vietnam* (New York: Henry Holt and Company, 1994), p. 512. Also see George W. Hopkins, "'May Day' 1971: Civil Disobedience and the Vietnam Antiwar Movement," in *Give Peace a Chance: Exploring the Vietnam Antiwar Movement*, ed. Melvin Small and William D. Hoover (Syracuse: Syracuse University Press, 1992), http://libcom.org/library/ending-war-inventing-movement-mayday-1971. While this event surely had an underappreciated effect historically, and rightfully deserved copying for years, it may not have been effective without the activist protest bombings also occurring at that time. The event reportedly shook up Nixon and his staff, and CIA Director Richard Helms said, "it was a very damaging kind of event [that] put increasing pressure on the administration [to end the war.]"

31 James Westheider, *Fighting on Two Fronts: African Americans and the Vietnam War* (New York: NYU Press, 1997). On fragging, see section "Black on White, White on Black." On de-escalation of war, see section "Racism at Sea." On historian saying assaults in thousands, see David Cortright, *Soldiers in Revolt: The American Military Today* (Garden City, NY: Anchor Press, 1975), p. 44. On only 10% of these ending up in court, see Eugene Linden, "The Demoralization of an Army: Fragging and Other Withdrawal Symptoms," in *Saturday Review*, 1/5/72, p. 12.

32 Lee and Shlain, *Acid Dreams*, p. 281. Also see, David Black, *Acid*, pp. 175, 186.

33 Black, *Acid*, p .63.

34 Black, *Acid*, p. 63.

35 See how the CIA's Operation Chaos joined forces with the FBI's Counterintelligence Program (Cointelpro) against activists such as Los Angeles Black Panther leader Geronimo Pratt, Alex Constantine, *The Covert War Against Rock* (Venice, CA: Feral House, 2000), pp. 15, 18; and Angus McKenzie, *Secrets: The CIA's War at Home* (Berkeley, CA: University of California Press, 1999), p. 69. On CIA spying on Americans, Seymour Hersh, "Huge C.I.A. Operation Reported in U.S. Against Antiwar Forces, Other Dissidents in Nixon Years," *New York Times*, 12/22/74, p.A1. For government documents on Operation Merrimac in *New York Times*, see http://graphics8.nytimes.com/packages/pdf/national/familyjewels/20070626_surveillances.pdf.

36 Lee, *Acid Dreams*, pp. 248-50. Black, *Acid*, p. 116.

37 Lee, *Acid Dreams*, p. 249.

38 Lee, *Acid Dreams*, pp. 250-51.

39 Lee and Shlain, *Acid Dreams*, p. 250. Lee and Pratt, *Operation Julie*, p. 79. Also see Black, *Acid*, p. 125.

40 Lee and Pratt, *Operation Julie*, pp. 332, 347. Black, *Acid*, p. 140. Lee said that he never heard anything from MI5 or MI6 about his investigation's findings, nor did he hear about them following up on his investigation. Black, p. 142.

41 Black, *Acid*, pp. 91-96, 140, 144, 189.

42 Black, *Acid*, p. 116.

43 Black, *Acid*, pp. 146, 159, 160.

44 Black, *Acid*, p. 183.

45 Black, *Acid*, pp. 160-62, 183. And finally, amongst many other contacts, Stark had documents that verified his contacts with the Italian political underworld. These included: mafia boss and former Prime Minister Giulio Anderotti associate Salvo Lima; "Prince Gianfranco di

Montereale, who had previously been implicated in coup plotting; and Graziano Verzotto, a former president of the State mining corporation, Ente Minerario. Verzotto had fled to Lebanon to escape a financial investigation of his association with Mafia banker and P-2 [Masonic] Lodge member, Nino Sindona." The P-2 Lodge was headed by a former Mussolini Blackshirt, Licio Gelli, who defected to U.S. Army intelligence at the end of WWII, becoming the main liaison between them and the Italian secret service.

46 Black detailed how when Stark went to prison, he pretended to be a Palestinian revolutionary. An undercover agent who worked for this "stay behind" intelligence network, Mario Moretti, joined the revolutionary leftist Red Brigade from its start. Morettti plotted the imprisonment of the group's leaders, orchestrated the kidnap of Prime Minister Moro and then murdered him. Black said Stark did key work on "the cover-up of the Moro affair in its aftermath, and possibly in the actual events of the kidnap and subsequent murder." Key players in that assassination linked Stark's work in the Italian prison system to Moretti's actions that smeared the Red Brigade and all leftist revolutionary groups. Black, *Acid*, pp. 169-81, quote from p. 181.

47 Lee and Shlain, *Acid Dreams*, p. 281.

48 Lee and Shlain, *Acid Dreams*, pp. 255-56, 281. Black, *Acid*, pp. 160, 175.

49 Black, *Acid*, pp. 175, 190.

50 Lee and Shlain, *Acid Dreams*, p. 282.

51 Lee and Shlain, *Acid Dreams*, pp. 255, 282.

52 Lee and Shlain, *Acid Dreams*, p. 143. H.P. Albarelli, *A Terrible Mistake: The Murder of Frank Olson and the CIA's Secret Cold War Experiments* (Waterville, OR: Trine Day, 2009), p. 291.

53 Lee and Shlain *Acid Dreams*, p.160. On report of many Human Be-Ins, Personal Interview with Warren Green, August 30, 2013.

54 Lee and Shlain, *Acid Dreams*, pp. 251-52. "State Investigating Handling of Tickets At Woodstock Fair," *New York Times*, August 27, 1969, p. 45. Michael Lang stated 400,000 attended; half of them did not have a ticket.

55 Lee and Shlain, *Acid Dreams*, pp. 251-52. Jane Alpert, *Growing Up Underground*, p. 205. On Kesey, Perry, *On the Bus*, p. 181.

56 Abbie Hoffman, high on acid, ran on stage to deliver a political rap about the plight of John Sinclair, the White Panther founder in jail for possession of two joints. His mike went dead and Pete Townshend reportedly hit him in the head with his guitar. This all happened just as Hoffman started to talk. Lee and Shlain, *Acid Dreams*, p. 253. While evidence supports that FBI undercover agent George Demmerle led the Yippie offshoot group, the Crazies, a man who called himself Karl Crazy sat on the Yippies steering committee. Karl Crazy's absurd name, and his statement, "Woodstock was political because everyone was tripping," is suggestive of his possibly assisting Demmerle in that offshoot group. Lee and Shlain, *Acid Dreams*, p. 255.

57 For example, personal interview with former "Friends of the Panthers" activist George Hurd, 3/20/11.

58 See Goode, 1972, in Stephen R. Kandall, *Substance and Shadow* (Harvard Univ. Press, 1999), p. 171. Another report noted that by 1970, between one and two million Americans had tried LSD: W.H. McGlothlin and D.O. Arnold, "LSD revisited (a ten-year followup of medical LSD use)," Archives of General Psychiatry (1971), 24: 35-49, 59 "Rise in Hallucinogen Use, National Institute of Justice Research in Brief," October 1997, in Kandall, *Substance and Shadow*.

60 Carl Oglesby, "The Acid Test and How It Failed," *The National Reporter*, Fall 1988, p. 10. See this excerpt on web at http://www.foreignpolicyjournal.com/2011/02/07/the-globalist-web-of-subversion/6/.

Brian Jones

Chapter Thirteen

Intelligence Targeting of the Rolling Stones & Other Bands

In the mid-'70s, the exposure of the FBI's Counterintelligence Program (Cointelpro) against leftist activists gained ground and led Senator Frank Church and other politicians to head up committees for investigation. These committees often fell short of exposing the full panoply of U.S. intelligence operations, and minimized the atrocities they did uncover. Nonetheless, they did publish their findings. A few independent journalists and media organizations reported on some of these findings. Future Undersecretary of Defense William Bader spearheaded the Senate Church Committee investigation, which included CIA officials admitting that well over 400 members of the media, and almost all the media ownership, lived dual lives in their work for the CIA.[1]

Another important finding by the Church Committee (officially, the U.S. Senate Select Committee to Study Governmental Operations with Respect to Intelligence Activities) was a document proving U.S. intelligence had a special longtime concern about political musicians, and sophisticated strategies for attacking them. In his book *The Covert War Against Rock*, Alex Constantine first published part of this document taken from a section on the FBI Cointelpro strategy. The memorandum detailed many tactics used against political musicians. It instructed agents:

> Show them as scurrilous and depraved. Call attention to their habits and living conditions, explore every possible embarrassment. Send in women and sex, break up marriages. Have members arrested on marijuana charges. Investigate personal conflicts or animosities between them. Send articles to the newspapers showing their depravity. Use narcotics and free sex to entrap. Use misinformation to confuse and disrupt. Get records of their bank accounts. Obtain specimens of their handwriting. Provoke target groups into rivalries that may result in death.[2]

While the FBI orchestrated lower-level targeting of political musicians in this regard, the CIA and MI6 appeared to have a slightly different agenda in their first work with musicians. Excepting the FBI, the CIA Director supervised all 14-plus intelligence agency directors. A goal of the CIA's MK-Ultra was to get popular musicians to use drugs and influence other musicians to do the same. This would provide easier manipulation of these musicians, and also aid the CIA's media assets in their goal of promoting drugs, as these musicians were often seen as role models.[3] It would influence the population in general, but particularly the more suggestible teens and young adults protesting racism and the war.

Did U.S. intelligence promote and elevate many American musicians in exchange for their collaboration with MK-Ultra goals? As previously detailed, Dave McGowan wrote about the inordinate number of musicians living in the Laurel Canyon area of Los Angeles whose parents had elite military and wealthy white Anglo-Saxon Protestant backgrounds. These bands and musicians included Jim Morrison (the Doors), David Crosby (the Byrds, and Crosby, Stills and Nash), Stephen Stills (Buffalo Springfield and Crosby, Stills and Nash), John Phillips (The Mamas and The Papas), Mike Nesmith (the Monkees), Gerry Beckley (America, of "Horse with No Name" fame). Some of these musicians appeared to aid MK-Ultra goals, such as Jim Morrison's popularizing of acid, along with Crosby holding the party where Beatle George Harrison tripped his second time and Ringo first tripped.[4]

Mae Brussells, a radio journalist in the 1970s, listed many famous musicians she believed the CIA targeted through MK-Ultra. She said, "All of these musicians were at the peak of a creative period and success at the time they were offered LSD. Their personalities altered drastically. Optimism and gratification were replaced with doubt and misery." Brussels included folk musician Phil Ochs in this list, while noting the incredible fact that he "just happened to be touring Africa when a native 'robber' jumped after him and cut his throat so that it affected his singing? [Ochs was] the most political symbol of protest against the war in Vietnam, [whose songs were sung by] Bob Dylan, Joan Baez, and many others, selected from millions of U.S. tourists for assault to his vocal chords." She included a timeline of MK-Ultra and linked murderous operations.[5]

Rolling Stones Targeted and Brian Jones Murdered

In 1968, Mick Jagger attended a demonstration against the Vietnam War. It inspired him to write and release a single, "Street Fighting Man," an ode to radical anti-War protesters.[6] It included the lyrics: "The summer's here and the time is right for fighting in the streets," as well as "Hey! Think the time is right for a palace revolution."[7]

After the previously discussed 1967 setup by undercover U.S. intelligence agent David Schneidermann to dose Mick Jagger, British police began regular stops and searches of Mick Jagger and Keith Richards from 1967 to 1969. Jagger's girlfriend, Marianne Faithfull, said there were "many, many busts." She said that on one of these searches of Mick Jagger's car, the police planted drugs during their search. After the police officer planted the drugs, Jagger then "set the guy up—the detective, whoever he was—to pay him off, and filmed the payoff with a hidden camera. Needless to say, all charges against Mick were immediately dropped. But all that persecution takes something vital out of an artist."[8]

Rolling Stones founder Brian Jones and lead singer Mick Jagger were outspoken against the Vietnam War.

Multi-instrumentalist Brian Jones, who founded the Rolling Stones, was the most publicly outspoken band member against British war policies supporting the U.S. in Vietnam, and as such, a prime target for MI6 and the rest of British intelligence. Jones's first arrest came on May 10, 1967, the day his bandmates Jagger and Richards went to trial on the Schneiderman setup.[9] Jones was convicted for possession and use of marijuana and received a nine-month jail sentence. He was arrested a second time in 1968, and this time sentenced to three years probation. About that arrest, Rolling Stones bassist Bill Wyman said that a dozen police officers entered Jones's home, "to bust another one and end the Stones for good."[10] Wyman said they found one planted vial of marijuana. Citing these two convictions, British authorities denied Jones a visa to leave the country with the Stones in 1969, on their first American tour in three years.[11]

By the summer of 1969, British intelligence appeared to target Brian Jones more severely. Nicholas Fitzgerald, a member of the Guinness beer family, was a longtime friend of Jones and wrote a book about him. Fitzgerald said that Jones had bought a new home at Cotchford Farm and had people hanging out there, supposedly working on the grounds. Fitzgerald said that Jones couldn't get rid of these people. Jones told Fitzgerald they were constantly answering his phone and saying it was the wrong number, and hiding his motorcycle from him. Jones also said his phone would go dead mid-conversation.[12]

Bandmate Bill Wyman said this group's intimidations led Jones to decay, "physically, mentally and musically." His inability to join the Stones' American tour and other factors led Jagger and Richards to at least temporarily ask Jones to resign from the Rolling Stones. After some initial depression, Brian Jones bounced back from this. In mortal fear of prison, he reportedly gave up all drugs except wine.[13]

Despite these setbacks, Brian Jones had good prospects for the future. Author A.E. Hotchner , the former longtime editor for Ernest Hemingway, said Jones "was enthusiastic about his band plans. He had talked to Jimi Hendrix and John Lennon, and both were seriously considering joining up with him to form a new band."[14]

This pairing of socialist John Lennon, with the increasingly politically radical Jimi Hendrix and Jones, would have been a British and U.S. intelligence nightmare because of the bandmates' universal appeal and leftist political influence. Top military strategists reported intelligence fears of black radicals and white antiwar radicals joining forces.[15]

On July 3, 1969, Brian Jones died, reportedly due to an "accidental drowning in his swimming pool." After reading the official reports from witnesses and the coroner about what happened that night, Hotchner found many inconsistencies. The official report was that Brian Jones died of an accidental drowning; the coroner said he might have had an asthma attack. Brian's father said Brian hadn't had an asthma attack in years. The coroner also found trace amounts of a speed-like drug and alcohol in his body, but not enough to explain accidental drowning. This led Hotchner to his own investigation, which led to many interviews.[16]

Rolling Stone guitarist Keith Richards said, "We were completely shocked about [Jones's] death. I got straight into it and wanted to know who was there and couldn't find out." Richards continued, "I've seen Brian swim in terrible conditions, in the sea with breakers up to here ... he was a goddamn good swimmer, and it's very hard to believe he could have died in a swimming pool." Richards concluded: "Some weird things happened the night Brian died ... We had some chauffeurs working for us, and we tried to find out. They had a weird hold over Brian. There were a lot of chicks there ... they were having a party ... It's the same feeling with who killed Kennedy. You can't get to the bottom of it."[17]

Hotchner detailed the statement of Brian Jones's close friend, Nicholas Fitzgerald, who gave an eyewitness account. Fitzgerald said he had been to Jones's home, and Jones asked him to pick up a friend in the nearby village. Fitzgerald said he and a friend had dinner in the village, but couldn't locate the person to pick up. They called Jones and a strange woman answered the phone. When Fitzgerald asked to speak to Jones, she wouldn't respond. Fitzgerald heard a lot of noise and loud music as if a party was going on. Jones hadn't mentioned having any party that night. So Fitzgerald and his friend went back to Jones's house.

A car was blocking Jones's driveway with its headlights on facing the road. The two walked around to the back where there were woods and a swimming pool. They came to a spot where they could see the pool and saw three men who looked like workmen, overseeing the drowning of a man. One had his hand on the swimmer's head while another commanded a third man to jump on the swimmer's back. The commanding man then ordered another man to jump in and help hold the swimmer under the water. Another woman and man watched.[18]

The man being drowned was Brian Jones. Suddenly, a large man came out of the bushes and said, "Get the hell out of here, Fitzgerald, or you'll be the next." Fitzgerald also couldn't understand how this stranger knew his name, unless he was part of a spy ring watching Jones. Fitzgerald further said he was too scared to tell police or anyone else until he published his account in a book years later.[19]

Hotchner also found and interviewed a man who had proof he worked at Brian Jones's house that night. The man agreed with Fitzgerald's account of seeing several men drown Brian Jones. Fitzgerald further said that after he witnessed the Jones murder with his friend, the friend went missing, never to be seen again.[20] The failure of police to detain the party members and investigate this as a murder, as well as the media cover-up of eyewitnesses' immediate accounts of a drowning, suggests this was an MI6 operation. MI6 has similar, though lesser, control over British media as its CIA counterpart's over American.[21]

EXCLUSIVE

Call to exhume Brian Jones in new death probe

'We believe he was killed in the house and thrown in pool'

Hemingway editor A.E. Hotchner was one of several Rolling Stones historians who quoted eyewitnesses saying they saw Brian Jones murdered.

Hotchner published his book with the above accounts around 1990, but more information came out by 1994. England's *Independent* reported that police were considering reopening the investigation into Jones's death, "after claims in two new books that he was murdered. The books both name Frank Thorogood, who died last year, as the man responsible for the killing." One of the authors, Geoffrey Guiliano, said an unnamed associate of Thorogood's admitted helping him hold Jones's head under the water. Witnesses added that Thorogood made a deathbed confession.[22] A third author talked to a murder witness who said someone from the group of electricians that murdered Jones may have slipped a drug in a brandy Jones was drinking to make the drowning easier to cover up.[23]

Altamont, Hell's Angels and the CIA

As discussed previously, undercover U.S. intelligence agents such as David Schneidermann pushed drugs on the Rolling Stones and other musicians. This appeared part of U.S. intelligence's systematic plan that was also reported by agent Steve Abrahms under MK-Ultra. Music industry workers such as attorney Dan Cronin, who used to work with top musicians for record companies, revealed one of his duties. He said he was told to regularly provide various drugs to the musicians with whom he worked. The question remains: why did drugs become the norm amongst so many musicians? Was this a "natural" phenomenon, or did U.S. intelligence promulgate this trend, not only with acid, but with cocaine, heroin, amphetamines and other drugs?[24]

By 1968, Mick Jagger gave the CIA and MI6 more reason to target him. Jagger had made political statements to the press, including: "War stems from power-mad politicians and patriots. Some new master plan would end all these mindless men from seats of power and replace them with real people, people of compassion."[25] Besides attending antiwar demonstrations and their lyrics calling "for a palace revolution," the Stones recorded the song, "Gimme Shelter," in 1969. This song included the antiwar lyrics, "War, children, it's just a shot away … murder, rape, it's just a shot away … Mad bull has lost its way."

In their promotion of that song and its album, *Let It Bleed,* the Stones scheduled a November 1969 American tour. At the end of this tour, they tacked on a free show in California at Altamont Race Track in a musical event billed as Woodstock West. It would be their first appearance in America since Britain allowed them to leave—the same tour that had planned to leave Brian Jones behind due to his drug charge. The Altamont show occurred five months after the murder of Brian Jones, and details suggest it was conceived by U.S. intelligence. For one thing, suspected MK-Ultra collaborators, the Grateful Dead, organized the event, and other bands in the line-up also had suspected intelligence links.[26]

The Altamont Music Festival took place in December of 1969. Mick Jagger flew to the show by helicopter with Tim Leary seated beside him. Similar to the 1967 San Francisco Human Be-In, Leary sat onstage in full view of the crowd throughout the Stones performance. The media's elevation of Leary as a figurehead of the anti-War movement must have made it easier for the Grateful Dead to convince the Rolling Stones to include him.[27] The Grateful Dead and agents instigated the large gathering of people to trip on acid while ostracizing any anti-War message.

Other evidence points to the Grateful Dead's collaboration with U.S. intelligence via the Hell's Angels, whom they had often used for security.

The Angels and similar biker gangs included ex-military and helped traffic guns between states. A London *Telegraph* article noted that the FBI had undercover agents working in Hell's Angels, purportedly to find and arrest subversives. An ATF (Alcohol, Tobacco and Firearms) agent testified in court that the ATF contracted with the Oakland Angels' leader Sonny Barger to murder Black Panther National Minister of Information, Eldridge Cleaver, as well as Cesar Chavez, who headed the migrant farmworkers union.[28]

The Grateful Dead once again enlisted Oakland's Hell's Angels to provide security at the Altamont Music Festival. The Angels were in charge of keeping people off the unusually low, 39-inch-high stage.[29] Someone supplied the Angels with 1,000 hits of amphetamine-laced LSD for the event.[30] The motorcycle gang guzzled beer and ate amphetamine-laced LSD by the handfuls throughout the day's festival, leading them to behave in brutal ways. They were well prepared, "loaded with weapons—knives, chains, lead pipes, tire irons and sawed-off pool [sticks] with lead-weighted ends."[31]

Dealers of acid and other drugs hawked their wares to concertgoers. It's likely these dealers included local undercover FBI and CIA agents, as had been the case at New York's Woodstock Fest. The crowd of 300,000 suffered so many bad trips, and broken bones from Angels' beatings, that physicians at nearby Haight-Ashbury and Berkeley free clinics ran out of the antipsychotic treatment for LSD, Thorazine, in half an hour.[32]

Filmmakers at the festival described many incidents of the Hell's Angels clubbing anyone who tried to get near the stage, or cameramen trying to take pictures of their bloody bludgeoning.[33] Yet cameramen did capture movie film of a murderous incident where someone managed to climb on stage for a moment. When the Rolling Stones were playing "Sympathy for the Devil," an eighteen-year-old black man, Meredith Hunter, stood near the stage, took out a gun and climbed onto the stage only a few yards from Mick Jagger. Before Hunter could fire the gun, a Hell's Angel named Alan Passaro pulled him down from the stage, grabbing his gun arm and stabbing him. Other Angels finished the job, killing Hunter.

While most accounts see this incident as part of the Angels' random violence, the film *Gimme Shelter* appeared to show Passaro and other Angels stepping out of line, away from the others to thwart what looked like a planned shooting of Mick Jagger and/or another Rolling Stone. It showed

Hunter holding a gun as if ready to shoot. An autopsy revealed he had methamphetamines in his system at the time. An Angel on the stage told Jagger, "You gotta get down ... that guy's got a gun out there and he's shooting at the stage." Actually shooting or not, the gun was large, visible and was reportedly loaded.[34]

What explanation could there be for Meredith Hunter to step up onto the stage with a gun? While theories abound, the notion that someone paid Hunter to do this is certainly possible. Those plotting to kill Jagger likely wanted to divide black activists and white activists. A black man shooting Mick Jagger could have helped drive a wedge between these groups.

Mick Jagger was sued by Meredith Hunter's family, and settled for $10,000. In either a bizarre coincidence, or purposeful action to warn others about thwarting a planned intelligence murder operation, some years later Hell's Angel Alan Passaro was found dead in the Anderson reservoir with $10,000 in his pocket.[35]

Attacks on the Rolling Stones continued after the Altamont Music Fest. The Associated Press reported that a former Hell's Angel named Butch was placed in the witness protection program when he testified to the Senate Judiciary Committee. He said the Angels had an "open contract" to murder Mick Jagger, purportedly for not defending them over the Altamont stabbing.[36]

Butch testified to at least two more Angels-planned attempts to murder Mick Jagger. In the mid-1970s they sent an Angel with a gun and a silencer to stake out a hotel Jagger was to stay in, but he didn't show. Later, when Mick Jagger stayed on Long Island, a Hell's Angels chapter tried to carry out a murder plan there. They piloted a boat and transported plastic explosives to Jagger's house, but were foiled by a storm just before Jagger left that location. The murder of bandmate Jones and the murder contracts given to the FBI-infiltrated Oakland Angels suggest these were a series of successful attempts to scare outspoken anti-War singer Mick Jagger into a lower profile politically.[37]

Both Keith Richards and Mick Jagger eventually abused or were addicted to such drugs as cocaine and heroin. The intelligence-manipulated mainstream media made them and the late Brian Jones poster children for drug abuse. During this time the Stones stopped writing political lyrics, but began again in the early 1980s with the song "Undercover of the Night," about the brutality of the U.S.-supported fascist regimes in South America. MTV banned the video for that song, purportedly due to its violent content.[38]

Notes

1 Carl Bernstein, "The CIA & the Media," *Rolling Stone*, October 20, 1977, http://www.carlbernstein.com/magazine_cia_and_media.php.

2 As noted above, one intelligence document a Senate committee found included strategies for use against political musicians such as "Intelligence Activities and Rights of Americans," Book II, April 26, 1976, Senate Committee with Respect to Intelligence, Report; excerpted in Alex Constantine, *The Covert War Against Rock* (Los Angeles: Feral House, 2001), p. 9. U.S. Senate Select Committee to Study Government Operations, *The FBI's Covert Program to Destroy the Black Panther Party* (Washington, DC: U.S. Government Printing Office, 1976).

3 On CIA Director supervising other intelligence agency directors, Victor Marchetti and John Marks, *The CIA and the Cult of Intelligence* (New York: Dell, 1974).

4 See David McGowan, *Weird Scenes Inside the Canyon: Laurel Canyon, Covert Ops & the Dark Heart of the Hippie Dream* (London: Headpress, 2014). Also see http://www.mygen.com/Laurel_Canyon-David_McGowan_report.htm. The Doors came up with the name as a shortened version of Aldous Huxley's famous book, *The Doors of Perception*, about Huxley's first use of the psychedelic mescaline. The Doors were major promoters of tripping in the Sixties. The media wrote about how Jim Morrison was an avid LSD user from 1965 on, and the Doors most popular songs, such as "People are Strange" and "Light My Fire," are supposed to be about a bad trip and getting high, respectively. Ben Fong-Torres, *The Doors* (New York: Hyperion, 2006).

5 http://www.maebrussell.com/Mae%20Brussell%20Articles/Operation%20Chaos.html.

6 Christopher Andersen, *Jagger* (New York: Delacorte Press, 1993), Introduction.

7 http://www.beatzenith.com/the_rolling_stones/rsingleslist.htm.

8 A.E. Hotchner, *Blown Away: A No-Holds-Barred Portrait of the Rolling Stones and the Sixties Told by the Voices of the Generation* (New York: Fireside, 1990) p. 231.

9 Constantine, *The Covert War Against Rock*, pp. 42-44. On Britain supporting the U.S. in the Vietnam War, see, for example, Sylvia Ellis, *Britain, America and the Vietnam War* (Westport, CT: Praeger, 2004). Also see Mark Curtis, "Britain's Secret Support of U.S. Repression: The Vietnam War," 3/3/06, http://markcurtis.wordpress.com/2007/02/01/britains-secret-support-for-us-aggression-the-vietnam-war/.

10 Constantine, *The Covert War Against Rock*, p. 45.

11 Bill Wyman and Richard Havers, *Rolling With The Stones* (New York: DK Publishing, 2003), pp. 324-26.

12 Nicholas Fitzgerald, *Brian Jones: The Inside Story of the Original Rolling Stone* (New York: Putnam, 1985), referenced in Hotchner, *Blown Away*, p. 296.

13 On Wyman account, see Wyman and Havers, *Rolling With The Stones*, p. 428, referenced in Constantine, *The Covert War Against Rock*, p. 47. On Jones giving up drugs except alcohol, see Hotchner, *Blown Away*, p. 286.

14 Hotchner, *Blown Away*, p. 296.

15 For example, Former Air Force Secretary Townsend Hoopes said one of the government's greatest fears was "the fateful merging of anti-war and racial dissension"; Todd Gitlin, *The Whole World is Watching* (Berkeley: University of California Press, 1980) p. 55, cited in Martin Lee and Bruce Shlain, *Acid Dreams: The Complete Social History of the CIA, LSD, the Sixties and Beyond* (New York: Grove Press, 1985), p. 210.

16 Hotchner, *Blown Away*, pp. 29-35, 298.

17 Hotchner, *Blown Away*, pp. 291-92.

18 Hotchner, *Blown Away*, pp. 297-98.

19 Hotchner, *Blown Away*, pp. 297-98.

20 Hotchner, *Blown Away*, pp. 298-301.

21 See, for example, MI5 agent Annie Machon's account of MI6 control over media, http://www.youtube.com/watch?v=XrNrSozjzDY. Also see, Chris Hastings, "How the BBC Used MI5 to Vet Thousands of Staff," *The Telegraph*, July 2, 2006, http://www.telegraph.co.uk/news/uknews/1522875/Revealed-how-the-BBC-used-MI5-to-vet-thousands-of-staff.html.

22 "Murder Claims Raise Doubt over Rolling Stone's Death," *The Independent*, 4/4/94, p. 2.

23 Constantine, *The Covert War Against Rock*, pp. 47-51. On biographers of Jones finding

investigation a whitewash, see Laura Jackson, *Golden Stone: The Untold Life and Tragic Death of Brian Jones* (New York: St. Martin's, 1992) p. 217.

24 Personal Interview with Dan Cronin, October 3, 2012, in Las Vegas, NV.

25 On Jagger's political statement, A.E. Hotchner, *Blown Away: A No-Holds-Barred Portrait of the Rolling Stones and the Sixties Told by the Voices of the Generation* (New York: Fireside, 1990), pp. 231-32. On regular police stops and Jagger setting up cop, see Constantine, *The Covert War Against Rock*, p. 46. He quotes Marianne Faithfull interviewed and in "Operation Chaos," unpublished manuscript by longtime radio journalist, Mae Brussells.

26 This was the first Rolling Stones single since 1964 to not break into the British top 10 on the sales charts. British radio stations appeared to censor it, as it came in at #21. See other suspected musician agents: http://www.mygen.com/Laurel_Canyon-David_McGowan_report.htm.

27 James Miller, *Flowers in the Dustbin: The Rise of Rock and Roll, 1947-1977* (Simon & Schuster, 1999), pp. 275-77

28 On Hells Angels providing security for the Grateful Dead, see Miller, *Flowers in the Dustbin*, pp. 275-77; and http://www.therollingstones-music.com/bio.html. On FBI in Hells Angels, see Brian Eden, "Hells Angels Plot to Kill Mick Jagger," *Telegraph* (UK), March 2, 2008, http://www.telegraph.co.uk/news/uknews/1580456/Hells-Angels-plotted-to-kill-Mick-Jagger.html. On Angels members and gun running, personal interview with Karen Sykes-Dill, a wife of a former biker gang member who was also a Vietnam War veteran. On ATF agent detailing murder contract offered to Barger, ATF agent Larry Shears stated this in court, reported by Channel 23, Los Angeles, news broadcast, 12/17/71. Drew McKillips, "Amazing Story by Hell's Angels Chief," *San Francisco Chronicle*, 12/12/72, p. 1, "ATF Agent Says He Was Part of Coast Plot to Kill Cesar Chavez," *New York Times*, 1/ 2/72, p. 31. All referenced in Alex Constantine, *The Covert War Against Rock*, pp. 55-59.

29 Miller, *Flowers in the Dustbin*, pp. 275-77.

30 Robert Sam Anson, *Gone Crazy and Back Again* (New York: Doubleday, 1981), p. 148, referenced in Constantine, *The Covert War Against Rock*, p. 57.

31 Hotchner, *Blown Away*, pp. 19-20.

32 Martin Lee and Bruce Shlain, *Acid Dreams: The Complete Social History of LSD, the CIA, the Sixties, and Beyond* (New York: Grove Press, 1994), pp. 256-57.

33 Hotchner, *Blown Away*, pp.19-20.

34 The Rolling Stones et al., *Gimme Shelter* (Criterion, 1970, Maysles brothers' DVD released 2000), http://www.youtube.com/watch?v=0qTKsylrpsg&feature=related. On methamphetamines in system and other details, also see Henry Lee, "Altamont 'Cold Case' is Being Closed," *San Francisco Chronicle*, 5/26/05, http://www.sfgate.com/cgi-bin/article.cgi?f=/c/a/2005/05/26/BAG3CCUE8997.DTL.

35 "Drowning death of ex-Hell's Angel probed," *Houston Chronicle*, October 4, 1985.

36 Associated Press, "Witness: Cyclists Can't Get No Satisfaction Until Stones are Slain." *Lakeland Ledger* (Florida) March 4, 1973, http://news.google.com/newspapers?nid=1346&dat=19830304&id=YbkwAAAAIBAJ&sjid=s_sDAAAAIBAJ&pg=7008,1232656.

37 Hotchner, *Blown Away*, p. 320. Also see, Brian Eden, "Hells Angels Plot to Kill Mick Jagger," *Telegraph* (UK), March 2, 2008, http://www.telegraph.co.uk/news/uknews/1580456/Hells-Angels-plotted-to-kill-Mick-Jagger.html.

38 R. Serge Denisoff, *Inside MTV* (New York: Transaction Publishers, 1988), p. 284, http://books.google.com/.

CHAPTER FOURTEEN

U.S. Intelligence Targets Joplin & Hendrix

U.S. and British intelligence appeared to target musicians from historically oppressed groups, particularly early in their careers. Examples of such early targeting arise in two trail-blazing activist rock musicians, one female and one black. Evidence suggests that intelligence agents entered the lives of musical prodigies Janis Joplin and Jimi Hendrix early in their careers.

"Queen of Rock" Janis Joplin Targeted with Speed & Heroin

Janis Joplin, whom National Public Radio would later dub the first queen of rock 'n' roll, had a typically hard time breaking into the male-dominated rock world of San Francisco, but she clearly had star talent early on.[1] After growning up in Texas, Joplin attended the University of Texas at Austin, where the school newspaper highlighted the bluesy white singer in the early 1960s. By 1963, she had moved to San Francisco, where musicians such as Toni Brown said, "The word was out that there was this singer ... who was going to be very big." Joplin also became a hit on the second stage of the 1963 Monterey Folk Festival, where she won three singing contests, and major label record companies soon wanted to sign her.[2]

By 1964 a U.S. intelligence-linked man entered Janis Joplin's life. In San Francisco that year, Joplin dated a man who called himself Michel Raymond,

Janis Joplin's fiancé has been reported as working for the FBI and leading Joplin to her amphetamine addiction.

and who had told another girlfriend he worked for the FBI. Raymond worked for the French Army during the Algerian conflict, and sold a communication system to revolutionary groups in the Middle East and North Africa.[3] Joplin's publicist said years later that neither Raymond's "name nor his history was his own." He had "a fraudulent international pharmaceutical company he set up in Canada to obtain drugs."[4] All of this suggests Raymond worked with intelligence agencies in general and likely had joined U.S. intelligence.

The physically attractive Michel Raymond was deceitful and manipulative. Raymond obtained pure amphetamines through his fraudulent pharmaceutical company. A musician friend of Joplin's said Raymond got Janis to use speed regularly until she was "totally strung out. She was emaciated ... almost catatonic, just not responding." Janis's publicist also said, "Her speed experience was induced by a man. *He* had been the cause of it. *He* had brought her lower than she had ever been in her life." Raymond asked Joplin to marry him and they were engaged for a while, until Joplin found out he already had a pregnant wife.[5]

Researcher Mae Brussells stated that Janis Joplin's first LSD was administered surreptitiously. When Joplin discovered what happened, she ran to spit it out. Her publicist described Janis Joplin's second acid trip. Someone was passing around a bottle of wine filled with acid and didn't tell her what was in it. Joplin took a big swig of the wine before someone revealed it was filled with LSD.

"'ACID,' Janis shrieked, ran to the bathroom, and forced herself to throw up."[6]

Biographer Alice Echols wrote that in 1965, during an amphetamine drought in San Francisco, Janis Joplin turned to heroin and became interested in George Hunter, who had moved from Los Angeles to San Francisco and started a band called the Mainliners. Echols related that Hunter's initial success was "due less to his musical ability than to his good looks and vision." Hunter also lured beatnik kids, "out of the coffeehouses and onto the dance floors," with bands and parties. Hunter admitted to Echols that he rejected Joplin's quest to join his band, saying, "I had no idea [Joplin] was a musician because the whole scene we were part of was connected to dope [heroin]." It's uncertain if the Mainliners name stood for "mainlining" (injecting) heroin. They later changed their name to the Charlatans, and some dubbed them the first psychedelic rock band when they started tripping in 1964.[7]

At the start of 1966, Janis Joplin joined the band Big Brother and the Holding Company. Despite the reports of her not liking LSD, she and the band attended the Trips Festival in early 1966.[8]

Janis achieved sobriety for a while, and her fame grew to the point where promoters scheduled her with Jimi Hendrix, The Mamas and The Papas and others at the Monterey Pop Music Festival in the summer of 1967.

That concert got Joplin's Big Brother and the Holding Company signed to Columbia Records, where a number of their recordings topped the charts.

During this time, Big Brother and the Holding Company moved near the Grateful Dead at Lagunitas, and, "Janis often hung out at the Dead's house." Biographer Echols said, "Not everyone in or around the band was shooting speed, but once Janis moved to Lagunitas, she found little support for staying clean."[9]

As previously mentioned, the Grateful Dead's first manager published a 1971 book revealing that the Grateful Dead dealt heroin in the 1960s, presumably to finance their early tours. But it may have had another purpose: to get many local musicians hooked to make it easier to get control over them.[10] Pushing speed, heroin and acid appeared to be mainstays in that MK-Ultra-linked crowd.

Janis Joplin's on-and-off struggles with heroin are well known. She joined a growing list of music stars who had either dabbled in or become strung out on it. While MK-Ultra undercover agents and scientists manipulated Janis Joplin's San Francisco home area in the 1960s, it's uncertain if any suspected agents besides Michel Raymond specifically targeted her. However, researchers filed Freedom of Information Act requests, and FBI documents revealed that surveillance and discussion of Joplin had begun by the time of Woodstock in the summer of 1969.[11]

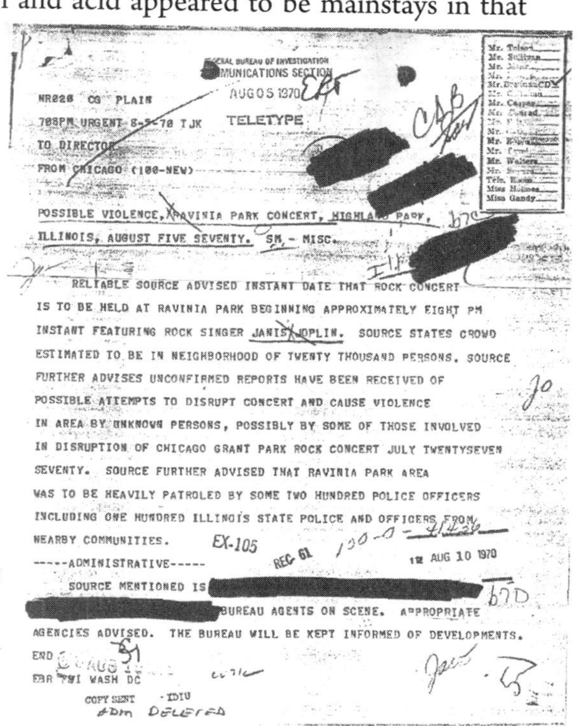

FEDERAL BUREAU OF INVESTIGATION
COMMUNICATIONS SECTION
AUG 05 1970
TELETYPE

NR028 CG PLAIN
708PM URGENT 8-5-70 TJK
TO DIRECTOR
FROM CHICAGO (100-NEW)

POSSIBLE VIOLENCE, RAVINIA PARK CONCERT, HIGHLAND PARK, ILLINOIS, AUGUST FIVE SEVENTY. SM - MISC.

RELIABLE SOURCE ADVISED INSTANT DATE THAT ROCK CONCERT IS TO BE HELD AT RAVINIA PARK BEGINNING APPROXIMATELY EIGHT PM INSTANT FEATURING ROCK SINGER JANIS JOPLIN. SOURCE STATES CROWD ESTIMATED TO BE IN NEIGHBORHOOD OF TWENTY THOUSAND PERSONS. SOURCE FURTHER ADVISES UNCONFIRMED REPORTS HAVE BEEN RECEIVED OF POSSIBLE ATTEMPTS TO DISRUPT CONCERT AND CAUSE VIOLENCE IN AREA BY UNKNOWN PERSONS, POSSIBLY BY SOME OF THOSE INVOLVED IN DISRUPTION OF CHICAGO GRANT PARK ROCK CONCERT JULY TWENTYSEVEN SEVENTY. SOURCE FURTHER ADVISED THAT RAVINIA PARK AREA WAS TO BE HEAVILY PATROLED BY SOME TWO HUNDRED POLICE OFFICERS INCLUDING ONE HUNDRED ILLINOIS STATE POLICE AND OFFICERS FROM NEARBY COMMUNITIES.

EX-105 REC 61 AUG 10 1970

-----ADMINISTRATIVE-----

SOURCE MENTIONED IS [redacted] BUREAU AGENTS ON SCENE. APPROPRIATE AGENCIES ADVISED. THE BUREAU WILL BE KEPT INFORMED OF DEVELOPMENTS.

END

FBI WASH DC

COPY SENT
ADM DELETED

A page out of Janis Joplin's FBI file shows surveillance of the singer, particularly after she announced a couple of anti-War fundraising stadium shows just before she died.

In 1970, Janis Joplin planned to participate in two huge, unprecedented anti-War music concerts. These "Festivals for Peace" raised a lot of money for the peace movement. In Joplin's third appearance on the nationally popular Dick Cavett television talk show, she announced two of these Peace Festivals, with the first scheduled in New York's Shea Stadium that August of 1970, and the second scheduled for Philadelphia. With a U.S. intelligence tactic used more often later, police refused to provide security for the latter show, and got it cancelled.[12]

By October of 1970, Janis Joplin had fallen back into using heroin again, which she exclusively bought from her usual dealer. That fall, the dealer's supplier had apparently given him a batch of heroin that was 40-50% pure, four to ten times purer than the average. Joplin died within ninety minutes of injecting it. All of the dealer's customers would die from that batch. Janis's sister Laura said rumors persisted that the CIA had arranged her sister's death, but she didn't know if there was any truth to them.[13]

Just before her death, Joplin, with a backup band, had recorded the album *Pearl.* It included a cover of a song by her one-time lover Kris Kristofferson, "Me and Bobby McGee," a co-written "Mercedes Benz," and a birthday song she recorded for famed Beatle John Lennon. *Pearl* sold over 4 million copies, topping the Billboard sales chart for nine weeks.[14]

Jimi Hendrix Drugged ... and Murdered?

In the U.S, Jimi Hendrix found little fame in the mid-1960s while he toured with music legends such as Sam Cooke, who was the first black musician to produce his own records before his career was cut short by his murder.[15] In 1966 Jimi Hendrix moved to England where he would initially reach stardom. In England, a "former" spy, Mike Jeffery, coerced his way into managing Hendrix. Jeffery had worked for British MI6. Jeffery's continued partnerships with CIA-linked figures, his sudden huge wealth, and his skills at acquiring CIA-type tax havens in the Bahamas suggests he maintained MI6 work undercover.[16]

Black artists were a particular intelligence focus because of left-wing radicalism among them. By 1968, Jimi Hendrix became popular worldwide. The assassination of Martin Luther King Jr. that year led Hendrix to actively support the Black Panthers and engage in more radical-left activism.[17] Former Air Force Secretary Townsend Hoopes said one of the government's greatest fears was "the fateful merging of anti-war and racial dissension." The widely admired Jimi Hendrix aided the bridge between the predominantly white anti-War movement and black civil rights activists.[18]

FBI and police targeting soon began against Hendrix in the U.S., and other countries aided their efforts when Hendrix went abroad. Such collaboration is common through the international police group Interpol. Also, while British and U.S. intelligence collaboration is well known, at least one former MI6 agent said the CIA actually looked to his agency for guidance, as American intelligence was partly created by British intelligence.[19] While this relationship isn't certain, and may have changed over the century, British intelligence's three-hundred-plus-year head start on the CIA supports the possibility of this claim.

The FBI started a closely guarded file on Hendrix and placed him on a security list of subversives to be rounded up for detainment in case of a national emergency.[20] Police detectives began round-the-clock surveillance of Hendrix and his band.[21]

When Hendrix traveled north of the U.S. border, Canadian federal police arrested him at an airport, claiming he transported drugs.[22] Biographers Harry Shapiro and Caesar Glebbeek cited Hendrix saying he'd never take such a risk and that his manager, Mike Jeffery, set up that airport arrest. The biographers described many ways Hendrix's manager stole from the famed guitarist and tried to sabotage him. Hendrix's biographers said that, contrary to popular belief, Hendrix produced his first classic album with virtually no drug use. Then, after getting into drugs for a while, Hendrix gave them up except for moderate alcohol and marijuana use.[23]

The media didn't give up on their manufactured image of Jimi Hendrix as a constant user of LSD. They also fabricated his having a heroin addiction. Various media sources claimed Hendrix was with different women all the time. In fact, Hendrix was living with his fiancée Monica Dannemann when he was only twenty-seven, contradicting this image.[24]

These Jimi Hendrix biographers and Monica Dannemann further claimed that Hendrix's manager Mike Jeffery consistently sabotaged the guitar legend's political activist work. Dannemann believed Hendrix when he said he thought Jeffery dosed his drink with a large amount of acid before one political benefit show that caused him to end his set early. Dannemann said Jeffery and his associates had also attempted to control Hendrix by constantly giving him drugs, in an unsuccessful attempt to get him addicted. In fact, she said, in his last year of life, Hendrix "spoke out against drugs in interviews, as well as some of his songs."[25]

After Mike Jeffery inserted himself as Jimi Hendrix's manager, he admitted his "former" MI6 (British CIA) work and proceeded to control Hendrix's career. Years later, one roadie claimed Jeffery made a drunken admission of having Hendrix killed.

According to the same sources, Mike Jeffery's Mafia connections were extensive. In 1969, a Mafia group kidnapped Hendrix for several days. Jeffery gained Hendrix's freedom by purporting to have help from a larger Mafia family.[26] Researchers have previously noted the CIA/FBI/Mafia links. Hendrix biographers Shapiro and Glebbeek believe Jeffery set up this Mafia kidnapping to intimidate Hendrix not to fire him, as Hendrix was reportedly trying to do at the time.[27] On another occasion Jeffery brought over a Mafia marksman to intimidate Hendrix regarding a business deal.[28] The Hendrix biographers also said Jeffery's business partner, band manager Jerry Morrison, was a former propagandist for a CIA-supported Haitian dictator.[29]

Jeffery controlled Jimi Hendrix in other key ways, besides just trying to keep Hendrix from participating in any political activism. Jeffery created a concert schedule that had Hendrix criss-crossing the country from one concert to the next, leaving him exhausted with jet lag. This helped Jeffery and others around Hendrix to more easily manipulate him and push drugs on him. When Jimi Hendrix finally fired the former MI6 agent, Hendrix was dead within forty-eight hours.[30]

Rumors still swirl about the manner of Hendrix's death, and none of the accounts are completely consistent. Monika Dannemann reported that on September 17, 1971, the day after Hendrix finally fired Jeffery, she found her fiancé unconscious in their London apartment bed before noon. Hendrix had been at a party the night before where people had given him pills. He showed her the handful then flushed them down the toilet. Unable to sleep, he took multiple doses of Vesperax sleeping pills. The next morning, she went out briefly and came back to find Hendrix unresponsive. Dannemann called an ambulance. Hendrix died either before arriving at the hospital or an hour after, according to differing reports. While biographers Shapiro and Glebbeek found some discrepancies within Dannemann's account of Hendrix's last twenty-four hours, most of their eyewitnesses' reports backed Dannemann's general description.[31]

The coroner reported that what Hendrix had in him—a non-fatal dose of sleeping tablets, a small amount of alcohol, a trace of the barbiturate Seconal, and 20 mg of amphetamine—shouldn't have killed him. So the official cause of death was described by one source as possibly being: "inhalation of vomit due to Barbiturate intoxication."[32] It is likely that at the party someone spiked Hendrix's drink with the amphetamine, and possibly the Seconal, found in his system.

Monika Dannemann's memoir and Shapiro and Glebbeek's biography described how official foul play was rife after Hendrix's death. Dannemann said that when police investigated her place, they failed to take anything, and warned her to not say anything about the death. An official British inquest resulted in the London coroner and the inquest members declaring an open, inconclusive verdict on Hendrix's death. The inquest called only three witnesses to testify: Dannemann, Hendrix's road manager and the coroner. They failed to have the ambulance workers, the people Hendrix saw at the party, or the hospital doctors testify. Additionally, when Dannemann traveled with reporters to whom she could give her opinions about Hendrix's last twenty-four hours and officials' foul play thereafter, someone damaged Dannemann's thinking and communication by dosing her with LSD.[33]

Police also presented false information on Hendrix, backing up erroneous media reports that Hendrix was suicidal and used drugs heavily.

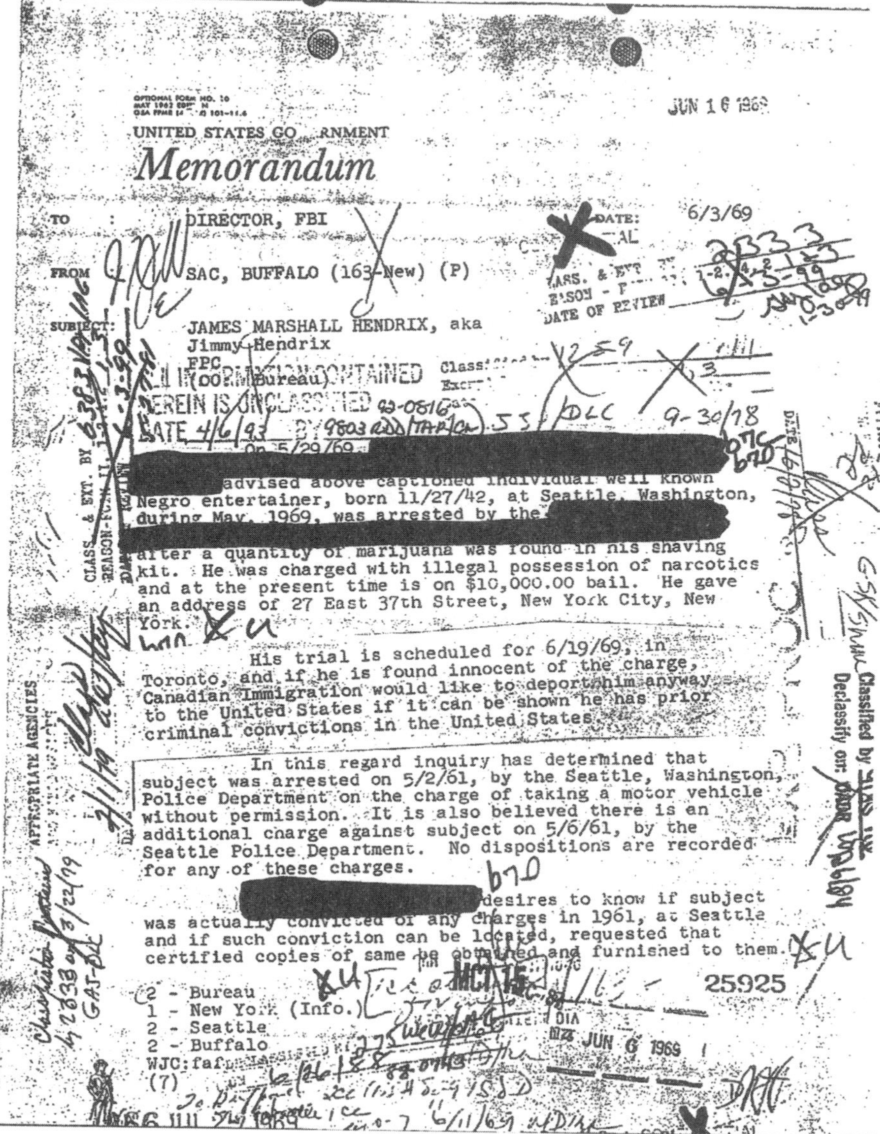
OPTIONAL FORM NO. 10
UNITED STATES GOVERNMENT
Memorandum

JUN 16 1969

TO : DIRECTOR, FBI
DATE: 6/3/69

FROM : SAC, BUFFALO (163-New) (P)

SUBJECT: JAMES MARSHALL HENDRIX, aka Jimmy Hendrix
FPC
(OO: Bureau)

ALL INFORMATION CONTAINED HEREIN IS UNCLASSIFIED
DATE 4/6/93 BY 9803 ADD/TAR/CAL

On 5/29/69 [redacted] advised above captioned individual well known Negro entertainer, born 11/27/42, at Seattle, Washington, during May, 1969, was arrested by the [redacted] after a quantity of marijuana was found in his shaving kit. He was charged with illegal possession of narcotics and at the present time is on $10,000.00 bail. He gave an address of 27 East 37th Street, New York City, New York.

His trial is scheduled for 6/19/69, in Toronto, and if he is found innocent of the charge, Canadian Immigration would like to deport him anyway to the United States if it can be shown he has prior criminal convictions in the United States.

In this regard inquiry has determined that subject was arrested on 5/2/61, by the Seattle, Washington, Police Department on the charge of taking a motor vehicle without permission. It is also believed there is an additional charge against subject on 5/6/61, by the Seattle Police Department. No dispositions are recorded for any of these charges.

[redacted] desires to know if subject was actually convicted of any charges in 1961, at Seattle and if such conviction can be located, requested that certified copies of same be obtained and furnished to them.

2 - Bureau
1 - New York (Info.)
2 - Seattle
2 - Buffalo
WJC:faf
(7)

25925
JUN 6 1969

This is one of many FBI documents on Hendrix, as they reportedly had him under 24-hour surveillance in his last years.

After his death, press accounts described Jimi Hendrix as an "overdosing … wild man," and a violent, hard drinking, drugged up sex maniac.[34] Police said that on the night he died, Hendrix left a message on the answering machine of his friend and former manager, Chas Chandler, in which he said, "Help me, man!" Chandler said he didn't own an answering machine.

Later on, Monika Dannemann came upon new and disturbing evidence. The coroner also found an unidentifiable compound in Hendrix's body.

Well-respected doctors told Dannemann that because the coroner waited several days to do Hendrix's autopsy, any poisons in his system might not have been in a detectable state.[35]

In 1975, the magazine *Crawdaddy* investigated and concluded that a death squad of undercover intelligence agents killed Hendrix.[36] While that magazine's sources aren't known, in 1992 England's Attorney General ordered an inquiry. Scotland Yard also re-examined the case, but failed to conclude that foul play occurred.

Dannemann, Shapiro and Glebbeek easily contradicted Scotland Yard, exposing their cover-up of contradictory evidence. Scotland Yard claimed to quote Hendrix's attending doctor, Dr. John Bannister, saying Hendrix was "dead on arrival ... [dying] in the ambulance or at home."[37] The ambulance workers denied this.[38] The hospital's official report had Hendrix's hospital arrival time as 11:45 A.M., and pronounced dead at 12:45 P.M.[39] Dannemann claimed Hendrix was alive when the ambulance workers took him from their apartment. Whether or not Hendrix was dead on arrival, what happened during that hour? Scotland Yard couldn't give Dannemann an answer. When she asked what Dr. Bannister had to say about it, Scotland Yard told her he had been struck off England's official medical register of all doctors in the country, without any further explanation.[40]

Mike Jeffery confiscated all of Hendrix's recordings and belongings in his New York studio. It took twenty-five years for Al Hendrix to gain the rights to his son's music from Warner Records. On albums and memorabilia, Warner records made over $100 million in sales, while Al Hendrix was only given $2 million.[41]

As happened in other targeted musicians' deaths, several close to Jimi Hendrix died in uncertain ways after him. Close friend Devon Wilson last saw Hendrix at the party the night before he died. Months later, she died of a reported overdose, but friends who saw the scene of her death said it looked like a violent murder.[42]

Several people sued Mike Jeffery for money he owed them. A judge allowed Jeffery to travel for business during the trial, and he reportedly died in a plane crash in 1973. Because a witness only saw Jeffery's jewelry to identify him, some believe he escaped with the shell company fortunes he amassed. Jeffery created his tax haven shell with the same Bahamas institutions that worked earlier with William Mellon Hitchcock and later with George H.W. Bush's CIA in the BCCI/Iran-Contra scandal.[43]

Another Hendrix-linked death occurred much later. Monica Dannemann said Jeffery threatened to kill her if she published the memoir about Hendrix she wrote in 1971. She said she lost her book manuscript twice between 1971 and 1973, first to a thief she believed Jeffery sent, and then to a Jeffery associate.[44] In 1995, she finally published a book about Hendrix's activist political plans, Jeffery's sabotage, and government cover-up. News reports said Dannemann killed herself in 1996. Her close friends believe she was murdered. They said Dannemann received death threats over the years, and had just finished a long interview for a film on Hendrix.[45]

In 2009, new information came to light regarding Mike Jeffrey's work on behalf of British and U.S. intelligence in their orchestration of Jimi Hendrix's murder. One of Jimi Hendrix's roadies, James "Tappy" Wright, published a memoir, *Rock Roadie*. Wright claimed that Mike Jeffery made a drunken confession in Wright's apartment one night in 1971. Wright said Jeffery confessed to having Hendrix murdered. The emergency room doctor, John Bannister, also said that after examining Hendrix it was "plausible" that Hendrix was murdered.[46]

Police investigating Hendrix's death failed to investigate Mike Jeffery despite Hendrix's lawyer, Henry Steingarten, and Monika Dannemann knowing that Hendrix had just fired him. While it's widely reported Jeffery "formerly" worked for MI6, a *London Times* reporter also wrote that Jeffery "flaunted his connections with organized crime and the FBI."[47]

Notes

1 Laura Sydell, "Janis Joplin: The Queen of Rock," *National Public Radio*, June 7, 2013, http://www.npr.org/2010/06/07/127483124/janis-joplin-the-queen-of-rock.

2 Alice Echols, *Scars of Sweet Paradise: The Life and Times of Janis Joplin* (New York: Henry Holt, 1999), pp. 75-76.

3 Echols, *Scars of Sweet Paradise*, pp. 87-88.

4 Myra Friedman, *Janis Joplin: Buried Alive* (New York: Three Rivers Press, 1973/1992), pp. 55-56.

5 Echols, *Scars of Sweet Paradise*, pp. 88, 89-94. On Janis's statement on speed experience, Friedman, *Janis Joplin*, p. 55.

6 Friedman, *Janis Joplin*, p. 78. On Joplin's first trip, see http://www.maebrussell.com/Mae%20Brussell%20Articles/Operation%20Chaos.html.

7 Echols, *Scars of Sweet Paradise*, p. 84. On Charlatans as first psychedelic rock band, Ronald M. James, *The Roar And The Silence: A History Of Virginia City And The Comstock Lode* (University of Nevada Press, 1998), p. 264.

8 Hank Albarelli, *A Terrible Mistake: The Murder of Frank Olson and the CIA's Secret Cold War Experiments* (Waterville, OR: Trine Day, 2009), p. 291.

9 Echols, *Scars of Sweet Paradise*, pp. 136-37.

10 Ian Halperin and Max Wallace, *Love and Death: The Murder of Kurt Cobain* (New York: Simon and Schuster/Atria, 2004), p. 29.

11 FBI Memorandum from SAC, New York (100-167072), dated 9/5/69.

12 Friedman, *Buried Alive*, p. 252.

13 Laura Joplin, *Love, Janis* (It Books, 2005), pp. 309-11.

14 "American album certifications – Janis Joplin – Pearl," Recording Industry Association of America.

15 On Hendrix, see Harry Shapiro and Caesar Glebbeek, *Jimi Hendrix: Electric Gyspy* (New

York: St. Martin's Press, 1995), pp. 70-71, 106-110. On Cooke, see Prakash Gandhi, "Sam Cooke," AMI Specials: Rock Secrets and Scandals, March 14, 2000, p. 30; Frederic Dannen, *Hit Men* (New York: Vintage, 1991), p. 34. Sam Cooke's popular songs included "You Send Me," "Chain Gang" and "Twistin' the Night Away." A hotel desk clerk claimed Cooke attacked her, so she shot him. Others believe the Mafia murdered Cooke for being the first black musician to take music ownership from Mafia hands and that police failed to investigate. On government-linked Mafia, see details on Genovese frontman Mo Levy's huge Black-recording-industry control in Dannen, *Hit Men*. On Genovese Mafia family's CIA links, see, for example, Vito Genovese as lieutenant for Charles "Lucky" Luciano, who worked with U.S. Naval Intelligence and then the CIA, in Alfred McCoy, *The Politics of Heroin: CIA Complicity in the Global Drug Trade* (New York: Lawrence Hill, 1991), pp. 36, 38, 43; and Clarence Lusane, *Pipe Dream Blues* (Boston: South End, 1991), p. 117.

16 On Jeffery's British MI6 work, possible continued MI6 work, and his later associates with likely CIA background, see Shapiro and Glebbeek, *Jimi Hendrix*, pp. 120-21, 280, 480-85; Alex Constantine, *The Covert War Against Rock* (Los Angeles, CA: Feral House, 2001), pp. 63-64. Mike Jeffery inserted himself into managing several other bands. They all reported Jeffery's negative manipulations and control over their careers. Mike Jeffery then developed Caribbean tax havens with banks that did U.S. intelligence work. He created similar shell companies as Death Row Records owner Dave Kenner. On such Caribbean bank work as CIA and Pentagon-type work through BCCI as part of the Iran-Contra scandal, see "Banks and Narcotics Money Flow in South Florida," US Senate Banking Committee report, 96th Congress, June 5-6, 1980, p. 201; Jonathon Kwitney, *The Crimes of Patriots: A True Tale of Dope, Dirty Money, and the CIA* (New York: Touchstone, 1987), p. 153. Both cited in Constantine, *The Covert War on Rock*, p. 64. On Jeffery associate Jerry Morrison likely being CIA, he had done five years of public relations work for Haiti's Pentagon-backed brutal dictator, "Papa Doc" Duvalier. See Shapiro and Glebbeek, *Jimi Hendrix*, pp. 279-80. The *New Columbia Encyclopedia* (William Harris and Judy Levey, eds., New York and London: Columbia University Press, 1975), described Duvalier as army-backed and in office through a "sham election," after which he declared himself "president for life." It further said he led a "reign of terror ... summarily executed his political opponents" and had his son succeed him in 1971. For Pentagon backing see, Noam Chomsky and Edward Herman, *The Washington Connection and Third World Fascism* (Boston: South End Press, 1979), chart: "The Sun and Its Planets: Countries Using Torture on an Administrative Basis in the 1970s, With Their Parent-Client Affiliations," which cites U.S. military training 567 Haitian military personnel from 1950-1975. U.S. also gave $4,200,000 in military aid. Their source: *Amnesty International Report on Torture* (U.S. edition, Farrar, Straus and Giroux, 1975), as backed by other extensive evidence. Amount of military aid obtained from Agency for International Development (A.I.D.*), U.S. Overseas Loans and Grants and Assistance from International Organizations*, 1976 ed.

17 In Monica Dannemann, *The Inner World of Jimi Hendrix* (New York: St. Martin's, 1995), pp. 40,116. Shapiro and Glebbeek, *Jimi Hendrix*, pp. 271-72. On interviews supporting the Black Panthers and political benefit for Bobby Seale and the Chicago 7, see "Jimi Hendrix, Black Power and Money," *Teenset*, January, 1969; and, Constantine, *The Covert War Against Rock*, p. 61. Dannemann also quoted from part of this interview, though she cited Jacob Atlas, *Circus*, March 1969, in Monica Dannemann, *The Inner World of Jimi Hendrix*, p. 123. It could have been a press conference quoted by both magazines. On Hendrix dedicating his last album to the Panthers, see Douglas Pringle, *The Jimi Hendrix Companion* (New York: Simon & Schuster, MacMillan, 1996), p. 63.

18 Todd Gitlin, *The Whole World is Watching* (Berkeley: University of California Press, 1980), p. 55, cited in Martin Lee and Bruce Shlain, *Acid Dreams: The Complete Social History of the CIA, LSD, the Sixties and Beyond* (New York: Grove Press, 1985), p. 210.

19 James Casbolt, "MI6 Are the Lords of the Drug Trade," 2006. Note that Casbolt's father Peter was also an MI6 agent. This article has been reprinted on a dozen or more websites. One is http://icssa.org, dated May 22, 2006. After this article, an article purportedly by Casbolt has appeared about extraterrestrials or UFOs. This has the look of a fake article planted by intelligence to discredit Casbolt.

20 Santa Barbara University campus newspaper filed a FOIA request and obtained this information in 1979, Constantine, *Covert War Against Rock*, p. 61. FBI surveillance of Hendrix also noted by Lee and Shlain, *Acid Dreams*, p. 226.

21 Dannemann, *The Inner World of Jimi Hendrix*, p. 78; Shapiro and Glebbeek, *Jimi Hendrix*, p. 360.

22 Shapiro and Glebbeek, *Jimi Hendrix*, pp. 359-61. Dannemann, *The Inner World of Jimi Hendrix*, pp. 48, 76-78.

23 Shapiro and Glebbeek, *Jimi Hendrix*, pp. 335, 361. Dannemann, p. 49. Dannemann claimed, and this was backed by Shapiro and Glebbeek, that Hendrix's first album, *Are You Experienced*, considered a masterpiece by most, was done six months before Hendrix ever used LSD. Purple Haze, for example, was the name of diffused light in a Hopi Indian folklore book. A batch of LSD out of San Francisco then took on that nickname. Shapiro and Glebbeek, p.148. Various media then turned this around, saying Hendrix's Purple Haze song was about LSD. For example, it's consistently referred to as "psychedelic" or "acid rock" and was played in the scene of the top movie, *Apocalypse Now*, when one of the characters is tripping, http://www.allmusic.com/style/acid-rock-ma0000012327/songs.

24 Dannemann, *The Inner World of Jimi Hendrix*, p. 177.

25 Dannemann, *The Inner World of Jimi Hendrix*, pp. 46-49.

26 Shapiro and Glebbeek, *Jimi Hendrix*, p. 280.

27 On Mafia kidnapping and Jeffery/Morrison freeing Hendrix, Shapiro and Glebbeek, *Jimi Hendrix*, pp. 393-96.

28 On Jeffery's association with Mafia and intimidation of Hendrix with Mafia, see Shapiro and Glebbeek, *Electric Gypsy*, pp. 294-96, Constantine, *The Covert War Against Rock*, p. 62. Also see Mafia intimidation account of Hendrix percussionist Juma Sultan in Shapiro and Glebbeek, p. 395.

29 Shapiro and Glebbeek, *Jimi Hendrix*, p. 280.

30 On Hendrix, see Dannemann, *The Inner World of Jimi Hendrix*, pp. 165-67. Hendrix firing Jeffery also in Shapiro and Glebbeek, *Jimi Hendrix*, pp.461-2. Note that rap icon Tupac Shakur was killed within 9 days of firing his lawyer, Death Row's umbrella company owner Dave Kenner, see Connie Bruck, "The Takedown of Tupac," *The New Yorker*, 7/2/97, p. 63.

31 Dannemann, *The Inner World of Jimi Hendrix*, pp. 165-67. Shapiro and Glebbeek, *Jimi Hendrix*, pp. 461-7, 473.

32 Dannemann, *The Inner World of Jimi Hendrix*, pp. 167-70, 175-78.

33 Dannemann, *The Inner World of Jimi Hendrix*, pp. 175-78. Shapiro and Glebbeek, *Jimi Hendrix*, pp. 463-67, 473.

34 Dannemann, *The Inner World of Jimi Hendrix*, pp.176-77. Shapiro and Glebbeek, *Jimi Hendrix*, pp. 468-472. On media smears to promote drugs, see Dannemann, p. 177 and Shapiro and Glebbeek, *Jimi Hendrix*, pp. 468, 473.

35 Dannemann, *The Inner World of Jimi Hendrix*, p. 178.

36 John Swenson, "The Last Days of Jimi Hendrix," *Crawdaddy*, January, 1975, p. 45, cited in Constantine, *The Covert War Against Rock*, p. 72.

37 Dannemann, *The Inner World of Jimi Hendrix*, pp. 188-89.

38 Dannemann, *The Inner World of Jimi Hendrix*, Shapiro and Glebbeek, *Jimi Hendrix*, p. 475, and Constantine, *The Covert War Against Rock*, pp. 65-66.

39 Dannemann, *The Inner World of Jimi Hendrix*, pp.188-89. Shapiro and Glebbeek, *Jimi Hendrix*, pp. 466-67.

40 Dannemann, *The Inner World of Jimi Hendrix*, p. 188.

41 Shapiro and Glebbeek, *Jimi Hendrix*, pp. 473, 477-91, particularly 490.

42 Shapiro and Glebbeek, *Jimi Hendrix*, pp. 473, 477-91. Wilson's death, also Dannemann, p. 185. Also see Chuck Phillips, "Father Gets Hendrix Song, Image Rights," *Los Angeles Times* (home ed.), 7/26/95, p.1, cited in Constantine, *The Covert War Against Rock*, p. 73.

43 On lawsuit trial and death, Shapiro and Glebbeek, *Jimi Hendrix*, pp. 479. On Bahama shell company, see Constantine and Swenson, "The Last Days of Jimi Hendrix." Also "Banks and Narcotics

Money Flow in South Florida," US Senate Banking Committee Report, 96th Congress, June 5-6, 1980, p. 201, and Jonathon Kwitney, *The Crimes of Patriots: A True Tale of Dope, Dirty Money, and the CIA* (New York: Touchstone, 1987), p. 153. All cited in Constantine, *The Covert War Against Rock*, pp. 63-64. Also, Shapiro and Glebbeek, pp. 484-88. On Wilson's death, also Dannemann, *The Inner World of Jimi Hendrix*, p. 185. Also see, Chuck Phillips, "Father Gets Hendrix Song, Image Rights," cited in Constantine, *The Covert War Against Rock*, p. 73.

44 Dannemann, *The Inner World of Jimi Hendrix*, pp. 184-85.

45 *Eastern Daily Press*, April 6, 1996, cited in Constantine, *The Covert War Against Rock*, pp. 66, 71.

46 Wright quoted Jeffery as saying, "I had to do it. You know damn well what I'm talking about." Jeffery reportedly said he had taken out a life insurance policy on Hendrix worth $2 million, with himself as beneficiary. Wright further quoted Jeffery as saying, "I was in London the night of Jimi's death and together with some of our old friends ... got a handful of pills and stuffed them into his mouth ... then poured a few bottles of red wine deep into his windpipe. I had to do it. Jimi was worth much more to me dead than alive. That son of a bitch was going to leave me." This appears as an actual drunken confession and then a lie as to why, to cover-up the confession. James "Tappy" Wright and Ron Weinberg, *Rock Roadie: Backstage Confidential with Hendrix, Elvis, The Animals, Tina Turner and an All-Star Cast* (New York: Thomas Dunne/St. Martin's, 2010), pp. 231-32. The emergency room doctor who worked on Jimi Hendrix backed this account. After James Wright's book release in 2009, reporters interviewed the emergency room doctor, John Bannister, who supported Wright's claim, saying it was "plausible" that he was murdered. Bannister said, "The amount of wine that was over [Hendrix] was extraordinary. Not only was it saturated through his hair and shirt, but his lungs and stomach were absolutely full of wine... He had really drowned in a massive amount of red wine." Aislinn Simpson, "Jimi Hendrix murder theory 'plausible' says ER doctor," *The Telegraph* (London), 7/2/09, http://www.telegraph.co.uk/news/newstopics/celebritynews/5869491/J.

47 Dominic Wells, "Was Jimi Hendrix Murdered?" *The Times* (London), 7/4/09.

Chapter Fifteen

The Assassination of John Lennon

While the Beatles officially broke up as a band around 1970, Beatles lead singer/songwriter John Lennon had a solo career from about 1968 until 1975. Lennon initiated his split with the Beatles after he started dating Yoko Ono and separated from his wife Cynthia in 1968. He began producing songs solo or with Yoko in late 1968, and married her a year later.[1]

Some say the fact that Yoko Ono's family was one of the wealthiest in Japan suggests her work for a collaborating Japanese intelligence agency. This is uncertain. John Lennon did say he was having a lot of bad acid trips and decided to stop taking it for a while, but both Ono and his Apple Record label press officer encouraged him to keep using acid.[2] John Lennon also started using heroin with Yoko Ono, who reportedly tried it before him.[3] Lennon ended up writing the songs "Me and My Monkey" and "Cold Turkey" about his heroin addiction, before detoxing from the drug in the 1970s.[4]

The Beatles' singer/songwriter John Lennon was a strident antiwar activist, and the U.S. government tried to deport him in the early 1970s.

John Lennon's drug use failed to stop him from developing radical leftist politics. He talked about being an atheist and started associating with nationally known anti-War activists Jerry Rubin, Abbie Hoffman and Rennie Davis. He held anti-War events and did a benefit concert to free imprisoned activist John Sinclair.

Lennon had sporadically written songs about radicalism with the Beatles, such as "Revolution." Once he went solo he continued to produce more-radical political songs including "Give Peace a Chance," "Working Class Hero," "Imagine," and "Power to the People." Lennon also paid for billboards in twelve countries announcing: "WAR IS OVER – IF YOU WANT IT."[5]

Despite stopping the use of LSD, Lennon's earlier use of acid had residual effects, appearing to cause him hallucinogen-induced anxiety disorder, a not-uncommon problem with heavy acid users. Lennon had toured comfortably with the Beatles for years, but on his own in the 1970s, he admitted he vomited for hours before taking the stage, due to performance anxiety.[6]

Lennon continued to write activist songs and, in 1972, he produced an album titled *Some Time in New York City*. The album was almost exclusively political, supporting feminists, Irish Nationalists and Black Panthers. Asked in 1971 if he was becoming increasingly radical and political, he said, "In my case I've never not been political, though religion tended to overshadow it in my acid days."[7]

Also in 1972, John and Yoko cohosted the Mike Douglas show for a week, where they introduced radical anti-War activists to a huge new audience of Americans.[8] Lennon further helped organize a planned disruption of the 1972 Republican National Convention.[9]

For four years Lennon fought with President Nixon's administration while they tried to deport him via extradition for a 1968 possession-of-marijuana charge in Britain.[10] Lennon believed the marijuana arrest was a frame-up. It occurred when John and Yoko took up temporary residence in Ringo Starr's London apartment. A reporter warned Lennon that a detective and his drug squad were after him. Lennon cleared the apartment of any drugs, but believed the drug squad planted some marijuana. The detective who was on the scene would later be charged with corruption. Lennon pled guilty and paid a 150-pound fine to avoid a conflict with the government that could have gotten Yoko deported.[11]

In 1972, when the FBI were following Lennon's activities prior to the Republican National Convention, a source told the feds that Lennon had contributed $75,000 to the group planning to disrupt the Republican's convention. About the same time, the FBI issued a memorandum—one of over hundreds of pages in his FBI file—stating a domestic arrest of Lennon on drug charges could make him deportable. The documents also revealed how the New York City Police Department was attempting to arrest both Lennon and Ono for narcotics use in 1972, "to neutralize any disruptive activities of" Lennon.[12]

Another biographer also lent credence to heavy intelligence involvement in Lennon's life. He wrote that FBI agents, "attended his concerts, studied his song lyrics ... CIA men shadowed him in his private life ... and tapped his phone." On the *Dick Cavett Show*, Lennon said what really scared him was how openly and brazenly he was harassed. Even so, Lennon continued to address peace rallies, including one in New York attended by 20,000 people in 1972.[13]

Lawyer's Conclusion: CIA Murdered Lennon

Fenton Bresler made broader claims in a 1989 book, *Who Killed John Lennon?* Bresler, a lawyer and top London legal reporter with decades of experience, conducted an eight-year investigation showing there was an extensive cover-up regarding Lennon's murder. Working as London's *Daily Mail* and *Sunday Express* legal correspondent, Bresler said he fought for years with functionaries of the Freedom of Information Act to get copies of 217 pages that the FBI had in their file on John Lennon, and four pages that the CIA had in their file on him. Bresler said the FBI pages alluded to many more pages in the CIA files that they wouldn't release.[14]

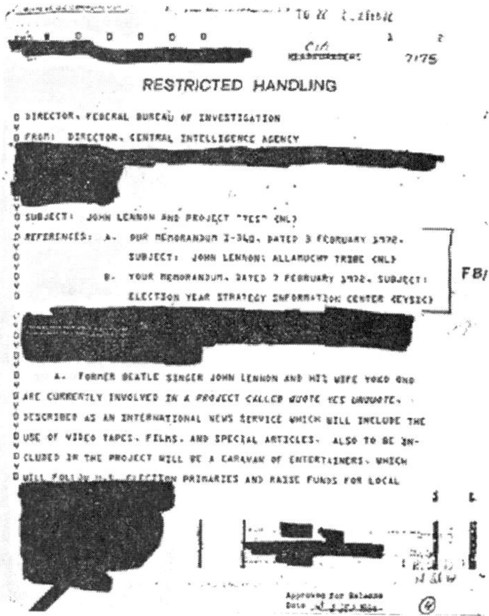

7175

RESTRICTED HANDLING

DIRECTOR, FEDERAL BUREAU OF INVESTIGATION

FROM: DIRECTOR, CENTRAL INTELLIGENCE AGENCY

SUBJECT: JOHN LENNON AND PROJECT "YES" (NL)

REFERENCES: A. OUR MEMORANDUM I-340, DATED 3 FEBRUARY 1972, SUBJECT: JOHN LENNON; ALLAMUCHY TRIBE (NL)

B. YOUR MEMORANDUM, DATED 7 FEBRUARY 1972, SUBJECT: ELECTION YEAR STRATEGY INFORMATION CENTER (EYSIC)

FBI

A. FORMER BEATLE SINGER JOHN LENNON AND HIS WIFE YOKO ONO ARE CURRENTLY INVOLVED IN A PROJECT CALLED QUOTE YES UNQUOTE, DESCRIBED AS AN INTERNATIONAL NEWS SERVICE WHICH WILL INCLUDE THE USE OF VIDEO TAPES, FILMS, AND SPECIAL ARTICLES. ALSO TO BE INCLUDED IN THE PROJECT WILL BE A CARAVAN OF ENTERTAINERS, WHICH WILL FOLLOW U.S. ELECTION PRIMARIES AND RAISE FUNDS FOR LOCAL

Approved for Release

This is one of many government documents on Lennon. He said government spies had him under constant surveillance.

These and other FBI Cointelpro documents, along with findings by a judge and former Cointelpro agent Wes Swearingen, indicate the ongoing political targeting of John Lennon.[15] Many other research investigations, including one by the *New York Times*, revealed how the CIA joined in these operations against American leftists in the 1970s with its Operation Chaos.[16] While Operation Chaos officially ended in 1973, former CIA agents such as John Stockwell reported its continuance. High-level CIA whistleblower Victor Marchetti also reported Operation MK-Ultra's continuance, and further evidence supports this.[17]

By 1973, public outcry along with overt and underground activists' work, led political leaders to investigate U.S. intelligence's corrupt activities. Congress began an investigation into U.S. intelligence's covert operations that year. Richard Helms, the CIA Covert Operations Director, feared people would find out about the MK-Ultra program. In the 1950s, Helms's CIA Director Allen Dulles had allowed him to run a percentage of the programs without a formal contract. This reportedly would help protect the reputations of academics running the program by having deniability that they officially worked for the CIA's MK-Ultra program. Helms at least temporarily stopped MK-Ultra in 1973 and destroyed all documents connected with it (though many remained in linked financial departments).[18]

Focusing more on Lennon's murder, Bresler uncovered evidence of much government foul play against the musical icon, and the author reviewed the known political activism of Lennon that put him in opposition to the incoming Ronald Reagan's right-wing presidential administration. By the early 1970s, Lennon considered himself a socialist and, "became more and more active in radical politics."[19]

Lennon stayed out of the public eye from 1975 to 1979, to focus on raising his new son Sean. In 1976, Lennon finally got his Green Card, allowing him to stay in the U.S. In 1980, Lennon released two albums of music that quickly rose to the top of the charts. [20] Lennon also signed a legal document about the Beatles agreeing to reunite for a concert within the next five years, partly to stop a stageshow called *Beatlemania*.[21]

While spying and threats of deportation led Lennon to closet his activism after the early seventies, this changed in 1980. Shortly after his musical comeback, Lennon sent press releases about his support for an important Teamsters strike. As noted by a *Newsweek* "Special Report" on Lennon, written after his murder, Lennon was scheduled to march with the striking workers and sing at their rally. The workers were Japanese-Americans striking for equal pay with their white counterparts. And, Lennon was just one month away from being allowed to become an American citizen when he was killed.[22]

The FBI and CIA files obtained by Fenton Bresler indicated the FBI had ordered their agents to keep Lennon under constant surveillance.[23] On December 8, 1980, at 10:50 P.M., John Lennon came home with Yoko Ono to their New York apartment in the Dakota building. Twenty-five year-old Mark Chapman was standing near the sidewalk entrance to Lennon's apartment as Lennon walked by. When Lennon was less than twenty feet away, Chapman took out a .38 caliber snub-nosed gun, crouched in a combat stance and fired at him. Chapman hit Lennon in the back and shoulder with four highly lethal hollow-point bullets. Chapman then dropped the gun, took off his jacket, folded it up next to his feet, took out the book *The Catcher in the Rye*, and read it until the police came. Lennon was rushed to the hospital where he died after doctors spent eleven hours trying to save him.[24]

In *Who Killed John Lennon?* Fenton Bresler cited evidence incriminating U.S. intelligence concerning Lennon's murder and investigation. Bresler detailed his evidence indicating that the CIA orchestrated Mark Chapman's assassination of John Lennon. In summary, Bresler documented how an Atlanta area police officer trained Chapman in shooting and gave him the bullets with which he killed Lennon, on behalf of U.S. intelligence.

Bresler showed how this could be easily done. He first cited a *New York Times* article discussing CIA training of local police officers in a dozen major cities including New York.[25] Bresler believes that the CIA worked with Atlanta police intelligence in commissioning help with the assassination.

Phil Strongman, a critically praised music writer who authored five books and edited another two, also investigated Lennon's murder for his book *John Lennon: Life, Times and Assassination*. Strongman agreed with Bresler about the Atlanta police officer, whom Strongman names as Dana Reeves. Bresler said Reeves had a pseudonym, Gene Scott, and only used that name (but Reeves will be used here). Fenton Bresler and Strongman separately gave provocative evidence that Reeves guided Chapman through his path of becoming a drugged and hypnotized CIA tool, in the way other investigators believed had been done with Robert Kennedy's assassin, Sirhan Sirhan. Bresler detailed how Reeves had first known the younger Chapman when he was still in high school. Bresler cited Chapman's history of drug use at that time, including the regular use of LSD beginning at age fifteen and heroin use while still a teenager.[26]

Dana Reeves was working as a Dekalb County sheriff's officer in the Atlanta area, where he developed a close relationship and extreme control over Chapman by the time he was nineteen years old. Chapman's parents feared Reeves's involvement with their son, and said the police officer changed their son's personality. For example, the parents and others described Chapman as anti-gun throughout his teens, but Reeves turned Chapman on to guns, training him to be a very competent shooter. Chapman had worked at a regular YMCA summer camp in Atlanta. In 1975, Chapman applied for exotic positions in YMCA's abroad program, first unsuccessfully in the Soviet Union, despite not speaking Russian, and then working in Beirut, Lebanon in June 1975. He had just turned twenty in May.[27]

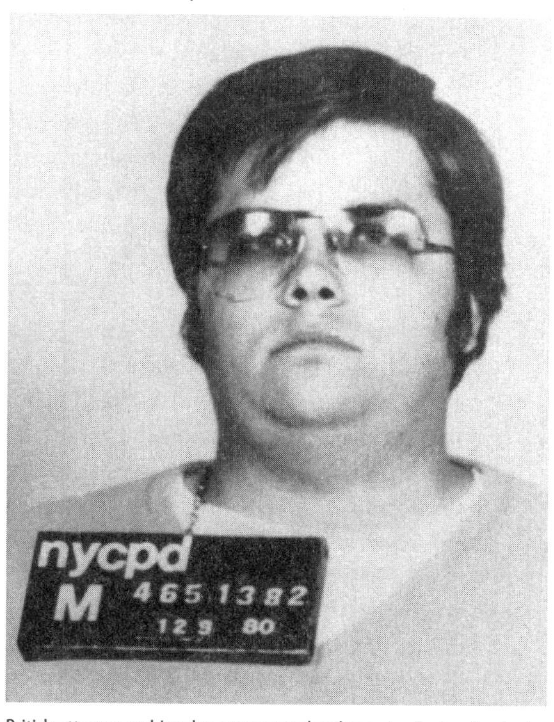

British attorney and London newspaper legal reporter Fenton Bresler investigated Lennon's murder for seven years. He concluded that the CIA used drugs and hypnosis on Mark David Chapman, pictured here, to kill Lennon.

Bresler believed that the CIA "blooded" Chapman in Beirut to aid his becoming a programmed killer. Bresler described this as exposing someone to the kind of constant gun murders going on in war-torn areas such as Beirut, in order to desensitize them to killing. Many researchers, such as Watergate muckraker Bob Woodward, described the massive CIA presence in mid-1970s Beirut. The country was involved in its second civil war at that time.[28] Beirut was also the site of a U.S. naval intelligence base and a CIA assassination training camp.[29]

Furthermore, Philip Agee, a leading CIA-whistleblower, cited the CIA's use of international YMCA facilities for their operations abroad, and said that at least two active CIA officers were on the YMCA's board of directors. Chapman had reportedly never heard gunfire before and brought home tape recordings of bombs, gunfire and screams from the wounded people just outside the windows of his temporary home, working for the YMCA in Beirut.[30] After about six months in that position, Chapman received a job, as special assistant to the director of the YMCA's camp, working with 5,000 South Vietnamese refugees for five months in Fort Chaffee, Arkansas. A percentage of these refugees had been working for the U.S. military's puppet leader of South Vietnam in the war that just ended.[31]

Fenton Bresler said that refugee camp placed thousands of refugees into homes and then closed up in December of 1975. Dana Reeves picked Mark Chapman up from Arkansas and took him back to Atlanta. They were living together in 1976, when Reeves suggested that the 21 year-old Chapman get a job as an armed security guard. Chapman had quickly turned from hating guns to scoring an 88 out of a 100 in a pistol-shooting test for which he only needed to score a 60.[32]

By January of 1977, Mark David Chapman decided to make a move halfway around the globe to Hawaii—a location with seven major military bases. On a security guard's salary, Chapman flew to Hawaii, came back again to Atlanta briefly and then was back in Hawaii again. This time, biographers purported that Mark David Chapman was diagnosed and treated for clinical depression at Castle Memorial Hospital, a Seventh Day Adventist hospital, in the summer of 1977. University of California Professor Peter Dale Scott stated that Chapman actually went through CIA-developed behavior modification at Castle Memorial Hospital.[33] Bresler and Strongman agree that in Castle Memorial and in other locales, the CIA was developing Chapman into an assassin. Bresler detailed how after two weeks of treatment at this private hospital, they released Chapman. Weeks later, Castle Memorial Hospital hired him to work in maintenance, and then in customer-relations there for the next 27 months, until November of 1979.[34]

In support of Bresler's, Strongman's and Prof. Scott's claims about Castle Memorial Hospital, Chapman's biographers reported Chapman flew around the country and around the world at least twice. In one of the trips he visited a dozen countries for over six weeks, at times staying in expensive hotels. This would have been highly improbable on his meager salary. Castle Memorial Hospital reportedly "gave him a loan" to do this.[35]

In late 1979, Chapman left his job at Castle Memorial for another security guard job in Hawaii. Soon after, Chapman started becoming very interested in a book, *The Catcher in the Rye.* Bresler and Strongman believe Chapman's CIA handlers used the book as one of their hypnotic triggers for Chapman. In 1980, shortly before Chapman came face to face with John Lennon, he was back living with police officer Dana Reeves, who trained him to improve his marksmanship. Reeves also gave Chapman special police hollow-point bullets. These bullets are extra-deadly as they expand upon impact and tear up the body more.[36]

Around the first week of December, an article said, Mark Chapman somehow attained a $2000 loan from the credit union of Castle Memorial Hospital again, despite not working there in a year. The article said he used it to travel to Chicago to see his grandmother, before heading to New York. On the night of December 8, 1980, Chapman came to John Lennon's New York City address and waited for Lennon to arrive late from his recording studio. When Lennon arrived, Chapman kneeled down in a combat stance and shot Lennon with four bullets closely cropped in a tight circle in Lennon's back, from about 20 feet away. Chapman shot a fifth bullet that missed Lennon falling to the pavement. A statement from the coroner at Lennon's autopsy reports it was difficult to distinguish the separate bullet holes.[37]

There were few at the scene. Yoko Ono had come home with John Lennon but had been far ahead of him, inside their apartment building when Chapman shot Lennon. She told the man at the desk to call the police and then came outside to kneel beside her husband. A witness from an apartment building across the street described only being able to see two people—Mark Chapman and the apartment's doorman, Jose Perdomo, at the gate of the apartment. Chapman could have escaped to a subway entrance just across the street. Instead he took off his coat, folded it up, and took *The Catcher in the Rye* out of the pocket.[38] Despite Lennon being declared dead on arrival at Roosevelt Hospital, a team of seven surgeons tried to resuscitate him, to no avail, as he had lost 80% of his blood.[39]

When Fenton Bresler investigated John Lennon's murder, he talked with Lieutenant Arthur O'Connor, who headed the New York police district of one million people, where Lennon had lived. Lt. O'Connor said he had never experienced such pandemonium: "Within two hours of Lennon's murder, there were literally 150 reporters at the station house. It was like we were under siege." This exemplified the international interest and influence of Lennon, underscoring why his leftist activism was a threat to the CIA and the oligarchy.[40]

Lt. O'Connor admitted to Bresler that someone could have programmed Chapman for the murder of Lennon. "I studied him intensely," he said. "[Chapman] looked like he could have been programmed, and I know what you are going to make of that word! That was the way he looked and that was the way he talked."[41] He was the second police officer to make this assessment.[42] After Chapman was arrested for killing Lennon, his bizarre behavior was never checked with a drug test.[43]

So, attorney and crime reporter Fenton Bresler believes the CIA's MK-Ultra program hypnotized Mark David Chapman, with the aid of drugs, to become an assassin. Author Phil Strongman agreed with Bresler's general assessment. Bresler reviewed the history of MK-Ultra, and quoted other researchers, such as former CIA official John Marks, and attorney Daniel Sheehan of the Christic Institute, who also investigated cases of MK-Ultra hypnotized assassins.[44]

Strongman had one different belief regarding the icon's assassination. Strongman believed that the CIA likely used a backup marksman to aid in the assassination of John Lennon. Strongman stated that the full name of the doorman seen with Chapman at the murder was Jose Joaquin Sanjenis Perdomo. Strongman said that "various other books, and newspaper accounts, have established links between the Dakota doorman 'Jose' and a Jose who was an active anti-Castro Cuban. Cuban Information Archives have shown that a 'Jose Joaquin Sanjenis Perdomo' was active during the CIA's 1961 Bay of Pigs invasion as an armed member of Brigade 2056." Other authors interviewed a CIA spy employee who said Perdomo had been on the CIA payroll for at least ten years, including involvement in the Nixon Watergate burglary. Strongman further claimed that one of the first policemen on the scene of the murder initially believed that Perdomo, rather than Chapman, killed Lennon.[45] Whoever actually fired the fatal bullets, evidence indicates that U.S. intelligence was involved.

Bresler said that government officials then took part in a cover-up. Various officials altered evidence and reported losing official documents to stymie his investigation. For example, when Bresler documented Chapman's exact travel in the days leading up to Lennon's murder, he found that officials altered some documents on Mark Chapman's itinerary, and reportedly "lost" other key official documents regarding the days just prior to the murder.[46] Bresler found many contradictions concerning Chapman's whereabouts in those days. When Bresler later asked for copies of the official record, government administrators first denied Bresler access, before the New York District Attorney's office said it had disappeared from the office records. Bresler noted that this was in line with the YMCA saying it couldn't find its records on Chapman's work with them, as well as the fact that many CIA and FBI documents in Chapman's file allude to particular pages that were never released.[47]

Millions grieved over John Lennon's death at the early age of forty. His widow Yoko Ono asked for people to conduct silent vigils on December 14. New York Mayor Ed Koch, actress Jane Fonda, and her husband, SDS leader-turned politician Tom Hayden, convened with an estimated 100,000 in Central Park. Estimated hundreds to thousands gathered in city squares all over the U.S. and around the world, including 20,000 in Liverpool, England,

and several thousand in Melbourne, Australia.[48] By that Christmas, radio stations worldwide played Lennon's anti-Vietnam War song, "Happy Xmas (War is Over)" multiple times daily.[49]

In line with Jimi Hendrix, the Rolling Stones and others, John Lennon's life and death presents another example of the way American and British intelligence targeted leftist musicians. They appeared to manipulate Lennon to promote certain drugs while he was alive. When he began moving away from drugs and more towards activism, evidence indicates that they murdered him.

CIA Families' Involvement in Music and Radio

Fenton Bresler's book *Who Killed John Lennon?* was panned in London's *Sunday Telegraph.* Miles Copeland III wrote the *Telegraph* review.[50] Copeland worked as an entertainment executive best known for founding I.R.S. Records. Copeland's father was a founding officer of the CIA. His mother worked for British intelligence. Miles Copeland's brother, Stewart, founded the band The Police in 1977. These names, I.R.S. and The Police, seemed either ironic or purposefully obvious in order to suggest no possible malfeasance from children of a high-level CIA officer.[51]

Stewart Copeland's father reportedly helped The Police get shows worldwide, while son Miles worked as their manager, making them famous fast. (Police lead singer Sting ran into conflicts with the Copelands, eventually starting a solo career in 1984.) Similar quick fame came to other sons of military intelligence and the wealthiest families, such as CSN's David Crosby, the Doors' Jim Morrison, and others mentioned previously. Miles Copeland also started at least three other record companies besides I.R.S.

Miles Copeland III further developed a huge music management roster of musicians he helped make into stars, such as Lou Reed, the Go Gos, Gary Numan, The Alarm, Squeeze, and Adam Ant. Copeland had graduated from college in 1966 and then promoted his first concert before getting a Masters degree in business at the American University of Beirut in 1969. He started British Talent Management in the 1970s. Copeland's immediate power and influence in the British music industry was similar to that of previously MI6-employed Hendrix manager Mike Jeffery.[52]

In 1975 Copeland started the first traveling music festival in Europe. These festivals included some of the people he was managing: Soft Machine, the Mahavishnu Orchestra, and Lou Reed. Copeland continued managing groups for the next decades.[53]

Another powerful member of the music industry, radio mogul John McCaw, a member of the U.S. intelligence umbrella group, the National Security Council, appeared to have his four sons follow in their U.S.

intelligence-advising father's footsteps. The McCaws gained influence over the media by way of large ownership in cable television networks and other communications companies. The sons accumulated a net worth of at least $750 million each.[54] Other U.S. intelligence leaders set up similar spheres of influence in music and entertainment.[55]

Parallel with U.S. intelligence using organized crime to aid in their assassinations and their programs pushing drugs, they appeared to allow organized crime figures to dominate in the ownership of music publishing, clubs, labels and promotion. Organized crime also controlled record distribution and music tours through its power in the Teamsters Union.[56] At least one publisher, Lou Wolfe of *Covert Action Quarterly*, said the Mafia also owned East/West, the sole magazine distributor to kiosks and newsstands. Wolfe believed East/West collaborated with the CIA in barring his and most other leftist magazines.[57]

In the 1990s, Time Warner expanded its music holdings. Warner Music merged with EMI music, and combined over six well-known music labels—Warner Brother Records, Elektra Entertainment Group, Atlantic Group, Capitol, Virgin, and Priority, which they aggregately called WEA. These companies each owned a multitude of independent labels. They made up nearly a quarter of the total music sales, with three other companies controlling the rest.

Warner EMI dominated the market along with three other companies—Universal Music, BMG entertainment, and Sony Music. They soon formed an oligopoly, acting as a unit to control an entire industry. Time Warner owned Warner Brothers motion pictures and WB Television, and had additional vast holdings in dozens of cable TV stations, book publishing, and video production. They had the most media holdings of the four companies that dominated what *The Nation* magazine called "The National Entertainment State."[58]

The ruling oligarchy and U.S. intelligence apparently pursued the goal of controlling music for several reasons. First, they recognized that musicians arguably had the greatest influence over people's hearts and minds. Secondly, U.S. intelligence believed that control over the entertainment state would allow them to censor leftist musicians, promote apolitical and right-wing musicians, or popularize musicians who promoted drug use. That is what they appear to have done.

Notes

1 In 1968, John Lennon left his wife of several years, Cynthia Lennon, for his future wife Yoko Ono. Some researchers believe that Yoko Ono was inserted into John Lennon's life to control him. While this theory remains somewhat dubious, a few aspects of John's life with Yoko support the

notion. First, Yoko One came from one of Japan's wealthiest families. Secondly, Yoko's actions were reportedly harmful to Lennon.

2 Lennon said that when he thought he had lost all confidence and thought he should stop tripping, Yoko joined in with his Apple press officer, Derek Taylor, in convincing him to trip again. 1971 interview with *Rolling Stone* magazine publisher, Jann Wenner, http://taz4158.tripod.com/johnint.html.

3 Several reports state that Yoko convinced Lennon to try heroin for the first time. Other reports depict Lennon's purported thousand hits of LSD led him to become increasingly dependent and subservient to Yoko. Yoko, in turn, used this to lead Lennon to become dependent on the guidance of occultists. Philip Norman, *Lennon: The Life* (Ecco/Harper Collins, 2008), p. 187.

4 1971 interview with *Rolling Stone* magazine publisher, Jann Wenner, in 1971.

5 Bill Harry, *The John Lennon Encyclopedia* (Virgin, 2000), p. 960. Note that in the first produced version of "Revolution," his chorus was "You say you want a Revolution ... don't you know you can count me out, *in*." The in was added in that version, but then taken out in later produced versions, reportedly by his record company.

6 See *Rolling Stone* interview with Jann Wenner at http://taz4158.tripod.com/johnint.html. On hallucinogen-induced anxiety disorder, see http://www.minddisorders.com/Flu-Inv/Hallucinogens-and-related-disorders.html#b. Also note that this writer has worked for over twenty years in addictions. Working in a mental health hospital, I saw at least several people vomiting each morning from anxiety, with much LSD use in their history. If there were a positive about Lennon's destructive heroin habit, it would be that low dose opiates temporarily aid focus for songwriting, but the active habit usually ruins lives.

7 Norman, *Lennon*, pp. 183-86.

8 "Lennon filmmakers credit campaign," *BBC News*, October 12, 2006.

9 Jon Wiener, "Give Peace a Chance," *The Nation*, October 20, 1997.

10 Jon Wiener, *Come Together: John Lennon in His Time* (University of Illinois Press, 1990), p. 204.

11 Phil Strongman, *John Lennon: Life, Times and Assassination* (Liverpool, England: Bluecoat Press, 2010), p. 152.

12 Jon Wiener, "Give Peace a Chance." On "FBI teletype" and Lennon "contributing $75,000" see Strongman, *Lennon*, pp.152-54. Strongman quoted an FBI teletype from April 17 and documents from February 29, and April 21 and 25, 1972.

13 Ray Coleman, *Lennon: The Definitive Biography* (New York: HarperCollins, 1992), pp. 577-78. On 20,000 at a peace rally Lennon addressed, see Strongman, *Lennon*, p.154.

14 On U.S. intelligence focus on music, Alex Constantine, *The Covert War Against Rock* (Los Angeles, Feral House, 2000), p. 12. Also see, Fenton Bresler, *Who Killed John Lennon* (New York: St. Marks, 1989), p. 9.

15 On Cointelpro's continuance, deposition of former FBI agent M. Wesley Swearingen, taken in October 1980, in Honolulu, Hawaii, p. 2. On judge on Cointelpro's continuance, *Handschu, et al. vs. Special Services Division a/k/a Bureau of Special Services, U.S. District Court*, S.D.N.Y., 71 Civ. 2203 (CSH) Memorandum Opinion and Order, Mar. 7, 1985, p. 26. Ibid, Memorandum Opinion and Order, May 24, 1979, p. 3. All cited in Ward Churchill and Jim Vander Wall, *Agents of Repression: The FBI's Secret Wars Against the Black Panther Party and the American Indian Movement* (Boston: South End, 1988), p. 62.

16 On CIA spying on Americans, Seymour Hersh, "Huge C.I.A. Operation Reported in U.S. Against Antiwar Forces, Other Dissidents in Nixon Years," *New York Times*, 12/22/74, p. A1.

17 On agents, see Victor Marchetti interviewed in 1977, in M. Cannon, "Mind Control and the American Government," *Lobster* magazine 23 (1992). Also see this interview of Marchetti: http://www.skepticfiles.org/socialis/marcheti.htm. On Marchetti's work: Victor Marchetti and John Marks, *The CIA and the Cult of Intelligence* (New York: Dell,1974). On CIA Operation Chaos continuance, see http://www.youtube.com/watch?v=SaQVX30ginQ.

18 Al McCoy, *A Question of Torture: CIA Interrogation, from the Cold War to the War on Terror*

(New York: Metropolitan, 2006), pp.29-31. Jo Thomas, "C.I.A Says It Found More Secret Papers on Behavior Control: Senate Panel Puts Off Hearing to Study Data Dozen Witnesses Said To Have Misled Inquiry C.I.A. Tells Of Finding Secret Data," *New York Times*, September 3, 1973.

19 Coleman, *Lennon*, pp. 559-60.

20 http://www.billboard.com/features/john-lennon-s-top-10-albums-singles-1004118689.story#/features/john-lennon-s-top-10-albums-singles-1004118689.story.

21 http://www.billboard.com/#/charts/billboard-200?chartDate=1981-02-14.

22 Fenton Bresler, *Who Killed John Lennon?* (New York: St. Martin's, 1989), pp. 180, 214-215.

23 Bresler, *Who Killed John Lennon?* p. 129.

24 Bresler, *Who Killed John Lennon?* pp. 1, 2, 229-30, 234.

25 Bresler, *Who Killed John Lennon?* p. 205. Also see Strongman, *John Lennon*, pp. 164-65.

26 Bresler, *Who Killed John Lennon?* p. 100. Strongman, *John Lennon*, pp. 159, 197, 210.

27 Bresler, *Who Killed John Lennon?* pp. 117-18, 125-26, 143, 177-80. On officer's name, Strongman, *John Lennon*, p. 197.

28 See Bob Woodward, *VEIL: The Secret Wars of the CIA* (New York: Simon & Schuster, 1987), referenced in Bresler, *Who Killed John Lennon?* pp. 118-20.

29 Bresler, *Who Killed John Lennon?* pp.154, 120-24.

30 Bresler, *Who Killed John Lennon?* pp. 32-34. A 1986 edition of Agee's CIA Diary has no indexed reference to the YMCA. As Agee's book was first published in Britain, the reference may have appeared in Bresler's British edition.

31 Bresler, *Who Killed John Lennon?* pp.121-24.

32 Bresler, *Who Killed John Lennon?* p.143.

33 Peter Dale Scott, "The Assassinations of the 1960s as 'Deep Events,'' *History Matters*, Oct. 17, 2008. http://www.history-matters.com/essays/jfkgen/AssassinationsDeepEvents/AssassinationsDeepEvents.htm.

34 Bresler, *Who Killed John Lennon?* pp. 148-49, 151-53.

35 Bresler, *Who Killed John Lennon?* pp.148-49, 152-33. Regarding the loan, Bresler cites Jim Gaines, *People* magazine, 1987, three articles written with Chapman's full cooperation.

36 Bresler, *Who Killed John Lennon?* pp. 158-60, 177-79.

37 Tony Rennell, "Was John Lennon's Murderer Mark Chapman a CIA Hitman? Thirty years on, there's an extraordinary new theory," *The Daily Mail* (London), December 4, 2010, http://www.dailymail.co.uk/news/article-1335479/Was-John-Lennons-murderer-Mark-Chapman-CIA-hitman-Thirty-years-theres-extraordinary-new-theory.html. Chapman's distance from Lennon in shooting is given as "less than 20 feet away" in Bresler, *Who Killed John Lennon?* pp. 208, 229. On article discussing Chapman getting loan from Castle Memorial Hospital, Bresler cited an article by Bill Montgomery, *Atlanta Constitution*, December 10, 1980.

38 Bresler, *Who Killed John Lennon?* pp. 228-30.

39 Bresler, *Who Killed John Lennon?* p. 234.

40 Bresler, *Who Killed John Lennon?* pp. 255-56.

41 Bresler, *Who Killed John Lennon?* p. 257.

42 Rennell, "Was John Lennon's Murderer Mark Chapman a CIA Hitman?"

43 Bresler, *Who Killed John Lennon?* p. 100. Strongman, *John Lennon*, pp. 159, 210.

44 Bresler, *Who Killed John Lennon?* pp. 40-56. Strongman, *John Lennon*, pp. 77-95, 253-56.

45 Strongman, *John Lennon*, pp. 253-54. Source on Perodomo's CIA work, Warren Hinckle and William Turner, *The Fish is Red: The Story of the Secret War Against Castro* (Martin & Row, 1981), pp. 307-08. Note that the authors reported interviewing CIA Watergate "plumber" Frank Sturgis. Sturgis claimed that Peromo died shortly after Watergate without giving proof. Some claim he was trying to cover up Perdomo's continued CIA work.

46 Bresler, *Who Killed John Lennon?* pp. 200-05. Evidence, including a ticket to Chicago and the altering of Lennon murderer Mark Chapman's baggage claim, shows how authorities tried to hide Chapman's three day Chicago stopover between Hawaii and New York from the official police chronology of Chapman's whereabouts leading up to Lennon's murder.

47 Bresler, *Who Killed John Lennon?* pp. 178, 206, 275.

48 Bresler, *Who Killed John Lennon?* p. 253.

49 Andy Greene, "Readers' Poll: The Best Christmas Songs of All Time," *Rolling Stone,* November 30, 2011.

50 Coleman, *Lennon,* p. 47.

51 Coleman, *Lennon,* pp. 46-47.

52 On Sting's conflicts with the Copelands, see Sam Adams, "The Police's Andy Summers on his songs, Sting, and being ripped off by Puff Daddy," The A.V. Club, December 24, 2012, http://www.avclub.com/article/the-polices-andy-summers-on-his-songs-sting-and-be-90184. Also see, Interview, *Revolver,* April 2000, http://www.thepolice.com/news/article/3765/news.

53 Phil Sutcliffe and Hugh Fielder, *L'Historia Bandido* (London and New York: Proteus Books, 1981), pp. 15-16.

54 Constantine, *The Covert War Against Rock,* pp. 22-23, cites *Forbes* magazine regarding the McCaw sons and also cites the McCaw family's billion-dollar investment in Nextel Communication.

55 For example, Miles Copeland Jr. was a founding member of the CIA. His son Miles Copeland III organized concerts starting in the 1960s, and started a record label that represented musicians such as Tina Turner and hundreds of others. He also produced dozens of movies. His brother, Ian Copeland, started Frontier Booking International (F.B.I.), representing hundreds of successful bands. Stewart Copeland started the band, The Police, as their drummer and songwriter. He cofounded a film company with his brothers, http://en.wikipedia.org. Also see "New Wave music impresario Ian Copeland dead at 57," 5/24/06, http://news.yahoo.com.

56 On label ownership and promotion, see Frederic Dannen, *Hit Men* (New York: Vintage Books, 1991), pp. 34, 59, 164n, 272-99. On Mafia control of Teamsters, Harry Shapiro and Caesar Glebbeek, *Jimi Hendrix: Electric Gypsy* (New York: St. Martin's Griffin, 1990), p. 295.

57 Personal interview with Louis Wolfe, 5/10/04. Wolfe has copublished *Covert Action Quarterly* for over twenty years. This leftist political magazine was cofounded by Phil Agee, a longtime CIA employee who published a memoir tell-all about the CIA, *Inside the Company: CIA Diary* (New York: Bantam, 1975). *Covert Action* has won numerous annual Project Censored awards and published this writer's Tupac article.

58 Mark Crispin Miller, "The National Entertainment State," pullout, *The Nation,* 1996. On supporting Republicans such as Rockefeller, see Morton Mintz & Jerome S. Cohen, *Power Inc.* (New York: Bantam Books, 1977), pp. 461-62, and Ben Bagdikian, *The Media Monopoly,* 5th ed. (Boston: Beacon Press, 1997), pp. 25, 94-95.

Klaus Barbie

Chapter Sixteen

Nazis & CIA Drug-Trafficking War on Latin American Leftists

When the American drug-trafficking oligarchy sought additional sources for drug weapons they found what they were looking for by turning their gaze southward to Latin America. U.S. intelligence then spent decades developing this locus of drug cultivation with the aid of Nazis whom it helped hide in Latin America. These Nazis helped U.S. intelligence gain increasing control of the region, in opposition to indigenous leftist movements.

While former Nazis developed communities in various Latin American countries, indigenous leaders had successfully begun shedding the shackles of the Spanish and Portuguese colonialists who dominated the region. One such leader, future Cuban revolutionary Ernesto "Che" Guevara, grew up in a leftist Argentine family. He then attended medical school and worked as a physician. Before Che finished medical school, he rode a homemade motorcycle around Latin America, where he saw the dominions of the United Fruit Company engender vast poverty, hunger and disease. Secretary of State John Foster Dulles was also a stockholder and attorney for the United Fruit Company while his brother, Allen Dulles, headed the CIA in the 1950s.[1]

By 1955, Che Guevara met Cuban attorney Fidel Castro and his brother Raoul. By January of 1959, Che Guevara and Fidel Castro had successfully led the revolution that drove Cuba's dictator, U.S. puppet Fulgencio Batista, out of Cuba.[2]

Che Guevara and Fidel Castro became iconic revolutionary leaders who redistributed land to the peasants, raised the literacy rate from around sixty-eight percent to ninety-six percent in two years, and introduced affirmative action programs in the universities.[3] Attacks on Cuba and its new leaders came immediately and often. In 1961, Cubans repelled 1,400 U.S.-trained Cuban exiles who landed by boat in the Bay of Pigs Invasion.[4] The CIA's Technical Services Division that ran MK-Ultra plotted ways to use psychedelics on Castro, his brother Raoul, and Che. They devised a psychedelic aerosol spray to use against them. The U.S. Senate's Church

Committee detailed how they plotted to spray Castro's "broadcasting booth with a chemical which produced similar effects to LSD." They also "impregnated a box of cigars with a chemical that produced temporary disorientation" to discredit Castro. The Church Committee further found at least eight CIA plots to assassinate Castro.[5]

In 1967, Che brought a battalion of fifty Cuban troops into the jungles of Bolivia.[6] Che had some early successes against the Bolivian army regulars in the spring and summer of that year. As a result, the CIA had brought on extra help from a local CIA asset with a history of expertise in counterinsurgency work, who helped the Bolivian army capture and execute Che Guevara in October of 1967. The asset also had a key job of organizing cocaine trafficking with local Bolivian drug lords.[7]

The CIA and Nazis Traffic Drugs & Murder Leftists

The person the CIA enlisted for aid in killing Che in 1967 was former Nazi Klaus Barbie, a top asset in Bolivia whom the CIA had transplanted from France after World War II—nicknamed the "Butcher of Lyons," for the genocide he perpetrated in Lyons, France. Barbie also killed every Communist and Jew he found without regard to age or sex when he participated in the invasion of the Soviet Union. He was reportedly responsible for 14,000 deaths.[8]

The CIA precursor, OSS, urged President Roosevelt to save Nazis like Barbie for U.S. intelligence work. By the late 1940s, CIA director Allen Dulles and fellow CIA associates, particularly Reagan/Bush's future CIA director William Casey, worked on transporting thousands of Nazis to Latin America under Operation Sunrise and similar plans. Operation Paperclip was another plan that saved Nazi scientists, and worked in part through a front group directed by Casey—the International Refugee Committee in New York.[9] In 1947, these CIA-backed groups helped transport Barbie to Latin America.[10]

By the late 1960s, U.S. intelligence had done everything it could to counter the socialist political developments in various Latin American countries. As international bestselling author Naomi Klein documented in her book *Shock Doctrine*, the U.S. funded universities and teachers who pushed hyper-capitalist economic philosophies. When such methods failed to stop leftists from winning elections, U.S. intelligence orchestrated coups of the democratically elected leaders who had socialist-leaning economic policies. In this they had the important help of their U.S. placed Nazi allies.[11]

CIA documents and accumulated evidence show U.S. intelligence's implication in the forced change of leftist governments of Guatemala, Guyana, Ecuador, Brazil, Dominican Republic, Peru, Uruguay, Chile, Bolivia, Argentina, Nicaragua, Honduras, Haiti, Panama, Mexico and Venezuela.[12]

Shock Doctrine, along with books by professors Noam Chomsky and Edward Herman, detailed the CIA's plot against elected Chilean president Salvadore Allende, who wanted to "nationalize" major resources in Chile, taking them from multinational corporations and giving them back to Chileans.[13] The CIA and U.S. military used the generals they had trained and kept on their payroll to launch a coup against Allende's government on September 11, 1973.[14] In the days following the coup, General Augusto Pinochet and his military henchmen arrested 13,500 civilians in Santiago, tortured "subversives" and traveled the country with death squads.[15]

Before he stepped down as Commander-in-Chief in the 1990s, Pinochet's military junta started Operation Condor— a joint effort by Latin American "right-wing governments to crush left-wing opposition." The U.S. Agency for International Development's own published reports revealed how the U.S. financed and trained General Pinochet and his military units.[16] *New York Times* articles disclosed declassified State Department and CIA documents that depicted U.S. intelligence aid in Operation Condor's history of political assassinations of Latin American leftists. Condor dispatched "death squads to kill critics at home and overseas. [Murder] victims included government officials ousted in United States-supported military coups, trade unionists, rights advocates and suspected socialists."[17] Two key CIA-paid assets worked on Condor: former chief of Chile's Directorate of National Intelligence (DINA), Manuel Contreras, from 1974-77, and U.S.-born DINA assassin Michael Townley.[18]

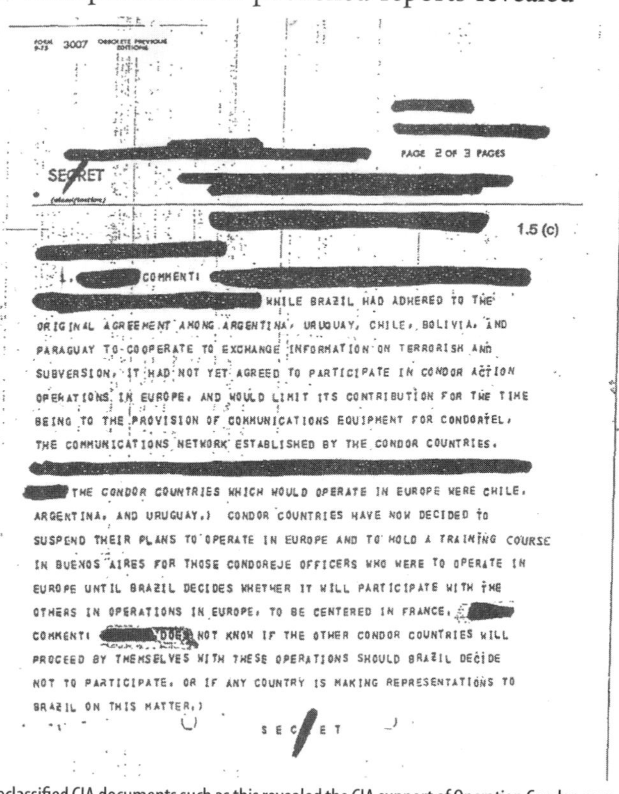

FORM 3007

PAGE 2 OF 3 PAGES

SECRET

1.5 (c)

1. COMMENT: WHILE BRAZIL HAD ADHERED TO THE ORIGINAL AGREEMENT AMONG ARGENTINA, URUGUAY, CHILE, BOLIVIA, AND PARAGUAY TO COOPERATE TO EXCHANGE INFORMATION ON TERRORISM AND SUBVERSION, IT HAD NOT YET AGREED TO PARTICIPATE IN CONDOR ACTION OPERATIONS IN EUROPE, AND WOULD LIMIT ITS CONTRIBUTION FOR THE TIME BEING TO THE PROVISION OF COMMUNICATIONS EQUIPMENT FOR CONDORTEL, THE COMMUNICATIONS NETWORK ESTABLISHED BY THE CONDOR COUNTRIES.

THE CONDOR COUNTRIES WHICH WOULD OPERATE IN EUROPE WERE CHILE, ARGENTINA, AND URUGUAY.) CONDOR COUNTRIES HAVE NOW DECIDED TO SUSPEND THEIR PLANS TO OPERATE IN EUROPE AND TO HOLD A TRAINING COURSE IN BUENOS AIRES FOR THOSE CONDOREJE OFFICERS WHO WERE TO OPERATE IN EUROPE UNTIL BRAZIL DECIDES WHETHER IT WILL PARTICIPATE WITH THE OTHERS IN OPERATIONS IN EUROPE, TO BE CENTERED IN FRANCE. COMMENT: DOES NOT KNOW IF THE OTHER CONDOR COUNTRIES WILL PROCEED BY THEMSELVES WITH THESE OPERATIONS SHOULD BRAZIL DECIDE NOT TO PARTICIPATE, OR IF ANY COUNTRY IS MAKING REPRESENTATIONS TO BRAZIL ON THIS MATTER.)

SECRET

Declassified CIA documents such as this revealed the CIA support of Operation Condor, managed from Chile and Argentina through more than half a dozen Latin American countries. It toppled elected leftists leaders and assassinated Latin American leftists worldwide.

FBI documents said Condor had several phases. Phase III murderously targeted "leaders especially feared for their potential to mobilize world opinion or organize broad opposition to the military states." This would include Chile's top folk singer, Victor Jara. Famed Chilean author Isabel Allende, Salvador's niece, believes that the Chilean military also hastened the death of Nobel Prize-winning poet Pablo Neruda. She said that Neruda was a Communist and had considered running for president.[19]

Another aspect of the Chilean-based Condor involved the Nazi intelligence enclave found there, called Colonia Dignidad. In 2005, the *New York Times* reported that a post-Pinochet government had arrested and was investigating a World War II Nazi doctor, Paul Schäfer, who founded the enclave in 1961. The enclave had several hundred German residents, a close partnership with the Pinochet dictatorship, intelligence files on political dissidents, an army's worth of military equipment, and underground torture chambers as part of Condor operations.[20] By 2006, Chile put Paul Schäfer on trial and convicted him of working with Pinochet's military and intelligence services to kidnap and torture leftists, along with sexually abusing twenty-six young boys.[21]

Other researchers reported how the Dignidad community was "a state within a state." It had its own airport, a locus for gun and drug trafficking, and could limit which planes were allowed to fly into its airspace. SS commandos and spies facilitated Schäfer's reign, which followed MK-Ultra techniques in keeping many in its community drugged. The Nazi spies secretly taped sex parties with prominent Chileans and its drugged youth in order to blackmail them.[22]

DINA Chief Manuel Contreras admitted that General Pinochet and his son were central to the manufacture and trafficking of cocaine in the region.[23] In this regard, Pinochet followed the right-wing dictators propped up by former Nazis throughout the region. The CIA's Operation Sunrise extended to most of the eight Condor-linked countries. The *New York Times* article on Chile's Nazi enclave supports other evidence that the CIA helped them direct the death-squad fascism in other Condor countries. Klaus Barbie's years in Bolivia exemplified this.[24]

CIA director Allen Dulles had helped smuggle some 5,000 Nazi Gestapo and SS agents to South America. Archival records show that the CIA-precursor OSS falsely claimed Nazis Adolph Eichmann, Joseph Mengele, and Klaus Barbie had died in the 1940s. In fact, Israelis kidnapped Eichmann from Argentina and put him on trial in Israel in 1961. U.S. intelligence had helped Auschwitz's "Angel of Death" Mengele and Barbie both gain safe passage to South America.[25]

It made sense that U.S. intelligence made Argentina the other founding center for Operation Condor's drug trafficking and genocide, as U.S. intelligence first helped transport many of these Nazis there.[26] Several veteran journalists published the controversial investigative conclusion that U.S. and British intelligence helped Adolph Hitler and his wife Eva Braun escape to Argentina. A 2011 London *Daily Mail* article summarized the investigation of television journalist (Reuters, BBC) Gerrard Williams and veteran military historian Simon Dunstan in their book, *Grey Wolf: The Escape of Adolph Hitler*. The article also summarized Argentinean journalist Abel Basti's 2003 book, *Hitler in Argentina*. Italian journalist Patrick Burnside wrote *Hitler's Escape*, which is being made into a movie. These researchers presented documents and eyewitness interviews backing their claims that Hitler died in Argentina in the 1960s.[27]

Longtime CBS Radio journalist Paul Manning, who worked with Walter Cronkite and Edward R. Murrow, also documented the history of Argentine Nazis in his book *Martin Bormann: Nazi in Exile*. He spent many years in Argentina solidifying his research findings that Martin Bormann, Adolph Hitler's Deputy, became the legal head of Germany's new state within Argentina.[28] In Argentina, Joseph Mengele, Klaus Barbie, and other top Nazis set up their first homes. Subsequently, they relocated to their new Latin American countries of Paraguay and Bolivia, respectively, to carry out their drug trafficking and coups. Manning found that Bormann's home in Argentina was part of a network of estates owned by at least eighty-two families, averaging 120,000 acres each—the largest landowners in South America. The Nazi enclave's World War II bounty and subjugation of Latin America helped prop up the American and German oligarchies.[29]

A Nazi flag in the Bolivian Andes when CIA Nazi assets aided a "Cocaine Coup" in that country. It helped keep cocaine trafficking steady in the Western hemisphere.

The *New York Times* stated, "As many as 30,000 people are thought to have been killed or disappeared," during Argentina's "Dirty War" years from 1976 to 1983. This article also emphasized that the dictatorship printed a list of names of artists and intellectuals deemed to have subversive leanings. This list totaled nineteen pages and included novelist Julio Cortazar and folk singer Mercedes Sosa.[30] This targeting of musicians in Chile and Argentina parallels similar targeting of musicians in the U.S.

Nazi-run German communities aided drug trafficking in many of the Operation Condor participating countries. A *New York Times* article recounted how notorious Nazi doctor Joseph Mengele moved from Argentina to Paraguay in 1959, living in a Nazi colony, Hohenhau. A right-wing dictator of German descent, Alfredo Stroessner, ruled Paraguay. Mengele then moved to Brazil before he died in 1979.[31]

In 1985, the Associated Press published the article "War Criminal Mengele Linked to Drug Trafficking," based on declassified CIA documents regarding Mengele's drug activity in Latin America in the 1970s.[32] Paraguayan intelligence documents found in 1993 detailed how President Stroessner worked with the CIA and the community of Nazis in Paraguay's southern region in the 1970s.[33]

Nazi Klaus Barbie directed CIA-supported operations in Bolivia. As a U.S. intelligence asset, Barbie helped coordinate six top drug lords in the overthrow of the government, in what the media dubbed as the first "Cocaine Coup," in 1980. Barbie directed security and aided the cocaine trafficking. *Covert Action,* a magazine started by CIA whistleblower Phil Agee, published a photo of a Nazi flag planted atop a Bolivian mountain at the time of that coup.[34]

Nazi Klaus "Butcher of Lyons" Barbie, pictured here in La Paz, Bolivia, helped the CIA hunt down Cuban revolutionary Che Guevara, while also later aiding the Bolivian Cocaine Coup.

Another cocaine coup had actually occurred two years earlier in Honduras. The drug trade started in Honduras at least as early as the 1930s. Standard Fruit gave a cut of its profits to the New Orleans-based Marcello crime family (involved in JFK's and MLK's assassinations) which trafficked enormous amounts of morphine and cocaine into the U.S.[35]

By 1975, Juan Alberto Melgar Castro had become President of Honduras. A coup by General Policarpo Paz Garcia ousted him in 1978. Researchers Peter Dale Scott and Jonathan Marshall said the rise of Paz Garcia cemented the power of the cocaine lords in Honduran politics. Even before this coup, "Honduras was a transfer point for half a billion dollars' worth of drugs bound for the United States each year."

After the coup, Honduras became "the largest recipient of U.S. aid in Central America." The CIA "relied totally on the cocaine-trafficking military of Honduras to back its plans to overthrow the Sandinista regime in Nicaragua." First, the CIA-backed Frente Democratico Nicaraguense Contras were based in Honduras as they tried to overthrow the socialist Sandinista regime. A U.S. Senate Foreign Relations Subcommittee report stated that Oliver North, who worked for the National Security Council starting in 1981 and as a U.S. Lieutenant Colonel in 1983, had set up the Contras' bank accounts. DEA Agent Thomas Zepeda, stationed in Honduras in 1981, documented the work of high-ranking Honduran military officers in drug trafficking. In this way, Honduran drug trafficking would help fund U.S. intelligence's war on other Latin American democracies.[36]

Role of Drugs in Banana Republics' Wars

Research uncovered the ways in which U.S. intelligence waged secret wars on people worldwide, but particularly in Latin American countries in the 1980s. In many Latin American countries, peoples' movements arose in a struggle to change their governments and their lives for the better; these included Colombia, Guatemala, El Salvador, Nicaragua and Panama, among others labeled "banana republics."[37]

Companies like Chiquita and Standard Fruit pushed U.S. intelligence to help them keep their workers' wages low. These workers wanted to change their governments and gain control over their own fruit production. U.S. intelligence aided corrupt governments in drug trafficking to keep the populace under control and raise money to fight those rebelling against their policies.

In 1954, when Guatemala had elected a left-wing democratic president, Jacobo Arbenz, United Fruit (its name later changed to Chiquita) pressured the U.S. government to engineer a coup. Many American officials "had a family or business connection to the company itself," while other Western corporations owned large amounts of various Guatemalan resources. United Fruit also funded paramilitary death squads there over the years.[38] CIA documents admitted backing a coup against Arbenz in 1954. CIA Director Allen Dulles orchestrated the round up of all suspected Communists in Guatemala, beginning a decades-long murderous political purge. From 1954 to 1990, the Guatemalan military was responsible for 100,000 deaths and 40,000 disappearances.[39]

Other so-called banana republics had lesser, though similar deaths and disappearances. U.S. intelligence helped one country develop into a central drug trafficking state—Colombia. Researcher Rensselaer Lee stated that at one point the Medellin and Cali crime syndicates of Colombia exported sixty to seventy percent of all cocaine sold in the United States. He added that, while these syndicates were certainly focused on making money, they had a political agenda that included "selectively persecuting the Colombian left."[40]

During President Jimmy Carter's administration, the U.S. Drug Enforcement Agency indicted Colombian drug lord Santiago Ocampo, who worked closely with Honduran and Mexican traffickers. Disgruntled DEA agents suspected they were stumbling onto a CIA connection when

President Ronald Reagan and Vice President George H.W. Bush came into office and their investigation was dismantled. Future researchers found Vice President Bush directing CIA and cocaine trafficking operations, which later became known during the Iran-Contra Scandal.[41]

While most people don't see marijuana as a dangerous drug, U.S. intelligence appeared to have several uses for it. It has been shown that a percentage of people develop marijuana abuse or dependence that could sidetrack productive achievement of higher goals such as antiwar activism. Also, the trafficking of marijuana provided more covert funds when, for example, a Democrat-controlled U.S. Congress cut off aid to brutal, right-wing Latin American governments in the new millennium.

Before the Sandanistas' revolution, the U.S. backed Nicaraguan dictator Anastasio Somoza. Authors Scott and Marshall said that, "Somoza was a partner of a major U.S. marijuana smuggler, Raymond Grady Stansel, Jr. in a Honduran Seafood Company." Somoza "made airplanes available to the smuggler."[42]

Mexico launched its own Operation Condor with CIA aid. It purported to go after drug traffickers, but only arrested poor farmers growing marijuana on tiny plots and those suspected of political organizing in the countryside. The State Department and CIA sent seventy-six airplanes and $115 million in aid for the aerial spraying of crops, though they carefully avoided all the large marijuana crops of drug chiefs.[43]

Another operation was "La Pipa" (The Pipe). The Mexican Security Organization, DFS, closely collaborated with current and "former" CIA agents on that operation in the late 1970s. DFS bought 600 tanker trucks, ostensibly for transporting natural gas from the U.S. to Mexico. DFS men packed the trucks with Mexican dealers' marijuana, running ten to twelve trucks a day into Phoenix and Los Angeles. Several Mexican and U.S. customs officials were bribed $50,000 a load to let the trucks pass. DFS also oversaw a $5 billion marijuana plantation in the province of Chihuaha.[44]

Another key group of CIA allies in Latin America were Cuban exiles. The Justice Department's Operation Eagle rounded up many CIA-trained Cubans as part of a drug trafficking syndicate in 1970, but saw their cases dropped on technicalities. Among them, Mario Escandar, Frank Castro, Ricardo Morales and others had long active careers in connection with the CIA. Frank Castro cofounded an anti-Communist group of twenty members called CORU. Ricardo Morales became a high-ranking officer in Venezuela's intelligence service DISIP, where he gave sanctuary to some CORU members.[45]

Ricardo Morales and CORU members took credit for exploding a bomb on a Cuban passenger jet, along with fifty other bombings in Miami, New York, Venezuela, Panama, Mexico, and Argentina in the first ten months of CORU's existence. In an interview with CBS News, CORU member Armando Lopez Estrada said, "We use the tactics that we learned from the CIA ... [we] are trained to set off a bomb, we were trained to kill."[46]

Scott and Marshall said financing for CORU came from WFC, a Florida-based financial conglomerate and drug-trafficking front that worked with the Restoy-Escandar-Trafficante organization. The researchers also quoted an unpublished congressional staff study saying the WFC corporation was involved in "political corruption, gun running, as well as narcotics trafficking on an international level." A CIA-trained Bay of Pigs veteran led the WFC. And, a Florida official directing an investigation of WFC found that one company subsidiary was "nothing but a CIA front."[47]

After a socialist revolutionary group, the Sandanista Liberation Front (FSLN), overthrew Nicaragua's Somoza in 1979, they won many international awards for their work on behalf of the masses of Nicaraguan people regarding health care for all, childcare, unions and land reform. The United Nations Educational, Scientific and Cultural Organization (UNESCO) gave the FSLN-led Nicaraguan government an award for miraculously decreasing the country's illiteracy rate from over fifty percent down to thirteen percent in only five months. They also won three other UNESCO awards in the 1980s.[48]

The CIA immediately organized a warring army against the Sandanistas' socialist Central American government. Frank Castro (no relation to Cuban leader Fidel) and four other CORU members joined the Nicaraguan opposition that the CIA continually aided—the Contras. As previously noted, the Contras were based in Honduras. Honduran military sources told American reporters that an airline company called SETCO was, "set up by the CIA to carry Contra forces and supplies." U.S. Senator John Kerry led a panel that issued a report stating, "One of the pilots ... for SETCO was Frank Moss ... who has been under investigation as an alleged drug trafficker since 1979."[49] This paralleled the CIA's use of Air America to traffic drugs during the Vietnam War.

Notes

1 Jon Lee Anderson, *Che Guevara: A Revolutionary Life* (New York: Grove Press, 1997). On CIA coup, Douglas Kellner, *Ernesto "Che" Guevara* (Chelsea House, 1989).

2 Sandison, David (1996), *The Life & Times of Che Guevara* (Paragon), p.36. Kellner, *Ernesto "Che" Guevara*, pp. 48, 112.

3 Kellner, *Ernesto "Che" Guevara*, pp. 57-58, 112. On affirmative action, see Anderson, *Che Guevara*, p. 449.

4 Anderson, *Che Guevara*, p. 509

5 U.S. Senate "Church Committee," *Interim Report: Alleged Assassination Plots Involving Foreign Leaders*, 1975, pp. 71-72, http://www.history-matters.com/archive/church/reports/ir/

html/ChurchIR_0043b.htm. On aerosol spray devised, but apparently abandoned, to be used against Fidel, Raoul and Che, see Hank Albarelli, Jr, *A Terrible Mistake, The Murder of Frank Olson and the CIA's Secret Cold War Experiments* (Waterville, OR: Trine Day, 2009), p. 338. Che also got his message out by writing books. In one essay, he described how capitalist propaganda portrayed Rockefeller as successful. "The amount of poverty and suffering required for the emergence of a Rockefeller, and the amount of depravity that the accumulation of a fortune of such magnitude entails, are left out." This essay ended with his most famous quote: "At the risk of sounding sappy, the true revolutionary is guided by great feelings of love": letter to Carlos Quijano, editor of *Marcha* a radical weekly published in Montevideo, Uruguay; published as "From Algiers, for *Marcha*: The Cuban Revolution Today" (12 March 1965); also published in *Verde Olivo*, the magazine of the Cuban armed forces "Socialism and Man in Cuba," variant translation by Margarita Zimmermann. Che Guevara also talked about the Northern Hemisphere countries exploiting the Southern Hemisphere countries. In that speech Che supported North Vietnam and urged developing countries to take up arms and create "one, two, three, many Vietnams"; Ernesto "Che" Guevara, *Che: Selected Works of Ernesto Guevara*, ed. Rolando E. Bonachea and Nelson P. Valdés (Cambridge, MA: MIT Press, 1969), pp. 352-59. Che also went to Africa to fight with Patrice Lumumba's former comrade, Laurent Kabila, in the Congo. On Congo, see William Gálvez, *Che in Africa: Che Guevara's Congo Diary* (Melbourne: Ocean Press, 1999).

6 All 50 members of Che Guevara's guerrilla movement in Bolivia are listed on a website compiled by the Latin American Studies Organization, http://www.latinamericanstudies.org/che/bolivia-guerrillas.htm.

7 According to Barbie's long-time confidante, Alavaro de Castro. See Oscar-winning director Kevin Macdonald's *My Enemy's Enemy* (2007); David Smith, "Barbie 'boasted of hunting down Che'" *The Observer* (London), 12/23/07.

8 "Ich bin gekommen, um zu töten," *Der Spiegel*, 2 July 2007. "Nazi war criminal Klaus Barbie gets life," BBC, 3 July 1987. In Lyons, Klaus Barbie earned his name more publicly by running a prison where he tortured and killed people in various creative ways. Barbie's personal work shackling Lise Leserve naked to a beam and beating her with a spiked chain failed to have her talk. Surviving his torture, she later testified against him. On torture and testimony of Lisa Leserve, see Alexander Cockburn and Jeffrey St. Clair, *Whiteout: The CIA, Drugs and the Press* (New York: Verso, 1999), p. 173.

9 Thierry Meyssan, "The Center for Security Policy: Washington's Manipulators," *Voltaire*, 11/13/02, www.voltairenet.org/article30118.html. Meyssan's citation for this appeared to be "Group Goes from Exile to Influence," *New York Times*, 11/23/81.

10 On Barbie's work with CIA, cocaine traffickers and coups in Bolivia, see Peter Dale Scott and Jonathan Marshall, *Cocaine Politics: Drugs, Armies and the CIA in Central America*, (Berkeley: University of California Press, 1991), pp. 44-46, 85.

11 Naomi Klein, *The Shock Doctrine: The Rise of Disaster Capitalism* (New York: Picador/Henry Holt: 2007).

12 William Blum, *Killing Hope: US and CIA Interventions Since World War II* (Common Courage Press, 2003). William Blum, *Rogue State: A Guide to the World's Only Superpower* (Common Courage Press, 2005). http://www.geopoliticalmonitor.com/us-interventions-in-latin-american-021/.

13 For many of these declassified CIA documents, see the archives at George Washington University's website: http://www.gwu.edu/~nsarchiv/NSAEBB/NSAEBB8/nsaebb8.htm. On U.S. coal giants, interview with Ricardo Lagos conducted 1/19/02. On 5,000+ U.S. companies, see Sue Branford and Bernardo Kucinski, *The Debt Squads: The U.S., the Banks, and Latin America* (London: Zed Books, 1988), pp. 40, 51-52. On Ad Hoc Committee, see Subcommittee on Multinational Corporations, "The International Telephone and Telegraph Company and Chile, 1970-71," Report to the Committee on Foreign Relations United States Senate by the Subcommittee on Multinational Corporations, 6/21/73, pp. 4, 18. All three sources cited in Klein, *The Shock Doctrine*, pp. 77-78.

14 On U.S. training of Pinochet and his military commanders, see *Amnesty International Report on Torture* (New York: Farrar, Straus and Giroux, 1975), p. 23. Cited in Noam Chomsky and Edward Herman, *The Washington Connection and Third World Fascism* (Boston: South End Press, 1979), pp. 47, 92 n4.

15 Peter Kornbluh, *The Pinochet File: A Declassified Dossier on Atrocities and Accountability* (New York: The New Press, 2004), pp. 155-56. Cited in Klein, *The Shock Doctrine*, p. 93.

16 Chomsky and Herman, *The Washington Connection and Third World Fascism*, p. 44.

17 "A Spymaster Joins the NYPD," *New York Times*, January 23, 2001, p. B3. Diana Jean Schemo, "New Files Tie U.S. to Deaths of Latin Leftists in 1970's," *New York Times*, March 6, 2001, p. A7. Orlando Letelier, the former Chilean foreign minister, and Ronni Mofit, an American colleague were killed by a car bomb while driving in Washington D.C. in 1976.

18 Damien Gayle, Michael Zennie and Associated Press, "Was Nobel Laureate poet poisoned by ed-CIA agent in 1973 on orders of Chilean Dictator?" *The Daily Mail* (UK), June 2, 2013, http://www.dailymail.co.uk/news/article-2334779/Pablo-Neruda-Chilean-poet-poisoned-American-CIA-agent-orders-Pinochet.html. Also see Prof. Patrice McSherry, "Operation Condor: Deciphering the U.S. Role," *Crimes of War*, July 6, 2001, pp. 1-6, http://www.crimesofwar.org/special/condor.html. McSherry is an Associate Professor of Political Science at Long Island University and author of *Incomplete Transition: Military Power and Democracy in Argentina* (New York: St. Martin's, 1997). She's written numerous articles on Condor and the Latin American military, conducting her research in Chile, Paraguay, Argentina and the U.S.

19 J. Patrice McSherry, "Operation Condor: Deciphering the U.S. Role" from her website, *Crimes of War*. On Jara, see *Amnesty International, Report on Torture*, pp. 206-07, cited in Chomsky and Herman, *The Washington Connection and Third World Fascism*, p. 9. On Neruda, Isabel Allende said this on Democracy Now, Isabel Allende on "'Maya's Notebook,' Drug Addiction, 1973 Chilean Coup & Death of Poet Pablo Neruda," April 30, 2013, http://www.democracynow.org/2013/4/30/isabel_allende_on_mayas_notebook_drug.

20 Larry Rohter, "At Cult's Enclave in Chile, Guns and Intelligence Files," *New York Times*, 6/17/05, p. A9.

21 Larry Rohter, "World Briefing; Chile: Cult Leader Gets 20 Years," *New York Times*, 5/25/06, p. A14. On sexually abusing young boys, see Becky Branford, "Secrets of ex-Nazi's Chilean Fiefdom," BBC News, March 11, 2005, http://news.bbc.co.uk/2/hi/americas/4340591.stm. Also, "New Charges for Cult Leader," BBCNews, March 22, 2005, and final sentencing on 5/24/06 for sexually abusing 25 children: 20 years in jail and a fine of the equivalent of $1.5 million, en.wikipedia.org, Paul Schaefer.

22 Marcello McKinnon, "Inside Chile's Colony of Terror," *Ohmy News*, 2/1/07, http://english.ohmynews.com/articleview/article_view.asp?no=342888&rel_no=1.

23 Larry Rohter, "Former Aide says Pinochet and a Son Dealt in Drugs," *New York Times*, 7/11/06, p.A3.

24 See, for example, U.S. government's Nazi hunter Allan Ryan's 600-page report, *Klaus Barbie and the United States Government* (Washington, D.C.: Government Printing Office, 1983) p. 212. And Allan Ryan, *Quiet Neighbors* (New York: Harcourt Brace Jovanovich, 1984), pp. 280-84. Also, correspondence obtained via Freedom Of Information Act (FOIA) for documentary background: Representative Peter Rodino to comptroller general, 2/17/83; Allan Ryan to Joseph Moore (FBI), 2/18/83; and GAO Director William Anderson to FBI Director William Webster, 3/2/83. A sanitized version of Barbie's FBI file available via FOIA includes similar internal DOJ correspondence on this investigation; see FBI File No. 105-221892 on Klaus Barbie. All cited in Christopher Simpson, *Blowback: The First Full Account of America's Recruitment of Nazis, and its Disastrous Effect on Our Domestic and Foreign Policy* (New York: Weidenfeld and Nicholson, 1988), pp. 192-93, nn 33, 34.

25 Peter Dale Scott, "How Allen Dulles and the SS Preserved Each Other," *Covert Action Information Bulletin* No.25, Winter 1986, pp. 4-14. Scott, a former Canadian diplomat with a Ph.D in political science, was a Professor of English at the University of California at Berkeley who has published numerous books. The 90 citations he used in this article include the following reference sources from around the world: U.S. National Archives, *Washington Post*, *Le Mond Diplomatique*, *Der Spiegel*, and whistleblowing books by Justice Department insiders such as John Loftus, *The Belarus Secret* (New York: Knopf, 1982). On Loftus's statement of "Dulles aided the smuggling of some

5000 Nazis," Jerry Meldon, *The Jewish Advocate*, 9/20/84, citing John Loftus, *Boston Globe*, 5/28/84. On O.S.S. false claims, U.S. National Archives, Record Group 165, 250.401. Sect. XIX; letter of 19 January 1948 from Brig. Gen. Telford Taylor, OCCWC, OMGUS. And U.S. National Archives, Record Group 319, CIC File No. V-2399, XE 012547 D20D216; *Washington Post*, 3/15/85, p. A10. The Simon Wiesenthal Center in Los Angeles released documents from the U.S. Army under the Freedom of Information Act saying Mengele "may have been arrested by U.S. authorities in Austria in 1947 and released," *The Nation*, 3/2/85, p. 231. Former WWII intelligence agent William Stevenson wrote about Mengele accumulating huge assets after gaining Parguayan citizenship in 1957: William Stevenson, *The Bormann Brotherhood* (New York: Harcourt, Brace, Jovanovich, 1973), p. 228. On Barbie and other Nazi's drug and arms trafficking, see, for example, "Barbie's reported dealings with August Joseph Ricord of Paraguay whose 'Corsican' drug ring was linked to networks of former Nazis in Europe and Latin America." Alain Jaubert, *Dossier D… comme drouge* (Paris: Alain Moreau, 1973), p. 296. In Scott, "How Allen Dulles…," p.9 n 33.

26 Peter Dale Scott and Jonathan Marshall, *Cocaine Politics: Drugs, Armies and the CIA in Central America* (Berkeley: University of California Press, 1991), p. 42.

27 Rick Dewbury, Allan Hall and Ellen Harding, "Did Hitler and Eva Braun flee Berlin and die (divorced) of old age in Argentina?" *The Daily Mail* (UK), October 18, 2011, http://www.dailymail.co.uk/news/article-2050137/Did-Hitler-Eva-Braun-flee-Berlin-die-old-age-Argentina.html On Abel Basti, see http://www.barilochenazi.com.ar/english/ On Dunstan and Williams, see http://www.amazon.ca/Grey-Wolf-Escape-Adolf-Hitler/dp/1402781393.

28 Paul Manning, *Martin Bormann: Nazi in Exile* (New York: Lyle Stuart, 1981). On Manning working with Walter Cronkite and Edward Murrow, see, for example, *The Writing 69th* (Green Harbor Publications). To read book online, see http://www.animalfarm.org/mb/mb.shtml Historians say people broke the legs of Paul Manning's publisher and then murdered his son after he published this book in 1981.

29 Manning, *Martin Bormann: Nazi in Exile*, see Ch. 8.

30 Simon Romero and Jonathan Gilbert, "Argentina Discovers Paper Trail to Brutal Era," *New York Times*, November 6, 2013. According to UC-Berkeley Professor Peter Dale Scott and former State Department official Jon Marshall, Argentina prepared computerized lists of opposition figures to imprison, torture and kill, and how other Operation Condor countries sent officers there to train. "At least 40 Bolivian officers have traveled to Argentina to train in 'antisubversive techniques,'" *Newsweek* reported in late 1981, "and Argentineans practiced in torture [are serving as] interrogators"; *Los Angeles Times*, 8/31/80, *Newsweek* 9/23/81. Both referenced in Peter Dale Scott and Jonathan Marshall, *Cocaine Politics: Drugs, Armies, and the CIA in Central America* (Los Angeles: University of California Press, 1991), p. 45.

31 James Brooke, "Hohenhau Journal; Sure, Mengele was at home here, but Bormann? *New York Times*, 6/1/93. http://www.nytimes.com/1993/06/01/world/hohenau-journal-sure-mengele-was-at-home-here-but-bormann.html At least one mainstream researcher believed Mengele didn't actually die in Brazil, he just moved again, to Nuevo Alamania, or "New Germany," in Paraguay. Graeme Wood, "Jose Mengele, Paraguayan" *The Atlantic*, 7/18/09, http://www.theatlantic.com/international/archive/2009/07/jose-mengele-paraguayan/21603/.

32 Associated Press, "War Criminal Mengele Linked to Drug Trafficking," *Gainesville Sentinel*, 2/27/85, http://news.google.com/newspapers?nid=1320&dat=19850227&id=bT1WAAAAIBAJ&sjid=z-kDAAAAIBAJ&pg=1553,4047151.

33 Glenn Yeadon and John Hawkins, *The Nazi Hydra in America: Suppressed History of the Century* (Palm Desert, CA: Progressive Press, 2008), pp. 409-10, http://books.google.com/books?id=vh7sx2xtjGEC&pg=PA409&lpg=PA409&dq=Nazi+drug+trafficking+in+South+America&source=bl&ots=DOYSKLjijq&sig=MmiU6wc-IjyFVSezSb0dIhA9hhA&hl=en&sa=X&ei=AVlvT46cLcqQ0QGlk9i2Bg&ved=0CCMQ6AEwAA#v=onepage&q=Nazi%20drug%20trafficking%20in%20South%20America&f=false.

34 On Barbie as U.S. intelligence agent and then Bolivian Coup co-orchestrator, see Magnus Linklater, Isabel Hilton and Neal Ascheron, *The Nazi Legacy* (New York: Holt, Rinehart,

and Winston, 1984), p. 280. On top drug lords meeting to help carry out coup, see *Sunday Times* (London), 8/10/80. On coup dubbed by media as the Cocaine Coup, see *Sunday Times* 6/29/80. All referenced and detailed in Scott and Marshall, *Cocaine Politics*, (Berkeley: University of California Press, 1991), pp. 44-46. On Nazi flags, see Kai Herman, "Klaus Barbie: A Killer's Career," *Stern*, May and June, 1984; this article was reprinted in *Covert Action Information Bulletin*, No. 25 Winter 1986, pp. 15-20. For some of Herman's sources, see interview with Argentinean intelligence agent, Alfredo Mingolla, pictures of Barbie in Bolivia, including his fake name on his intelligence ID, Klaus Altmann Hansen. On post-coup Nazi flags in Bolivia, see *Covert Action Information Bulletin*, No. 25 Winter 1986, pp. 3, 17.

35 John Davis, *Mafia Kingfish* (New York: McGraw-Hill, 1989), p. 36. In Scott and Marshall, *Cocaine Politics*, p. 54

36 On Honduras as transit point for cocaine, see *Facts on File*, 8/11/78. On Oliver North setting up FDN accounts, see U.S. Senate Foreign Relations Subcommittee on Narcotics, Terrorism, and International Operations chaired by Senator John F. Kerry of Massachusetts. "Drugs, Law Enforcement, and U.S. Foreign Policy," April 1989, p. 44. Scott and Marshall, *Cocaine Politics*, pp. 54-56. On Oliver North's career, see John Greenwald, David Beckwith and David Halevy, "Washington's Cowboys," *Time*, November 17, 1986.

37 The term was reportedly first used in the 1904 book by O. Henry, *Cabbages and Kings* (New York: Doubleday, 1904). Also see "Latin American Report," 4/7/99, http://www.converge.org.nz/lac/articles/news990407a.htm

38 Daniel Kurtz-Phelan, "Big Fruit," *New York Times*, 3/2/08. This article reviewed the book *Bananas* about United Fruit, http://www.nytimes.com/2008/03/02/books/review/Kurtz-Phelan-t.html. Two percent of the population owned 70% of the land in 1954, Thomas G. Paterson et al., *American Foreign Relations: A History, Volume 2: Since 1895* (Cengage Learning, 2009), p. 304. On U.S. owning Guatemalan electrical utilities, Stephen M. Streeter, *Managing the Counterrevolution: The United States and Guatemala, 1954-1961* (Ohio University Press, 2000), pp. 8-10.

39 On U.S. Military and CIA backing a coup and then roundup of Communists, Chomsky and Herman, *The Washington Connection and Third World Fascism*, p. 277. On 100,000 deaths, see *Los Angeles Times*, 4/14/90, in Scott and Marshall, *Cocaine Politics*, p. 189. For an excellent film on decades of Guatemalan genocide, see Granito: *How to Nail a Dictator*, http://skylightpictures.com/films/granito. On United Fruit continuing the murders over the years, see http://www.democracynow.org/2009/7/21/from_arbenz_to_zelaya_chiquita_in.

40 Rensselaer W. Lee III, *The White Labyrinth: Cocaine and Political Power* (New Brunswick, NJ: Transaction, 1988), pp. 8-9. Cited in Scott and Marshall, *Cocaine Politics*, p. 80.

41 James Mills, *The Underground Empire: Where Crimes and Governments Embrace* (New York: Dell, 1987), pp. 917-20, 1089. In Scott and Marshall, *Cocaine Politics*, pp. 88-89. Colombian traffickers worked with Honduran drug lord Juan Ramon Matta Ballesteros.

42 Messick, *Of Grass and Snow*, pp. 174-78; Penny Lernoux, *In Banks We Trust* (Garden City, NY: Anchor Press, 1984), pp. 152-53; *Tampa Tribune*, 6/9/74. Scott and Marshall said they were quoting trial testimony. Somoza claimed he was being "framed" by all the evidence at Stancel's trial. All in Scott and Marshall, *Cocaine Politics*, p. 53.

43 On Mexico's Condor, see *Proceso*, 4/17/89. On details of $115 million in aid and watering drug fields, see *Oregonian*, 8/14/88; Elaine Shannon, *Desperados: Latin Drug Lords, U.S. Lawmen, and the War America Can't Win* (New York: Viking, 1988), pp. 62-63; *Time*, 4/7/86. All referenced in Scott and Marshall, *Cocaine Politics*, pp. 37-38.

44 *Time*, 3/17/88; cf. Shannon, *Desperados*, pp.186-87. Referenced in Scott and Marshall, *Cocaine Politics*, p. 40.

45 Interview with CORU member Orlando Bosch, New Times, 5/13/77. In Scott and Marshall, *Cocaine Politics*, p. 30.

46 Estrada quoted in CBS special report, 6/10/77.

47 On Escandar, see Hinckle and Turner, *The Fish is Red*, p. 314. On "other CIA trainees," former CIA commando Grayston Lynch, quoted in *St. Petersburg Times*, 5/30/82. On congressional

staff study quote, see John Cummings, "Miami Confidential," *Inquiry*, 8/3/81, p. 20; cf. Lernoux, *In Banks We Trust*, Ch. 8. On Bay of Pigs veteran leadership of WFC, see *Miami Herald*, 5/4/86 and 7/1/89. On Dade County investigator quote, see *Providence Sunday Journal*, 6/22/80. All referenced in Scott and Marshall, *Cocaine Politics*, pp. 26-27, 30-31.

48 Dr. Ulrike Haneman, "Nicaragua's Literacy Campaign," (Background Paper Prepared for) Education for All Global Monitoring Report, 2006, http://unesdoc.unesco.org/images/0014/001460/146007e.pdf. On international awards in other areas, see http://www.stanford.edu/group/arts/nicaragua/discovery_eng/timeline/.

49 Scott and Marshall said that the founding members of the Contras were Frank Castro, Luis Posada Jose Dionisio Suarez, Armando Lopez Estrada, and Juan Perez Franco. See *Wall Street Journal*, 1/16/77. On SETCO airlines, John Dillon and Jon Lee Anderson, "Who's Behind the Aid to the Contras," *The Nation*, 10/6/84, p. 318. Senate Committee on Foreign Relations, Subcommittee on Terrorism, Narcotics and International Operations, report, Drugs, Law Enforcement and Foreign Policy (a.k.a. Kerry Report) (Washington, DC: U.S. Government Printing Office, 1989), pp. 44-45, 296. All in Scott and Marshall, *Cocaine Politics*, pp. 30 n46, 56-57.

Chapter Seventeen

FBI Targets Black Panthers & Young Lords

Huey Newton and Bobby Seale first launched the Black Panther Party for Self-Defense in Oakland, California in October of 1966. It distinguished itself from a lesser-known Black Panther Party. Within several years of its founding, the Oakland-based Black Panthers grew to over a hundred chapters and over ten thousand members across the country.[1]

Huey Newton and Bobby Seale cofounded the national Black Panther Party for Self Defense. They were groundbreaking community organizers who also armed themselves for battling police brutality.

Huey Newton and Bobby Seale officially registered the Black Panther Party for Self-Defense as a political organization. The "Self Defense" strategy was a response to the rampant racist police brutalization of their black Oakland community that they experienced personally. They called for gun possession by civilians for defense against police. Newton was taking law classes at the time and instructed Panthers on the law. He led them in countering local police brutality incidents by having his Panthers surround the police with guns pointed while he recited the brutality victim's legal rights.[2]

The Black Panthers further had a socialist "free services for the poor" philosophy that they outlined in a "Ten Point Plan." They enacted their Ten Point Plan through free breakfast programs for poor children, free health clinics, and free political education programs. In 1970 their national newspaper had a circulation of 125,000 copies a week.[3]

The Panthers' political education taught their members about changing society to change their situation. They based their teachings on books by writers like black liberation theorist Franz Fanon, Chinese revolutionary Communist leader Mao Zedong and Cuba's socialist revolutionary Che Guevara, along with speeches by Malcolm X. Newton, Seale and later Panther leaders required a lot of reading by incoming members.[4]

Huey Newton and Bobby Seale impressed a number of national black activists and writers, and influenced them to join the Panthers. Best-selling author Eldridge Cleaver, who worked as editor of the San Francisco-based *Ramparts* magazine, joined the Panthers as their Minister of Information in 1967.[5] That year, Bobby Seale and Huey Newton made Student National Coordinating Committee leaders Stokely Charmichael and H. Rap Brown honorary Panther leaders on the East Coast. Other SNCC members began starting Panther chapters in Chicago and eastern cities.[6]

The Black Panther Party's goal of economic power for minorities and the poor posed a threat to the capitalist oligarchy. The oligarchy's foot soldiers, the cliques of U.S. intelligence's real leadership, waged war on leftist groups in general, though they used particularly murderous tactics against the Black Panthers through the FBI's Counterintelligence Program.[7]

In the days after Martin Luther King's 1968 assassination, in Oakland, California, a city with one of the country's largest urban African-American populations, the Black Panthers successfully quelled rioting. They feared police would use rioting as an excuse to murder national Panther leaders. Despite this, police quickly found a way to set up the shooting of Eldridge Cleaver and shot what some said were thousands of bullets into the home where Cleaver and Bobby Hutton cowered. During a lull in the shooting barrage, Cleaver came up with a plan. He suggested they both take off all their clothes and go out of the house naked so police couldn't use the excuse that they were concealing weapons and shoot them. Cleaver, already wounded, came out naked and survived. The more modest Hutton came out shirtless and was quickly shot dead.[8]

Assassination of Black Panther Leaders

The Black Panthers evolved into a vanguard organization that had a "no drugs" policy and had some leaders that had formerly led large gangs. The year after Bobby Hutton was killed by police, authorities initiated a string of successful assassinations beginning with Los Angeles Black Panther leader Alprentice "Bunchy" Carter and his coleader, Jon Huggins. Carter had previously led the 5,000-strong Slauson gang.[9]

Former L.A. FBI Cointelpro agent Wes Swearingen described his unit's murderous machinations against Carter and Huggins. He said the FBI paid undercover agents in the United Slaves Organization, a Black cultural nationalist group, to murder the two leaders. The killers, reportedly George and Larry Stiner, shot them on the UCLA campus in January of 1969.[10]

Whistleblowing author and former L.A. police intelligence agent Louis Tackwood also revealed he regularly gave money, guns, drugs and orders to United Slaves leader Ron Karenga to attack the Panthers.[11]

Tackwood testified to this before a Senate intelligence committee, and he passed a polygraph test.[12] After the Carter and Huggins murders, the FBI's undercover agents inside the United Slaves murdered four more Black Panthers, including John Savage. Savage witnessed the United Slaves murder of Carter and Huggins and was scheduled to testify soon after.[13]

Swearingen verified claims that the FBI then engineered the prison break of several United Slaves murderers.[14] And, New Haven Panther George Edwards said he acquired a U.S. intelligence document reporting Karenga's meetings with Governor Ronald Reagan, funding by the Rockefellers, and the Stiners' work with U.S. intelligence.[15]

Huggins and Carter had left a tape saying if anything happened to them, they wanted Panther Elmer "Geronimo" Pratt to take over as L.A. Panther leader, and he did.[16] Years later, Pratt said the United Slaves organization shouldn't be held accountable for the FBI agent infiltrators who carried out the Panther murders. Pratt, who later changed his last name to Ji Jaga, said that new Panther Elaine Brown was an undercover agent who started the conflict leading to the Carter and Huggins murders, and that the Stiners of the United Slaves were falsely accused of involvement (Panthers George Edwards and Kathleen Cleaver also support Pratt's take on Elaine Brown's undercover agent role).[17]

FBI whistleblower Swearingen supported Pratt in many ways, though he disagreed about Pratt's assessment of the Stiners' innocence in the murders. Swearingen said that an FBI agent named Eric Galt arranged the Stiners' murder of Carter and Huggins, and that "Darthard Perry, a self-admitted and publicly acclaimed informer for the FBI, filed an affidavit in a Black Panther Party lawsuit against the government, charging he knew the United Slaves members responsible for the murders of the Panthers were FBI informers."[18] While Pratt's account may be held in higher regard than all others, and whether the United Slaves were a U.S. intelligence-created group or not, many agree about the FBI's orchestration of the murders.[19]

Evidence also indicates that the FBI used undercover agents in the United Slaves to target both the New York and Los Angeles Panthers. FBI informant D'Arthard Perry said that the FBI used United Slaves infiltrator Claude Hubert to kill several L.A. Panthers and then transferred him to New York City.[20]

On January 17, 1969, the day United Slave FBI infiltrators murdered L.A. leaders Carter and Huggins, police shot at Bronx Panther leader Sekou Odinga.[21] Around this same date, undercover police agent Ralph White shot a gun in the Black Panther office, within several feet of Harlem leader Lumumba Shakur.[22] The police officers' shooting at Odinga and Shakur were part of the FBI Cointelpro attacks against the New York Panthers.[23]

AS with Bunchy Carter's leadership of the Slauson gang, the FBI's targeting of the New York Panther leaders may have partially stemmed from fears they would politicize the gangs they had formerly led.

New York prosecutors indicted Lumumba Shakur, his wife Afeni (rap icon Tupac's mother), Odinga and nineteen other leading Panthers for planning to bomb and shoot at police precincts and public places around New York.[24] These proved to be fantastical charges with no merit, but kept many of the New York Panther leaders in jail for up to two years. Despite the government keeping the New York Panther 21 in jail for a trial that dragged on for two years, a record amount of time in New York state history up to that period, the jury deliberated for approximately two hours to find the defendants not guilty of all the charges.[25]

While U.S. intelligence targeted members of the Black Panther national leadership early on, a question remains about whether they orchestrated large-scale murderous operations against Panther leaders who could politicize urban youth and gangs in major cities. Did they first focus on Bunchy Carter due to fears about his former leadership of the 5,000-strong Slauson gang and his potential to politicize them?[26]

At least one historian, University of Southern California Professor Laura Pulido, interviewed people who said Carter led many Slauson gang members to convert to activist Panthers. One interviewee said, "What happened in Los Angeles was a unique experience ... What [Carter] did was make his gang [the Panthers] the only gang." Pulido said that because so many of the Panthers were "underground" or hid their membership, estimates of the Southern California Panther chapter membership "ranged from five hundred to several thousand."[27]

Afeni Shakur had formerly led the Disciples Debs gang of girls. Lumumba Shakur had led the Bishops gang and Sekou Odinga had been part of the Sinners gang.[28] Were they partly attacked on such a huge scale because of fears over their converting many former gang members into activist Panthers? Whether they were or not, Malcolm X envisioned this potential in referring to urban youth in their teens and twenties as "Black social dynamite."[29]

Fred Hampton Murdered by Police after Converting Gangs

U.S. intelligence murdered Illinois Panther leaders Fred Hampton and Mark Clark in 1969. Hampton headed the Illinois Black Panthers statewide from his home in Chicago. Mark Clark led the Southern Illinois chapter of Black Panthers.

Hampton had achieved a lot by the time he was twenty-one years old. He had risen to a leadership position of the Chicago Black Panthers.

Fred Hampton headed the Chicago Black Panthers. Evidence indicates that an undercover agent drugged Hampton so police could shoot him in his bed.

He organized the Rainbow Alliance of leftist groups: Students for a Democratic Society, the Hispanic Young Lords, and the Panthers. Hampton was an inspirational speaker, firing up his audiences with statements such as: "You can kill the liberator but you can't kill liberation."[30] Possibly the most important concern was Hampton's ability to appeal to Chicago's gang leaders. Hampton convinced Chicago's largest gang, the Blackstone Rangers, to merge with the Black Panthers. In the process of this merger, the Blackstone Rangers had already changed their name to the Black P. Stone Nation.[31]

U.S. intelligence may have been particularly concerned about the merger of the Blackstone Rangers and the Panthers, because of the Panthers' no-drugs policy. The Blackstone Rangers were said to be involved in drug dealing. Stopping their involvement would have provided a major blow to the money laundered by local banks and corporations.[32] FBI undercover agents and tactics sabotaged the Blackstone Rangers joining with the Panthers. These FBI agents also sabotaged Hampton's progress with Chicago's Vice Lords gang.[33]

By October of 1969, various FBI Cointelpro units had successfully acted on FBI Director J. Edgar Hoover's goal of "neutralizing" the Black Panther national leadership. Police and FBI had shot and arrested Panther national cofounder Huey Newton in 1967. They arrested Panther national cofounder Bobby Seale for the Chicago Democratic Convention "police riot" in 1969, and again in New Haven, Connecticut that year.[34]

The Black Panthers appointed new leaders to take their place. Fred Hampton was to replace Oakland's David Hilliard as the Chief of Staff. With Bobby Seale and Huey Newton in jail, Hampton and Los Angeles Panther leader Geronimo Pratt were in line to succeed them. [35]

Court transcripts suggest that the FBI orchestrated Hampton's murder on December 4, 1969. The night before, FBI undercover agent William O'Neil had slipped a substantial dose of the tranquilizer, secobarbital, into the drinks of Chicago Black Panther leaders Hampton and Southern Illinois Panther leader Mark Clark during dinner. Hampton's mother said he passed out mid-sentence while he was in bed talking to her on the phone that night.[36]

At 4:30 A.M., the FBI and police led a brutal raid on Hampton's home that left him murdered in his sleep. The police intelligence unit had obtained a floor plan from Panther infiltrator William O'Neal. Court transcripts indicate that police kicked in the townhouse door and shot Mark Clark fatally in the chest. They shot unarmed Panther Brenda Harris, and pumped forty-two bullets through the wall of Hampton's bedroom and into his bed's headboard. Court testimony revealed police fired a submachine gun at the remaining Panthers, who tried to cover themselves.[37] Hampton's wife, pregnant Panther Deborah Johnson, along with two other Panthers, failed to rouse the unconscious Panther leader as dozens of bullets came through the walls of their bedroom. Police then shot Hampton in his bed. They shot Hampton twice more in the head at pointblank range.[38]

In all, the police injured many in firing at least eighty-two shots, while a shot fired by Clark was the only round fired by the Panthers during the raid, and only one policeman was even slightly wounded. Even Clark's shot was said to be an unconscious response that his drugged body made when police shot him while he was passed out on security duty holding his shotgun. Police arrested the surviving Black Panther members on charges of aggravated assault and attempted murder.[39]

FBI cover-up, media discrepancies and a lawsuit ensued. A *Chicago Tribune* editor considered a "friend of the FBI" presented the Chicago-police version of the raid being conducted out of self-defense. Only later did another media outlet show that photos supporting the police story, one of being shot at, were fabricated.[40] FBI luminary Richard G. Held took over the Chicago FBI office at this time and supervised the cover-up.[41] The survivors sued the Chicago police and FBI. It took fourteen years of appeals and arbitration to win a $1.85 million settlement.

Huey Newton Targeted with Drugs

Harassment arrests and a near-fatal shooting were among the first of several tactics used against Black Panther national cofounder Huey Newton.[42] When Bobby Seale went to bail Newton out on one specious charge, police arrested Seale for breaking a law that bars even a legally concealed weapon near a jail.[43]

Police failed to keep Newton and Seale imprisoned for long, but attacks continued. On October 27, 1967, the last night of Newton's probation for a 1964 conflict, one of a long line of bizarre shootings involving Panthers occurred. An Oakland police officer with a list of Black Panther license plates pulled over the car Newton was driving. Another police car followed him. While accounts differ on the details of what happened, a shoot-out ensued that left one officer dead, another officer and Newton wounded. Newton left the scene for a hospital, where police soon found, beat and jailed him. Details of the incident support Newton's claim of not having a gun when police shot him.[44]

Elaine Brown, left, was reported to have entered the life of Huey Newton, center, with cocaine and beautiful women, leading him into a drug problem.

In 1968, Huey Newton was convicted of involuntary manslaughter and sentenced to two-to-fifteen years in prison. In 1970, the California Appellate Court reversed the conviction and ordered a new trial. After two more subsequent mistrials, the Superior Court dismissed the charges when the district attorney decided not to pursue a fourth trial in December of 1971, and prison officials released Newton.[45]

U.S. intelligence continued its war on Black Panther leadership. While Panther cofounders had originally barred the use of drugs, the attitude changed with the huge use of marijuana among youth. However, no reports have been found of Panthers receiving drug-dealing charges in the early years of the organization.

CIA agent John Stockwell said the CIA waged psychological warfare on Huey Newton from the time he left prison until his death. Reports support this. Various CIA undercover agents tried to get close to Newton. One, Earl Anthony, said he worked for the FBI and CIA as an undercover agent in the Black Panthers, using cocaine around Newton, and trying to sell him bulk weed.[46]

Bobby Seale said Newton started selling cocaine at this time. Newton claimed he wasn't involved in heavy drugs, and cited the FBI's failed attempts to arrest him for drugs.[47] Several sources claim Panther Elaine Brown helped get Newton using cocaine. L.A. Panther leader Geronimo Pratt said Newton told him in 1988 that when he first got out of prison in 1970, Brown, "kept cocaine and sexy women on him everyday/night."[48] Evidence supports Pratt's allegation that Brown, previously mentioned as being associated with the Los Angeles Black Panthers before becoming Huey Newton's lover, was an undercover agent.[49]

Other evidence that Elaine Brown helped influence Huey Newton's drug involvement includes her arrest for cocaine possession in 1976. Unlike other Panthers who often received heavy sentences for small charges, Brown was only sentenced to complete a series of yoga lessons.[50]

Geronimo Pratt, Panther National Spokesperson Kathleen Cleaver, New Haven Panther leader George Edwards and others stated the belief that Brown's possible spy work led to the murders of Panthers. Many Panthers believed

Brown influenced Newton to expel Pratt and his wife, Nsondi (Sandra "Red" Pratt), from the Black Panther Party. After the Pratts' expulsion, pregnant Nsondi was found bullet-riddled and stuffed in a sleeping bag on a roadside. Reportedly there was no serious police investigation of her murder.

Evidence supports claims that U.S. intelligence further orchestrated the murder of writer and Panther "Field Marshal" George Jackson by prison guards after he was trying to escape from San Quentin prison. Jackson was originally convicted of a $70 armed robbery when he was eighteen. He became highly radicalized during his imprisonment. Professor Angela Davis headed his defense committee, and he wrote a book, *Blood in My Eye*.[51]

Regarding Huey Newton and Elaine Brown, Geronimo Pratt reported Newton told him it took many months for him to come out of his drug and sex euphoria that Brown had cultivated, and realize he was surrounded by agents. Newton said he first began to suspect that Brown was an agent when it came out during Pratt's trial that Brown's name was on a receipt from a paint shop that changed the color of Pratt's car to implicate Pratt in a murder of which he was falsely accused. When the court overturned Pratt's case twenty-seven years later, the government settled with Pratt for $4.5 million in a false imprisonment lawsuit.

Newton also said Brown testified against the United Slaves members who weren't the ones who pulled the trigger on murdered former Panther leaders Carter and Huggins. Newton said he became convinced she was an FBI asset and had fellow Panthers take custody of Brown, but his "advisors" eventually got her back and involved in the Panthers against his wishes.[52]

Another point of evidence supporting Elaine Brown's possible work for U.S. intelligence was her relationship with Jay Richard Kennedy before she joined the Black Panthers. A Pulitzer Prize-winning book, David Garrow's *Bearing the Cross: Martin Luther King, Jr. and the Southern Christian Leadership Conference,* named J.R. Kennedy as a top CIA informant. Released CIA documents back this claim, as does the King family lawyer William Pepper in his book *Orders to Kill*. Brown said that before Newton, Jay Kennedy had been her lover for two years.[53]

The CIA documents, Brown's incidental disclosures, and whistleblower reports give additional credence to Brown's possible U.S. intelligence work. In the 1990s, Brown cited Jay Kennedy as a lifelong mentor, despite reports on his CIA connection having appeared in the mid-'80s.[54] Jay Kennedy was verified as a CIA-supported writer who infiltrated the civil rights movement early in the 1960s. One of his positions was as a manager for entertainer Harry Belafonte, a longtime MLK supporter. Belafonte later fired Kennedy when his suspicions grew about Kennedy's true allegiance.[55]

Elaine Brown went on to lead the only still active section of the Black Panthers, in Oakland. She had them endorse Jerry Brown in his successful run for governor in 1974. She also lectured, wrote books and wrote a newspaper column. Her negative reflections on Huey Newton in *A Taste of Power: A Black Woman's Story* contradict accounts by Afeni Shakur and Kathleen Cleaver. Many other books on the Panthers also contradict Brown's accounts.[56]

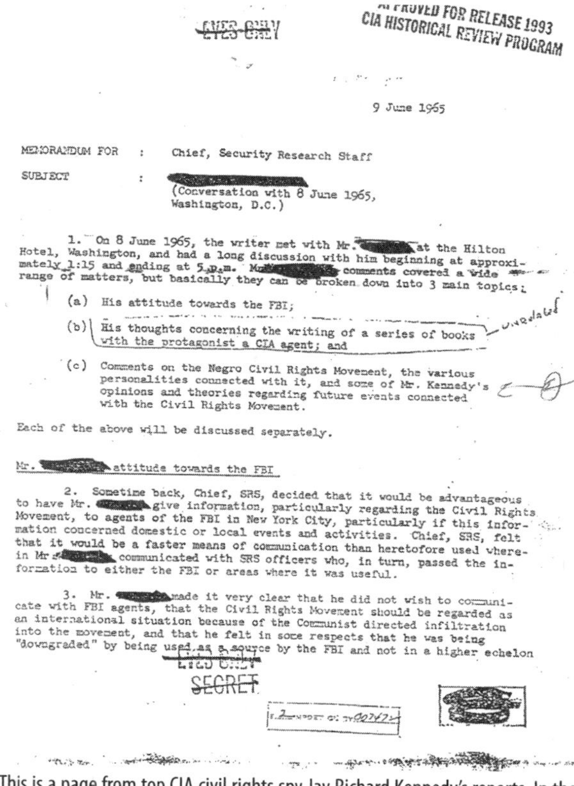

APPROVED FOR RELEASE 1993
CIA HISTORICAL REVIEW PROGRAM

~~EYES ONLY~~

9 June 1965

MEMORANDUM FOR : Chief, Security Research Staff

SUBJECT : [redacted]
(Conversation with 8 June 1965, Washington, D.C.)

1. On 8 June 1965, the writer met with Mr. [redacted] at the Hilton Hotel, Washington, and had a long discussion with him beginning at approximately 1:15 and ending at 5 p.m. Mr. [redacted] comments covered a wide range of matters, but basically they can be broken down into 3 main topics:

(a) His attitude towards the FBI;

(b) His thoughts concerning the writing of a series of books with the protagonist a CIA agent; and

(c) Comments on the Negro Civil Rights Movement, the various personalities connected with it, and some of Mr. Kennedy's opinions and theories regarding future events connected with the Civil Rights Movement.

Each of the above will be discussed separately.

Mr. [redacted] attitude towards the FBI

2. Sometime back, Chief, SRS, decided that it would be advantageous to have Mr. [redacted] give information, particularly regarding the Civil Rights Movement, to agents of the FBI in New York City, particularly if this information concerned domestic or local events and activities. Chief, SRS, felt that it would be a faster means of communication than heretofore used wherein Mr [redacted] communicated with SRS officers who, in turn, passed the information to either the FBI or areas where it was useful.

3. Mr. [redacted] made it very clear that he did not wish to communicate with FBI agents, that the Civil Rights Movement should be regarded as an international situation because of the Communist directed infiltration into the movement, and that he felt in some respects that he was being "downgraded" by being used as a source by the FBI and not in a higher echelon

~~EYES ONLY~~
~~SECRET~~

This is a page from top CIA civil rights spy Jay Richard Kennedy's reports. In the 1990s, Elaine Brown publicly said J.R. Kennedy was her lover for two years and her lifelong mentor.

Elaine Brown's later statements and activist work provide additional clues to her real motives. In a 2003 lecture, she rejected the notion of many undercover agents infiltrating the Panthers, even though a significant number of them had openly testified against the Panthers in trials, and further evidence showed there were many others. Brown also unsuccessfully sued Geronimo Pratt (now Geronimo Ji Jaga) and Kathleen Cleaver for libel regarding these accusations in 2008. Brown's defenders might say her work of heading the Oakland Panthers when Newton fled the country in the '70s, her work on behalf of prisoners, and her writing on behalf of black activists show good intentions. However, evidence of Brown's past misdeeds make it necessary to carefully scrutinize her.[57]

For public relations' sake, the FBI officially ended their Counterintelligence Program in 1971, after activists broke into an FBI office and stole thousands of documents revealing it.[58] However, former Cointelpro agent Wes Swearingen said the FBI continued the program under different names.[59] Various judges who oversaw trials of black activists agreed that an FBI/police Cointelpro continued.[60]

Through all their travails, the Black Panthers did receive some help from many citizens of all ethnicities, including white celebrities. Among them were actors Jane Fonda, Donald Sutherland, Jean Seberg and Marlon Brando. Brando, upon hearing of MLK's assassination, immediately asked his assistant to call the Panthers' Los Angeles office and made a speech at a rally on their behalf. New York Symphony orchestra leader, and writer of *West Side Story*'s music, Leonard Bernstein held benefit parties for the Black Panthers in New York. These celebrities helped the Panthers raise money for their legal defense committees.[61]

CIA Floods American Urban Areas with Asian Opium

U.S. intelligence repressed American leftists as their agents pushed heroin along with the other drugs. Janis Joplin's biographer Alice Echols said heroin became a regular part of the San Francisco music scene as early as 1965, when Joplin and many others "turned to heroin to help them come down" from speed. Organized-crime figures such as the Genovese mafia family, who worked with U.S. intelligence from at least World War II trafficking heroin, also worked closely with top jazz club owner and publisher Morris Levy. The top black jazz musicians who played regularly in his club, such as Charlie "Bird" Parker, got hooked on heroin and also served as role models in their communities. Other jazz greats who got hooked on heroin include Billie Holliday and Miles Davis.[62]

The trafficking of heroin from the Golden Triangle into American cities increased tenfold during the 1960s, in seeming proportion to the increase in anti-War and black radical activism. A U.S. narcotics agent summarized this in respect to the amount of heroin coming into New York. He said, "In 1961 when we ... seized fifteen kilos there was street panic in New York City. Junkies were lined up in front of doctors' offices begging for the stuff.... Now [in 1971] we seize five hundred kilos in three weeks, and it has no effect whatsoever."[63]

In 1971, a CIA leak to the *New York Times* reported that laboratories in the Golden Triangle region around Vietnam produced more than enough tons of Western-grade heroin a year to satisfy the ten tons of heroin Americans consumed annually.[64] Americans living in black urban communities reported a sudden flood of heroin into their neighborhoods. Crime skyrocketed as junkies stole to support their heroin habits. Suburban and small-town American streets soon succumbed to this scourge, as heroin use filtered down to their "safe" white neighborhoods. Peter Arnett of the Associated Press reported that heroin "flooded America in the late 1960s, causing the first nationwide epidemic."[65]

In 1970, a conflict occurred between the CIA and President Nixon's Justice Department. On a June day that year, Attorney General John Mitchell announced that his Bureau of Narcotics and Dangerous Drugs had arrested

150 suspects around the country. Its aforementioned Operation Eagle was deemed "the largest roundup of major drug traffickers in the history of federal law enforcement." Mitchell said these wholesalers handled "about 30% of all heroin sales" and about "80% of all cocaine sales in the United States."[66]

Reviewing Operation Eagle, University of California-Berkeley Professor Peter Dale Scott and State Department researcher Jonathan Marshall found that, "as many as seventy percent of those arrested had once belonged to the Bay of Pigs invasion force." This was the CIA's amassed army of Cuban expatriates launched against the socialist government of Cuban revolutionary leaders Fidel Castro and Ernesto "Che" Guevara. Mario Escandar and other Operation Eagle defendants had their court cases thrown out on a technicality. Escandar "went on to become one of Miami's most powerful and untouchable traffickers." Other CIA trainees enjoyed similar status in the drug trade throughout the 1970s.[67]

American University Professor Clarence Lusane joined Professor Alfred McCoy in reporting that U.S. intelligence supplied drugs to organized crime families who carried out most of the street-level drug dealing. By the later 1960s, the CIA began using other major dealers as well. The first black high-level drug dealer, Frank Matthews, grossed over $100 million by 1971, with over one hundred people cutting and bagging heroin, and then cocaine, in New York City.

Early in 1973, Matthews was arrested. He gained bail and, by that July, left the game, disappearing with his bodyguard, mistress, and $20 million. Lusane stated that a "Top Secret" Justice Department report cited how nine of Matthews' drug suppliers had their drug importation charges dropped because of their ties to the CIA, illustrating the CIA's dominance in drug trafficking.[68]

Young Lords Find Activism after Detoxing

Puerto Rican teenagers founded the Young Lords as a Chicago gang in 1959. Jose "Cha-Cha" Jimenez led the gang in 1964 when they were protecting Latino teens from white ethnic gangs. By 1968, the gang had gotten involved with heroin, cocaine, acid and other drugs. Jimenez was jailed for heroin possession that year. While in jail he read Martin Luther King, Malcolm X and Black Panther Party literature.

When Jimenez got out of jail, he consulted with Chicago Panther leader Fred Hampton on how to turn the Young Lords into a similar organization as the Panthers, but for the Latino community. Jimenez went to Oakland and shadowed Black Panther national cofounder Bobby Seale for a month. Jimenez ran his Young Lords Organization with similar community organizing activities, such as free breakfast programs for the poor, free health care programs, anti-police brutality programs, women's rights programs and political education through their own newspaper.[69]

The Young Lords grew so popular that in 1969 they led a march of 10,000 calling for Puerto Rico's independence. The FBI's Counterintelligence Program was targeting the Young Lords at this time. Police arrested Jimenez and other Young Lords multiple times for many false charges, including marijuana possession. Cointelpro later attacked all Young Lords chapters with false arrests, infiltrators and sabotage.

In 1975, Jose Cha-Cha Jimenez ran for 46th ward Alderman, as an organizing tactic. Despite only 1000 Latinos registered to vote there, Jimenez won 36% of the vote, with 51% needed to win. Also that year, police arrested Jimenez after a protest action he led in support of recently arrested members of FALN, an armed Puerto Rican liberation group that had conducted protest bombings.

By 1983, Jimenez had joined with Puerto Rican activist groups that helped gain black politician Harold Washington's election as Chicago's mayor. On a June day that year, Jimenez introduced Washington to a Puerto Rican crowd of 100,000. The following day Jimenez and other Latino activists met in the Chicago FBI office with the director to demand that the government stop the mistreatment and torture of jailed FALN. The day after this meeting, a drug dealer assassinated Rudy Lozano, a Mexican activist and fellow Mayor Washington supporter, in his home.[70]

The Young Lords Organization in Chicago inspired Latino communities nationwide. Young Lords chapters formed in Milwaukee, Philadelphia, Bridgeport, Newark, Boston, Los Angeles, San Diego and other cities. A particularly large group formed in New York City. The New York City Young Lords elected Felipe Luciano as their founding chairman. Luciano was also a poet and member of the Last Poets musical group in the 1970s. Many consider them the godfathers of political rap music.

Luciano and his Young Lords first surveyed their East Harlem neighborhood for the top problem to work on, and found it was trash not getting picked up. Sanitation services didn't take care of the poorer neighborhoods like the rest of the city. The Young Lords first tried to clean up neighborhoods themselves. They then built the uncollected garbage into a five-foot tall barricade across Third Avenue in East Harlem and set it ablaze. It stopped traffic and finally brought on improved sanitation services.

Among other New York Young Lords actions, they physically took over the First Spanish Methodist Church, providing a free breakfast program inside of it, as well as a clothing program, free health services, day-care services and a liberation school. They took a mobile chest x-ray machine and brought it to where it was more needed. They later took over Lincoln Hospital in the Bronx for 12 hours and demanded door-to-door preventive health services, maternal and childcare aid, drug addiction treatment, senior care services, and testing for lead paint poisoning and tuberculosis. They carried out many of these services themselves until they could get the city's help.[71]

One Young Lords member, Vincent "Panama" Alba, had a heroin problem as a teenager in the South Bronx, before Black Panther Cleo Silvers helped to get him clean and sober. She also turned him on to activism.[72] Alba played a key role in politicizing the Latin Kings street gang. Other prominent Young Lords leaders included Juan Gonzalez, who had also been part of the Columbia Students for a Democratic Society (SDS). Gonzalez later became an award-winning journalist, a longtime columnist for the *New York Daily News* and a co-host of *Democracy Now!* Other famous New York Young Lords include longtime television talk show host Geraldo Rivera and Young Lords documentary filmmaker Iris Morales.

Notes

1 Another Black Panther Party had started that same year out of Maxwell Stamford and Herman Ferguson's Revolutionary Action Movement in Philadelphia and New York. While also doing lasting work, they used more discreet tactics and remain lesser known. Muhammad Ahmad (Maxwell Stanford Jr.) *We Will Return in the Whirlwind: Black Radical Organizations 1960-1975* (Chicago: Charles H. Kerr, 2007), pp. 120-24. Ward Churchill and Jim Vander Wall, *Agents of Repression* (Boston: South End Press, 1990), pp. 44-46. Michael Newton, *Bitter Grain: Huey Newton and the Black Panther Party* (Los Angeles: Holloway House, 1980), pp. 12-15 (author no known relation to Huey Newton).

2 See, for example, , Bobby Seale, *Seize the Time:The Story of the Black Panther Party and Huey P. Newton* (Baltimore: Black Classic Press, 1996), pp. 28-29.

3 Seale, *Seize the Time*, pp. 28-29. Huey Newton, *To Die for the People: Selected Writings and Speeches*, ed. Toni Morrison, (New York: Writers and Readers Publishers, 1972, 1999), pp. 3-6. Also see Newton, *Bitter Grain*. Churchill and Vander Wall, *Agents of Repression*. Also, Lumumba Shakur, Afeni Shakur, et al., *Look for Me in the Whirlwind: The Collective Autobiography of the New York 21* (New York: Vintage, 1971). On Panther newspaper circulation, see Seale, *Seize the Time*, p. 179.

4 Ex-Panther Lee Lew-Lee's *All Power to the People* (documentary, 1996). On political organization and philosophy, see Huey Newton, *War Against the Panthers: A Study of Repression* (New York/London: Writers and Readers Publishing, 1981/96), pp. 28-35. Also see, Seale, *Seize the Time*, p. 82; and Afeni Shakur, "We Will Will," in Phil Foner, ed., *The Black Panthers Speak* (New York: Di Capo/Perseus, 1970), p. 161.

5 Cleaver's detailed description in Newton, *Bitter Grain*, p. 24.

6 M. Newton, *Bitter Grain*, pp. 38, 173. Churchill and Vander Wall, *The COINTELPRO Papers: Documents from the FBI's Secret Wars Against Dissent in the United States* (Boston: South End Press, 1991), p. 126; *Agents of Repression*, p. 64.

7 For more information on the general targeting of black Americans, see the excellent film on DVD by directors Deb Ellis and Denis Mueller: *The FBI's War on Black America* (Maljack Productions, 1990. DVD Createspace, 2009), http://www.youtube.com/watch?v=Zwdx1ewLBYA.

8 M. Newton, *Bitter Grain*, pp. 74-78.

9 Nikhil Pal Singh, The Black Panthers and the 'Undeveloped Country' of the Left," in Charles Earl Jones, ed., *The Black Panther Party (Reconsidered)*. Also, Elaine Brown, *A Taste of Power: A Black Woman's Story* (New York: Anchor/Doubleday, 1992), caption.

10 Note that the FBI commonly calls these undercover agents "informants"—a cover-up name that hides both their employment by the FBI and the insidious nature of their murderous actions. M. Wes Swearingen, *FBI Secrets: An Agent's Expose* (Boston: South End Press, 1995), pp.82-84.

11 The irony of the United Slaves abbreviation as US is apparent. This work with Karenga came from undercover police Louis Tackwood and Citizens Research-Intelligence Committee, *The Glass House Tapes: The Story of an Agent Provocateur and the New Police-Intelligence Complex* (New York: Avon Books,1973), cited in *Agents of Repression*, p. 63. The "drugs" provided by Tackwood were reported in M. Newton, *Bitter Grain*, p. 97.

12 M. Newton, *Bitter Grain*, pp. 95-97.

13 Swearingen, *FBI Secrets*, pp. 82-84. Kit Kim Holder, "The History of the Black Panther Party 1966-1972: A Curriculum Tool for Afrikan Amerikan Studies," dissertation 1990, Amherst College Library, Amherst, MA, p. 62. *Rolling Stone*, September 9, 1976, p. 47.

14 From two affidavits, one given to attorney Fred Hiestand and the other to Charles Garry, filed in Black Panther Party v. Levi, No. 76-2205 and interview with Fred Hiestand, 1/9/80. Also cited in information given to Ernest Volkman, *Penthouse* magazine, April 1980. All cited in H. P. Newton, *War Against the Panthers*, pp. 81, 101n. FBI undercover agents George and Larry Stiner were tried and convicted of the murders. They did four years in prison before escaping and not being heard from again. Hubert was never apprehended: *War Against the Panthers*, p. 81; and Swearingen, *FBI Secrets*, p. 84.

15 Personal Interview with George Edwards, 7/24/07.

16 Churchill and Vander Wall, *Agents of Repression*, p. 79.

17 *Human Rights in the United States: The Unfinished Story, Current Political Prisoners—Victims of Cointelpro*, Issue Forum, U.S. Congressional Hearing, 9/14/00, 1:25 P.M. Rayburn House Office Building, Washington, D.C. Room 2000, http://www.ratical.org/co-globalize/CynthiaMcKinney/news/if000914HR.html. Also, personal interview, Michael Warren, attorney for Tupac Shakur and Mutulu Shakur in New York, September 2, 2003.

18 Swearingen, *FBI Secrets*, pp. 82-84.

19 Greg Land, "Former Black Panther to Appeal Dismissal in Libel Case," *Law.com* 1/26/2009, http://www.law.com/jsp/article.jsp?id=1202427713045&Former_Black_Panther_to_Appeal_Dismissal_in_Libel_Case&slreturn=20130425141020.

20 From two affidavits, one given to attorney Fred Hiestand and the other to Charles Garry, filed in *Black Panther Party v. Levi*, No. 76-2205 and interview with Fred Hiestand, 1/9/80. Also cited in information given to Ernest Volkman, *Penthouse* magazine, April, 1980. All cited in Huey P. Newton, *War Against the Panthers*, pp. 81,101n. FBI undercover agents George and Larry Stiner were tried and convicted of the murders. They did four years in prison before escaping and not being heard from again. Hubert was never apprehended. H. Newton, *War Against the Panthers*, p. 81.

21 Murray Kempton, *The Briar Patch: The People of the State of New York v. Lumumba Shakur Et Al.* (New York: Dell, 1973), pp. 77-78. Peter Zimroth, *Perversions of Justice* (New York: Viking Press, 1974), pp. 179-83. M. Newton, *Bitter Grain*, p. 182. Police also shot at two other Panthers while they were parked near the Harlem river. Odinga and Panther Kuwasi Balagoon escaped. Police arrested 19-year-old female Panther Joan Bird, whom they found cowering in the shot-up car. They then beat her up in the precinct.

22 An attempt by the FBI to murder Lumumba that day is uncertain but possible. BOSS undercover agent Ralph White admitted shooting his gun *inside* the Harlem office with Lumumba there, though he said it was several days before the 17th. White said Lumumba warned him to never do that again, but White made the false claim Shakur said this due to his storing dynamite in the office. Zimroth, *Perversions of Justice*, p. 187

23 M. Newton, *Bitter Grain*, pp. 181-55. Kempton, *The Briar Patch*, pp. 75-78. Zimroth, *Perversions of Justice*, pp. 179-83. Note that police said they only accidentally came upon Odinga and the other Panthers, who were there to shoot at a police precinct. Evidence suggests this was a complete fabrication.

24 The indictment stated that the Panthers planned to bomb public places such as The Botanical Gardens. M. Newton, *Bitter Grain*, pp. 181-85. Kempton, *The Briar Patch*, pp. 2-12, 75-78. Zimroth, *Perversions of Justice*, pp. 3-5, 179-83. Lumumba Shakur, Afeni Shakur, et al., *Look For Me In the Whirlwind.* Only Sekou Odinga evaded the April 2 police sweep by climbing out of his third story window and escaping to Algeria. Once there he joined Eldridge and Kathleen Cleaver. Eldridge had jumped bail on his previous frame-up, and Kathleen went with him to the African country that granted them asylum.

25 Note from publisher of Lumumba Shakur et al, *Look For Me in the Whirlwind: The Collective Autobiography of the New York 21* (New York: Vintage/Random House, 1971), p. 363. Also see Jasmyn Guy, *Afeni Shakur: Evolution of a Revolutionary* (New York: Atria, 2004), pp. 110-11. On courtroom scene, jury time of deliberations, etc., see quoted trial transcript and spectator Zimroth in Zimroth, *Perversions of Justice*, pp. 308-09.

26 Nikhil Pal Singh, "The Black Panthers and the 'Undeveloped Country' of the Left," in Charles Earl Jones, ed., *The Black Panther Party (Reconsidered)*. Also, Brown, *A Taste of Power*, caption.

27 Laura Pulido, *Black, Brown, Yellow and Left: Radical Activism in Los Angeles* (Los Angeles: University of California Press, 2006), p. 103.

28 L. Shakur et al., *Look For Me in the Whirlwind*, pp. 139, 148-50. Lumumba believed the police and power structure encouraged these gangs to get people of color killing each other, but with memberships of ten thousand each, "the gangs were actually apolitical small armies better equipped than some African and Latin American states when they first got so-called independence."

29 Malcolm X, with Alex Haley, *The Autobiography of Malcolm X* (New York: Ballantine, 1965), pp. 317-19.

30 Fred Hampton, 1970, speech excerpt from Foner, *The Black Panthers Speak.* See documents and evidence in the case of *Iberia Hampton, et. al. Plaintiffs-Appellants v. Edward V. Hanrahan, et al., Defendants-Appellees*, Transcript at 21741-62 and 21807-18 (hereinafter cited as *Transcript*). Churchill and Vander Wall, *Agents of Repression*, pp. 64-65, nn5, 8. *Appeal*, #26-30 and WON 5. Also see *Transcript* at 6579 and 8907. Churchill and Vander Wall, *Agents of Repression*, p. 66, nn22-23.

31 On Hampton gaining conversion of Blackstone Rangers, see Transcript, pp. 21741-62 and 21807-18. Churchill and Vander Wall, *Agents of Repression*, pp. 64-65 nn5, 8.

32 On Blackstone Rangers selling drugs, Ann D. Witte, "Beating the System?" in *Exploring the Underground Economy*, ed. Susan Pozo, 1996, cited in Christopher Thale, "Underground Economy," *Encyclopedia of Chicago*, http://www.encyclopedia.chicagohistory.org/pages/1280.html.

33 On sabotage of gang conversions, see *Transcript.* Churchill and Vander Wall, *Agents of Repression*, pp. 64-65, nn5, 8.

34 M. Newton, *Bitter Grain*, pp. 29-31, 42-65. For lesser details, see Churchill and Vander Wall, *Agents of Repression* and their *The COINTELPRO Papers.* On CIA file and "hit list," see "National Security, Civil Liberties and the Collection of Intelligence: A Report on the Huston Plan," reported in *U.S. Congress, Senate, Book III. Final Report of the Select Committee to Study Government Operations with Respect to Intelligence Activities*, 94th Cong. 2d sess., 1976, pp. 936-60. Cited in H. Newton, *War Against the Panthers*, pp. 43, n93. On charges dismissed see, M. Newton, *Bitter Grain*, p. 65.

35 Churchill and Vander Wall, *Agents of Repression*, p. 69. *Transcript*, pp. 29037-8 and 29183-4. David Hilliard was the current Chief of Staff of the Panthers' Central Committee.

36 On secobarbital in Hampton's system from O'Neil's likely drugging, see thin-layer chromatography examination performed on Hampton's blood by Cook County Chief Toxicologist Eleanor Berman. There was no known drug use amongst these Panthers at this time. On Hampton

falling asleep mid-sentence, see *People's Law Office vs. Edward V. Hanrahan et al.*, Transcript at 25398; Brief at p. 36. Churchill and Vander Wall, *Agents of Repression*, pp. 71, 401 n78, 402 n88. Also see Churchill and Vander Wall, *The COINTELPRO Papers*, p. 140.

37 *Transcript*, p. 33716. In Churchill and Vander Wall, *Agents of Repression*, pp. 73, n403. Also see, Jeffrey Haas *The Assassination of Fred Hampton: How the FBI and the Chicago Police Murdered a Black Panther* (Chicago: Lawrence Hill Books, 2010), pp. 92, 299, 353.

38 Churchill and Vander Wall, *Agents of Repression*, p. 402 n88. Also see Churchill and Vander Wall, *The COINTELPRO Papers*, p. 40.

39 Churchill and Vander Wall, *Agents of Repression*, p. 402, from *Transcript*, pp. 33842-33855, 33970, 17810. On many shots fired and injuries, see Zimroth, *Perversions of Justice*, p. 87; Foner, *The Black Panthers Speak*, p. 137; Churchill and Vander Wall, *Agents of Repression*, p. 73. On Clark shot pointblank in the chest, Churchill and Vander Wall, *The COINTELPRO Papers*, p. 358 n93.

40 Brief of documents from *Transcript*, pp. 58-59. Also Tackwood, *The Glass House Tapes*, p. 100, cited in Churchill and Vander Wall, *Agents of Repression*, pp. 73, 403 nn101, 105.

41 For example, Chicago Police Captain Harry Ervanian and Lt Robert Kukowski were forced to say in court under oath that the investigation was a "whitewash" and the "worst investigation" they had ever seen. *Transcript*, pp. 174, 177, in Churchill and Vander Wall, *Agents of Repression*, pp. 74, 403 n107.

42 Seale, *Seize the Time*, pp. 106-07.

43 M. Newton, *Bitter Grain*, pp. 31, 35-36.

44 For details, see M. Newton, *Bitter Grain*, pp.29-31, 42-65. For lesser details, see Churchill and Vander Wall, *Agents of Repression.*

45 UPI, "Case Against Newton Dropped," *The Dispatch*, December 15, 1971.

46 Earl Anthony, *Spitting in the Wind: The true story behind he violent legacy of the Black Panther Party* (Malibu, CA: Roundtable, 1990), p122. Published following Churchill and Vander Wall's extensively more revealing accounts, Anthony's book appears as part fact and part subterfuge. Among other undercover agents who got involved with the Oakland Black Panther office, LA Panther Melvin "Cotton" Smith eventually admitted he had been an undercover police intelligence agent. Smith traveled up to Oakland and worked in that Panther office before then traveling to the New York office, where Assata Shakur said he continually tried to get Panthers drinking liquor with him. See Churchill and Vander Wall, *Agents of Repression*, pp. 86, 404 n130, 408 n166. Also Assata Shakur, *Assata: An Autobiography*, pp. 228-230. On psychological warfare, see John Stockwell saying this in the documentary by Lee Lew-Lee, *All Power to the People* (1996).

47 Stated by Bobby Seale at the first Black Panther Film Festival, New York, 1999. On Newton's claims, for example, see "Teletype from FBI San Francisco to director, 2/16/74. FBU "Informative Notes," 2/16/74, prepared for "J.L.B." FBI Memorandum from Supervisor Gary L. Penrith to SAC San Francisco, 4/13/73. Newton noted that these documents said he might be "shaking down" drug dealers to donate money rather than buying or selling drugs with them, H. Newton, *War Against the Panthers*, pp. 48-49.

48 Also see personal interview, Watani Tyehimba, 5/10/00. Tyehimba, was a former Los Angeles-based Black Panther in a chapter started by a different national activist group, the Revolutionary Action Movement. Tyehimba supported Geronimo Pratt's defense and said he understood that Pratt helped Newton with cocaine withdrawal symptoms when they ended up in prison together, but the actual extent of Newton's cocaine use is uncertain. See more notes below on agents trying to get Newton using drugs.

49 Personal interviews with Kathleen Cleaver, 10/5/02 and George Edwards, 8/20/00. Cleaver also made a strong implication of Brown's spy work when directly asked about it by an audience member at the 2nd Black Panther Film Festival. Churchill and Vander Wall also stated that "Elaine Brown, widely suspected among former [Panther] party..." *The COINTELPRO Papers*, pp. 153, 362 n131. Note also the FBI memos on that discuss the split in Panther factions, which Brown was believed to have influenced, between Newton's Oakland office and the still united Cleaver faction in Algeria, Pratt in LA, and the Shakur-led chapter in New York. These memos discussed trying to stop Kathleen Cleaver coming from

Algeria to re-unify Huey Newton's national Oakland office with these other key chapters. "FBI Memo, 2/17/71, To: Director (100—448006) From: San Francisco (157-601) COINTELPRO—BLACK EXTREMISTS, RM.," *The COINTELPRO Papers*, pp. 151-52. On Brown as Newton's one-time lover, she also apparently visited Newton in prison before that: Brown, *A Taste of Power*, pp. 242, 246, 258. Much thanks to Kathleen Cleaver for her information and support..

50 On Brown's cocaine conviction, this author has a Xeroxed clipping of a California news article from April 24, 1976, supplied by ex-Panther George Edwards, one of New Haven's former top Black Panthers. His very compelling stack of evidence first was compiled for and reported in Lee Lew-Lee's documentary *All Power to the People* (1995). Edwards then kindly donated his information, time, and insights to this author. Personal interview, George Edwards, 8/22/00.

51 On Pratt and his wife's expulsion and murder see, Churchill and Vander Wall, *Agents of Repression*, pp. 87-88; *The COINTELPRO Papers*, pp. 153, 362 n131. Researchers also claim that Brown heavily aided the FBI's manufacture of the split between Newton and New York Panthers, as well as Newton's split with LA Panther leader Geronimo Pratt. Former Panther National Communications Director Kathleen Cleaver further cited belief in Brown's possible connection to the murder of two LA Panther leaders and Black revolutionary George Jackson. Personal interviews with Kathleen Cleaver, 10/5/02 and George Edwards 8/22/00. See Tackwood, *Glass House Tapes*, and note that Tackwood also passed a polygraph about his account, as cited in Churchill and Vander Wall, *Agents of Repression*, p. 95 n205. This source also cites former FBI agent M. Wesley Swearingen's deposition taken in Honolulu, Hawaii, October 1980, p. 2 in his discussions with FBI undercover agent Darthard Perry, a.k.a. Othello.

52 Newton quote from a description written by Geronimo Pratt and sent by Kathleen Cleaver's email, http://whosemedia.com/drums/2007/05/09/was-elaine-brown-an-agent/. Pratt also noted Brown receiving psychiatric treatment at UCLA. Pratt called this a "prerequisite for patsies of Elaine's type." This suggests Brown was being manipulated with some kind of MK-Ultra conditioning in a psychiatric hospital and that Pratt had seen others go through this. On Pratt's legal settlement, Todd Purdum, "Ex Black Panther Wins Long Legal Battle," *New York Times*, April 27, 2000, p. A18. Douglas Martin, "Elmer G. Pratt, Jailed Panther Leader, Dies at 63," *New York Times*, June 3, 2011, http://www.nytimes.com/2011/06/04/us/04pratt.html?_r=0.

53 This writer's copies of CIA documents on Jay Kennedy, for example, were FOIA-obtained by ex-Panther turned filmmaker Lee Lew-Lee and given to George Edwards and then to this writer. See, for example, CIA internal memorandum in CIA file for Chief, Security Research Staff, from Allan Morse, one Jay R. Kennedy report, 6/9/65, p. 7. On Jay Kennedy as Brown's ex-lovers, Elaine Brown, *A Taste of Power* (New York: Doubleday, 1992), pp. 79-86. Earl Anthony, *Spitting in the Wind: The True Story Behind the Violent Legacy of the Black Panther Party* (Malibu, CA: Roundtable, 1990), pp. 79, 151. Jay Kennedy as CIA's "Principal source," David Garrow, *Bearing the Cross: Martin Luther King, Jr. and the Southern Christian Leadership Conference* (New York: Quill, William Morrow, 1986), p. 285. William Pepper, *Orders to Kill: The Truth Behind the Murder of Martin Luther King, Jr.* (New York: Warner Books, 1995), pp. 82, 445.

54 Rosemary Bray, "A Black Panther's Long Journey," *New York Times Magazine*, 1/31/93, p. 68. J.R. Kennedy as "Principal source," Garrow, *Bearing the Cross*, p. 285. Brown's *A Taste of Power* also mentions discussion with Jay Kennedy, while she was a Panther, several times in the book, see pp. 175, 262.

55 See, for example, CIA internal memorandum in CIA file for Chief, Security Research Staff, from Allan Morse, one Jay R. Kennedy report. 6/9/65, p.7. Memorandum from Howard Osborn, Director of Security to Deputy Director of Support. 3/27/68. Also see Pepper finding that Jay Kennedy was the CIA's "Informant A," Pepper, *Orders To Kill*, p. 82.

56 In *A Taste of Power*, Brown's 1992 published account, she said Newton physically abused her, which no other source has corroborated Newton having done to anyone. Newton wrote his doctoral thesis in 1980, based on his FBI and CIA file. His surviving wife published it in 1991. One FBI document detailed the kind of smear campaign they would attempt on Newton. In Brown's later memoir, she described Newton's early '70s, post-prison apartment as a "twenty-fifth-floor penthouse...

[with] many balconies." An FBI document described how an FBI media collaborator, Ed Montgomery, helped the FBI in one of its "counter-intelligence activities," smearing Newton with a false report in a front-page *San Francisco Chronicle* article. The article characterized Newton's apartment as "luxurious," in contrast to "the ghetto-like BPP 'pads' and community centers." Other FBI memorandums detailed their intent to carry out this smear campaign. The FBI also created a fake letter from an anonymous Panther they sent from the Oakland Panther office to Panther offices nationwide, complaining about Newton's alleged luxurious apartment. Brown, *A Taste of Power*, p. 9. FBI memorandum from San Francisco to hqtrs., 11/24/70, and from SAC New Orleans to director, 12/11/71, in H. Newton, *War Against the Panthers*, pp. 61-62. Afeni Shakur in Jasmine Guy, *Afeni Shakur: Evolution of a Revolutionary* (New York: Atria, 2004), p. 77, and Kathleen Cleaver, personal interview, 10/5/02. Many other books on the Panthers also contradict Brown's accounts.

57 This writer attended one of Brown's 2004 lectures in Washington D.C. Brown wrote an article and signed an advertisement on behalf of former honorary Black Panther, Imam Jamil Al-Amin (formerly H. Rap Brown), Elaine Brown, "Black Panther Party Long Victimized by Campaign of Lies," *Atlanta Journal-Constitution*, 3/25/00.

58 On Media, Pennsylvania break-in, Churchill and Vander Wall, *The COINTELPRO Papers*, pp. xi, 332. See for, example, *The FBI's Covert Program to Destroy the Black Panther Party*, 94th Congress, 2nd Session, U.S. Government Printing Office, Washington, D.C., 1976. Seymour Hersh, "CIA Reportedly Recruited Blacks for Surveillance of Panther Party," *New York Times*, March 17, 1978, p. A1, A16. quoted in H. Newton, *War Against the Panthers*, p. 90.

59 Deposition of former FBI agent M. Wesley Swearingen, taken in October 1980, in Honolulu, Hawaii, p. 2, in Churchill and Vander Wall, *Agents of Repression*, p. 62

60 *Handschu, et al. vs. Special Services Division a/k/a Bureau of Special Services, U.S. District Court*, S.D.N.Y., 71 Civ. 2203 (CSH) Memorandum Opinion and Order, Mar. 7, 1985, p. 26. Ibid, Memorandum Opinion and Order, May 24, 1979, p. 3. Connie Bruck, "The Takedown of Tupac," *New Yorker*, 7/7/97, p. 54.

61 On stars in general, *Elle* editors, "Protesting with the Stars" *Elle* magazine. October 14, 2011, http://www.elle.com/life-love/society-career/protesting-the-stars-608996-10#slide-10. On U.S. intelligence targeting Fonda and Seberg, see Churchill and Vander Wall, *The COINTELPRO Papers*, pp. 214-16.

62 On Jewish and Italian organized crime figures working with U.S. intelligence, see Henrik Kruger, *The Great Heroin Coup* (Boston: South End Press, 1980), pp.14, 33. Referenced in Clarence Lusane, *Pipe Dream Blues: Racism and the War on Drugs* (Boston: South End Press, 1999), p. 117. On undercover agents in San Francisco music scene pushing drugs, see Martin Lee and Bruce Shlain, *Acid Dreams: The Complete Social History of LSD: The CIA, the Sixties, and Beyond* (New York: Grove Press, 1994), pp.188-9. On popularity of speed and heroin in music scenes in LA, NYC and San Fran, see Alice Echols, *Scars of Sweet Paradise: The Life and Times of Janis Joplin* (New York: Metropolitan/Henry Holt, 1999), pp. 82-83. On Morris Levy see Fredric Dannen, *Hit Men* (New York: Vintage, 1991), pp. 36-38. On jazz artists such as Billy Holiday and heroin addiction, see for example, "Billy Holiday: About the Singer," *American Masters*, PBS, 6/8/2006, http://www.pbs.org/wnet/americanmasters/episodes/billie-holiday/about-the-singer/68/.

63 Alfred McCoy, *The Politics of Heroin: CIA Complicity in the Global Drug Trade* (New York: Lawrence Hill, 1972/1991), p. 260.

64 *New York Times*, 6/6/71, p. 2. Also see *Evening Star* (Washington, DC), 6/19/72. On CIA support of other military leaders in region: Interview with Elliot K. Chan, Vientiane, Laos, 8/15/71. (Chan was a USAID police adviser to the Royal Laotian government.) Interview with an agent, U.S. Bureau of Narcotics and Dangerous Drugs, New Haven, CT, 11/18/71. All referenced in McCoy, *The Politics of Heroin*, pp. 286-89.

65 Peter Arnett, AP Special Correspondent, "Heroin War: National Epidemic Feared as Illicit Drugs Pour into U.S." *The Free-Lance Star*, 11/18/80. His story diverted from the top culprits, in laying the blame on the "French connection."

66 *BNDD Bulletin*, September-October 1970; cf. Hank Messick, *Of Grass and Snow*

(Englewood Cliffs, NJ: Prentice-Hall, 1979), p. 6. On Mitchell quote, Warren Hinckle and William Turner, *The Fish is Red* (New York: Harper & Row, 1981), p. 314. Referenced in Peter Dale Scott and Jonathan Marshall, *Cocaine Politics: Drugs, Armies, and the CIA in Central America* (Los Angeles: University of California Press, 1991), p. 26.

67 On Escandar, see Hinckle and Turner, *The Fish is Red,* p. 314. On "other CIA trainees," former CIA commando Grayston Lynch, quoted in *St. Petersburg Times,* 5/30/82. Referenced in Scott and Marshall, *Cocaine Politics,* pp. 26-27.

68 On Matthews disappearance with mistress and money, see Messick, *Of Grass and Snow,* pp. 36-37. On nine suppliers tied to CIA, see Jefferson Morley, "The Kid Who Sold Crack to the President," *City Paper* (Washington, DC), 12/15/89, p. 31. Both referenced in Lusane, *Pipe Dream Blues,* pp. 41-42.

69 On newspaper, see http://libcom.org/history/latin-liberation-news-service-newspapers-young-lords-organization. On other programs and history of Young Lords in Lincoln Park, see Frank Browning, "From Rumble to Revolution: The Young Lords," *Ramparts* (October 1970). On Jimenez and heroin, jail stint, shadowing Seale, https://www.youtube.com/watch?v=vayeZc5YsMc. On Young Lords and Jimenez involved in and arrested for drugs, see http://nationalyounglords.com/?page_id=15.

70 http://nationalyounglords.com/?page_id=15.

71 Jennifer B. Lee, "The Young Lords Legacy of Puerto Rican Activism," *New York Times,* August 24, 2009, http://cityroom.blogs.nytimes.com/2009/08/24/the-young-lords-legacy-of-puerto-rican-activism/?_r=0. Also see, David Gonzalez, "Young Lords: Vital in the '60s, a Model Now," *New York Times,* October 18, 1996; and Iris Morales, *Palante Siempre Palante: The Young Lords* (Documentary). *The Last Poets, made in Amerikkka* (Documentary, 2008), dir. Claude Santiago, France.

72 "Seize the Hospital to Serve the People: An Interview with Activist Cleo Silvers, 2009," www.socialmedicine.org/media/.

Bob Marley

Chapter Eighteen

Drugs and Murder of Jamaica's Bob Marley

Bob Marley and Peter Tosh both grew up in squalid Jamaican homes. They met and formed a singing group called the Wailers in the mid-1960s. By the mid-'70s they broke into the American and British music world as a hot new band playing reggae, a unique sound derived from various elements of music from Black communities worldwide, filtered through Jamaicans' Rastafarian community influence. Their 1974 *Burnin'* album was particularly known for its Black Power songs such as "I Shot the Sheriff," "Burnin' and Lootin'," and "Get Up, Stand Up." The album's "Revolution" was a particularly incendiary song in saying there was no political change without revolutionary struggle.[1]

By 1980, Bob Marley had become a hero for Africans. He played concerts for leftist leader Robert Mugabe in Zimbabwe and supported leftist struggles in Angola, Mozambique and South Africa. New York's Black Liberation Movement-aligned station, WLIB radio, worked to get Marley's next album, *Uprising,* nationwide play on mostly politically conservative Black radio.[2]

Right-Wing Attacks on Jamaica and Marley

In the 1970s, democratic socialist leader Michael Manley took the office of Prime Minister in Jamaica. Researchers uncovered covert U.S. interventions that included arson, bombing and assassination The U.S. told Prime Minister Manley they weren't involved in covert actions against the Jamaican government. However, Manley's forces intercepted at least one shipment containing 500 machine guns that came from a right-wing Jamaican paramilitary faction with CIA roots and leaders convicted of drug trafficking. This right-wing group also reportedly aided the trafficking of cocaine and heroin into Jamaica.[3]

Pulitzer Prize-winning journalist Gary Webb said that, in 1977, two investigative reporters found the CIA's Jamaican station chief waged a destabilization program against democratic socialist leader Michael Manley. Cuban Bay of Pigs veteran Luis Posada Carriles helped the CIA make covert shipments of arms to Manley's opponents and sponsored violence against Manley's supporters that included bombings, assassinations, inciting labor unrest and giving financial support and bribes to the conservative Jamaican Labour Party.[4]

Marley, Peter Tosh and their Rastafarian friends preached that Jamaicans should resist American interventions, and resist using heroin and coke, limiting drug use to marijuana. Although their loyalty generally seemed aligned with Manley's government, right-wing officers arose within the police department. There is documentation that in 1972 right-wing police officers knocked down Tosh's door, and in 1975 beat him badly, dislocating several ribs.[5]

In 1976, when right-wing militia attacks on the government and its allies escalated, the Governor-General of Jamaica declared a state of emergency. Upcoming national elections saw the rise of right-wing militia-backed Edward Seaga as the opposition. Prime Minister Michael Manley said the CIA helped stir up armed unrest due to the upcoming elections. He said government police loyal to him fought this calculated unrest organized by his political opponents.

Several writers, including Gary Webb and former CIA agent Philip Agee, documented how the CIA used money, guns and cocaine to undermine Michael Manley's administration. The CIA station chief in Jamaica, with the help of some opposition groups, began a program that included assassinations. The Jamaican Labour Party and their supportive gangs were part of this cabal. At least one member later claimed he was trained by the CIA to fight political wars for the JLP.[6]

The CIA's concern about Bob Marley's influence in Jamaica increased after his 1976 song "Rat Race" stated, "Rasta don't work for no CIA!"[7] As elections neared, Manley spent several long nights at Marley's house. The two planned a free concert sponsored by the Jamaican Ministry of Culture just before the elections. The CIA undoubtedly feared Jamaicans would see this as a Marley endorsement of the socialist prime minister.

The CIA-backed Jamaican Labour Party's paramilitary force, the Shower Posse, attacked Marley a week before the concert, holding him at gunpoint, and successfully extorted money from him, an intimidation tactic to get him to withhold any endorsement. Manley's People's National Party responded by sending a cadre of gunmen to guard Marley's home twenty-four hours a day.[8]

Then, on the Friday night before the show, at a home where Marley was holding a meeting, Shower Posse gunmen interrupted the meeting by firing a barrage of bullets at the house. One gunman raced to the kitchen and shot at Marley five times. One bullet went through Bob Marley's chest and arm, but did not kill him. The gunman hit Marley's manager Don Taylor four times, but he survived. Another bullet from the outside gunmen embedded in the head of Bob's wife, Rita Marley, and another went into a friend's stomach. All the victims survived the attack.[9]

Don Taylor said Rastafarians eventually captured several of the gunmen who shot Marley. When confronted by Marley and Taylor, the attackers confessed. Taylor described the situation: "Three young men were tied and bound in the gully when we arrived. One, a young man I knew only as Leggo Beast, told the ghetto court that four of them had been trained by the CIA and given guns and unlimited supplies of cocaine to do the assassination."[10]

CIA Director's Son Poisoned Bob Marley?

After the attack, police and Rastafarians escorted the Marleys and their band members to a secluded mountain encampment. Armed government soldiers and machete-toting Rastas patrolled the encampment, successfully protecting Bob Marley before the concert. Marley appeared at the concert on stage with Prime Minister Manley and Manley's PNP handedly won the election.

Rastafarians such as Bob Marley said that they resisted CIA-trafficked cocaine and heroin through smoking marijuana. A gunman admitted that the CIA paid him to shoot Bob Marley, and evidence suggests that a CIA Director's son poisoned Marley with a cancer-causing agent.

However, those present at the encampment said an unarmed right-wing agent, cameraman Carl Colby, attacked Marley in an unforeseen way. Colby's group was making a film of Marley's concert. Unknown to anyone on the film crew, Carl Colby was the son of CIA director William Colby.[11] Manager Don Taylor also claimed in his memoirs that a "son of a prominent CIA official" had been planted among the pre-election concert film crew as part of a plan to assassinate Marley. Taylor said he was convinced that "the CIA had been behind the plot to kill Bob Marley due to his possible influence on Jamaican politics and the wider world." Taylor further said that the U.S. "behind Seaga and the JLP, frowned on Bob's close association with Michael Manley, whose own friendship with Fidel Castro was regarded as disturbing as Bob's strong appeal to white American youths."[12]

Researcher Alex Constantine interviewed former Black Panther and cinematographer Lee Lew-Lee, who was also a friend of some of the Wailers. Lew-Lee said that Colby brought a new pair of boots for Marley, and Marley immediately tried the boots on, a reported customary gesture of appreciation among Rastafarians when receiving a gift. Sticking his foot in, the singer exclaimed "Oww!" as something jabbed him. Marley pulled out a length of metal wire embedded in the boot.

Lew-Lee said he thought nothing of the boot incident at the time but then became suspicious when Marley was playing soccer and broke his toe on that same foot several months after receiving the boots. When the bone wouldn't mend, doctors found it had cancer. Many suggested the wire in Colby's gift boots had a carcinogenic chemical compound on it. The cancer eventually spread to Marley's brain, lungs and liver.[13]

CIA documents from its MK-Ultra program detailed the program's focus on using methylcholanthrene, the most potent known carcinogen, to assassinate its targets.[14] On a Jamaican doctor's advice, Marley traveled to Germany and received treatment for eight months from Dr. Josef Issels, without realizing Issels had previous worked alongside Nazi Dr. Joseph Mengele. Constantine detailed the account of Marley's mother, Cedella Booker, who described how she visited her son when he was being treated by Issels with a needle. She said Issels "plunged the needle straight into Nesta's [Marley's] navel right down to the syringe. Nesta grunted and winced. He could only lie there helplessly, writhing on the table, trying his best to hide his pain." Issels ridiculed Marley for grimacing, yanked out the needle and strolled casually out of the room.[15]

In his last days, Marley toured the world, playing shows in pain, and still had run-ins with CIA forces bent on defeating Manley's democratic socialist party. CIA operatives made additional threats against Marley if he returned to Jamaica before the 1980 election in which Manley was seeking a third term. The CIA also reportedly used their work inside the Inter-American Press Association to influence the right-wing transformation of the Jamaican *Daily Gleaner* newspaper. A Drug Enforcement Agency intelligence report said that during the election campaign, political gangs akin to the CIA-backed Shower Posse killed more than 700 people. Manley lost the 1980 election. Bob Marley died of cancer in May of 1981 at the age of thirty-six. Some 30,000 mourners attended his Jamaican wake.[16]

After that, former Wailer Peter Tosh collaborated with Rolling Stone Mick Jagger. Tosh continued his political message music until 1987, when gunmen who were part of the CIA-backed Jamaican Labour Party murdered Tosh and a friend of his in Jamaica. Tosh's producer, Wayne Johnson, cited an unnamed Jamaican government official who told him one of the gunmen was a police officer. Journalist Eric Williams reported that Tosh also owned an apartment in New York. Williams said that purported burglars cleared out that apartment, and a NYC public administrator somehow gained possession of Tosh's master tapes. In a 1994 article, Williams claimed that an administrator hid them in a warehouse for years, barring the public from hearing the political songs of one of the world's most influential reggae artists.[17]

Notes

1 Timothy White, *Catch a Fire: The Life of Bob Marley* (New York: Henry Holt, 1996), pp. 260-61, 268.

2 White, *Catch A Fire*, pp. 304, 317-18.

3 Ellen Ray and Bill Schaap, "Massive Destabilization in Jamaica," *Covert Action Information Bulletin*, no. 10 (August-September 1980), pp. 13, 16; William Blum, *The CIA: A Forgotten History* (London: Zed Books, 1986), p. 301; Jerry Meldon, "The CIA's Dope-Smuggling 'Freedom Fighters,' Veterans of the CIA's Drug Wars, Profile: Luis Posada Carriles," *High Times*, December 18, 1998. All three cited in Alex Constantine, *The Covert War Against Rock* (Los Angeles, Feral House, 2000), pp. 137-38.

4 Gary Webb, *Dark Alliance* (New York: Seven Stories, 1998), p. 144. Webb's endnote citations on CIA destabilization of Jamaica and work against Manley, are Ernest Volkman and John Cummings, "Murder as Usual," *Penthouse*, December 1977. The plots against Manley are also summarized in William Blum, *Killing Hope* (Monroe, Maine: Common Courage Press, 1995), pp. 263-67. On Jamaican trafficking groups, Webb cites U.S. Department of Justice, Drug Enforcement Administration, Intelligence Division, *Crack Cocaine, Drug Intelligence Report*, DEA-94016, 1994, p. 8.

5 White, *Catch a Fire*, p. 268.

6 Casey Gane-McCalla, "How the CIA Created the Jamaican Shower Posse," *News One*, 6/3/10.

7 White, *Catch a Fire*, pp. 285, 304.

8 White, *Catch a Fire*, p. 318.

9 White, *Catch a Fire*, pp. 268, 285-291.

10 Don Taylor, *Marley and Me: The Real Bob Marley Story, Told by his Manager* (Fort Lee, NJ: Barricade Books, 1995), pp. 168-69.

11 White, *Catch a Fire*, pp. 268, 285-91.

12 Taylor, *Marley and Me*, p. 143, 149. Also see, White, *Catch a Fire*, p. 291.

13 Alex Constantine interview with Lee Lew-Lee, Los Angeles, October 30, 1997, in Alex Constantine, *The Covert War Against Rock* (Los Angeles, Feral House, 2000), pp. 135-36, 140-41.

14 Hank Albarelli Jr., *A Terrible Mistake: The Murder of Frank Olson and the CIA's Secret Cold War Experiments* (Waterville, OR: Trine Day, 2009), p. 292. Albarelli cited a "CIA Memorandum for the Record for DD/P through C/SE, Subject: Radiological Warfare, 28 October 1954."

15 Cedella Booker and Anthony Winkler, *Bob Marley: An Intimate Portrait by his Mother* (New York: Viking, 1996), pp. 189-91; Bob Marley's mother to Lew-Lee, interviewed, 10/30/97; Michael H. Kater, *Doctors Under Hitler* (Chapel Hill, NC: University of North Carolina Press, 1989), p. 235. All three sources cited in Constantine, *The Covert War Against Rock*, pp. 141-42. The Jamaican doctor who referred Marley was Dr. Carl "Pee Wee" Fraser, p. 140.

16 On DEA report, Gary Webb, *Dark Alliance: The CIA, the Contras and the Crack Cocaine Explosion* (New York: Seven Stories, 1998), p. 144. Webb's endnote citations on CIA destabilization of Jamaica and work against Manley are Ernest Volkman and John Cummings, "Murder as Usual," *Penthouse*, December 1977. Summarized in William Blum, *Killing Hope* (Monroe, Maine: Common Courage Press, 1995), pp. 263-67. On Jamaican trafficking groups, Webb cites U.S. Department of Justice, Drug Enforcement Administration, Intelligence Division, *Crack Cocaine, Drug Intelligence Report*, DEA-94016, 1994, p. 8. On CIA's influence over *Daily Gleaner*'s transformation, and Marley's wake: White, *Catch A Fire*, pp. 304, 317-18. In his bibliography, White cites Fred Landis, "The CIA and The Media: IAPA and the Jamaican *Daily Gleaner*," *Covert Action Information Bulletin* no. 7 (December 1979-January 1980), and "CIA Media Operations in Chile, Jamaica and Nicaragua." *Covert Action Information Bulletin* no.16 (December 1981).

17 Eric Williams, "Who Killed Peter Tosh?" *High Times* no. 221 (January 1994), p. 18, for warehoused tapes. This and other facts cited in Constantine, *The Covert War Against Rock*, p. 144.

Huey Newton

Chapter Nineteen

Drugs & CIA Targeting of Newton, Shakurs & Other Panthers

Chemical warfare began to change the shape and attitude of the brothers and sisters who participated in, what we called then, the revolution. Whether it be the civil rights aspect of integrating into or assimilating into America, or the revolutionary nationalist fight for self-determination and/or liberation by nationhood.... [Our] ability to fight chemical warfare was a significant contribution.... So the Lincoln Detox became not only recognized by the community as a political formation, but for its work in developing and saving men and women ... we began to move around the country and educated other communities around acupuncture drug withdrawal.

– Mutulu Shakur, cofounder of the Republic of New Afrika and Assistant Director of Lincoln Detox.[1]

The Shakurs: Black Liberation Leaders

In the U.S. during the 1970s, the Weather Underground activists and the Black Liberation Movement began to cooperate more closely. FBI documents stolen in 1971 show the FBI used their Counterintelligence program to target both groups, but waged particularly brutal attacks on the Black Liberation Movement.[2]

A revered family had arisen amongst the East Coast Black Liberation Movement—the Shakurs. El Hajj Sallahudin "Abba" Shakur and his wife gave birth to Lumumba and Zayd Shakur (born Anthony and James Coston). They also adopted and raised Mutulu Shakur, amongst other black children. Abba Shakur was an organizer in Marcus Garvey's United Negro Improvement Association and later in Malcolm X's Organization of Afro-American Unity in New York City, where he was one of several in Malcolm X's inner circle of confidantes.[3]

Lumumba, Zayd and Mutulu Shakur joined Malcolm X's group just before the leader's death. After that, Lumumba founded the Harlem Black Panther Party chapter. Lumumba's childhood friend, Sekou Odinga, founded the Bronx Black Panther chapter with Zayd Shakur. Abba and Mutulu Shakur became active in the Revolutionary Action Movement.[4]

Lumumba Shakur married Afeni Shakur in 1968. In the same year, Mutulu Shakur became a cofounder of the Republic of New Afrika. The RNA was politically aligned with the Panthers, had similar goals and experienced similar police repression. The RNA formed when five hundred grassroots activists from around the country met in Detroit to declare independence for the black nation inside the U.S. The following year, police attacked the RNA convention at Rev. C.L. Franklin's (father of "Queen of Soul" Aretha Franklin) New Bethel Church in Detroit. Police fired 800 rounds in the church, and held 150 people incommunicado before a judge set up court in the police station and got most of them released.[5]

In April 1969, New York's police intelligence unit, the Bureau of Special Services, obtained an indictment for the arrest of Lumumba, Afeni, Sekou Odinga, and eighteen other Black Panther leaders who were dubbed the New York 21. Odinga escaped police pursuit on the morning of the New York 21 arrest.[6]

The imprisoned Black Panthers chose Afeni Shakur to gain release on bail first to speak and raise bail for the other Panthers. The Panthers elected her the new Harlem Panther leader.[7] A judge then revoked her bail and she returned to jail. After what was the longest New York court case of its time, a jury acquitted the remaining thirteen Panthers on trial. Several jurors cited Afeni Shakur's work as her own lawyer for their acquittal of the Panthers in 1971.[8]

Afeni had become pregnant with another Panther's child when out on bail in 1970, and Lumumba divorced her. A few months after Afeni's 1971 court acquittal, she gave birth to Tupac Shakur, the future rap icon.[9] By 1973, Afeni moved in with Lumumba's adopted brother Mutulu Shakur.[10] Mutulu Shakur also worked as a political education instructor at Lincoln Detox in the Bronx in the early 1970s. He got a degree in acupuncture by the mid-1970s and used it to successfully treat drug addicts. It still remains the most nationally reknowned center for acupuncture drug treatment training. Mutulu started national acupuncture groups and lectured on the subject worldwide.

One-time Harlem Black Panther leader Afeni Shakur addressing a large crow

Describing his work, Mutulu said, "Chemical warfare began to change the shape and attitude of the brothers and sisters who participated in what we called then, the revolution. Whether it be the civil rights aspect of integrating into or assimilating into America, or the revolutionary nationalist fight for self-determination and/or liberation by nationhood.... [Our] ability to fight chemical warfare was a significant contribution.... So the Lincoln Detox became not only recognized by the community as a political formation, but for its work in developing and saving men and women ... we began to move around the country and educated other communities around acupuncture drug withdrawal."[11]

While Mutulu worked at Lincoln Detox, other Shakurs contributed significantly as Black Liberation Movement leaders. Afeni accepted invitations to speak at Harvard, Yale, and other colleges nationwide.

Before the Panther 21 gained their acquittal, Bronx Black Panther Minister of Information Zayd Shakur had made progress in mending the feud between the New York Panthers and the Oakland, California Panther leadership. The FBI's Counterintelligence Program had manufactured this rift between Huey Newton's Oakland National Panther Office and Panther Minister of Information, Eldridge Cleaver, then exiled in Algeria. Some New York Panther 21 members aligned themselves with Cleaver. The FBI accomplished this with fake letters and undercover agents.

Zayd had gone underground after he felt that FBI undercover agents were threatening his life and he saw some of his fellow Panthers killed. After Sekou Odinga returned to America, he and Zayd started a new militant self-defense group, the Black Liberation Army, which reportedly protected activist leaders from armed police assault by regularly positioning snipers on various black neighborhood rooftop locations.[12]

Zayd's close Panther friend, Assata Shakur (born Joanne Chesimard), quit the Panthers because of the New York/Oakland feud. The respect Assata attained among other Panthers led to continued targeting anyway. Seeing her picture on the front page of the *Daily News* with the notice that she was wanted for questioning about a policeman's murder scared her into joining Zayd in his underground hideout.[13]

The FBI started a propaganda campaign against Assata Shakur, calling her "the revolutionary mother hen" of the Black Liberation Army, which was accused of murdering a number of New York City police officers. Most of these accusations came with little evidence and few valid convictions. The FBI conducted a nationwide manhunt for Assata in 1972, and put her on their Most Wanted list with her picture plastered in police precincts and banks as a shoot-to-kill target.[14]

In May of 1973, New Jersey police pulled over Zayd and Assata Shakur's car. Police fatally shot Zayd, while wounding Assata and former NY Panther

Sundiata Acoli. One of the police officers was also shot and killed. Assata said police beat her at the scene, then tortured her in a hospital and in custody.[15]

New Jersey police charged Assata with killing the police officer. The case didn't reach trial for four years because prosecutors brought Assata to trial six times for alleged involvement in half a dozen other major criminal actions spanning several years. They failed to gain a conviction at any of those venues.[16]

By 1976, Assata's lead trial lawyer, Stanley Cohen, reported several breakthroughs in her case, and was found dead from a physical attack soon after, with all his papers stolen.[17] At the trial, Assata's other lawyers presented tests and medical experts to prove her innocence in court. For example, Assata's fingers tested negative for gun residue, and police shot Assata while she had her hands raised. Doctors said the bullet immediately severed a median nerve that wouldn't have allowed Assata to pull a trigger. Nonetheless, prosecutors won a conviction against her for killing the police officer during that 1973 stop.[18]

Within the next few years, a group labeled the Black Liberation Army's Multinational Task Force took on a daring operation. This group reportedly consisted of members from the Weather Underground, the Puerto Rican group the Young Lords, and the Black Liberation Army. They broke Assata Shakur out of prison and helped her gain political exile status in Cuba. She remained there in 2015, despite million dollar bounties being placed on her capture, and having been the first woman placed on the FBI's list of most wanted terrorists in 2013.[19]

Mutulu Shakur's life-long activism put him under constant FBI surveillance. The FBI had developed a file on Mutulu, and agents delivered reports on him to the FBI Director every three months since he was nineteen years old.[20]

Mutulu Shakur also cofounded and directed the National Task Force for Cointelpro Litigation and Research.[21] Afeni Shakur, Mutulu's live-in partner, worked with Mutulu on this project. Afeni's activism particularly focused on a New York City lawsuit started by a wide array of antiwar activists, including Abbie Hoffman. This historic lawsuit accused the New York City police department of violating the legal rights of New York activists with everything from illegal spying to murder.[22]

After close to a decade, a judge agreed with most of the lawsuit's charges. The suit's lead lawyer, Barbara Handschu, helped the group gain the most restrictions on police intelligence of any city nationwide. This forced the NYPD to officially end its police Cointelpro activities.[23] However, in the 1980s, the same judge ruled in a later case involving Mutulu Shakur that the NYPD had actually continued its Cointelpro activities.[24]

By the 1970s, Mutulu Shakur had become the Assistant Director of Lincoln Detox in the Bronx. Others working with Lincoln Detox included Black Liberation movement activists, members of the Latino community's version of the Panthers, the Young Lords, and white SDS/Weather Underground activists, such as Bernardine Dohrn's sister, Jennifer Dohrn.[25]

Mutulu Shakur was assistant director of Lincoln Detox and cofounded the Republic of New Afrika, before U.S. intelligence targeted his clinic and then him.

The National Acupuncture Detoxification Association (NADA) attributes its birth to Lincoln Detox (later changed to "Lincoln Recovery"). The clinic started after a group of activists formed the United Bronx Drug Fighters to demand drug detox at Lincoln Hospital, which didn't have it in 1970. At this time clinicians agreed with addicts' account of having to wait up to a year to get into addiction treatment programs in New York City. While starting with the innovative use of methadone for detox instead of maintenance, both staff and addicts desired a non-drug method of detox. Around late 1973, a Chinese doctor published his findings of acupuncture's success with opiate detox, and Lincoln Detox began using it with great results. While some research questions acupuncture's success with addiction, studies out of Yale University and Britain's top medical journal, *The Lancet*, support its efficacy.[26]

NADA cited three key people amongst Lincoln Detox's rise: Jose Aponte, Mutulu Shakur and Richard Taft, MD. NADA gave details supporting Mutulu Shakur's description of how conservative forces conducted "low-intensity warfare" against Lincoln Detox. Medical Director Richard Taft began receiving death threats and somebody shot at him, leading him to start carrying a gun. Dr. Taft was then found dead. The NADA description suggested that he was murdered. Mutulu Shakur said somebody tried to make it look like a heroin overdose to discredit the clinic. The drug was found in his skin, but not in his blood. Mutulu said Taft's was just one of at least several early murders among targeting tactics. Mutulu said that Assata's lawyer, Stanley Cohen, "the best attorney that the clinic and revolutionaries had," was found dead in a similar state as Taft, physically attacked and found by the coroner to have an "overdose" of cocaine in him.[27]

Despite its reported success, Lincoln Detox was defunded by New York City in 1978. The clinic continued without funding. Reports vary on numbers, but estimates of 50-200 police were sent to close Lincoln Detox and physically force Mutulu and other workers out of the Lincoln Hospital area. Mutulu continued his work anyway, founding a national acupuncture group, the Black Acupuncture Advisory Association of North America (BAAANA). He was invited to China, Zimbabwe and Europe to further his work. In an interview decades later, Mutulu described many top activists who took part in BAAANA, but were then targeted by U.S. intelligence. For example, he said that Nehanda Abiodun "is still being hunted by the law, the FBI, CIA, Interpol. She was a sister who helped start BAAANA on 129th St. between 7th and 8th Avenue in Harlem. She was a part of the Republic of New Afrika's cadre and was one of the first organizers of the New Afrikan People's Organization."[28]

The FBI said Mutulu founded the Black Liberation Army's Multinational Task Force (MTF).[29] Researchers said some MTF members, the multi-ethnic activist group that included Weather Underground members, worked at Lincoln Detox and took extreme measures when the city tried to close it. The government charged the group with robbing banks to support Lincoln Detox when the city barred its funding. The FBI also charged the MTF with breaking Assata Shakur from jail. A judge convicted members of the MTF on a failed Brinks bank truck robbery in 1981 that killed two police officers and a guard. Police went after Mutulu, not for any involvement in the actual crime, but for being a "co-conspirator." Mutulu went underground but was caught and brought to trial in 1986. In 1988 he was convicted and sentenced to 60 years in prison.[30]

Mutulu Shakur remains imprisoned as a purported co-conspirator in the attempted robbery, while other MTF members closely involved have gained their freedom. For example, white Weather Underground member Kathy Boudin sat in the front of the getaway truck with Black Liberation Army members in the back. She was released in 2003 after two decades in prison.

Weather Underground member Marilyn Buck was also convicted of involvement in the Brinks truck robbery and Assata's prison break. She had cancer, was released in July of 2010, and died the following month. White Weather Underground member David Gilbert remains in jail for aiding the Black Liberation Army in that incident.[31] Others convicted for that incident, among other charges, include former Black Panther 21 members-turned BLA members Kuwasi Balagoon and Sekou Odinga. Balagoon died in prison in 1986. The courts also convicted Odinga regarding Assata's prison break. He was released from prison in November of 2014.[32]

Overall, these radical leftists received hugely disproportionate sentences compared to right-wing radicals. For example, researchers Ward Churchill and Jim Vander Wall pointed out how MTF supporters Susan Rosenberg and Tim Blunk were captured at a cache of explosives in 1984 and received unprecedented 58-year prison sentences. In comparison, Dennis Malvesi, a right-wing fanatic convicted of actually using explosives to blow up abortion clinics in the early 1980s, only received a seven-year prison sentence.[33]

In 1971, New York City had closed its Bureau of Special Services Cointelpro unit but some of the activities continued, according to a federal judge's report. Police whistleblowers reported working in New York City Police Department's Protective Research Unit, inside the Intelligence Unit, which they called the "Black Desk," to spy on political black leaders. Another unit created in 1980 was the Joint Terrorist Task Force that New York and U.S. intelligence started in response to the Black Liberation Army and the Multinational Task Force. California started a similar ad hoc unit out of Los Angeles. The FBI utilized these Task Forces as open amalgams of national, state and city police units formerly run covertly.[34]

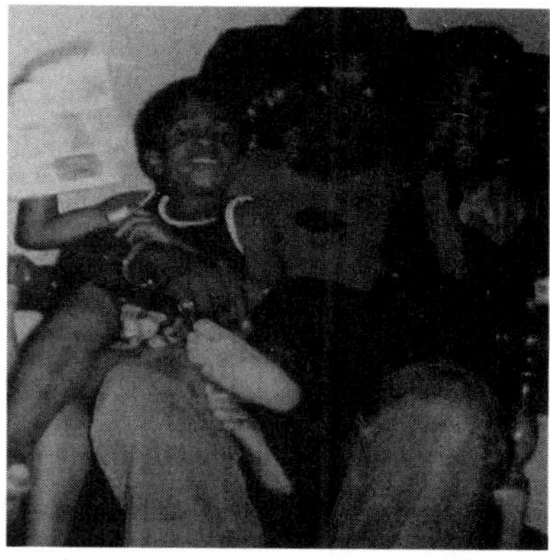

Mutulu Shakur with his stepson, future rap icon Tupac, on his lap, and his biological son Maurice.

A judge acknowledged Cointelpro's continuance against Mutulu despite the FBI's claim that it disbanded. At the end of Mutulu's trial, the federal district court judge said, "The rights of Mr. Shakur ... were violated by the Cointelpro program."[35] Still, Mutulu started serving a sixty-year sentence in August of 1988 for conspiracy to commit armed robbery and murder, and aiding Assata Shakur's prison escape. The parole board repeatedly denied parole for Mutulu, partly because he refused to renounce his politics, repeating the pattern of L.A. Panther leader Geronimo Pratt.[36]

U.S. Continues Targeting Afeni Shakur

The FBI never stopped targeting Afeni Shakur, probably using agents within their cocaine distribution network for some tasks. Initially, and for many years, the FBI visited Afeni's job sites and intimidated employers into firing her or not hiring her. Afeni, her son Tupac, and her daughter with Mutulu, Sekyiwa, moved dozens of times, often sleeping on friends' floors.[37]

Despite this destitution, Afeni managed to stay politically active in the 1970s and early 1980s. For example, she continued her work on the Handschu lawsuit against New York City.[38] Afeni also wrote a chapter of a book, *Human Rights for Everybody*. The book was co-written by other activists including her ex-husband Lumumba Shakur, Howard Zinn, Noam Chomsky, Grace Paley, and Juan Jose Pena.[39]

The FBI, under the Reagan/Bush administration, had a motive to neutralize Afeni Shakur to stop her successful work in helping restrict New York police intelligence. By 1982, within a year of Mutulu Shakur going underground, a drug dealer named Kenneth "Legs" Saunders entered Afeni's life. After moving through dozens of homes and homeless shelters, Afeni moved into Legs's home.[40] Legs eased Afeni's poverty while she tried to raise Tupac and Sekyiwa. Afeni said Legs got her to use crack cocaine. "That was our way of socializing," she said. "He would come home late at night and stick a pipe in my mouth."[41]

Research suggests that U.S. intelligence inserted Legs into beleaguered Afeni's life. Radio reporter Richard Boyle, who covered the trial of Vietnam Veterans Against the War leaders in the '70s, found it wasn't uncommon for U.S. intelligence to use "women or men, to get in personal relationships with their targets."[42]

Legs's connections indicate this was his role in 1982. He was an associate of New York drug lord Nicky Barnes.[43] Barnes assisted the first national "Black drug kingpin," Frank Matthews, who worked untouched for years. As mentioned, the Justice Department indicted Matthews's entire network in 1973, but dropped charges on nine of them due to their CIA ties. Matthews left the U.S. with millions of dollars. Barnes took Matthews's place from 1973 into the late 1980s. Barnes's ability to remain jail-free suggested he was either one of the nine with CIA ties or he had similar U.S. intelligence support. Professor Clarence Lusane found Barnes won so many "acquittals on gun, narcotics, bribery and murder charges," the *New York Times* called him "Mr. Untouchable."[44]

Afeni Shakur's relationship with Legs Saunders ended several years later, when she moved to Baltimore and he went to prison for credit card fraud. When she called to talk to him, a prison official claimed he died of a crack-induced heart attack.[45]

Afeni reportedly relapsed with her cocaine addiction when living in Baltimore from approximately 1984 until 1987. She further used crack cocaine for four years after she moved herself, her son Tupac Shakur, and his half-sister Sekyiwa, to Marin City, outside Oakland, California in 1987. She moved into the home of Geronimo Pratt's wife, Linda Pratt.[46]

In 1991 Afeni finally gained long-term sobriety. The wife of another Panther 21 defendant first tricked Afeni into attending inpatient drug treatment.[47] Afeni then started attending Narcotics Anonymous (NA) at the urge of the Panther 21 comrade's adult daughter. She gained her long-term sobriety that year with the help of a sponsor and support network through NA.[48]

Afeni Shakur's other activism had included her work on Black Panther Geronimo Pratt's defense team, which she returned to with her sobriety. Former Los Angeles FBI Cointelpro agent Wes Swearingen and other agents testified that L.A. FBI informants set Geronimo Pratt up on a murder frame-up.[49] An FBI-paid lawyer had infiltrated Pratt's defense counsel, according to the California Attorney General's office in a declaration filed in court, and the FBI paid another person on Pratt's defense team. This led to Pratt's conviction and imprisonment for over 25 years.[50]

While Afeni Shakur and Geronimo Pratt's defense team initially failed to have Pratt acquitted, the lawyers did uncover how he had been targeted by joint efforts of the CIA's Chaos program, and the FBI's Cointelpro. Pratt's defense team eventually gained his release from prison. The U.S. awarded Pratt several million dollars as compensation for false imprisonment in 1997.[51]

Six years later, reporters revealed another example of U.S. intelligence using an undercover agent to exploit the weakness of a black woman activist. In 2003, the *New York Times* described how an FBI informant became the boyfriend of Malcolm X's daughter, Qubilah Shabazz, and then ensnared her in a plot to assassinate Nation of Islam leader Louis Farrakan. The boyfriend convinced Shabazz that Farrakan plotted against her mother, Betty Shabazz. The article claimed that Betty Shabazz blamed Farrakan for some aspect of Malcolm X's death. It's possible that the boyfriend also contributed to Qubilah Shabazz's apparent drug problem, as the government agreed to drop the charges if Shabazz agreed to see a psychiatrist and to get drug treatment (the government also switched custody of her 12 year-old son Malcolm to Betty Shabazz).[52]

The Assassination of Huey Newton

As documented earlier, the CIA waged psychological warfare on Black Panther national cofounder Huey Newton his entire life after prison until his death at the age of forty-seven.[53] In the 1970s, a U.S. Senate Committee published an admission that as early as 1970 the FBI, the Central Intelligence Agency, the Defense Intelligence Agency and the National Security Agency began cooperatively targeting Newton as part of their "Enemy's List."[54] In one example described earlier, U.S. intelligence appeared to have also used the tactic of an undercover agent acting as a romantic partner and using drugs to undermine an activist when Elaine Brown brought cocaine into Newton's life just after he came out of prison in 1970.[55]

The exact extent of Huey Newton's involvement with cocaine still remains up for debate. National Black Panther cofounder Bobby Seale said he split with Newton by 1973, as Newton had started dealing cocaine by that time. On the other hand, Newton wrote and published his autobiography, *Revolutionary Suicide*, in 1973, suggesting he was more functional than most full-fledged addicts. Huey Newton also worked towards attaining a doctorate in the 1970s. In his doctoral dissertation, *War Against the Panthers*, published in 1980, Newton meticulously detailed U.S. intelligence's unsuccessful attempts to arrest him for drug involvement.[56]

In *War Against the Panthers*, Newton also detailed how the FBI tried to kill him in 1973 by having police shoot up the door of his next-door neighbor at 5 A.M. one day. He knew the neighbor was dealing drugs, but only later found out the FBI was paying the neighbor's rent. Newton believed it was an attempt to lure him into defending the neighbor and getting shot in the process.[57]

By 1988, Newton had started a Panther-inspired school for children in Oakland, California. That year, police arrested Huey Newton on a minor charge that put him in prison with former Los Angeles Panther leader Geronimo Pratt.[58] In prison, Pratt took Newton under his wing while Newton was reportedly in drug withdrawal, and the two compared their intelligence files. They saw how the FBI and CIA set them against each other and manufactured the war between Newton's Oakland Office and the New York Panthers, with whom Pratt had been close.

On August 22, 1988, the day officials were to release Newton from prison, he chose to remain incarcerated and announced a press conference for the following day. There, he said he wouldn't leave prison until officials freed Pratt. However, Pratt asked Newton to leave and help him from the outside.[59]

Once out, Huey Newton worked with Pratt's lawyer and made speeches for his release. In the summer of 1989, East Coast Black Panthers had restarted a Black Panther newspaper. Newton called them and said he wanted to reunite and restart the East Coast and West Coast Black Panthers.[60] U.S. intelligence reportedly still had Newton under surveillance, and these moves likely contributed to his early death.

On August 22, 1989, on the one-year anniversary of Newton's refusal to leave prison on Geronimo Pratt's behalf, a gunman murdered Newton in Oakland. A minor conviction for gun possession had left Newton unarmed. The assailant shot Newton three times, including twice in the head as he lay on the ground.[61]

In addition to its anniversary timing, many other aspects of Newton's murder suggest it was a U.S. intelligence assassination. The *San Francisco Examiner* caught Oakland Police Lt. Mike Sims in a number of lies about the murder. When Sims repeatedly said the police had "no suspects, no clues," the *Examiner* reported police had been videotaped arresting three men near the scene within minutes of the murder. Sims later said only two were arrested, neither of whom were linked to Newton's murder. Oakland Police corrected Sims the following day, saying the two were suspects, though they only named and charged one. It is important to note that FBI Special Agent in Charge, Richard Held, spoke with Sims at this press conference.[62]

The FBI and police claimed the accused shooter, Tyrone Robinson, appeared to have acted in self-defense when Newton pulled a gun after an argument over money he owed Robinson for cocaine. The earlier police statement that they didn't find a gun belonging to Newton at the scene contradicts this claim. The account also doesn't explain why the shooter would put two extra bullets in Newton's head as he lay on the street from the first bullet. As a Special Forces commando described for an unrelated article, putting two extra bullets in the head is a signature move in a combat military execution.[63]

Richard Held headed the San Francisco Bay area FBI office and was caught lying about Huey Newton's murder in Oakland.

Witness Michelle Johnson, who lived just across the street from where Newton was killed, gave a description of the killing consistent with a murder setup. Johnson heard a brief argument and recognized one of the two men as Huey Newton. The other man ordered Newton into a car. Newton protested, "Man, I ain't getting in your car." She next heard shots, peeked out her window and saw Newton slumped on the sidewalk. This firsthand account refutes the notion that-Newton was killed over drugs, but rather that Newton's assailants had kidnapping and murder plans.[64]

Johnson's description, along with other aspects of the murder, bolsters the contentions of Newton's brother and area activists that the FBI murdered Newton.[65] Several writers support the accounts of Newton's close friends who said the police had Newton under constant surveillance. These factors strongly indicate U.S. intelligence set up his assassination.[66]

The assassination of other black leaders came with similar anniversary or threat timing. Martin Luther King's family lawyer, William Pepper, made it clear that U.S. intelligence orchestrated Martin Luther King's assassination exactly one year after he officially announced his opposition to the Vietnam War.[67] A gunman assassinated Congo president Laurent Kabila on January 16, 2001, exactly forty years after the U.S. aided the assassination of Kabila's former comrade, and Congo's first independently elected president, Patrice Lumumba.[68] This tactic offers an implicit warning to those of similar leftist persuasions.

Notes

1 "Interview from Lompoc Federal Prison with Tyehimba Jess of WHBK Radio in Chicago," www.mutulushakur.com/lompoc.html.

2 On Media break-in, Ward Churchill and Jim Vander Wall, *The COINTELPRO Papers: Documents from the FBI's Secret Wars Against Dissent in the United States* (Boston: South End Press, 1991), pp. xi, 332. See, for example, "The FBI's Covert Program to Destroy the Black Panther Party," South End Press, 1991), pp. xi, 332. See, for example, "The FBI's Covert Program to Destroy the Black Panther Party," Final Report of the Select Committee to Study Governmental Operations with Respect to Intelligence Activities, 94th Congress, 2nd Session (U.S. Government

Printing Office, Washington, DC, 1976). This study was issued by the United States Senate Select Committee that included: Frank Church, Idaho, Chairman; John Tower, Texas, Vice-Chairman; future vice-president Walter Mondale, Minnesota; and eight other senators, https://archive.org/stream/finalreportofsel03unit/finalreportofsel03unit_djvu.txt. Seymour Hersh, "CIA Reportedly Recruited Blacks for Surveillance of Panther Party," *New York Times,* March 17, 1978, p. A1, A16. All quoted in Huey P. Newton, *War Against the Panthers* (New York: Harlem River Press/Writers and Readers Publishing, 1996), p. 90.

3 Personal Interview with Afeni and Mutulu Shakur's close associate, Watani Tyehimba, 5/10/00. Also see, Kalonji Jama Changa, "Tupac and the Revolutionary Shakur Family," Interview with former Black Panther who also worked with legendary musician, Gil Scott Heron, Bilal Sunni-Ali, 7/13/06, http://www.thuglifearmy.com/interviews/3578-tupac-2pac-and-the-revolutionary-shakur-family.html.

4 Peter Zimroth, *Perversions of Justice: The Prosecution and Acquittal of the Panther 21* (New York: Viking, 1974), pp.16, 48. Also see http://www.mutulushakur.com/about.html.

5 On RNA alignment with Panthers, see Huey Newton, "To the Republic of New Afrika: September 13, 1969," *To Die for the People* (New York: Writers and Readers Publishing, 1972, 1999), pp. 96-101. On RNA founding, Chokwe Lumumba, "20th Anniversary Commemoration of the Historic New Bethel Incident," *By Any Means Necessary!* Vol. 5, No.2, 1989, p.11. On New Bethel Attack, Dan Georgakas and Marvin Surkin, *Detroit: I Do Mind Dying* (New York: St. Martin's, 1975), pp. 664-68. Both of these last two sources and their information was contained in the essay "A Brief History of the New Afrikan Prison Struggle," by Sundiata Acoli, pp.10-11. Acoli is an imprisoned former New York Panther 21 member who was attacked in a car with Zayd and Assata Shakur. This essay can be found at www.prisonactivist.or/pubs/brief-mst-naps.html. His bio and contact info can be found in Committee to End the Marion Lockdown (CEML), *Can't Jail the Spirit: Political Prisoners in the U.S.* (Chicago: Committee to End the Marion Lockdown, 2002), p. 65.

6 Odinga was said to have jumped 35 feet down to the ground to make his escape. Murray Kempton, *The Briar Patch: The People of the State of New York v. Lumumba Shakur Et Al.* (New York: Dell, 1973), pp. 2-12; and Michael Newton, *Bitter Grain: Huey Newton and the Black Panther Party* (Los Angeles: Holloway House, 1980), p. 185. Also see Zimroth, *Perversions of Justice,* pp. 3-5. Lumumba Shakur, Afeni Shakur, et al., *Look For Me In the Whirlwind: the Collective Autobiography of the New York 21* (New York: Vintage, 1971).

7 Connie Bruck, "The Takedown of Tupac," *The New Yorker,* 7/7/97, p. 47. On Assata Shakur, see editorial, "Thoughts and Notes on Tupac," *Amsterdam News* (New York), 12/17/94, p. 24.

8 On courtroom scene, jury time of deliberations, etc. see quoted trial transcript and spectator Zimroth in Zimroth, *Perversions of Justice,* pp. 308-09. On jury and writer's opinions crediting Afeni with winning case for Panthers, see Zimroth's interviews, pp. 310, 367-68, 377; and Connie Bruck "The Takedown of Tupac." On Lumumba and others' stay in jail after verdict, Zimroth, *Perversions of Justice,* p. 310.

9 Bruck, "The Takedown of Tupac." On Assata Shakur, see editorial, "Thoughts and Notes on Tupac," *The Amsterdam News,* 12/17/94, p. 24.

10 Personal interview, Watani Tyehimba, 5/10/00. Former Panther Tyehimba is a friend of Afeni's since that time. Also see, CEML, *Can't Jail the Spirit,* p. 65.

11 "Interview from Lompoc Federal Prison with Tyehimba Jess of WHBK Radio in Chicago," www.mutulushakur.com/lompoc.html.

12 On Zayd Shakur and Sekou Odinga as founding the BLA, see Churchill and Vander Wall, *The COINTELPRO Papers,* pp. 306-07. On snipers, Lee Lew-Lee, *All Power to the People.* After a 2013 conversation with Panther National Secretary of Communication Kathleen Cleaver, this author has rejected his earlier belief in an "East Coast versus West Coast" Panther fued, as Los Angeles Panther leader Geronimo Pratt sided with the New York Panthers.

13 Assata Shakur, *Assata: An Autobiography* (Chicago, IL: Lawrence Hill, 1987), pp.231-34. On Tupac's aunt Assata, Scott, *The Killing of Tupac Shakur* (Las Vegas: Huntington Press, 1997), p. 65.

14 Churchill and Vander Wall, *The COINTELPRO Papers*, p. 308. Lennox Hinds, on behalf of the National Conference of Black Lawyers, in a petition to the United Nations Commission on Human Rights, 12/11/78. Lennox Hinds, "The Injustice of the Trial," *Covert Action Quarterly* #65, Fall 1998, p. 43.

15 Shakur, *Assata*, pp. 3-11, 82-83. Assata said that while in the hospital, she was only saved from more torture when a white nurse intervened. But, she said, prison officials used torturous tactics on her thereafter.

16 See chart of trial charges and outcomes in Shakur, *Assata*, p. xiv.

17 Shakur, *Assata*, p. 247.

18 Hinds, "The Injustice of the Trial," *Covert Action Quarterly* #65, Fall 1998, p. 43.

19 Churchill and Vander Wall, *The COINTELPRO Papers*, p. 309. On BLA Multinational Task Force, see Sundiata Acoli, "A Brief History of the New Afrikan Prison Struggle," 2/19/92, www.prisonactivist.org. Tim Griego, "Cuba still harbors one of America's most wanted fugitives. What happens to Assata Shakur now?" *Washington Post*, December 20, 2014.

20 CEML, *Can't Jail the Spirit*, pp. 147-50.

21 CEML, *Can't Jail the Spirit*, pp. 147-50.

22 Handschu, et al. vs. Special Services Division a/k/a Bureau of Special Services, U.S. District Court, S.D.N.Y., 71 Civ. 2203 (CSH) Memorandum Opinion and Order, December 16, 1981, p. 6.

23 Ibid, Memorandum Opinion and Order, May 24, 1979, p. 3. Also see, Handschu, et al. vs. Special Services Division a/k/a Bureau of Special Services, U.S. District Court, S.D.N.Y., 71 Civ. 2203 (CSH) Memorandum Opinion and Order, Mar. 7, 1985, p. 26. And on widest restrictions, *New York Sun*, 12/5/02, and Benjamin Weiser, "Threats and Responses: Law Enforcement" *New York Times*, 2/12/03, p. 17. Also, Associated Press, "Judge Backs Expanded Police Surveillance," *New York Times*, 3/22/03, p. 2.

24 Barbara Handschu et al., plaintiffs, Rev. Calvin Butts, Sonny Carson, C. Vernon Mason, Michael Warren, Intervenors v. Special Services Division a/k/a Bureau of Special Services et al., Memorandum Opinion and Order, Kudge Charles Haight, U.S. District Court, Southern District of New York, 71 Civ.2203-CSH, p. 34.

25 See CEML, *Can't Jail the Spirit*, pp. 147-50. And, for example, Alfred McCoy, *The Politics of Heroin: CIA Complicity in the Global Drug Trade* (New York: Lawrence Hill, 1972,1991). Also see interview with Mutulu Shakur, http://www.mutulushakur.com/interview-lompoc.html.

26 Milton L. Bullock, Patricia D. Culliton, and Robert T. Olander, "Controlled Trial of Acupuncture for Severe Recidivist Alcoholism," *The Lancet*, June 24, 1989, pp. 1435-1438. S. Kelly Avants, PhD; Arthur Margolin, PhD; Theodore R. Holford, PhD; Thomas R. Kosten, MD, "Randomized Controlled Trial of Auricular Acupuncture for Cocaine Dependence," *Arch Intern Med* 2000, 160 (15): 2305-2312. Lena Bergdahl, A. H. Berman and Kristina Haglund, "Patients' experience of auricular acupuncture during protracted withdrawal," *Journal of Psychiatric and Mental Health Nursing* (2013). See more at: http://www.healthcmi.com/Acupuncture-Continuing-Education-News/705-acupuncturedrugalcoho-withdrawal#sthash.29DZPbGy.dpuf.

27 On NADA description, see Ellinor R. Mitchell, "The Lincoln Story," with excerpts from *Fighting Drug Abuse with Acupuncture*, http://www.acudetox.com/nada-resources/15-online-resources/50-the-lincoln-story. And, Mutulu Shakur, "Live from Lompoc Federal Prison with Tyehimba Jess of WHBK Radio in Chicago: On the History of the Use of Acupuncture by Revolutionary Health Workers to Treat Drug Addiction, and US Government Attacks Under the Cover of the Counterintelligence Program (COINTELPRO), www.mutulushakur.com/lompoc.html.

28 On Lincoln Detox success, it was reportedly "recognized as the largest and most effective of its kind by the National Institute on Drug Abuse [NIDA], National Acupuncture Research Society, and the World Academic Society of Acupuncture." This and Zimbabwe travels, CMEL, *Can't Jail the Spirit*, pp. 147-48. Also see Churchill and Vander Wall, *The COINTELPRO Papers*, pp. 309, 411-12.

29 Churchill and Vander Wall, *The COINTELPRO Papers*, pp. 309, 410-11, note 24. Ward Churchill and Jim Vander Wall, *Agents of Repression: The FBI's Secret Wars Against the Black Panther*

Party and the American Indian Movement (Boston: South End, 1988), p. 364. Assata Shakur, "Assata Shakur: The life of a revolutionary," *Covert Action Quarterly* #65, Fall 1998, p. 36. Some reportedly linked to RATF and serving long political prisoner sentences include white Weather Underground radicals Kathy Boudin, Dave Gilbert, Sara Evans, Susan Rosenberg, Marilyn Buch and Judy Clark. A doctor who aided some of the wounded RATF members, Allan Berkman, MD, was jailed. This was the first time a doctor was jailed for such a charge since the doctor who aided John Wilkes Booth after he shot Abraham Lincoln. Italian activist Silvia Baraldini was arrested as linked to RATF, as were black activists (mostly former Panthers) Sekou Odinga, Chui Ferguson, Edward Joseph Anthony Laborde, Bilal Sunni-Ali, Iliana Robinson and Kuwasi Balagoon. The Puerto Rican independistas who formed the Movimiento de Liberacion National (MLN) were Ricardo Romero, Maria Cueto, Steven Guerra, Julio Rosado and Andres Rosado. All from Churchill and Vander Wall, *COINTELPRO Papers*, pp. 310-11, 322, 411-12.

30 Churchill and Vander Wall, *The COINTELPRO Papers*, p. 309. On BLA Multinational Task Force, see Sundiata Acoli, "A Brief History of the New Afrikan Prison Struggle," 2/19/92, www.prisonactivist.org. Note that this group has also been called the Revolutionary Armed Task Force.

31 Information regarding the trial of a white woman providing an escape car for some of the BLA in this Brinks truck incident suggests a loss of nuance in decision making likely due to the lingering effects of too much LSD use. An article on former Students for a Democratic Society member Judy Clark said that she had joined the Weather Underground's Days of Rage, before joining a group called the May 19 Communist Organization. The article described how in the 1970s, The writer said he saw Clark in the 1970s pointedly reprimand a Vietnam War veteran suffering from Post-Traumatic Stress Disorder. Clark said, "You were the invading army. How many did you kill?" At the Brinks truck trial, she told the jury, "Revolutionary violence is necessary, and it is a liberating force." The article described an incredible transformation Clark made in prison to present herself as a constantly warm and inspirational, but trial statements like this one contributed to her getting a 75-year prison sentence. Tom Robbins, "Judith Clark's Radical Transformation," *New York Times*, 1/12/12, http://www.nytimes.com/2012/01/15/magazine/judith-clarks-radical-transformation.html?pagewanted=all.

32 Harvey E. Klehr , *Far Left of Center* (New Brunswick, NJ: Transaction, 1988), pp. 115-18. NewsOne Staff, "Black Panther Convicted of Trying to Kill Six Cops Released from N.Y. Jail," *NewsOne*, November 26, 2014.

33 "[These 58-year sentences] were 38 years longer than the longest sentence imposed on any defendant in 1982 or 1983 for violation of *any* section of the federal explosives act." It said the sentences were three times the 1985 average for second degree murder and four times the average for bank robbery. See "Defendants Motion to Dismiss the Indictment for Governmental Misconduct," *U.S. v. Laura Whitehorn, et al.* CR. No. 88-145-05 (HHG), United States Court for the District of Columbia, January 3, 1989, pp.55-56. Churchill and Vander Wall, *The COINTELPRO Papers*, pp. 309-10, 412 n30.

34 On New York units that continued carrying out political spying, see *Barbara Handschu et al. v. Special Services Division, a/k/a Bureau Of Special Services, et al.,71 Civ. 2203 (CSH) Memorandum Opinion and Order*, United States District Court Southern District of New York, July 18, 1989, Charles S. Haight, Jr. U.S. District Court Judge. On Joint Terrorist Task Force, see Churchill and Vander Wall, *The COINTELPRO Papers*, pp. 309-11. One source said that federal marshals captured Mutulu in 1986, in his brother Lumumba Shakur's new hometown. Lumumba, Afeni's ex-husband and the founding Harlem Panther leader, was found dead in that Louisiana town within days of Mutulu's capture. Mutulu suspected that a police informant learned of his whereabouts, decided to target both brothers and killed Lumumba, http://www.hitemup.com/tupac/family.html. For other info, Churchill, *The COINTELPRO Papers*, pp. 411-12nn. On the Protective Research Unit, known as the Black Desk, see Leonard Levitt, "Secret Cop Squad," *New York Newsday*, April 29, 1999, p. A42. Cited in Frank Morales, *Covert Action Quarterly*, "Special Edition," July 1, 1999.

35 Connie Bruck, "The Takedown of Tupac," *The New Yorker*, 7/7/97, p.54.

36 Scott, *The Killing of Tupac Shakur*, p. 66. A year before Mutulu's capture government agents

had seized Marilyn Buck and Dr. Allan Berkman, a well-known activist doctor who worked at Lincoln Detox. A court convicted Dr. Berkman for giving medical assistance to Buck. He was the first individual convicted for giving medical aid since Dr. Mudd was charged with giving medical aid to John Wilkes Booth after his assassination of Abraham Lincoln. Churchill, *The COINTELPRO Papers*, p.311.

37 Scott, *The Killing of Tupac Shakur*, p.66. On FBI visiting Afeni's employers and potential employers, Michael Warren in trial documents: "Motion" at Sentencing, *New York vs. Tupac Shakur*, December 1994.

38 Speaking at colleges, Connie Bruck, *The New Yorker*, p. 47. *Handschu, et al. vs. Special Services Division a/k/a Bureau of Special Services*, U.S. District Court, S.D.N.Y., 71 Civ. 2203 (CSH) Memorandum Opinion and Order, December 16, 1981, p. 6. Benjamin Weiser, "Threats and Responses: Law Enforcement" *New York Times*, 2/12/03, p. 17. Also, Associated Press, "Judge Backs Expanded Police Surveillance," *New York Times*, 3/22/03, p. 2. Connie Bruck, "The Takedown of Tupac," *The New Yorker*, 7/7/97.

39 On FBI keeping Afeni unemployed, see Testimony of Tupac Shakur's attorney, Michael Warren, former Black Liberation Movement leader, New York vs. Tupac Shakur, sentencing hearing transcript, pp. 46-50. The use of this FBI tactic is backed by Michael Swearingen, *FBI Secrets: An Agent's Exposé* (Boston: South End Press, 1995), p. 116. On Afeni moving dozens of times, see Scott, *The Killing of Tupac Shakur*, p. 66. On Afeni writing chapter of book with Chomsky et al., see Marilyn Vogt, "Letter: Re: *Human Rights for Everybody*," *New York Review of Books* Vol. 24, Nos. 21 & 22, January 26, 1978. Other authors included poet Allan Ginsberg, Latino activists Armando Gutierrez and Juan Jose Pena; as well as feminist activist Kate Millet .

40 "Legs" referred to as Legs McNeil in Scott, *The Killing of Tupac Shakur*, p. 66. On Legs McNeil referred to as Legs Saunders, the major motion picture release, *Tupac: Resurrection* (Paramount/MTV Films, 2003). Latter is likely better source, as it was co-produced by Afeni Shakur.

41 Ronin Ro, *Have Gun Will Travel: The Spectacular Rise and Violent Fall of Death Row Records* (New York: Doubleday, 1998), p. 139.

42 KSAN radio reporter Richard Boyle, on the CD, *Me and My Shadow: Investigation of the political left by the United States Government*, producers Tarabu Betserai and Adi Gevins, from "The Pacifica Radio Archives," Track 3.

43 Robert Sam Anson, "To Die Like A Gangsta," *Vanity Fair*, March 1997, p. 248. Also Scott, *The Killing of Tupac Shakur*, p. 66.

44 Many linked to CIA, according to a 1976 "Top Secret" Justice Department report. Jefferson Morley, "The Kid Who Sold Crack to the President," *The City Paper*, 12/15/89, p. 31. On Barnes's acquittals and *New York Times* label, "Mr. Untouchable," see Hank Messick, *Of Grass and Snow* (Englewood, CA: Prentice-Hall, 1979), p. 148. Both cited in Clarence Lusane, *Pipe Dream Blues: Racism and the War on Drugs* (Boston: South End Press, 1991), pp. 41-42 nn 76, 79. Mutulu Shakur also alluded to Nicky Barnes as a "rat," suggesting that he, too, thought Barnes worked for the government. See the momentary display of Mutulu's Thug Life Code in *Tupac: Resurrection* DVD at the Mutulu Shakur interview.

45 Scott, *The Killing of Tupac Shakur*, p. 66

46 Michael Eric Dyson, *Holler If You Hear Me* (New York: Basic Civitas Books, 2001), pp. 84.

47 Afeni said that a white female married to another Panther defendant drove her to an upstate residential drug treatment facility and, despite her kicking and screaming, put her inpatient. Anson, "To Die Like a Gangsta."

48 Jasmine Guy, *Afeni Shakur: Evolution of a Revolutionary* (New York: Atria, 2005).

49 Swearingen, *FBI Secrets: An Agent's Exposé*, p. 86.

50 Amnesty International, *Proposal for a commission of inquiry into the effect of domestic intelligence activities on criminal trial in the United States of America* (New York: Amnesty International, 1980) p. 25. Cited in Churchill and Vander Wall, *Agents of Repression*, p. 91.

51 On Pratt's legal settlement, Todd Purdum, "Ex Black Panther Wins Long Legal Battle," *New York Times*, April 27, 2000, p. A18. On CIA joining forces with FBI against Pratt, with Chaos

against Pratt, see Alex Constantine, *The Covert War Against Rock* (Venice, CA: Feral House, 2000), pp. 15, 18; and Angus McKenzie, *Secrets: The CIA's War at Home* (Berkeley: University of California Press, 1999), p. 69. CIA spying on Americans, Seymour Hersh, "Huge C.I.A. Operation Reported in U.S. Against Antiwar Forces, Other Dissidents in Nixon Years," *New York Times*, 12/22/74, p.A1.

52 Mike Wilson, "For Malcolm X's Grandson, a Clouded Path," *New York Times*, September 6, 2003, p. A1.

53 Ex-CIA agent John Stockwell, in Lee Lew-Lee's *All Power to the People* documentary film, 1996. Lee previously worked as the cinematographer for the Academy Award winning documentary *The Panama Deception*.

54 "National Security, Civil Liberties and the Collection of Intelligence: A Report on the Huston Plan," reported in *U.S. Congress, Senate, Book III. Final Report of the Select Committee to Study Government Operations with Respect to Intelligence Activities*, 94th Cong. 2d sess., 1976, pp. 936-60. Cited in H. Newton, *War Against the Panthers*, pp. 43, 93n.

55 Newton quote from a description written by Geronimo Pratt and sent by Kathleen Cleaver's email, http://whosemedia.com/drums/2007/05/09/was-elaine-brown-an-agent/.

56 On Newton dealing cocaine, Seale said this at the podium of the April 1999 Black Panther Film Festival in New York City. This author was in the audience for that event. Regarding FBI trying to kill Newton while raiding neightbors home, see teletype from FBI San Francisco to director, February 16, 1974. FBI "Informative Note," 2/16/74; FBI Memorandum from Supervisor Gary Penrith to SAC San Francisco, 4/13/73; FBI memorandum from Special Agent Stephen Kies to SAC San Fran, 10/11/73. All cited at length in H. Newton, *War Against The Panthers*, pp. 48-50.

57 *Oakland Tribune*, 2/22/73, p. 1. FBI occupancy seen in memorandum from J.G. Deegan to W. R. Wannall, 8/26/74, saying, "There has been no indication that the BPP was aware of our occupancy of the apartment next door to Newton's." The apartment tenant, Don Robert Stinette, reportedly fired two shots through the door after police knocked, but didn't hit cops before his rifle jammed, according to FBI memorandum from Special Agent Wilbert J. Weiskrich to SAC San Francisco, 2/28/73. Also see, Interview of attorney Charles Garry reviewing FBI file made available in Dellinger v. Mitchell, Civ. Action No.1768-69, Fed. Dist. Ct. (D.C. 1969). All in H. Newton, *War Against the Panthers*, pp. 64, 98n.

58 Huey Newton, *To Die for the People* (New York: Random House/Writers and Readers, 1972/95), ed. Toni Morrison. Huey Newton, *Revolutionary Suicide* (New York: Harcourt Brace/ Writers and Readers, 1973/95). Erik Erickson and Huey Newton, *In Search of Common Ground* (New York: W. W. Norton & Co., 1973).

59 Jack Olson, *Last Man Standing: The Tragedies and Triumphs of Geronimo Pratt* (Anchor, 2001). Personal interviews with former Black Panthers Watani Tyehimba, and George Edwards. Torri Minton, "Prison Protest by Ex-Panther Newton," *San Francisco Chronicle*, August 24, 1988, p. B8. Torri Minton, "Huey Newton Gives In, Gets Out of Quentin," *San Francisco Chronicle*, August 27, 1988, p. A3. Paul Liberatore, "How Huey Newton Let a Panther Down," *San Francisco Chronicle*, September 16, 1988, p. A13. On the continued targeting of Newton with seeming frame-ups, see examples in M. Newton, *Bitter Grain*, pp. 210-16. On doctorate, see his published doctoral thesis, *War Against the Panthers*, which gained him his doctorate at the University of California at Santa Cruz in the History of Conscience. On Panther school, M. Newton, *Bitter Grain*, p. 218..

60 On black political prisoner starting to identify themselves as New Afrikans, see CEML, *Can't Jail the Spirit. On* Newton's work for Pratt, see Paul Liberatore, "How Huey Newton Let a Panther Down," *San Francisco Chronicle*, 9/16/88, p.A13. On Tupac's quote, see *Tupac Shakur, Thug Angel, Life of an Outlaw*, QD3 Entertainment, 2002. On Newton reuniting Panthers, personal interview, Billy Johnson, *Black Panther* newspaper editor, 2nd International Black Panther Film Fest. Also, Newton attended African People's Socialist Party (a.k.a. Uhuru Movement) meetings. Personal interview of Watu of Afrikan People's Socialist Party, 10/28/03.

61 On shooting details, Lori Olszewski and Rick DelVecchio, "Huey Newton Shot Dead On West Oakland Street," *San Francisco Chronicle*, Wednesday August 23, 1989, pp. A1, A14. Clarence Johnson and Lori Olszewski, "Friends Say Huey Newton Had Financial Problems." *San Francisco*

Chronicle, 8/24/89.

62 Churchill and Vander Wall, *The COINTELPRO Papers*, pp. 320, with many more details in long endnote 90, pp. 417-18. The authors cite more information from Saxifrage Group, "Huey P. Newton: Tribute to a Fallen Warrior," *New Studies on the Left*, Vol. XIV, Nos. 1-2 (Spring-Summer 1989), pp. 45-69. .

63 Churchill and Vander Wall, *The COINTELPRO Papers*, pp. 417-18 n90. On military-style execution, a Special Forces Group commander described how after dropping an assassination victim with the first shot, he then puts two bullets in the victims head: Stephen Kinzer, "Commandos Left a Calling Card: Their Absence," *New York Times*, 9/26/01, p. B6.

64 Michelle Johnson quoted in Clarence Johnson and Lori Olaszewski, "Friends Say Huey Newton Had Financial Problems," *San Francisco Chronicle*, 8/24/89, A1.

65 Newton's bother, Melvin Newton said this, as did Omali Yeshitela, a leader of the Uhuru House, a Black nationalist group in Oakland. Yeshitela dismissed the police version of Newton's murder as ludicrous. Omali believed that the government signed Newton's death certificate when they pressed the weapons charges, leaving him unarmed and defenseless. Both cited in Sharon McCormick, "Mourners Pay Respects to Huey Newton," *San Francisco Chronicle*, August 28, 1989, p. A3

66 Newton's friend Pat Wright, in Johnson and Olszewski, "Friends Say Huey Newton Had Financial Problems." *San Francisco Chronicle*, 8/24/89. CIA agent John Stockwell in Lee Lew-Lee, *All Power to the People* (Documentary, 1996).

67 William Pepper, *Orders to Kill: The Truth Behind the Murder of Martin Luther King, Jr.* (New York: Warner Books, 1995) p. 5.

68 Antoine Roger Lokongo, "Hands Off the Democratic Republic of Congo, Now!" *The Burning Spear*, October 2003, p. 17. Also heard on Pacifica's WBAI radio in New York. On CIA assassinating Lumumba, see, for example, James DiEugenio and Lisa Pease, eds., *The Assassinations: Probe Magazine on JFK, MLK, RFK, and Malcolm X* (Los Angeles, CA: Feral House, 2003), pp. 162-63. Also see Alexander Cockburn and Jeffrey St. Clair, *White Out: The CIA, Drugs and the Press* (New York: Verso), excerpted in Dave Greaves, "The CIA, Drugs and Big Media," *Our Times Press*, 9/98, p. 8. On CIA attempting/aiding Patrice Lumumba assassination, see Mark Mazetti and Tim Weiner, "Files on Illegal Spying Show CIA Skeletons from Cold War," *New York Times*, p. A1, 6/27/07.

A MERCURY NEWS SPECIAL REPORT
'Crack' plague's roots are in Nicaraguan war
Colombia-Bay Area drug pipeline helped finance CIA-backed Contras
'80s effort to assist guerrillas left legacy of drugs, gangs in black L.A.
THE KEY PLAYERS

Gary Webb

Chapter Twenty

U.S. Intelligence Drug Trafficking: Cocaine & Heroin

In a 1988 report, the panel documented that covert networks supplying arms to the Contras with the blessing of U.S. officials were also bringing narcotics to American cities at the height of the urban drug epidemic. (A decade later, a CIA inspector general's report concluded the same.)

– Findings of U.S. Senate foreign relations investigative subcommittee, reported in the *Washington Post*.[1]

The CIA payroll in Jamaica included many political operatives who later, "immigrated to the United States. They settled into the large Jamaican and Caribbean communities in Miami and New York City. In the early 1980s, the [Shower] Posse leaders ... evolved from small-time marijuana sellers into nationwide cocaine and crack distributors."[2]

In 1983, Vice-President George H.W. Bush ordered Oliver North and the CIA to set up drug shipments from Latin America to the U.S. east coast. North reportedly contracted with the chief cocaine producer in Bolivia that year to airlift over 500 tons of cocaine to the east coast for distribution by a Columbian cartel.[3] The Shower Posse members apparently served as some of their lower-level dealers before their roles grew larger in time.

Iran-Contra Cocaine & the War on Ethnic Groups

So much information was made public about the CIA paying Nicaraguan Contras and aiding them in the trafficking of cocaine, it led to nationally televised Congressional hearings in the 1980s. One insider, Al Martin, a retired U.S. Navy Lt. Commander and former officer in the Office of Naval Intelligence, testified as a whistleblower about his involvement. Pulitzer Prize-winning investigative reporter Gary Webb also investigated these CIA covert operations and published a week of front-page articles in the *San Jose Mercury News*. Webb detailed them more extensively in his book *Dark Alliance: The CIA, the Contras, and the Crack Cocaine Explosion*.[4]

While Webb's 1996 *San Jose Mercury News* articles gained mass dissemination through the Internet, veteran journalists such as the Associated Press's Robert Parry first broke the story in 1986. This contributed to the U.S. Congress holding hearings in the 1980s. Much of mainstream media ended up attacking Webb and the *San Jose Mercury News,* pressuring the publisher to stop the series with only half of the articles printed. Nonetheless, the aforementioned 1998 report by the CIA Inspector General stated the CIA did work with the Contras in trafficking cocaine, vindicating Webb and backing his findings.[5]

In 1986, the Nicaraguan military shot down a counter-revolutionary Contra supply plane laden with drugs, flying over Nicaragua. Southern Air Transport, a Florida-based cargo airline once controlled by the CIA, provided the plane. The event unraveled U.S. intelligence's secret war on Nicaragua, with investigations prompting Congressional hearings. It was found that the Contras were being illegally funded by the U.S. through cocaine trafficking, as well as the sales of arms to Iran. When the public first found out about these operations in the late 1980s, the media dubbed it the Iran-Contra scandal.

The seeds for Iran-Contra were planted seven years earlier, when Ayatollah Khomeini led the faction to overthrow the U.S-backed Shah of Iran. Khomeini's government whipped up hatred towards the U.S. and took hostages whom they freed the day of President Ronald Reagan's inauguration. Credible books claim weapons company owners who supported Reagan promised the Iranians arms sales if they held the hostages past election day, to help Reagan defeat President Carter. This secret agreement has been called the October Surprise.[6] Congress said Reagan authorized such deals several years later.

Reagan and Bush then used the money received from these arms sales for the illegal funding of a counter-revolutionary army against Nicaragua. In 1980, newly elected President Reagan and Vice President George H.W. Bush began building support for the Nicaraguan Contras, after the socialist Sandanista government had seized power the year before. Early in the '80s, Congress cut off U.S. government funding of the Contras due to their human-rights abuses, but Bush illegally reinstated it with the Iran-Contra cocaine operations. George Washington University archived the Reagan administration government documents on this part of the scandal, as well as the illegal, covert war against the Nicaraguan government.[7]

By 1986, the shot-down CIA plane that the Reagan/Bush operation used had secretly transported drugs and guns for years.[8] In the early 1980s, Barry Seal, "one of the biggest cocaine and marijuana importers in the southern United States," had piloted the plane. Louisiana's attorney general said Seal smuggled "between $3 billion and $5 billion worth of drugs into the U.S."[9]

Barry Seal had many connections to the CIA. Seal officially worked for the Agency in 1984, purportedly for a drug sting. Seal transported drugs through a small airport that was federally confirmed as a "joint training operation with another federal agency." A National Security Council staffer said Seal's "records showed him to be a contract CIA operative both before and during his years of drug running in Mena, Arkansas in the 1980s."[10]

Writer Michael Montalvo documented how Marine Lt. Col. Oliver North's own diary entries disclosed much of his role supervising the transportation of "over 500 tons of cocaine ... to the poor masses of the inner cities and across the USA." North purported the shipments were only trying to save Central America from Communism by funding the anti-Sandanista Contras.[11]

Reporter Webb and others described how the CIA operation accomplished this massive cocaine distribution by luring low-level drug dealers into high-level national trafficking. These CIA-backed suppliers trafficked the largest amounts of cocaine ever in this country, dropping kilogram prices from $60,000 to $12,000 in a year.[12] Although the method of turning cocaine into more affordable and addictive "crack" first got the government's attention in 1979, widespread marketing was not achieved until the early 1980s. Evidence indicates that U.S. intelligence used Los Angeles-based national crack cocaine traffickers, giving them virtual legal immunity for years.[13]

Oliver North oversaw the Contra operation with his direct supervisor, Vice President George H.W. Bush. North worked as National Security Advisor to Bush while Bush headed the National Security Council. They kept documentation of these operations under wraps through President Reagan's Executive Order 123333. The order "'privatized' NSC intelligence operations and permitted agencies other than the CIA to carry out special operations without reporting its activities ... [allowing] any private enterprise the NSC set up, to carry out covert operations." This barred researchers from attaining any government documentation through Freedom of Information Act filings.[14]

Mike Levine was one of several DEA agents who blew the whistle on CIA cocaine trafficking in Latin America.

A long list of other researchers and people investigating aspects of the drug trade and drug war backed Gary Webb's account. Besides Professor Peter Dale Scott, Drug Enforcement Agency veteran Mike Levine wrote about his findings of CIA drug trafficking in his exposé *Deep Cover.* He repeated the allegations for years in his weekly Pacifica radio program, *Expert Witness.*[15]

At least one other DEA agent, Celerino Castillo, testified to the House Permanent Select Committee on Intelligence about the CIA drugs- and arms-trafficking. A Senate committee chaired by Sen. John Kerry also interviewed key witnesses such as imprisoned drug dealers and money launderers, who disclosed their roles in the huge cocaine-trafficking scheme. Senior DEA supervisory agent Dennis Dayle said, "In my thirty-year history in DEA, the major targets of my investigations almost invariably turned out to be working for the CIA." And finally, Leslie Cockburn exposed similar information in her book *Out of Control,* as did *Nation* columnist Alexander Cockburn, in *White Out.*[16]

Los Angeles Police Department narcotics detective Michael C. Ruppert reported giving over two hundred and fifty pages of documents to members of the U.S. Senate Select Committee investigating CIA drug dealing. In his 1997 testimony to that committee, Ruppert said that his evidence showed

> conclusively that, as a matter of national policy, set at the National Security Council—the White House—elements of the CIA, in concert with elements of the military, and other federal agencies, have dealt drugs to Americans for at least three decades. Major defense contractors like E-Systems have also engaged in such traffic.

Ruppert further said his evidence indicated "that the CIA has infiltrated and established illegal relationships with a number of police departments around the country. One of the purposes of this has been to protect CIA drug operations from law enforcement. I have personal knowledge of this activity in Los Angeles and New Orleans and have documented such a case in New York City."[17]

The *Washington Post* summarized confirmation of what the U.S. Senate's foreign relations investigative subcommittee found:

> In a 1988 report, the panel documented that covert networks supplying arms to the Contras with the blessing of U.S. officials were also bringing narcotics to American cities at the height of the urban drug epidemic. (A decade later, a CIA Inspector General's report concluded the same.)[18]

Associated Press and *Newsweek* journalist Robert Parry documented how George H.W. Bush was CIA Director in 1976, and how he continued to run intelligence operations for three decades through CIA staff that remained loyal to him. A congressional committee noted how when President Carter nominated Stansfield Turner as CIA Director to succeed Bush, Bush loyalist William Casey helped engineer a secret CIA office behind President Carter's back from 1977-1981. Casey ran operations for the wealthiest conservative families without President Carter's knowledge.[19]

Parry detailed how Casey then became President Reagan's CIA Director, working under Vice President Bush. Casey proceeded to create a clique of CIA officers who maintained decades of dominance, including his key assistant, Robert Gates, head of the Defense Intelligence Agency. Parry also described many others as "Gates's clones," such as George Tenet (CIA Director 1997-2004, straddling the terms of presidents Clinton and George W. Bush), David Cohen and John McLaughlin, among others. These figures remained in top U.S. intelligence positions until at least 2009. Gates became George H.W. Bush's CIA Director, George W. Bush's Secretary of Defense and President Barak Obama's Secretary of Defense for several years.[20]

U.S. Navy Lt. Commander Al Martin, the whistleblower involved in the Iran-Contra crack affair, showed letters from Congressmen thanking him for his testimony regarding the Iran-Contra crack hearings. He had testified about how Vice President Bush appointed CIA and FBI personnel to have direct contact with narcotics traffickers. Martin also testified that U.S. intelligence manipulated U.S. Customs to ensure certain aircraft and ships were not inspected. Martin further stated that U.S. intelligence maintained secured shipping routes and narcotics storage facilities.[21]

Closer to the street level of drug dealing, about the same time as Nicky Barnes and Legs Saunders dealt cocaine, the CIA was running a California-based cocaine-trafficking operation with a similar network. During that mid-'80s time period, U.S. intelligence-paid operatives supplied the nation's west coast-based premier drug trafficker, "Freeway" Ricky Ross. Before his arrest in 1989 by an apparently honest federal agent, prosecutors said, Ross bought and resold several metric tons of cocaine. This earned the equivalent, in 2013 dollars, of a $2.5 billion gross profit and $850 million net profit.[22]

CIA Contra Crack Operations Under Bush and Gov. Clinton

While the Iran-Contra scandal was an obvious reflection of Reagan/Bush politics on behalf of the ruling oligarchy, most of the media hid politically-hot aspects of the scandal. One such aspect involved future president Bill Clinton, who either cooperated with the CIA on the drug-trafficking operation, or at least turned a blind eye while he was governor of Arkansas. Trafficker Barry Seal's primary airport of entry was Mena, Arkansas. Reporter Gary Webb said, "Clinton's critics have charged that it was impossible for the governor of Arkansas to have been unaware of Seal's activities at Mena."[23]

Terry Reed, an Air Force intelligence officer and FBI informant, wrote in his memoir *Compromised* that he aided the CIA Contra project under Clinton's watch. This project facilitated gun- and drug-smuggling, with a weapons manufacturing company inside a fake "parking meter" factory in Arkansas. Other CIA-connected individuals set up similar front companies in the U.S. and in Nicaragua's neighbor, El Salvador.[24] This trafficking fueled a covert war on the Sandinistas, while massive inner-city crack cocaine distribution triggered a proliferation of gang wars in the U.S.

It is interesting to note that a court convicted Clinton's brother Roger and a high-powered supporter, Danny Ray Lasater, as co-conspirators with twenty-four other codefendants for drug trafficking out of Little Rock, Arkansas. Lasater was an investment bond broker in Little Rock, the largest bond community in the U.S. outside of New York City. This was probably due in part to laundered drug money, since bond brokers can play an intermediary role to keep the investors anonymous.[25]

The CIA Inspector General's office confirmed that the CIA ran a joint training operation with another federal agency at Mena's airport. Thus Clinton, reported as knowingly allowing Lasater's trafficking, either colluded with the CIA's operation or looked past it. An Arkansas State Police intelligence unit officer said that he was then ordered to shred nearly a thousand documents related to Mena and Iran-Contra.[26]

This foreshadowed how President Bill Clinton would tolerate intelligence operations during his presidency in the 1990s. Indeed, America increased its operations and military aid in Columbia in that decade. Accordingly, Columbia increased its coca leaf production fields from 3.8 to 12.3 thousand hectares from 1991 to 1999.[27]

Drug War Against Poor People of Color

As the 1980s came to a close, in many American cities cocaine and its cheaper and quicker delivery system, the rock-like smokeable "crack," had risen in popularity to at least equal the problem of heroin addiction.[28] In African-American and Latino neighborhoods, gangs increased in numbers, with the largest being Los Angeles's rival Bloods and Crips. A Hollywood film, *Colors,* the title coming from their opposing red and blue bandana colors, made them well known worldwide.

In communities where these drugs were sold, users developed addictions to them that resulted in loss of money, jobs and families. Addicts developed tolerances to the drugs, and had to use more to get the same effect. Men often had to deal and/or steal to afford them. Women had to deal, steal or prostitute themselves.[29]

The violence stemming from these gang wars for command of drug-dealing turf harmed communities around the country. Many people were killed in these wars, including innocent adults and children who were in the wrong place at the wrong time. As fear rose, those who could flee from crime-ridden urban areas did so, bringing down the tax base and impoverishing inner city areas with abandoned buildings and limited revenue to pay for services.

Law professor Michelle Alexander studied the issue of drugs for years. In a review of Alexander's book *The New Jim Crow*, magazine writer Arnie Cooper said,

> The "War on Drugs" was the creation of conservative political strategists.... That it resulted in disproportionate drug-arrest rates in poor communities of color may even have been part of the plan.... Alexander's statistics [show that] in 2004, 75 percent of all people imprisoned for drug offenses were black or Latino, despite the fact that the majority of the country's illegal-drug users and dealers are white.[30]

Supporting Michelle Alexander's conclusions, a *New York Times* column noted that President Clinton signed a law (originally formulated under President G.H.W. Bush) establishing the 100-to-1 punishment ratio for crack cocaine possession versus powder, meaning sentencing guidelines of six months for possession of a small amount of powder cocaine were six hundred months (50 years) for possession of the same amount of crack cocaine. The *Times* column said, "Clinton signed this despite the pleas of civil rights leaders who correctly predicted that this would be an anvil dropping on the black community." Alexander's *The New Jim Crow* spent ten months on the *New York Times* bestseller list. In her introduction, Alexander wrote,

> Few legal rules meaningfully constrain the police in the drug war, and enormous financial incentives have been granted to law enforcement to engage in mass drug arrests through military-style tactics. Once swept into the system, one's chances of ever being truly free are slim, often to the vanishing point ... [*The New Jim Crow*] debunks the notion that rates of black imprisonment can be explained by crime rates and identifies the huge racial disparities at every stage of the criminal justice process—from the initial stop, search, and arrest to the plea bargaining and sentencing phases. In short, [*The New Jim Crow*] explains how the legal rules that structure the system guarantee discriminatory results. These legal rules ensure that the undercaste is overwhelmingly black and brown.[31]

A number of other sources supported Alexander's conclusions. For example, a documentary, *Kids for Cash*, highlighted how corporations gave kickbacks to two judges for sending thousands of kids to the corporation's private prisons for minor offenses. The Pennsylvania courts found both judges guilty, and stated that one of the judges had violated the constitutional rights of thousands of kids. A number of these kids were sent to juvenile prisons after first-time minor offenses such as marijuana paraphernalia possession.[32]

Another example of systemic corruption that is incarcerating people en masse comes from documents released by National Security Agency whistleblower Edward Snowden. Reuters detailed how the Drug Enforcement Agency had a Special Operations Division that partnered with over two dozen other agencies, including the CIA, the FBI, the NSA and Homeland Security. The DEA trained federal agents in falsifying their investigative trail, what they did in their investigation and how they came to find evidence, which they called a "parallel construction"—a false story about how and when they obtained evidence. This opens the door for planting false evidence without being caught. As Reuters detailed:

> A secretive U.S. Drug Enforcement Administration unit is funneling information from intelligence intercepts, wiretaps, informants and a massive database of telephone records to authorities across the nation to help them launch criminal investigations of Americans. Although these cases rarely involve national security issues, documents reviewed by Reuters show that law enforcement agents have been directed to conceal how such investigations truly begin – not only from defense lawyers but also sometimes from prosecutors and judges.
>
> The undated documents show that federal agents are trained to "recreate" the investigative trail to effectively cover up where the information originated, a practice that some experts say violates a defendant's Constitutional right to a fair trial. If defendants don't know how an investigation began, they cannot know to ask to review potential sources of exculpatory evidence – information that could reveal entrapment, mistakes or biased witnesses.
>
> "I have never heard of anything like this at all," said Nancy Gertner, a Harvard Law School professor who served as a federal judge from 1994 to 2011. Gertner and other legal experts said the program sounds more troubling than recent disclosures that the National Security Agency has been collecting domestic phone records.[33]

U.S. Attorney General Ramsey Clark remains one of many prominent people who backed Alexander's general view even before these revelations about bribed judges and the DEA's systemic cover-ups. After working under Presidents Kennedy and Johnson, Clark became a more radical activist, and gave his opinion of U.S. intelligence's use of drugs. As noted earlier, he said, "I think the government uses drugs to sedate and divide the masses."[34]

The Opium War on Afghanistan, Pakistan & Opposition Abroad

When U.S. military forces could not beat back the North Vietnamese, they lost control over the Southeast Asian area around Vietnam. After

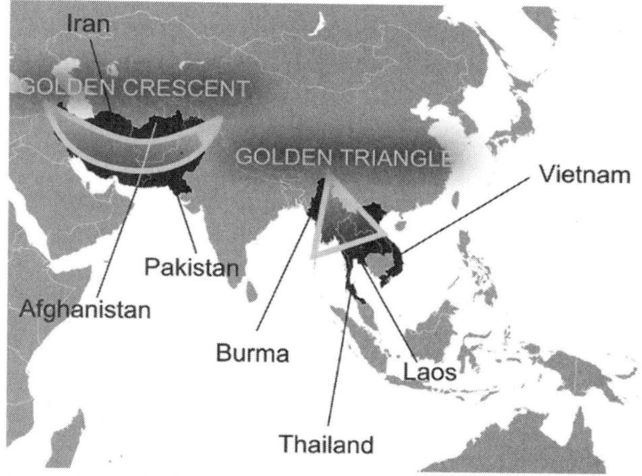

The world's most fertile poppy fields for heroin-producing opium exist at the two ends of the same mountain range, which stretches from the Golden Triangle of the Vietnam area near China up to Afghanistan, sites of America's longest wars.

this loss of easier access to inexpensive Golden Triangle opium crops, opium production declined. One of the top producers of the Golden Triangle, the country of Laos, produced 200 tons of opium in 1975 and only 30 tons by 1984. U.S. intelligence proceeded to increase activities in the "Golden Crescent" region where Pakistan borders Afghanistan, lying at the other end of the same mountain range containing the Golden Triangle. A *World Opium Survey* reported the Pakistani-Afghan opium harvest rose from 400 tons in 1971 to 1,200 tons in 1978.[35]

Afghanistan has historically been one of the most underdeveloped of third-world countries. By 1973, the Soviet Union had given Afghanistan, its neighbor, close to a billion dollars in civilian aid, accounting for sixty percent of its foreign aid.[36]

American oligarchs started meddling around the border of Pakistan and Afghanistan in the early 1970s. The U.S. has been giving military and economic aid to neighboring Pakistan at least since then.[37] Professor Peter Dale Scott holds that Pakistan had started to increase its "support for Afghan Islamic resistance movements following a left-wing coup [in Afghanistan] in 1973." The Pakistan-Afghan three-fold increase in opium production coincided with this support for Afghanistan's Islamic resistance to the more leftist Afghan coup leaders.[38]

The CIA cultivated key Pakistani assets who assisted in an arms pipeline to the Afghan Islamic resistance.[39] One of these assets was the Gulf Group shipping line of the Gokal brothers. Another was the Bank of Credit and Commerce International (BCCI). While researchers suspected CIA ties to the bank's future officers before its founding in 1972, in 1976 CIA Director George H.W. Bush strengthened the CIA's ties to various Arab intelligence agency figures who were all BCCI insiders.[40]

When President Carter took office in 1976, he did not reappoint Bush as CIA Director. It was then that Bush and William Casey set up the secret CIA office and worked with British intelligence. They set up a Bank of Credit and Commerce International affiliate in the Cayman Islands. During the Iran-Contra crack hearings, it came out that BCCI was the top conduit for laundering money in these 1980s dealings.[41]

In April of 1978, a newly formed, pro-Soviet, socialist-leaning People's Democratic Party overthrew Mohammad Daud's leadership in Afghanistan. They seized the land from its wealthiest overseers and redistributed it to the people. They also nationalized farm credit.[42]

This, along with the fall of the longtime CIA-supported Shah of Iran, put the CIA into intensive planning mode, figuring how to gain more control in Pakistan and Afghanistan, neighboring Iran's oil-rich Middle East region. President Carter's National Security advisor Zbigniew Brzezinski made important disclosures confirmed by U.S. intelligence reports. In an interview with a French media organization he said he advised Carter to start arming and funding radical fundamentalist Islamic fighters (the mujaheddin) to wage war on the People's Democratic Party of Afghanistan in early 1979.

President Carter armed and funded the mujaheddin's war on Afghanistan's leftist leadership, and the Soviet Union invaded Afghanistan about eight months later. According to Afghan expert Dr. Barnett Rubin in testimony before Congress, the U.S. proceeded to pay and arm Afghan mercenaries to fight the Soviet Union. The same American oligarchs involved in opium trafficking in the Vietnam area were now trafficking opium out of Afghanistan.[43]

Afghanistan, the size of Texas, shared its northern border with the Soviet Union. For ten years the Soviet Union sent troops into Afghanistan to help fight the Islamic mujaheddin. All the while, the Reagan and Bush administrations continued a proxy war for that decade, arming and paying the mujaheddin to keep fighting.

The CIA considered the Golden Crescent a new Golden Triangle. Heroin factories popped up on the Afghan-Pakistan border to help process the opium for local sales, while raw opium traveled globally. "By 1980 Pakistan-Afghan opium dominated the European market and supplied sixty percent of America's illicit demand."[44]

Professor McCoy wrote that 1979 to 1989 encompassed "ten years of CIA covert support for the mujaheddin resistance." He detailed how this resistance involved Afghan guerillas and Pakistani military intelligence. The *Washington Post* noted that CIA Director William Casey advised Pakistani Inter-Services Intelligence (ISI) to train mujaheddin resistance for attacks upon the Soviet Union, which they eventually carried out. McCoy added that during this time, the "U.S. government and media sources were silent about the involvement of leading Afghan guerillas and Pakistan military in the heroin traffic."[45]

Veteran *Daily Telegraph* journalist Ahmed Rashid, whose best-selling books include *Jihad: The Rise of Militant Islam in Central Asia,* wrote, "In 1986 the secret services of the United States, Great Britain and Pakistan agreed to launch guerilla attacks in [Soviet territories] Tajikistan and Uzbekistan. [The task] was given to [Pakistan's] favorite mujaheddin leader, Gulbuddin [Hekmatyar]." Reuters, the British version of the Associated Press, also confirmed that a guerilla warfare training camp in Afghanistan was "set up in the early 1980s by the CIA and ISI and run by ... Hekmatyar." Hekmatyar was supplementing his CIA and Pakistani ISI income with profits from his heroin labs in the Pakistani intelligence-controlled area at this time. Hekmatyar, who founded the Muslim Brotherhood, became Afghanistan's leading drug lord.[46]

CIA-Pakistani intelligence strategy included heavy control over the drug flows. Professor Peter Dale Scott believed that CIA Director William Casey followed through on a plan promoted "to him by an Alexandre de Marenches, that the CIA supplied drugs on the sly to Soviet troops." While Marenches denied it went through, reports came in that "Heroin, hashish, and even cocaine from Latin America soon reached Soviet troops." These reports said the CIA-ISI-linked Bank of Credit & Commerce International, along with several American intelligence operatives, were deeply involved in the drug trade before the war was over. Scott wrote, "Maureen Orth heard from Mathea Falco, head of International Narcotics Control for the State Department under Jimmy Carter, that the CIA and ISI together encouraged the mujaheddin to addict the Soviet troops."[47]

Professor McCoy cited that they had hundreds of heroin refineries, and they targeted the Pakistani people, increasing heroin addiction there from 5,000 users in 1980 to 1.3 million by 1986. By 1990, mainstream media substantiated Gulbuddin Hekmatyar's Afghan heroin trafficking. A front-page article in the *Washington Post* stated that a senior administration official in the White House confirmed Hekmatyar and the Pakistan ISI as American allies involved in heroin trafficking.[48]

The increased CIA involvement in the Golden Crescent area along the border of Pakistan and Afghanistan contributed to the ever-increasing opium production there. After a growth to 1,200 tons in 1978, it almost quadrupled in the next twenty years. The United Nations said Afghanistan's opium production had risen to 4,600 tons in 1999, or seventy percent of the world's total.[49]

Notes

1 Dale Russakoff, "Shifting Within Party to Gain His Footing," *Washington Post*, pp. A1, A8, 7/26/04.

2 Gary Webb, *Dark Alliance: The CIA, the Contras, and the Crack Cocaine Explosion* (New York: Seven Stories, 1998), p. 144. Webb's endnote citations on CIA destabilization of Jamaica and work against Manley are Ernest Volkman and John Cummings, "Murder as Usual," *Penthouse*, December 1977. Summarized in William Blum, *Killing Hope: U.S. Military and CIA Interventions Since World War II* (Monroe, ME: Common Courage, 1995), pp. 263-67. On Jamaican trafficking groups, Webb cites U.S. Department of Justice, Drug Enforcement Administration, Intelligence Division, *Crack Cocaine, Drug Intelligence Report*, DEA-94016, 1994, p. 8.

3 Michael Montalvo, M.B.A, J.D., "Prisoner of the Drug War: An Inside Report from a former Inside Player," *Prevailing Winds*, No. 8, 2000, p. 77.

4 Webb, *Dark Alliance*. Al Martin, *The Conspirators: The Secrets of an Iran-Contra Insider* (Pray, MT: National Liberty, 2001).

5 Russakoff, "Shifting Within Party to Gain His Footing."

6 See, for example, Gary Sick, *The October Surprise* (New York: Three Rivers Press, 1992). Sick was on President Carter's National Security Council and was a professor at Columbia University School for International and Public Affairs. Also see Barbara Honneger, *October Surprise* (New York: Tudor, 1989), and Associated Press veteran Robert Parry, *Trick or Treason: The October Surprise Mystery* (Sheridan Square Publishing, 1993). Note that the head of the Iranian Wrestling Federation, the country's top sport, told this writer in 1990 that leading Iranian intellectuals believe the Ayatollah Khomeini was inserted by the U.S. as the best of the alternatives to the Shah.

7 "The Iran-Contra Affair Twenty Years On: Documents Spotlight Role of Reagan, Top Aides," http://www.gwu.edu/~nsarchiv/NSAEBB/NSAEBB210/.

8 Webb, *Dark Alliance*, p. 120. U.S. Congresswoman Maxine Waters wrote the book's foreword, and the book was a finalist for the PEN/Newman's Own First Amendment Award.

9 Webb, *Dark Alliance*, p. 119. Webb was quoting a letter from Louisiana's attorney general to U.S Attorney General Ed Meese.

10 Webb, *Dark Alliance*, pp. 117, 119. Webb quoted former National Security Council staffer Roger Morris's 1996 book on the Clintons, *Partners in Power, The Clintons and Their America* (Henry Holt, 1986).

11 Montalvo, "Prisoner of the Drug War," pp. 76-82. Montalvo was imprisoned as part of the drug war but got a law degree in prison, then litigated a double jeopardy/forfeiture case, winning in the Supreme Court, http://u2.lege.net/whale.to/b/montalvo.html.

12 Montalvo, "Prisoner of the Drug War," p. 77.

13 On government's initial attention to new crack cocaine, Webb, *Dark Alliance*, pp. 144-45. On virtual immunity for years, see, for example, stories of "Freeway" Ricky Ross and Ron Lister in *Dark Alliance*. Los Angeles police detectives searching Lister's home found evidence that Lister had regular contacts with Scott Weekly, who ran at least two covert operations involving the National Security Council and a special unit inside the U.S. State Department. That unit worked with Ollie North and the CIA: *Dark Alliance*, p. 339.

14 Montalvo, "Prisoner of the Drug War."

15 Michael Levine, *Deep Cover: The Inside Story of How DEA Infighting, Incompetence and Subterfuge Lost Us the Biggest Battle of the Drug War* (New York: Delacorte Press, 1990). "Expert Witness" is on Pacifica's WBAI 99.5 FM in New York City.

16 "The Global Narco-Nexus: An Interview with Peter Dale Scott," pp. 46-51. "'Heads Have to Roll": Testimony of a DEA Agent," pp. 68-75. Mike Levine, "I Volunteer to Kidnap Oliver North," pp. 84-91. "'So in your view, we're sort of wasting our time?': Excerpts from the Kerry Hearings, 1989," pp. 64-67. All Articles in *Prevailing Winds*, No. 8, 2000. Also, Alfred McCoy, *The Politics of Heroin: CIA Complicity in the Global Drug Trade* (New York: Lawrence Hill Books, 1991). On DEA supervisor Dennis Dayle, see Mike Ruppert, "The CIA, Iran-Contra and the Narcotics Money Laundering Nexus," originally 1997, reprinted by *Global Research News*, April 24, 2014, http://www.globalresearch.ca/the-cia-iran-contra-and-the-narcotics-money-laundering-nexus/5379003. Leslie Cockburn, *Out of Control* (New York: Atlantic Monthly Press, 1988). Alexander Cockburn and Jeffrey St. Clair, *White Out: The CIA, Drugs and the Press* (New York: Verso, 1999).

17 Ruppert, "The CIA, Iran-Contra and the Narcotics Money Laundering Nexus."

18 Russakoff, "Shifting Within Party to Gain His Footing."

19 Craig Unger, *House of Bush, House of Saud: The Secret Relationship Between the World's Two Most Powerful Dynasties* (New York: Scribner, 2004), pp. 41, 50-51, 309-10n. Unger noted how Carter's CIA Deputy Director set up a separate Arlington complex to run these operations. Other key figures in these operations included Reagan/Bush's future CIA director William Casey, Republican congressman Dick Cheyney, Zbigniew Brzezinski, and James Baker. Unger's sources include Sick, *October Surprise*, p. 24; "Unauthorized Transfers," Committee on the Post Office and Civil Service, pt. 1, pp. 36, 39, 55, 100, 102, 124, 1086, 1105; United Press International, July 24, 1983; Laurence I. Barrett, *Gambling with History* (New York: Doubleday, 1983), p. 383; and former congressman Donald Albosta, telephone interview.

20 Robert Parry, "The CIA's DI Disgrace," 7/13/04, www.consortiumnews.com. This article was adapted from Parry's book, *Secrecy and Privilege: Rise of the Bush Dynasty from Watergate to Iraq* (2004). Parry said that before George Bush left the presidency in '92, he appointed Robert Gates as CIA Director and David Cohen as deputy director of the Directorate of Intelligence. Many CIA administrators petitioned President Bill Clinton for a housecleaning of all the Bush/Reagan leftover intelligence leaders. While Clinton let go of Gates, he left Cohen and others in their powerful positions. He also appointed a neo-conservative Democrat who was close to Bush, James Woolsey, as CIA director. Clinton then appointed another Gates ally, George Tenet, as CIA director in his second presidential term.

21 Martin, *The Conspirators*, p. 162.

22 On CIA's California-based trafficking, see Webb, *Dark Alliance*. The CIA's trafficking revealed by Webb was later disclosed in the CIA's Inspector General Report of 1998, cited in Dale Russakoff, "Shifting Within Party to Gain His Footing." On Rick Ross profits, Mike Sager, "Say Hello to Rick Ross," *Esquire*, September 13, 2013.

23 Webb, *Dark Alliance*, pp. 117-18.

24 Webb, *Dark Alliance*, pp. 113-15.

25 Webb, *Dark Alliance*, pp. 118-19.

26 Webb, *Dark Alliance*, p. 119.

27 Peter Dale Scott, "Honduras, the Contra Support Networks, and Cocaine: How the U.S. Government has Augmented America's Drug Crisis," in Alfred McCoy and Alan A. Block, eds., *War on Drugs: Studies in the Failure of U.S. Narcotics Policy* (Boulder, CO: Westview, 1992), pp. 126-27.

28 This author began working as an addictions counselor in 1989 in a Baltimore City addictions agency. Our director's statistics on our client addicts saw crack addiction rise to equal heroin addiction for the first time that year.

29 *Colors* (Dir. Dennis Hopper, 1988). On effects of drugs on addicts' behaviors, over 20 years of addicts' narratives in counseling attest to these.

30 Arnie Cooper, "Throwing Away the Key: Michelle Alexander on How Prisons Have Become the New Jim Crow," *The Sun Magazine*, February 2011, #422.

31 Michelle Alexander, *The New Jim Crow: Mass Incarceration in the Age of Colorblindness* (New York: The New Press, 2012), Introduction.

32 "Court Tosses Convictions Of Corrupt Judge," CBSnews.com, March 26, 2009. Jennifer Learn-Andes, "Juvenile records to be erased," *Wilkes-Barre Times Leader*, March 27, 2009. Scott Schaffer, *Kids for Cash* (Documentary,1994). On marijuana paraphernalia possession first-time charge, see case of child whose father had police friend frame his star wrestler son for this, which led to four months of juvenile detention and his son committing suicide, http://www.democracynow.org/2014/2/4/kids_for_cash_inside_one_of.

33 John Shiffman and Kristina Cooke, "Exclusive: U.S. directs agents to cover up program used to investigate Americans," *Reuters*, August 5, 2013.

34 Personal interview with Ramsey Clark at "Beyond Terror" conference held by the Maryland Institute College of Art, 1991.

35 On drop in Laos opium, Peter Dale Scott, *Drugs, Oil, and War: The United States in*

Afghanistan Colombia, and Indochina (New York: Rowman and Littlefield, 2003), p. 40. On rise in Pakistan-Afghan opium, Malthea Falco, "Asian Narcotics: The Impact on Europe," *Drug Enforcement* (February, 1979), pp. 2-3; U.S. CCINC, *World Opium Survey* 1972, pp. A-7, A-14, A-17. Both cited in Alfred McCoy, *The Politics of Heron: CIA Complicity in the Global Drug Trade* (New York: Lawrence Hill Books, 1991), p. 446.

36 Hafizullah Emadi, *State, Revolution, and Superpowers in Afghanistan* (New York: Praeger, 1990), pp. 3, 52-53. John K. Cooley, *Unholy Wars: Afghanistan, America and International Terrorism* (Virginia: Pluto Press, 1999), p. 3. Both cited in Katherine Harvey, "Afghanistan, the United States, and the Legacy of Afghanistan's War," *EDGE*, 5/6/03, http://www.stanford.edu/class/e297a/Afghanistan,%20the%20United%20States.htm#_ftn9.

37 John P. Lewis, *New York Times*, Op-Ed, 9/12/71. Referenced in Noam Chomsky and Edward Herman, *The Washington Connection and Third World Fascism* (Boston: South End Press, 1979), pp. 105-06.

38 M. Emdad-ul Haq, *Drugs in South Asia: From the Opium Trade to the Present Day* (New York: St. Martin's, 2000), pp. 175-86; Ahmed Rashid, *Taliban: Militant Islam, Oil, and Fundamentalism in Central Asia* (New Haven, CT: Yale University Press, 2001), pp. 12-13.

39 M. Emdad-ul Haq, *Drugs in South Asia: From the Opium Trade to the Present Day* (New York: St, Martin's, 2000) pp.175-86; Ahmed Rashid, *Taliban: Militant Islam, Oil, and Fundamentalism in Central Asia* (New Haven: Yale University Press, 2001) pp.12-13.

40 U.S. Congress, Senate, Committee on Foreign Relations, *The BCCI Affair*, by Senators John Kerry and Hank Brown [the "Kerry-Brown Report"](Washington, D.C.: GPO, 1992), pp. 27-28. Peter Truell and Larry Gurwin, *False Profits: The Inside Story of BCCI, the World's Most Corrupt Financial Empire* (Boston: Houghton Mifflin, 1992), pp. 123, 130. In Scott, *Drugs, Oil, and War*, pp. 46-47.

41 Joseph J. Trento, *The Secret History of the CIA* (New York: Forum/Crown/Random House, 2001), pp. 410, 466-67. John Loftus and Mark Aarons, *The Secret War Against the Jews* (New York: St. Martins, 1994), p. 395. In Scott, *Drugs, Oil, and War*, p. 47.

42 Emadi, *State, Revolution, and Superpowers in Afghanistan*, pp. 3, 52-53. Cooley, *Unholy Wars*, p. 3. Both cited in Katherine Harvey, "Afghanistan, the United States, and the Legacy of Afghanistan's War," *EDGE*, 5/6/03, http://www.stanford.edu/class/e297a/Afghanistan,%20 the%20United%20States.htm#_ftn9.

43 On interview with media in France, see "How Jimmy Carter and I Started the Mujahideen: Interview with Zbignew Brzezinski," *La Nouvelle Observateur*, January 15-21, 1998, p. 76, http://www.proxsa.org/resources/9-11/Brzezinski-980115-interview.htm. On U.S. intelligence reports, see Digital National Security Archive, 12 May 2003, http://nsarchive.chadwyck.com/afinitio.htm. Barnett R. Rubin, testimony before the House Foreign Affairs Committee, Subcommittee on Europe and the Middle East and Subcommittee on Asia and the Pacific, "Answers to Questions for Private Witnesses," March 7, 1990, p. 5. All cited in McCoy, *The Politics of Heroin*, p. 449.

44 U.S. intelligence Agency, memorandum, "Subject: Iran—An Opium Cornucopia," Sept. 27, 1997. Malthea Falco, "Asian Narcotics: The Impact on Europe," *Drug Enforcement* (February 1979), pp. 2-3; U.S. CCINC, *World Opium Survey 1972*, pp. A-7, A-14, A-17. U.S. State Department, Bureau of International Narcotics Matters, *International Control Strategy Report* (1984) pp.4, 7-8. William French Smith, Drug Traffic Today: Challenge and Response," *Drug Enforcement* (Summer 1982) pp.2-3. All referenced in McCoy, *The Politics of Heroin*, pp. 446-47. After two years of droughts in the original Golden Triangle of Southeast Asia, it re-emerged to equal the production of the Southern Asian Pakistan-Afghan border. The Golden Triangle produced about 1,000 tons of opium to equal the same amount produced along the Pakistan-Afghan border each year. During the 1980s the Golden Triangle shared half of the First World markets with the Pakistan-Afghan area "Golden Crescent." U.S. State Department, Bureau of International Narcotics Matters, *International Control Strategy Report* (1984), pp. 4, 7-8. U.S. State Department, Bureau of International Narcotics Matters, *International Control Strategy Report* (1990), pp. 19-20. Both cited in McCoy, *The Politics of Heroin*, p. 447.

45 All from McCoy, *The Politics of Heroin*, p. 447, except the section on Casey. That is from the *Washington Post*, July 19, 1992, referenced in Scott, *Drugs, Oil, and War*, p. 49.

46 On guerilla attacks, Ahmed Rashid, *Jihad: The Rise of Militant Islam in Central Asia* (New Haven: Yale University Press, 2002), p. 43. On Hekmatyar leading them, Ahmed Rashid, *Taliban: Militant Islam, Oil and Fundamentalism in Central Asia* (New Haven, CT: Yale University Press/Nota Bene, 2001), p. 129. On heroin labs, M. Emdad-ul Haq, Drugs in *South Asia: From the Opium Trade to the Present Day* (New York: St. Martin's, 2000), p. 189. All cited in Scott, *Drugs, Oil, and War*, pp. 49-50. On leading drug lord, founder of Muslim Brotherhood, see Steven Galster, "Biography: Hekmatyar, Gulbuddin," National Security Archives, Washington, DC, March 14, 1990; Tariq Ali, *Can Pakistan Survive?* (Penguin, 1983), pp. 139-42. Note that Hekmatyar was said to have followers throw vials of acid in the faces of women who didn't wear veils, when he organized opposition to a king who allowed secular reforms. John F. Burns, "Afghans: Now They Blame America," *New York Times Magazine*, February 4, 1990, p. 37. On Reuters quote, see Levon Sevunts, "Who's Calling the Shots? Chechen conflict finds Islamic roots in Afghanistan and Pakistan," *The Gazette*, Montreal, October 26, 1999. On these Hakmatyar-trained Chechen leaders leading Chechens in 1995 war, see Vitaly Romanov and Viktor Yadukha, "Chechen Front Moves to Kosovo," Rossiya Segodnya (Moscow), February 23, 2000. These last two articles were referenced by Prof. Michel Chossudovsky, "The Sochi Olympic Games and the Threat of a Terrorist Attack. Who is Behind the Caucasus Terrorists?" *Global Research*, February 6, 2014, http://www.globalresearch.ca/the-sochi-olympic-games-and-the-threat-of-a-terrorist-attack-who-is-behind-the-caucasus-terrorists/5367601.

47 On Marenches plan, Cooley, *Unholy Wars*, pp. 128-29; Jonathan Beaty and S.C. Gwynne, *The Outlaw Bank: A Wild Ride in the Heart of the BCCI* (New York: Random House, 1993), pp. 305-06. On reports of drugs reaching Soviet troops and American intelligence operatives, Beatty and Gwynne, *The Outlaw Bank*, pp. 82, 306; also Stephane Allix, *La petite cuillere de Scheherazade, sur la route de l'heroine* (Paris: Editions Ramsay, 1998), pp. 35, 95. On Orth and Falco's statement, Maureen Orth, *Vanity Fair*, March 2002, pp. 170-71. A Tajik sociologist added that she knew "drugs were massively distributed at that time," and that she often heard how Russian soldiers were "invited to taste." All cited in Scott, *Drugs, Oil, and War*, p. 49.

48 *Washington Post*, May 13, 1990. On increase of addicts in Pakistan, Pakistan Narcotics Control Board, *National Survey on Drug Abuse in Pakistan* (Islamabad: Narcotics Control Board, 1986), pp. iii, ix, 23, 108; Zahid Hussain, "Narcopower: Pakistan's Parallel Government?" *Newsline* (Karachi), December 1989, p. 17. McCoy, *The Politics of Heroin*, pp. 453, 455

49 On 1971-78, see McCoy, *The Politics of Heroin*, p. 446. On 1999, see Cooley, *Unholy Wars*, p. 139. Cited in Scott, *Drugs, Oil, and War*, pp. 40-41.

Chapter Twenty-One

Kurt Cobain's Death: Love, Heroin & Police Cover-Up

Punk rock expressed the way I feel socially and politically.... Drugs are a waste of time. They destroy your memory and your self-respect and everything that goes along with your self-esteem. They're no good at all.... The duty of youth is to challenge corruption.... Rap music is the only vital form of music introduced since punk rock.... I would like to get rid of the homophobes, racists and sexists in our audience. I know they're out there and it really bothers me.

– Kurt Cobain, various quotes.

"Nevermind" came without a lyric sheet.... At first he wanted to print some of his poems, then some "revolutionary debris."... Kurt says "revolutionary debris" meant "all kinds of anarchistic, revolutionary essays and diagrams about how to make your own bomb. And I just thought we better hold off on that," he says. "If we ever really want to do that, we'd be more effective if we gained popularity first."

– From *Come As You Are: The Story of Nirvana*, published shortly before Cobain's death.

Kurt Cobain sang, wrote the lyrics and played guitar for the band Nirvana. They were widely considered the most influential band of the 1990s, despite Cobain's death at the age of twenty-seven in 1994. While the band topped the music charts for sales, its music, then considered "punk rock," fell into the all-purpose genre of "alternative." Later music critics considered Nirvana the founders of the "grunge" music sound. Cobain, like a number of other grunge musicians, developed a heroin problem in the early 1990s.

Heroin & Alternative/Punk Musicians

As the Afghan heroin-producing opium supply grew in the 1990s, American and European consumption also grew. While a number of mainstream musicians developed heroin problems, heroin use appeared even more popular among a fringe collection of artists and musicians who lived in urban areas. From the 1960s to the 1990s, a number of these musicians who became influential in alternative music developed heroin problems. Some of them also crossed paths with members of U.S. intelligence.

In the 1960s, John Lennon, who had glorified heroin use with his Beatles' *White Album* song "Me and My Monkey," referring to the slang "monkey on my back" for addiction, had spies watching him closely. Velvet Underground lead-singer songwriter Lou Reed, managed by suspected spy Miles Copeland III, wrote "Heroin" and "Waiting for My Man." White House physician Max "Dr. Feelgood" Jacobson regularly gave psychedelics and amphetamines or cocaine-with-heroin "speedballs" to people who attended Andy Warhol's parties, where the Velvet Underground first performed as the house band. Jacobson had also frequented Timothy Leary's gatherings. World-renowned artist Warhol produced the Velvet Underground's influential first albums.[1]

In the 1970s, one of the first American punk icons, Iggy Pop, had a known heroin addiction while his band, the Stooges, popularized aggressive, intelligent, "pre-punk" rock music. Anarchist punk-rock icon Sid Vicious, of early '70s British punk-rock band, the Sex Pistols, reportedly died of uncertain causes after a slip-up with heroin following some clean time. His girlfriend Nancy Spungeon developed her heroin addiction when living in New York prior to their meeting. She traveled to England and moved in with Vicious. Spungeon died of a knife wound four months before Vicious. Vicious had at one point been implicated in her death, but British investigators never came to a conclusion about who killed her.[2]

By the 1980s, more punk-inspired musicians developed heroin problems. For example, Australian punk singer Nick Cave started using heroin and glorified the drug with compelling lyrics and music for his band, The Birthday Party. In Sydney, Australia, CIA and Special Forces veteran Michael Hand joined businessman Frank Nugan to form Nugan Hand Bank. Nugan had notes from CIA Director William Colby, and other top CIA help, in aiding heroin traffickers. Prof. Peter Dale Scott said that Nugan Hand Bank financed the first major drug imports, "organized by veterans of U.S. Special Forces and CIA in Laos." Australian heroin addiction rose dramatically in the late 1970s.[3]

Researchers argued that drug dealers directed much of the cocaine and heroin mostly to urban American black and Hispanic communities.

Urban whites were more likely to try heroin and cocaine if they lived in these racially mixed neighborhoods.[4] With top music magazines *Rolling Stone* and *Spin* calling Nirvana the most influential band of the 1990s, its frontman Kurt Cobain had the greatest effect in popularizing heroin to the white community.[5]

Cobain as Radical Political Leftist

Kurt Cobain grew up in a middle-class neighborhood of Aberdeen, Washington, where artists and musicians in his family helped cultivate his early development. By the age of twenty, Cobain started the band Nirvana and had a relationship with Tobi Vail, who was in the all-female, radical political band Bikini Kill. Vail and Bikini Kill singer Kathleen Hanna helped influence Cobain's increasingly radical leftist politics.[6]

Bikini Kill's feminist politics followed the lineage of radical-leftist punk rockers, The Clash.[7] Post-punk bands such as Washington DC's "hardcore" band Fugazi continued in this vein, and was well known for its "straight edge" anti-drug lifestyle. This term came from the song "Straight Edge," by Fugazi singer Ian McKaye's former band, Minor Threat (without co-lead singer Guy Picciotto).

As a teenager, Kurt Cobain recreationally used alcohol and marijuana, and soon used psychedelic drugs a few times. By the late 1980s, Cobain loved Fugazi, and even had their name written on his shoes. In 1989, Nirvana had produced its first album *Bleach,* for local Seattle independent record label Sub Pop.[8]

Soon, major labels courted Nirvana, and the band decided to sign with Geffen. Sonic Youth, another Geffen client, took Nirvana with them on their European tour as the opening act in 1991, filming it for the movie *1991:The Year that Punk Broke.*[9]

An MTV video, "Smells Like Teen Spirit," helped Nirvana break out globally in the late summer of 1991. Their album *Nevermind* hit the top of the pop charts in the U.S. and seven other countries by the beginning of 1992, selling five million copies in four months. *Nevermind* would go on to sell 10 million copies in the U.S. and 30 million worldwide by 2011.[10]

Journalists noted how *Nevermind*'s unmatched success changed the course of music, the recording industry and even fashion.[11] The "grunge" look of jeans, t-shirts, or flannel shirts to keep warm, were popularized by the clothing Kurt Cobain and his fellow band members continued to wear even after they began making lots of money.

Nirvana's album covers presented subtle and not-so-subtle political statements. The cover of *Nevermind* had a baby submerged in a pool reaching for a dollar bill on a fishhook. The album *In Utero,* banned by

Wal-Mart and K Mart supposedly for Cobain's sculpture of fetuses on its cover, also contained four pictures of the burnt-out Los Angeles Republican Party Headquarters during the 1992 Los Angeles riots. Cobain further forced *Rolling Stone* magazine to display his t-shirt in their cover picture of him. He had written on the shirt: "Corporate Magazines Still Suck."[12]

Leftist Nirvana frontman Kurt Cobain wore a shirt stating "Corporate Magazines Still Suck" on the cover of *Rolling Stone*. Police whistleblowers say their supervisor ordered them only to investigate his death as a suicide, not the murder that evidence suggested.

Not everyone was aware of Kurt Cobain's left-wing political passions. Michael Azzerad published a biography of the band, *Come as You Are,* six months before Cobain's death, revealing Cobain's politics that ranged from pro-Democrat to radical anarchist. On the mainstream side, Cobain urged his fans to vote for Bill Clinton in 1992, and was credited with making the difference in Clinton's win over George H.W. Bush. In that election, youth came out to vote in the largest percentages since the voting age was first lowered in the 1960s.[13]

Cobain's political actions were often discreet, such as putting an anonymous track on an AIDS benefit album, and participating in benefits for abortion rights groups, anti-bigotry organizations, and anti-censorship organizations. He also battled prejudice by publicizing his hypothetical bisexuality and hatred of homophobia.[14]

More radically, Cobain was quoted as saying he originally wanted to put "revolutionary debris" inside his hugely popular album *Nevermind.* He said this meant "all kinds of anarchistic, revolutionary essays and diagrams about how to make your own bomb. And I just thought we better hold off on that ... we'd be more effective if we gained popularity first. Then people might actually think twice about it."[15]

While Cobain's lyrics remained more personal and apolitical, he consistently made liberal-to-revolutionary political statements in other public forums. In the band's first biography, Cobain said his popular single "Lithium" was an update on *Communist Manifesto* author Karl Marx's statement on religion as the opiate of the masses.[16] In interviews he took a leftist perspective, mocking the American economic system, saying if major record labels bought up all the alternative bands, then, "Chalk one up for capitalism. Let's get our top hats and tails and have a cigar."[17]

Love, Marriage and Heroin

Canadian award-winning writers Max Wallace and Ian Halperin spent years investigating Cobain's death, after musicians they knew said it was suspicious. Wallace wrote for the *New York Times* and contributed to the British Broadcasting Corporation. Halperin co-authored two best-selling books, was a regular correspondent on Court TV and contributed to *60 Minutes 2*. Their first book, *Who Killed Kurt Cobain,* came out in 1998. They published *Love and Death: The Murder of Kurt Cobain* in 2004. They gained much assistance from a police detective-turned private investigator, Tom Grant, whom Cobain's wife Courtney Love had hired in early April of 1994. Grant started investigating her on his own, after he found evidence of foul play.

Wallace and Halperin chronicled how Kurt Cobain met his wife, singer Courtney Love, after his first album with major label Geffen Records was released. Love, who had left another husband a year before, became pregnant with Cobain's child within several months of their meeting. Some of Cobain's close friends, such as Dylan Carlson, said Love's pregnancy prompted Cobain to propose to her. They were married in February of 1992 with a prenuptial agreement, which barred either getting the other's money via divorce. By that time some band members had become unhappy with Cobain's budding heroin addiction and disapproved of Courtney Love. Nirvana bassist Krist Novoselic and all family members of Cobain and Love were absent from the wedding.[18]

Cobain's wife Courtney Love hired private detective Tom Grant to look for Cobain. Grant reported finding that Cobain was leaving her and that she played a part in his murder.

Most reports had Cobain's regular heroin use starting at the same time he started dating Courtney. Love's father and ex-husband both said she had a regular heroin addiction while she lived with them. After the birth of Cobain and Love's child, *Vanity Fair* published an article about Love, describing her heroin addiction.[19] Kurt Cobain's heroin addiction reportedly reached its peak when he almost failed to complete a *Saturday Night Live* performance. Cobain went to detox in September 1992.[20]

Kurt Cobain apparently relapsed with heroin after his detox. In an incident less than a year prior to his death, on May 2, 1993 Cobain had shot up heroin in what private detective Tom Grant reported as an accidental overdose. Grant obtained the police report, and reprinted a copy of it in his *Case Study Manual.* It says that after Cobain became semiconscious from the accidental overdose, Courtney claimed to have tried to revive him by injecting him with buprenorphine. She also force-fed him Valium and four codeine-based Tylenol pills, containing acetaminophen and Benadryl. Grant said that adding these drugs to Cobain's system put him at much greater risk of death.[21]

While the full extent of Cobain's heroin addiction remains uncertain, reports suggest that a stomach problem he had since he was a teenager was the trigger for his continued drug use. The stomach ailment left him vomiting, starving and in bed for weeks. The most commonly prescribed medication for stomach ailments, Paragoric, included a tincture of opium, as it relieved intestinal problems. Cobain ended up trying morphine and then used heroin. However, in the summer of 1993, a doctor diagnosed Cobain's problem as a pinched nerve and successfully treated it, along with prescribing a medication that helped sustain his treatment. Virtually all reports supported Cobain's abstinence from heroin while on this medication.[22]

By September 1993, Nirvana released their second album with Geffen Records, *In Utero*, which topped the pop sales charts its first week out. Shortly before the album's release, Kurt Cobain increased his share of the band's formerly equally divided royalties, since he had written most of the songs. Friends said Love had nagged him repeatedly for almost two years to make these changes with his bandmates. Cobain reluctantly threatened to quit the band unless his bandmates accepted his getting 100% of money from the lyrics and 75% of royalties from the music, to be applied retroactively to *Nevermind*'s sales. This caused a rift between Cobain and his band.[23]

Now that they were rich, Courtney Love insisted she and Cobain live in an expensive house in the wealthiest neighborhood, the polar opposite of their apartment in the seedy university district of Seattle. Living across a lake from billionaire Bill Gates, Cobain complained to friends he was embarrassed by the house's extravagance. Cobain's friend Peter Cleary said the singer booked a 38-day European tour partly because he "was like an emotional cripple around his wife, but on tour … he was the boss." Cobain was certain to gain some independence, since Courtney couldn't accompany him while she was mixing her band Hole's upcoming album.[24]

A recent American tour had exhausted Cobain, but he felt ready for the European tour, as he was "exhilarated by the absence of his stomach problems." However, after the first show in Munich, Germany, a doctor diagnosed Cobain with bronchitis and suggested he take two months off from his tour.[25]

Kurt Cobain had gotten into increasing conflicts with his wife by this time. Their lawyer, Rosemary Carroll, said they had become hateful towards each other. Cobain had finally decided to leave Love, wanting a divorce. Love called and asked Carroll to find her, "the meanest, most vicious divorce lawyer" she knew.[26]

Nonetheless, Cobain adored his one-and-a-half year-old daughter Frances, and missed her on his music tours. So he asked Love to bring Frances and meet him in Rome. Love had flown to London for publicity regarding her upcoming album. Love and Frances met with Cobain in a hotel in Rome on March 3, 1994.[27]

Around 6:15 A.M. the next day, Love called the front desk and asked them to get an ambulance, as she had found Cobain unconscious on the floor. Twenty-four hours later, Cobain woke up from what the doctor described as a pharmacological coma "due not to narcotics, but the combined effect of alcohol and tranquilizers which had been medically prescribed by a doctor [to Love]." Everyone called it an accidental overdose. No one but Love ever referred to it as a suicide attempt.[28]

Back home in Seattle two weeks later on March 18, Courtney Love called 911 and said her husband had locked himself in a room with a gun and was threatening to kill himself. When police arrived at their Lake Washington estate, they found Cobain behind a locked door, but their report said he told them he was in there "to keep away from Courtney." The report further said he insisted that he didn't want to hurt himself and that he didn't have a gun in the room with him. When the police questioned Love about her false report, she apparently admitted not seeing him take a gun, and said she didn't hear him say he was going to kill himself. The officers confiscated Cobain's four guns from the house, a box of ammunition and, importantly, Cobain's stomach medication pills. Cobain bought another rifle at the end of March.[29]

In late March, Cobain and Love reportedly battled over his wanting to back out of the scheduled headlining of the Lollapalooza tour, which would have made him millions of dollars, along with millions for others. Soon after this conflict, Cobain called his fellow bandmembers to announce he was breaking the band up. Subsequently, Love and several of Cobain's management executives did an intervention on Cobain, during which Love threatened to limit Cobain's access to his daughter unless he went into rehab. Much evidence suggests that Cobain had largely gotten away from narcotics at this time. But whether or not he had a "slip" with his heroin use, he felt threatened enough to enter Exodus residential treatment in Los Angeles on March 30.[30]

Murder and Heroin Chic

Private detective Tom Grant said that on Friday, April 1, Courtney Love called the Exodus pay phone thirteen times. Kurt Cobain left rehab

Courtney and Kurt in happier times?

later that day. Exodus and most other long-term residential drug treatments centers are not locked-down facilities. Cobain entered under his own volition, so he could have told staff he wanted to leave and walked out the door without a problem, ignoring their suggestions for him to stay. Instead, he avoided talking to staff about deciding to leave early, and climbed over a six-foot wall in the back, according to journalists Wallace and Halperin.[31]

Soon after leaving rehab that Friday night at 8:47 P.M., Cobain called the Peninsula Hotel in L.A., where Courtney Love was staying, and left a message for her. The message said he was staying with a friend, leaving Love the number of the friend, a woman named Elizabeth in California. Cobain then took a plane flight to Seattle early the next morning. From her Peninsula Hotel room, Love called private detective Tom Grant on April 3, purportedly to hire him to look for her husband, alleging she didn't know where he was.

According to Grant, he brought another investigator with him and they met with Love in her hotel room, where she told them about having a phony story planted with the Associated Press, saying she had overdosed on drugs and was in the hospital. Grant claimed Love said she did this to get Cobain's attention.[32]

On that day, Love also evidently told Grant she had Cobain's credit card canceled and wanted Grant to call the credit card company to find out about attempted activities on the card. The following day, Grant said Love told him that she had called in a missing person's report pretending to be Kurt's mother, Wendy O'Connor. On April 6, Love sent Grant to Seattle to look for Cobain, but Grant had no luck finding him.[33]

Just a few days later, on April 8, 1994, an electrician found Kurt Cobain dead in a sunroom above the garage of his home. The coroner said he had been dead since April 5. Most reports say he committed suicide by shooting himself in the mouth with a shotgun. However, evidence points to high-level police and media cover-up of a murder scenario in which Cobain's wife Courtney took part.

Cobain's death made front-page news worldwide. Virtually all the stories repeated a Seattle police spokesman's account that Cobain had been shooting heroin intravenously in the sunroom, then used a shotgun to commit suicide. Media looked for suicidal statements, magazines lauded his musical influence, but most mainstream investigative reporters did little-to-no investigation of a possible homicide.

Investigators Say Cobain Was Murdered

During the next ten years, independent investigations about Cobain's "suicide" found links to U.S. intelligence foul play, but there was extremely sparse mainstream media coverage until the new millennium. Award-winning investigative journalist Duff Wilson published a story in the *Seattle Times* a month after Cobain's death. Wilson's sources in the Seattle Police Department told him that many facts in Cobain's case didn't add up. For example, private detective Tom Grant found and shared with police that someone tried to use Cobain's credit card between the time of his death and his body being found. Additionally, the suicide note didn't appear to be about suicide at all, and the handwriting changed part way through it. With the knowledge from his former police detective work, Grant said the police also made the highly doubtful claim that there weren't any legible fingerprints on the shotgun.[34]

After publishing these inconsistencies, neither Wilson nor the *Seattle Times* followed up with a long-term investigation. More importantly, a police officer investigator working at the scene said his supervisor told the team of police investigators that they were not to investigate Cobain's death as a homicide, making it clear from the start that the so-called homicide investigation was just a show. The officer said this highly surprised him and other police investigators, especially with the change in handwriting on the suicide note at a particularly important point. That part of the note was only a goodbye to fans; the band acknowledged that Cobain was breaking them up.[35]

Grant, Wallace and Halperin investigated Cobain's death as a homicide for years. Grant continued to communicate with Love for some months after Cobain's body was found. She then stopped talking to Grant after she realized he had started investigating her.[36]

After refusing countless lucrative financial offers for over fifteen years, Tom Grant eventually came out with his own independently published books on this subject. He had formerly only shared much of his work with authors Max Wallace and Ian Halperin, for their books. Wallace and Halperin also produced a film, *The Cobain Case,* based on these books. It was released in Europe, while American media refused to even make mention of it, except on YouTube. It includes recorded conversations between Tom Grant and Courtney Love, along with their lawyer, Rosemary Carroll. This film further shows Cobain's grandfather Leland Cobain, the relative to whom Cobain was closest. Leland Cobain and his wife Iris didn't believe Kurt was suicidal. Leland also believes his grandson was murdered.[37]

The books and movie offer extensive evidence that someone murdered Kurt Cobain by first giving Cobain an extremely pure dose of heroin that left him unconscious within seconds. That person or another then put a shotgun in Cobain's hands and shot him in the mouth to make it look like a suicide.

Some of the accumulated evidence supporting this murder scenario includes the amount of opiates in Cobain's corpse, accompanied by Valium, which potentiates heroin. Cobain had a morphine level seventy times higher than the amount that would kill the average person, and three times the amount of heroin that would *immediately* incapacitate and kill even a severe addict.[38] This suggests that someone gave Cobain a "hot shot"—a dose many times the normal 5% purity of street-bought heroin.[39]

Most importantly, Cobain's and Love's lawyer of two years, Rosemary Carroll, said it was obvious Cobain didn't write the last part of his "suicide" note, which, as mentioned, appeared to be a goodbye to fans regarding the band's breakup.[40]

In 1997, the NBC-TV show *Unsolved Mysteries* released Cobain's autopsy report findings to Cyril Wecht, President of the American Academy of Forensic Science. He said, "For most people, including addicts, [this] is a significant level. And for most of them, the great percentage, it will be a level that will induce a state of unconsciousness quite quickly. We're talking about seconds, not minutes." He continued, "I just can't tell you that it would have been impossible" that Cobain then pulled the trigger of the shotgun, "but it does raise a question as to whether or not *he* shot that shotgun."[41]

Wecht went on to say, off camera, "If it *was* suicide, he probably would have had to be holding the gun in his hand while he was injecting himself with the heroin, and then shot himself immediately after the injection." As seen in the trailer for an important movie on Cobain's murder, *Soaked in Bleach*, Dr. Wecht said, "I can not think of a case in which someone injects himself with a large amount of heroin and then proceeds to kill himself. It just doesn't make sense."[42]

Denise Marshall, a deputy coroner in Colorado who has investigated hundreds of deaths said, "When I saw the blood morphine results of the toxicology tests [I asked myself] how could he have pulled the trigger? ... It would have been virtually impossible."[43]

Did Courtney Love Help Set Up Cobain's Murder?

Ian Halperin, Max Wallace and Tom Grant found particularly strong evidence that Courtney Love helped set up her husband's murder, partly to get his money, since the prenuptial agreement would have nullified any alimony she could have gotten with a divorce.[44] Attorney Rosemary Carroll, whom the couple had also named godmother to their daughter, first raised the possibility of Love setting up Cobain's murder. Cobain had felt so close to Carroll, he told friends he regarded her as a surrogate mother. Carroll said Cobain wasn't suicidal, and that Cobain was divorcing Love. Carroll discussed her suspicions with Grant, who taped most of his phone conversations about the case. They are summarized in *Love and Death,* can be heard on Grant's website, and were played for reporters in April 2004.[45]

Grant said Love originally told him that Cobain had prematurely left a residential drug treatment facility and that she was looking for him. Within twenty-four hours she apparently changed her story, saying first she thought Cobain was suicidal, and then that Cobain was divorcing her and leaving her for another woman.[46]

Besides Love asking Carroll to find her the "most vicious divorce lawyer," she wanted to know if her prenuptual agreement could be voided. Meanwhile, Cobain had called Carroll and asked her to take Courtney out of his recently drafted will, which was still unsigned. Award-winning filmmaker Nick Broomfield interviewed a young female nanny the couple employed, who also said Love was obsessed with Cobain's will, in Broomfield's film *Kurt and Courtney*.[47]

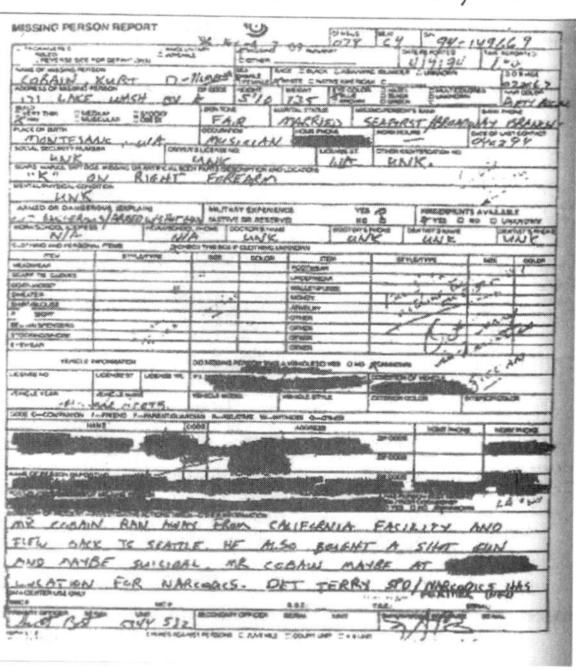

MISSING PERSON REPORT

94-149669

COBAIN, KURT

171 LAKE WASH BV E

5'10 135

FAIR

MARRIED

MONTESANO, WA

MUSICIAN

UNK

UNK

UNK.

"K" ON RIGHT FOREARM

UNK

N/A

N/A

UNK

UNK

UNK

UNK

MR COBAIN RAN AWAY FROM CALIFORNIA FACILITY AND FLEW BACK TO SEATTLE. HE ALSO BOUGHT A SHOT GUN AND MAYBE SUICIDAL. MR COBAIN MAYBE AT [redacted] LOCATION FOR NARCOTICS. DET TERRY SPD/NARCOTICS HAS

Grant said Love filed this false missing person's report, which was taken by Det. Antonio Terry. When Terry defied his supervisors and investigated Cobain's death as murder, he became the first Seattle cop gunned down in seven years.

On April 6th, two days prior to the discovery of Cobain's body, Love visited Carroll and accidentally left behind her backpack. After Cobain's corpse was found, Carroll looked through Love's backpack and found two pieces of paper. One was a "to do" note that read, "Get Arrested." (On April 7, Love was arrested after a reported overdose. It gave her an alibi for where she was when her husband was found dead.) The second piece of paper looked like handwriting practice, as if to forge a letter. Carroll took the backpack to private detective Grant, who secretly copied the suicide note that Love refused to show anyone after the police investigation. After Grant showed Carroll the note, Carroll said she didn't believe Cobain killed himself, and added that Love "planned the whole thing."[48]

Carroll gave Grant other contents of Love's backpack, including an itemized hotel bill, phone records and messages from where she stayed the week that Cobain died. It seemed that Love lied to Grant about her many contacts with Cobain the day he left rehab.[49]

Many believe Love lied in saying Cobain was suicidal. Besides Carroll's statement, Cobain's closest friend, Dylan Carlson, told Grant that Cobain was confronting some issues, but was optimistic about them, not suicidal. Two psychologists who evaluated Kurt Cobain in the rehabilitation center didn't find him suicidal either. Friends who visited Cobain in rehab saw him happily playing with his infant daughter.[50] Cobain's grandfather, Leland, said Kurt wasn't suicidal, and had asked Leland to help him choose a new pick-up truck to buy. Even Courtney admitted once, "I don't think he was really suicidal when he came home [from drug rehab]."[51]

Though Courtney Love said Kurt Cobain's brief coma due to accidentally overdosing on her sleep medication in Rome was a suicide attempt, details suggest it was another attempt by Love to kill him. When the hospital pumped Cobain's stomach they found evidence of Rohypnol, the infamous "Roofie" drug used to dope and rape women, as the drug leads them not to remember anything that happened. In Rome these are most commonly known as sedatives or sleeping pills.[52] Love's very questionable behavior around Cobain's death a month later, and the impending divorce, suggests Love may have slipped a massive amount of Rohypnol in Cobain's drink that night in Rome.

Love and several others had pressured Cobain to go into drug rehab. After Cobain left rehab early and got back to Seattle, he talked to Michael "Cali" Dewitt, another live-in nanny for the couple's infant daughter. Hotel phone records show Love talked to Dewitt continuously that week, even though she had her daughter with her in an L.A. hotel.[53]

Dewitt was a former boyfriend of Love's and a known heroin user. Grant and Carroll stated suspicions about Dewitt's role in Cobain's murder. Grant found a note Dewitt wrote to Cobain at Cobain's home, in the time between the singer's presumed death (April 5) and finding his body in a room above the home's garage (April 8). Grant found the note the night of April 7, and believed it sounded like an attempt to cover up Dewitt's knowledge of Cobain's death. He'd later learn police had taxi records showing Dewitt left from the Cobain home for a plane flight to L.A. several hours earlier, before Grant arrived.[54]

Phone records and Love's payments to Dewitt and his family point to Dewitt as a suspect in Cobain's death. Phone records place Dewitt in Cobain's home until April 5, when he left to stay at a friend's place. Dewitt returned briefly on April 7. Love got Dewitt a high-paying job at Geffen Records. Love also paid several hundred thousand dollars to Dewitt's father to renovate her house, and she paid for many of Dewitt's drug detoxes, along with detox for his girlfriend.[55]

Additionally, a Los Angeles-based musician and acquaintance of Love's, Eldon Hoke, made the claim on television and film that Courtney Love had come to his workplace at a record store and offered him $50,000 to kill Cobain. He said she provided him with a plan to make the killing look like a suicide. Hoke's statement was backed by his boss, who overheard part of the conversation, and Hoke passed a lie detector test about this statement with a nationally renowned polygrapher. Many knew Hoke as having a drinking problem, and as someone who would do anything for money. Hoke, however, never followed through on Courtney's offer.[56]

U.S. Intelligence Connection to Cobain's Murder

There is considerable evidence to suggest that Kurt Cobain's wife, Courtney Love, planned her husband's murder. However, investigations fell short in failing to explore why police superiors and mainstream media helped cover up the murder (and why the FBI never investigated). They also failed to explore evidence of possible U.S. intelligence aid in the murder. The only explanation given by Tom Grant for police failures are "professional pride, city politics and potential lawsuits." He claims there were copycat suicides within days of Cobain's death that led police to not reinvestigate whether Cobain was murdered.[57]

Evidence suggests that, unknown to Cobain, U.S. intelligence used him to promote heroin use, similar to the way U.S. intelligence and media assets helped promote acid in the 1960s. Suppressed evidence indicates that U.S. intelligence helped orchestrate Cobain's murder due to his anti-materialistic, radical leftist politics, along with his implicit threat to promote sobriety when he stopped using drugs.

Police foul play started as early as what appeared to be Love's first attempt to kill Cobain. While it's not certain if Love gave Cobain the overly pure batch of heroin he nearly overdosed on in Seattle in May 1993, she was with him and immediately injected him and force-fed him more drugs that could have caused his death. Private Detective Tom Grant asked why Love wasn't "arrested for possessing, injecting and administering illegal drugs." While Grant suggested that it was due to her friendship with certain Seattle Police Department officers, the police department blacked out an entire paragraph of the police report that described Love's actions.[58]

By most accounts, Kurt Cobain finally found abstinence from heroin by the summer of 1993. Ironically, Cobain's near-death experience on March 4 of 1994 actually offered evidence of this. The doctor in Rome found no narcotics in Cobain's system besides the prescription tranquilizer Rohypnol. Cobain's tourmates through Europe said he was not using any drugs, and wouldn't even participate in "the very mild debauchery that went on."[59] Courtney Love said that Kurt Cobain barely drank in his last months alive.[60]

Police also failed to charge Love with any crime in what appeared to be a false report. That was the incident where Love claimed Cobain had locked himself in a room and said he was going to kill himself. Police confiscation of Cobain's prescribed stomach medication could have caused him a setback. Two weeks later she allegedly filed another false police report mentioning that Cobain was suicidal, pretending she was Cobain's mother. Police again failed to charge her, nor investigate why she did this, despite Tom Grant sharing his information with them.[61]

Seattle police have a substantial record of working closely with U.S. intelligence, including acting as provocateurs to infiltrate radical left political groups and promoting illegal drug use among them.[62] Such a history helps make more sense of foul play around Kurt Cobain's death. A source in the Seattle Police Department told researchers he and others in the department had serious doubts about the investigation, especially when the medical examiner declared Cobain's death a suicide immediately upon viewing the corpse. The officer said, "The clincher for many of us was the note. Anybody who saw it thought it was strange."[63] Several years later, the *Unsolved Mysteries* television show hired two national handwriting experts to examine the note. They both confirmed the top part of the note was in Cobain's handwriting, but the bottom was not.[64]

This same police officer also reported that photos taken at the scene of Cobain's death were not developed. Wallace and Halperin obtained an internal memo of this officer's supervisor stating to his superior that he planned never to develop the film.[65]

When authors Wallace and Halperin filed a Freedom of Information Act request for police department internal documents regarding the Cobain investigation, the Seattle Police refused to confirm or deny whether the photos remained in their files.[66] Photo results could have been critical to the case. One of America's most respected forensic pathologists noted, "If somebody actually held Kurt [Cobain]'s hand around the gun and pulled the trigger, some of the blood would probably have splattered on their hand, leaving a void on Kurt's."[67]

Police delayed even a fingerprint analysis on the gun, only to declare nearly a month later there were no legible prints.[68] Similarly, they did not check prints on shell casings or the note until three years later, when a television show about Cobain's death was about to air.[69] And, no follow-up was ever reported on who tried to use Cobain's credit card after his death.

As previously detailed, toxicology reports showed Cobain would most likely have died within seconds from the "hot shot" opiate overdose. Wallace and Halperin cited top medical journals and quoted national forensic pathologists in support of Cobain's having three times the level of opiates in his blood stream than what would immediately kill even a severe addict. A *CIA Assassination Manual* discussed the use of heroin for assassination by causing an overdose.[70]

Detective Grant believed addict Mike Dewitt, one of the nannies for Frances Cobain who was dependent on and close to Love, was involved in Cobain's murder. Colorado deputy coroner Denise Marshall believes that someone drugged Cobain, first with Valium (present in the autopsy report), possibly using the soda can found near him but never tested by police. Either Cobain then relapsed, or the killer injected the lethal dose of heroin in Cobain, before shooting him to create the appearance of a suicide.[71]

The purity of the heroin was one of the first pieces of evidence that U.S. intelligence might have played a part in the actual murder. Whoever gave him the drug would have had to have access to rare, pure heroin, which the government and some police departments have, but which is virtually impossible to find on the street. The extreme degree of police cover-up behavior further supported U.S. intelligence involvement.[72]

Police avoidance of following up on a top witness's account put more of a spotlight on possible police intelligence involvement in Cobain's murder. Eldon Hoke had appeared on the TV show *Hard Copy*, saying Courtney Love asked him to kill Kurt Cobain. *Hard Copy* paid for America's leading polygraph examiner, Dr. Edward Gelb, to administer a polygraph to Hoke about this statement. Hoke's score fell "beyond possibility of deception," twice. Just after that appearance, Hoke and his friends called both Los Angeles and Seattle police departments in an attempt to get the case reopened.[73] This led Seattle police to briefly reopen the Cobain case, saying they would investigate Hoke's report, but no documents show any follow-up.[74]

Policeman Investigates, Becomes Next Victim

One police officer, Detective Antonio Terry, refused to abide by his boss's orders to not conduct a homicide investigation. A month after Cobain's death, *Newsweek* and the *Seattle Times* reported that Det. Terry spent nearly two hundred hours investigating the source of heroin found in Cobain's corpse.[75] A month later, Terry was driving home from work in civilian clothes in an unmarked car when a stranded motorist flagged him down at his known regular exit off the highway. When Terry pulled over and got out of his car to help, two gunmen shot him.[76]

When the case went to trial eighteen months later, it suggested high-level cover-ups of the incident. Although mortally wounded, Terry shot one of his assailants. He then got back into his car, drove to his South Precinct, and made a statement in which he reported one of the shooters saying, "He's a cop." Terry bled to death after making the statement. He was the first police officer killed in the state of Washington in seven years. Someone in the police department then forged Terry's personnel records that day. These details support the gunmen's knowing who he was despite the absence of police trappings, that they tracked his home route, and then squashed any investigation of his murder. And that Det. Terry was murdered for bucking a much higher authority's orders.[77]

The officer who supervised Cobain's death scene also supervised Terry's homicide case.[78] In 1994, it appears, Courtney Love "quietly paid a significant amount of money to Terry's widow," seemingly to help keep Terry's widow from making press statements about her husband's death.[79]

Ongoing Media Coverage Uncovers Facts

Prior to Cobain's death, Love had evidently made a number of false reports to the Seattle police about Cobain's mental health, which she later retracted. And during the investigations afterward, overwhelming evidence emerged of Love's motives for killing her husband, yet she was never investigated.

Cobain was internationally known, a lifestyle image-maker whose music, dress, and even heroin usage influenced millions. So it is almost unbelievable that after his death so few major media organizations ever reported Grant's or Halperin and Wallace's findings. Only after a decade did some broadcast media briefly permit these researchers to present what they found, but none allowed any in-depth investigations. The years-long media cover-up of the evidence indicates CIA involvement, because of the Agency's ability to censor such politically sensitive issues.

As stated previously, U.S. intelligence aided in manufacturing and trafficking massive amounts of heroin from the Pakistan-Afghanistan border.[80] Cobain's heroin use, amongst others', helped popularize the drug for many Americans. Movies that featured white people using heroin began to appear in the 1990s, including *Trainspotting, Permanent Midnight, The Basketball Diaries,* and the Academy Award-winning *Pulp Fiction*. The fashion industry popularized "heroin chic."[81] Overall, the rate of long-term heroin users increased almost ten percent annually from 1990 to 1995.[82] A heroin-using Kurt Cobain helped popularize this trend. A sober Cobain might have turned the trend around, while also turning many on to radical-left politics.

Within five years of Cobain's death, activists embodied the anarchism that Kurt Cobain said he wanted to support with the original idea of essays inside of Nirvana's album *Nevermind,* and the pictures of burnt-out Los Angeles Republican Headquarters after the riots inside their album cover of *In Utero*. Radical activists gathered from around the country in Seattle to protest the World Trade Organization (WTO) summit. The activists claimed the WTO and the International Monetary Fund (IMF) were representing the wealthiest corporations in exploiting people globally. Left-wing groups for which Nirvana held benefits, such as Fairness and Accuracy In Reporting (FAIR), gave much advance promotion to the anti-WTO protests, which ended up including marches, rallies, and ensuing riots. These Seattle protests sparked similar anti-WTO and anti-IMF protests for at least a couple of years, though they were more common abroad than in the U.S.[83]

Kurt Cobain's cofounder of Nirvana, Krist Novoselic, for the occasion formed a band he called No WTO, with Kim Thayil of Soundgarden, and Jello Biafra, the former frontman of the Dead Kennedys. They only released one album, *Live from the Battle in Seattle,* on Biafra's independent Alternative Tentacles label.[84] However, without Kurt Cobain, this musical support for the anti-WTO protest went virtually unnoticed.

Notes

1 On Jacobson, see Martin Lee and Bruce Shlain, *Acid Dreams: The Complete Social History of LSD, the CIA, the Sixties and Beyond* (New York: Grove/Weidenfeld, 1985, 1992), p. 102.

2 Karen Schoemer, "The Day Punk Died," *New York,* Oct. 19, 2008, http://nymag.com/arts/popmusic/features/51394/.

3 Alfred McCoy, *The Politics of Heroin: CIA Complicity in the Global Drug Trade* (New York: Lawrence Hill Books, 1972/1991), pp. 461-78. Peter Dale Scott, *Drugs, Oil and War: The United States in Afghanistan, Colombia and Indochina* (New York: Rowman and Littlefield, 2003), pp. 40-41. On Nick Cave, Simon Hattenstone, "Old Nick," *The Guardian* (London), Feb. 22, 2008, http://www.guardian.co.uk/music/2008/feb/23/popandrock.features.

4 On cocaine and heroin directed into urban communities of color, see Clarence Lusane, *Pipe Dream Blues: Racism and the War on Drugs* (Boston: South End Press, 1999). Also see Gary Webb, *Dark Alliance: The CIA, the Contras and the Crack Cocaine Explosion* (New York: Seven Stories, 1998), particularly the Foreword by U.S. Congresswoman Maxine Waters.

5 Rolling Stone Staff, "Rock Fisticuffs: Nirvana vs. Radiohead," *Rolling Stone,* February 12, 2007, http://www.rollingstone.com/music/blogs/staff-blog/rock-fisticuffs-nirvana-vs-radiohead-20070212.

6 Michael Azerrad, *Come as You Are: The Story of Nirvana* (New York: Doubleday, 1994), pp. 67-68. Charles R. Cross, *Heavier Than Heaven: A Biography of Kurt Cobain* (New York: Hyperion, 2001), p. 152.

7 Steve Hochman, "Can Lollapalooza Cure The Clash?" *Los Angeles Times,* March 12, 1995, http://articles.latimes.com/1995-03-12/entertainment/ca-41764_1_lollapalooza-lineup.

8 On Fugazi on shoes, Darcey Steinke, "Smashing Their Heads on that Punk Rock," *Spin,* October 1993; in John Rocco, ed., *The Nirvana Companion* (New York: Schirmer, 1998), http://www.nirvanafreak.net/art/art36.shtml. On teen and possibly twenties drug use, Brian Libby. "Even in His Youth," AHealthyMe.com. Also, Cross, *Heavier Than Heaven,* p. 75. Note, this author does have some uncertainties about the validity of Cross's information.

9 On Sonic Youth, Michael Azerrad, *Our Band Could Be Your Life* (New York: Little, Brown, 2001). On Sonic Youth recommending Geffen, http://altmusic.about.com/od/artists/a/nirvana.htm. Director David Markey, *1991: The Year Punk Broke* (We Got Power Films, 1992), http://wegotpowerfilms.com/films/punk.html.

10 James Montgomery with Vanessa WhiteWolf, "Nirvana's Big Break with a Smashing Pumpkins Assist," MTV.com News, Sept. 23, 2011, http://www.mtv.com/news/articles/1671270/

kurt-cobain-nirvana-smashing-pumpkins.jhtml. Also Steinke, "Smashing Their Heads on that Punk Rock," in Rocco, *The Nirvana Companion*, p. 82. On 10 million and 30 million albums sold, James Montgomery, "Nirvana's Nevermind By the Numbers," MTV.com News, September 24, 2011, http://www.mtv.com/news/articles/1671298/nevermind-nirvana-album.jhtml.

11 Darcey Steinke, "Smashing Their Heads on that Punk Rock," in Rocco, *The Nirvana Companion*, p. 82.

12 Cover photo, "Nirvana: Inside the heart and mind of Kurt Cobain," *Rolling Stone*, April 16, 1992.

13 Max Wallace and Ian Halperin, *Love & Death: The Murder of Kurt Cobain* (New York: Atria/Simon and Schuster, 2004), p. 196. Census Bureau statistics, from interview with Joanne Chasmire, Human SERVE, 9/2/98. Human SERVE wrote and then promoted the National Voter Registration Act, enacted by Congress in 1993.

14 Azerrad, *Come As You Are*, pp. 241, 312.

15 Azerrad, *Come As You Are*, p. 209.

16 Azerrad, *Come As You Are*, p. 218. Before *Nevermind*, he spray-painted revolutionary and feminist graffiti with Bikini Kill lead singer Kathleen Hanna. *Come As You Are*, p. 211.

17 Bob Gulla, "Architects of Grunge," *Guitar One*, May 2004 (reprinted 1991 interview), p. 90.

18 Wallace and Halperin, *Love and Death*, pp. 44-46. On prenuptual, p. 136.

19 Wallace and Halperin, *Love and Death*, pp. 38-41.

20 Wallace and Halperin, *Love and Death*, pp. 44-45, 48-49, 69.

21 Tom Grant, T*he Kurt Cobain Murder Investigation Case Study Manual* (Lompoc, CA: The Grant Company, 2012,), pp. 68-69.

22 David Fricke, "Kurt Cobain: The Rolling Stone Interview," 1/27/94, in *Rolling Stone* ed.s *Cobain* (New York: Little, Brown, 1994), p. 65. Wallace and Halperin, *Love and Death*, p. 210. Friends also visited him in the drug rehab and reported being surprised by how happy he was. On answer to stomach ailment, Max Wallace and Ian Halperin, *Who Killed Kurt Cobain? The Mysterious Death of an Icon* (Secaucus, NJ: Birch Lane/Carol, 1998), p. 86. More on stomach ailment, *Love and Death*, p. 44.

23 Wallace and Halperin, *Love and Death*, pp. 63-4.

24 Wallace and Halperin, *Love and Death*, pp. 64-5.

25 Wallace and Halperin, *Love and Death*, pp. 65-6.

26 Wallace and Halperin, *Love and Death*, pp. 135-36.

27 Wallace and Halperin, *Love and Death*, pp. 65-66.

28 Wallace and Halperin, *Love and Death*, pp. 65-66.

29 Wallace and Halperin, *Love and Death*, pp. 193-94. On Cobain buying another rifle, see Grant, *The Kurt Cobain Murder Investigation Case Study Manual*, p. 38. Grant included a copy of the receipt that Cobain had his closest friend, Dylan Carlson, put in his name on March 30. Carlson confirmed this to police detective-turned private investigator Grant.

30 Halperin and Wallace, *Love and Death*, pp. 67-69.

31 Halperin and Wallace, *Love and Death*, p. 70.

32 Grant, *The Kurt Cobain Murder Investigation Case Study Manual*, pp. 12-13.

33 Grant, *The Kurt Cobain Murder Investigation Case Study Manual*, pp. 14-15.

34 Linda Keene, Duff Wilson, Ferdinand M. De Leon, Vanessa Ho, Patrick Macdonald, Kery Murakami, Peyton Whitely, "Questions Linger After Cobain Suicide – Credit-Card Activity, Details Of Last Days Intrigue Investigators," *Seattle Times*, May 11, 1994, http://community.seattletimes.nwsource.com/archive/?date=19940511&slug=1909954. Grant provided a copy of the credit card record, noting that the credit card company explained that the listed time of attempted usage was accurate within one hour. Grant, *The Kurt Cobain Murder Investigation Case Study Manual*, pp. 116-17.

35 Wallace and Halperin, *Who Killed Kurt Cobain?* pp. 124, 141-42. On internal memo of police supervisor to his superior, see Wallace and Halperin, *Love and Death*, p. 229. Note that

Wallace and Halperin obtained this police memo through a Freedom of Information Act (FOIA) request. Bandmate Dave Grohl admitted on the Howard Stern Show in 1998 that the band had split up at that time. And other Nirvana bandmate Krist Novoselic told Cobain biographer Charles Cross that they had broken up before his death. Cross, *Heavier Than Heaven*, p. 174.

36 Wallace and Halperin, *Who Killed Kurt Cobain?* pp. 94-95.

37 Keene et al., "Questions Linger After Cobain Suicide." Leland Cobain said this in a documentary, not released in the United States, by Max Wallace and Ian Halperin. Director Ian Halperin, *The Cobain Case* (Canada: Rottin' Rolling Films, 2005), http://www.youtube.com/watch?v=Wjv5zZpA7dQ.

38 On credit card, Wallace and Halperin, *Who Killed Kurt Cobain*? p. 101. On two handwritings, *Love and Death*, pp. 146-49. On Cobain's toxicology, *Love and Death*, p. 75

39 This writer is an addictions counselor who has heard many stories of low purity, and drug-counseling textbooks cite the average purity of street-bought heroin as ranging between 3-5%. Weldon Witters and Peter Venturelli, *Drugs and Society* (Boston: Jones and Bartlett, 1988), p. 233.

40 Wallace and Halperin, *Love and Death*, p. 174.

41 *Unsolved Mysteries*, narrator Robert Stack, Season 9, Episode 13 (total episode #262), aired February 7, 1997, NBC-TV, http://www.youtube.com/watch?v=d7mhtGOfk2s&feature=relmfu Note that Wallace and Halperin appeared to get the quote slightly wrong, but they may have seen extra footage of the taped segment that wasn't aired.

42 Wallace and Halperin, *Love and Death*, p. 85. This author's personal interview with Cyril Wecht via Skype, from the JFK Assassination Conference November 23, 2011. Wecht would later repeat this comment for the film *Soaked in Bleach* (Suburban Hitchhiker/Daredevil, 2014), in a trailer for the film at 3:12: https://www.youtube.com/watch?v=Hyww88llLjc.

43 Wallace and Halperin, *Love and Death*, pp. 77-87.

44 Wallace and Halperin, *Love and Death*, pp. 46, 107, 136, 176, 219, 281.

45 For Tom Grant's website, see http://www.cobaincase.com.

46 Ian Halperin and Max Wallace, *Love and Death*, pp. 102-09.

47 Wallace and Halperin, *Love and Death*, pp. 135-36. This young female nanny can also be seen saying this when interviewed by award-winning filmmaker, Nick Broomfield for his documentary, *Kurt and Courtney* (Strength Ltd, 1998).

48 Wallace and Halperin, *Love and Death*, pp. 148-50.

49 Wallace and Halperin, *Love and Death*, pp. 151-52.

50 Neil Strauss, "The Downward Spiral," in Rolling Stone eds., *Cobain*, p. 83.

51 Wallace and Halperin, *Love and Death*, pp. 211, 220.

52 Wallace and Halperin, *Love and Death*, pp. 197-201.

53 Wallace and Halperin, *Love and Death*, pp. 153, 192.

54 Wallace and Halperin, *Love and Death*, p. 191

55 Wallace and Halperin, *Love and Death*, pp. 190-2.

56 Wallace and Halperin, *Love and Death*, pp. 249-54. Also see Hoke interviewed in Broomfield, *Kurt and Courtney* (Documentary 1988).

57 Grant, *The Kurt Cobain Murder Investigation Case Study Manual*, p. 109.

58 Grant, *The Kurt Cobain Murder Investigation Case Study Manual*, pp. 68-70. It includes a duplicate of the "Seattle Police Report, Drug Overdose, Incident Number 93-191695."

59 Wallace and Halperin, *Love and Death*, p. 80.

60 Wallace and Halperin, *Love and Death*, p. 202.

61 Wallace and Halperin, *Love and Death*, pp. 193-94.

62 Robert Justin Goldstein, *Political Repression in America, 1870 to the Present* (Cambridge/London: Schenckman/Two Continents, 1978), pp. 473-75. *Seattle Times*, December 7, 1970. Referenced in Ward Churchill and Jim Vander Wall, *The COINTELPRO Papers* (Boston: South End Press, 1990), pp. 34-35, 222-23.

63 Wallace and Halperin, *Who Killed Kurt Cobain?* p. 124.

64 Wallace and Halperin, *Love and Death*, p. 176.

65 Wallace and Halperin, *Who Killed Kurt Cobain?* pp. 124, 141-42. On internal memo of police supervisor to his superior, see Wallace and Halperin, *Love and Death,* p. 229. Note that Wallace and Halperin obtained this police memo through a Freedom of Information Act (FOIA) request. Keene et al., "Questions Linger after Cobain Suicide," http://community.seattletimes.nwsource.com/archive/?date=19940511&slug=1909954.

66 Wallace and Halperin, *Love and Death,* p. 229.

67 Wallace and Halperin, *Love and Death,* pp. 228-29.

68 A copy of this actual police document can be found at www.justiceforkurt.com.

69 Grant, *The Kurt Cobain Murder Investigation Case Study Manual,* 1997.

70 On heroin overdose for assassination, see H.P. Albarelli Jr, *A Terrible Mistake: The Murder of Frank Olson and the CIA's Secret Cold War Experiments* (Walterville, OR: TrineDay, 2009), p. 723. It cites a draft CIA Assassination Manual from 1952. On fatal level of opiates in Cobain's bloodstream, journal and pathologist reports, see Wallace and Halperin, *Love and Death,* pp. 81-85.

71 Halperin and Wallace, *Who Killed Kurt Cobain?* pp. 113-14; Wallace and Halperin, *Love and Death,* pp. 75, 77, 93, 188-92.

72 Witters and Venturelli, *Drugs and Society,* p. 233. Many examples of police cover-up include police blacking out report, see Grant, *The Kurt Cobain Murder Investigation Case Study Manual,* pp. 68-70. It presents a duplicate of the "Seattle Police Report, Drug Overdose, Incident Number 93-191695."

73 Wallace and Halperin, *Love and Death,* pp. 253-55.

74 Wallace and Halperin, *Love and Death,* pp. 253-55.

75 Wallace and Halperin, *Love and Death,* p. 247. Wallace and Halperin, *Who Killed Kurt Cobain?* p. 107.

76 Wallace and Halperin, *Love and Death,* p. 245.

77 Later, Terry's personnel records were altered to make it appear he was on duty when murdered, insuring that the killers got life imprisonment if convicted. Wallace and Halperin, *Love and Death,* pp. 246-47.

78 A Washington State Patrol crime lab reported someone altered Terry's checkout sheet in six places. The Seattle police never determined who was responsible nor disciplined anyone for the offense. Wallace and Halperin, *Love and Death,* pp. 246-47.

79 Wallace and Halperin, *Love and Death,* p. 247.

80 Russil Durrant and Jo Thakker, *Substance Use & Abuse: Cultural and Historical Perspectives* (Sage, 2003), p. 87.

81 Jonathan Peterson, "Clinton Dresses Down Fashion Industry for 'Heroin Chic,'" *Los Angeles Times,* May 22, 1997.

82 "Drug Trafficking—Criminal Penalties for Trafficking, Is the Profit Worth the Risk? Substantial World and U.S. Trade," which cites Substance Abuse and Mental Health Administration (SAMHSA) data, http://www.libraryindex.com/pages/2361/Drug-Trafficking-HEROIN.html.

83 On FAIR and WTO protests, Norman Solomon, "Media Beat: Nearing Global Summit, WTO on High Media Ground," FAIR's *Extra!* November 11, 1999, http://fair.org/media-beat-column/nearing-global-summit-wto-on-high-media-ground/. On Nirvana doing benefit for FAIR, Robert Hillburn, "Smells Like Rock Classics: Nirvana's Forum concert demonstrates why the Seattle group may be the most important American rock band since R.E.M," *Los Angeles Times,* January 4, 1994. On Seattle sparking more protests, Geov Parrish, "Is This What Failure Looks Like? Five years after the Battle in Seattle, results are mixed. Third World delegates have gridlocked the WTO but in the U.S. anti-globalization organizers have struggled to convert street heat into policy." *Seattle Weekly,* October 9, 2006.

84 No WTO, *Live from the Battle in Seattle* (Alternative Tentacles, 1999).

Chapter Twenty-Two

Courtney Love: Drugs and Death

Along with the death of Detective Antonio Terry, the officer investigating Kurt Cobain's death, several other deaths were linked to Cobain's. Courtney Love's life and possible links to these deaths give further credence to the idea that she knowingly or inadvertently collaborated with U.S. intelligence. Did U.S. intelligence manipulate the popular Seattle music scene to promote heroin to activist youth, while trying to silence influential leftist musicians such as Cobain?

Witness Dies. Is Wrench a Spy Tool?

Eldon Hoke's claim about Courtney Love trying to inveigle him into murder-for-hire continued to gain importance after his TV interview. In April of 1997, Sundance award-winning documentarian Nick Broomfield interviewed Hoke for his film *Kurt and Courtney.* Hoke repeated his claim about Love's offer. In that interview, Hoke started to pronounce the name of someone he believed did accept Love's offer, saying "Allen ..." before stopping short and laughing nervously. A different interviewer, Brent Alden, said that on April 18 he talked with Hoke, and he was very frightened because he knew who killed Cobain: a local Los Angeles musician, Allen Wrench.[1]

Eldon Hoke died within a week of making this statement; Allen Wrench was the last person seen with Hoke before he died. But private detective Tom Grant said he believes the whole Wrench story is a "hoax." While Grant is one of the best investigators of the Cobain case, he doesn't state why he's so sure Wrench being a suspect is a hoax. Writers Halperin and Wallace took Wrench somewhat seriously. They interviewed Wrench for their book *Love and Death,* and their film *The Cobain Case.* In those interviews, Wrench admitted to killing Cobain.[2]

Information about Wrench both from film and book suggests that he was an undercover U.S. intelligence agent. On film, Wrench, an articulate, clean-cut man, admits to carrying out Cobain's murder. Even if facetious, such an admission would normally be investigated by police, but never was.[3]

Other evidence raises the question of whether U.S. intelligence inserted Allen Wrench into the Los Angeles punk music scene. A number of leftist political punk bands had sprung up in the Los Angeles area, including Black Flag, the Minutemen, and Rage Against the Machine, providing the impetus for U.S. intelligence to open operations there in an attempt to counter leftist political musicians. Allen Wrench clearly had designs to try and depoliticize punk rock. Although Wrench didn't have any visible source of income, he came into wealth soon after Cobain's death. With a house full of expensive recording equipment, he started his own barely profitable label, Devil Vision Records. He also bought a brand new Lexus soon after Cobain's death. Wrench had a few minor arrests in his background, and was a master of Brazilian jiu jitsu.[4]

Wrench also had a surprisingly elaborate website for his local band, Kill Allen Wrench. The band, it declared, is all about "all four rock essentials: Satanic Worship, Alcoholism, Spousal Abuse, and Self Destructive Drug Use!" The website included transcribed interviews from female groupies. It also had an exhaustive gallery of frequently updated pornography. Concert photos of Wrench had him decked out in devil's horns, pentagrams, red glop, and half-naked young groupies. Furthermore, despite suspicions of Wrench murdering Mentors lead singer Eldon Hoke, the two groups toured together with their similar apolitical, female defouling, pseudo-punk, supposedly humorous bands in 2012. Wrench's Facebook pictures include many with Mentors founding bassist Steve Broy playing in Wrench's band.[5]

As previously detailed, Los Angeles had a history of vast U.S. intelligence operations overlapping the entertainment industry, particularly in Laurel Canyon, where the U.S. Air Force's Lookout Mountain Laboratory film studio started in the 1940s, and military folks-turned musicians flocked in the 1960s. Allen Wrench reported regularly playing with Eldon "El Duce" Hoke's band, the Mentors, on the Riverside, California ranch property of Mentors bassist Steve Broy. By 2003, Broy played both in Wrench's band and the Mentors. Riverside lies near Los Angeles, within 70 miles of Laurel Canyon. The Mentors' first album was *Live at the Whiskey*, referring to the Whiskey A-Go-Go, which launched the Laurel Canyon bands in the 1960s. Also, Broy's Riverside property lies in the general vicinity of various Teledyne Technologies military contracting facilities. Riverside lies adjacent to both the Naval Surface Warfare Center and the March Air Reserve Base.[6]

Bassist Steve Broy's biography stated that he started the Mentors with Hoke in Seattle in 1976. They later moved to Los Angeles, though Broy had taken time off from the band to get a degree in engineering. Steve Broy has worked as a "Director of Engineering at Teledyne Analytical Instruments," with a Bachelors degree from the "University of Washington in Electrical Engineering." Prior to Teledyne, Broy worked on military equipment for "TRW in Redondo Beach," in the Los Angeles area, where

TRW has a Heliport (helicopter airport). Mentors bassist Broy confirmed in a 2010 interview that he still worked as an engineer in his day job. MK-Ultra "superspy" Captain Alfred Hubbard also worked for Teledyne while distributing LSD worldwide.[7]

In his aforementioned book *Weird Scenes Inside the Canyon,* Dave McGowan detailed another key aspect of the Laurel Canyon rock scene. In a chapter titled, "Dig! The Laurel Canyon Death List," McGowan reported that at least twenty-seven longtime, or one-time residents of Laurel Canyon, mostly musicians, ended up dead for mysterious reasons. McGowan noted that Laurel Canyon musician "Mama" Cass Elliott reportedly died of "heart failure" at the age of thirty-two. Others died of overdoses, murders, traffic accidents, "natural causes," and purported suicides.[8]

Alex Constantine, author of *The Covert War Against Rock,* believed U.S. intelligence killed Elliott for knowing too much and getting too politically progressive, unlike her previous Mamas and Papas bandmate, former military officer "Papa" John Phillips. Cass apparently had dinner with Bobby Kennedy, Roman Polanski and his actress partner, Sharon Tate, at film director John Frankenheimer's home in 1968. Strangely enough, the followers of musician and sociopath Charles Manson murdered Tate along with coffee heiress Abigail Folger, who had met Manson years earlier in Cass's home and later gave money to Manson and the Process Church cult, of which he was a member.

The only Mamas and Papas member to become successful solo, "Mama" Cass Elliot sold millions of albums while she was getting active in liberal politics. Her early death seemed to involve foul play.

Mama Cass was the only member of The Mamas and The Papas to launch a successful solo career following the group's break up. Cass had been dating Pic Dawson at the time of her death. Scotland Yard had been investigating him for international drug smuggling. Dawson's father worked for the U.S. State department under Henry Kissinger. A Mama Cass biographer filed a FOIA request for FBI documents on her and published twelve pages from her FBI file that were almost entirely redacted, obscured by black ink.

Constantine noted that one report on Mama Cass was marked "urgent" and "confidential," stating that she attended a fundraiser in Hollywood that included Jack Nicholson, Ryan O'Neal, Marlo Thomas, Tuesday Weld, Burt Lancaster and Jane Fonda. The Entertainment Industry for Peace and Justice Committee (EIPJ) organized the event. Cass told television host Mike Douglas about her political ambitions as she organized against the Vietnam War from within the Democratic Party. Leftist writer Paul Krassner said that "Cass was a friend," and believed "she may have been killed." Pathologists in London, where Cass died, refused to specify the cause of death at a public hearing.[9]

David McGowan reviewed some particularly important characters of Laurel Canyon who carried out many murders. Charles Manson befriended Dennis Wilson of the Beach Boys. Manson murderer Charles "Tex" Watson also hung out with Manson at many Laurel Canyon musicians' parties. Watson further handled large drug transactions for Manson. Another Manson murderer, musician Bobby Beausoleil, had the job of driving girls to topless dance clubs and to shoots for porno films. Many of these girls also became part of Manson's acid-drenched "family," similar to Vito Paulekas's acid-fueled dance troupe of proto-hippies who frequented the rock clubs and provided Laurel Canyon parties with orgies. Several of these Manson girls were accomplished musicians and, apparently, murderers.[10]

Courtney Love & MK-Ultra

Courtney Love has lived a bizarre life filled with suspicious overlaps with the goals of the CIA's Operation MK-Ultra. Despite some singing talent, much of Love's life makes her appear a fantasy-driven drug addict seeking glory by marrying a rock star or becoming one. However, closer scrutiny suggests she may have been groomed or conditioned from an early age to carry out some U.S. intelligence tasks.

Courtney Love's father Hank Harrison described his daughter's apparent dissociative identity disorder (previously known as multiple personality disorder) in a book, *Love Kills: The Assassination of Kurt Cobain*. Love had invited Harrison to attend a Hole show in 1993, where Harrison talked with Hole bass player Kristen Pfaff. The bass player told Harrison she feared that Love was going in and out of various personalities as if she appeared "dissociative," and was going through "fugue state amnesia." Harrison said that over the years he also saw Courtney progress through various dissociative states. How she may have gotten this way deserves much consideration.

Linda Carroll (no relation to Rosemary Carroll) was an adopted daughter of a family who had major stock holdings in the Bausch and Lomb eye-care business and in gold mining. Carroll gave birth to Courtney Michelle Harrison on July 9, 1964, in San Francisco, California. Hank Harrison was attending graduate school and working as a counselor, while also managing the Warlocks for six months after they formed in the San Francisco Bay community of Palo Alto in May of 1965. The band soon changed its name to the Grateful Dead. Harrison lived with members of the Grateful Dead, and its bassist, Phil Lesh, became Courtney's godfather. Interestingly, Carroll named her friend, Del Nan Winblad-DeMarco, Courtney's godmother. Winblad-DeMarco's right-wing husband had a huge ranch in Delano and was one of migrant farm workers organizer Cesar Chavez's biggest foes. Courtney was born about sixteen months before the first Acid Tests at which the Grateful Dead performed.[11]

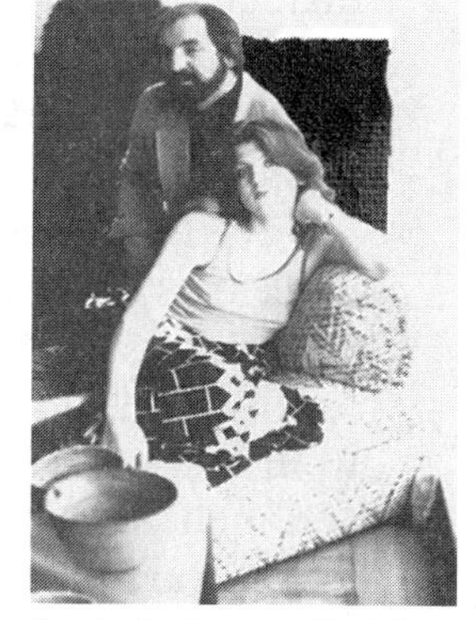

Grateful Dead manager Hank Harrison with his teenage daughter, the future Mrs. Kurt Cobain, Courtney Love, after her incarceration in Oregon. Harrison said she became a prostitute by sixteen and was traveling with a CIA agent at seventeen.

Courtney's parents' history appears to link with MK-Ultra's. In the early 1970s, the Grateful Dead turned against Hank Harrison, as he published a book asserting that the band sold heroin. Linda Carroll was also intimately connected to drug users in Ken Kesey's acid test scene, where high-level CIA MK-Ultra scientists such as John Gittinger attended several Acid Test parties.[12]

Courtney's statement that several witnesses claim she was given LSD at the age of three remains hard to verify. Love said the acid came from her father, but Harrison presented a polygraph test that he passed stating he never gave Courtney acid. Carroll did send her daughter to psychotherapy at the age of three, a strange and uncontested biographical note. Carroll was raising Courtney in San Francisco at that time, near Santa Clara Valley Medical Center, where CIA MK-Ultra scientists conducted narco-hypnosis and behavior modification in association with the Stanford Research Institute. Ken Kesey had also taken part in CIA MK-Ultra experiments at a Stanford-based research program.[13]

Hank Harrison said that Linda Carroll's parents pushed their adopted daughter to separate from him by 1967, when Courtney was three. Linda Carroll said in a memoir that her alcoholic adopted father, Jack Risi, regularly sexually molested her when she was very young. It's unknown what was happening to Courtney, either in childcare, where Carroll said Courtney may have gone through "child abuse," or her "therapy" at that age. But Harrison noted being puzzled as to why Courtney threw tantrums each time he had to take her back to Carroll's home at the end of his weekend custody.

Carroll divorced Harrison by 1968 and took him to court for full custody in 1970. Harrison said her parents used their wealth to extend the hearings for a year and to secretly bribe his lawyer, leading him to lose all rights. He said he went into a deep depression in the following years, as Carroll kept him from seeing Courtney.[14]

In federal hearings on CIA projects in 1995, two women, Chris De Nicola and Claudia Mullen, testified that they were victims of MK-Ultra experiments in subproject "Monarch," starting at three years old, during the same 1967 time period Courtney Love attended psychotherapy. De Nicola's and Mullen's therapist, Valerie Wolfe, also testified, stating that forty other therapists contacted her, with remarkably similar stories from their patients, when they learned she was giving testimony. De Nicola and Mullen testified that LSD, trauma, and hypnosis were used on them from infancy until the age of sixteen, to help turn them into prostitutes and assassins for the CIA. Mullen said that MK-Ultra's John Gittinger and Sidney Gottlieb did the experimental training on her. Other female agents wrote memoirs with similar stories.[15]

The late Jim Keith transcribed much of Claudia Mullen's account in his book *Mass Control*. Keith presented similar public testimony of self-reported CIA victims Katherine Sullivan and the pseudonymous Brice Taylor. Keith further detailed a 1992 speech given by psychologist Dr. Corydon Hammond to an audience of psychology professionals at a regional conference on abuse and multiple personality. Hammond interviewed therapists nationwide to find that in about two-thirds of ritual abuse cases, perpetrators used "a highly developed and uniform technology of mind control."

Hammond said many of these cases had connections to the CIA and military, and employed a type of technology originally created by the CIA. He said one group that practiced this was the Process Church associated with the Manson family. In 1967, Charles Manson lived several blocks from the Process Church headquarters in the CIA- and Prankster-filled Haight Ashbury neighborhood of San Francisco. Process leaders visited Manson in jail.[16]

All this deserves consideration when reviewing further aspects of Courtney Love's life, raising the question of whether Courtney's "psychotherapy" at three was part of a CIA-type victimization. Harrison believes that Carroll sent Courtney to therapy in order to "brainwash" her. He doesn't know if the therapy had anything to do with MK-Ultra, but he said that Linda Carroll kept Courtney away from him for years. Carroll had dated Frank Rodriguez in the late 1960s, married him in 1969, and moved to Eugene, Oregon with him near the Acid Test crowd.

This crowd had followed Ken Kesey when he moved to his hometown near his brother Chuck Kesey. The transplanted Acid Test crowd who called themselves "Merry Pranksters" included Kesey, Ken Babbs and "Spider Lady" Nancy Van Brasch Hamren. Nancy Hamren had a boyfriend whose sister was married to Grateful Dead frontman Jerry Garcia. Chuck Kesey had a business, the Springfield Creamery, which hired Hamren as an assistant, and then named their new yogurt, Nancy's Yogurt, after her. Hank Harrison said that Linda Carroll became close with Hamren, while the Grateful Dead played benefit shows for the Springfield Creamery that popularized it.

About a year after Carroll's marriage to Frank Rodriguez, Rodriguez filed for divorce, claiming Carroll was sleeping with Courtney's psychiatrist. In a memoir, Linda Carroll said she then moved to New Zealand in 1973 and left Courtney in Oregon. Within a year, Courtney was brought to New Zealand, but then sent back to Oregon again. Carroll claimed a former "family therapist" took the bizarre action of flying to New Zealand to pick Courtney up and take her back to the U.S. This is an extreme breach of boundaries, and of time and expense for a therapist.

Most importantly, Courtney found Harrison when she was fourteen years old in 1979, and in Hillcrest Youth Correctional Facility in Salem, Oregon. Harrison got her out of Hillcrest and housed her for a while. Courtney evidently told Harrison that she was sexually molested by Frank Rodriguez and the psychiatrist. She also said that the doctor hypnotized her and gave her the psychohypnotic drugs Tuinal and Seconal, starting at least as early as age seven. Harrison said he met Rodriguez, and didn't believe he would molest Courtney, but he never understood her tantrums over returning to her mother's at three and four years old. Harrison said he didn't know the psychiatrist, and believed Courtney was telling the truth about him, particularly knowing such exotic drugs at such a young age.[17]

MK-Ultra researchers Lee and Shlain cited CIA documents detailing their psychiatrists' use of Seconal, in similar fashion to Scopolamine, as a narcohypnotic to gain trance states. Also, as noted earlier, one of the CIA MK-Ultra "leading psychologists" John Gittinger accompanied two other MK-Ultra scientists to several Acid Tests, before the acid test crowd moved with Ken Kesey to the Eugene, Oregon area, and Linda Carroll ended up following them. MK-Ultra victim Claudia Mullen's federal hearing testimony regarding Gittinger is supported by many victims who testified before the Australia Royal Commission. Gittinger took his split personality experiments to Australia by the mid-1970s. John Marks, a former U.S. State Department Director of the Bureau of Intelligence and Research, obtained 16,000 FOIA-released CIA documents, some of which showed Gittinger's work with drugs and hypnosis. Gittinger was also publicly accused of hypnosis and drug experimentation by Vermont dissociative identity (multiple personality) disorder victim Karen Wetmore.[18]

Another claim about Courtney appeared in a biography, *Courtney Love: The Real Story*, by Poppy Z. Brite. At sixteen years of age Courtney apparently worked for organized crime in Japan as a stripper in what Courtney called "the white slave trade," implying it included prostitution. Hank Harrison said Courtney had found out how to become legally emancipated that year. Harrison said Courtney was beyond his control, and that he saw her start prostituting with a San Francisco madam he knew, who became a longtime advisor to Courtney. Harrison claims she introduced Courtney to high-paying clients such as Hewlett Packard scion David Packard (also a former U.S. Deputy Secretary of Defense). Harrison said Courtney went overseas with the Japanese Mafia both before and after meeting the madam. Courtney biographer Melissa Rossi also said Courtney reported prostituting in Taiwan as a teen.[19]

After her first six months in Japan, Courtney came back and gained access to a trust fund left by her maternal family. In 1980, while Courtney was in Japan, Harrison got a book deal to research a project in Dublin, Ireland. While still sixteen, Courtney evidently bought a thousand hits of LSD and stopped at her father's temporary home in Dublin for several months. While there, she took acid with Steve O'Leary, who was working for the CIA. She and O'Leary then traveled to Liverpool, England, as well as Ockendon Vietnamese Refugee Camp in London's suburbs. (A strange echo of Lennon assassin Mark Chapman spending time at the Arkansas Fort Chaffee Vietnamese Refugee camp. Harrison said Ockendon was known as a CIA-owned group.)[20]

The Liverpool music scene was experiencing the biggest explosion in bands since the Beatles put that city on the map twenty years earlier. Perhaps this is why Courtney brought the thousand hits of acid to Liverpool, where she certainly expected to distribute them, according to Wallace and Halperin in their book *Love and Death: The Murder of Kurt Cobain*. If so, she followed in the same path as CIA MK-Ultra and British intelligence agents ready to introduce LSD and manipulate the minds of young, impressionable music industry leftists while also popularizing the drug.[21]

It is reported that Love quickly became a groupie for many of the United Kingdom's top bands (Pogues, Adam Ant, Flock of Seagulls, Echoe and the Bunnymen), comically claiming to have lost her virginity to several different music stars. One of these music stars, Julian Cope of The Teardrop Explodes, described Courtney as destructive. For example, Hank Harrison said his daughter aborted a pregnancy after sex with the drummmer for the Pogues, breaking up his marriage. Reports of her destructiveness all over the city surely contributed to what researchers describe as her being "no longer welcome in Liverpool" by 1982.[22]

Years later, during Courtney's marriage to Kurt Cobain, Cope went so far as to take out a large advertisement in the music press. His ad made an allusion to Love: "Free us from Nancy Spungen-fixated heroin A-holes who cling to our greatest rock groups and suck out their brains." Cope was referring to the wife of Sex Pistols guitarist, Sid Vicious,[23] who had a heroin problem when she met Vicious in New York and reportedly turned him on to the drug, before they both died young. Love physically resembled Spungeon and had unsuccessfully auditioned to play Spungeon in the film *Sid and Nancy*.[24]

Reports continued of Courtney Love next traveling to Portland, Oregon where she also pushed drugs and caused chaos in that music scene. Many said Courtney was always "popping huge amounts of pills" including barbiturates, speed, and opiates: "[When] she had extra, she'd distribute them around as if they were candy." There is no mention of how she could be able to get so much to distribute freely. As in Liverpool, she latched onto potential music stars. Rozz Rezabek, of the new-wave band Theater of Sheep, said she tried to mold him.[25]

Eventually tiring of the Portland scene, Courtney moved to Los Angeles, where she worked as a stripper. While there she tried to become a rock star, joining a band with Kat Bjelland and Jennifer Finch. Bjelland soon formed Babes in Toyland and moved to Minneapolis. They quickly kicked Courtney out of the band for being a sub-standard instrumentalist.[26]

When Courtney Love was nineteen, she went back to Portland to live with her father, but he soon kicked her out for having heroin parties and leaving syringes all over the basement. She then moved to Alaska where she stripped in a club and reportedly prostituted at the local Army base. Years later she is said to have told her first husband, James Mooreland, that she "slept with generals at the Army base who told her secret information that proved that the wars they got us into were for our own good."[27]

By 1985 Courtney returned to Los Angeles and began a sexual affair with director Alex Cox. She gained a small role in his movie *Sid and Nancy*, about the Sex Pistols, and a starring role in another film. During this time she became friendly with more United Kingdom rock stars, including Elvis Costello and Joe Strummer. Courtney reportedly lived briefly in Strummer's house with him and his wife. Strummer's band, The Clash, is considered by many as one of the top radical leftist punk bands in music history.[28]

Courtney Love went on to spend some time in the New York music and film scene before moving back to Los Angeles in the late 1980s and starting a punk band, Hole, with Eric Erlandson. There she latched onto L.A.'s local punk music star James Mooreland and convinced him to marry her. Mooreland said he thought he was marrying a radical punk feminist, but instead ended up with a "right-wing Phyllis Diller." He said he soon realized Courtney was a "junky stripper and prostitute," who had used hired thugs to beat people, as various underworld characters were beholden to her. Similar to Kristen Pfaff's and Hank Harrison's descriptions, Mooreland said Courtney seemed "as if she had another personality" capable of extreme violence. He was constantly threatened by Love, and when he refused one of her demands, a stranger actually beat him into submission.[29]

Love and Mooreland broke up after she got pregnant, used drugs during her pregnancy, and got an abortion. Around 1986, Courtney Love reportedly went into surgery for a nose job. Within the next five years she had added breast implants and liposuction. After the divorce from Mooreland, she dated Trent Reznor of Nine Inch Nails (one time and then stalked him) and was dating Smashing Pumpkins' lead singer Billy Corgan, whose album *Gish* was heading to the top of the charts just before Nirvana's *Nevermind*. Former bandmate Lori Barbero said Love left Corgan for Cobain in late summer 1991, immediately after being introduced to him.[30]

Kurt's friends said Cobain had only tried heroin a few times before he met Courtney, but she apparently got Cobain into a daily intravenous habit. For example, Cobain's longtime friend Alice Wheeler said Courtney did this "to control him. She's very sophisticated that way."[31] During Cobain's last 12 months, Love supplied many addicts with money and heroin, surrounding Cobain with them. This included "nanny and gun nut," Mike "Cali" Dewitt, who admitted his "spy role" for Love to author Everett True. Cobain fired Dewitt but Love rehired him. Love also forced Cali's friend, Rene Naverette, on Cobain as a bodyguard. Love finally had Eric Erlandson at the house often, even during Cobain's last days, making the scene similar to Rolling Stone Brian Jones's death scene. Well-documented evidence suggesting Courtney's role in Cobain's death, along with the total lack of police investigation about it, speaks to a high level of U.S. intelligence protection.[32]

Following Cobain's death, Courtney Love promoted LSD and crack cocaine. Barbara Walters conducted a high-profile interview of Love in 1995 for a TV audience of 25 million viewers. Love made bizarre statements lauding LSD, telling Walters her father gave her acid as a kid, stating, "He wanted to make a superior race, and by giving children acid you could do that."[33]

In 2012, Love discussed crack cocaine in a biography. Love said while crack cocaine "screwed me up in a lot of ways, it improved me in certain others ... I've never been good at numbers, but when I was on crack, I could do math really, really well. I became a fucking wiz at calculus."[34]

Immunity from criminal prosecution continued. Love physically attacked numerous people, both men and women, with few or no legal repercussions, leading many to avoid discussing her out of fear. These attacks included some women who had been close to Cobain, such as singer Mary Lou Lord and Kathleen Hanna, lead singer of the seminal "riot grrl" band Bikini Kill. Riot grrl was a movement of female empowerment through punk music and zines (small-press magazines). Love punched Hanna in the face at the 1995 Lollapalooza Fest. She pled guilty and was ordered to receive anger management counseling.

Love also attacked journalist Victoria Clarke and media photographer Belissa Cohen. In separate incidents, she punched them in the face and dragged them by their hair. Cohen sued Love in a civil trial. Out of these multiple physical assaults, reports claim Love only received one misdemeanor sentence.[35]

By 2012, Courtney Love's actions were so injurious that her daughter Frances filed a protective order against her. The judge granted the order to Frances Cobain and several of her relatives, including Frances's aunt, Kimberly Cobain, who had previously gained legal custody of then 17-year-old Frances in 2009.[36]

Love Leaves a Trail of Death

While one musician died of a heroin overdose in 1990, much of the chaos in the Seattle music scene started after Courtney Love arrived in the early fall of 1991. Susan Silver, who helped manage Soundgarden, Alice In Chains and the Screaming Trees, said, "After Courtney hooked up with Kurt, it was the first time anyone had ever publicly trash-talked anybody in the community. It was really awful to have somebody with this addict behavior of divide-and-conquer. We had this really lovely, cohesive, supportive community, and this tornado came and started blowin' things apart."[37]

In late October of 1991, noted Seattle poet, and Cobain's friend, Steve Bernstein reportedly committed suicide by slitting his throat. Bernstein's friend, film director Oliver Stone, believed he was murdered. It must be emphasized that though there is no direct evidence implicating Love at the scene of Cobain's death, the violence was not the first in a series of sinister events involving individuals with whom she had some connection. By early 1993, the frontman for Mudhoney, Mark Arm, and the bassist for Alice In Chains, Mike Starr, both near-fatally overdosed, after reportedly shooting up with Courtney in separate incidents.[38]

One singer, Mia Zapata, had come to Seattle and was considered the "queen of the scene" for her inspirational singing and guidance of other female musicians. She had leftist roots as a relative of the famous Mexican revolutionary Emilliano Zapata. By 1993 Mia Zapata's band, the Gits, had toured with Nirvana, and were about to sign a major-label record deal. The Gits organized a tour to shadow the U.S. tour of Pope John Paul II, to denounce the church's politics. One month prior to the tour, on July 7, 1993, Zapata was found laid out in a street with her arms straight out and legs together, forming a cross. She had been raped and murdered.

Seattle musicians didn't trust the police investigation, and hired a private detective. The band Tad organized a benefit show to raise money for that purpose. Nirvana joined in and was scheduled to co-headline with Tad. Backstage before the show, Courtney Love started a physical fight with the girlfriend of Tad's lead singer, knocking over a lamp that started a fire, and nearly sabotaged the benefit concert.[39]

Another close friend of Cobain's, Kristin Pfaff, had briefly joined Courtney Love's band Hole for their hit album *Live Through This*. Pfaff, who was reportedly happy to leave Seattle and Hole, died ten weeks after Cobain. A friend found her dead in her bathtub, of an alleged overdose. Pfaff had formerly been in the Minneapolis band Janitor Joe, who wrote antiwar songs such as "Big Metal Birds."

Wallace and Halperin quoted many who knew Pfaff. Everyone reported how peaceful, friendly and talented she was. Her band Janitor Joe had received critical acclaim. Courtney Love and her ex-boyfriend, Eric Erlandson, talked Pfaff into joining Hole for their major-label debut with Geffen Records. Pfaff's family tried to talk her out of it, concerned about Erlandson's and Love's drug use. But with a generous financial offer made to her, Kristen Pfaff saw a chance to make a living with music, so she decided to join Hole on a temporary basis.[40]

Erlandson soon coupled with Pfaff romantically. Within weeks Pfaff was hooked on heroin. Her brother, who relocated to Seattle, said Courtney Love supplied Pfaff with heroin and syringes. A good friend said Love emotionally traumatized Pfaff, who would make musical suggestions only to have Love scream at her and threaten to fire her.[41]

It didn't help Love and Pfaff's relationship that Kurt Cobain was attracted to Pfaff, with her beautiful long black hair, striking figure, and similar passions. Cobain said in confidence to his close friend Dylan Carlson, "She's a fucking talented musician. She's also a beautiful soul. I think she's so beautiful, but if I ever told her that and Courtney found out, it would be hell."[42] Pfaff and Cobain spent hours talking about similar interests, but when Cobain gave Kristen a copy of the novel *Perfume*, which had greatly inspired him, "Courtney hit the ceiling."[43]

When Hole's *Live Through This* eventually came out, critics credited Pfaff's bass playing for the band's unique sound. Even Erlandson told *Spin* magazine, "The day Kristen joined Hole is when we took off." But Pfaff didn't care. She had already quit her "nightmarish" relationship with Erlandson around Christmas of 1993, and, with Hole's *Live Through This* completed, she left Seattle and moved back to Minneapolis.[44]

In Minneapolis, Pfaff awaited the start of Hole's summer tour, to which she was still contractually committed. Pfaff's mother Janet said that Cobain asked Pfaff to join him in a new band he wanted to start without the rest of Nirvana. When Kristen heard about Kurt Cobain's death in April of 1994, "she was devastated. She stopped doing drugs the day Kurt died." Pfaff entered a detox center and started straightening out her life. She then rejoined her old band, Janitor Joe, and "was adamant she would never go back to Hole."[45]

Kristen Pfaff went on tour in Europe with Janitor Joe, but still needed to clear her things out of her Seattle apartment. Pfaff got a Minneapolis friend,

Paul Erickson, to drive a storage truck with her to Seattle. According to *Love and Death* authors Wallace and Halperin, in 1994 in Seattle there were "said to be more heroin addicts per square foot in Kristen's Capitol Hill neighborhood ... than in any other district in the United States." Pfaff's friend Erickson slept in the truck with Pfaff's belongings to protect them from junkie thieves. A bandmate of Pfaff's said she called him that night sounding "as chipper and happy as she's ever been."[46]

Hole's bass player Kristen Pfaff attracted Cobain's attention. After he died, she rejoined her old band, refusing to play with Love. Police denied requests for an investigation into Pfaff's own strange death.

At 8:30 P.M., Erickson said, he saw Eric Erlandson enter Pfaff's apartment and leave again roughly half an hour later. Erickson found Pfaff unconscious in an inch of water in the tub the next morning. She was dead before police arrived. Police said they found "syringes and narcotics paraphernalia in the bathroom," and pages were ripped out of Pfaff's journal. The same coroner who had declared Kurt Cobain's death a suicide claimed Pfaff died of "Acute Opiate Intoxication" caused by an accidental "[injectable] use of the drug."[47]

Police rebuffed Kristen's mother's requests to investigate her daughter's death as a possible homicide. Kristen's brother Jason suggested Erlandson may have killed Pfaff. "It could have been a dose of dirty [overly pure] heroin. The fact that Kristen was clean for so long combined with a dose of dirty heroin would have been enough to kill her." Jason was explaining how her tolerance to heroin was likely lower, and it wouldn't have taken as much heroin to get high, but that it being overly pure would have killed her more easily.[48]

Evidence suggests Eric Erlandson as a suspect in Pfaff's death, yet there is no mention of police investigating him. Again, police inaction appears purposeful. With the mass of evidence that Courtney Love carried out MK-Ultra-type activities with criminal impunity, Erlandson's actions regarding Pfaff and his partnership with Love at this time suggest his collaboration.

Notes

1 Nick Broomfield, *Kurt and Courtney* (Strength Ltd., Documentary, 1998). Max Wallace and Ian Halperin, *Love & Death: The Murder of Kurt Cobain* (New York: Atria/Simon and Schuster, 2004), pp. 249-54, 258-59.

2 Wallace and Halperin, *Love and Death*, pp. 258-61. *The Cobain Case* (film) by Ian Halperin and Max Wallace, http://www.youtube.com/watch?v=Wjv5zZpA7dQ. Note that this film has only been available in Europe.

3 Wallace and Halperin, *Love and Death*, pp. 258-61. Halperin and Wallace, *The Cobain Case*.

4 Wallace and Halperin, *Love and Death*, pp. 261, 267-70. Halperin and Wallace, *The Cobain Case.*

5 Wallace and Halperin, *Love and Death*, pp. 259-60, 267-70; https://www.facebook.com/pages/Kill-Allen-Wrench/182148178469543.

6 For Broy having a "ranch" in Riverside, CA, and playing with both the Mentors and Kill Allen Wrench, Wallace and Halperin, *Love and Death*, pp. 261, 269. Authors note that Allen Wrench's real name is Richard Allen Wrench, and he was born on August 4, 1967.

7 ISA EXPO 2009 Technical Conference 10/6/2009-10/8/2009. Steve Broy, Teledyne Analytical Instruments, Biography, http://expoexhibitor.isa.org/isa09/CC/forms/attendee/index.aspx?content=speakerInfo&speakerId=211 Also, Steve Broy profile on Linked In. Wikipedia has band starting in 1976; Broy interview said 1977, Robin Schroffel, "The Mentors Interview with Steve Broy, Founder and Bassist," *Suite*, September 8, 2010, https://suite.io/robin-schroffel/45em2ke. On Captain Al Hubbard as "superspy," Martin Lee and Bruce Shlain, *Acid Dreams: LSD, the CIA, the Sixties and Beyond* (New York: Grove Weidenfeld, 1985, 1992), p. 198.

8 Dave McGowan, *Weird Scenes Inside the Canyon: Laurel Canyon, Covert Ops & the Dark Heart of the Hippie Dream* (London: Headpress, 2014), pp. 22-40.

9 On Folger meeting and funding Manson, Maury Terry, *The Ultimate Evil: An Investigation into America's Most Dangerous Satanic Cult* (New York: Dolphin, 1987), pp. 494-96. Paul Krassner in Craig Karpel, "The Power of Positive Paranoia," *Oui*, May 1975, p. 111. Much else from John Johnson, *Make Your Own Kind of Music: A Career Retrospective of Cass Elliot* (Los Angeles: Music Archives Press, 1987), pp. 71-72. Karpel and Johnson sources cited in Alex Constantine, *The Covert War Against Rock* (Los Angeles: Feral House, 2000), pp. 38-41.

10 McGowan, *Weird Scenes Inside the Canyon*, pp. 137-39.

11 Max Wallace and Ian Halperin, *Who Killed Kurt Cobain? The Mysterious Death of an Icon* (Secaucus, NJ: Birch Lane/Carol, 1998), pp. 42-43. Several personal interviews with Hank Harrison, 11/2014, and Hank Harrison, *Love Kills: The Assassination of Kurt Cobain* (San Francisco: Arkives Press, 2013), pp. 67, 73. "Dissociative Identity Disorder (Multiple Personality Disorder)," WebMD.

12 Wallace and Halperin, *Love and Death*, pp. 28-29. On Carroll's history, see Wallace and Halperin, *Who Killed Kurt Cobain?* p. 43.

13 On MK-Ultra behavioral modification, H.P. Albarelli Jr, *A Secret Order* (Walterville, OR: TrineDay, 2013), pp.253-4. On Courtney Love therapy at 3, Wallace and Halperin, *Love and Death*, pp. 28, 31. Interviews with Hank Harrison, 11/2014, and Harrison, *Love Kills*, polygraph results copied at end of book.

14 On Harrison's accounts of Risi's wealth, divorce, Warlocks/Grateful Dead, personal interviews, 11/2014, and Harrison, *Love Kills*, pp. 67, 137, 152, 172-73. On Carroll sexually molested by adopted father, Linda Carroll, *Her Mother's Daughter: A Memoir of the Mother I Never Knew and of My Daughter, Courtney Love* (New York: Doubleday, 2005), pp. 30-31, 187. Note that the Presidio military base's child-care center in San Francisco had a long history of mass sexual abuse that finally had it closed down by 1987. Harrison believes Courtney attended that day-care center. AP, "Army Will Close Child Care Center," *New York Times*, 11/16/87. Note that acccused former Lt. Colonel in the DIA's Psychological Warfare Division, Michael Aquino, worked at the Presidio, Linda Goldstein, "Child Abuse at Presidio," *San Jose Mercury News*, 7/24/88.

15 Wallace and Halperin, *Love and Death*, pp.28-31. On MK-Ultra hearings, see victim testimony, Chris De Nicola, here: http://www.youtube.com/watch?v=RRkrgDQqVXc&feature=related this testimony came at the Human Radiation Experiment Hearings in 1995. Therapist Valerie Wolfe testified about 40 therapists contacting her with similar stories from the clients they counseled. On Wolfe's testimony, see http://www.youtube.com/watch?v=MSesgGc4nwI&feature=relmfu. Note that Wolfe named MK-Ultra Director, Dr. Sidney Gottlieb, as one of the doctors working on these experiments. On victim Claudia Mullen testifying about being turned into a CIA asset as a prostitute, see http://www.whale.to/b/wolf3.html#toc. Note that De Nicola's birthdate appears transcribed wrong here as 1952 instead of 1962. Claudia Mullin is particularly interesting because she carried out CIA tasks as a prostitute and discusses Drs. Gottlieb, Gittinger, and other key MK-

Ultra agents as participating in her torture to shape her mind. Also note numerous other similar female victims of MK-Ultra have spoken out publicly and written memoirs. For example, see Cathy O'Brien with Mark Phillips, *Trance: Formation of America* (Reality Publishing, 2005). Brice Taylor, *Thanks for the Memories* (Brice Taylor Trust, 1999). And see book by veteran writer Donald Bain, *The Control of Candy Jones* (Playboy Press, 1976).

16 Jim Keith, *Mass Control: Engineering Human Consciousness* (Kempton, IL: Adventures Unlimited Press, 1999/2003). On Hammond, pp. 135-40; Mullen, pp. 142-48; Taylor and Sullivan, pp. 149-65. Regarding Manson and Process Church, see Barnes and Noble E-book with these page numbers for book reprinted in hard copy by Bantam Books. Maury Terry, *The Ultimate Evil*, Ebook pp. 1001-02, 1004, 1006, 1008-09.

17 Harrison's accounts on Courtney's tantrums, brainwashing, Courtney's godmother Winblad-DeMarco, and Courtney telling him of molestation, hypnosis, and drug "therapy," personal interviews, 11/2014, and Harrison, *Love Kills*, pp. 67, 78-79, 96, 116. Note that a 14-year-old Courtney said in a letter to Harrison that she began seeing the psychiatrist somewhere between 3 and 7 years old, and that her mother's affair with him caused the break-up with her stepfather, Frank Rodriguez. In that letter Courtney also implies Rodriguez and the psychiatrist were molesting her. Courtney further said Carroll left her in the U.S. at 8 years old. Letter reprinted in back of Harrison's book, pp. 483-39. Also on Carrol leaving Courtney in Oregon, and on therapist picking up in New Zealand a few years later, Carroll, *Her Mother's Daughter*, p. 224, 248-49. Carroll (p. 227) described Courtney, at age 9, as "a zombie" from psychiatrists' tranquilizers. On Nancy Van Brasch Hamren, Acid Test crowd, and Springfield Creamery, Hank Harrison's account, and Katy Muldoon, "Nancy's Yogurt has the Grateful Dead, Haight-Ashbury, Oregon and those Keseys in the mix," *The* (Portland) *Oregonian*, March 27, 2010.

18 On Seconal (Tuinal is Seconal plus the sedative hypnotic, Amobarbital), untitled CIA document, June 8, 1954, and Gittinger as one of "CIA's leading psychlogist," all in Martin Lee and Bruce Shlain, *Acid Dreams: The Complete Social History of LSD, the CIA, the Sixties and Beyond* (New York: Grove Weidenfeld, 1985), pp. 7, 16, 299. On Australian victims testifying against Gittinger, an article by victim, Fiona Barnett, "Trapped Inside Australia's Vast Child Abuse Network," *Independent Australia*, May 9, 2014, https://independentaustralia.net/life/life-display/trapped-inside-australias-vast-child-abuse-network-part-1,6460. Regarding John Marks citation on Gittinger, see, for example, CIA document #433, August 21, 1959, "Possible Use of Drugs and Hypnosis in [deleted] Operational Case, MK-Ultra Subproject 128," and interviews with Gittinger, all in John Marks, *The Search for the "Manchurian Candidate": The CIA and Mind Control: The Secret History of the Behavioral Sciences* (New York: W. W. Norton, 1979), pp. 202, 244. Regarding Wetmore, Karen Wetmore, *Surviving Evil: CIA Mind Control Experiments in Vermont* (Burlington, VT: Manitou Communications, 2014).

19 Wallace and Halperin, *Love and Death*, p. 33. Also Poppy Z. Brite, *Courtney Love: The Real Story* (New York: Simon and Schuster/Touchstone, 1998), pp. 48-49. Personal interviews with Hank Harrison, 11/2014, and Harrison, *Love Kills*, pp. 181-85. Melissa Rossi, *Courtney Love: Queen of Noise* (New York: Pocket Books, 1996), p. 63.

20 Wallace and Halperin, *Love and Death*, p. 34. On O'Leary, personal interview, Hank Harrison, 11/13/14. Harrison, *Love Kills*, pp. 174, 223-24, 231, 501-505. Harrison said O'Leary wrote him six months before he died, admitting he and his brother worked for the CIA at the time they were hanging out with Courtney around her 17th birthday. Harrison said he visited Courtney and O'Leary in London and Ockendon.

21 Wallace and Halperin, *Love and Death*, pp. 34-35.

22 Wallace and Halperin, *Love and Death*, pp. 34-35. On Love and Pogues drummer, Hank Harrison interview, 11/13/14. Harrison said a friend of the drummer's ex-wife described the situation to him.

23 Wallace and Halperin, *Who Killed Kurt Cobain?* p. 48. *Love and Death*, p. 35.

24 Wallace and Halperin, *Who Killed Kurt Cobain?* pp. 51-52. For more on Sid Vicious and Nancy Spungeon's bizarre deaths, see Paul Scott, "Did Sid really kill Nancy? Explosive new evidence

suggests the punk rocker my have been innocent," *The Daily Mail* (London), January 23, 2009, http://www.dailymail.co.uk/femail/article-1127035/Did-Sid-really-kill-Nancy--Explosive-new-evidence-suggests-punk-rocker-innocent.html.

25 Wallace and Halperin, *Who Killed Kurt Cobain?* p. 49. Wallace and Halperin, *Love and Death*, pp. 35-37.

26 Wallace and Halperin, *Love and Death*, pp. 37-38.

27 Wallace and Halperin, *Love and Death*, pp. 39, 41.

28 Wallace and Halperin, *Who Killed Kurt Cobain?* pp. 51-52. On living with Strummer, see film by director Julien Temple, *Joe Strummer: The Future is Unwritten* (2007).

29 Wallace and Halperin, *Love and Death*, pp. 41-42. . On Mooreland's comments regarding Courtney and "another personality," underworld characters, and being beaten, see Hank Harrison's taped interview of Mooreland quoted in, Harrison, *Love Kills*, pp. 143-44.

30 Mark Yarm, *Everybody Loves Our Town: An Oral History of Grunge* (New York: Random House/Crown Archetype, 2011), pp. 294-98. . On stalking Reznor, Harrison, *Love Kills*, p. 177. On plastic surgery, nose job and breast implants, Rossi, *Courtney Love*, pp. 77, 114. On liposuction, Hank Harrison personal interview, 11/13/14.

31 Wallace and Halperin, *Love and Death*, p. 44.

32 Wallace and Halperin, *Love and Death*, p. 45. On Cali as "gun nut" and telling True he was a spy, and on Naverette and Erlandson, Harrison, *Love Kills*, pp. 187, 289, 437, 456-57, 461, 463. Also Rossi, *Courtney Love*, p. 160.

33 Wallace and Halperin, *Love and Death*, p. 28.

34 Mike Larkin, "'She Killed the family pets:' Frances Bean Cobain Slams Mum Courtney Love Bizarre Behavior in Damning Testimony," *The Daily Mail* (London), February 2, 2012, http://www.dailymail.co.uk/tvshowbiz/article-2095142/Frances-Bean-Cobain-slammed-Courtney-Loves-behaviour-restraining-order-testimony.html

35 On attacks of Lord, Hanna and Clark, see Wallace and Halperin, *Love and Death*, pp. 52, 272-73. On attacking Cohen, see Daniel Frankel, "Writer Sues Courtney Love for Alleged Attack," *EOnline*, May 29, 1998, http://www.eonline.com/news/writer_sues_courtney_love_alleged_attack/36483. On those avoiding discussing Love out of fear, see *Love and Death*, p. 35. Associated Press, "Courtney Love Loses Custody of Frances Bean," *Today.com*, 12/14/2009, http://www.today.com/id/34420813/ns/today-today_entertainment/t/courtney-love-loses-custody-frances-bean/#.UxOzIP1tfCQ. Harrison said Love was also kicked off planes twelve times, once including the need by fire marshals to stop her tantrums at gunpoint. One time she was with baby Frances, and Harrison's daughter-in-law was a hostess on the flight. Regarding this, and Love attacking men but being acquitted in court, Harrison, *Love Kills*, pp. 170, 178, 180.

36 Larkin, "She Killed the family pets."

37 Yarm, *Everybody Loves Our Town*, p. 365.

38 Regina Hackett, "A Legacy of Poetic Provocation," *Seattle Post-Intelligencer*, October 9, 2003, http://www.seattlepi.com/ae/article/A-legacy-of-poetic-provocation-1126584.php. On musicians overdosing after using with Courtney Love, see Yarm, *Everybody Loves Our Town*, pp. 397, 401. Starr's near death occurred when Nirvana and Alice In Chains played at a rock festival in Brazil on January 23, 1993.

39 Yarm, *Everybody Loves Our Town*, pp. 321-22. Mia said her father, true to their name, had a strong social conscience around activist causes. Mia attended the very liberal Antioch College in 1984. That school involved cooperative education of working six months and studying six months. Mia Zapata and two classmates did their work at an urban farm that also held punk music shows. Yarm, *Everybody Loves Our Town*, pp. 322-33. See her bandmate Selene Vigil-Wilk and boyfriend Matt Dresdner in Yarm, *Everybody Loves Our Town*, pp. 331-22. On major-label Atlantic Records offer, see Rachiel Arief, "Interview with The Gits drummer, Steve Moriarty," *Popular 1* (Spain), February 2009, http://popular1.com/revista/articlesinterviews/articles-in-english/interview-steve-moriarty-of-the-gits-by-rachel-arieff/. On anti-pope tour, Gits drummer Steve Moriarty in Yarm, *Everybody Loves Our Town*, p. 416.

40 Wallace and Halperin, *Love and Death,* pp. 232-33.
41 Wallace and Halperin, *Love and Death,* pp. 233-34.
42 Wallace and Halperin, *Who Killed Kurt Cobain?* p. 149.
43 Wallace and Halperin, *Love and Death,* p. 235.
44 Wallace and Halperin, *Love and Death,* pp. 235-36.
45 Wallace and Halperin, *Love and Death,* pp. 235-36, 239. Hank Harrison told me Janet Pfaff described her daughter's professional and lifestyle changes in detail, personal interview, 11/13/14. Also Harrison, *Love Kills,* p. 331.
46 Wallace and Halperin, *Love and Death,* p. 237.
47 Wallace and Halperin, *Love and Death,* p. 238.
48 Wallace and Halperin, *Love and Death,* p. 244.

Chapter Twenty-Three

Police Attacks on Tupac Shakur and Activist Gangs

Couldn't survive in this capitalistic government,
'Cause it was meant to hold us back with ignorance.
Drugs and sneak attacks in my community, they killed our unity.
But when I charged them, they cried immunity.

– Tupac Shakur, "Panther Power" (1989), from *The Lost Tapes*, 1998

A review of rap icon Tupac Shakur's radical leftist lineage and leadership provides the first motive of the ruling oligarchy to push U.S. intelligence to target Tupac at the beginning of his career. Soon after beginning his solo rap career, Tupac developed a plan to aid the movement of gangs away from drug dealing and into leftist politics, making him a more major target. As Tupac's talent propelled his fame in a meteoric fashion, his increasing success at converting gangs to activists would put major dents in the oligarchy's fortunes and threaten their control over society.

Tupac's Leftist Lineage and Teen Leadership

Tupac Amaru Shakur was born in 1971 to former Harlem Black Panther leader Afeni Shakur, who named him after the last Incan leader to die trying to fight off the Spanish invaders in the 1500s.[1] She named Bronx Panther Assata Shakur as Tupac's godmother and L.A. Panther leader Geronimo Pratt his godfather. Afeni's partner, Mutulu Shakur, regularly took Tupac to activist meetings and to the Lincoln Detox drug treatment clinic in the Bronx, where Mutulu was Assistant Director. After the FBI put Mutulu on its most wanted list and he went underground, the FBI visited Tupac in school to ask if he had seen his leftist stepfather.[2]

Tupac never veered from the political path onto which his family set him. When twelve-year-old Tupac was asked what he wanted to be when he grew up, he immediately said, "A revolutionary." Mutulu came out of hiding every so often just to wave to Tupac and acknowledge how much he meant to him.[3]

While the FBI kept Afeni from gaining employment, Tupac took up acting at the age of thirteen. His good looks and ability landed him the lead child's role in *A Raisin in the Sun*. The play showed at the Apollo Theater as a fundraiser for Jesse Jackson's presidential campaign.[4]

In the mid-1980s, Afeni Shakur moved Tupac and his sister Sekyiwa to Baltimore, where she had family. There, Afeni fought successfully for her son's admission into the Baltimore School for the Arts, where he excelled. Baltimore teachers described Tupac as a natural leader, chosen to represent the school at citywide forums. One teacher reported Tupac was the best actor they ever had. [5]

By then, Tupac had begun to attend national activist meetings. His mother's close friend, Watani Tyehimba, was a former Revolutionary Action Movement-based Black Panther in Los Angeles and cofounded the New Afrikan People's Organization as their National Security Director. Tupac attended their young adult group, the New Afrikan Panthers.[6]

When Tupac was about seventeen, their Baltimore neighborhood was experiencing a major crack epidemic, and a teenager was shot. Afeni took Tupac and Sekyiwa to Marin City, near Oakland, California, to protect them.[7] There they moved in with imprisoned Panther leader Geronimo Pratt's second wife, Linda. Afeni didn't know that people called the neighborhood "Cokeland," and U.S. intelligence had developed a hotspot for cocaine trafficking in the same San Francisco Bay area.[8]

The New Afrikan Panthers, active in eight cities nationwide, had many members in their teens and twenties, reflecting the ages and actions of Black Panthers when that group first organized. They made 17-year-old Tupac Shakur their youngest-ever elected national chairman.[9]

FBI's Richard Held Targets Huey Newton, Judi Bari

Someone else had moved to the San Francisco Bay area soon before the Shakurs. Richard W. Held, who once headed the L.A. Cointelpro unit, became the San Francisco FBI office chief. Held's father had been an FBI Assistant Director, helping to cover up Panther Leader Fred Hampton's murder, and leading attacks on the American Indian Movement. Following in his father's political footsteps, Richard Held had arranged for police snipers to shoot Geronimo Pratt in his bed, where they thought he was sleeping. They failed to hurt Pratt at that time, but later Held successfully framed Pratt for an L.A. murder. With Afeni's continuing addiction, Tupac took her place working hard on Pratt's defense team, which was soon infiltrated and sabotaged, apparently with Held's help.[10]

In August of 1988, Panther cofounder Huey Newton worked on Pratt's Defense Committee.[11] In his position of New Afrikan Panther Chairman, Tupac said he consulted with Geronimo as well as with Newton, who talked to East Coast former Black Panthers about reuniting. Tupac also started rapping and performing at benefits for Pratt. Huey Newton was assassinated in 1989, under Held's watch.[12]

The year after Newton was murdered, a bomb went off under the car seat of environmentalist Judi Bari, leader of the environmental organization Earth First! Evidence and disclosures eventually indicated the FBI was most likely behind this bombing. The car bomb paralyzed Bari from the waist down. She and her wounded fellow activist passenger launched a lawsuit. A reporter asked Bari about the FBI's search for the bomber. Reflecting her label as "queen of the quip," she said, "I hope the FBI find their man. And when they do, I hope they fire him." [13]

After the bombing, Judi Bari chronicled dozens of murderous Cointelpro-type tactics the FBI used against her and Earth First! leading up to the car bomb incident.[14] The research gave credence to Bari's lawsuit against FBI supervisor Richard Held and his collaborator in the Oakland police. Congressional support helped bring it to trial and, eventually, jurors awarded $4.4 million to Bari's partner, Darryl Cherney, and Bari's estate after she died in 1997.[15]

Police Armed Attacks on Tupac & Other Foul Play

Former colleagues and writers say the Bari suit sent Held into early retirement in 1993, though not before three armed and murderous attacks took place on new entertainment star Tupac Shakur, who lived in Held's area.[16] Evidence suggests that U.S. intelligence tried to "neutralize" Tupac with imprisonment or murder, using increasingly sophisticated strategies in direct proportion to his ever-increasing wealth and fame in the first four years of Tupac's entertainment career. They targeted Tupac both as a leftist black leader and for using his new wealth to fund former Black Panthers and other FBI targets. This targeting included arresting Tupac on drug charges several times.

Due to both Afeni Shakur's crack addiction and Linda Pratt's alcohol addiction, Tupac left home and moved in with a fellow leftist named Leila Steinberg. Steinberg managed Tupac and introduced him to Grammy-nominated rap artists Digital Underground. Tupac decided to leave his New Afrikan Panther leadership to tour with Digital Underground through the U.S. and Europe, thinking he might be able to reach more people with his politics through rap.[17]

Tupac's debut CD, *2Pacalypse Now*, was picked up by major label Interscope Records. Tupac also landed an acting role in the film *Juice*.

Tupac's debut CD included political songs such as "Wordz of Wisdom," in which he calls out to various members of his Panther extended family, while blaming the government for bringing drugs into his community, and rapping, "The war on drugs is a war on you and me." In another track he says, "Fuck you to the FBI ... the CIA and ... B-U-S-H."[18]

In late 1991, several days after MTV released Tupac's solo debut music video "Trapped," two white Oakland police officers stopped him for jaywalking before physically assaulting him. In a legal testimony printed and presented in court by Tupac's lawyer, Tupac (cited as "claimant") detailed Oakland Police officer, Alexander Boyovich, "putting him in a chokehold" and then taking him down to the ground. The document said, "Officer Boyovich repeatedly slammed claimant's face upon the pavement while Officer Rodgers held claimant's body down. Officer Boyovich continued to choke claimant until he lost consciousness. At no time did the claimant assault or resist the officers while they were physically attacking him." These police tactics have led to other victims' deaths. Tupac sued for $10 million but settled for $42,000 several years later.[19]

In August of 1992, Tupac accepted an invitation by politicians in Marin City to be the honored guest at their annual music fest back in his old neighborhood on the exact three-year anniversary of Huey Newton's assassination. Eyewitness Marku Reynolds said that someone named Demetrius with a group of other guys "punched Tupac," while "he was signing autographs." Reynolds then re-enacted seeing Mutulu Shakur's son, Maurice "Mopreme" Harding, shooting a warning shot straight up to the sky. Reynolds further described how other shots were fired, and, "after I didn't hear no more shots, I raised my head and they were already chasing [Tupac] and Harding." Later witnesses said these other shots didn't come from Harding, thus they must have come from the attackers, who hit a six-year old boy two blocks away. The attacking group convinced a mob to attack Tupac, all in front of passively watching police officers, according to Reynolds. Bay Area FBI Director Richard Held specialized in various tactics used in that attack.[20]

After that incident, important politicians began to vilify Tupac, and conservative companies censored him. Vice President Dan Quayle condemned Tupac's lyrics in a well-publicized speech in 1992.[21] When Tupac's debut album approached gold, Time Warner bought a controlling interest in Interscope Records, and they proceeded to censor many of Tupac's lyrics on his second CD, *Strictly 4 My N.I.G.G.A.Z,* (his code for Never Ignorant Getting Goals Accomplished), not allowing Tupac's political song, "Holler If You Hear Me," to be his released single. They also delayed the release of this CD for a year.[22]

After Quayle's public denouncement, police appeared to use the same FBI harassment arrest strategy against Tupac as they used against his Black Panther extended family.[23] In line with Tupac's quote, "I never had a record until I made a record," police arrested him close to a dozen times on dubious charges, most of which were dismissed. In Los Angeles, the FBI would accumulate a 4,000-page file on Tupac.[24]

Police arrested Tupac several times for marijuana possession to gain his temporary imprisonment. The aforementioned intelligence memorandum on musicians leaked by the Senate Intelligence Committee spelled out "Have members arrested on marijuana charges ... Use narcotics ... to entrap." Police arrested Tupac several times for such specious claims as smoking marijuana in the lobby of a hotel at a political rap convention in Atlanta. While that 1992 charge was dismissed, it did drain Tupac of time and money. A later marijuana possession charge almost landed Tupac in jail long-term.[25]

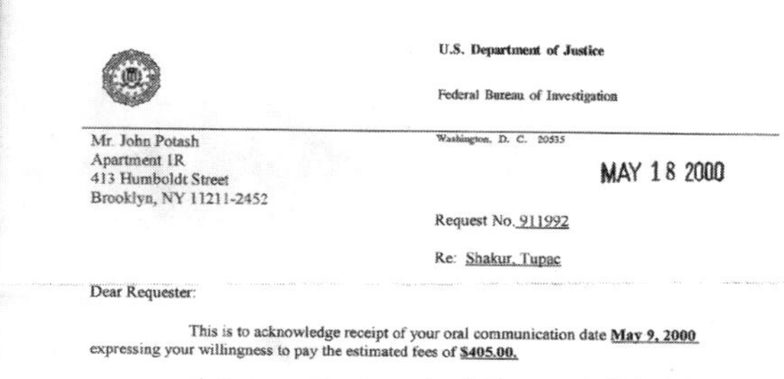

U.S. Department of Justice

Federal Bureau of Investigation

Washington, D. C. 20535

MAY 18 2000

Mr. John Potash
Apartment IR
413 Humboldt Street
Brooklyn, NY 11211-2452

Request No. 911992

Re: Shakur, Tupac

Dear Requester:

This is to acknowledge receipt of your oral communication date **May 9, 2000** expressing your willingness to pay the estimated fees of **$405.00.**

This letter confirms the author's conversation with a Dept. of Justice FOIA representative, who admitted that there were over 4,000 pages in the FBI's file on one-time New Afrikan Panther leader-turned rapper Tupac Shakur.

By the end of 1991, Afeni Shakur had finally begun her recovery from crack addiction. She started helping with Tupac's life work in 1992. She handled Tupac's public relations and other aspects of his music and film career.[26]

By 1993, Tupac bought his mother a house in Atlanta. Former Panther Watani Tyehimba, Tupac's business manager, had already moved there as Security Director for the New Afrikan People's Organization. Afeni rejoined Tyehimba in their work for gaining the freedom of Geronimo Pratt (now Geronimo Ji Jaga), which finally succeeded in 1997, with his gaining a multimillion-dollar settlement from the government for false imprisonment. Tupac planned to move to Atlanta even though he had been hit there with trumped up drug charges in 1992.[27]

Politicized Gangs Worry U.S. Intelligence

About the same time he produced his first CD, Tupac Shakur came up with his Thug Life Movement. Tupac's manager and longtime political mentor, Watani Tyehimba, confirmed that Tupac had decided to pretend to be a "gangsta" in order to appeal to gangs and then politicize them. This was part of his Black Panther extended family's work in helping local Bloods and Crips gangs stop fighting each other over drug dealing turf and fight instead for leftist political change.[28]

In the early 1990s, someone had filmed Los Angeles police beating unarmed motorist Rodney King. It made nightly news and some of the police officers went on trial. Their acquittal sparked the Los Angeles riots. Just days before, former Black Panthers and other activists successfully developed a gang truce between several sections of the Bloods and the Crips, who vowed to fight police racism instead of each other.[29] Former Panthers and civil rights activists like singer Harry Belafonte helped the peace truce, and activist conversions spread to Oakland, which worried the intelligence community.[30]

The Bloods and Crips not only encompassed the majority of the estimated 100,000 gang members in Los Angeles, but reports also acknowledged the two gangs had spread to states across the U.S. from Texas to New York.[31] Studies found 1,100 individual Bloods and Crips gangs active in 115 cities.[32] By 1995, the Bloods and Crips were reportedly active in all four branches of the armed services and at more than 50 military bases around the U.S.[33]

Tupac Shakur helped host gang-peace truce picnics and also fashioned a "Code of Thug Life" plan with his imprisoned stepfather Mutulu Shakur. Their plan sought to reduce the harm that drug-dealing gangs caused in the community.[34] Mutulu further helped organize a gang truce between the Crips and the Bloods in the federal prison system.[35]

In the summer of 1992, *The Nation* published a plan promoted by one former gang leader-turned-socialist writer, "Monster" Kody Scott. In the article, Scott discussed the Bloods/Crips truce and their plan that included a proposal for Los Angeles's budget to improve poor communities' education and economy, as well as getting drug lords to convert to legitimate businesses.[36]

Over the following years, the gang unity movement gained top political allies, including Congresswoman Maxine Waters.[37] The gang unity movement raised funds for legitimate businesses with profits going toward rebuilding recreational centers, drug treatment, and community centers.[38] These converted gangs also may have posed a threat to mainstream political leadership, as many credited Jose "Cha-Cha" Jimenez and his converted Chicago gang, the Young Lords, with helping elect Chicago's first black mayor, Harold Washington, in the 1980s.

The Los Angeles Police Department responded to this development with several operations and the bolstering of their specialized anti-gang units. U.S. Attorney General William Barr, of President George H.W. Bush's administration, said the Crips and Bloods, together with criminal illegal aliens, replaced Communism as the major domestic subversive threat. The U.S Justice Department deployed Marines and the 82nd Airborne in the streets during the L.A. riots. They also had the FBI and the Immigration and Naturalization Services working against these gangs.[39]

The FBI deployed a 100-agent unit to investigate the Crips and Bloods. They worked with the L.A. Police Department in Operation Hammer, a program that had police raiding activists' gang-truce meetings and framing the gang-truce leaders.[40] Bush also initiated a second program, Weed and Seed, that coincided with his administration's statements that gangs led the L.A. riots. Bush said drug dealers and gang members needed to be weeded out for a neighborhood to get seed money.[41] Activists claimed the name applied to undercover agents weeding into the Bloods and Crips to seed conflict.[42]

Gunmen soon murdered gang-truce leaders, causing few repercussions. Tony Bogard, one of the gang leaders acclaimed nationally for championing the Watts neighborhood Bloods/Crips truce of 1992, was murdered in January of 1994. Bogard was considered a hero in Watts for forming the non-profit Hands Across Watts, which promoted business ventures for reformed Bloods and Crips. Reputed drug dealer Rodney Compton fatally shot Bogard six times and was released from jail after pleading no contest to one count of voluntary manslaughter. Police said gunpowder residue was found on Bogard, who was caught without his bulletproof vest on. Compton, shot once in the arm, said Bogard fired first, though no witnesses confirmed his account.[43]

Other gang leaders were targeted. Police arrested Dewayne Holmes, the gang-truce leader who finalized the '92 truce, for an alleged "crime" of a ten-dollar robbery at a gang-unity dance. Despite personal appearances on his behalf by California Congresswoman Maxine Waters and once-and-future governor Jerry Brown, Holmes received a near-maximum sentence, and the courts sent him to a remote prison in the Sierra Nevada mountains.[44]

In spite of these problems, over the next few years activists helped the gang truce spread throughout Los Angeles. While the 1992 gang truce reportedly started with the three largest housing project gangs, primarily in the Watts section of L.A., by the spring of 1994 more than two-dozen other L.A. rival gang factions joined the truce. The gang-peace activists also reached out to the Mexican gangs and other ethnic groups. Latinos played a huge part in the rioting, and Latino rappers publicly supported the rebellion of blacks in L.A.[45]

Gang truces and activist conversions eventually spread nationwide, and were talked about internationally. In 1993, activists like Common Ground Foundation director Fred Williams helped organize a national gang-truce summit in Kansas City, Missouri.[46] L.A. Blood Omar Portee took Black Panther books to New York, starting the gang in Rikers prison to fight oppression.[47] And in 1994, leaders of the Bloods and the Crips addressed rallies in England's Manchester and London, organized by the black British organization Panther—a subsection of a socialist group, the Militant.[48]

Young Lord Vincent "Panama" Alba leaves the stage to the Latin King Antonio "King Tone" Fernandez at Columbia University in the mid-'90s after Alba influenced King Tone (far right) to have his gang, New York's largest, stop drug dealing and start community organizing.

New York saw the conversion of the state chapter of the Latin Kings into the Almighty Latin King and Queen Nation (ALKQN). In *The Almighty Latin King and Queen Nation: Street Politics and the Transformation of a New York City Gang*, published by Columbia University, it was reported that the 3,000-strong group stopped drug dealing and started to get involved in activism.[49] Former Young Lords activist, Vincent "Panama" Alba influenced Latin Kings leader, Antonio "King Tone" Fernandez, to make this conversion.[50]

After King Tone converted the Latin Kings into an activist group, the NYPD arrested King Tone on many charges, but courts failed to convict him. Prosecutors finally sent King Tone to jail long-term for "conspiracy to sell and distribute heroin" in 1998. Alba and other prominent leaders believe it was a frame-up, after the FBI and New York police spent a million dollars on Operation Crown that year but failed to find evidence against 91 other ALKQN leaders. One single raid during that operation was reportedly the largest in NYC since alcohol prohibition.[51]

Gang Conversions Cost Money Launderers Billions

The profits of the drug trafficking, ruling oligarchy were decreased by billions of dollars due to the gang-peace truce movement and conversion to activism between 1993 and 1996. The United Nations Drugs and Crime czar, Antonio Maria Costas, told the London *Observer*, "Inter-bank loans were funded by money that originated from the drugs trade." The *Observer* went on to state that, "Gangs are now believed to make most of their profits from the drugs trade and are estimated to be worth £352bn, the UN says ... evidence that drug money has flowed into banks came from officials in Britain, Switzerland, Italy and the US."[52] U.S. intelligence surely knew of this, as some of their top leaders also had leadership in the finance industry.

Recent articles have covered drug money laundering by major banks. In 2010, Wachovia (now part of Wells Fargo) admitted to not following the law that guarded against laundering narcotics traffickers money, when they were caught doing so in a 2006 incident. Bloomberg News reported that an airplane involved in this trafficking was one of four that transported twenty-two tons of cocaine. In working with Mexican currency exchange houses from 2004 to 2007, Wachovia allowed $378 billion of laundered money to go unexamined.[54] Furthermore, in 2012 a "Senate inquiry found that HSBC, England's largest bank, accepted more than $15 billion in cash between 2006 and 2009, much of it thought to be connected to drug gangs."[55]

Drug money is also allegedly laundered through the profit reports of local chain stores and restaurants whose parent companies are on the New York Stock Exchange. As detailed earlier, Catherine Fitts, former top-level Wall Street insider and former U.S. Deputy Housing Commissioner, explained the huge boost street level drug dealing gives to banks and other companies on the stock exchange that launder the money (hide it as cash profits in their businesses). The business, often a restaurant that deals in cash, may see a 20-fold increase in the stock value of the company that owns the business.

Fitts gave a concrete example of how a drug dealer's sales convert into millions of dollars on the stock market.

> Every day there are two or three teenagers on the corner dealing drugs across from our home in Philadelphia. We figured that if they had a 50% deal with a supplier, did $300 a day of sales each, and worked 250 days a year that their supplier could run his net profits of approximately $100,000 through a local fast food restaurant that was owned by a publicly traded company.
>
> Assuming that company has a stock market value that is a multiple of 20-30 times its profits, a handful of illiterate teenagers could generate approximately $2-3 million in stock market value for a major corporation, not to mention a nice flow of deposits and business for the Philadelphia banks and insurance companies.[56]

The gang conversion movement in which Tupac participated with his Black Panther extended family and the Young Lords was leading thousands of gang members to stop drug dealing in each of dozens of cities nationwide. The Latin Kings 3,000-member gang stopping dealing would have cost New York money launderers billions of dollars from their conversion alone.

Some fast-food restaurants have been charged with money laundering for drug dealers, and some chain fast-food restaurants have major stockholders who headed U.S. intelligence. Davco Restaurants bought the franchise rights for Wendy's fast food chain in the cities of Baltimore and Washington.[57] Davco Restaurants, one of the world's largest Wendy's franchisees, with over 150 restaurants in the mid-Atlantic region, has significant U.S. intelligence connections. One of its major stockholders is Citibank director John Deutch, the Director of Central Intelligence for two years under President Clinton.[58] Deutch also was a director of the following corporations at the same time: Ariad Pharmaceuticals, CMS Energy Corp., Cummins Engine Co., Raytheon Co., and Schlumberger Ltd, NY. The *New York Times* noted how Citibank worked with Cayman Island banks, transferring at least hundreds of millions of dollars for over two years, despite the Cayman banks' known drug money laundering.[59]

Police Shoot at Tupac; Tupac Shoots Back

U.S. intelligence responded in a number of ways to these gang conversion developments. To lessen Tupac's regular talks with his stepfather, they transferred Mutulu Shakur to the highest security prison in the country, located underground in Florence, Colorado. Federal prison officials have a history of collaborating with U.S. intelligence objectives. According to a warden's memo, prison officials put Mutulu in the country's most restrictive confines due to concern over his "outside contacts and influence over the younger black element."[60]

In response to the work of Tupac Shakur and other rappers with leftist political agendas, politicians were officially brought into the tactical strategy in 1993. According to Sundance Award-winner Nick Broomfield, who produced the documentary *Biggie and Tupac*: "In 1993, a Senate Select Committee was set up to look into the hip-hop movement. Fear of its inflammatory qualities led to FBI surveillance." The FBI were actually watching at least one rap group, N.W.A, since 1988.[61]

After a late October 1993 concert in Atlanta, Tupac's road manager drove the rapper in a motorcade following his business manager Watani Tyehimba's car. Several cars of guards and friends followed them. Just as Tyehimba went through an intersection, Tupac's car was stopped at a red light. Tupac saw two white men punching a black man in his car in an adjacent hotel driveway. The rapper rolled down his window and asked what was happening.[62]

A random bystander, Edward Fields, stated that he saw one of the white men, Mark Whitwell, point a gun at Tupac's group, and he screamed "Get Down! Get Down! Get Down!" at which point Tupac and many in his entourage quickly rolled up their windows.[63] A white couple from Cherokee County in a car facing Tupac's at the corner said in an interview that they looked up to see two white men and a white woman rush across the street to Tupac's car looking like a white gang attacking a black man.[64] When the white husband saw that at least one of the men had a gun, he told his wife to duck her head down.[65]

Watani Tyehimba got out of his car and said he "saw Mark Whitwell smash the Mercedes front passenger window with the handle butt of a gun and shoot at Tupac who was sitting behind the driver." Bystander Edward Fields also said he saw "one of the White males ... pull out and point a black handgun ... and then fired one shot" into the Mercedes.[66]

Tupac's biological cousin, Billy Lesane, described seeing Tupac roll out of his Mercedes and grab a gun from another of his cousins. Likely due to the surprise of there being several cars with Tupac's that included guards with guns, the outnumbered attackers started running away, while Mark Whitwell kept his arm extended with the gun pointed behind him at the group. Lesane said that Tupac had gotten down on one knee "like a soldier and fired three rounds," hitting Mark Whitwell in the small of the back and Scott Whitwell in the butt.[67]

While these accounts alone support a planned attempt to murder Tupac, the Whitwells' behavior following the incident further suggests such a plan in their attempted cover-up. The Whitwells were police officers, purportedly off-duty at this time, and they filed a written police report that included the statement, "Niggers came by and did a drive-by shooting."[68] Also, despite the many eyewitnesses, the Whitwells told a police division that they didn't have any guns on them.[69] The two were treated at a hospital and released the following day.

Tupac was arrested, charged with attempted murder and brought to trial. At some time between Tupac's arrest and the trial, Tupac's lawyers, Chokwe Lumumba and Ken Ellis, found out that the Whitwells were police officers. These cops never identified themselves as such at the scene, suggesting they were trying to hide the fact, as it could have protected them from the potentially fatal retaliatory shooting.[70]

It appears this was another U.S. intelligence attempt to assassinate the rap and film star. Tupac's lawyer found that one of the men who shot at Tupac used a gun the other had stolen from a police evidence locker. In a separate trial, another police officer said such a gun is known as a "throwaway gun," one that could be put down after murdering someone and couldn't be traced back to the officer.

Police also came to Tupac's hotel room immediately after the shooting. Since the rooms were reserved under several false names, it shows the police had always had Tupac under close surveillance. When the evidence mounted against the wounded police officers, Atlanta prosecutors dropped their charges against Tupac for shooting them.[71]

Notes

1 Connie Bruck, "The Takedown of Tupac," *The New Yorker*, 7/7/97, p. 47. On Assata Shakur, see editorial, "Thoughts and Notes on Tupac," *The Amsterdam News*, (New York), 12/17/94, p. 24. On Afeni leading Harlem Black Panthers while Lumumba was in jail, see Jasmine Guy, *Afeni Shakur: Evolution of a Revolutionary* (New York: Atria, 2004), p. 82.

2 Ward Churchill and Jim Vander Wall, *The COINTELPRO Papers: Documents from the FBI's Secret Wars Against Dissent in the United States* (Boston: South End, 1991), pp. 309, 410-11, note 24. Ward Churchill and Jim Vander Wall, *Agents of Repression: The FBI's Secret Wars Against the Black Panther Party and the American Indian Movement* (Boston: South End, 1988) p.364. On Mutulu underground on FBI's Most Wanted list, see Cathy Scott, *The Killing of Tupac Shakur* (Las Vegas, NV: Huntington Press, 1997), p. 65. On Tupac attending political meetings with Mutulu: *Resurrection* (Documentary, Amaru Entertainment/MTV Films, 2003).

3 On FBI queries of Tupac and Mutulu keeping in touch with him, see Scott, *The Killing of Tupac Shakur*, p. 65. On Rev. Daughtry's quotes, see transcript of his 1996 memorial speech, Armond White, *Rebel for the Hell of It: The Life of Tupac Shakur* (New York: Thunder's Mouth Press, 1997), p. 2.

4 On FBI keeping Afeni unemployed, see Testimony of Tupac Shakur's attorney, Michael Warren, former Black Liberation Movement leader, New York vs. Tupac Shakur, sentencing hearing transcript, pp. 46-50. The use of this FBI tactic is backed by Michael Swearingen, *FBI Secrets: An Agent's Exposé* (Boston, MA:South End,1995), p. 116. On Afeni moving dozens of times, see Scott, *The Killing of Tupac Shakur*, p. 66. On Harlem acting, see Michael Eric Dyson, *Holler If You Hear Me: Searching for Tupac Shakur* (New York: Basic Civitas, 2001), p. 33. 17 year-old Tupac Shakur in video, *Tupac Shakur, Thug Angel, Life of an Outlaw* (QD3 Entertainment, 2002).

5 Dyson, *Holler If You Hear Me*, p. 33.

6 Personal interview, Watani Tyehimba, 5/2/00. Personal interview with Chokwe Lumumba, 5/10/00. Tyehimba was a former Revolutionary Action Movement-based Los Angeles Black Panther who befriended Afeni Shakur working on Geronimo Pratt's case.

7 Dyson, *Holler If You Hear Me*, p. 84. After Tupac got there, he found out that two of his friends were fatally shot in Baltimore

8 Dyson, *Holler If You Hear Me*, p.84. Personal interviews, W. Tyehimba, 5/10/00 and C. Lumumba, 5/5/00. On poetry see Tupac Shakur, *The Rose That Grew from Concrete* (New York: MTV Books, 1999), p. 111. Tupac Shakur, *The Lost Tapes* (Herb N' Soul, 2001). On cocaine trafficking in San Francisco, Gary Webb, *Dark Alliance: The CIA, the Contras, and the Crack Cocaine Explosion* (New York: Seven Stories, 1998), p. 559.

9 Personal interview, Watani Tyehimba, 5/2/00. Personal interview with Chokwe Lumumba, 5/10/00. Michael Eric Dyson, *Holler If You Hear Me*, p. 84. White, *Rebel for the Hell of It*, also claimed that Tupac was the New Afrikan Panthers youngest-ever elected chairman.

10 Churchill and Vander Wall, *The COINTELPRO Papers*, pp. 320, 417-18.

11 Jack Olson, *Last Man Standing: The Tragedy and Triumph of Geronimo Pratt* (Anchor, 2001). Personal interviews with former Black Panthers Watani Tyehimba and George Edwards. Torri Minton, "Huey Newton Gives In, Gets Out of Quentin," *San Francisco Chronicle*, August 27, 1988, p. A3. Torri Minton, "Prison Protest by Ex-Panther Newton," *San Francisco Chronicle*, August 24, 1988, p. B8. Paul Liberatore, "How Huey Newton Let a Panther Down," *San Francisco Chronicle*, September 16, 1988, p. A13.

12 On FBI/Held's work against Pratt and his legal team in 1985, see *Pratt V. D.J. McCarthy, et al.*, NO. CR. 81-3407-PAR (K), United States District Court, Central District of California, 1985; Vol.3[A], pp. 452-53. Cited in Chuchill and Vander Wall, *Agents of Repression*, p. 92 note 195. Also see Swearingen, *FBI Secrets*, p. 167. On music benefits for Pratt, see Bruck, "The Takedown of Tupac," *The New Yorker*, 7/7/97, p. 49. Newton's work for Pratt, see Liberatore, "How Huey Newton Let a Panther Down." On Tupac's quote, see *Tupac Shakur, Thug Angel, Life of an Outlaw*. On Newton reuniting Panthers, personal interview, Billy X Jennings, *Black Panther* newspaper editor, first International Black Panther Film Fest , New York City, April 8, 2000. Also, Newton attended African

People's Socialist Party (a.k.a. Uhuru Movement) meetings. Personal interview of Watu of Afrikan People's Socialist Party, 10/28/03. Churchill and Vander Wall, *The COINTELPRO Papers*, pp.320, 417-18. On Tupac consulting with Newton, he said he was consulting "with the Panther Minister of Defense," Huey Newton's official position: Dyson, *Holler If You Hear Me*, p. 54.

13 On the Bari quote, this writer heard it on tape of her played on WBAI radio, NYC, 3/3/00. On other information, see Ward Churchill, "The FBI Targets Judi Bari" *Covert Action Quarterly*, Winter 1993-94, Number 47. Robert J. Lopez, "Bomb victims jailed," *Oakland Tribune*, May 26, 1990; and Dean Congblay, "Police Say Car Bomb in the Back Seat: How Earth First! victims became suspects," *San Francisco Chronicle*, May 28, 1990. Sgt. Michael Sitterud, Oakland Police Follow-Up Investigation Report (1) RD No. 90-57171, May 2, 1990, pp.1, 3.

14 See her five-page printed speech, Judi Bari, "Community Under Siege," 5/8/91, in which she details Held's Cointelpro tactics against the Panthers, the American Indian Movement and then her Earth First! She listed and described a least 8 key tactics against her and her group: www.things.org/~jym/ef/community-under-siege.html. As this book was going to press, a Native American who worked with the American Indian Movement, Jesse Chi-Makwa Smith, contacted this author. He said his rap group, Savage King Ent, has experienced many attacks due to their activist songs, particularly their song "The Rez."

15 Held's former colleague M. Wesley Swearingen called the Bari bombing another example of the FBI's continued Cointelpro as "an effort by the FBI to neutralize Judy Bari." Swearingen, *FBI Secrets*, p. 106. Richard Held later leading a top credit card company; see *Covert Action Quarterly*'s founding co-publisher Louis Wolfe, *Human Rights in the United States: The Unfinished Story, Current Political Prisoners—Victims of Cointelpro*, Issue Forum, U.S. Congressional Hearing, 9/14/00, http://www.ratical.org/co-globalize/CynthiaMcKinney/news/if000914HR.html. Wolfe said his investigation led him to discovering that Held was CEO of a major credit card company in California. This underscores the revolving door between U.S. intelligence and the wealthiest families in the United States.

16 Swearingen, *FBI Secrets*, p. 106. On Bari's lawsuit leading to Held's early retirement, see Swearingen quote in Ward Churchill, "The FBI Targets Judi Bari" *Covert Action*, Winter 1993-94, Number 47. Louis Wolfe, *Human Rights in the United States: The Unfinished Story, Current Political Prisoners—Victims of Cointelpro*, Issue Forum, U.S. Congressional Hearing, 9/14/00, 1:25 P.M. Rayburn House Office Building, Washington, D.C. Room 2000.

17 Bruck, *The New Yorker*, 7/7/97, pp. 50, 52.

18 Tupac Shakur, *2Pacalypse Now* (Interscope,1991)

19 "Claim Against the city of Oakland, California, Claimant: Tupac Shakur" by John Burris, Esq. Photocopied for Jacob Hoye and Karolyn Ali, eds., *Tupac: Resurrection* (New York: Atria Books, 2003), pp. 78-79. Danyel Smith "Introduction," Vibe editors, *Tupac Shakur* (New York: Crown Publishing, 1997), p. 17. Personal interview, Watani Tyehimba, December 11, 2002. Robert McFadden, "At Two Rallies, Protesters Accuse Police in Killings," *New York Times*, 8/3/03, p. 32. Several other deaths in police custody have occurred via choking, with the most recent case being caught on video: Barry Paddock, Rocco Parascandola and Corky Siemaszko, "Homicide: Medical Examiner Says NYPD Chokehold Killed Staten Island Dad Eric Garner," *New York Daily News*, August 21, 2014, http://www.nydailynews.com/new-york/nyc-crime/eric-garner-death-ruled-homicide-medical-examiner-article-1.1888808. Note that one source here said Tupac's settlement was for only $15,000, but Tupac's business manager Watani Tyehimba said that it was for $42,000, Personal Interview, 5/1/00.

20 Mostly Marku Reynolds in video, *Thug Immortal* (Sunset Home Entertainment/Xenon/Don't Back Down Productions, 1998, DVD 2202). Veronica Chambers, "Ain't Nothing Changed but the Weather," *Premiere*, August, 1993, p. 84. Also, Robert Sam Anson, "To Die Like A Gangsta," *Vanity Fair*, March 1997, p. 248. Connie Bruck, "The Takedown of Tupac," *The New Yorker*, July 7, 1997, p. 47. On Harding living in Marin, Attorney Michael Warren, personal interview, 4/10/00. Reprinted from a Booneville, CA speech, Judi Bari, "Community Under Siege," 5/8/91, www.things.org/~jym/ef/community-under-siege.html. Michael Newton, *Bitter Grain: Huey Newton and the*

Black Panther Party (Los Angeles: Holloway House, 1980), p. 224

21 Chris Morris, "Quayle's 2Pac/Interscope Attack Puts New Heat On Time Warner," *Billboard*, October 3, 1992, pp. 5, 86.

22 Anson, "To Die Like a Gangsta," p.251. Bruck, "The Takedown of Tupac," p.57. Tupac lyric from "Keep Ya Head Up," *Strictly 4 My N.I.G.G.A.Z* (Interscope, 1993). Tupac Shakur, *2Pacalypse Now* (Interscope, 1992). The *Strictly...* CD was ready for release, but held up for a year by Time Warner; Personal interview, Watani Tyehimba, 5/5/00.

23 See August 30, 1967 FBI Memorandum from Philadelphia's Special Agent in Charge to the FBI Director, reprinted in Churchill and Vander Wall, *Agents of Repression*, pp. 44-47.

24 Associated Press, "Rapper Shakur Hit with a Gun Arrest Encore," *New York Daily News*, May 1, 1994. Personal interview with Tupac's Atlanta trial lawyer Ken Ellis, 5/20/00. On celebrities and guns, see, for example, "Names and Faces: Pistol Packing Big Shots," compiled by Chris Richards, *Washington Post*, 8/5/03, p. C3. While it names many celebrities among the 3,600 New Yorkers with licenses to carry a loaded weapon, its interesting that Steven Seagal was denied a permit renewal after his films exposed much U.S. intelligence drug trafficking. On Tupac's many arrests for mostly minor charges, see "Rapper's Rap Sheet: 10 Arrests," *New York Post*, 12/22/93 . On FBI's 4,000-page file, a Department of Justice incidentally revealed this in a phone conversation with this author. She also revealed it would be 10 cents a page to copy. See Freedom Of Information Act (FOIA) correspondence, John M. Kelso Jr., Section Chief, Freedom of Information-Privacy Acts Section Office of Public and Congressional Affairs, to John Potash, May 18, 2000, regarding estimated fees of $405.

25 "Intelligence Activities and Rights of Americans," Book II, 4/26/76, Senate Committee with Respect to Intelligence Report, reprinted in Alex Constantine, *The Covert War Against Rock* (Los Angeles, Feral House, 2000), p. 9. On marijuana charges, personal interview with Tupac's Atlanta trial lawyer Ken Ellis, 5/20/00.

26 Jasmine Guy, *Afeni Shakur: Evolution of a Revolutionary* (New York: Pocket Books, 2005).

27 On Geronimo, see Douglas Martin, "Elmer G. Pratt, Jailed Panther Leader, Dies at 63," *New York Times*, June 3, 2011, http://www.nytimes.com/2011/06/04/us/04pratt.html?_r=0. Personal interview with Tupac's Atlanta trial lawyer, Ken Ellis, 5/20/00.

28 From literature, "Code of THUG LIFE" by Tupac Shakur and Mutulu Shakur. Provided to author by former New Haven Black Panther George Edwards. Alexander Cockburn, "Beat the Devil," *The Nation*, June 1, 1992, pp. 738-39. See "Code of Thug Life" reprinted in Jamal Joseph, *Tupac Shakur: Legacy* (New York: Atria, 2006), pp. 37-38.

29 Lucille Renwick, "Gang Members Are Not the Only Ones Who Benefit from the Truce Between Bloods and Crips factions," *Los Angeles Times*, 6/5/94, p. 14. Jesse Katz, "Crips and Bloods Factions Prepare Ground for Widespread Gang Truce Cease-fire: More Than two dozen rival groups plan to raise funds to support legitimate businesses. The profits would go toward recreational centers, drug treatment and community facilities," *Los Angeles Times*, 5/19/94, p. 1. Efrain Hernandez Jr. and David Ferrell, "March a Tribute to Fragile Truce," *Los Angeles Times*, 4/29/95, p 1. Joe Garofoli, "Singer Belafonte feels the beat of antiwar sentiment/ Keynote speaker at Oakland rally hears international criticism," *San Francisco Chronicle*, 4/5/03, p. A15. This truce partly started with the reported Los Angeles police (LAPD) execution-style shooting of a top Crip in 1991. His cousin, Dewayne Holmes, worked with ex-Black Panther Michael Zinzun and local Shiite Muslim leader Mujahdid Abdul-Karim to rally Bloods and Crips factions against the LAPD instead of each other. Mike Davis, "Who Killed LA: Part Two: the Verdict is Given," *New Left Review* 198, pp. 34-35.

30 Garofoli, "Singer Belafonte feels the beat of antiwar sentiment." Also on Jesse Jackson's aid, Davis, "Who Killed LA: Part Two," pp. 34-35.

31 Mitchell Landsberg and John Mutchell, "In Gang's Territory, a Weary Hope," *Los Angeles Times*, 12/5/02, p. A1.

32 "Rival Gangs Extend Reach to Small Cities," *Houston Chronicle*, 9/20/94, p. 20.

33 Reuters, "Gangs Found in Military, Magazine Says," *St. Louis Post – Dispatch*, 7/17/95, p. A4.

34 http://www.hitemup.com/tupac/family.html.

35 Bruck, "The Takedown of Tupac," *The New Yorker*, 7/7/97, p. 53. He reportedly started organizing the truce in the Lompoc Penitentiary, http://www.hitemup.com/tupac/family.html.

36 On Scott's conversion, see Kody Scott (aka Sanyika Shakur), *Monster: The Autobiography of an L.A. Gang Member* (New York: Penguin, 1994), pp. vii-viii, 347-49. Tupac planned activist projects with Scott, Vibe eds., *Tupac*, '97, p. 51. On *Nation* article, Alexander Cockburn, "Beat the Devil," *The Nation*, June 1, 1992, pp.738-9. Also hear Kody/Sanyika's 20+ minute phone conversation at https://www.youtube.com/watch?v=BO0mI5AbTc4.

37 Davis, "Who Killed Los Angeles? Part Two," pp. 36-37.

38 Jesse Katz, "Crips and Bloods Factions Prepare Ground for Widespread Gang Truce Cease-fire: More Than two dozen rival groups plan to raise funds to support legitimate businesses. The profits would go toward recreational centers, drug treatment and community facilities." *Los Angeles Times*, 5/19/94, p. 1.

39 Mike Davis, "Who Killed LA? A Political Autopsy," *New Left Review* 197, 1993, p. 7.

40 Mike Davis, "In L.A., Burning All Illusions," *The Nation*, 6/1/92, p. 745. Davis, "Who Killed Los Angeles? Part Two," pp. 34-35. WBAI Radio, 4/15/02. FBI work with LAPD in Operation Hammer in Megan Garvery and Rich Winton, "City Declares War on Gangs," *Los Angeles Times*, 12/4/02. One activist was taped speaking to a large assembly and broadcast on the Pacifica Radio Network. He told how the LAPD's Operation Hammer—an "anti-gang operation"—disrupted the gang peace summit meetings, breaking up one meeting with a charge of "unlawful assembly," heard by this writer on 99.1, WBAI radio in New York City, April 29, 2001.

41 Davis, "Who Killed LA? A Political Autopsy," p.7.

42 Tupac's manager Watani Tyehimba also reported a lecture on an anti-gang peace summit operation "Weed and Seed." He said that undercover police agents were paid to "weed" their way into the two gangs and then attempt to sew seeds of dissension between them. Personal interview, Watani Tyehimba, 12/14/02.

43 Jesse Katz, "Man Freed in Death of Gang Leader, Courts: Rodney Compton is to get one year probation in the slaying of Tony Bogard, who helped reach a truce between the Crips and Bloods," *Los Angeles Times*, 6/1/94, p. 3.

44 Davis, "Who Killed Los Angeles? Part Two," p. 35

45 Katz, "Man Freed in Death of Gang Leader."

46 Renwick, "Gang Members Are Not the Only Ones Who Benefit from the Truce Between Bloods and Crips factions," p. 14.

47 Chris Hedges, "Old Colors, New Battle Cry; Gang Founder Calls for Focus on the Community, Not Crimes," *New York Times*, 1/31/2000, pp. B1, B6.

48 Tim King, "US street gang leaders to address London rally," *The Guardian* (London), 10/28/94.

49 David Brotherton and Luis Barrios, *The Almighty Latin King and Queen Nation: Street Politics and the Transformation of a New York City Gang* (New York: Columbia University Press, 2004). On membership, p. 199. Also on Latin Kings, see Jennifer Gonnerman, "Throne Behind Bars: The Latin King Leader on Love, Law Enforcement, and Landing Back in Jail," *Village Voice*, 4/7/98, p. 61. Further see video, *Black and Gold: The Latin King and Queen Nation*, a documentary (Big Noise Films, 1999), which is probably the best account. On New York Bloods, Hedges, "Old Colors, New Battle Cry ...". Personal interviews with Vincente Panama Alba, 10/35/1996 and 5/1/1998.

50 "Seize the Hospital to Serve the People: An Interview with Activist Cleo Silvers, 2009," www.socialmedicine.org/media/.

51 Personal interview with Hector Torres, 9/12/98. Torres, called the "elder spokesman" for the Latin Kings and Queens, also worked for New York activist Reverend Al Sharpton Sharpton and headlined a seminar at John Jay College of Criminal Justice. In describing how King Tone's probation officer didn't believe Tone's probation should be violated, Torres described a similar situation as had happened to Tupac before his sentencing hearing. Torres said that the probation officer's high level superiors came in and took the case from her, rewrote her report to the judge and recommended

that Tone be violated and imprisoned. For Tupac's case, see Sentencing hearing transcript—New York vs. Tupac Shakur and Charles Fuller, defendants, February 14, 1995, pp. 8-9. Torres said he would travel nationwide to transform gangs "into positive political voices for disenfranchised communities," Maki Becker, "Latin King vows to aid gang kids," *Daily News*, 7/9/01. Arrest of King Tone and 23 other Latin Kings also reported in Gonnerman, "Throne Behind Bars."

52 Rajeev Sayel, "Drug Money Saved Banks in Global Crisis, Says UN Adviser," *The Guardian/The Observer* (London), December 12, 2009, http://www.guardian.co.uk/global/2009/dec/13/drug-money-banks-saved-un-cfief-claims.

54 Michael Smith, "Banks Financing Mexico Gangs Admitted In Wells Fargo Deal," *Bloomberg News*, June 29, 2010, http://www.bloomberg.com/news/2010-06-29/banks-financing-mexico-s-drug-cartels-admitted-in-wells-fargo-s-u-s-deal.html.

55 Harry Wilson, "HSBC to Set Aside $600 million to Cover Mis-selling and Money Laundering Scandals," *The Telegraph* (UK), July 29, 2012, http://www.telegraph.co.uk/finance/newsbysector/banksandfinance/9436539/HSBC-to-set-aside-600m-to-cover-mis-selling-and-money-laundering-scandals.html.

56 Catherine Austin Fitts, "Narco Dollars for Beginners; How the Money Works in the Illicit Drug Trade; Part II: The Narco Money Map, *Narco News Bulletin*, October 31, 2001, http://www.narconews.com/narcodollars2.html.

57 On McDonalds franchises charged with money laundering, Jesse Garza, "Owner of 3 North Shore Restaurants charged with Conspiracy to sell marijuana," *Journal Sentinel*, October 12, 2013, http://www.jsonline.com/news/indictment-connects-north-shore-mcdonalds-to-drug-conspiracy-b99122166z1-228109891.html. Note that these franchises were also laundering proceeds from opiates. On Davco history, see www.wendavco.com/davco-history-wendys-history.

58 On 150 restaurants, see Davco history on above website. On Deutch as part of Citibank directors invested in Davco, see http://edgar.brand.edgar-online.com/EFX_dll/EDGARpro.dll?FetchfilingHTML1?ID=514923&SessionID=bcuSHe9tsQt4pA7. On his CIA Director status, https://www.cia.gov/library/center-for-the-study-of-intelligence/csi-publications/books-and-monographs/directors-and-deputy-directors-of-central-intelligence/deutch.html.

59 Tim Golden, "Citibank Criticized for Slow Response to Drug Laundering Scheme," *New York Times*, February 27, 2001, http://www.nytimes.com/2001/02/27/world/27LAUN.html.

60 A warden's memo said that Mutulu's transfer was due to "outside contacts," Bruck, "The Takedown of Tupac," p. 54.

61 Nick Broomfield, *Biggie and Tupac* (documentary, 2002). Broomfield had previously won a best documentary award at the Sundance Film Festival.

62 Personal interview with Tupac's Atlanta trial lawyer, Ken Ellis, 5/12/00. Partly from eyewitness Watani Tyehimba, parked next to black motorist first focused on by the plainclothes cops. Personal interview, 11/5/03. Danzy Senna, "Violence is Golden," *Spin Magazine*, April, 1994, pp. 43-47. Also, personal interview with Tupac's other lawyer, Chokwe Lumumba, 5/5/00.

63 Personal interview with Tupac's Atlanta trial lawyer, Ken Ellis, 5/12/00. Ellis reported that his investigator interviewed the black motorist, Fields and the white couple. Partly from eyewitness Watani Tyehimba, parked next to black motorist first focused on by the plainclothes cops. Personal interview, 11/5/03. Fields and Chokwe Lumumba also in Danzy Senna, "Violence is Golden," p. 46. Personal interview with Ken Ellis, 5/12/00.

64 Reported from interview of couple by Tupac's lead lawyer, Chokwe Lumumba, Senna, "Violence is Golden," p. 46.

65 Personal interview with Ken Ellis, Tupac's Atlanta trial lawyer, with whom Tupac's national lawyer, Chokwe Lumumba, was working.

66 Personal interview, Watani Tyehimba. From witness interviews: personal interview, Ken Ellis. Edward Fields cited in Senna, "Violence is Golden." The daily *Atlanta Journal Constitution* also provided portions of the police report in which Edward Fields is quoted as saying this, in Scruggs and Marshall, "Witness says off-duty cops fired first shot."

67 Personal interview, Billy Lesane, April, 10, 1999.

68 Ronin Ro, *Have Gun Will Travel* (New York: Doubleday, 1998), p. 146.

69 Scruggs and Marshall, "Witness says off-duty cops fired first shot."

70 Partly from eyewitness Watani Tyehimba, parked next to black motorist first focused on by the plainclothes cops. Personal interview, 11/5/03. Both attorneys, Ellis and Lumumba, seperately asserted that Atlanta cops would normally say "police," off duty or not, for protection, unless they wanted to hide the fact, personal interviews, Ken Ellis, 5/12/00, Chokwe Lumumba, 5/5/00. Senna, "Violence is Golden." Personal interview, eyewitness Billy Lesane, 4/10/98. Scruggs and Marshall, "Witness says off-duty cops fired first shot."

71 On white officers' account, see their lawyer in Scruggs and Marshall, "Witness says off-duty cops fired first shot." Personal interviews with Ellis, 5/20/00; Lumumba, 5/5/00; Lesane, 4/10/99; and Tyehimba, 5/10/00. On gun stolen from evidence locker, Scott, *The Killing of Tupac Shakur*, p. 77, and Senna, "Violence is Golden," p. 46. On "throwaway gun," New York City police officer Craig McKernan, *People of the state of New York vs. Charles Fuller and Tupac Shakur*, Indictment no. 11578-93, Trial Excerpt of People's Witness—Officer McKernan cross-examination, pp. 8-9, by Michael Warren, Esq.

Chapter Twenty-Four

Spy Targets & Tupac: Weed Promotion, Rap War & Gangs

More evidence regarding attacks on two other black leaders, Mumia Abu-Jamal and Imam Jamil Al-Amin, would suggest that U.S. intelligence orchestrated the 1993 incident where Atlanta police shot at rap icon Tupac Shakur. After that incident, Tupac was arrested on a forced sodomy accusation (anal or oral sex), before being shot in New York. Evidence then indicated that U.S. intelligence ran a sophisticated operation through the Death Row Records label that involved manipulating Tupac to promote marijuana use and promulgate a war between rappers. An investigation also found Death Row trafficking guns and cocaine, before using Tupac's last days to end the Bloods/Crips gang truce.

Spy Targets: Mumia Abu-Jamal & Imam Jamil Al-Amin/H. Rap Brown

Evidence that U.S. intelligence attempted to orchestrate Tupac Shakur's murder in Atlanta is bolstered by U.S. intelligence attacks on other black leaders, particularly former Black Panther Mumia Abu-Jamal and former Student Nonviolent Coordinating Committee leader Imam Jamil Al-Amin. U.S. intelligence appeared to use psychological profiling in their targeting of both Tupac and Mumia. Regarding Imam Al-Amin, the FBI had worked with Atlanta police intelligence in the same 1990s time period, using undercover agent infiltrators in the Imam's Muslim group at that time, before framing Imam Al-Amin for murder.

U.S. intelligence appeared to have used psychological profiling to set up Tupac by having white police in street clothes attack a black man in front of the rapper to try and draw him out of his car. Black Panther Huey Newton wrote that U.S. intelligence used a similar ploy on him when police shot up the door of his next-door neighbor to unsuccessfully try to lure Newton out so he could be killed. As noted, that neighbor was dealing drugs and renting the apartment from the FBI when police shot up his door.[1]

Evidence also indicates the use of similar psychological profiling in a murder attempt of Mumia Abu-Jamal (born Wesley Cook). Mumia had been Minister of Information for the Philadelphia Black Panthers as a teen. Mumia then became an award-winning journalist after the Panthers disbanded. Mumia worked for WUHY-FM in Philadelphia, as well as writing and reading stories on National Public Radio. Respect from his journalism peers led them to elect Mumia as the head of the Philadelphia Black Journalists Association.[2]

Mumia covered many police-brutality cases, particularly assaults on the activist group MOVE, who forbade drug use. MOVE taught how an oppressive U.S. government cultivated addiction in America. Reports claim Mumia strongly supported MOVE by 1981, and later joined them.[3]

On December 9, 1981, Mumia Abu-Jamal and police officer Daniel Faulkner were shot in what evidence showed to be an attempt to murder Mumia or jail him for Officer's Faulkner's murder. When top bands and international groups around the world supported Mumia in the 1990s, he became the most famous political prisoner in the world. On his CD cover and in his songs, Tupac Shakur promoted Mumia's freedom.[4]

In the following years, many witnesses gave testimony that not only exonerated Mumia Abu-Jamal, but reinforced the understanding that the incident he was accused of was part of a huge operation.[5] Police tried to hide the medical examiner's report that the fatal .44 caliber bullet that killed officer Faulkner could not have been fired from Mumia's .38 caliber gun. Years after the shooting, Arnold Beverly, a career hit man serving time in jail, signed an affidavit saying the Mafia paid him and another gunman to shoot Faulkner. Other police were at the scene to back Beverly up and provide help with his getaway.[6] Beverly passed two lie detector tests regarding this affidavit.[7]

More affidavits supported witness testimony that Ken Freeman, a friend of Mumia's brother Billy Cook, was the other gunman identified by Beverly and worked undercover for U.S. intelligence to help kill Faulkner. Without each shooter's full knowledge, this operation targeted Mumia with murder or imprisonment. In an affidavit, Mumia Abu-Jamal said he heard gunshots, heard his brother scream after being beaten by Officer Faulkner, and ran to the scene where he saw a uniformed policeman turn toward him, gun in hand. Mumia said he then saw a flash and went down on his knees, severely wounded.[8]

According to Billy Cook, that night Ken Freeman was armed with a .38 caliber gun. Apparently, after Mumia's conviction, Freeman told Billy about a plan to kill Faulkner and that he participated in the shooting of Officer Faulkner. Freeman also said he was, "connected, and knew all kinds of people" after being in the Army.[9]

Further cover-ups ensued. Three years later, Philadelphia police tried to serve an illegal warrant on MOVE, the activist organization Mumia supported. Then, police infamously dropped a C-4 military explosive from a helicopter onto the roof of the row house that was MOVE's home and headquarters. The FBI and Bureau of Alcohol, Tobacco and Firearms gave Philly police the explosive. The explosion caused raging flames, but police wouldn't let firefighters put hoses on the fire for several hours. Eleven men, women, and children, and their pets, burned to death. The spreading flames also burned down two whole city blocks. Only two survived, Ramona Africa and thirteen-year-old Birdie Africa. Police jailed Ramona.[10] Ken Freeman was "discovered dead in Philadelphia under mysterious circumstances" the following day.[11]

In the 1960s, the FBI's Cointelpro murderously targeted H. Rap Brown. He worked as a Student National Coordinating Committee (SNCC) leader and honorary Panther, before changing his name to Imam Jamil Al-Amin at the time of Mumia's imprisonment in the 1980s.[12]

In 1967, an hour after H. Rap Brown spoke at a summer rally in Maryland, two black auxiliary police officers shot at the SNCC leader, grazing his head. Blacks reacted by rioting. When later asked about the truth of rumors that organizers snuck him out of town in a coffin, Brown replied, "I've never said. The government probably would have liked me to leave in a coffin." The U.S. Congress then passed the Rap Brown Amendment, making it illegal to go across state lines and give a speech that "provokes" a riot.[13] Though the FBI Counterintelligence Program had supposedly ended, agents said it continued into the 1990s under different names.[14]

In Atlanta, Imam Jamil Al-Amin presided over the second largest community of traditional Muslims in the United States.[15] Most Muslims in the world belonged to Al-Amin's sect of Islam.[16] Al-Amin's work included successfully clearing drugs out of neighborhoods of Atlanta.[17]

In 1993, when Atlanta police attacked Tupac, they also targeted Imam Jamil Al-Amin in several ways. From 1992 to 1995, Atlanta police intelligence worked with the FBI to infiltrate Al-Amin's mosque, allegedly to investigate a possible homicide. Several years of spying and tens of thousands of documents failed to produce any charges.[18] In 1995 a man was shot in a park near Al-Amin. Police first pressed charges against Al-Amin for the shooting, but dropped the charges when the man claimed police forced him to say that Al-Amin shot him.[19]

U.S. intelligence appeared to wage their largest attack on Imam Jamil Al-Amin in 1999. Police claimed he fatally shot a police officer.[20] The problem began when Al-Amin was driving a friend's car, and a police officer pulled him over. Al-Amin had a police badge that a local mayor had given him as an honorary auxiliary officer for helping to get drug dealers out of a neighborhood. When Al-Amin presented the badge to the officer, the officer charged him with theft and impersonating a policeman.[21]

Soon after, police sent two black police officers to arrest Al-Amin, with a warning that the Iman was armed and dangerous. One of these policemen said Al-Amin fatally shot his fellow officer.[22] A large body of evidence indicates this was not Al-Amin, and the officers were sent after, or must have come upon, a different person. The officer said he shot and wounded Al-Amin. Police investigators also said Al-Amin left a trail of blood from where he was shot. Upon arrest several days later, Al-Amin didn't have a mark on his body, but he still ended up on death row for his alleged killing of a police officer. Tupac Shakur's manager, Watani Tyehimba, and Tupac's New York trial lawyer both worked to help Imam Jamil Al-Amin's defense appeals, but he remains in prison.[23]

FBI Escalates Attacks on Tupac

The sophistication of attacks on Tupac Shakur continued to develop in proportion to his increasing wealth and fame. While Tupac was working on his third film, *Above the Rim,* with Woody Harrelson, a Haitian music promoter named Jacques Agnant (a.k.a. Ricardo "Nigel" Brown) befriended the rap star. In November of 1993, two weeks after the Atlanta cops shot at Tupac, Agnant introduced Tupac to a woman named Ayanna Jackson in a New York dance club. She admitted in court to having unzipped Tupac's pants and "kissed" Tupac's penis in the middle of a crowded dance floor, before having sex with him in his hotel.[24] Several nights later, she stated she came back to Tupac's hotel room and had oral sex with him, but this time Jackson accused Tupac, Agnant and two other associates of forced sodomy and sexual abuse. She filed charges with police.[25]

Tupac Shakur's description of the night indicates that Jacques Agnant had set him up, perhaps by slipping a drug in his drink. Tupac said he was having drinks with his road manager, Agnant and one of Agnant's associates when Agnant called to get Ayanna Jackson over to the hotel room. Tupac messed around with her in his room, and then Agnant came in with his associate. Tupac reported walking out of the room and going into another room before passing out. Tupac said that when he woke up, "I felt like I was drugged." Jackson's accusations against Shakur and Agnant included forced sodomy, assisting forced sodomy, and gun possession.[26]

Evidence accumulated to indicate U.S. intelligence set up the Ayanna Jackson incident. A U.S. intelligence memorandum regarding political musicians specifically addressed this tactic. It instructed agents to: "Send in women and drugs ... [use] free sex to entrap."[27] Police also tampered with evidence, "accidentally" destroying tapes of Ayanna Jackson on Tupac's hotel voicemail that supported his defense of a consensual sexual experience.[28]

Other evidence indicated Jacques Agnant worked for U.S. intelligence. A Policemen's Benevolent Association lawyer bailed Agnant out of jail and represented him in court.[29] Tupac's trial lawyer, Michael Tarif Warren, acquired Agnant's rap sheet, which showed a long list of major charges up and down the East Coast, all dismissed, which Warren said was "a sure sign that Agnant was a police agent." Warren also said that Agnant successfully had his case severed from Tupac's, which the attorney said was highly unusual.[30]

Towards the end of Tupac's trial, the case was looking so bad for the prosecution they said they'd be willing to accept a mistrial for having withheld evidence: photographs of Ayanna Jackson at the hotel scene.[31] Tupac rejected the offer, wanting to clear his name. To prevent Tupac from continuing his meteoric career trajectory, police intelligence apparently tried another plan.

While the jury was still out at the end of November 1994, an associate of Jacques Agnant's, Jimmy "Henchman" Rosemond (a.k.a. Booker), called Tupac. Rosemond said he'd give him $3,000 to record a song with another rapper. Wary of Rosemond because of Agnant, Tupac said he'd only come for $7,000. Rosemond complied and Tupac came to the New York recording studio in Times Square.[32]

In an interview for *Vibe* magazine, Tupac detailed how, "I felt nervous because this guy knew somebody I had major beef with ... Nigel [Agnant] had introduced me to Booker [Rosemond]. Everybody knew I was short on money. All my shows were being canceled." This was reportedly due to police groups calling concert venues and saying they wouldn't provide security due to Tupac shows being a riot risk.[33]

But Tupac suffered through many legal charges as well as many lawsuits, leading him to say, "All my money from my records was going to lawyers; all the movie money was going to my family. So I was rapping for guys and getting paid."[34]

Tupac had always avoided hard drugs, a reaction to his mother's addiction. However, perhaps not realizing that the genetics of addiction could predispose him to cannabis dependence, Tupac developed a marijuana habit. He said that he was "smoking chronic [strong marijuana] daily."[35]

Tupac reported that when he walked up to the studio, a thirty-something-year-old black man was hanging out in army fatigues and didn't acknowledge him. Tupac later said he was too stoned to realize how suspicious that was, since black men in that age group usually recognized and acknowledged him due to his film and music fame. Inside the building, that man, and another who had been waiting indoors, shot Tupac once to put him on the ground, then twice in the skull, according to a doctor's affidavit.[36] Amazingly, though Tupac was seriously wounded, he survived.

Tupac's plan to clear his name became more complicated, as mainstream media twisted the facts of the incident to state that the shooters were only mugging Tupac, and Tupac reached for his gun to shoot them. A security camera pointed at the lobby doors for buzzing people in had a videotape, which police didn't confiscate. Instead, they abruptly halted the investigation.[37]

Years later, Dexter Isaac signed a letter saying, "James Rosemond hired me to rob 2Pac Shakur at the [mispelled in letter] Quad Studio. He gave me $2,500, plus all the jewelry I took," which amounted to tens of thousands of dollars. Either Isaac or the gunman with Isaac had the more serious mission of killing Tupac, seemingly for U.S. intelligence. Government documents showed Rosemond had been charged with a crime in 1994, before Tupac's shooting. Rosemond met with U.S. prosecutors as an apparent informant from that time until at least June of 1998. Documents included an "Agreement" that Rosemond's ongoing "statements" to the District Attorney and U.S. State's Attorney would not be used against him regarding the 1994 criminal case, the prosecution of which was put on indefinite hold.[38]

It would not be surprising to learn the FBI used the 1994 criminal case against James Rosemond to turn him into an "informant" (collaborating agent). The FBI had a pattern of doing this. Noted FBI researchers Ward Churchill and Jim Vander Wall described this scenario. The FBI approached FBI infiltrator William O'Neal just after he was arrested twice for car theft. "Apparently in exchange for a monthly stipend and the dropping of these charges, O'Neal agreed to infiltrate the Chicago [Black Panther Party] as a counterintelligence operative."[39]

By 2011, James Rosemond was indicted for trafficking "numerous kilos of cocaine."[40] A *Village Voice* article claimed a jury convicted Rosemond of trafficking "thousands of kilos of drugs and dirty cash between Los Angeles and New York." The article further stated that "Prosecutors proved" that these shipments included "machine guns" and were in "music crates to recording studios and record labels owned by or affiliated with Vivendi's Universal Music Group, the largest music corporation in the world." The article further reported that Rosemond admitted his part in the assault on Tupac at Quad Studio, in a "cooperation deal that might lead to a reduced sentence, according to federal prosecutors." Rosemond wouldn't do time for that crime as "in New York, the statute of limitations on robbery is seven years, which means the time to prosecute anyone for the Quad case expired 11 years ago."[41] U.S. intelligence appeared to give up on Rosemond, as he received a long jail sentence for the trafficking.

On December 1, 1994, the day after the Quad shooting, a jury found Tupac innocent on all charges including forced sodomy and assisting forced sodomy. They only found him guilty of "touching Jackson's butt" against her will and assisting suspected police agent Jacques Agnant of doing the same. For that offense, Tupac received a sentence of one to four years in jail. For virtually the same charges, Agnant's indictment was dismissed and he pled guilty to two misdemeanors (the equivalent of a reckless driving and a public intoxication charge).[42] Tupac had been hospitalized for his shooting wounds, recovered, and then began serving his sentence.

Tupac started serving time on Riker's Island, New York City's central jail complex. While there, Interscope released his next CD, *Me Against the World,* and it topped the pop charts for two weeks. This coincided with the time President Bill Clinton ordered the bombing of Bosnia. Reporters interviewed Tupac in jail about his chart-topping success, and Tupac questioned the government's treatment of Cuba and bombing of other countries while people go hungry on American streets.[43]

Tupac admitted that after developing a daily marijuana habit before prison, it was hard to stop abruptly. "My brain was half dead from smoking so much weed ... drinking, going to clubs, just being numb," he said. Tupac vowed to quit smoking marijuana.[44]

From Riker's, prison officials shipped Tupac nine hours north to the maximum security Clinton Correctional facility in Dannemora, New York. There, guards subjected Tupac to the full gamut of penal coercion tactics. These are tactics identified by Amnesty International as designed for manipulating political prisoners. Prison guards conducted rectal exams on Tupac every time someone visited him, saying they were searching for contraband, despite that they watched each visit. They also kept him in solitary confinement during ten of his eleven months in prison. An American Civil Liberty Union (ACLU) report stated the purpose of these tactics were to "reduce [prisoners] to a state of psychological incompetence sufficient to neutralize them."[45]

These tactics aided U.S. intelligence's next possible goals for Tupac. They apparently decided to manipulate Tupac and use him to both target the rap community and to influence his fans in several negative ways. These included using Tupac's gangsta façade to promote gang behaviors, manufacturing an East Coast versus West Coast rap war, and promoting marijuana use.

Evidence suggests that media assets and intelligence agents were deployed to help set up the East Coast vs. West Coast rap war between Tupac and his rap star friend, Biggie Smalls (a.k.a. Notorious B.I.G., born Christopher Wallace). An intelligence document discussing how to target political musicians stated, "Provoke target groups into rivalries that may result in death." FBI documents and former Panthers detailed how the

FBI used similar tactics to set up the New York-based Black Panthers that include his mother, Afeni Shakur, and California-based Panther cofounder, Huey Newton.[46]

It appears U.S. intelligence also wanted Tupac to sign with Death Row Records, a new rap label that evidence suggests was a U.S. intelligence front company. In line with Time Inc.'s extensive history of work with the CIA, Time Warner gave Death Row a substantial amount of start-up money. Tupac's case was being appealed, and bail was set at $3 million. Normally, only 10% of bail is necessary to secure a bail bond and release from imprisonment. While the Court of Appeals would not accept Tupac's offer of 45% of the bail money, the Court immediately accepted a similar offer from Death Row within days of Tupac signing to them, releasing Tupac from jail while the appeals case was ongoing.[47]

Death Row Had CIA Drug Goals?

A reported drug kingpin, Michael "Harry-O" Harris, started Death Row Records with the help of his attorney, Dave Kenner, who owned its umbrella company.[48] Journalist Gary Webb quoted national drug trafficker "Freeway" Ricky Ross's probation officer, who said that Harris was one of Ross's two understudies. Ross regularly attained cheap cocaine from the CIA Nicaraguan Contra network, before distributing it nationally.[49]

Tupac Shakur with his Death Row Records produc Suge Knight and lawyer Dave Kenner. Kenner founde the record label with Michael "Harry-O" Harris, one two understudies of the CIA-collaborating cocair trafficker Freeway Ricky Ross.

Dave Kenner allowed former football player Marion "Suge" Knight to direct Death Row Records. Knight had a number of convictions with increasingly harsher sentences until suddenly, while still committing crimes, he seemed untouchable. Similar to Jacques Agnant and Eugene O'Neil, the agent infiltrator of the Chicago Panthers, it is most likely that Knight made a deal with police, as they failed to arrest him while he ran Death Row Records, until he completed his most important tasks. These tasks appeared to overlap U.S. intelligence's agenda.[50]

Death Row Records also filled its ranks with police officers. High-level Los Angeles Police detective, Russell Poole, along with detective Ken Knox, discovered "dozens and dozens of police officers were working" at all levels of Death Row Records. Det. Poole was told these officers could be considered "troubleshooters or covert agents." Death Row's Security chief, Reggie Wright Jr., "formerly" employed by the LAPD, admitted to having many LAPD officers working for him. Wright's father headed the Compton, California police gang unit at this time. Compton, part of the greater Los Angeles area, launched both top rap group N.W.A. and one of the first Bloods/Crips truces.[51]

Suge Knight and Death Row appeared to continue U.S. intelligence's work against Tupac Shakur. Death Row's suspicious criminal history led Watani Tyehimba to have his New Afrikan People's Organization completely disconnect with Tupac, who cried on Tyehimba's shoulder about it, saying, "I know I'm selling my soul to the devil."[52]

Knight also helped break up top rap groups that had any type of message U.S. intelligence opposed. He lured rappers DOC and Andre "Dr. Dre" Young away from the chart-topping group N.W.A. The group's songs included "Fuck the Police," which the FBI sent warning letters about to their record label in 1988.[53] The FBI further sent letters to concert hall owners and police, working to get N.W.A.'s concerts cancelled by having police refuse to work security. They repeated this tactic against Tupac and top radical music group, Rage Against the Machine.[54]

Death Row, it seems, also got well-known rappers to promote marijuana. Prior to joining that label, Dr. Dre wrote the song, "Express Yourself," saying, "I still express, yo. I don't smoke weed or sense/ Cause it's known to give a brother brain damage, and brain damage on the mic don't manage." After signing with Death Row, Dr. Dre's first CD was named *Chronic,* the slang for strong weed. Knight also started public brawls around Dre, in which only he, not Dre, avoided arrest. But Knight was unsuccessful when he tried to coerce top New York politically-linked rap groups such as Public Enemy and Wu Tang Clan to switch to his label.[55]

While Dr. Dre's statement that weed causes brain damage may be a bit exaggerated, several studies show the harm regular marijuana smoking can cause to mental abilities. One study reported that seven days after their last heavy marijuana use, subjects showed cognitive deficits, but that those problems were reversible twenty-eight days after last use. Another study showed that the more weed smoked, the more negative effects on "verbal and visual memory, executive functioning, visuoperception, psychomotor speed and manual dexterity" even after twenty-eight days of not smoking. Of greater concern, a 2013 study showed that teens who were heavy marijuana smokers—smoking it daily for about three years—"had abnormal changes in their brain structures related to working memory and performed poorly on memory tasks ... two years after they stopped smoking marijuana."[56]

Although study outcomes can differ, and it's hard to be sure one is definitive, did the CIA's MK-Ultra work with marijuana mid-century continue with promotion to teens, particularly black teens in the 1990s and beyond? The National Institute on Drug Abuse stated that marijuana is addictive to 9% of users in general, and 17% of users who start using in their youth. In 2000, an estimated "7 million people in the US population used marijuana at least weekly." The latest figures for 2013 cited "12% of eighth graders and 36% of seniors at public and private schools said they had smoked marijuana in the past year."[57]

With about five million American students in each grade, was the CIA trying to promote marijuana and get millions of kids, particularly black kids, addicted to weed each year? If so, weed's common effect of producing apathy could raise their dropout rate and keep most of them in lower paying jobs. Along with people addicted to other drugs, unemployed people addicted to weed may resort to crime for money to survive as adults, contributing to the private prison industry, or exclusion from voting if they picked up felonies, such as for possession or distribution of weed. With the title of her book, law professor Michelle Alexander said imprisonment for drugs turned into *The New Jim Crow* for blacks, as it replaced the "Jim Crow" laws that controlled blacks after slavery ended. She said more blacks are in prison today than were enslaved in 1850.[58]

If Death Row was furthering this goal for U.S. intelligence, they did so alongside other goals. Police Detective Russell Poole, who had gotten himself assigned as co-lead investigator of the 1997 Biggie Smalls murder investigation, said in the film *Biggie and Tupac*: "It was no secret that Death Row was involved in drug trafficking." Poole presented writer Randall Sullivan many police reports detailing this, discussed in Sullivan's book *LAbyrinth*. Poole also found that Death Row Records was trafficking guns.[59] Death Row insiders said that Death Row director Suge Knight and other top Death Row staff were provoking murderous fights between the Bloods and Crips gang members it employed. In doing so, Death Row appeared to aid the U.S. intelligence operation to end the gang-peace truces that were part of the radical politicization of these gangs achieved by Tupac and the Panthers.[60]

Det. Poole's investigation would eventually launch a task force investigating the infamous Los Angeles Rampart Division Scandal. Assistant District Attorney Richard Rosenthal said that "the connections that Russ Poole had made ... including the possibility that an LAPD officer, or officers, might be involved, were the origin of the task force." In that scandal, over seventy undercover members of the Community Resources Against Street Hoodlums (CRASH) unit were implicated in corruption that included unlawful shootings of drug dealers, as well as stealing and dealing their drugs. Death Row-linked cop Raphael Perez was a lead witness-turned prosecuted perpetrator in that scandal. Death Row bodyguard Kevin Hackie said Perez and LAPD cop David Mack were at many Death Row private parties. It wasn't a coincidence that the undercover CRASH unit targeted the gang truces.[61]

Death Row Records owner Dave Kenner and director Suge Knight had picked Tupac up from jail, and evidently wasted no time in drinking and smoking weed with him, leading Tupac to break his publicly printed vow not to smoke weed again. Kenner and Knight also convinced Tupac to enter the recording studio the same day as his prison release, while he was drunk and stoned. This resulted in Tupac's producing his most negative lyrics. These included a double album of lyrics that almost exclusively promoted smoking weed and selling drugs, and served to increase tensions in the East Coast versus West rap war U.S. intelligence appeared to orchestrate.[62]

Knight, Kenner and Death Row's undercover police agents also appeared to continue some of the penal coercion tactics on Tupac outside of prison. For example, Knight had his guards, mostly "moonlighting" cops, beat people "disloyal" to Death Row in front of Tupac. Witnesses claimed that Death Row employees who were also in the Bloods killed some Crips at a Snoop Dogg rap show without getting arrested. Police on duty, as opposed to those cops in Death Row at the event, came to the show but didn't detain most of the potential witnesses. At least one police officer reportedly working with Death Row, David Mack, was "also a self-confessed MOB Piru" Bloods gang member. Death Row further disrupted political rap conventions, such as Atlanta's annual Jack the Rapper hip-hop conference where Tupac had previously given speeches.[63]

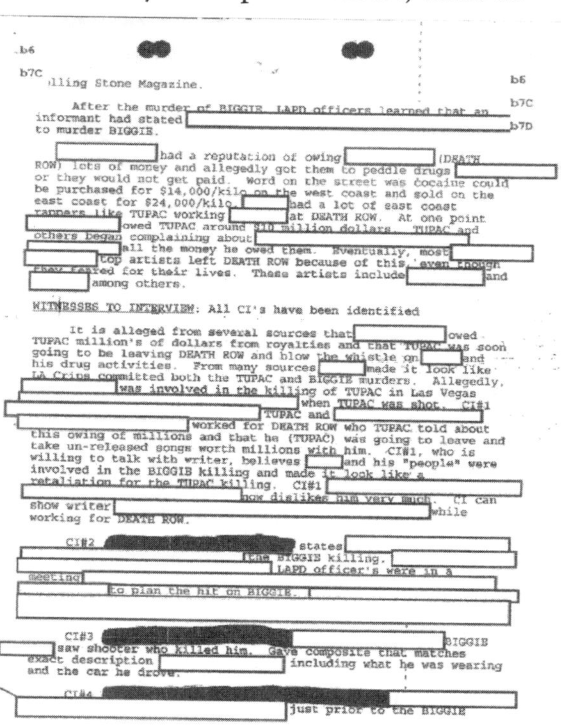

b6 b7C

...lling Stone Magazine.

b6 b7C b7D

After the murder of BIGGIE, LAPD officers learned that an informant had stated to murder BIGGIE.

had a reputation of owing (DEATH ROW) lots of money and allegedly got them to peddle drugs or they would not get paid. Word on the street was cocaine could be purchased for $14,000/kilo on the west coast and sold on the east coast for $24,000/kilo. had a lot of east coast rappers like TUPAC working at DEATH ROW. At one point owed TUPAC around $10 million dollars. TUPAC and others began complaining about all the money he owed them. Eventually, most top artists left DEATH ROW because of this, even though they feared for their lives. These artists include and among others.

WITNESSES TO INTERVIEW: All CI's have been identified

It is alleged from several sources that owed TUPAC million's of dollars from royalties and that TUPAC was soon going to be leaving DEATH ROW and blow the whistle on and his drug activities. From many sources made it look like LA Crips committed both the TUPAC and BIGGIE murders. Allegedly, was involved in the killing of TUPAC in Las Vegas when TUPAC was shot. CI#1 TUPAC and worked for DEATH ROW who TUPAC told about this owing of millions and that he (TUPAC) was going to leave and take un-released songs worth millions with him. CI#1, who is willing to talk with writer, believes and his "people" were involved in the BIGGIE killing and made it look like a retaliation for the TUPAC killing. CI#1 now dislikes him very much. CI can show writer while working for DEATH ROW.

CI#2 states the BIGGIE killing. LAPD officer's were in a meeting to plan the hit on BIGGIE.

CI#3 BIGGIE saw shooter who killed him. Gave composite that matches exact description including what he was wearing and the car he drove.

CI#4 just prior to the BIGGIE

These FOIA-released FBI documents reveal more evidence that LA police officers worked for Death Row Records as covert agents, trafficking drugs and disrupting Tupac's work politicizing gangs.

Death Row contributed to yet another U.S. intelligence goal. In the 1960s, the FBI had sent fake letters between Afeni Shakur's East Coast New

York Panthers and Huey Newton's West Coast Oakland Panther National Office, dividing these groups. The FBI also used undercover agents to create these divisions, and appeared to use similar tactics against Tupac. After strangers in prison and anonymous letter writers told Tupac that his friend Biggie helped set up his shooting in New York, Tupac didn't first believe it. Death Row's Suge Knight constantly hyped their conflict with Biggie's label, Bad Boy Records, and physical attacks began to occur, with most coming from Death Row's police corps. Tupac then began writing lyrics attacking Biggie and Bad Boy Records producer, Sean "Puffy" Combs.[64]

Death Row Uses Tupac's Exit to End Gang Truce?

By the summer of 1996, the now 25-year-old Tupac had released a double CD for Death Row, *All Eyez on Me*. It was the world's second fastest selling CD ever, going triple platinum within months. Tupac also finished co-starring in two more major motion pictures. His personal life improved as well. He became engaged to Kidada Jones, daughter of music mogul Quincy Jones. Kidada said Tupac started staying home with her, and they planned to have a child and move out of their Death Row-leased apartment. [65]

In another major change, Tupac broke from Death Row's influence. While still required by contract to complete another CD with Death Row, Tupac started his own record label, Euphenasia, and his own publishing company. He returned to leftist activism, including attending Central American solidarity benefits, speaking for groups such as the Brotherhood Crusade, and continuing his work to spread peace truces between the Bloods and Crips gangs. In his efforts to improve the lives of the disadvantaged, Tupac planned to finance a chain of day care centers for low-income women, and fund sports leagues for poor children in Los Angeles.[66]

Regarding the gang-peace work, Tupac discussed plans for community centers with former Crips gang leader-turned author Kody Scott. Kody Scott's best-selling book, *Monster*, documented his and other prison inmates' ideological conversion to socialism. Scott had been a spokesman for the Los Angeles gang-peace truce movement with an article in *The Nation* magazine. By this time Scott had changed his name to Sanyika Shakur in deference to the Shakur family.[67] Tupac and Sanyika planned to spread activism into various Los Angeles communities together, strategizing on various community projects that were to include other rap stars and celebrities.[68] The government would imprison Sanyika at least two more times, including at least once due to a positive urinalysis for marijuana.[69]

In that summer of 1996, many noticed Tupac's attempts to stop smoking weed and stop drinking. Music mogul Russell Simmons said that at a party, while everyone else was smoking weed and drinking, Tupac didn't. Instead, he spent the whole night dancing with his bodyguard Frank Alexander's wheelchair-bound neice.[70]

A video offered further evidence of Tupac's efforts to stop smoking weed. It showed Tupac at a concert talking to a fan while smoking a cigarette. At one point, a white roadie came up to Tupac and offered a joint. Tupac shook his head "no" to the marijuana and kept smoking his cigarette.[71]

With Tupac slipping away from Death Row's control, police and prosecutors brought a marijuana-possession charge against Tupac, a violation of his release on bail during appeal of the sexual-abuse jail sentence. A judge showed mercy. Tupac's lawyer had filed for Tupac to plead guilty, "open to the judge," which required the lawyer to commission a report on Tupac for the judge to read. After reading the report, which recommended Tupac give a free benefit concert, the judge said in court, "This young man seems to me to be absolutely remarkable." He agreed to the benefit concert sentencing, which would take place in Las Vegas on September 7, 1996, on the same night and in the same city as Mike Tyson's heavyweight boxing match.[72]

Tupac had strong disagreements with Suge Knight that summer, insisting the CD he finished in August, *Makaveli: Killuminati, The Seven Day Theory,* satisfied their three-CD contract agreement. At the end of August, Tupac fired his lawyer, Death Row owner Dave Kenner. Kenner had written the contract Tupac signed with Death Row, which also made him Tupac's lawyer, flouting the obvious conflict of interest.[73]

Tupac Shot in Las Vegas

Undercover police agent Kevin Hackie said in a public forum that he was working "as an FBI agent" for the four years he was working for Death Row Records, including when he became one of Tupac's three personal bodyguards. Hackie appeared to turn his back on the FBI when he urged Tupac not to go to Las Vegas that weekend in early September 1996. Knight and his security director, Reggie Wright Jr., immediately fired Hackie the day before the Vegas trip. Tupac almost took Hackie's advice and backed out of Las Vegas, but his friend Tyson's boxing match and the court-ordered benefit concert there that night likely led him to attend the Vegas event.[74]

Additional undercover Las Vegas police joined the police ranks working in Death Row Records for this night. Death Row held a pre-bout party with plenty of people drinking liquor and smoking weed. People said Tupac took part in both. With Knight and others from Death Row, he attended the boxing match at the MGM Grand hotel arena. Afterwards, in the hotel's lobby, Tupac got into a scuffle with a stranger, Orlando Anderson. Witnesses said they believed Suge Knight helped set it up, partly by describing Anderson as a Crips gang member who stole a Death Row chain from an associate of Tupac.[75]

After leaving the hotel, Knight, with Tupac in his passenger seat, set out with an entourage of Death Row cars to their company-owned Club 662, where Tupac was to give his midnight benefit concert. On the way there, just off of the Las Vegas strip, Tupac was murdered in what police Detective Russell Poole described as a police-orchestrated drive-by shooting, within nine days of his firing Death Row owner Dave Kenner. Poole said that an eyewitness, Tupac bodyguard Frank Alexander, "believed the entire assault on Anderson had been staged ... it was entirely possible Suge had paid the Crip to take that beating and then kill Tupac ... as the white Cadillac [with the shooters] ... was actually a little bit ahead of the BMW when the killer opened fire, allowing him to shoot at an angle that made it possible to avoid hitting Suge with a stray bullet."[76]

Las Vegas Times crime reporter Cathy Scott reported the FBI had Tupac under surveillance the night he was murdered. Along with rampant police foul play around Tupac's murder scene, police superiors squashed any real investigation. Scott detailed a page-and-a-half list of police improprieties in the investigation. Kevin Hackie said he had documents to prove his FBI employer had undercover agents, along with Alcohol Tobacco and Firearms agents, in that entourage. Hackie said on film that Knight was involved in "the orchestration of the shooting of Tupac." LAPD Det. Russell Poole said he was shocked when Las Vegas police showed him a closet full of evidence regarding Tupac's murder case, and their superiors told them not to investigate.[77]

While Tupac Shakur fought for his life in a Las Vegas hospital, Death Row spread the word that the Crips shot Tupac. Death Row also distributed guns to gang members in L.A. Fatal shootings began, ending the Blood/Crips peace truce. Suge Knight talked to both the police and the FBI during this time. After many gang members were killed, activists spread the word that it wasn't the Crips who shot Tupac. The violence stopped just after Tupac died on September 13, 1996.[78]

Police lied in saying there were no forthcoming witnesses among the hundreds of people outside the Maxim Hotel on the busy heavyweight-title fight night. Comedian Chris Rock would later mock U.S. intelligence, as Tupac was killed just off the strip "during a Mike Tyson fight! And they say there were no witnesses! More people watched Tupac get shot than watched the last episode of Seinfeld! The government hates rappers!"[79]

Two of Tupac's backup rappers, one of whom was Yafeu Fula, told police they thought they could identify the shooter. Police failed to follow up with either of them. The night of the next Tyson fight on November 10, 1996, someone put two bullets in Fula's head. Like Tupac having a Panther mother, Fula's father was Bronx Panther leader Sekou Odinga. Police pretended Fula's murder had no relation to Tupac's. *Time* magazine called it "drug related." But Fula had no prior criminal record, and even the FBI somehow released an unredacted document stating that, "Fula was killed mob style ... executed from point blank range ... the murder was done professionally."[80]

Many others linked to Tupac also died around this time. Tupac's former business manager, ex-Panther Watani Tyehimba, said that as national security director of the New Afrikan People's Organization, he had to distance himself from Tupac after he signed with Death Row, so as to not put the group in jeopardy. Tyehimba added that his oldest son, Yakhisizwe, had followed Tupac to keep working with him after he signed to Death Row Records. Yakhisizwe also turned up dead around the time of Tupac's murder.[81] This left three former Black Panthers with the loss of a child.

After Tupac's death, the leading theories put forth by mainstream media included the idea that Tupac was killed as part of the East Coast versus West Coast rap war. In that scenario, writers said that Biggie Smalls and his producer, Sean "Puffy" Combs, played a part in Tupac's murder. Writers presented these theories with little-to-no evidence.[82]

Det. Russell Poole, the co-lead investigator of the murder of rap star Biggie Smalls, had to resign from the Los Angeles police force and hold a press conference to get his investigative information out. Poole stated "Knight's people killed Tupac," and that Biggie's and Tupac's murders were "well orchestrated well planned out, radios being used ... experienced police officers knew exactly what to do." Poole also substantiated Kevin Hackie as "a main source of information and his information was worthy of follow-up," but "I was ... ordered not to go any further." Hackie believed Death Row killed Biggie "to throw the attention off Death Row [for killing Tupac] ... make it look like the East West rivalry ... make it look like Bad Boy Records ... which wasn't remotely the case."[83]

The murders of Tupac and Biggie remained in the news for years. Journalists identified New York FBI and ATF agents taking pictures of Biggie just before his murder. This included FBI agent Oldham who simultaneously worked as a New York police detective and monitored a later trial of Sean Puffy Combs. Biggie's mother used this and much more evidence to pursue a lawsuit against the LAPD for her son's murder. Despite initial success with that suit, including a $1.1 million award for legal fees, a judge ultimately dismissed the case.[84]

Notes

1 *Oakland Tribune,* 2/22/73, p. 1. FBI occupancy seen in memorandum from J.G. Deegan to W. R. Wannall, 8/26/74, Description of incident, FBI memorandum from Special Agent Wilbert J. Weiskrich to SAC San Francisco, 2/28/73. In Huey Newton, *War Against the Panthers* (New York: Harlem River Press/Writers and Readers, 1991), p. 64 n98. Also see, Interview of attorney Charles Garry reviewing FBI file made available in Delligner v. Mitchell, Civ. Action No.1768-69, Fed. Dist. Ct. (D,C.1969), *Oakland Tribune,* 2/22/73, p. 1.

2 J. Patrick O'Connor, *The Framing of Mumia Abu-Jamal* (Chicago: Chicago Review Press, 2008). Mumia Abu-Jamal's journalism accomplishments included becoming chairman of the Pensylvania Black Journalists Association and publishing articles in prestigious journals such as the *Yale Law Review.* On FBI targeting: picture with "dead" written on back, personal interview with Mumia's European spokesperson, Michael Warren (Tupac's lawyer), 2/5/96. Also see, C. Clark Kissinger, "Why Mumia Abu-Jamal Deserves a New Trial," a compilation of articles that originally appeared as a series in the *Revolutionary Worker,* January-April, 2000.

3 On The MOVE, personal interviews with Pam Africa, a MOVE spokesperson and leader of International Concerned Family and Friends of Mumia Abu-Jamal, 9/15/07.

4 For some examples, see Jill Smolowe "Mumia on Their Mind," *Time,* 8/7/95, p. 33. Peter Noel and Danielle Douglas, "The Fleeing Man," *Village Voice,* 11/30/99, Vol. 44, #47, pp. 61-65. Don Terry, "Key Witness Alters her Testimony in Death Row Case," *New York Times,* 10/2/96.

5 Common Pleas court Petition, Pennsylvania v. Mumia Abu-Jamal, Petition for Post Conviction Relief. Also see longtime legal writer and investigator Michael "Affidavit of George Michael Newman," Court of Common Pleas, Commonwealth, Case No. 8201-1357-59 vs. Mumia Abu-Jamal. Noel and Douglas, "The Fleeing Man." Police had pressured prostitutes to falsely testify against both Newton and Mumia. On Newton, see Michael Newton (no relation), *Bitter Grain: Huey Newton and the Black Panther Party* (Los Angeles: Holloway House, 1980), pp. 213-14, and H. Newton, *War Against the Panthers.* On Mumia, see Don Terry, "Key Witness Alters her Testimony in Death Row Case," *New York Times,* October 2, 1996.

6 On Mumia's .38 caliber gun and a .44 fatal bullet, see Smolowe "Mumia on Their Mind," p. 33. On not testing Mumia's gun, nor his hand for residue to show he fired a gun, or hiding the results, see "Petition for Post-Conviction Relief" Court of Common Peas of Philadelphia v. Mumia Anu-Jamal. Criminal Division Nos 1357-1358 (January Sessions, 1982), pts. 37-39. "Executive Summary," C. Clark Kissinger, 9/01. Helen Halyard, "Live from Death Row: Political prisoner Mumia Abu-Jamal speaks from prison," 4/21/99, World Socialist Website. On getaway, Affidavit by Arnold R. Beverly on the Events of December 9, 1981, U.S. District Court, Eastern District of Pennsylvania, *Mumia Abu-Jamal, Case N. 99 Civ 5089 (Yohn) vs. Marin Horn, Commissioner, Pennsylvania Department of Corrections,* 6/8/99.

7 Personal interview, Pam Africa, 1/4/08.

8 "Affidavit by William Cook on the Events of December 9, 1981." U.S. District Court, Eastern District of Pennsylvania, *Mumia Abu-Jamal, Case No. 99 Civ 5089 (YOHN) Petitioner, vs. Martin Horn, Commissioner, Pennsylvania Department of Corrections, and Connor Blaine, Superintendent of the State Correctional Institution at Greene, Defendants* (hereafter, "U.S, District Court, Abu-Jamal vs. Horn & Blaine"). Affidavit by Mumia Abu-Jamal on the Events of December 9, 1981," *Mumia Abu Jamal vs. Martin Horn, Commissioner, Pennsylvania Dept. of Correstions,* U.S. District Court, Eastern District of Pennsylvania. Posted, 5/5/01.

9 "Affidavit by William Cook on the Events of December 9, 1981." "U.S, District Court, Abu-Jamal vs. Horn & Blaine."

10 See "Technology Transfer From Defense: Concealed Weapons Detection," *National Institute of Justice Journal,* Issue #229, Aug. 1995, pp. 42-43. Frank Donner, *Protectors of Privilege: Red Squads and Police Repression in Urban America* (Berkeley: University of California Press, 1990), pp. 242-43. "25 Years on the Move," published by MOVE, P.O. Box 19709, Philadelphia, PA 19143, p. 49. Richard Poe, "Preemptive Strike: A New Kind of Policing, " *East Village Eye,* June 1986, p. 12.

11 Noel and Douglas, "The Fleeing Man."

12 Brown as Cointelpro target while he led SNCC with Stokely Charmichael in the late '60s, and an honorary Panther leader: FBI memorandum from SAC Albany to Director, FBI, August 25, 1967, "COUNTERINTELLIGENCE PROGRAM, BLACK NATIONALIST-HATE GROUPS," Copied in Ward Churchill and Jim Vander Wall, *The COINTELPRO Papers: Documents from the FBI's Secret Wars Against Dissent in the United States* (Boston: South End, 1991), pp. 92-93. Also see important FBI document expressing concern that SNCC's Charmichael or Brown, SCLC's MLK, RAM's Max Sanford, or NOI's Elijah Muhammad could become the new black "messiah." See "AIRTEL, To: SAC Albany, From: Director, FBI (100-448006), COUNTERINTELLIGENCE PROGRAM, BLACK NATIONALIST HATE GROUPS, RACIAL INTELLIGENCE, 3/4/68, in *The COINTELPRO Papers*, pp. 108-11, particularly Brown et. al. at p. 111. On Brown's honorary East Coast Panther status, *The COINTELPRO Papers*, p. 126.

13 On black officers shooting Brown, see eyewitness Gloria Richardson, interviewed by Gil Noble on ABC television's *Like It Is*, March 17, 2002. This, Rap Brown's quoted response, and Rap Brown Amendment discussed in Carl Schoettler, "A Whole New Rap," *Baltimore Sun* , 8/19/95, p. 1D.

14 Deposition of former FBI Cointelpro agent M. Wesley Swearingen, taken in October 1980, in Honolulu, Hawaii, p. 2, in Churchill and Vander Wall, *Agents of Repression*, p. 62. Also see Swearingen interviewed in award-winning documentary by Lee Lew-Lee, *All Power to the People* (1996).

15 Schoettler, "A Whole New Rap." Also see Peter Slevin, "Police Seek Ex-Militant in Slaying," *Washington Post*, 3/18/00, pp. A1, 12.

16 Fareed H. Numan, a consultant for the American Muslim Council, in Schoettler, "A Whole New Rap." Also see David Firestone, "For Former Radical, Old Battleground Became a Refuge," *New York Times*, March 22, 2000, p. A21.

17 Joshua B. Good and Richard Whitt, "Eye on Al-Amin: FBI, Police Tracked Militant, Inner Circle in '90s Homicides," *Atlanta Journal-Constitution*, April 1, 2000, http://www.accessatlanta.com/partners/ajc/newsatlanta/alamin/0402.htm.

18 Good and Whitt, "Eye on Al-Amin."

19 Schoettler, "A Whole New Rap."

20 Evidence contradicted police claims. For example, see Peter Slevin, "Police Seek Ex-Militant In Slaying," *Washington Post*, March 18, 2000, p. A12. Gloria Richardson on *Like It Is*, March 17, 2002. Fareed H. Numan in Schoettler, "A Whole New Rap." Also, see David Firestone, "For Former Radical, Old Battleground Became a Refuge," *New York Times*, March 22, 2000, p. A21. Good and Whitt, "Eye on Al-Amin." 4/1/2000. *The Revolutionary Worker*, April 9, 2000, p. 7. Associated Press, "Former Black Panther May have Fled Georgia," *New York Times*, March 20, 2000, p. A10. Jack Warner, "Note Had Warning on Al-Amin," *Atlanta Journal-Constitution*, 4/1/2000. Kevin Sack, "A Legacy of Achievement and Also of Investigation," *New York Times*, January, 15, 2001, p. A10. Personal interview, Watani Tyehimba, 10/15/02. Ernie Suggs, "Trial of Al-Amin May Test Community," *Atlanta Journal-Constitution*, 9/9/2001. Alvin Benn, "Former Black Panther Arraigned," *Montgomery Advertiser*, October 2, 2002, http://lw3fd.hotmail.msn.com/cgi-b… SG1034043255.239&start=1554351&len=9272.

21 Honorary officer, *The Revolutionary Worker*, April 9, 2000, p. 7. Theft, impersonation charge, AP, "Former Black Panther May have Fled Georgia."

22 Slevin, "Police Seek Ex-Militant in Slaying." Warner, "Note Had Warning on Al-Amin."

23 Firestone, "For Former Radical, Old Battleground Became Refuge." Also, personal interview with Watani Tyehimba, 11/2/02.

24 See Ayanna Jackson in *New York v. Charles Fuller and Tupac Shakur*, Indictment No. 11578-93. Also Det. Slimak, People's Witness, p. 352. *New York v. Tupac Shakur*, Notice of Motion Pursuant to CPL 530.45 Ind. No. 11578/93 by Michael Warren, p. 8, cites trial testimony at pp. 33-38, 40, with Jackson's confirming consensual oral and vaginal sex at hotel room.

25 Cross-examination of Ayanna Jackson, by Ken Ellis, Esq. *New York v. Charles Fuller and Tupac Shakur*, Indictment no. 11578-93, Nov. 14, 1994.

26 Kevin Powell, "Ready to Live: Post-trial Tupac Interview," *Vibe* April 1995, in Vibe editors, *Tupac Shakur 1971-1996* (New York: Crown, 1997), p. 50. On charges, see *New York v. Tupac Shakur*, Notice of Motion Pursuant to CPL 530.45 for Bail Pending Sentence, Indictment No. 11578/93.

27 As noted above, one intelligence document a Senate committee found included strategies for use against political musicians such as "Intelligence Activities and Rights of Americans," Book II, April 26, 1976, *Senate Committee with Respect to Intelligence Report*. Excerpted in Alex Constantine, *The Covert War Against Rock* (Los Angeles: Feral House, 2001), p. 9. U.S. Senate Select Committee to Study Government Operations, *The FBI's Covert Program to Destroy the Black Panther Party*, U.S. Government Printing Office, Washington. D.C. 1976.

28 Al Guart, "Tupac-tape Tamper Alleged," *New York Post*, November 24, 1993. Salvatore Arena, "Sex Tapes Erased, Says Shakur Lawyer," *New York Daily News*, November 24, 1993. Cross-examination of Ayanna Jackson, by Ken Ellis, Esq. *New York vs. Charles Fuller and Tupac Shakur*, Indictment no. 11578-93, Nov. 14, 1994, p. 232.

29 Personal interviews, Michael Warren, 12/25/94, 10/15/96, 11/8/98. Also see Connie Bruck, "The Takedown of Tupac," *The New Yorker*, 7/7/97, p. 55.

30 Personal interviews, Michael Warren, 12/25/94, 10/15/96, 11/8/98. On ADA Mourges and judge allowing Agnant's case to be severed from Tupac's, see Connie Bruck, "The Takedown of Tupac," *The New Yorker*, 7/7/97, pp. 54-55.

31 Richard Perez-Pena, "Wounded Rapper Gets Mixed Verdict In Sex-Abuse Case," *New York Times*, 12/2/94, pp. A1, B4. Also, Personal interview, Michael Warren, 4/7/99.

32 Rosemond referred to as "Booker" in this interview—Powell, "Ready to Live" *Vibe* April 1995, in Vibe editors, *Tupac Shakur*, p. 46. On Rosemond's details about luring Tupac to the studio, see Jason Rodriguez with Sway Calloway, "Game Manager Jimmy Rosemond Recalls Events the Night Tupac was Shot, says Session was 'All Business,'" *MTV News*, April 1, 2008, http://www.mtv.com/news/articles/1584524/game-manager-jimmy-rosemond-recalls-night-tupac-was-shot.jhtml. On Rosemond cocaine trafficking, Greg Wallace, "Exclusive: Jimmy Henchmen Associate Admits to Robbery/Shooting of Tupac; Apologizes to Pac and B.I.G.'s Mothers," *AllHipHopNews*.com June 15, 2011.

33 Tupac said shows cancelled in Vibe eds., *Tupac Shakur*, p. 46. Rage Against the Machine lead singer Zach De La Rocha detailed how police used this tactic against his group when they went on tour with rap group Wu Tang Clan, personal interview, Zach De La Rocha, 5/5/98. On the FBI and N.W.A. shows, see Bruce C. Brown, "Quayle Boosts 'Cop Killer' Campaign," *Washington Post*, 6/20/92, pp. B1, 5. Cited in Barry Shank, "Fears of the White Unconcious: Music, Race, and Identification in the Censorship of 'Cop Killer.'" *Radical History Review* #66, Fall 1996. This writer attended a Rage Against the Machine benefit concert for Mumia, just outside New York City in New Jersey, and heard radio stations such as K-Rock 92.3 FM discuss police attempts to cancel the show in 2000.

34 Powell, "Ready to Live," in Vibe eds., *Tupac Shakur*, p. 46.

35 Powell, "Ready to Live," in Vibe eds., *Tupac Shakur*, p. 46.

36 On bullets through head while on ground, see Deposition of Barbara Justice, MD, *New York v. Tupac Shakur*, December 21, 1994. That is a military execution tactic, see Stephen Kinzer, "Commandos Left a Calling Card: Their Absence," *New York Times*, 9/26/01, p. B6. On jewelry worth, see Cory Johnson, "Sweatin' Bullets," February 1995, in Vibe eds., *Tupac Shakur*, p. 41. Agnant bought jewelry for Tupac, Powell, *"Ready to Live,"* in Vibe eds.,*Tupac Shakur*, pp. 46-47. Agnant referred to as Nigel.

37 Cathy Scott, *The Murder of Biggie Smalls* (New York: St. Martin's Press, 2000), p. 65.

38 Greg Wallace, "Exclusive: Jimmy Henchmen Associate Admits to Robbery/Shooting of Tupac; Apologizes to Pac and B.I.G.'s Mothers," *AllHipHopNews.com* June 15, 2011. http://allhiphop.com/2011/06/15/exclusive-jimmy-henchman-associate-admits-to-role-in-robberyshooting-of-tupac-apologizes-to-pac-b-i-g-s-mothers/. Regarding Rosemond corroborating with the government, see, *U.S. v. James J. Rosemond*, case # 7:94-CR-36-1-BR, this shows a criminal case from 1994. The notice is dated February 8, 1997 scheduling a "proceeding" to take place on February 24, 1997. An "Agreement" on April 24, 1997, that "prosecution will not offer in evidence on its case-in-chief, or in connection with any sentencing proceeding ... any statements made by Client at the meeting." It was signed by the Asst. District Attorney, Diane Kiesel, on behalf of Robert Morgenthau, District Attorney of New York, and also signed by James Rosemond. A second, "Proffer Agreement," used similar language and was dated 6/18/98.

39 See *Ibera Hampton, et al., Plaintiffs-Appellants v. Edward Hanrahan, et al., Defendants-*

Appellees (Nos. 77-1968, 77-1210 and 77-1370) Transcript at 21741-62 and 21807-18. FBI SAC Mitchell posted bail for O'Neal on one charge and O'Neal never prosecuted on either charge. In *Agents of Repression*, p. 65 n8.

40 Greg Wallace, "Exclusive: Jimmy Henchmen Associate Admits to Robbery/Shooting of Tupac; Apologizes to Pac and B.I.G.'s Mothers," AllHipHopNews.com June 15, 2011.

41 Chuck Philips, "James 'Jimmy Henchman' Rosemond Implicated Himself in 1994 Tupac Shakur Attack: Court Testimony," *Village Voice*, June 12, 2012, http://blogs.villagevoice.com/runninscared/2012/06/jimmy_henchman_implicated.php.

42 On ADA Mourges and judge allowing Agnant's case to be severed from Tupac's, along with Agnant's indictment being dismissed in favor of two misdemeanors, see Connie Bruck, "The Takedown of Tupac," *The New Yorker*, 7/7/97, pp. 54-55. On Warren's comment, personal interview, 11/8/98. On Tupac and Agnant's charges and sentencing, see *New York v. Tupac Shakur, Ricardo Brown (a.k.a. Jacques Agnant) & Charles Fuller*, Exhibit A. 2. PL 130.65 Sexual Abuse 1st Degree "forcing contact between the... buttocks of informant and the hands of defendant Shakur, Brown." Also, Richard Perez-Pena, "Wounded Rapper Gets Mixed Verdict in Sex Abuse Case," *New York Times*, 12/2/94, p. B4. Tupac's criminal record of two misdemeanors were for weapons possession and simple assault when someone came on his stage in Lansing, Michigan and tried to take the microphone away from him. Notice of Motion or Bail Pending Sentence *New York v. Tupac Shakur*, Indictment no. 11578/93, Michael Warren, Attny for Defendant-Petitioner Tupac Shakur, p. 19 point 48.

43 On sales, see Vibe editors, *Tupac Shakur*, p. 140. On quote, see Michael Eric Dyson, *Holler If You Hear Me: Searching for Tupac Shakur* (New York: Basic Civitas, 2001), p. 125.

44 Powell, "Ready to Live," in Vibe editors, *Tupac Shakur*, p. 46.

45 On Clinton, see Jacob Hoye and Karolyn Ali, eds., *Tupac: Resurrection* (New York: Atria, 2003), p. 153. Cathy Scott, *The Killing of Tupac Shakur* (Las Vegas: Huntington Press, 1997), p. 83. Tupac's prison card, *Tupac: Resurrection*, p. 152. Album release date, Vibe eds., *Tupac Shakur*, p. 140. Reporter Mark Schwartz, covering prison legislative reform, CD, *Me and My Shadow: Investigation of the political left by the United States Government*, producers Tarabu Betserai and Adi Gevins from "The Pacifica Radio Archives." U.S. intelligence influence on judges and prisons, see Mike Ryan, "The Stammheim Model: Judicial Counterinsurgency," *New Studies on the Left*, Vol. XIV, Nos. 1-2, Spring-Summer 1989, pp. 45-69. On political prisoners and "torture," see *Amnesty International Report on Torture, 1983*. Also see, Thomas Benjamin and Kenneth Lux, "Soliltary Confinement as Psychological Torture," *California Western Law Review*, 13(265), 1978, pp. 295-96. Also, Dr. Edgar Schein discussing methodology with federal maximum-security prison wardens in 1962, quoted in National Committee to Support the Marion Brothers, *Breaking Men's Minds* (Chicago: 1987). "Biderman's Chart on Penal Coercion," *Amnesty International Report on Torture, 1983*. All reproduced and discussed in Churchill and Vander Wall, *The COINTELPRO Papers*, pp. 321-24. Caryn James, "The Things That People Say," *New York Times*, December 15, 1995, pp. C15, C19. On length of time, see Hoye and Ali, *Tupac: Resurrection*, p. 162. On rectal examinations of Tupac with gloved fingers as humiliation and possible torture, see eyewitness, attorney Stewart Levy, in Bruck, "The Takedown of Tupac."

46 Personal interviews with Tupac manager Watani Tyehimba, 5/10/00, national lawyer Chokwe Lumumba, 5/5/00 and New York lawyer, Michael Warren, 11/8/00. Nick Broomfield also said this after discussions with Tyehimba, noted in his credits, Nick Broomfield, *Biggie and Tupac* (Film Four/Lafayette Films, 2002). On FBI's use of fake letters and undercover agents to set up conflict between Afeni Shakur's New York Panthers and Huey Newton's West Coast Panthers, see Bronx Black Panther Assata Shakur, *Assata: An Autobiography* (Chicago: Lawrence Hill, 1987), pp. 230-32. Some of these were reprinted in Churchill and Vander Wall, *The COINTELPRO Papers*, pp. 160-61, such as, "From: Director, FBI (100-448006) COINTELPRO – BLACK PANTHER PARTY (BPP) – DISSENSION RACE MATTERS 2/10/71," and "Airtel to Albany et al. Re: COINTELPRO – Black Panther Party (BPP) – Disssension 100-448006 Newton's ... (deletions) ... New York 21 ... San Francisco and New York are already involved in counterintelligence operations ... creating dissension between local branch and/or its leaders and BPP national headquarters." Also see FBI undercover agent Louis Tackwood's admissions in Churchill and Vander Wall, *Agents of Repression*, p. 80; and Lewis E.

Tackwood, "My Assignment was to Kill George Jackson," *Black Panther*, April 21, 1980. See former FBI Cointelpro agent M. Wesley Swearingen, *FBI Secrets: An Agent's Expose* (Boston: South End, 1995) pp. 82-83. Regarding intelligence document "Provoke target groups," "Intelligence Activities and Rights of Americans," Book II, April 26, 1976, *Senate Committee with Respect to Intelligence Report*; excerpted in Alex Constantine, *The Covert War Against Rock* (Los Angeles: Feral House, 2001), p. 9. Scott, *The Killing of Tupac Shakur*, p. 153. On anonymous letters, see Tupac's road manager, Charles "Man-Man" Fuller, in Bruck, "The Takedown of Tupac," p. 58. Mark Schwartz, *Me and My Shadow: Investigation of the political left by the United States Government*, Tarabu Betserai and Adi Gevins from "The Pacifica Radio Archives." Track 5. Personal interview, Tupac's biological cousin Billy Lesane, 3/26/99. On media role, see, for example, Cheo Hodari Coker, "How the West was Won," Vibe eds, *Tupac Shakur*, p. 39. Also, suspected intelligence agent "Booker" (Rosemond) "spun" Tupac's first interview to push the rap war's start, in Vibe eds, *Tupac Shakur*, p. 59. Adario Strange, "Death Wish," *The Source*, March 1996, pp. 87-88, in Ronin Ro, *Have Gun Will Travel, The Spectacular Rise and Violent Fall of Death Row Records* (New York: Doubleday, 1998), p. 163.

47 One source said Time Warner's initial funding of Death Row was $10 million. Robert Sam Anson, "To Die Like a Gangsta," *Vanity Fair*, March 1997, p. 252. Ronin Ro reported a $1.5 million initial financing from Michael Harris, along with "millions" from Time Warner and others, Ronin Ro, *Have Gun Will Travel*, p. 315. Time Warner said it sold all links to Death Row in late '95, but it still keeps publishing rights, Randall Sullivan, *Labyrinth: A Detective Investigates the Murders of Tupac Shakur and Notorious B.I.G., the Implication of Death Row Records' Suge Knight, and the Origins of the Los Angeles Police Scandal* (New York: Atlantic Monthly Press, 2002), p. 173. Penal Coercion goal, Amnesty International Report on Torture, 1983 in Churchill and Vander Wall, *The COINTELPRO Papers*, p. 323. Death Row gave Tupac $200,000 for one song in 1993, Ro, *Have Gun Will Travel*, p. 146. Time Warner push for Tupac on Death Row, Bruck, "The Takedown of Tupac," p. 57. On Tupac's bail money, Tupac's aunt, Jean Cox, and mother, Afeni, put up personal bonds; actress friend Jasmine Guy put up $350,000. Tyehimba got Atlantic Records to put up $850,000 against Tupac's next CD to bring it to $1.2 million. See, *New York v. Tupac Shakur*, sentencing hearing transcript, p. 70 and Affidavits from Tupac Shakur, 2/2/95, Watani Tyehimba, Ahadi Tyehimba. On Tupac's release just after signing to Death Row, see Hoye and Ali, *Tupac: Resurrection*, pp. 193-94, and Bruck, "The Takedown of Tupac," p. 58. On Death Row's bail offer, Ro, *Have Gun Will Travel*, p. 250.

48 On Kenner owning umbrella company and more on Harris, Ro, *Have Gun Will Travel*, pp. 76-80.

49 On Harris as Ross understudy, Gary Webb, *Dark Alliance*, p. 148. On Harris as silent partner, Ro, *Have Gun Will Travel*, pp. 76-80. Bruck, "The Takedown of Tupac,", p. 58. Ross worked with Ron Lister who worked with CIA ex-Deputy Director William Nelson. See Department of State's Biographical Register, 1973, and CIA-BASE, a database operated by former CIA officer Ralph McGehee, in Webb, *Dark Alliance*, pp. 196-97, 513 n197, 558.

50 Some cite government lawyer Larry Longo keeping Knight jail-free. Lawyers working on the case said Longo had nothing to do with the settlement because he was "the low man on the totem pole" in that case, Ro, *Have Gun Will Travel*, pp. 36-37, 130-31, 197. Death Row hadn't signed a contract with Longo's daughter Gina, until January of '96, while Knight's continued arrests, convictions, and jail-free suspended sentences included several as early as 1990, Sullivan, *LAbyrinth*, pp. 107, 300-03.

51 Police Detective Russell Poole said this on film in Broomfield, *Biggie and Tupac*, as well as in Sullivan, *LAbyrinth*. Poole names many of the cops working in Death Row throughout this book. Sullivan, *LAbyrinth*, pp. 40, 124, 166, 169-70, 191. On Wright, Jr. working with his father on Compton police force, Sullivan, *LAbyrinth*, p. 191. On Wright, Sr. as Gang chief, see Broomfield, *Biggie and Tupac*.

52 On tearful parting between Tupac and Tyehimba, Personal Interview with Tyehimba, 5/10/00. Also discussed in Bruck, "The Takedown of Tupac," p. 58. On Death Row continuing what appeared to be U.S. intelligence work against Tupac, see Ro, *Have Gun Will Travel*, pp. 271-272, 319-20, Sullivan, *LAbrynth*, pp.35-38. Also see, "Biderman's Chart on Penal Coercion," Amnesty International Report on Torture, 1983. Reproduced in Churchill and Vander Wall, *The*

COINTELPRO Papers, pp. 321-23. Anson, "To Die Like a Gangsta," p. 280.

53 Ro, *Have Gun Will Travel*, pp. 122-23, 158, 174-76. On Death Row and Wu Tang, also see Sullivan, *LAbyrinth*, p. 85. On the FBI's fax campaign to get police canceling N.W.A. shows, see Bruce C. Brown, "Quayle Boosts 'Cop Killer' Campaign," *Washington Post*, 6/20/92, pp. B1, 5. Cited in Barry Shank, "Fears of the White Unconcious: Music, Race, and Identification in the Censorship of 'Cop Killer,'" *Radical History Review* #66, Fall 1996.

54 Personal interview with Rage Against the machine lead singer, Zach De La Rocha, May 5, 1999. This writer attended that Rage Against the Machine benefit concert, just outside New York City in New Jersey. Radio stations such as KROK discussed police attempts to cancel the show in 2000.

55 Alcohol and weed at Death Row, see Ro, *Have Gun Will Travel*, pp. 104, 110. 116. On Tupac and weed before Death Row, Kevin Powell interview with Tupac, Vibe editors, *Tupac Shakur*, pp. 45-46. Also see Ro, *Have Gun Will Travel*, pp. 83-84, 122-23, 158, 174-76. On Death Row and Wu Tang, Sullivan, *LAbyrinth*, p. 85. Wu Tang was co-produced by Black Liberation Movement leader Sonny Carson, who had a recording studio. He worked with Tupac's New York lawyer Michael Warren when New York police illegally targeted them with their Black Desk unit.

56 On memory problems reversible after 28 days, HG Pope Jr, AJ Gruber, JI Hudson, MA Huestis and D. Yurgelun-Todd, Neuropsychological performance in long-term cannabis users," *Archives of General Psychiatry*, 2001 Oct; 58(10):909-15, www.bcbi.blm.gov/pubmed/11576028. On cognitive problems lasting over 28 days, K.I. Bolla, PhD, K. Brown, MPH, D. Eldreth, BA, K. Tate, BA and J.L. Cadet, MD, "Dose-related neurocognitive effects of marijuana use," *Neurology*, November 12, 2002, col. 59 no. 9, 1337-1343, http://www.neurology.org/content/59/9/1337.full. On brain changes and poor memory 2 yrs later, Marla Paul, "Marijuana Users have Abnormal Brain Structure and Poor Memory," *Northwestern News*, December 16, 2012. Matthew J. Smith, Derin J. Cobia, Lei Wang, Kathryn K. Alpert, Will J. Cronenwett, Morris B. Goldman, Daniel Mmah, Deanna M. Barch, Hans C. Breiter and John G. Csernansky, "Cannabis-Related Working Memory Deficits and Associated Subcortical Morphological Differences in Healthy Individual and Schizophrenia Subjects," *Schizophrenia Bulletin*, December 15, 2013, http://schizophreniabulletin.oxfordjournals.org/content/early/2013/12/10/schbul.sbt176.abstract.

57 On NIDA statement, www.drugabuse.gov/publications/drugfacts/marijuana. On 7 million weekly users, US Department of Health and Human Services Substance Abuse and Mental Health Services Administration Office of Applied Studies, *National household survey on drug abuse* (Washington, DC: US Government Printing Office, 1999). Quoted in K.I. Bolla, PhD et al. "Dose-related neurocognitive effects of marijuana use," *Neurology*, vol. 59 no.9, 11337-1343, http://www.neurology.org/content/59/9/1337.full. Anahad O'Connor, "Increasing Marijuana Use in High School is Reported," *New York Times*, December 18, 2013, p. A15.

58 http://nces.ed.gov/fastfacts/display.asp?id=372 National Center of Education Statistics, "Fast Facts," 21013. Michelle Alexander, "Michelle Alexander: More Black Men are in Prison Today than were Enslaved in 1850," *Huffington Post*, October 12, 2011, http://www.huffingtonpost.com/2011/10/12/michelle-alexander-more-black-men-in-prison-slaves-1850_n_1007368.html. Note that this author also barely missed failing a class and not graduating from high school, as his weed problem led to doing little-to-no homework for months.

59 Stated by Poole in the Nick Broomfield documentary, *Biggie and Tupac*. Of the many examples, see Sullivan, *LAbrynth*, pp. 40, 124.

60 Ro, *Have Gun Will Travel*, pp. 261-64, 270-72, 319-20. Sullivan, *LAbrynth*, pp. 35-38.

61 On Poole and Rampart, Sullivan, *LAbrynth*, pp. 207-08. On real Death Row-linked illegalities and gangs, ibid., pp. 37-39, 40, 124, 169-70, 191, 192, 197, 201-07. Mike Davis, "Who Killed Los Angeles? Part 2," *New Left Review*, #199, 1993, p. 34-35. Davis authored the best-selling book *City of Quartz* on the history of Los Angeles. Jesse Katz, "Man Freed in Death of Gang Leader Courts: Rodney Compton is to get one year probation in the slaying of Tony Bogard, who helped reach a truce between the Crips and Bloods," *Los Angeles Times*, 6/1/94, p. 3. Mike Davis, "In L.A., Burning All Illusions," *The Nation*, 6/1/92, p. 745. FBI work with LAPD in Operation Hammer in Megan Garvery & Rich Winton, "City Declares War on Gangs," *Los Angeles Times*, 12/4/02. OJJDP Summary, August 2000—Youth Gang Programs and Strategies, "Suppression Programs," www.ncjrs.org/html/ojjdp/

summary_2000_8/suppression.html. Also see, Ro, *Have Gun Will Travel*, pp. 166, 208-11.

62 Ro, *Have Gun Will Travel*, pp. 250, 252. Anson, "To Die Like a Gangsta," p. 280. Also Afeni Shakur in Hoye and Ali, *Tupac: Resurrection*, pp. 198, 206.

63 Scott, *The Killing of Tupac Shakur*, p. 86. Ro, *Have Gun Will Travel*, pp.261-64, 270-72, 319-20. Sullivan, *LAbrynth*, pp. 35-38. On Mack, Nick Broomfield stated this in *Biggie and Tupac*, at about 1:01:40.

64 Ro, *Have Gun Will Travel*, pp. 156-57, 226-27, 232, 258, 280-82. Cathy Scott, *The Murder of Biggie Smalls* (New York: St. Martin's, 2000), pp. 54-55. *Vibe* editors, *Tupac Shakur*, pp. 80, 101-02. Also see copies of FBI correspondence in Ward Churchill and Jim Vander Wall, *The COINTELPRO Papers* (Boston, MA: South End Press, 1990), pp.160-61. Such as, "From: Director, FBI (100-448006) COINTELPRO – BLACK PANTHER PARTY (BPP) – DISSENSION RACE MATTERS 2/10/71," and "Airtel to Albany et al Re: COINTELPRO – Black Panther Party (BPP) – Disssension 100-448006 Newton's ... (deletions) ... New York 21 ... San Francisco and New York are already involved in counterintelligence operations ... creating dissension between local branch and/or its leaders and BPP national headquarters." Also see former FBI Cointelpro agent M. Wesley Swearingen, *FBI Secrets: An Agent's Exposé* (Boston: South End, 1995, pp.82-3.

65 On second fastest selling CD ever, in first week out, Ro, *Have Gun Will Travel*, p. 281. On companies Tupac started, Anson, "To Die Like a Gangsta," pp. 280-81. Also, personal interview with Tupac's personal assistant, Molly Monjauze, 12/2/98. Scott, *The Killing of Tupac Shakur*, pp.81, 89.

66 Anson, "To Die Like a Gangsta," pp. 246, 280, 281. Armond White, *Rebel for the Hell of It* (New York: Thunder's Mouth Press, 1997), p.193. Also, Personal Interview in 12/2/98 with Tupac's personal assistant, Molly Monjauze, who then became Afeni Shakur's personal assistant. On sports leagues, see note below.

66 Anson, "To Die Like a Gangsta," pp. 246, 280-81. Armond White, *Rebel for the Hell of It* (New York: Thunder's Mouth Press, 1997), p. 193. Also, Personal Interview on 12/2/98 with Tupac's personal assistant, Molly Monjauze, who then became Afeni Shakur's personal assistant. On sports leagues and gang peace work, Tupac can be heard saying this on a recording of his talk with Sanyika Shakur, Dannielle Harling, "Tupac Says Quad Shooting, Sexual Assault Case were 'All Connected' In Previously Unheard Phone Call," *HipHopDx.com* June 6, 2014, recorded October 18, 1995, http://www.hiphopdx.com/index/news/id.29135/title.tupac-says-quad-shooting-sexual-assault-case-were-all-connected-in-previously-unheard-phone-call.

67 Sanyika Shakur (a.k.a. Kody Scott), *Monster: The Autobiography of an L.A. Gang Member* (New York: Penguin, 1994), pp. vii-viii, 347-49. Tupac planned activist projects with Scott, Vibe eds., *Tupac Shakur*, p. 51. Personal correspondence with Kody Scott/Sanyika Shakur, from 2009-2011.

68 Personal interview with Sanyika Shakur in September 2012. Sanyika Shakur also provided a taped conversation of himself and Tupac discussing these plans just before Tupac's death.

69 Email from Sanyika Shakur to this author on September 24, 2013.

70 Anson, "To Die Like a Gangsta," pp. 246, 280-81.

71 Live footage of Tupac following a show in 1996 and viewed by this author.

72 Dyson, *Holler If You Hear Me*, pp. 247-48. Another "Proffer Agreement" document, dated 6/18/98.

73 Tupac's personal bodyguards, Frank Alexander and Kevin Hackie, said this in Det.Poole's interviews, Sullivan, *LAbyrinth*, pp. 188, 192. Bruck, "The Takedown of Tupac," pp. 61-63. See copy of handwritten contract, signed in jail, in Hoye and Ali, *Tupac: Resurrection*, pp. 192-93. Kidada Jones in Anson, "To Die Like a Gangsta," p. 281.

74 Sullivan, *LAbyrinth*, pp.192-3. On Hackie stating publicly that he was being paid by the FBI, see Jullianne Shepherd, "Death Row Bodyguard=Undercover FBI Agent," Vibe.com, http://www.vibe.com/news_headlines/2007/10/death_row_undercover/. Also see, TMZ staff, "Tupac's Former Bodyguard: I Was Undercover FBI," TMZ.com, 10/20/2007. The article said, "During a Q&A screening for the new DVD, *Tupac Assassination - Conspiracy or Revenge?...* Kevin Hackie revealed for the first time that he was an FBI agent -- not an informant, which had been previously reported. Hackie worked undercover as a bodyguard for Death Row from 1992-1996."

75 On alcohol and weed at party, Anson, "To Die Like a Gangsta," p. 282. On the Vegas moonlighting cops joining the LA moonlighting cops, Scott, *The Killing of Tupac Shakur*, p. 6. Eyewitness Frank Alexander in Sullivan, *LAbyrinth*, p. 188. Tupac was likely more easily influenced to get involved in this scuffle partly because of his probable post-party intoxicated state and partly because he had previously been punched by some Crip gang members for no reason, Dream Hampton, "Hellraiser," *The Source*, September 1994, p .85. Broomfield, *Biggie and Tupac*. Sullivan, *LAbyrinth*, p.p 188-89.

76 Frank Alexander quoted in Det. Poole's interviews, Sullivan, *LAbyrinth*, pp. 188-89. On Hackie's belief in this, ibid., p. 192. On film, at about 40:00 minutes, in Broomfield, *Biggie and Tupac*, Hackie said he believes Death Row orchestrated Tupac's murder. Connie Bruck, "The Takedown of Tupac," pp. 61-63.

77 Scott, The Killing of Tupac Shakur, pp. 8-9, 39, 40, 42-43, 59. Also see, "Investigative Reports: Interview with Cathy Scott," XXL Magazine, October, 2000, p. 131. Sullivan, LAbyrinth, p. 143. Hackie said this in Nick Broomfield, Biggie and Tupac (Documentary, 2002)

77 Scott, *The Killing of Tupac Shakur*, pp. 8-9, 39, 40, 42-43, 59. Also see, "Investigative Reports: Interview with Cathy Scott," *XXL Magazine*, October 2000, p. 131. Sullivan, *LAbyrinth*, p. 143. Hackie said this in Broomfield documentary *Biggie and Tupac*.

78 Sullivan, *LAbyrinth*, pp. 141-43, 145. On Death Row's Travon Lane reporting Anderson and Crips killing Tupac, *Tupac Assassination* (2007, documentary), Rich Bond and Frank Alexander producers. Crip Darnell Brims was shot three times on 9/9/96. A Blood working for Death Row's Wrightway security was shot several times by a Crip. Thirty-year-old Bobby Finch was fatally shot on Compton's Southside. Anson, "To Die Like a Gangsta," p. 282.

79 Scott, *The Killing of Tupac Shakur*, pp. 18-19, 35-39, 112. Scott, *The Murder of Biggie Smalls*, p. 89. Chuck Phillips, "2 Say They Saw Attackers of Slain Rapper; Members of Tupac Shakur's entourage say they haven't been asked to view photos of suspects." *Los Angeles Times*, 2/28/97, p. A3. On Chris Rock, http://www.youtube.com/watch?v=q-YrEc5ve3Y.

80 FOIA obtained FBI document from file# 194C-LA-232722 FOIAPA Coumputer # 1027308-1. On Biggie Smalls, aka Notorious B.I.G. born Christopher Wallace. Document dated January 28, 2004.

81 Personal Interview with Watani Tyehimba, 3/10/2003.

82 See, for example, Chuck Phillips, "Who Killed Tupac Shakur? How a fight between rival Compton gangs turns into a plot of retaliation and murder." *Los Angeles Times*, September 6, 2002. This article made worldwide news, but was easily debunked by other veteran researchers in *Vibe* magazine, Sam Anson, "Reasonable Doubt," *Vibe*, December, 2002, pp. 148-56. Another similar story by Phillips was officially retracted by the *Los Angeles Times* after it was easily debunked by Thesmokinggun.com. "For the Record: Times Retracts Shakur Story," *Los Angeles Times*, April 7, 2008.

83 In *Biggie and Tupac* film, Poole said Knight's people killed Tupac at 38:75; Poole on Hackie, 54:45; Poole on police in orchestrated hit, 56:35-58:30; Wright at about 40:00-42:10 and again at 109:00.

84 Sullivan, *LAbyrinth*, pp. 208-09. Broomfield, *Biggie and Tupac*. Chuck Phillips, "Officers May Have Seen rap Killing; Crime: Off-duty Inglewood police member was behind vehicle when rap star Notorious B.I.G. was slain and undercover New York agents were trailing the singer that night, sources say." *Los Angeles Times*, 4/23/97, pp. B1-2. Broomfield, *Biggie and Tupac*. Scott, *The Murder of Biggie Smalls*, pp. 94, 128-29. "Investigative Reports: Interview with Cathy Scott," *XXL Magazine*, October, 2000, p. 131. "LAPD photocopies of business cards of Det. Oldham, New York Police Department, and Timothy Reilly, Special Agent, U.S. Department of Treasury, Criminal Investigation Division, with handwritten notes, dated 3/9/97 1 page." This was under section, "Documents: Biggie Smalls Murder," in Sullivan, *LAbyrinth*, pp. 136, 313-14. ATF as Division of the Treasury Department, Christopher Lee, "ATF Eyes Bargaining Exemptions," *Washington Post*, 6/24/03, p. A19. On Biggie lawsuit, Dave Itzkoff, "F.B.I. Files Reveals Details of the Investigation of the Notorious B.I.G.'s Killing," *New York Times*, April 7, 2011.

Jam Master Jay

Chapter Twenty-Five

Rap Targeting and Ecstasy: Eminem & Wu Tang; POCC

Eventually, word got out that the New York and Los Angeles police departments were training police units around the country to target rappers. The training included FBI Counterintelligence Program tactics.[1] Police foul play surrounded deaths and dubious charges against many rappers who had become activists in New York. For example, the execution-style shooting of Run DMC's Jam Master Jay in October of 2002 was caught on surveillance video camera, similar to how surveillance video had Tupac Shakur's New York shooters on tape. While police rejected the videotape covering Tupac's shooting, in the case of Jam Master Jay, it's unknown if police ever did anything with the tape. No one was ever convicted of Jam Master Jay's murder.[2]

Targeting also included top rappers who had become involved with the HipHop Summit Action Network, which had developed a radical leftist 15-point plan to reform society.[3] It had top rappers, leftist academics and activists on its board, including the late Columbia University Professor Manning Marable, former NAACP Director Ben Chavis, and Congressman Kweisi Mfume. Rappers such as Shawn "Jay Z" Carter, Sean "P. Diddy/ Puffy" Combs, Marshall "Eminem" Mathers, and rap producer Russell Simmons, who was founder of the group, all appeared to get targeted and scared away from more leftist activism after their involvement.[4]

Evidence Reveals Ecstasy Brain Damage

By the mid-to-late 1980s, a new drug, MDMA or "ecstasy," began to get popular. MDMA is a "methyl analog" of MK-Ultra drug MDA. The media quoted celebrities about ecstasy, and its popularity increased into the 1990s. Evidence points to U.S. intelligence and other Western country intelligence agencies having a hand in popularizing the drug as a weapon against potentially activist young adults and cultural leaders.

By 2001, significant studies had been published regarding ecstasy. The National Institute on Drug Abuse in its Research News wrote that ecstasy "damages the brain and impairs memory in humans." Johns Hopkins neurologist, Dr. George Ricaurte, was the principal investigator in this National Institute on Drug Abuse joint study. Ricaurte also led a second study showing dark areas in positron emission tomography (PET) images of MDMA users' brains that represented damage due to chronic use.[5]

British professor A.C. Parrott published a review of fifteen years of research in the journal *Human Psychopharmacology,* citing numerous studies that found ecstasy use led to neurocognitive deficits. "Memory deficits," he wrote, "have been demonstrated in light users with an average lifetime ecstasy consumption of 10-20 occasions."[6] He further stated the worst cognitive function damage was generally found in heavier users.[7] Studies from many countries have shown how ecstasy damages selective memory and causes learning deficits, as demonstrated on a wide variety of tasks.[8]

Ecstasy a Weapon in South Africa

The CIA's Operation MK-Ultra had originally used the metabolite for ecstasy, MDA, in its experiments on American citizens, resulting in the death of unknowing patients.[9] Later, foreign intelligence agencies used ecstasy as a weapon against their own people, as happened in South Africa during its racist apartheid regime. The apartheid government made people of color second-class citizens by law. In 1994, apartheid had finally fallen and the majority of citizens, who were black or of mixed race, elected the pro-black African National Congress (ANC) to its top offices.

The new ANC government arrested Wouter Basson in 1997. Basson had been the Director of Chemical and Biological Warfare (CBW) for South Africa's former white apartheid regime. The ANC government charged Basson with selling 1,000 ecstasy tablets in South Africa's black neighborhoods, and far worse crimes, as part of CBW's "Project Coast." Basson's former research manager admitted that he was told to manufacture more than a ton of ecstasy crystals.[10]

Wouter Basson has been dubbed "Dr. Death" in the South African press. In the AN[illegible] post-apartheid spirit of amnesty, he somehow avoided conviction on war-crime charg[illegible] In 2015 Basson was still fighting to keep his medical license.

Evidence suggests that Western intelligence agencies also started promoting and trafficking ecstasy to youth worldwide around 1990. The campaign was similar to that of LSD by the CIA's MK-Ultra Program and collaborating intelligence agencies in the 1960s and beyond. Techno music and midnight "raves" began to take hold in dance clubs during the 1990s, bringing scores of young people together for this underground experience. Soon "astroturf," or fake grassroots promotion, could be seen in this movement. Incomprehensibly expensive, glossy cardboard invitations sometimes circulated regarding these events. Clubs were bought out and transformed, with techno DJs replacing former dance clubs' DJs. The old DJs had played dance songs by bands that had lyrics and messages that occasionally promoted leftist causes, such as top leftist group Rage Against the Machine. The scene was transformed by repetitive techno music with minimalist, shallow lyrics.[11]

While drug dealing existed in the old clubs, the rave or "techno" clubs that replaced many of them had many more drug dealers making sales. These new dance forums popularized "club" drugs such as ecstasy and ketamine (Special K), as well as "poppers" (amyl nitrate) and acid. One drug dealer, working with a partner from a Baltimore Mafia family, described what happened when he asked his partner if the Mafia was collaborating with government agents in distributing mass quantities of these drugs. He said his partner panicked and turned shaky, stating, "You don't want to be asking those kinds of questions."[12]

FBI Dealer-Agents Trap Wu Tang Clan

The techno/rave community tried to reach out and appeal to people of all races. U.S. intelligence appeared to accomplish this in several ways. In 1999, circumstantial evidence started to accumulate. That year, an attractive young white woman stated she brought ecstasy to use with some of the most popular New York rap groups. Also at that time, rappers started discussing their ecstasy use in top magazines, and the drug increased in popularity.[13]

Strong evidence of U.S. intelligence involvement in the distribution of ecstasy came in a front-page *Village Voice* article in 2000. It discussed how the FBI and ATF worked on a joint operation employing a Mafioso wholesale ecstasy kingpin, Michael Caruso. The article claimed Caruso "first brought techno music to Manhattan and turned Staten Island on to ecstasy." Caruso had been sentenced for a string of crimes that included drug pushing, bank robbery, kidnapping and extortion. The government drastically reduced his sentencing on the ecstasy charges, after which the FBI and ATF hired him to work as an undercover agent with the goal of getting close to the rap group Wu Tang Clan.[14]

The targeting of Wu Tang Clan had a history. U.S. intelligence unsuccessfully tried to get Wu Tang's 1998 concert tour with Rage Against the Machine cancelled. Rage Against the Machine threatened to file a lawsuit and got the tour shows re-instated.[15] Police previously used this tactic against rappers N.W.A, Tupac Shakur and Paris.[16]

U.S. intelligence had a number of reasons to put heavy focus on Wu Tang Clan. Besides touring with Rage, the Grammy nominated Wu Tang Clan worked with a founding member of the Republic of New Afrika, Brooklyn's Sonny Carson. Carson had worked with Tupac's New York lawyer, Michael Tarif Warren, on black liberation causes. Papa Wu, the brother of Wu Tang rapper Ol' Dirty Bastard (ODB, birth name, Russell Jones), founded a music studio with Carson in the Bedford-Stuyvesant neighborhood of Brooklyn. Wu Tang also worked with the Panther-inspired, worldwide hip-hop activist organization Zulu Nation.[17]

U.S. intelligence had many reasons for concern over Sonny Carson's work with rappers topping the pop charts. Zulu Nation revered Carson, and the group was inspiring new chapters worldwide. Also, Carson's son, Lumumba Carson, started an influential Brooklyn group called Blackwatch. That group was one of the first to explicitly meld Black Nationalist politics with Hip Hop. Blackwatch spawned many activist rappers, including Lumumba Carson's next group, X-Clan, where Carson took on the moniker "Professor X" in the 1980s.[18]

Rap activists reported that the music industry aided the more subtle attacks on rappers. Public Enemy's former member Professor Griff said people in the record industry tried to create a conflict between his group and X-Clan.[19] Also, politically conservative Time Warner bought up a majority of rap labels.

In the late '90s, events supported Wu Tang Clan rapper ODB's claims that the FBI had targeted him. While ODB was the most eccentric of the group, his brother Papa Wu kept ODB joining activist causes. ODB told friends and relatives that the FBI killed Tupac Shakur for being a rap activist. ODB changed his name in the futile hope of avoiding being framed or murdered due to his own activism. From 1998-99, police arrested ODB four times around the country on trivial charges. In the summer of '98, strangers broke into ODB's New York home and shot him, but he survived.[20]

Later, possibly using a version of the U.S. intelligence threat-timing tactic, police orchestrated their most blatant and deadly attack on ODB and his rapper cousin Fred Cuffie on Martin Luther King's birthday. The NYPD rap intelligence unit had a file on Cuffie. On a mid-January night in 1999, two plainclothes New York Street Crime Unit police, wearing bulletproof vests and driving an unmarked car in Brooklyn, sirened ODB to pull over. One of the officers put a gun to the head of ODB's passenger, Cuffie. The

May 30, 2000 • Vol. XLV No. 21 • America's Largest Weekly Newspaper • www.villagevoice.com • FREE

the village VOICE

The Rap Group & the Rat

Gunrunning, the Feds, and the Wu-Tang Clan

By Frank Owen p43

This *Village Voice* cover story revealed that the FBI paid Mafia-connected ecstasy kingpin Michael Caruso to work undercover as the manager for two members of the rap group Wu Tang Clan when Black Liberation leader Sonny Carson worked as their producer.

other cop told ODB to get out of the car. Out of fear, ODB stepped on the gas and fled. The police then fired at the rappers.[21]

A different group of uniformed police then came upon the rappers, surrounding ODB's car just outside his aunt's boarding home. While they didn't find a gun on ODB or Cuffie, they did arrest the two based on the claim that ODB was driving with his headlights off, and that the rapper fired at the undercover cops first. A police source said ODB's lights were on, and a grand jury ruled in favor of ODB and Cuffie's account. Months after that New York shooting, police arrested ODB and held him on $115,000 bail for wearing a bulletproof vest.[22]

In 2000, the aforementioned *Village Voice* article said the FBI had paid ecstasy-dealing young Mafia kingpin Michael Caruso to work undercover. Caruso's work appeared to include becoming a personal manager for two Wu Tang rappers. It's uncertain how much Caruso influenced Wu Tang to use and promote ecstasy, but the *Voice* reported Caruso organizing sex and drug parties for Wu Tang members. The FBI said they and the Bureau of Alcohol, Tobacco and Firearms were investigating Wu Tang on suspected gunrunning, but the FBI never charged anyone with a crime.[23] Months later, *The Source* rap magazine ran an interview of Mike Caruso joking about the allegation of his FBI spy work, but Caruso failed to say Wu Tang fired him after reading the *Voice* article.[24]

From 1999-2004, police subjected ODB to trivial arrests, and prison officials reportedly forced ODB to take psychiatric medications while he was incarcerated. ODB put out solo CDs at this time, and most topped the pop music sales charts. In 2004, after his prison release, ODB died just before his 36th birthday. Mysteriously, it took over a month for a coroner to announce that ODB died from a heart attack due to mixing cocaine with a prescription painkiller.[25] ODB's brother disagreed with the coroner's report, saying ODB was drug free at the time of his death. He also implied political reasons for his brother's death, saying he and ODB were attending activist rallies together at that time.[26]

Eminen Promotes Ecstasy Before Promoting Recovery

In 1999, white rapper Eminem (Marshall Mathers) came out with *The Slim Shady LP*. The CD made constant references to drug use and rose to the top of the rap charts. During an interview with *Rolling Stone* magazine, Eminem reportedly took hits of ecstasy as he talked to the reporter. He also promoted it in his songs. Other rappers, in magazine interviews, started discussing ecstasy use, increasing the drug's popularity.

Eminem had risen from an independent label-produced rapper to rap prominence, just as top rap industry figures had formed the Hip-Hop Summit Action Network (HSAN) that was then attacked by conservative forces.[27] Eminem supported HSAN. In 2003, Eminem also produced, for free, many of Tupac's songs for Afeni Shakur, and supported her major motion picture release, *Tupac: Resurrection*.[28] At about the same time, Eminem wrote a song saying he didn't care about "dead presidents" (cash), he only wanted to see the president (George W. Bush) dead. The Secret Service launched an investigation.[29]

Eminem had multiplatinum sales on his 2004 release *Encore*. Eminem had tried to sway the presidential election in the fall of 2004 by releasing another song and video highly critical of Bush. The CD's song "Mosh," and its accompanying video, encouraged young people to storm the White House and get Bush out of office for lying about the reasons for the Iraq war. Eminem produced this album just before he volunteered his time to produce a whole album of Tupac Shakur's unreleased music, *Loyal to the Game*. It topped the music sales charts.[30] Additionally, Eminem worked on a collaborative song with Mos Def and Jadakiss in a rap written by Immortal Technique, wherein the Bush administration is blamed for bringing down the World Trade Center on 9/11/01.[31]

Starting at the close of 2005, strangers shot members of Eminem's rap group, D12, whose CDs had sold over four million copies each since 2001. In December of 2005, someone shot and wounded D12 rapper Obie Trice as he was driving on a Detroit-area highway. On April 12, 2006, someone fatally shot D12 rapper Proof, Eminem's best man at his wedding and his right-hand man onstage. Proof had a musical legacy; his father played in Marvin Gaye's band. Less than a week before Proof's murder, *Rolling Stone* published an article about him and his new solo CD. In that article Proof made reference to his song "Kurt Kobain," with this assertion: "The circumstances of Kurt's death are freaky to me. I don't think he killed himself."[32]

Details on rapper Proof's shooting show signs of intelligence targeting. One of the people involved in the shooting was a former U.S. Army sergeant, as had been the case in another circumstance of political targeting. Secondly, the gunman shot Proof three times in the head and chest, a military-execution style used on Black Panther national founder Huey Newton, and unsuccessfully on Tupac Shakur.[33] It's interesting that this occurred just after Eminem first got clean and sober. In 2005, the year before Proof's death, Eminem faced his addiction and went to residential treatment. Eminem said that Proof's murder triggered his relapse, and he eventually needed to go back into rehab after overdosing on methadone in 2007. His friend Elton John mentored him through rehab in 2008, and he stayed sober thereafter, promoting it with a 2010 album: *Recovery*.[34]

By 2012, articles discussed the prevalence of ecstasy in the Hip Hop music world, including one rap label's involvement in trafficking the drug. In April 2012, articles stated that prosecutors were charging a rap label, Thizz Entertainment ("thizz" is another slang name for MDMA/"ecstasy") with trafficking the drug nationwide, along with cocaine, heroin, and marijuana. While the evidence was strong to support the notion that Death Row Records was a U.S. intelligence front company, some evidence also suggests that Thizz Entertainment was doing U.S. intelligence bidding.

The *Los Angeles Times* stated that the rap label started in 1999, and at some point started dealing ecstasy, until it was trafficking nationwide around 2010.[35] Court documents associated with the article show the government had a paid informant within Thizz Entertainment as early as 2004. In U.S. intelligence operations, "informant" usually means "paid agent" who takes on activities that range from drug dealing to helping set up murders. The court documents list many other U.S. intelligence undercover agents, including a key informant who began his work in 2006. So, the traffickers spread their operations nationwide years *after* Drug Enforcement Agency-paid infiltrators became part of that group. This suggests that DEA agents were helping to traffic ecstasy in wider and wider areas for at least those six years, until more honest police agents found out about it and pressed criminal charges against the rap label.[36]

Chicago Police Use Drugs to Target Hampton Jr.'s POCC

Fred Hampton Jr., son of the Chicago Black Panther leader, had first become a leader of Chicago's National People's Democratic Uhuru Movement when he was twenty-two years old in 1992. Blacks in Los Angeles rioted that year, following the acquittal of police who were filmed beating black motorist

Rodney King. Hampton Jr. organized a rally to protest that police acquittal. Hampton said that a day after his rally, police officer Joseph Grubesette, who led FBI agents in arresting Hampton's father before murdering him, picked Hampton Jr. up as he was walking with his three-year-old daughter. Evidence indicates that they framed Fred Hampton Jr. for firebombing a store that never even experienced a fire. Hampton spent nine years in prison.[37]

Both in and out of prison, Fred Hampton Jr. experienced murderous attacks, as he founded the Prisoners of Conscience Committee (POCC).[38] The brutal Chicago political establishment continuously attacked the POCC. A former Vietnam War military policeman, Jon Burge, headed a Chicago Police tactical squad implicated in torture interrogation tactics. These tactics included suffocation as well as the use of electric cattle prods on the ears and genitals of over one hundred black and Latino suspects. A groundswell of bad publicity eventually led Chicago police chiefs to suspend Burge by 1991.[39]

POCC's Minister of Defense Aaron Patterson spent seventeen years on death row after a confession gained through Burge-supervised suffocations and beatings. Illinois Governor George Ryan pardoned Patterson in January of 2003, at which time he jumped into his activist leadership position. By that year, Richard Daley Jr. had kept a longtime position as Chicago's mayor. Patterson regularly spoke at anti-war rallies and anti-police brutality forums, while organizing with POCC.[40]

Within twenty months, Chicago police culminated an operation with Federal Alcohol and Tobacco and Firearms agents against Patterson. POCC Chairman Fred Hampton Jr. said they labeled this "Operation Revolving Door," and Joe Gorman Jr. headed it. Hampton also named the connections to his father's murder in this operation. He said that Mayor Richard Daley Sr. had personally hired Michael Cronin, who headed the gang narcotics unit, while Joe Gorman Sr. used a machine gun to help kill Panther Chairman Fred Hampton Sr. and Mark Clark. The ATF, the same group involved in murderously targeting Tupac, Biggie, Wu Tang Clan, MOVE, Panther leader Eldridge Cleaver and Cesar Chavez, arrested Patterson with Michael Cronin present. They had paid someone to offer Patterson guns and drugs for sale.

Judge Rebecca Pallmeyer, who had presided over a corruption trial that removed Gov. Ryan from office, sentenced Patterson to thirty years in jail. Prosecutors did not charge Patterson with selling drugs or guns, nor possession of drugs and guns, but merely "conspiracy" to do so. Prosecutors alleged Patterson intended to become involved in these activities.[41]

In September of 2007, Fred Hampton Jr. said that he and his fellow POCC members heard that Chicago police shot two black youths. The POCC decided to conduct a people's investigation of it. They came upon the police and got out of their cars to observe what was happening. The police reportedly beat Hampton and other POCC members for "attempting to disrupt the police investigation of an aggravated battery." Hampton was acquitted in mid-October of 2007.[42]

Notes

1 Andrew Lee and Carl Swanson, "NYPD Raps," *New York*, 4/30/01, p. 13. Nicole White and Evelyn McDonnell, "Police Secretly Watching Hip-Hop Artists," *Miami Herald*, 3/9/04, p. 1A. Nicole White and Evelyn McDonnell, "Monitoring of Rap Stars Disputed," *Miami Herald*, 3/17/04, p. 1B. Dasun Allah, "NYPD Admits to Rap Intelligence Unit," *Village Voice*, 3/23/04. Evelyn McDonnell and Nicole White, "Arresting Data in Rap Binder," *Miami Herald*, 5/14/04, p. 1B. Dasun Allah & Joshua Fahiym Ratcliffe, "Law and Disorder," *The Source*, June 2004, p. 44. Randall Sullivan, *LAbyrinth: A Detective Investigates the Murders of Tupac Shakur and Notorious B.I.G., the Implication of Death Row Records' Suge Knight, and the Origins of the Los Angeles Police Scandal* (New York: Atlantic Monthly Press, 2002), pp. 208-09, 313-14. Chuck Phillips, "Officers May Have Seen rap Killing; Crime: Off-duty Inglewood police member was behind vehicle when rap star Notorious B.I.G. was slain and undercover New York agents were trailing the singe that night, sources say," *Los Angeles Times*, 4/23/97, pp. B1-2.

2 From Wire Reports, "Run-DMC D.J. Killed in Shooting at Studio," *The Sun* (Baltimore), October 31, 2002, p. 3A. Andy Newman and Al Baker, "Was It a Bad Business Deal or a Music Industry Feud," *New York Times*, November 1, 2002, http://www.nytimes.com/2002/11/01/nyregion/was-it-a-bad-business-deal-or-a-music-industry-feud.html. Also see, Anthony Florence, "AllHipHop.com: Jam Master Jay's Killer Caught on Tape," *New York Amsterdam News*, November 17, 2002, Vol. 93 Issue 45, p. 34.

3 HSAN's Board of Directors consisted of a multiracial group of top rap record label owners. These included a Def Jam director, Kevin Liles, and Damon Dash of rapper Jay-Z's Roc-a-Fella Records, as Simmons' co-chairs. The board also included Bad Boy Entertainment founder Sean "Puffy" Combs (name later changed to P. Diddy) and white Warner executive, Lyor Cohen. HSAN developed a 15-point goal statement similar to the Black Panthers' Ten-Point Program, called "What We Want." While not containing all of the overt socialist politics nor the militant self-defense tactics of the Panthers' Program, their statement included Panther-like radical leftist ideas such as "the total elimination of poverty ... racism and ... bigotry." It also called for universal health care, equal justice without discrimination, African American reparations, voter enfranchisement and the end of companies' environmental polluting of poor neighborhoods. Hip-Hop Summit Action Network, www.hsan.org/Content/main.aspx?pageid=27. Kristin Jones, "Rocking the Hip-Hop Vote," *The Nation*, 12/1/03, pp. 7-8. Hip-Hop Summit Action Network, www.hsan.org/Content/main.aspx?pageid=27.

4 On Hiphop Summit Action Network, Felicia R. Lee, "Hip-Hop is Enlisted in Social Causes," *New York Times*, June 22, 2002. Cathy Scott, *The Murder of Biggie Smalls* (New York: St. Martin's, 2000), pp. 94, 129. Rock and Rap Confidential's Dave Marsh reported that New York cops put rappers under surveillance and quoted hip-hop journalist, Davey D, about national rap surveillance and banning of rap shows. On Combs, Dan Barry and Juan Forero, "Between High Life and Street Life," *New York Times*, December 29, 1999, p. B1. Katherine Finkelstein, "Judge in Combs Case Permits Statement by Missing Witness," *New York Times*, 3/6/01, p. B2. Peter Noel, "Daddy Under the Gun," *Village Voice*, January 9, 2001, p. 21. Simmons: Nolan Strong, "Kimora Lee Simmons Arrested," 7/28/04, All HipHop.com: News. Jay-Z: Personal interview with attorney, Murray Richman. Articles covering videotape supporting Jay-Z include kris ex, "Jay Z: The Trial and Tribulations of S. Carter," Vibe, February 2000, p. 136. The record producer was Lance "Un" Rivera. Kim Odorio, "Police is Watching," *The Source*, July 2001, p. 49. Eminem, *Washington Post*, 12/6/03, p. C3.

5 Robert Mathias, "'Ecstasy' Damages the Brain and Impairs Memory in Humans." *NIDA Notes* Vol. 14 #4, 9/99. http://archives.drugabuse.gov/NIDA_Notes/NNVol14N4/Ecstasy.html.

6 Andrew C. Parrott, "Human psychobiology of MDMA or 'Ecstasy': an overview of 25 years of empirical research," *Human Psychopharmacology* 07/2013; 28(4):289-307.

7 Karen I. Bolla, PhD; Una D. McCann, MD; and George A. Ricaurte, MD, PhD, "Memory Impairment in Abstinent MDMA ("Ecstasy") Users," *Neurology*, 1998; 51: 1532-7. Robert J. Verkes et al., *Psychopharmacology* (2001) 153: 196-202.

8 Parrott, "Human psychopharmacology of MDMA." *Human Psychopharmacology*, 2001: 16; 557-577, see Table 2. Also see this study by Parrott in 2002 in *Pharmacology, Biochemistry and Behavior* 71, 837-844. See Table 3 in Michael John Morgan, "Ecstasy (MDMA): a review of its possible psychological effects," *Psychopharmacology* (2000) 152:230-248. Example: http://www.erowid.org/archive/rhodium/pharmacology/PBB-71-837.pdf.

9 Declassified Army document, "Inspector General's Report of Inquiry into the Facts and Circumstances surrounding the Death of Mr. Harold Baluer at the New York State Psychiatric Institute (NYSPI) and Subsequent Claims and Actions, DAIG-IN 27-75, 1975. From Martin Lee and Bruce Shlain, *Acid Dreams: The CIA, LSD, the Sixties and Beyond* (New York: Grove Press, 1985/1992), p. 38, 302n.

10 Chris Opperman, "Basson's Army Buddy Blows the Whistle," *Mail & Guardian*, 6/27/97 in De Wet Potgieter, "Apartheid's Poison Legacy: South Africa's Chemical and Biological Warfare Program," *Covert Action Quarterly* #63, Winter 1998, p. 33, http://mediafilter.org/CAQ/caq63/caq63apartheid.html.

11 On change in dance clubs, this writer frequented these dance clubs in various American cities and saw the changes starting in the early-to-mid 1990s. Perry Farrell displayed his leftist beliefs in touring the nation with Zach De La Roca's (lead singer of Rage Against the Machine) Spitfire Spoken Word tour. This writer attended one of Spitfire's events in New York around 1999.

12 Personal interview with an admitted drug dealer whom this writer counseled regarding his addictions in 1995. The client visited me for advice at my office several times after his completion of group treatment, when he told this story. Due to confidentiality laws, the client must remain anonymous.

13 On acquiring ecstasy for rap artists, this author was told this by a woman in a Williamsburg, Brooklyn café in 1999. Chris Lee, "Hip Hop's Chemical Romance with Ecstasy," *The Los Angeles Times*, September 24, 2010. http://articles.latimes.com/2010/sep/24/entertainment/la-et-rappers-ecstasy-0924.

14 Frank Owen, "The Rap Group and the Rat; Gunrunning, the Feds, and the Wu-Tang Clan," *Village Voice*, May 30, 2000, pp. 43-48. Caruso disclosed being personal manager for two Wu Tang rappers. "Music Matters; Family Ties," *The Source*, October 2000, p. 56, http://www.villagevoice.com/2000-05-23/news/wu-tang-clan-is-sumthing-ta-fuck-wit/.

15 Personal interview with Rage Against the Machine lead singer, Zach De La Rocha, May 5, 1999. Stadium managers first canceled their shows when police wouldn't provide security, stating too much risk of a riot, but Rage Against the Machine collaborated with several rappers, such as Public Enemy's Chuck D at a Mumia Abu-Jamal benefit that police also unsuccessfully tried to cancel. This writer attended that Rage Against the Machine benefit concert, just outside New York City in New Jersey. Radio stations such as KROK discussed police attempts to cancel the show in 2000.

16 They tried to get N.W.A.'s rap shows canceled in '88 and Tupac's concerts cancelled in '93. They also worked to cancel the shows of Oakland-based political rapper Paris, according to at least one news article, likely due to his 1992 lyrical attack on the President, "Bush Killa." On the FBI's fax campaign to get police canceling N.W.A. shows, see Bruce C. Brown, "Quayle Boosts 'Cop Killer' Campaign," *Washington Post*, 6/20/92, pp. B1, 5. Cited in Barry Shank, "Fears of the White Unconcious: Music, Race, and Identification in the Censorship of 'Cop Killer.'" *Radical History Review* #66, Fall 1996. On Tupac, see Vibe eds., *Tupac Shakur* (New York: Crown, 1997), p. 46. On Paris, see "Sonic Jihad release from Paris," http://polsong.gcal.ac.uk/news_archive.html. Also see this attempted use against Jimi Hendrix, Harry Shapiro and Caesar Glebbeek, *Jimi Hendrix: Electric Gyspy* (New York: St. Martin's Griffin, 1995), pp. 190, 426.

17 On Carson as founding member of Republic of New Afrika, see Dasun Allah, "Sonny Carson Dies: Legendary Black Nationalist Figure in Bedford-Stuyvesant," *Village Voice*, 12/31/02, www.villagevoice.com On, Zulu Nation, personal interview: this author heard Zulu nation founder

Afrika Bambata say this at the Third Black Panther Film Festival at CUNY in New York City, 2002, then talked briefly with him afterwards. On Zulu's worldwide status see, Shaila Dewan, "At a Live Homage, Hip-Hop Is King but 'Rapping" is Taboo," *New York Times,* November 13, 2000, p. B3. Also see articles on Zulu Nation at www.daveyd.com, which said the Zulu Nation had 10,000 members.

18 Andy Soages, "Hip Hop Fridays: Vibes of the Pro Black: A Conversation of Brother J. of X-Clan Part 1" (May 27-30), 2005, www.blackelectorate.com

19 Personal interviews with June of Shaka Shakur's Maroon Records and "Panther Cub" Orlando Green, who also organizes the Hip Hop Convention, www.hiphopconvention.org, 3/4/06. In an interview with Davey D, Professor Griff also claimed that Public Enemy's former Def Jam label claimed that the group owed them $2 million. He further said that the industry changed the laws making sampling of other's music require royalty payments, and that this went into effect retroactively, http://odeo.com/audio483066/view.

20 Peter Noel, "A Bullet for Big Baby Jesus," *Village Voice,* 2/2/99, pp. 45-46.

21 Most details of this event described in Noel, "A Bullet for Big Baby Jesus." On cops shooting at ODB in Street Crime Unit, see *Vibe,* May 1999. Noel cited a Criminal Court complaint saying that these cops were part of the Street Crime Unit. Note that the Street Crime Unit was also implicated as the first to arrive at the shooting of Tupac in New York, as well as his year-earlier purported sexual assault scene. Writers have stated the belief that Street Crime Unit took over for the NYPD's Cointelpro BOSS unit in starting the year Cointelpro and BOSS 'officially' end. For one, see Frank Morales, "The Militarization of the Police," *CovertAction Quarterly,* no. 67, Spring/Summer, 1999, p. 48.

22 Patrice O'Shaughnessy, "Rapper Vows Suit, Sez Cops Did Him Dirty in Shooting," *New York Daily News,* February 5, 1999, p. 4. *Vibe,* May 1999. Noel, "A Bullet for Big Baby Jesus." On arrest for vest, Associated Press, "Rapper's in the Clink," *New York Daily News,* 3/11/99, p. 3.

23 Owen, "The Rap Group and the Rat. Caruso disclosed being personal manager for two Wu Tang rappers. "Music Matters; Family Ties," *The Source,* October 2000, p. 56

24 "Music Matters; Family Ties." Frank Owens, "Letters: Response," *Village Voice,* June 13, 2000, p. 6.

25 Nolan Strong, "Ol' Dirty Bastard Dead," 11/12/04. Roman Wolfe, "Ol' Dirty Died From Cocaine and Prescription Painkillers," 12/15/04. Both from *AllHipHop.com*: News. The listed painkiller was Tramidol.

26 Odd names do run in the family, but his appears to have a positive purpose. Remmie Fresh, "Family, Friends, Say Goodbye to Ol' Dirty Bastard," *AllHipHop.com*: News, 11/19/04.

27 On HSAN, Hip-Hop Summit Action Network, www.hsan.org/Content/main.aspx?pageid=27. Kristin Jones, "Rocking the Hip-Hop Vote," *The Nation,* 12/1/03, pp. 7-8. For more on HSAN and top rap industry figures as part of it, see note 3. On Eminem and ecstasy, "Down and Dirty White Boy Rap: The Twisted Life of Eminem," *Rolling Stone,* April 29, 1999.

28 Shaheem Reid, with Larua Lazin, "Eminem: Reconstructing Tupac," mtv.com. www.mtv.com/bands/t/tupac/news_feature_102703/. On Tupac film in top 10, Nielson, *New York Times,* movies.nytimes.com/pages/movies/boxofffice/weekend_us/index.html.

29 "Names and Faces,"*Washington Post,* 12/6/03, p. C3.

30 Reid, with Lazin, "Eminem: Reconstructing Tupac."

31 Michael Kane, "Hip-Hop and the 911 Truth Movement," *Guerilla News Network,* 12/22/04. This article discusses many rappers who blamed the Bush administration for 9/11 in their raps, including Jadakiss, Paris, Immortal Technique, Mos Def, etc. Immortal Technique did a particularly eloquent job in his rap with samples of Mos Def, Eminem, Jadakiss, etc, titled "Bin Laden," http://www.gnn.tv/print/1016/Hip_Hop_and_the_9_11_Truth_Movement.

32 On Obie Trice, *Associated Press,* "Emimen's friend killed in nightclub shooting on Eight Mile Rd," *Star Tribune,* 4/11/06, www.StarTribune.com . On Proof, see EM News, "Proof Shot to Death Outside Detroit Club," 4/11/06, www.allabouteninem.com/news.html. On 4 million in sales, AP, "Rapper killed in nightclub shooting," *CNN.com* 4/11/06. Proof on Cobain, Christina Fuocco, "D12's Proof Channels Jerry Garcia," *Rolling Stone,* August 8, 2005.

33 On former U.S. Army, Nolan Strong, "Man Suspected of Fatally Shooting Rapper Proof Surrenders, Pool Game May Have Sparked Fight," www.allhiphop.com/hiphopnews, 4/12/06. On three shots fired in chest and head, Lawrence Van Gelder, "Arts, Briefly: Rapper Who Was Killed Fired First Shot, Police Say," *New York Times*, 4/14/06, p. E5. In the other instance, a former member of the army murdered an influential black New York City councilman—the first such shooting ever in City Council chambers. On Askew leaving Air Force in North Carolina in the summer of 2001, Michael Daly, "Rev. Moon Son Made Gun," *New York Daily News*, 7/27/03, p. 7. On prominent black activist putting Davis's assassination on par with MLK's, Alton Maddox, Jr. "Something Smells in Councilman Davis' Assassination," *Amsterdam News*, 7/31/03, p. 12.

34 Monica Herrera, "Eminem, Clean and Sober, Draws on New Inspiration," *Reuters*, June 25, 2010, http://www.reuters.com/article/2010/06/25/us-eminem-idUSTRE65N09720100625. Josh Eells, "Eminem on the Road Back From Hell," *Rolling Stone*, November 25, 2010.

35 Lee, "Hip Hop's Chemical Romance with Ecstasy." On Thizz starting to spread their trafficking nationwide around 2010, see Mathew Gafni, *Contra Costa Times*, "Feds Bust Supected Ecstasy drug Ring centered around Bay Area rap label founded by Mac Dre," *San Jose Mercury News*, April 25, 2012, http://www.mercurynews.com/twitter/ci_20469324/feds-bust-suspected-ecstasy-drug-network-centered-around.

36 Mathia Gafni/Media News Group, "Thizz Entertainment Involved in a Lot More than Rap, Federal Drug Authorities Say," *The Times Herald*, April 24, 2012, http://www.timesheraldonline.com/news/ci_20473073/. On court documents, see United States District Court, Eastern District of California. These papers are shown below on above *Times Herald* website. They were stamped, "Original Filed April 16, 2012. Case number 2:12 MJ 0101," under "Affidavit of DEA Special Agent Brian Nehring in Support of Criminal Complaint and Arrest Warrants." At point #14, Nehring discussed Thizz artists promoting ecstasy consistently in their lyrics from their founding in 1999. At point #16, the affidavit said that "Confidential Source 1" started working for the DEA in 2004 and continued until at least 2006. The documents also show many more paid informants.

37 Personal interview, Fred Hampton Jr. at Third Black Panther Film Festival, New York City, 8/1/03. Also written about in "Framed! For Defending the Rights of the Black Community," www.inpdumchicago.com/framed.html. Fred Hampton Jr., as told to Heru, "Assassination Attempt on Fred Hampton, Jr.," 10/2/02, *Davey D's Hip-Hop Corner: the New Source for the Hip-Hop Generation*, http://www.daveyd.com/FullArticles/articleN1274.asp. On walking with daughter, Heru, "Fred Hampton, Jr. Interview," *AWOL Magazine*, 2002.

38 Personal interview, Fred Hampton Jr., 8/1/03. On pictures of assassination attempts, Minister of Information J.R. (Valrey), "Young Chairman Fred Hampton Jr. Pictorial," *San Francisco Bay View*, www.sfbayview.com/022603/manyhaveforgotten022603.shtml. On Hampton citing Tupac's importance, see reprint of Vibe Online Exclusive: "Interview with Chairman Fred Hampton, Jr.," 12/3/04, https://groups.yahoo.com/neo/groups/openyourthirdeye/conversations/topics/13196.

39 Sasha Abramsky, "Trial by Torture," *Mother Jones Online*, 3/3/00, http://www.truthinjustice.org/chicops.htm. On number of black and Latino suspects tortured, see Caryl Sortwell, "Aaron Patterson Targeted in Police and Fed Frame-up," *Fightback News*, Oct-Nov 2004, http://www.fightbacknews.org/2004/04/aaronpatterson.htm.

40 John Conroy, "Aaron Patterson," *The Chicago Reader*, 12/3/99, www.ccadp.org/aaronpaterson-reader.htm. Sortwell, "Aaron Patterson Targeted in Police and Fed Frame-up."

41 Conroy, "Aaron Patterson." Sortwell, "Aaron Patterson Targeted in Police and Fed Frame-up." Minister of Information J.R. (Valrey), "POCC Min. of Defense Aaron Patterson Sentencing Hearing Update: The Saga Continues in the Legal Lynching of Aaron Patterson; and Interview wit' Chairman Fred Hampton Jr., 8/31/07.

42 Personal Interview of Fred Hampton Jr., 10/10/07, and myspace.com/ChairmanFredpart_2 .

Chapter Twenty-Six

CIA, MAPS & Heffter; Embalming The Dead

In the new millennium, the *New York Times*, the *Baltimore Sun* and other large circulation daily newspapers highlighted research on psychedelics and ecstasy. Doctors at prestigious university medical schools produced studies promoting positive aspects of these drugs. These studies often mentioned an affiliated funding source research group—the Multidisciplinary Association of Psychedelic Studies, Inc. (MAPS).

Founded in 1986, MAPS received early aid from MK-Ultra participants such as Timothy Leary. The former CIA-contracted inventor of LSD, Albert Hoffman, also donated to the funding of MAPS. The year before, the Food and Drug Administration had classified ecstasy as a Schedule I drug. This made ecstasy illegal as an addictive substance without clinical value.[1]

Rick Doblin founded MAPS. Doblin described his first acid trip, which reportedly led him to say he had "been fortunate to be able to combine psychedelics with the pursuit of the American dream." The Reagan-Bush administration's IRS granted 501c3 tax-exempt charity status to Doblin's North Carolina-based MAPS. MAPS received large contributions from billionaire George Soros, the multi-billionaire Pritzker family, and an anonymous British foundation. In the new millennium, MAPS listed major contributions from families and groups, including the Pritzker family, who had a net worth in the tens of billions of dollars.[2]

The Multidisciplinary Association for Psychedelic Studies (MAPS) got start-up help from the administration of former CIA Director George H. W. Bush. MAPS funds studies supporting LSD and ecstasy use worldwide.

Back in 1993, Rick Doblin had already received attention from the Associated Press when they covered the 50th anniversary of LSD's discovery. A conference was held, and many of the LSD luminaries were quoted there, including Timothy Leary. The relatively short article devoted about two paragraphs to MAPS founder Doblin.[3]

MAPS's start during the Reagan-Bush presidential administration seemed no coincidence. In 1986, Vice President George H.W. Bush's aide Oliver North jump-started the Iran-Contra scandal, involving the CIA in trafficking cocaine. Once former CIA Director Bush reached the presidency, he appointed Dr. David Kessler as Food and Drug Administration Commissioner. Harking back to the MK-Ultra days of testing LSD in schools, Kessler approved university testing of psychedelics again in 1990, just after his U.S. Senate confirmation.[4]

This approval marked the FDA's first for psychedelic research in over twenty years. Dr. Kessler remained FDA Commissioner for the next five years, including three years under President Clinton. President Bush also had Kessler fill the FDA with a like-minded research staff favorable to psychedelics. In an interview, Rick Doblin said one of these leading doctors in the FDA was Dr. John Harter, whose "vision was to train me to understand how the FDA worked so that I could try to mobilize the demoralized psychedelic community to submit protocols."

Doblin went on to describe the history of his work, which inadvertently revealed his unusual power in the FDA, even after Kessler's resignation under President Clinton: "There was a short period after he resigned in 1995 during which lower level FDA officials made it difficult to move forward with psychedelic and medical marijuana research. However, I filed a complaint with the ombudsman and the policies established by 'Pilot Drug' were reaffirmed in 1999 by FDA upper management." Doblin further said Clinton's successor, President George W. Bush, also picked an "FDA commissioner, Dr. Jane Henney, [who] is supportive of psychedelic research."[5]

From 2000 to 2011, MAPS articles showed up in newspapers worldwide. With MAPS funding of Harvard and Johns Hopkins researchers, the idea of LSD and ecstasy having health benefits spread. The *New York Times, Baltimore Sun* and other newspapers helped spread MAPS propaganda, further legitimizing the group.[6]

Studies Prove Ecstasy Dangerous in Any Amount

By 2007, the danger of ecstasy came out more broadly outside of MAPS's circles. Two British researchers, Keith Laws and Joy Kokkalis of Hertfordshire University School of Psychology, led a meta-study of 26 previous studies involving 600 ecstasy users. They found ecstasy had a "medium to large effect on impairing short and long-term memory." The study also found the number of ecstasy tablets taken over a lifetime didn't have much effect on the results. Regarding memory impairment, Professor Laws said, "Essentially it's the same if you take only a few, or an extremely large amount of tablets."[7]

Health correspondent Jane Kirby, of the British newspaper, *The Independent*, published her review of the study. Kirby added, "[Other] studies have shown long-term or heavy ecstasy use can damage neurons in the brain and cause depression, anxiety and difficulty sleeping."[8]

A journal, *The Psychologist*, quoted a MAPS researcher, Dr. Ilsa Jerome, critiquing British researcher Keith Laws's meta-study. Jerome said the studies Laws analyzed had methodological problems. Jerome said these problems related to polydrug use, uncertain dosage, and drug purity.

Laws answered, saying the main polydrug use was cannabis and was dealt with in their paper. He said cannabis use with ecstasy led to long-term visual memory deficit, while ecstasy alone caused only verbal memory problems. Laws also said purity and dosage amounts were not a problem in analyzing the effects of street ecstasy on memory.[9]

But, similar to the evidence of U.S. intelligence's media assets promoting marijuana and LSD in the 1960s and '70s, ecstasy promotion gained renewed strength after 2000.[10] MAPS researchers and staff also understood the power of repetition and wider information dissemination. In 2011 another article quoted Harvard MAPS-funded researcher John Halpern. In the journal *Addiction*, Halpern published a study that received $1.8 million from the U.S. National Institute on Drug Abuse. An article in *The Guardian*, a London newspaper, repeated Halpern's dubious claims that the other studies had "methodological drawbacks [that] bedeviled" them.

John Halpern continued churning out similar critiques. "Too many studies," he stated, "have been carried out on small populations while overarching conclusions have been drawn from them." Halpern further said that different populations were compared in prior studies—ravers with non-ravers. *The Guardian* stated as fact that, "All-night dancing … exposed these individuals to sleep and fluid deprivation—factors that are themselves known to produce long-lasting cognitive effects."[11] With a simple third control group of non-rave participants, Halpern could have proved this alleged methodological problem, but he never did so, and that is significant.

Halpern also said in 2011 that he used his almost $2 million for his study to whittle down 1,500 potential participants to only 52 users and 59 non-users. Thus, *The Guardian*, and surely other mainstream media, failed to note that many other studies, with subjects ranging from 15 to 150, showed long-term memory and psychological problems from ecstasy use. For example, the *Archives of General Psychiatry* noted in 2007 how Thelma Schilt and her colleagues compared 58 individuals before and after their ecstasy use, to 60 individuals with the same age, sex and intelligence score, but who did not use ecstasy in the same two year period. They found "that low doses of ecstasy are associated with decreased verbal memory function." Another study followed 109 individuals who took a little more than one ecstasy pill every other week for a year; they had similar declines in their relational memory. A final study worth mentioning compared control groups of marijuana users and found that ecstasy caused its own unique memory problems, with users of only ten ecstasy pills in a year.[12]

CIA MK-Ultra's Fifty Years of Involvement

The strongest evidence of the CIA continuing MK-Ultra was revealed in the November 2000 arrest of 55-year-old William Pickard, deputy director of UCLA's Drug Policy Research Program, for running one of the nation's largest LSD laboratories. Drug Enforcement Agents would also eventually implicate Prof. John Halpern and another psychedelic think tank, the Heffter Institute, which had worked on many projects with MAPS. The DEA arrested Pickard at the laboratory site: a decommissioned missile silo. DEA agents found enough raw materials there to make over fifteen million hits of acid.

Comprehensive articles in *Rolling Stone* and the *San Francisco Chronicle* cite evidence suggesting that Halpern, Pickard, and others were involved in a continuing MK-Ultra operation. This operation had links to the original MK-Ultra LSD laboratories and to universities involved in MK-Ultra, top government officials, and LSD-promoting think tanks.

First, *San Francisco Chronicle* reporter Seth Rosenfeld described William Pickard as meeting with top LSD chemist Tim Scully in 1974. Scully had worked with former top acid trafficker August Owsley Stanley III, as well as the Grateful Dead with the Acid Tests. Scully then worked with William and Peggy Mellon Hitchcock's family and ran the American LSD laboratory for the world's top LSD trafficker, U.S. intelligence agent Ronald Stark. According to Rosenfeld, during their 1974 meeting, Pickard handed Scully a U.S. Army Chemical Warfare Group pin, before giving him thousands of dollars for his legal defense.

William Pickard grew up in a wealthy suburb of Atlanta. He developed an early expertise in chemistry, but dropped out of Princeton and traveled to the San Francisco Bay area in 1967. There he befriended Talitha Stills, sister of Crosby, Stills and Nash singer Stephen Stills. She said Pickard had a trust fund and didn't work in the late 1960s. The Bureau of Narcotics Enforcement said Pickard was working with the Brotherhood of Eternal Love's LSD laboratory.[13]

U.S. intelligence agent Ronald Stark based his American operation at that laboratory. *Rolling Stone* reporter Peter Wilkinson said that in 1978, police found Pickard's fully functioning MDA laboratory, and Pickard admitted he tried to sell some of the Brotherhood's lab gear that had traces of MDA (ecstasy/MDMA analogue) on it. In 1980, Pickard was arrested for manufacturing amphetamines, and a few months later for manufacturing MDA again.[14]

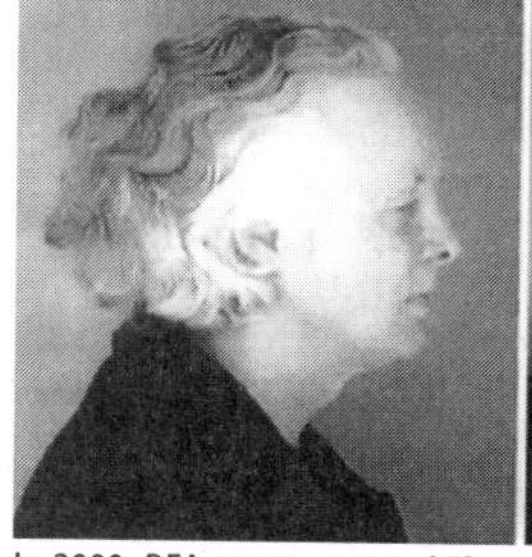

In 2000, DEA agents arrested "former" informant Leonard Pickard with 90 pounds of raw materials for making millions of hits of LSD. None of Pickard's highly connected associates went to jail with him.

Prior to that, William Pickard had worked as a research manager at University of California Berkeley from 1971 until 1974. The *San Francisco Chronicle* stated that Pickard's academic résumé contains a 20-year gap from 1974 to 1994. Some records placed him at other universities, such as MK-Ultra hot spot Stanford University in the San Francisco Bay area. The *Chronicle* noted that when Tim Scully got out of the prison in the early 1980s, Pickard consulted with him on manufacturing LSD. It should be remembered that the government isn't monolithic, as every agency has different factions, including honest DEA agents who will arrest chemists such as Scully. It only appears that the most powerful factions are able to keep the top acid traffickers, such as Ron Stark and William Mellon Hitchcock, from receiving prison sentences.[15]

In the mid-1980s, Pickard took a course on "social drugs" with Alexander Shulgin. Shulgin worked for Dow Chemical in the 1960s, where he synthesized some of MK-Ultra's newest super-hallucinogens, such as DOM (street name: STP). He then gave samples to the CIA to experiment with at Edgewood Arsenal in Maryland, who released its chemical makeup to the public soon after.[16] The *New York Times* called Shulgin "Dr. Ecstasy," and said he created over two hundred psychedelic compounds from 1960 to 2005. Shulgin further reportedly "advised" LSD manufacturer Owsley for years, including hanging out with him at Grateful Dead shows.

By 1988, William Pickard's neighbor had called police about odors coming from a shop Pickard ran in a San Francisco Bay area industrial park. DEA agents found two hundred thousand doses of LSD, including blotter paper featuring Grateful Dead album covers. Pickard had "state-of-the-art equipment, including a roto-evaporator, heating mantles and a pill press, an item that DEA restrictions make almost impossible to obtain." Pickard served part of a five-year sentence. Officials later revealed Pickard had been on their payroll as an "informant" for state and federal drug agents at that time.[17]

By 1992, William Pickard was out of jail and attending monthly meetings with Shulgin and other important figures, like Harvard public policy professor Mark Kleinman. Pickard enrolled at Harvard, another MK-Ultra hot spot, in Kleinman's John F. Kennedy School of Government. During that period, Pickard married Deb Harlow, who pioneered the use of MDMA in therapy before it became illegal in 1985 (reminiscent of LSD used to aid "therapy" before 1966). Pickard also wrote papers reviewed by Robert Gelbard, then Assistant Secretary of State for International Matters and Law Enforcement Affairs.[18] Rick Doblin, director of the Multidisciplinary Association of Psychedelic Studies, socialized with Pickard in Cambridge, Massachusetts and Shulgin's home in Northern California.[19]

It's surely not coincidental that Pickard started mass-manufacturing LSD again in this mid-1990s time period. Pickard went to former MK-Ultra subject Al Salvinelli's home in New Mexico, where he met with Harvard Medical School resident John Halpern, who conducted the ecstasy-promoting studies for MAPS. They conferred regularly over the coming months, and revisited in Salvinelli's home before Halpern introduced Pickard to Stefan Wathne, a Manhattan blue-blood socialite and trustee of the American Ballet Theatre. The DEA helped attain an indictment on Wathne for his laundering of millions of dollars for Pickard's LSD operation. *San Francisco Chronicle* reporter Seth Rosenfeld also said that Pickard admitted giving Halpern $299,000 in cash in 1998, without explaining why.[20]

LSD Network a CIA MK-Ultra Drug War on Russia?

The *San Francisco Chronicle* learned Prof. John Halpern had told the DEA that Pickard admitted he was working for the FBI, the DEA and American spy agencies. An informant also claimed that Pickard had sent close to a $100,000 in just one shipment of LSD profits to the Heffter Research Institute. The *Chronicle* said that Heffter financed "federally approved human experiments with psilocybin at the University of Arizona, as well as studies at Harvard and universities in Switzerland and Russia."[21]

Heffter's funding of MK-Ultra programs against America's cold war enemy, Russia, may be particularly significant. Heffter also received money from Laurence Rockefeller, the brother of David Rockefeller who was on the National Security Council's Operations Coordinating Board. David Rockefeller informed President Eisenhower of all of the CIA's covert activities during MK-Ultra's first decade. The Rockefeller Foundation also went from funding Germany's Nazi eugenics institutes to funding the CIA's MK-Ultra Human Ecology Fund.[22] The *San Francisco Chronicle* said that as of 2001, the Heffter Institute included "respected scientists at the University of California and other schools. Halpern is a consultant; Shulgin is an advisor."[23]

Mark Kleinman left Harvard to head UCLA's Drug Policy Analysis Program, naming William Pickard assistant director. While there, Pickard did research in Russia. A Harvard source said Pickard befriended law enforcement in Russia, including the Federal Security Services, the successor to the KGB. Kleinman had overseen Pickard's research at Harvard and UCLA. Pickard's main focus at UCLA was the Future and Emerging Drugs Study (FEDS), a proposal for an international group of experts to monitor new drugs that could purportedly have novel positive effects.[24] Were spy agencies paying corrupt Russian FSB agents to aid their attempt to popularize acid in Russia?

The final three years of this operation began in 1997. That year, William Pickard began working with Gordon Skinner, who had telltale signs of long-term work with U.S. intelligence. Skinner owned Porsches and a missile silo in Kansas. Skinner's history included getting caught selling very large quantities of marijuana in 1989. While authorities usually use smaller dealers to entrap larger dealers, in Skinner's case they allowed him to avoid much jail time by having him do the opposite. He sold thirty pounds of weed to three people and turned them in. Skinner also beat an involuntary manslaughter charge the following year. Similar to other cases, this history suggests that U.S. intelligence at least turned Skinner into a paid informant, if he wasn't already an agent for them. Skinner also had a link to the Grateful Dead, renting Jerry Garcia's home in 1999.[25]

Furthermore, high-level military figures met with Skinner and Pickard. Moise Seligman reported meeting with them in Las Vegas months before Pickard's arrest. Seligman, an Army Reserves Major General, had led the 122nd Army Reserves Command covering Arkansas, Louisiana, Texas, Oklahoma and Mississippi during the Vietnam War. Seligman claimed he came as a family friend to discuss an invention, but U.S. intelligence has historically used Army Reserve units in Special Forces Group (Green Beret) covert operations.[26]

In November 2000, as noted, some apparently non-complicit DEA agents raided William Pickard's laboratory. It was estimated that Pickard produced a kilogram (ten million hits) of LSD every five weeks. While some DEA officials may have aided Pickard's operations, others authorized the raid and arrest. Drug Enforcement Agents seized ninety pounds of reagents for making LSD—the largest such seizure in DEA history. Pickard's co-conspirators apparently allowed him to be the fall guy.

One of Pickard's best customers reportedly sold a majority of his LSD to dealers in Europe. Pickard had befriended members of the British House of Lords, while also working with State Department officials and the district attorney of San Francisco, Terrence Hallinan. While William Pickard ended up getting jail time for this last operation, Professor Halpern, MAPS, the Heffter Institute and others remained untarnished as they continued their drug promotion work.[27] Skinner set up Pickard and gained criminal immunity despite admitting to high-level functions of laundering drug money, securing LSD laboratory sites, and delivering thousands of LSD doses.[28]

Honest law enforcement would later catch other military figures involved in ecstasy trafficking. Within five years of Pickard's arrest, authorities would charge an Air National Guard captain and master sergeant of importing 290,000 ecstasy pills worth $11.6 million from Germany to New York on a military cargo plane. The *New York Times* reported that federal agents said these two military officials had carried out at least three earlier flights that moved drugs worth $10 million or more.[29]

LSD Officially Weaponized. Is Burning Man an Acid Test?

In 1998, the United States Air Force published an influential report outlining the use of LSD and other drugs as weapons. The author, Air Force Major Mark R. Thomas, provided an extensive bibliography on how these Non-Lethal Weapons have "been a material element of civilian law enforcement for many years." Two policy analysts also detailed non-lethal weapons for combat use in the Air Force Academy's *Journal of Policy Analysis and Management*. They discussed the cooperation between the Department of Defense and the Department of Justice on this tactic.

Air Force Major Thomas's report, *Non-Lethal Weaponry: A Framework for Future Integration*, summed up the American and global use of nonlethal weapons. It said soldiers might oppose "lethal military force ... against [their fellow citizens]." So, "from Seattle to Philadelphia, from D.C. to Prague and most recently Davos, Switzerland, 'non-lethal confrontation' has become second nature to U.S. fighting forces and those inspired and trained by U.S. affiliates." The non-lethal weapons listed in this report included "club drugs" listed as "Disassociative hallucinogens: LSD and Ketamine." It also listed "Calmative Agents: Sedatives, Tranquilizers, and Hypnotics."[30]

Army intelligence and other parts of the U.S. military had previously been involved in MK-Ultra's use of LSD on Americans. Also, high-level CIA MK-Ultra scientists reported their cross-country attendance of Acid Test parties. That, along with other evidence, suggests they supported such projects to promulgate LSD use. These evolved into the many thousand-strong Human Be-Ins and other similar gatherings where MK-Ultra project psychedelics appeared in abundance. Evidence suggests that U.S. intelligence continued influencing such gatherings at raves and techno parties, and possibly at new outdoor gatherings such as "Burning Man."

The Burning Man event started as a gathering of artists with unknown funding who got together and threw a party in the middle of a desert area near Black Rock City, Nevada. It may be noteworthy that MK-Ultra also included radiation experiments centered in Nevada in the 1950s, and the first "psychedelic saloon" was started in Nevada in the 1960s.

The event got its name from the burning of a huge wooden sculpture of a man as the culmination of the party. Art attracts some people to the event, while others come for DJs playing techno music, and still others for optional open nudity. People with unknown motives acting as grassroots promoters of the event have been seen in disparate cities, such as Seattle, New York and Barcelona, Spain, showing photographs with nude participants and giving long descriptions while trying to lure strangers to the annual event in Nevada.[31]

The *New York Times* Arts section and other mainstream media eventually gave the Burning Man event huge publicity. Mini Burning Mans started popping up in cities all over the country. Burning Man has elaborate websites with videos and pictures and interviews. It has grown to attract tens of thousands of people each year.

Evidence arose that some people at the main Burning Man event forced involuntary doses of LSD on others. A woman who DJ'd at the event wrote a blog titled, "Stay Out of Our Camp, Acid-Assault Hippie!" The DJ started her blog extolling the good aspects of the event. The DJ said, "All in all it was a very successful year and well worth all the hard work .... I could very well say this was the best 'burn' we have had in at least ten years except for one blight on our otherwise wonderful experience: acid assaults by complete strangers."

On a night she had been working, the blogger said one of the bartenders complained he had been doped by a "hippie dude" who had slipped acid into a sip of "special" bourbon he offered. "From that night on," the blogger continued, "we had to institute a policy that nobody could accept food or drink from strangers unless they were willing to take a chance on being dosed."

"We were not alone in being targeted," the blogger wrote. "The next evening I was having dinner with friends from a neighboring camp, and was informed that a medic for Burning Man had been dosed with acid via a spray bottle while he was on shift." After another campmate related a similar story, the DJ went to a radio station and made an announcement that, "some hippie or group of hippies were roaming Burning Man assaulting people with LSD."

The writer concluded with a message to the perpetrators, blaming them for "fucking up other people's Burning Man, and destroying the sense of community that we 'burners' try to preserve."[32]

National and Global LSD Promotion Continues

It is well known that the Grateful Dead shows increased the availability of LSD. One LSD dealer reported buying a supply directly from the Grateful Dead band members.[33] High-level MK-Ultra scientists like John Gittinger attended the Grateful Dead's earliest mid-1960s "Acid Test" shows.[34] Grateful Dead frontman Jerry Garcia's longtime heroin addiction may have also helped popularize that drug among its devoted following of "Deadheads."[35]

After Ken Kesey and the Merry Pranksters moved to Oregon, former Marine Ken Babbs followed him there. His Prankster brother John Babbs also moved nearby. Ken Babbs started a literary journal with Kesey. With a grant from the Grateful Dead, Babbs also catalogued the Prankster bus trip film and audiotape, taking it on the road to show to former and new fans.[36]

Timothy Leary commented that the Grateful Dead kept the acid tests going for over twenty years thereafter. Leary seemed proud that the Pranksters initiated thousands of people to LSD, and said, "By the way, I never heard of any casualties from it. There were 3,000 people in one of those warehouses with electric Kool-Aid, and I never heard of any casualty rate.... Out of those Acid Tests we have a living, growing flower known as the Grateful Dead. Several hundred thousand people go to see them each year."[37] But studies show there were many acid casualties.

As previously noted, the Grateful Dead have had many links to the CIA's MK-Ultra and later MK-Ultra-type operations. MK-Ultra scientists attended the Dead's early Acid Tests, and the U.S. intelligence-collaborating Oakland Hell's Angels provided security at their shows. U.S. intelligence's top global trafficker, Ron Stark, also had the phone numbers for Grateful Dead band members on him when he was arrested in Italy, and top 1990s acid-trafficking collaborator Gordon Skinner rented Dead frontman Jerry Garcia's home.[38]

In 1995, Jerry Garcia died of heroin-related problems, which ended the Dead's relentless touring. There was a major drop in LSD use the first year without the Grateful Dead tours. *Slate* magazine writer Ryan Grim wrote, "For thirty years, Dead tours were essential in keeping many LSD users and dealers connected, a correlation confirmed by the DEA in a divisional field assessment from the mid-1990s. The spring following Garcia's death (the season the MTF [Monitoring the Future] surveys are administered), annual LSD use among 12th-graders peaked at 8.8 percent and began to slide."[39]

Radio station owners and producers kept the Grateful Dead extremely popular by continuing to play their music on stations nationwide. By 2011, over a hundred stations around the country had "Grateful Dead Hour" as part of their weekly radio schedule. Some radio stations of the left-leaning Pacifica radio network devote two to three hours a week to the Grateful Dead.[40] No other band has ever attained a fraction of that much airtime on radio stations nationwide.

Many former Deadheads became devoted to Phish in the mid-1990s. *Slate*'s Ryan Grim noted, "Phish picked up part of the Dead's fan base—and presumably vestiges of the LSD delivery system. At the end of 2000, Phish stopped touring for several years, and perhaps not coincidentally, the MTF numbers for LSD began to plummet."[41] At an end of 2013 New Years Eve, Phish held several nights of concerts at Madison Square Garden. A 52-year-old dealer was arrested with 424 capsules of MDMA, 71 strips of LSD and 14 bags of mushrooms. He was one of 228 arrested or receiving summons, mostly for drugs, at the three straight nights of Phish shows.[42]

Groups continued to promote LSD, along with ecstasy, nationally and globally. By 2009, the two key MK-Ultra-linked research groups, the Multidisciplinary Association for Psychedelic Studies (MAPS) and the Hefter Institute, gained increasing mainstream news acceptance in legitimizing LSD and ecstasy, leading to an increase in use by impressionable youth.[43] In 2012-13 alone, MAPS financial pages detail the funding of at least nine conferences on psychedelics, three LSD studies and twenty-three MDMA studies around the world. They earmarked $5 million for just one of these ecstasy studies.[44]

As of early 2014, a Burning Man website boasted of regional chapters and events on six continents. The website listed forty-six articles featuring Burning Man in 2013 alone, from sources such as CNN, NBC, ABC, the *Huffington Post* and the *Moscow Times*. The website influences press coverage, with a very sophisticated and extensive guide for media coverage of Burning Man. While Burning Man has maintained itself as a grassroots phenomenon, and some are likely sincere about their involvement, the vast financial resources apparent from its website suggests its use of public relations "astroturf": faking a grassroots phenomenon.[45]

Notes

1 On founding, http://www.maps.org/about/mission/. On Hoffman and Leary contributions, http://www.maps.org/news-letters/v14n1-html/lsd_blotter_art.html.

2 Scott Thompson, "Is a New MK-Ultra drug plague afoot?" *EIR* vol. 24, March 21, 1997. http://www.larouchepub.com/eiw/public/1997/eirv24n13-19970321/eirv24n13-19970321_044-is_a_new_mk_ultra_drug_plague_af.pdf. For donations to MAPS, see http://www.maps.org/about/fiscal/.

3 Associated Press, "Psychedelic Summit marks hallucinogen's 50th birthday," *Galveston Daily News*, Friday Morning, 4/16/93, p. A11.

4 Thompson, "Is a New MK-Ultra drug plague afoot?"

5 Rick Doblin in conversation with RU Sirius, "The FDA Trip or How Psychedelic Research was Revived in the 90s." Dr Curtis Wright was a "Trekkie" who had his computer make Star Trek sounds, http://www.maps.org/media/thresher.html.

6 For example, see John Tierney, "Hallucinogens Have Doctors Tuning In Again" *New York Times*, April 11, 2010, http://www.nytimes.com/2010/04/12/science/12psychedelics.html?_r=0, and David Kohn, "Ecstasy Researchers Look for Benefits" *Baltimore Sun*, July 25, 2004, http://www.baltimoresun.com/news/health/bal-te.ecstasy25jul25,1,3903594.story?coll=bal-home-headlines.

7 Keith Laws and Joy Kokkalis, "Ecstasy and Memory Function: A Meta-Analytic Update,"

Human Psychopharmacology, 2007, vol. 22, pp. 381-88, http://herts.academia.edu/KeithLaws/Papers/260387/Ecstasy_MDMA_and_Memory_Function_a_Meta-Analytic_Update.

8 Jane Kirby, "Ecstasy linked to 'significant' memory loss," *The Independent* (UK), 6/25/07, http://drugprevent.org.uk/ppp/2010/05/ecstasy-linked-to-significant-memory-loss/.

9 Tejinder Kondel, "Ectasy and Memory Loss," *The Pychologist*, 8/14/07, www.thepsychologist.org.uk/publications/thepsychologist/extras/.

10 David Black, *Acid: the Secret History of LSD* (London: Satin/Vision, 1998), pp. 65-66.

11 Robin McKie, "Ecstasy does not wreck the mind, study claims." *The Guardian* (London), 2/19/11, http://www.guardian.co.uk/society/2011/feb/19/ecstasy-harm-brain-new-study.

12 Fabrizio Schifano, "Potential Human Neurotoxicity of MDMA ('Ecstasy'): Subjective Self-Reports, Evidence from an Italian Drug Addiction Centre and Clinical Case Studies," *Neuropsychobiology* Vol. 42, 2000, pp. 25-33. "Study Finds Long-Term Ecstasy Use Leads to Memory Loss," *ScienceDaily*, 4/10/01. This cites Konstantine K. Zakzanis, PhD and Donald A. Young, PhD, "Memory impairment in abstinent MDMA ("Ecstasy") users: A longitudinal investigation," *Neurology* vol. 56 no. 7, April 10, 2001, pp. 966-69. Also see, "Low Doses of Ecstasy Associated with Decline in Verbal Memory," *ScienceDaily*, 6/5/07, citing Thelma Schilt, *Archives of General Psychiatry, 2007; 64:728-736.* Euphrosyne Gouzoulis-Mayfrank, Jorg Daumann, Fran Tuchtenhagen, Susanne Pelz, Steffanie Becker, Hans-Jurgen Kunert, Bruno Fimm, Henning Sass, "Impaired congnitive performance in drug free users of recreational ecstasy (MDMA)," *Journal of Neurology, Neurosurgery and Psychiatry*, 2000; 68: 719-25. L. Reneman, J. Booij, B. Schmand, W. van den Brink, B. Gunning, "Memory disturbances in 'Ecstasy' users are correlated with an altered brain serotonin neurotransmission," *Psychopharmacology* (Berlin) 2000 Feb; 148(3): 322-24. J. Rodgers, "Cognitive performance amongst recreational users of 'ecstasy,'" *Psychopharmacology* (2000) 151: 19-24. This study by Rodgers concluded: "The present study provides additional evidence for longterm neuropsychological sequelae associated with the use of ecstasy, particularly with regard to delayed memory ability." Megan Brooks, "Short-term, Recreational Ecstasy Use May Damage Memory," *Medscape.com*, July 26, 2012. Brooks cites a study by Dr. Daniel Wagner using 109 participants, who used no more than 10 ecstasy pills in a one-year period, published in *Addiction*, July 26, 2012.

13 Seth Rosenfeld, "William Pickard's long, strange trip: Suspected LSD trail leads from the Bay Area's psychedelics era to a missile silo in Kansas," *San Francisco Chronicle*, June 10, 2001.

14 Peter Wilkinson, "The Acid King," *Rolling Stone*, July 5, 2001, http://tahoejimbo420s.blogspot.com/2010/01/acid-king-by-peter-wilkinson-rolling.html.

15 Rosenfeld, "William Pickard's long, strange trip."

16 On Shulgin first synthesizing DOM/STP, see http://www.websters-online-dictionary.org/definitions/2%2C5-Dimethoxy-4-Methylamphetamine. On DOM/STP as an MK-Ultra deployed drug, see Burton Wolfe, *The Hippies* (New York: New American Library, 1968), p. 149, as referenced in Martin Lee and Bruce Shlain, *Acid Dreams: The Complete Social History of the CIA, LSD, the Sixties and Beyond* (New York: Grove Press, 1985), pp. 187, 312.

17 On state of the art equipment, see Wilkinson, "The Acid King." On Grateful Dead cover art, DEA informant, and sentencing, see Rosenfeld, "William Pickard's long strange trip." Drake Bennett, "Dr. Ecstasy," *New York Times*, January 30, 2005. Personal interviews with Hank Harrison, November 2014.

18 Rosenfeld, "William Pickard's long strange trip."

19 Wilkinson, "The Acid King."

20 Rosenfeld, "William Pickard's long strange trip." On Wathne's LSD money laundering, see Chris Vogel, "Valerie Srofim Says She was Taken to the Cleaners: The socialite sure to get back her investment from an alleged money launderer," *Houston Press*, 2/7/08.

21 Rosenfeld "William Pickard's long strange trip."

22 H.P. Albarelli Jr., *A Terrible Mistake: The Murder of Frank Olson and the CIA's Secret Cold War Experiments* (Waterville, OR: TrineDay, 2009), pp. 161, 464-65.

23 Rosenfeld "William Pickard's long strange trip."

24 Wilkinson, "The Acid King."

25 Wilkinson, "The Acid King."

26 On Seligman meeting with Skinner and Pickard, and what he said about it, see Wilkinson, "The Acid King." On Seligman's history, see http://www.ruebelfuneralhome.com/obituaryindividual.php?id=654. Attorney William Pepper, a friend of Martin Luther King Jr., wrote that reservists trained in Mississippi were involved in the covert operation to assassinate MLK in 1968. See Mississippi reservist in Special Operations Group assigned to aid MLK's assassination, in William Pepper, *Orders to Kill: The Truth Behind the Murder of Martin Luther King, Jr.* (New York: Warner Books, 1995), p. 418.

27 Wilkinson, "The Acid King." On largest seizure in DEA history, see Vogel, "Valerie Srofim Says She was Taken to the Cleaners."

28 Rosenfeld "William Pickard's long strange trip."

29 Julia Preston, "2 Charged With Smuggling Ecstasy Pills on Military Jets," *New York Times*, March 14, 2005, p. B6. For a shorter report on this incident, see Associated Press, "Air Force jet was used for drug run, authorities say," *USA Today*, 4/14/2005, http://usatoday30.usatoday.com/news/nation/2005-04-14-jet-bust_x.htm.

30 Mark R. Thomas, Major, USAF, *Non-Lethal Weaponry: A Framework for Future Integration*, Air Command and Staff College, Air University (Maxwell Air Force Base, Alabama), April 1998, http://tuvok.au.af.mil/au/database/projects/ay1998/ascs/98-279.pdf. And, David Hemenway and Douglas Weil, "Phasers on Stun: The Case of Less Lethal Weapons," *Journal of Policy Analysis and Management*, Vol.9, No.1, Winter 1990. Both cited in Frank Morales, "Non-Lethal Weapons: Welcome to the Free World," *CovertAction Quarterly*, April-June 2001, pp. 10-11, 13.

31 On the "psychedelic saloon," see Alice Echols, *Scars of Sweet Paradise: The Life and Times of Janis Joplin* (New York: Holt, 1999), pp. 115-16. On Burning Man, this writer talked to one of these people, and witnessed them spending long periods of time promoting the event, acting like new friends to strangers in a coffeehouse in Seattle in 1999. A bleached-blonde guy had a photo album from Burning Man that he showed to many there. I saw another, older looking bleached-blonde man in Barcelona striking up a conversation with a young college couple at a popular, hip Gaudi tourist attraction, where he described Burning Man in glowing terms. A third experience saw an artist display photos of nude people taken at Burning Man. She presented them at a big party she threw in Brooklyn.

32 "Stay Out of Our Camp, Acid Assault Hippie!" *Commentary*, September 10, 2010. *Burncast.tv*, http://burncast.tv/blog/index.php?id=6772098479204493167.

33 Personal interview with an LSD dealer who stated this anonymously.

34 Albarelli, *A Terrible Mistake*, pp. 187, 291-92, 297.

35 Steve Dougherty, "What a Long, Strange Trip," *People*, August 21, 1995, http://www.people.com/people/archive/article/0,,20101375,00.html.

36 Paul Perry, *On the Bus: The Complete Guide to the Legendary Trip of Ken Kesey and the Merry Pranksters and the Birth of the Counterculture* (New York: Thunder's Mouth Press, 1990), p. 185.

37 Perry, *On the Bus*, pp. 166-67.

38 The other bands whose phone numbers were found with Stark were Faces, Deep Purple, and The Family: Black, *Acid*, pp. 146, 159-60.

39 Ryan Grim, "Who's got the acid?" *Slate*, April 1, 2004, http://www.slate.com/articles/news_and_politics/hey_wait_a_minute/2004/04/whos_got_the_acid.html.

40 See http://www.gdhour.com/stations.html.

41 Grim, "Who's got the acid?" On switch from Grateful Dead to Phish, this author has talked to many Deadheads who have developed a devotion to Phish.

42 Eli Rosenberg and Michael Schwirz, "Drug Use Runs Wild as Phish Rocks City," *New York Times*, January 1, 2014, p. A14.

43 See, for example, Tierney, "Hallucinogens have doctors tuning in again." On drug use trends, see http://www.samhsa.gov/data/DAWN.aspx.

44 Rick Doblin, "Annual Financial Report: Fiscal Year 2012-13 (June 1, 2012-May 31, 2013)," http://www.maps.org/news-letters/v23n3/v23n3_4-12.pdf.

45 http://www.burningman.com/. On "astroturf" propaganda, see John Stauber and Sheldom Rampton, *Toxic Sludge is Good for You: Lies, Damn Lies, and the Public Relations Industry* (New York: Common Courage, 2002), pp. 13-14.

Chapter Twenty-Seven

International Drug Wars; Occupy Wall Street

It's worth repeating that two of the longest running wars of the last hundred years, Vietnam and Afghanistan, had the same major commonality—both involved vast drug crops. Afghanistan, in central Asia, has the largest expanse of poppy fields for heroin-making opium crops. As part of the "Golden Crescent," the Afghanistan region would end up producing more opium than the Southeast Asian "Golden Triangle" area around Vietnam, at the other end of the same mountain range, after the U.S. took over many of Afghanistan's opium fields. Another area of conflict, Colombia, a South American country to which the U.S. increased its military aid by billions of dollars in the late 1990s, had some of the largest cocaine-making coca crops in the world. Colombia offers a prime example of the numerous covert operations that have continued in Latin American for over six decades.

Plan Colombia: Control of Coca Crops

In 1991, President George H.W. Bush launched the "Andean Initiative" for drug eradication in Central and South American countries. These countries mostly produced coca crops from which cocaine is produced, while they also had a small amount of opium-producing poppy plants. U.S statistics showed that by 1999, Colombia's cultivation of coca actually tripled, rising from 3.8 to 12.3 thousand hectares, and the cultivation of opium increased from .13 thousand hectares to .75 thousand hectares.[1] As previously discussed, the illicit drug sales, both locally and globally, artificially prop up stock markets.

The Revolutionary Armed Forces of Colombia (FARC) started in 1964 as a military wing of the Colombia Communist Party, after the military of Colombia's Conservative Party government attacked the Communist Party members in their rural enclaves. Following decades of fighting between FARC and government forces, in the late 1990s Colombian president Andres Pastrana granted FARC over 15,000 square miles of land as a peace settlement.[2]

President Clinton's "Plan Colombia" followed the military path of President G.H.W. Bush in "combating cocaine" by actually combating Colombia's leftist rebels while increasing cocaine trafficking to the U.S.

While the CIA and other U.S. governmental groups had supported cocaine trafficking in Latin America for decades, President Bill Clinton's administration significantly increased its support of this top cocaine-exporting country. In 1998, the Clinton administration announced its Plan Colombia would give $7.5 billion in economic, military and social aid to the country. The European Union was supposed to collaborate in this program, but pulled back and criticized its military emphasis, when thirty-seven Colombian human rights groups and non-governmental organizations signed a statement rejecting the plan. Professor Peter Dale Scott said, "Plan Colombia was, like so many aid programs in the past, 90 percent military."[3]

The Clinton administration claimed most of the money went to combating drug trafficking. Scott detailed how this explanation was a farce. He said the Colombian military and their paramilitary allies "have been directly involved in drug trafficking, as opposed to FARC guerillas who until recently merely taxed the trade. In November, 1998, for example, a Colombian Air Force plane landed at Fort Lauderdale ... with ... sixteen hundred pounds of cocaine."[4]

Plan Colombia appeared to be a hugely escalated war against FARC and the other largest Colombian Marxist rebel groups, such as the National Liberation Army (ELN). Carlos Castana headed the top Colombian paramilitary group aiding the Colombian government, the United Self-Defense Forces of Colombia (AUC). He stated his group was financed 70% through drug trafficking. *Newsweek* and the *San Francisco Chronicle* reported the Colombian government's own intelligence agency estimate in 2001 that the responsibility for drug trafficking fell 40% to right-wing paramilitary groups and only 2.5% to FARC. Yet, Plan Colombia focused primarily on the FARC-controlled regions and not the areas controlled by the AUC and the other top right-wing paramilitary drug-trafficking groups.[5]

By the end of 2013, Dana Priest reported in the *Washington Post* that the CIA and the National Security Agency helped the Colombian military kill at least two-dozen FARC and ELN leaders. In that article, Priest confirmed this through interviews of thirty former and current Colombian and American officials. Priest further reported that Clinton's Plan Colombia package had increased to $9 billion, but that the aid given by the CIA is an additional "secret assistance, which also includes substantial eavesdropping help from the National Security Agency, [that] is funded through a multibillion-dollar black budget." The additional CIA and NSA aid was started under President Bush in 2000 and continued under President Obama.[6]

Afghanistan Invaded for Access to Drugs & Oil

On September 11, 2001, planes hit the World Trade Center in New York City, one side of the Pentagon in Washington D.C. experienced destruction, and an airplane went down in Pennsylvania. President George W. Bush's administration quickly blamed Osama Bin Laden and Al-Qaeda. Bush just as quickly blamed the Taliban of Afghanistan for harboring Bin Laden, and started a war there on October 7, 2001.[7]

Professor Peter Dale Scott and others have unearthed evidence that the Bush administration's real reason for invading Afghanistan was access to its poppy fields and its proximity to oil resources. Scott quoted a Foreign Military Studies Office of Fort Leavenworth article published three months before the World Trade Center destruction. The article discussed the large inland sea to the west of Afghanistan, through which oil companies proposed a key pipeline: "The Caspian Sea appears to be sitting on yet another sea—a sea of hydrocarbon." Scott added that those oil reserves played an important part in America's strategic concerns and military plans. America's ruling oligarchy apparently identified several key reasons for invading Afghanistan, with the top two being drugs and oil.[8]

American troops are often seen patrolling opium/heroin-producing poppy fields. After the Taliban outlawed opium production in 2000, Afghanistan became the world's largest supplier of heroin following the U.S. invasion.

The U.S. had also identified vast mineral resources, including copper, cobalt, gold and, perhaps most importantly, critical industrial metals like lithium. The Pentagon stated that lithium deposits they found could lead the country to equal or surpass the world-leading supply found in Bolivia, recently led by the anti-corporate Evo Morales. Lithium is increasingly used in batteries of all kinds, from household to auto and airplane, and in various types of electronic equipment.[9] Additionally, a number of sources, such as Minot University's Rural Methamphetamine Education Project, offer an interesting side note regarding lithium's use in underground methamphetamine labs: "Lithium metal is a key element in the clandestine production of methamphetamine. Lithium is used as a reducing agent during the chemical process."[10]

Before September 11, 2001, a major change took place in Afghanistan that affected the world's opium trade. The Taliban controlled most of the country at that time, and by 1999 they were profiting the most, in supplying nearly 5,000 tons of heroin annually, or 70-75% of the world's heroin. In July of 2000, as confirmed by a United Nations report printed in the *Washington Post*, the Taliban supreme leader, Mullah Mohammad Omar, imposed a ban on opium production in Afghanistan. The *New York Times* also printed a 2001 headline: "Taliban's Ban on Poppy a Success, U.S. Aides Say." That ban "resulted in 70% of the world's illicit opium production [4,600 tons] being virtually wiped out at a stroke" that year. The Taliban reportedly did this for religious reasons.[11]

The Northern Alliance, also known as the United Front for the Salvation of Afghanistan, had formed in 1996 as an opposition group to the Taliban. The CIA backed them as they tried to counter the opium ban in Afghanistan in 2000. The Northern Alliance increased its own opium production and trafficking. The London *Observer* wrote: "During the ban the only source of poppy production was territory held by the Northern Alliance. It tripled its production … for 83% of the total Afghan production of 185 tons of opium during the ban."[12]

Given the timing of the Afghanistan invasion, the Bush administration might have invaded to regain control over the opium-producing poppy fields. Besides illicit opium and heroin, opiates are used in various medicines.[13]

The Northern Alliance's drastically low production went on for only fifteen months, before the U.S. and other Western countries invaded on October 2, 2001. After the Afghanistan invasion, the U.S, and British forces put Hamid Karzai in power. Karzai had represented the Northern Alliance/ United Front. In early October 2008, the *New York Times* published evidence suggesting that Hamid's brother, Ahmed Wali Karzai, protected caches of heroin found by lower-level Afghan authorities. The article claimed solid evidence of Ahmed Karzai's drug trafficking, and noted that even the "White House believes Ahmed Wali Karzai is involved in drug trafficking," though they only talked about him being a political liability.[14]

Several weeks later, the *New York Times* printed another article stating that Ahmed Karzai had been on the CIA's payroll for the prior eight years.[15] *BBC News* reported that by 2007, the 8,000-plus tons of Afghan opium production almost doubled any previous production.[16]

The head of the United Nations Drugs and Crime office noted that during the bank crisis of 2008 and 2009, a number of "inter-bank loans were funded by money that originated from the drugs trade ... some banks were rescued that way."[17] The International Monetary Fund stated, "The amount of money laundering occurring on a yearly basis could range between ... $600 billion and $1.5 trillion." U.S. lawmakers believe that "half is being laundered through U.S. banks." A majority of this money revolved around the drug trade.[18]

U.S. Intelligence Uses Drugs in Targeting Occupiers

On September 17, 2011, the first "Occupy" protest took place in Zucotti Park in New York City's Wall Street financial district. A Canadian activist group, Adbusters, initiated the protest. People gathered there to protest the corrupt influence of banks and corporations on the U.S. government, as well as the general economic inequalities in the U.S. The Bush and Obama administrations' bailout in giving over $700 billion to the top bank owners instead of to struggling Americans was just one example of their grievances. Their popular chant, "We are the 99%," suggested that 1% or less of the wealthiest Americans controlled the rest of people's lives in negative ways.[19]

Some people filmed the protest and the police brutality that occurred there, and posted the videos on YouTube. Those videos became popular and inspired many around the country to duplicate the Occupy Wall Street protests. They also offered inspiration to activists in other Western countries experiencing austerity measures imposed by U.S-linked global banks such as the International Monetary Fund. The term "austerity" acted as code for making most citizens work more hours for less money. Austerity measures sought to erode pollution laws, undermine national health care systems, and cut retirement pensions. They made life harder for the majority of people, while benefiting multinational corporations.[20]

When the Occupy Wall Street movement began, many prominent economists agreed with their stance of opposing the massive bank "bailouts." For example, Nobel Prize-winning economist Joseph Stiglitz was highly critical of $700 billion of taxpayer money used to bail out the banks. Stiglitz said little of this money actually went to helping out the average American.[21]

The Occupy movement reached many American cities and inspired camping out in public places in solidarity with the Wall Street protesters. Police used various means to counter and repress the protests. In Oakland, police attacked protesters with tear gas, clubs, and explosive flashbombs, forcing them out of their encampment.[22]

Media groups such as London's *Guardian* reported that U.S. intelligence began infiltrating Occupy Wall Street in New York City with undercover agents, whom the reports named. An undercover Army agent had previously infiltrated the Students for a Democratic Society, restarted in 2006, and framed some of them around 2009. The Partnership for Civil Justice obtained FBI files in 2012 and released documents describing how U.S. intelligence actually worked with the banks against Occupy Wall Street. For example, an FBI document dated November 3, 2011 showed how the FBI worked with the Joint Terrorist Task Force on targeting Occupy groups around the country. The FBI also formed "working groups" with both Homeland Security and bank representatives in this targeting. The FBI files further revealed that they had uncovered a plan to attack Occupy leaders in Houston with sniper fire, "if deemed necessary." What might make such action "necessary" in Texas was not detailed.[23]

In Minneapolis, police were caught using drugs to target Occupy activists. A team of videographer activists filmed police officers going to an Occupy encampment and offering activists free food and money to take part in a drug study. The officers escorted the Occupy activists to their car parked around the block. The Occupiers who went with the police said the police took them to a giant indoor warehouse, where they saw many other participants talking with police.

When the Occupy activists got back from the study hours later, the videographers interviewed some of them. They said police officers gave them a bag of marijuana and a pipe with which to smoke it. They smoked for about an hour. One said that once he was high, police asked him a lot of questions about himself and the other Occupy activists. They also independently described a mass of both state and county police in the giant warehouse to which the police took them.

Videographers created a documentary they titled *MK-Occupy*, capturing police bribing Occupy Wall Street activists in Minneapolis with drugs and trying to get information from them while they were high.

One Occupy activist who got stoned that way said, "People were smoking K2 and Spice, that synthetic [marijuana]. People were drinking and smoking." All activists agreed that police coerced them into using the drugs by buying them lunch and giving them free cigarettes, and even offering to pay the activist participants back for any kind of drugs they bought off the street. Police also asked other participants many questions about the Occupy movement, and offered drugs in exchange for participants' spying on the Occupy movement. Asking them questions about Occupy when stoned is reminiscent of early U.S. intelligence use of a potent marijuana extract as a "truth drug" for interrogations.[24]

Minnesota authorities eventually decided to close down the unit conducting these activities, run by the State Patrol. An article said they made the decision after the Minnesota Public Safety Commissioner issued a press release stating that a police officer involved in the program reported the police unit's drug exchange activities to the Minnesota State Patrol. But the incidents and film created by Minneapolis activist groups spawned many more investigative disclosures.[25]

The disclosures revealed the length and international scope of the program. A local mainstream Minneapolis news organization revealed that the police officers offering drugs to Occupy activists were part of a unit involved in the Drug Recognition program, started in 1991. A CBS News affiliate report said the Drug Recognition program involved police from around the state. It quoted a member of the Minnesota State Patrol, who said, "190 officers at 85 Minnesota agencies are Drug Recognition-trained officers at their departments."[26]

The Minneapolis daily newspaper, the *Star Tribune,* came out with an investigative article about police drugging Occupy participants, revealing that state police departments nationwide had been conducting these same types of programs. The *Star Tribune* discussed the debate in Maryland courts about the Drug Recognition program in that east coast state.[27] The Drug Recognition program began as part of the Drug Evaluation and Classification (DRE) program, which started in the early 1970s in California. It expanded to forty-nine states, Canada and other countries, according to its own website. The International Drug Evaluation and Classification Program office is in Alexandria, Virginia, a Washington D.C. suburb.[28] The *Star Tribune* article cited Earl Sweeney as the chair of the local DRE's oversight panel. He also was a member of the International Association of Chiefs of Police.[29]

The participant descriptions of massive police involvement in the Minnesota DRE program are suggestive of a new national MK-Ultra type program that uses various forms of regular and synthetic marijuana. Many people have suffered days, if not weeks or more, of psychosis after smoking "synthetic marijuana," sold in convenience stores under the names Spice or K2.[30] The Drug Recognition program started around the time the CIA's MK-Ultra and FBI's Counterintelligence Program were shut down. While this evidence calls for more investigation, the Occupy videographer activists also underscored their belief that this was a new version of MK-Ultra with the name of their film: *MK Occupy Minnesota.*[31]

Most Top Banks Launder Drug Money?

Many news sources, including *Forbes* magazine, Reuters, the *Wall Street Journal* and *Bloomberg News,* covered President Obama's administration fining of Wachovia, America's fourth largest bank, and HSBC,

Europe's largest bank, for allowing money laundering. *Bloomberg News* reported that HSBC failed to monitor more than $670 billion in wire transfers and $9.7 billion in purchases of U.S. currency, "allowing money laundering, prosecutors said." The *Wall Street Journal* reported prosecutors saying in 2010 that Wachovia (acquired by Wells Fargo in 2008), "processed $420 billion without using proper money laundering detection." U.S. investigators found that some of this money was used to buy planes caught trafficking vast amounts of cocaine, while other money was from laundered drug proceeds.[32] This money laundering allowed for money made from drug sales to be counted as legitimately made profits.

HSBC

The world's local bank

HSBC is Europe's largest bank, getting its start from the Chinese opium trade as the Hongkong and Shanghai Banking Company shortly after the second Opium War. In 2013 HSBC was fined $1.9 billion for massive Latin American money laundering.

In the Mexican journal *La Jornado,* Binghamton University Sociology Professor James Petras detailed how a majority of the largest American banks participated in these activities: "There is a consensus among U.S. Congressional investigators, former bankers and international banking experts, that U.S. and European banks launder between $500 billion and $1 trillion of dirty money each year." Petras cited U.S. Senator Carl Levin, who summarized that "half of that money comes to the United States."[33]

In a 2001 report, *Correspondent Banking: A Gateway for Money Laundering,* Senator Levin of Michigan, the Ranking Democrat on the U.S. Senate Permanent Subcommittee on Investigations, released the results of a yearlong investigation on how foreign banks use U.S. banks to launder money. The report additionally implicated Bank of America, Bank of New York, Barnett Bank, Chase Manhattan Bank (now J.P. Morgan Chase), Citibank, First Union National Bank, Harris Bank International, Popular Bank of Florida, Security Bank N.A, and Toronto Dominion Bank (New York branch) in money launderering.[34]

Professor Petras detailed an even larger scope of money laundering by American and European banks. Petras wrote, "Every major bank in the U.S. has served as an active financial partner of the murderous drug cartels—including ... JP Morgan, as well as overseas banks operating out of New York, Miami and Los Angeles, as well as London." The *Los Angeles Times* noted that the European banks involved in this money laundering included Credit Suisse, Barclays, Lloyds and ING.[35]

Julius Pierpont "J.P." Morgan was a descendant of the Pierpont family intermarried with the Russells, the top opium-trafficking Americans who started Yale's Skull and Bones secret society. By 2013, *Bloomberg News* reported that JP Morgan Chase & Co. was the largest bank in the world.[36]

The amount of HSBC's settlement with the Obama administration for money laundering was record-breaking in 2013. At that time, HSBC was the world's third largest bank and sixth largest public company. It's interesting to note the chronology of HSBC's start. In 1842, the British gained control of Hong Kong from China after the first Opium War, before another Opium War in 1860 forced China's legalization of opium trading. A Scottish Lord founded the Hongkong and Shanghai Banking Corporation (HSBC) in the British colony of Hong Kong in 1865.[37] HSBC appeared to be founded on opium profits, and it seems the bank never completely abandoned the advantages that could be maintained from links to opium and its derivatives.

Notes

1 Peter Dale Scott, "Honduras, the Contra Support Networks, and Cocaine: How the U.S. Government Has Augmented America's Drug Crisis," in Alfred McCoy and Alan A. Block, eds., *War on Drugs: Studies in the Failure of U.S. Narcotic Policy* (Boulder, CO: Westview, 1992), p. 161. Also International Narcotics Control Strategy Report, 1999, released by the Bureau for International Narcotics and Law Enforcement Affairs, U.S. Department of State, Washington, D.C., March 2000, www.state.gov/www/global/narcotics_law/1999_narc_report. Both referenced in Peter Dale Scott, *Drugs, Oil and War: The United States in Afghanistan, Colombia and Indochina* (New York: Rowman and Littlefield, 2003), p. 76.

2 Larry Rohter, "Colombia Rebels Reign in Ceded Area," *New York Times*, May 16, 1999, http://www.nytimes.com/1999/05/16/world/colombia-rebels-reign-in-ceded-area.html?pagewanted=all&src=pm.

3 By a vote of 474-1, the European Parliament adopted a resolution that was sharply critical of the U.S. emphasis on military measures and crop-spraying in Plan Colombia: *The Nation*, March 19, 2001. Transnational Institute, "Drugs and Democracy, " February 1, 2001, www.tni.org/drugs. Both cited in Scott, *Drugs, Oil and War*, p. 73.

4 *Miami Herald*, November 11, 1998, referenced in Scott, *Drugs, Oil and War*, p. 74.

5 *Newsweek*, May 21, 2001; *San Francisco Chronicle*, June 21, 2001; both referenced in Scott, *Drugs, Oil and War*, p. 75.

6 Dana Priest, "Covert Action in Colombia," *Washington Post*, December 21, 2013, http://www.washingtonpost.com/sf/investigative/2013/12/21/covert-action-in-colombia/.

7 *CBS News* timeline, http://www.cbsnews.com/2100-501704_162-5850224.html.

8 Lester W. Grau, "Hydrocarbons and the New Strategic Region: The Caspian Sea and Central Asia." *Military Review*, May-June 2001, cited in Scott, *Drugs, Oil and War*, p. 31. On proposed oil pipelines, see Paul Mathieu and Clinton R. Shiells, "The Commonwealth of Independent States Troubled Energy Sectors," *Finance and Development* (a quarterly magazine of the International Monetary Fund) Vol. 39 No. 3, September, 2002, http://www.imf.org/external/pubs/ft/fandd/2002/09/mathieu.htm.

9 James Risen, "U.S. Identifies Vast Mineral Riches in Afghanistan," *New York Times*, June 13, 2010, http://www.nytimes.com/2010/06/14/world/asia/14minerals.html?pagewanted=1&_r=1. On lithium, http://www.energizer.com/learning-center/pages/battery-comparison.aspx.

10 See the Rural Methamphetamine Education Project at Minot State University: http://www.minotstateu.edu/rcjc/rmep_chem.shtml.

11 Barbara Crossette, "Taliban's Ban On Poppy A Success, U.S. Aides Say," *New York Times,* May 20, 2001, http://www.nytimes.com/2001/05/20/world/taliban-s-ban-on-poppy-a-success-us-aides-say.html. Also see Paul Salopek, "With Taliban gone, poppy crops return," *Chicago Tribune,* December 26, 2001, http://articles.chicagotribune.com/2001-12-26/news/0112260209_1_poppies-taliban-regime-bernard-frahi. Jim Teeple, "Taliban Wipes out Afghanistan's Opium Production," Jalalad, Institute for Afghan Studies, April 8, 2001, http://www.institute-for-afghan-studies.org/AFGHAN%20CONFLICT/Drugs/Taliban%20Wipes%20Out%20Opium.htm. For quote, see *Jane's Intelligence Review,* October 22, 2001, cited in Scott, *Drugs, Oil and War,* p. 33. Scott also, p. 43, cites reference for the UN report on Taliban banning opium for the year: *Washington Post,* December 10, 2001. On 4,600 tons of opium, Scott, *Drugs, Oil and War,* p. 41.

12 Paul Harris, "Victorious Warlords Set to Open the Opium Floodgates," *The Observer/The Guardian* (London), November 24, 2001, http://www.guardian.co.uk/world/2001/nov/25/afghanistan.drugstrade.

13 On dollar per milligram for opiates such as Oxycontin: http://www.sfhp.org/InforMed/2010Q4/PitfallsofOxycontin.aspx.

14 James Risen, "Reports Link Karzai's Brother to Afghan Heroin Trade," *New York Times,* October 4, 2008, http://www.nytimes.com/2008/10/05/world/asia/05afghan.html.

15 Dexter Filkins, Mark Mazetti and James Risen, "Brother of Afghan Leader Said to Be Paid by C.I.A." *New York Times,* October 27, 2009.http://www.nytimes.com/2009/10/28/world/asia/28intel.html?_r=2.

16 Alastair Leithead, "Afghanistan Opium Production at Record High," BBC News, August 27, 2007. http://news.bbc.co.uk/2/hi/6965115.stm.

17 Rajeev Sayel, "Drug Money Saved Banks in Global Crisis, Says UN Adviser," *The Guardian/The Observer* (London), December 12, 2009, http://www.guardian.co.uk/global/2009/dec/13/drug-money-banks-saved-un-cfief-claims.

18 "Money Laundering," FBI Law Enforcement Bulletin vol.70, no.5 (May 2001), pp. 1-9. In Michigan State University Libraries, Criminal Justice Resources: Money Laundering: http://staff.lib.msu.edu/harris23/crimjust/moneylau.htm . Note that the U.S. General Accounting Office wrote a report in the new millennium outlining the huge scope of money laundering. It stated that "$500 billion to $1 trillion is laundered worldwide annually, according to the United Nations Office of Drug Control and Prevention." United States General Accounting Office, "Report to Congressional Requesters: Combating Money Laundering," September 2003, http://www.gao.gov/new.items/d03813.pdf. Also see Catherine Austin Fitts, "Narco Dollars for Beginners; How the Money Works in the Illicit Drug Trade; Part II: The Narco Money Map, *Narco News Bulletin,* October 31, 2001, http://www.narconews.com/narcodollars3.html.

19 Dan Berret, "Intellectual Roots of Wall Street Protest Lie in Academe," *Chronicle of Higher Education,* October 16, 2011, http://chronicle.com/article/Intellectual-Roots-of-Wall/129428/.

20 On police brutality and being caught on video spread on YouTube, see Ariel Finegold, "Swat Alums Face Police Brutality During 'Occupy Wall Street,'" *Swarthmore College Daily Gazette,* October 3, 2011, http://daily.swarthmore.edu/2011/10/03/swat-alums-face-police-brutality-during-occupy-wall-street-2/. On meaning of "austerity measures," see, for example, Mike Whitney, "The Meaning of Austerity Measures," *Counterpunch,* April 27-29, 2012, http://www.counterpunch.org/2012/04/27/the-meaning-of-austerity-measures/. On austerity measures often leading to "deregulation of industries," meaning allowing industry to pollute the environment, see for example, http://sarcasticliberal.blogspot.com/2012/03/liberty-right-wing-perspective.html.

21 Ed Vulliamy, "Global Banks are the Financial Services Wing of the Drug Cartels," *The Observer* (London), July 21, 2012. On bailouts, see Joseph Stiglitz, "The Book of Jobs," *Vanity Fair,* January 12, 2012, http://www.vanityfair.com/politics/2012/01/stiglitz-depression-201201.

22 MSNBC Staff and News Services, "Occupy Oakland: 400 Arrested after Violent Protest," MSNBC.com, January 20, 2012, http://usnews.msnbc.msn.com/_news/2012/01/30/10268080-occupy-oakland-400-arrested-after-violent-protest?lite.

23 Naomi Wolf, "Revealed: How the FBI coordinated the crackdown on Occupy," *The*

Guardian (London), December 29, 2012, http://www.guardian.co.uk/commentisfree/2012/dec/29/fbi-coordinated-crackdown-occupy. For the original FBI documents, see http://www.justiceonline.org/commentary/fbi-files-ows.html. As of early 2015, the FBI had successfully resisted appeals for additional information regarding the threats against Houston's Occupiers.

On agents infiltrating and framing SDS members, see "Exclusive: Inside the Army Spy Ring & Attempted Entrapment of Peace Activists, Iraq Vets, Anarchists," *Democracy Now!* February 25, 2014, http://www.democracynow.org/2014/2/25/exclusive_inside_the_army_spy_ring. The FBI and Homeland Security forming a working group with bank representatives suggests an element of fascism.

Occupiers on this book's cover were arrested on drug charges, though it's uncertain if government foul play was linked to their arrests. News groups reported police arresting at least three Occupy "leaders" on drug-possession charges, including Iowa Occupy organizer David Goodner, Charlotte Occupy organizer Gifford Cordova, and Utah Occupy organizer Tyler Galovich. Cordova also participated in Occupy sites in Atlanta and Washington D.C. Police apparently found ecstasy-coated chewing gum on Utah Occupy organizer Tyler Galovich. On Iowa's Goodner, see "Iowa Occupy Organizer Leaves Group After Drug Arrest,", ABC affiliate KORG, Nov. 20, 2011, http://www.kcrg.com/news/local/Iowa-Occupy-Organizer-Leaves-Group-After-Drug-Arrest-134214913.html. On Charlotte's Cordova, see "Occupy Leader Arrested On Weapons and Drug Charges," July 12, 2012. http://weaselzippers.us/2012/07/12/occupy-leader-arrested-on-weapons-and-drug-charges/. On Utah organizer Jay Hamburger, "Occupy Park City leader arrested on drug charge," May 11, 2012, *The Park* [City] *Record*, http://www.parkrecord.com/ci_20604447/park_city-contact_us.

It was also said that "ravers" brought drugs into the Occupy site in New York City, Hannah Roberts, Paul Bentley and Mark Duell, "Sex and Drugs on tap, who says it's not a political partaaay? Occupy Wall Street protesters make love as well as class war," *Daily Mail* (UK), October 10, 2011. http://www.dailymail.co.uk/news/article-2047168/Occupy-Wall-Street-protesters-make-love-class-war-sex-drugs-tap.html. Also see http://www.youtube.com/watch?v=d_IMeTaKHEU&feature=share&noredirect=1.

24 Twin Cities Indymedia, Rogue Media, Communities United Against Police Brutality & Occupy Minneapolis, *MK Occupy Minnesota: Drugs & the DRE program at Peavey Plaza* (2012), a 35-minute rough cut documentary, http://www.youtube.com/watch?feature=player_embedded&v=vTgN17FZGKE. Also see Matt McKinney, "Cops Drug Program Spawns More Questions," *Star Tribune*, May 11, 2012, http://www.startribune.com/local/minneapolis/151213325.html. Other perspectives on the incident can be found in S.E. Cupp, "Having Minnesota Cops Been Drugging Occupy Activists? There is Some Interesting Video," *The Blaze*, March 15, 2012. On marijuana as truth drug, see Martin Lee and Bruce Shlain, *Acid Dreams: the Complete Social History of LSD, the CIA, the Sixties and Beyond* (New York: Grove, 1992), pp. 4-5.

25 Aaron Rupar, "Police did indeed give Occupiers free pot, new evidence suggests; DRE program suspended," *City Pages*, May 9, 2012, http://blogs.citypages.com/blotter/2012/05/police_did_indeed_give_occupiers_drugs_new_evidence_suggests_dre_program_suspended.php.

26 Rupar, "Police did indeed give Occupiers free pot, new evidence suggests." For Sgt. Don Marose quote, Lindsey Seavert, "Drug Users Recruited to Help Police with Hands-On Training," WCCO-TV (CBS local affiliate), May 9, 2011, http://minnesota.cbslocal.com/2011/05/09/drug-users-recruited-to-help-police-with-hands-on-training/.

27 McKinney, "Cops Drug Program Spawns More Questions."

28 See Drug Evaluation and Classification Program website at www.decp.org.

29 McKinney, "Cops Drug Program Spawns More Questions."

30 On people showing psychotic symptoms after smoking spice, this author has seen many cases of it in the mental health hospital he has worked in over the last five years. Also on Spice causing psychosis, see Deborah Brauser, "Synthetic Cannabis May Pose an Even Greater Psychosis Risk: 'Spice' Packs a Bigger Punch than Natural Cannabis," *Medscape Medical News/Psychiatry*, December

13, 2011, http://www.medscape.com/viewarticle/755325.

31 Twin Cities Indymedia et al., *MK Occupy Minnesota: Drugs & the DRE program at Peavey Plaza.*

32 Christie Smythe, "HSBC Judge Approves $1.9 B Drug Money Laundering Accord," bloombergnews.com July 3, 2013, http://www.bloomberg.com/news/2013-07-02/hsbc-judge-approves-1-9b-drug-money-laundering-accord.html. Tim Worstall, "HSBC's $1.9 Billion Money Laundering Fine and the Somalian Cost of Bank Regulation," *Forbes*, August 8, 2013, http://www.forbes.com/sites/timworstall/2013/08/08/hsbcs-1-9-billion-money-laundering-fine-and-the-somalian-cost-of-bank-regulation/. Evan Perez and Carrick Mollenkamp, "Wachovia Settles Money-Laundering Case," *Wall Street Journal*, March 18, 2010. http://online.wsj.com/news/articles/SB10001424052748704059004575128062835484290.

33 James Petras, "'Dirty Money' Foundation of U.S. Growth and Empire," *La Jornado* (Mexico), May 19, 2001. Translated for globalresearch.ca, August 29, 2001, http://globalresearch.ca/articles/PET108A.html.

34 "Levin Shows How U.S. Banks are Used to Launder Drug Money and Fraud Proceeds: Findings of Year-Long Staff Investigation into High Risk Foreign Banks Released Today," February 5, 2001, http://www.levin.senate.gov/newsroom/press/release/levin-shows-how-us-banks-are-used-to-launder-drug-money-and-fraud-proceeds/?section=alltypes.

35 Associated Press, "HSBC to Pay $1.9 Billion to Settle Money-Laundering Case," *Los Angeles Times*, December 11, 2012, http://www.latimes.com/business/la-fiw-hsbc-to-pay-19b-to-settle-moneylaundering-case-20121211,0,3224744.story. Also, Petras, "'Dirty Money' Foundation of U.S. Growth and Empire."

36 Jonathan Well, "It's Official (Sort of): JPMorgan is World's Biggest Bank." Bloomberg News, May 13, 2013. http://www.bloomberg.com/news/2013-05-13/it-s-official-sort-of-jpmorgan-is-world-s-biggest-bank.html.

37 "The World's Biggest Public Companies," compiled annually in Forbes Global 2000. Vulliamy, "Global Banks are the Financial Services Wing of the Drug Cartels." On HSBC history, see Patricia Lim, *Discovering Hong Hong's Cultural Heritage* (Hong Kong: Oxford University Press, 2002).

Index

C

D

E

F

G

H

I

J

K

L

M

N

O

P

Q

R

S

T

Y

Z

Publisher's Afterword

There and Back Again

Excite the membrane, when the sense has cooled,
With pungent sauces, multiply variety
In a wilderness of mirrors. What will the spider do
Suspend its operations, will the weevil delay?

– T. S. Eliot, *Gerontion*

Most of my understanding of history has come from books, films, electronic media and other ephemera. A small amount has been derived from personal experience: first-person witness or firsthand knowledge. There are many items of history in *Drugs as Weapons Against Us* where my awareness comes solely from what I have read, seen or heard through media. But there are some things within the book of which I have direct knowledge and/or experience. I do not discount our author's main thesis, just that there may be nuances that one might see and experience that don't translate well into the history books.

It is not our role as a publisher to "deep" edit an author's work, to make his book conform to our beliefs and understandings. We can cajole a bit, make suggestions and do our diligence, but since much of "history" is open to interpretation and we are all peering backwards through the mists of time, sometimes all we can do is to try to help craft, hopefully, an honest discussion about difficult and vital subjects. Our First Amendment is not a guarantor of truth, and gives us a right to be wrong. But, at least, it allows us the opportunity to try.

***

"They are trying to opiate your whole generation."

I'll never forget those words. My father and I were having a mild argument in the driveway beside the family home in the late '60s. It was the first time I had ever heard the word opiate. I knew what it meant, but did not truly understand what he was talking about.

"How come all you kids are doing this: growing hair, wearing wild clothes, shouting slogans, doing dope … all at the same time. What's up?"

"Dad, I am not worried about heroin," I said. "I don't like needles, the nurse had to chase me all around; just to get a tetanus shot. I just smoke some pot, I don't even see any of that stuff."

"Still, all you are doing is making money for *them!*" He spat out the last word with such vituperation that the whole scene has never left me. The impression was most definite, my father felt a deep disgusting contempt for whoever "they" were.

It is my recollection (there was a lot going on) that this conversation occurred before Dad had a more serious chat with me on the day before my twentieth birthday.

"The Vietnam War is about drugs," he began. "There are these secret societies behind it."

Then he said, "And Communism is all a sham, these same secret societies are behind it all. It is all just a big game."

I was floored .... Well, actually I was sitting on a chair in a small bedroom downstairs, with Dad and a friend of his, Dr. D.F. Flemming, a professor from Vanderbilt University. I thought my father was nuts; I was young and knew way more about drugs than he did. At the time, I was married with a baby daughter, was a partner in a record store and was producing rock & roll shows. It was 1969, things were happening and the boomer generation was creating a counterculture – we were going to change the world.

A light bulb came on in my head, "Oh, Dad is having the 'drug talk' with me." So, I proceeded to sit up straight, preparing to say, "Yes, sir," and such. But my dad didn't say a word about marijuana. He told me about his twenty years or so working with American intelligence.

Dad had first become involved in 1936 as an eighteen-year-old exchange student to China. Then after graduating from college he went to work in Washington DC and abroad, serving with OSS, G-2 and the CIA. He told me he had left the Agency, in stages, in the late '50s, because he didn't like what was going on. He could talk now because his non-disclosure agreement time limit was up.

I was told, "*They* are playing out a lose scenario in Vietnam." Soon the professor and my dad were schooling me about propaganda and psychological warfare, but it became readily apparent that I had no idea what they were talking about. I had no frame of reference, and the conversation quickly ended, leaving me dazed and confused.

My father's intelligence career had *never* been mentioned before. It just wasn't talked about. I knew he had been in the CIA, but that had been gleaned from conversations with older siblings. It had never, until then, been spoken about to me by either parent. I was stunned and bewildered, but shrugged it off and went on with my life.

That discussion engendered a quest to understand *what had been said,* and I started to research a subject I call "CIA-Drugs." Early in the '70s, I mentioned to a friend of mine some of my research on what my father had said, and he looked at me and told me I was a conspiracy theorist. I scratched my head and wondered, "What the heck is a conspiracy theorist?" I decided to take on "conspiracy theory" as an intellectual discipline for study, and soon found myself in every bookstore I could find, asking to be led to their conspiracy section. I have always been a voracious reader, and before long found myself with more than enough to read, with stacks in every corner.

Each store at least had one book. I found differing books that would "blame it all" on the Jews, or the Catholics, or the Mormons, or the Masons, or the Communists, or the Illuminati, or the secular humanists, or the hippies, or the homosexuals, or the trade unions, etc. Or various combinations of these, and on and on. It soon became apparent to me that a conspiracy theory did not have to be true to have an effect. Matter-of-fact, some of these books seemed to be rhetorically designed to use ignorance, prejudices and disrespect to create division, hatred and social strife.

One method of research I employed was to read a book, look at the bibliography, and then get those books, etc. Before long, I found myself turning away from sketchy screeds and toward reading dusty tomes about banking, intelligence, politics, economics, war, the drug trade and such. Finding good information about secret societies was the most difficult.

I finally came across Antony Sutton's 1986 work, *America's Secret Establishment: An Introduction to the Order of Skull and Bones,* in late 1988. It had been almost twenty years since that weighty chat with my father, and I was *finally* beginning to understand some of what he had been talking about. It had been so hard to accept any type of co-operation between the U.S. and our enemy, the U.S.S.R. After all, I had been stuffed under my school desk as a young student because the Ruskies were going to bomb us to smithereens. (As if the desk was going to shield us!) That part of my father's talk had simply never computed for me.

But by then Dad had been ill with Parkinson's disease for years, was heavily medicated, and soon passed away in early 1990 from pancreatic cancer. I never got to ask him the many questions I had.

***

Later, when I had the opportunity, I did ask some questions.

In the late '60s I had married, left college, started a record store, and along with many of my generation, became a "hippie" and joined the counter-culture.

I was highly involved with producing music festivals, concerts and dances, including three Grateful Dead shows (one was written up in *Rolling Stone*), and attended many more. The first time I had seen the Dead was in 1967 at the Monterey Pop Music Festival as a seventeen-year old.

And I write songs, and perform at clubs and festivals. So I have some "experience" (as Mr. Hendrix once said), and have been studying the subject of intelligence agencies, black-market drugs and social dynamics for over forty years.

I personally knew and know some of the people mentioned in this book, not intimately, but socially, and encouraged our author to talk with those still with us, so as to elicit a truer understanding of those tumultuous times. He was able to speak with some and made changes in his interpretations, but not all would answer his calls or emails. Our author was left with unanswered questions and a less than complete record. And as stated before, there is a difference between researching history and actually being there.

***

One day in the mid-'90s, I took an opportunity and directly asked Ken Kesey about what I had read years before in a conspiracy screed: claims that Kesey and Jerry Garcia, guitar player for the Grateful Dead, were FBI agents.

Kesey laughed, "Naw."

I too snorted out a laugh.

He then said, "Hijack. I hijacked it."

He told me about how, because of his high-school and college wrestling career, he had learned to count his pulse at various parts of his body. When he was given LSD by the doctors, one of their questions was: "How long is a minute?" Kesey would slyly press some point on his body, count his pulse and tell them when a minute was up. The doctors were amazed and kept giving him higher and higher doses, really "tripping him out." He said he then decided to share it with his friends, and "hijacked" some to take home. The rest, as they say, is history ...

***

Well, there seem to be several differing viewpoints of that history: from one extreme view of absolute control to the other where everything was merely happenstance – simply evolution. As with many questions of history, the truth of the matter, I believe, is found somewhere in the middle.

A friend of mine who went through the similar generational and cultural dynamics in the '60s, but in the Washington DC area, noted, "LSD does not grow on trees.... My high-school crowd had 100 sources, but somehow ran across Hawaiian woodrose and morning glory seeds. And DMT was recommended as 'de-militarizing tea.' Coincidence? After a while ... I learned ... [about] the early managed experiment stage [of LSD], where there would be a sober psychiatrist guiding the group. We were not guided in that sense, but government agents were all around the edges."

From my perspective, we are dealing with a "wilderness of mirrors," a term added to our lexicon by James Jesus Angleton, the CIA's paranoid Chief of Counterintelligence from 1954 to 1974. He appropriated the phrase from T. S. Eliot's poem, *Gerontion*. As a former special assistant to the Deputy Director of the CIA, Victor Marchetti, noted about Angelton in *The CIA and the Cult of Intelligence*: "He wrote that the 'wilderness' consists of the myriad stratagems, deceptions and all the other devices of disinformation ... used to confuse and split ... producing an ever-fluid landscape where fact and illusion merge."

In other words, unraveling history can be a minefield of both witting and unwitting mis- and dis-information all roiled together with what actually happened, making it very hard to have an accurate understanding of what truly went down. And as any investigator knows, people experience the same events differently. And then you are also dealing with memories, agendas, and many unknowns that may color understandings.

Before things get black and white there is a gray area where only the actual participants may be aware of the reasons for their actions. And within the intelligence milieu comes compartmentalization, extraordinary funding and massive dissembling. So these participants themselves may not even have an accurate understanding, especially the farther they get away from "official" agents, and into the netherworld of undercover agents/assets, who many times may have no idea for whom they are working, what they are doing, or even that they are actually carrying water for somebody. Plus, generally, there are others throwing mud (lies and misdirection) around to cover tracks, and a clean-up crew following behind. *A situation ripe for hijacking.*

***

You see, the boomer generation was not supposed to cohere. We were being conditioned to be a peaced-out/drugged-out generation. *But* something happened and ultimately we did cohere, as "hippies" smoking a joint around a circle (with a little LSD thrown in). Sinister forces had been trying to establish the boomers as an anti-thesis to our parent's "war" generation. It was a secret-society/intelligence protocoled psychological warfare operation designed to create a problem, which then *allowed* "them" to deploy pre-constructed solutions: the War on Drugs, a polarizing divisive culture war, the shredding of our Constitution and the continued diminishment of our liberties. The social dynamics of what actually happened in a nutshell: the "monster" that the "evil" scientists hoped to create turned on its "master," and has been running pell-mell towards freedom ever since.

The boomers hijacked the "op," became hippies, and along the way helped foster the personal computer and the Internet, which are the tools we as a society are using to combat the corruption in which we are enmeshed.

***

Thomas Jefferson wrote to John Norvell in 1807, "The real extent of this state of misinformation is known only to those who are in situations to confront facts within their knowledge with the lies of the day."

And not only had Dad told me some outrageous things, but I began to notice on my own during the late '60s that everything wasn't "organic." I remember reading contemporary books that I felt to have an air of falseness, trying to manufacture my beliefs about what was happening. And once I began to research Skull & Bones, intelligence operations and psychological warfare, understanding how the world really works got easier

Consider the fact that I, as a teen in the '60s, in a small town, learned all about the "drugs," and such, from my parent's weekly *Life* magazine. I was exposed to what was "happening": LSD, mushrooms, and marijuana, including one issue that taught me how to clean the weed with a shoe-box lid, roll a joint and smoke it. I and many others were off and running ...

Life magazine was started by Henry Luce, a member of the Order of Skull & Bones at Yale. There were many other Bonesmen also working at Time-Life. The Order's families have been involved in, among other things, the illicit opium market since the secret society's founding in 1832. Theirs was the largest concern in the U.S., the third largest in the world. As detailed herein by John Potash, opium was and is big business and spawns huge revenue. Australian Professor Carl Trocki put it eloquently: "Opium created pools of capital and fed the institutions that accumulated it: the banking and financial systems, the insurance systems and the transportation and information infrastructures.... Drug trades destabilized existing societies ... they have the power to undercut the existing political economy of any state. They have created new forms of capital; and they have redistributed wealth in radically new ways."

Drugs, hmm. Hippies had been well schooled. And one particular event appears to have happened multiple times, in many places: all of a sudden all the pot would vanish, but plenty of speed, cocaine and heroin would be available. And the purity of the "white dope" would be up, and the cost of it would go down.

All this while marijuana was becoming more expensive, going from a nominal $10 an ounce, to $35, to $70. This encouraged folks to begin to grow cannabis in earnest for themselves and for sale. A new "business" was created and hippies began to take the marijuana trade *away* from the control of nefarious smugglers in the shadows ... releasing a genie from his lamp.

We colored out of the lines, didn't follow instructions, and instead of getting lost in the opiated haze, we never went all the way to the syringe or sniffing-straw, but stopped at the Zig-Zags.

There had been a disturbance in our four-generational cycle before. According to the book, *Generations: A History of America's Future, 1584 to 2069,* during the mid-nineteenth century Civil War Cycle, the "Civic" cohorts didn't cohere. Some joined the generation before, some the one after, others just went out in the woods and did weird stuff. I believe the main causes of the non-cohesion were war, a presidential assassination and opium. It appears a similar scenario was scripted for my generation in the late twentieth century.

The proper cycling of generations helps propel us forward, with the interactions among four cohort groups, Idealist, Reactive, Civic and Adaptive, forming a "constellation" that navigates through the eras and phases of life. When one of the generations of the constellation doesn't cohere, it makes all social, economic and political units more susceptible to corrupting covert machinations, leaving our "history" easier to manipulate.

The loss of the Civic cohort group during the Civil War Cycle resulted in fundamental changes in our Republic and its democratic institutions.

Primarily, in 1886 the United States Supreme Court in the case of *Santa Clara County v. Southern Pacific Railroad Company,* Supreme Court Justice Morrison R. Waite calmly proclaimed at the start of the case that:

> The court does not wish to hear argument on the question whether the provision in the Fourteenth Amendment to the Constitution, which forbids a State to deny to any person within its jurisdiction the equal protection of the laws, applies to these corporations. We are all of opinion that it does.

This two-sentence pronouncement by a single judge gave corporations the status of persons under the law, preparing the way for the rise of global corporate rule – changing the course of history.

Judge Waite was a member of the Order of Skull & Bones.

Then, through yellow journalism and a false-flag event ("Remember the Maine"), our country was misled into the Spanish-American War, and became an empire. And coincidently (fortunate for some), opium was made illegal once more. After the Second Opium War in 1860, opium had become legal, effectively corralling a very consistent *covert* cash cow.

American forces took the Philippines from Spain, and William Howard Taft, member, and son of a founder, of the Order of Skull & Bones, while serving as Governor-General of the Philippines, declared opium illegal there. As both Vice President and President, Taft later initiated calls for the Shanghai and Hague Conventions, commencing the steps towards our modern prohibition – again creating black-market profits and corruption.

Soon there was a spate of U.S. legislative chicanery and other world events that have helped "bind" us to an extra-Constitutional corporate cryptocracy ever since:

1913 - Sixteenth Amendment: income taxes.
1913 - Federal Reserve Act: specious corporate currency.
1917/1941 - WWI and WWII: debt, war industry, and jingoism.
1947 - National Security Act: creation of the CIA and the NSC.

To again accomplish the task of effecting a non-cohering generation, there needed to be in place by 1950 three main things: television, the "modern" education system and a nascent drug culture. As our author documents regarding the latter, these would have taken some years to establish.

In my opinion, a fly developed in the ointment – LSD. It wasn't discovered until 1938, and took awhile to develop any notoriety. LSD isn't as easy to control as opiates, and it got out of control. Yes it was used, but with opiates you can simply give out a few free samples and soon have a dynamic market. Psychedelics do not lend themselves to such simplistic measures. They can cause intense, life-changing experiences, endearing them to users, many to the point of becoming proselytizers. Psychedelics are nothing to be taken lightly, and as with things in general they may produce good or ill.

***

In 1970 I helped with Vortex I, a state-sponsored rock festival. The American Legion convention and President Nixon were coming to Portland, Oregon. For several years there had been violent confrontations wherever the convention was held, and national groups were gearing up for another round. We had marched against the war, but many of us locals didn't want violence. So instead of a riot there was a week-long party, and a strong identity was forged. The Rainbow Family was formed there.

We were becoming our own "community," instead of fodder for a police state and escalating violence. We were hijacking ourselves out of a scripted dialectic and stretching for a completely different synthesis. We were coming together as a generation. We were cohering as hippies.

To connect all the dots would take another book in itself, the short version goes like this:

Yes, there was a "plan," but as Robbie Burns has so wonderfully said,

The best-laid schemes o' mice an' men
Gang aft agley [Go often awry].

Onward to the Utmost Future!

Peace,
R.A. Kris Millegan
Publisher, TrineDay
April 5, 2015

Phil Lesh, Jerry's more explosive and dogmatic other half, comes right out and says that the Grateful Dead "are trying to save the world," but Jerry is more cautious. "We are trying to make things groovier for everybody so more people can feel better more often, to advance the trip, to get higher, however you want to say it, but we're musicians, and there's just no way to put that idea, 'save the world,' into music; you can only be that idea, or at least make manifest that idea as it appears to you, and hope maybe others follow. And that idea comes to you only moment by moment, so what we're going after is no farther away than the end of our noses. We're just trying to be right behind our noses.

"My way is music. Music is me being me and trying to get higher. I've been into music so long that I'm dripping with it; it's all I ever expect to do. I can't do anything else. Music is a yoga, something you really do when you're doing it. Thinking about what it means comes after the fact and isn't very interesting. Truth is something you stumble into when you think you're going some place else, like those moments when you're playing and the whole room becomes one being, precious moments, man. But you can't look for them and they can't be repeated. Being alive means to continue to change, never to be where I was before. Music is the timeless experience of constant change."

– Michael Lyndon, "Good Old Grateful Dead"
RollingStone #40, August 23, 1969